OXFORD STUDIES IN ANCIENT PHILOSOPHY

OXFORD STUDIES IN ANCIENT PHILOSOPHY

EDITOR: DAVID SEDLEY

VOLUME XXXII

SUMMER 2007

OXFORD
UNIVERSITY PRESS

Great Clarendon Street, Oxford OX2 6DP

Oxford University Press is a department of the University of Oxford.
It furthers the University's objective of excellence in research, scholarship,
and education by publishing worldwide in

Oxford New York

Auckland Cape Town Dar es Salaam Hong Kong Karachi
Kuala Lumpur Madrid Melbourne Mexico City Nairobi
New Delhi Shanghai Taipei Toronto

With offices in

Argentina Austria Brazil Chile Czech Republic France Greece
Guatemala Hungary Italy Japan Poland Portugal Singapore
South Korea Switzerland Thailand Turkey Ukraine Vietnam

Oxford is a registered trade mark of Oxford University Press
in the UK and in certain other countries

Published in the United States
by Oxford University Press Inc., New York

© Except where otherwise stated, Oxford University Press, 2007

The moral rights of the authors have been asserted
Database right Oxford University Press (maker)

First published 2007

All rights reserved. No part of this publication may be reproduced,
stored in a retrieval system, or transmitted, in any form or by any means,
without the prior permission in writing of Oxford University Press,
or as expressly permitted by law, or under terms agreed with the appropriate
reprographics rights organization. Enquiries concerning reproduction
outside the scope of the above should be sent to the Rights Department,
Oxford University Press, at the address above

You must not circulate this book in any other binding or cover
and you must impose the same condition on any acquirer

British Library Cataloguing in Publication Data

Data available

Library of Congress Cataloging in Publication Data

Oxford studies in ancient philosophy.—
Vol. xxxii (2007).—Oxford: Clarendon Press;
New York: Oxford University Press, 1983–
v.; 22 cm. Annual.
1. Philosophy, Ancient—Periodicals.
B1.O9   180.'5—dc.19   84-645022
AACR 2   MARC-S

Typeset by John Waś, Oxford
Printed in Great Britain
on acid-free paper by
Biddles Ltd, King's Lynn, Norfolk

ISBN 978-0-19-922731-0
ISBN 978-0-19-922738-9 (Pbk.)

1 3 5 7 9 10 8 6 4 2

ADVISORY BOARD

Professor Jonathan Barnes, *Université de Paris-Sorbonne, Paris IV*

Professor Michael Frede, *University of Athens*

Professor A. A. Long, *University of California, Berkeley*

Professor Martha Nussbaum, *University of Chicago*

Professor Richard Sorabji, *King's College, University of London, and Wolfson College, Oxford*

Professor Gisela Striker, *Harvard University*

Contributions and books for review should be sent to the Editor. Until 30 September 2007 this is Professor D. N. Sedley, Christ's College, Cambridge CB2 3BU, UK (e-mail dns1@cam.ac.uk); after that date it will be Professor Brad Inwood, Department of Classics, University of Toronto, 97 St George Street, Toronto M5S 2E8, Canada (e-mail brad.inwood@utoronto.ca).

Contributors are asked to observe the 'Notes for Contributors to Oxford Studies in Ancient Philosophy', printed at the end of this volume.

Up-to-date contact details, the latest version of Notes to Contributors, and publication schedules can be checked on the *Oxford Studies in Ancient Philosophy* website:

www.oup.co.uk/philosophy/series/osap

CONTENTS

Socrates' Profession of Ignorance 1
MICHAEL N. FORSTER

The Development of Plato's Theory of Ideas and the
'Socratic Question' 37
FRANCESCO FRONTEROTTA

Persuasion and the Tripartite Soul in Plato's *Republic* 63
R. F. STALLEY

Plato's *Phaedrus* and the Problem of Unity 91
DANIEL WERNER

Aristotle on the Necessity of Opposites in *Posterior
Analytics* 1. 4 139
RICHARD TIERNEY

Organic Unity and the Matter of Man 167
CHRISTOPHER FREY

The Union of Cause and Effect in Aristotle: *Physics* 3. 3 205
ANNA MARMODORO

Aristotelian Infinity 233
JOHN BOWIN

Listening to Reason in Aristotle's Moral Psychology 251
GÖSTA GRÖNROOS

Phronēsis as a Mean in the *Eudemian Ethics* 273
GILES PEARSON

Aristotle and the Problems of Method in Ethics 297
MARCO ZINGANO

Enquiry and Discovery: A Discussion of Dominic Scott,
Plato's Meno 331
GAIL FINE

viii   *Contents*

Philosophy, History, Anthropology: A Discussion of
Bernard Williams, *The Sense of the Past*   369
    G. E. R. LLOYD

Index Locorum   379

SOCRATES' PROFESSION OF IGNORANCE

MICHAEL N. FORSTER

I N a previous article in this journal[1] I developed an account of the historical Socrates' demand for definitions of ethical terms. The present article is interdependent with the previous one, but turns to a further topic. It is a well-attested fact that Socrates professed ignorance about the matters on which his enquiries focused, and indeed about all matters of real importance. Among those who knew him personally, both Plato and Aeschines of Sphettus depict this profession of ignorance, and a generation later Aristotle reports it as well.[2] What are we to make of this profession of ignorance?

For the most part, the explanations of it in the secondary literature fall into three classes. First, there are scholars who dismiss it as disingenuous, and who explain it as a sort of trick used by Socrates either in order to lure those guilty of the false conceit of knowledge into a conversation so that they can be refuted, or in order to hide his own ethical knowledge so that his interlocutors are forced to achieve such knowledge for themselves.[3] Second, there are scholars

---

© Michael N. Forster 2007

I would like to express deep gratitude to the late Arthur Adkins (University of Chicago), John Cooper (Princeton University), Vassiliki Kindi (University of Athens), Richard Kraut (Northwestern University), Ian Mueller (University of Chicago), Alexander Nehamas (Princeton University), and David Sedley (Cambridge University) for comments on this and related material which helped me to improve it in various ways.

[1] 'Socrates' Demand for Definitions', *OSAP* 31 (2006), 1–47.

[2] PLATO: *Ap.* 19 C, 20 C, 20 E, 21 B, 21 D, 22 D, 23 A–B; *La.* 186 B–E, 200 E; *Lys.* 212 A, 223 B; *Chrm.* 165 B–C; *H.Ma.* 286 C–E, 304 D; *H.Min.* 372 B; *Gorg.* 506 A, 509 A; *Meno* 71 A, 80 C–D; *Rep.* 337 E; *Sym.* 216 D; *Theaet.* 150 C–D, 210 C. AESCHINES OF SPHETTUS: 'Though I possess no knowledge which I might teach a man in order to benefit him . . .' (fr. 12 Nestle). ARISTOTLE: 'He used to confess that he did not know' (*SE* 183^{b}7–8).

[3] Examples of the former view: C. Ritter, *Sokrates* (Tübingen, 1931), 33–5, esp. n. 51; R. Robinson, *Plato's Earlier Dialectic* (Oxford, 1953), 8–9; N. Gulley, *The Philosophy of Socrates* (New York, 1968), 64. Examples of the latter view: F. M.

2   *Michael N. Forster*

who allow that the profession of ignorance is sincere, and who explain it as the result of Socrates' having set up exalted standards for ethical knowledge (for example, certainty and precision, the possession of scientific definitions, the discovery of the function of human life, or a grasp of everything about the subject in question), striven to meet these standards, made some progress, but not yet met them to his own satisfaction.[4] Third, there are a few scholars who allow that the profession of ignorance is sincere, and who explain it by saying that Socrates aimed primarily at dispelling the false conceit of knowledge in others and did not attain the (no doubt, in his view desirable) further end of affirmative belief.[5] In short, we are offered Socrates the sly, Socrates the student, and Socrates the sceptic.

In what follows I would like to indicate some reasons for thinking that none of these explanations of Socrates' profession of ignorance is adequate, and to offer an alternative explanation. This alternative explanation will appeal not to Socrates the sly, Socrates the student, or Socrates the sceptic but instead to a fourth, and less often considered, Socrates, whom we may as well, for alliteration's sake, call Socrates the saint.

I

Plato's *Apology* records two important facts about Socrates which bear directly on his profession of ignorance. It is, I think, reasonable to expect any account of his profession of ignorance to do justice to

---

Cornford, *Plato and Parmenides: Parmenides' Way of Truth and Plato's* Parmenides (London, 1939), 245; L. Veresenyi, *Socratic Humanism* (New Haven, 1963), 118, 120–1.

[4] 'Certainty and precision': J. Stenzel, 'Sokrates (Philosoph)', in A. F. Pauly, rev. G. Wissowa *et al.*, *Real-Encyclopädie der classischen Altertumswissenschaft* [*RE*] (Stuttgart, 1894–1980), ii/5. 811–90 at 823. 'Scientific definitions': E. Zeller, *Socrates and the Socratic Schools* (New York, 1962), 101–11 (who seems to hold that Socrates *eventually did* meet his standards, however); T. H. Irwin, *Plato's Moral Theory: The Early and Middle Dialogues* (Oxford, 1985), 39–40; R. Kraut, *Socrates and the State* (Princeton, 1984), 283–4. 'The function of human life': W. K. C. Guthrie, *Socrates* (Cambridge, 1971), 127. 'A grasp of everything about the subject in question': T. Penner, 'Socrates and the Early Dialogues', in R. Kraut (ed.), *The Cambridge Companion to Plato* (Cambridge, 1999), 121–69 at 145.

[5] G. Grote, *Plato and the Other Companions of Sokrates* (London, 1865), 373–4, 400. This was apparently also the interpretation given by those sceptics in the ancient world who interpreted Plato and Socrates as sceptics (see S.E. *PH* 1. 221–2; Cic. *Acad.* 1. 16, 44–6).

Socrates' Profession of Ignorance 3

both of these facts. Moreover, since they appear to be inconsistent with each other, they form a sort of *aporia* which any account must solve.

The first fact is Socrates' commitment to the message from the Delphic oracle which began his philosophical career. The oracle, it will be recalled, said that there was no one wiser than Socrates, which puzzled him because he was aware both that he knew nothing and that the god of the oracle could not be mistaken (21 A–B). His eventual interpretation of the oracle, to the verification and dissemination of which he henceforth devoted his life, was that, god being really wise, human wisdom was worth little or nothing— Socrates being taken as a mere example to make the point that that human being was wisest who, like Socrates, recognized that he was worthless in respect of wisdom (23 A–B). This message of universal human ignorance did not exclude everyday knowledge about non-evaluative matters—Socrates in particular recognized that the artisans had such knowledge (22 C–E; cf. *Euthph.* 7 B–C; *Alc. I* 111 B–D; *Phdr.* 263 A–B; Xen. *Mem.* 4. 6. 2–8). Rather, it concerned knowledge of 'the other matters of most importance [τἆλλα τὰ μέγιστα]' (22 D–E), of what was 'fine [καλὸν κἀγαθόν]' (21 D), i.e. the ethical matters with which, as Plato and Xenophon both show, and as the latter also explicitly says (*Mem.* 1. 1. 16), Socrates' conversations were always concerned. It is, I think, beyond reasonable doubt that Socrates' profession of ignorance in other Platonic texts, in Aeschines of Sphettus, and in Aristotle must be understood in connection with his commitment to this oracular message of universal human ignorance concerning ethics.

That this is so immediately makes highly implausible the *first* explanation of his profession of ignorance offered in the secondary literature, according to which it is an insincere trick used by Socrates to lure interlocutors into a conversation so that they may be refuted, or to mask his own knowledge and thus force interlocutors to achieve knowledge for themselves.[6]

Furthermore, as I argued in 'Socrates' Demand for Definitions', it is clear that Socrates understands this oracular message that, god being really wise, human wisdom is worth little or nothing (23 A) as a timeless statement about the human condition in comparison with the divine (not merely an unfavourable report on *human beings*

---

[6] Cf. G. Vlastos, 'Socrates' Disavowal of Knowledge', *Philosophical Quarterly*, 35/138 (1985), 1–31 at 5.

4   *Michael N. Forster*

at the moment or *human beings so far*). And if that is so, then this evidence also makes it very difficult to believe the *second* explanation of his profession of ignorance offered in the secondary literature, according to which he has a demanding ideal of ethical knowledge which he is striving to achieve, though as yet without complete success. For if he is sure that it belongs to the human condition to be without ethical knowledge, and has indeed devoted his life to verifying and disseminating just this message, then it is very difficult to believe that he is striving to achieve ethical knowledge *at all*. Moreover, as I argued in 'Socrates' Demand for Definitions', there is, on closer inspection, nothing in the *Apology* or in other early dialogues before the *Gorgias* that really suggests that he is so striving.

The second fact revealed by the *Apology* seems at first sight to conflict sharply with that first one (i.e. with Socrates' commitment to the oracle's message of universal human ignorance concerning 'the . . . matters of most importance', or ethical matters). The second fact is that *Socrates has perfectly confident beliefs about ethical matters which he considers of the utmost importance*. Thus he is clearly in no doubt, and has indeed made it his life's work to impress on people (29 D–30 B, 32 B–D, 38 E–39 B), that one should pursue practical judgement ($\phi\rho\acute{o}\nu\eta\sigma\iota s$), truth, perfection of the soul, and virtue, since these are 'the things that are of greatest value [$\tau\grave{a}$ $\pi\lambda\epsilon\acute{\iota}\sigma\tau o\upsilon$ $\mathring{a}\xi\iota a$]', before wealth, honour, reputation, and the body, which are 'less valuable' (29 D–30 A). And he has further confident beliefs about ethical matters which he considers vitally important as well. For example, he insists that one must be guided in one's actions by one's judgement of what is right and wrong, not by fear of death (28 B–29 A, 32 B–D, 38 E–39 B; cf. *Crito* 48 B, 48 D, 54 B; *Gorg.* 512 D–E, 522 E). He insists that it is worse to do than to suffer injustice (30 D; this thesis is treated in more depth in the *Gorgias*). He insists that it is bad to disobey a better, whether man or god (29 B; cf. 28 D–29 A; *Crito* 50 E–51 C). He insists that it is impious to break, or encourage someone else to break, an oath (35 C–D). He insists that one must respect the law, even at the cost of one's own well-being (32 B–C; this doctrine is treated in more depth in the *Crito*). Finally, as religious principles closely bound up with his ethics, he insists that it is not divine law that a better man should be injured by a worse (30 D), and that the gods never allow harm to come to a good man in life or after death (41 C–D; cf. *Gorg.* 527 C–D).

Socrates' Profession of Ignorance

This second fact from the *Apology* makes very implausible the *third* explanation of Socrates' profession of ignorance offered in the secondary literature, according to which he was primarily motivated by a concern to remove the false conceit of knowledge and did not arrive at the additional (and no doubt desirable) end of affirmative belief. For it seems that, on the contrary, he held many affirmative beliefs about ethical matters which he considered of the utmost importance.

Thus our two facts from the *Apology* appear between them to have excluded all three of the standard lines of interpretation of Socrates' profession of ignorance found in the secondary literature.

It is important, however, to recognize the full force of the *aporia* which arises when the second fact is set beside the first. The first fact tells us that Socrates believes in universal human ignorance on the matters of most importance, i.e. ethical matters, and that his profession of his own ignorance must be understood in this light; the second fact then tells us that he has perfectly confident beliefs about ethical matters which he considers of the utmost importance.[7] This *aporia* does not admit of any easy solution. In particular, these two facts cannot be reconciled by suggesting that Socrates considers his confident ethical beliefs to be too commonplace to count as significant exceptions to his denial of ethical knowledge. In his time they were actually far from commonplace, and the circumstance that he felt that he had to make it his life's work to impress them upon his fellow men (29 D–30 B, 30 D–31 C) shows that he did not consider them such either. Nor can these two facts be reconciled by suggesting that Socrates' achievement of confident ethical beliefs postdated and outdated the oracular message. Socrates actually gives no indication that he first came by these beliefs *after* receiving the oracular message. More importantly, he clearly implies that they did *not* outdate the message, for he says that he is *still now* verifying and disseminating it (22 B). Moreover, since (as has already been mentioned) the message is meant timelessly, it could not in any

---

[7] In 'Socrates' Demand for Definitions' I argued that Socrates understands the oracle's message to deny *any* ethical knowledge to people. Notice, however, that there would be an *aporia* here even if that were incorrect. A version of this *aporia* was noted by T. C. Brickhouse and N. D. Smith, *Socrates on Trial* (Oxford and Princeton, 1989), 100 ff. Their account also agrees with the solution that I shall be offering here in suggesting that Socrates understands his ethical beliefs to have a divine source (105 ff.).

6 *Michael N. Forster*

case be outdated (only refuted). The *aporia*, then, still awaits a solution.[8]

A satisfactory account of Socrates' profession of ignorance must therefore do justice to these two hard facts, and to the challenge of reconciling them.[9] None of the standard accounts of Socrates' profession of ignorance in the secondary literature seems capable of achieving this. Can we find one that is?

II

Such an account, I believe the correct one, can be distilled from three sources. First, there is a set of early Platonic texts—the *Apology*, the *Ion*, and the *Crito*—which collectively point to it, though without stating it explicitly. Second, there is Plato's early middle dialogue the *Meno*, which states it explicitly. Third, there are the

---

[8] Xenophon was evidently so impressed by the fact of Socrates' confident beliefs on important ethical and religious matters, and by its apparent irreconcilability with a profession of ignorance, that he made no room at all for such a profession in his portrait of Socrates, and indeed went out of his way to make his Socrates deny his own ignorance. Thus, Xenophon's pages are full of illustrations of Socrates giving confident ethical and religious instruction. And Xenophon is not shy about calling this knowledge; according to him, once Socrates had convinced an interlocutor of his ignorance, 'he began to expound very plainly and clearly the knowledge that he thought most needful [ἅ τε ἐνόμιζεν εἰδέναι δεῖν] and the practices that he held to be most excellent' (*Mem.* 4. 2. 40). Moreover, in the *Memorabilia* Xenophon has Hippias raise a suggestion of Socratic ignorance, accusing Socrates of mocking others, 'questioning and examining everybody, and never willing to render an account of yourself or to state an opinion about anything', and has Socrates retort to this: 'Indeed, Hippias! Haven't you noticed that I never cease to declare my notion of what is just?' (6. 4. 9–10). Xenophon's account should not, I think, cause us to question the weightier testimony of Plato, Aeschines of Sphettus, and Aristotle that Socrates professed ignorance. But it does show that Xenophon was so impressed by the fact of Socrates' confident beliefs on important ethical and religious matters and by its apparent inconsistency with a profession of ignorance that he could make no sense of such a profession.

[9] A special case of this antinomy is Socrates' commitment to both (1) the priority of a grasp of definitions to any knowledge of a general quality or of its particular instances, and consequently, since he and others lack definitions in ethics, his own and others' lack of the latter sorts of knowledge in ethics as well, and (2) his own possession of authoritative insights into the character of ethical qualities and into their particular instances, on which insights he often relies in order to refute proposed ethical definitions and other ethical theses. Concerning this sort of problem, see J. Beversluis, 'Socratic Definition', *American Philosophical Quarterly*, 11/4 (1974), 331–6. The solution to the general antinomy which I shall offer in this article also solves this special case of it.

Socrates' Profession of Ignorance

fragments from the *Alcibiades* of Aeschines of Sphettus, which also state it explicitly.

We have just seen that Plato's *Apology* imposes the constraint on any satisfactory account of Socrates' profession of ignorance that it must reconcile Socrates' sincere belief in his own ignorance about all matters of most importance, ethical matters, with his possession of confident beliefs about ethical matters which he considers of the utmost importance. We might, therefore, usefully begin by asking whether the *Apology* or any other early work of Plato's indicates a way in which such a reconciliation might be possible.

The only route for a reconciliation to take, it seems, would be via a distinction between *knowledge* and *true belief*. For if Socrates recognized such a distinction, he might consistently hold both that he had no knowledge about (important) ethical matters and that he none the less had true beliefs about such matters.[10] Do Plato's early texts anywhere record Socrates' recognition of such a distinction? They do in connection with one class of beliefs: the beliefs of poets, prophets, and oracle-givers, which come to them as a result of divine inspiration or possession. According to the *Apology* and the *Ion*, such people do state many truths (πολλὰ καὶ καλά, *Ap.* 22 C; *Ion* 534 B; cf. ἀληθῆ καὶ πολλά, *Meno* 99 C), but they make their statements 'not by wisdom [οὐ σοφίᾳ]' (*Ap.* 22 C; cf. *Ion* 536 C) nor 'from art [ἐκ τέχνης]' (*Ion* 533 E) nor with 'understanding [νοῦς]' (*Ion* 534 B, D), but instead 'because they are divinely inspired [ἐνθουσιάζοντες]' (*Ap.* 22 C) or 'divinely inspired and possessed [ἔνθεοι ὄντες καὶ κατεχόμενοι]' (*Ion* 533 E) or 'by a divine dispensation [θείᾳ μοίρᾳ]' (*Ion* 534 C).

Now in the *Apology* and the *Crito* we find two crucial passages in which Socrates shows that he understands his own ethical beliefs and the arguments which support them to be the result of divine inspiration as well. One of these passages occurs at the end of the *Apology*, where he infers that (his) death is a good thing from (1) the fact that the divine sign, which normally intervenes when he is about to do something that would result in bad consequences, has let him speak before the law court in such a way as to earn himself the death penalty, along with (2) an argument prompted by that divine hint to the effect that death is either the extinction of consciousness, and hence like a long dreamless sleep, in which

---

[10] Cf. Irwin, *Plato's Moral Theory*, 39–41, who begins from the same idea but in the end gives a very different account from the one developed here.

8   *Michael N. Forster*

case it is preferable to most of our life, or else a passage to an afterlife which promises divine judgement and, for the virtuous like himself, happy encounters with dead heroes and others from the past, in which case it is even better (40 A–41 D).[11]

The other passage occurs in the *Crito*, an early dialogue which, like the *Apology*, depicts Socrates both expressing and arguing for confident ethical beliefs. After making an extended case for the moral necessity of obeying the laws of the state, Socrates closes the dialogue as follows:

> soc. Be well assured, my dear friend Crito, that this is what I seem to hear, as the frenzied Corybantian worshippers seem to hear the flutes, and the sound of these words re-echoes within me and prevents my hearing any other words. And be assured that, so far as I now believe, if you argue anything against these words you will speak in vain. Nevertheless, if you think you can accomplish anything, speak.
>
> crito. No, Socrates, I have nothing to say.
>
> soc. Then, Crito, let it be, and let us act in this way, since it is in this way that the god leads/instructs us [ταύτῃ ὁ θεὸς ὑφηγεῖται].   (54 D–E)

Socrates here likens his belief in the moral necessity of obeying the laws of the state and the argument which he has given in support of that belief to the divine tune that lays hold of a Corybantian worshipper. And that this suggestion of a divine origin for his own ethical belief and argument is not merely metaphorical is made clear by the last sentence, in which he unambiguously assigns responsibility for them to the god (*which* god we shall consider later). The more specific point of the simile of the Corybantian worshipper is made clearer by a remark in the *Ion*: 'The Corybantian worshippers are keenly sensible of that strain alone which belongs to the god whose possession is on them, and have plenty of gestures and phrases for that tune, but do not heed any other' (536 c). Thus Socrates' idea here at the end of the *Crito* is that the god's inspiration of him with the argument for obedience to the laws of the state is of such a character as to make him unable to take seriously any other argument or an argument from any other source (so that he is 'prevent[ed] [from] hearing any other words' and 'if [Crito] argue[s] anything against these words [he] will speak in vain'). It is probably also significant that Socrates had presented his argument for the moral

---

[11] In the *Gorgias* Socrates explicitly characterizes a version of the latter account as true belief, rather than knowledge (523 A, 524 A–B, 526 D; cf. the distinction between (true) belief and knowledge at 454 D).

Socrates' Profession of Ignorance

necessity of obeying the laws of the state as though it were spoken by the personified, or deified, laws themselves (50 A ff.). For the essential dependence of the *content* of the argument on a conception of the laws as persons (and hence as possessing moral claims on an individual) suggests that this personification, or deification, is more than a mere literary conceit.[12]

From the *Apology*, the *Ion*, and the *Crito*, then, one would have fairly good reason to infer that the correct account of Socrates' profession of ignorance about ethical matters is as follows: he draws a distinction between knowledge, on the one hand, and true belief resulting from divine inspiration or possession, on the other; he understands his own ethical beliefs to be true beliefs resulting from divine inspiration or possession, not knowledge; and this explains why there is no inconsistency between his profession of ignorance about the matters of most importance, ethical matters, and his indulgence in confident beliefs about ethical matters which he considers of the utmost importance.[13]

[12] It is no objection to the interpretation of the two passages from the *Apology* and *Crito* which I am giving here that Socrates develops *arguments* for his ethical conclusions in both cases. For, as B. Snell pointed out in *The Discovery of the Mind in Greek Philosophy and Literature* (New York, 1960), 148–9, the absence of any sense of a tension between reliance on argument and reliance on divine inspiration is a characteristic feature of Greek culture in this period—visible, for example, in Parmenides' poem, where Parmenides relies *both* on the authority of the goddess's instruction *and* on the force of her argument (concerning the incoherence of the notion of not-being). Much of the recent secondary literature that deals with Socrates, religion, and reasoning—certainly work by Vlastos, but even M. L. McPherran, *The Religion of Socrates* (University Park, PA, 1999), ch. 4—seems to me vitiated by a failure to take this deep insight of Snell's sufficiently to heart, by an anachronistic assumption of a more modern conception of reasoning and divine inspiration as standing in natural opposition to one another. (Plato's own position is much closer to that modern conception, however—concerning which, see M. F. Burnyeat, 'Socratic Midwifery, Platonic Inspiration', *Bulletin of the Institute of Classical Studies*, 24 (1977), 7–16 at 13.)

[13] Two additional points to note: (1) at *Euthph.* 5 B Socrates implies a slightly different version of a distinction between knowledge/wisdom and true belief. There he envisages himself becoming Euthyphro's pupil concerning piety and religion and on that ground saying to his accuser Meletus: 'Meletus, if you acknowledge that Euthyphro is wise [σοφὸν] in such matters, then believe that I also hold correct opinions [ὀρθῶς νομίζειν].' This evidence coheres well with the account of Socrates' conception of his own ethical beliefs which I am giving here, for on this account with respect to such beliefs he will in effect be a pupil of the σοφός god whom he mentions at *Ap.* 23 A.

(2) It is significant that when Socrates comes to express and describe his confident ethical beliefs in the *Apology*, his description of his possession of them almost completely avoids the words which he had used to mean wisdom or knowledge throughout the oracle story: σοφία entirely disappears from view, and so does εἰδέναι

10   *Michael N. Forster*

This account of Socrates' profession of ignorance inferred from Plato's early dialogues is confirmed by a slightly later Platonic work which explicitly attributes to Socrates all of the essential views in question: the *Meno*. There Socrates explicitly draws a distinction between knowledge (ἐπιστήμη, σοφία, φρόνησις) and true or right belief (ἀληθὴς δόξα, ὀρθὴ δόξα, εὐδοξία), pointing out that both are equally good as guides to right action (96 E ff.); he indicates that the paradigm example of true or right belief which is not knowledge is the divinely inspired belief of oracle-givers and prophets (99 B–C); and he says that virtue or ethical insight is not knowledge but true or right belief resulting, like that of oracle-givers and prophets, from divine inspiration:

SOC. Well now, since virtue is not taught, we no longer take it to be knowledge?

MENO. Apparently not.

SOC. So of two good and useful things [i.e. knowledge and true or right belief], one has been rejected: knowledge cannot be our guide to political conduct.

MENO. I think not.

SOC. Therefore it was not by any wisdom, nor because they were wise, that the sort of men we spoke of controlled their states—Themistocles and the rest of them . . . And if not by knowledge, as the only alternative it must have been by right belief. This is the means which statesmen employ for their direction of states, and they have nothing more to do with wisdom than oracle-givers and prophets; for these people utter many a true thing when inspired, but have no knowledge of anything they say . . . And . . . we can say of the statesmen that they are divine and inspired, since they are under the influence and possession of the god [θείους τε εἶναι καὶ ἐνθουσιάζειν, ἐπίπνους ὄντας καὶ κατεχομένους ἐκ τοῦ θεοῦ] when they succeed in speaking many great things . . . Virtue

(with the explicable exception of just two passages, as already discussed in my 'Socrates' Demand for Definitions'). The word that replaces them is φρόνησις (29 E; cf. 36 C)—a word which continues to be preferred to σοφία, εἰδέναι, and other epistemic words in ethical contexts throughout Plato's works (see e.g. *Prot.* 352 C; *Meno* 88 B ff.; *Phaedo* 69 A–C; *Sym.* 209 A; *Laws* 631 C). Does Plato here echo a linguistic distinction which Socrates had used in order to mark the difference between knowledge, on the one hand, and ethical true belief resulting from divine inspiration, on the other? If so, then it must be admitted that Plato does not stay faithful to Socrates' usage—for example, at *Meno* 97 B ff. Plato groups φρόνησις together with σοφία and ἐπιστήμη and *in contrast to* true belief through divine inspiration. However, Aristotle may be staying more faithful to Socrates' usage in *NE* bk. 6, where he draws a sharp distinction between φρόνησις, on the one hand, and both ἐπιστήμη and τέχνη, on the other.

Socrates' Profession of Ignorance

is found to be . . . imparted to us by a divine dispensation [θείᾳ μοίρᾳ] without understanding in those who receive it. (99 B–100 A)

These doctrines in the *Meno* are, of course, usually interpreted as *Platonic* rather than Socratic. On what grounds do I reject that usual view? Briefly: (1) my main ground is that, as we saw, the same doctrines already seem to be implicit in the *Apology*, the *Crito*, and the *Ion*, and that moreover, as we are about to see, they are also explicitly ascribed to Socrates by an independent authority of weight, Aeschines of Sphettus. (2) The idea that virtue is true belief through divine inspiration seems much more likely to come from Socrates, who places great weight on divine inspiration in other connections, and indeed accepts it as the very source and basis of his philosophical mission, than from Plato, who is generally disinclined to accord it such importance.[14] (3) As far as I can see, the strongest argument *against* the doctrines being Socratic is that they seem to contradict Socrates' identification of virtue with knowledge, which is strongly attested both by Plato's early dialogues and by Aristotle.[15] However, this contradiction is more apparent than real. For the *Meno* not only says that virtue is true belief through divine inspiration rather than knowledge; it also implies that if anyone had *real* virtue, it would be he whose virtue was indeed knowledge—that such a man would be, compared to those whose virtue consists merely in true belief through divine inspiration, 'in respect to virtue, . . . a real substance among shadows' (99 E–100 A). Socrates' full position, as reflected in the *Meno*, is thus that the merely human virtue which men sometimes possess consists in true belief through divine inspiration, although *real* virtue, which no man has (only god—*Ap.* 23 A–B), consists in knowledge. When Plato in the early dialogues makes his Socrates identify virtue with knowledge, he oversimplifies that position, but he does not deeply contradict it. (4) In so far as the denial that these doctrines from the *Meno* are Socratic stems from a general assumption that doctrines which appear for the first time in relatively late works of Plato's are not Socratic, it stems from an assumption which, besides being intrinsically dubious on reflection, is, I think, demonstrably false. For example, Socrates' doctrine that he is a sort of philosophical midwife famously first appears in Plato as late as the *Theaetetus*; yet at Ar. *Clouds* 135–9

[14] Cf. E. de Strycker, 'Die historischen Zeugnisse über Sokrates', in A. Patzer (ed.), *Der historische Sokrates* (Darmstadt, 1987), 323–54 at 328–30.

[15] See e.g. Kraut, *Socrates and the State*, 303–4.

12   *Michael N. Forster*

we already find a joke about the miscarriage of an idea in Socrates' Thinkery (φροντιστήριον), which shows the midwife metaphor to have been genuinely Socratic (cf. *Theaet.* 149 D for a similar reference to 'miscarriages' of ideas).[16] Or to cite another instance, Plato for the first time in the *Meno* with its slave-boy example gives a clear portrayal of Socrates as using a method of education that involves *drawing* insights *from* an interlocutor rather than *communicating* them *to* him, and yet the *Clouds* already ascribes just such a method to Socrates,[17] and it is further confirmed as genuinely Socratic by the fragments of Aeschines' *Alcibiades* (as quoted next).[18]

The explanation of Socrates' profession of ignorance which I have given above receives further confirmation from an independent source of considerable weight: the extant fragments of Aeschines of Sphettus' *Alcibiades*. At the end of this dialogue Socrates lays claim to an ethical capacity. But he draws a distinction between, on the one hand, those capacities which consist in knowledge (or

---

[16] This has been questioned by Burnyeat in 'Socratic Midwifery, Platonic Inspiration', 7, 14 n. 4. But Burnyeat overlooks the (in my opinion) clinching facts that the *Clouds* not only contains the revealing joke just mentioned but also, like the *Theaetetus* and its midwife metaphor, (1) portrays Socrates as using a method of education which involves *drawing* theses *from* an interlocutor rather than *conveying* them *to* him (385 ff., beginning with Socrates' proposal 'I shall teach you from yourself [ἀπὸ σαυτοῦ 'γώ σε διδάξω]'; 695–782, beginning with Socrates' injunction 'Excogitate one of your own concerns [ἐκφρόντισόν τι τῶν σεαυτοῦ πραγμάτων]'), and (2) depicts Socrates as examining and rejecting as worthless the results produced by the interlocutor (that is what happens in the play when Socrates applies the method to Strepsiades; cf. *Theaet.* 149 D, 150 B–C, 151 C–D, and the overall negative outcome of the dialogue as summed up at 210 B).

[17] See the preceding footnote.

[18] Plato's late interest in Socrates' midwife metaphor and in Socrates' method of educating by drawing insights from an interlocutor was presumably sparked by his own development, beginning in the *Meno*, of the doctrine of knowledge as recollection, with which Socrates' metaphor and method then appeared to cohere so well. One may speculate that Plato's late interest in Socrates' doctrine that human virtue is true belief through divine inspiration rather than knowledge was sparked in a rather similar way: in the *Protagoras* Plato, by oversimplifying Socrates' position in the manner indicated in (3) above, had run into the paradox 'Virtue is knowledge, knowledge is by its very nature teachable, yet virtue is not teachable.' Since Socrates' doctrine offered a way out of this paradox, Plato now saw a merit in it that he had not seen before, and therefore presented it as a solution to the paradox in the *Meno*. I suspect that a second and much less textually obvious paradox played an analogous role as well: the *Protagoras* had implied not only that virtue is knowledge but also that virtue is unstable, something people can lose again (344 B–345 C). How could this be, given that knowledge is of its very nature stable (see *Alc. I* 116 E–117 A; *Meno*, 98 A)? The solution in the *Meno*: strictly speaking, human virtue is not quite knowledge but only true belief, and as such lacks the anchorage in a definition [αἰτίας λογισμός] which would render it stable (97 D–98 A).

Socrates' Profession of Ignorance 13

art), and, on the other hand, those which one enjoys through divine dispensation or inspiration. He denies adamantly that his ethical capacity consists in any knowledge (or art). And he insists that he instead enjoys it through divine dispensation or inspiration. His words are as follows:

> If I thought that I could help someone by means of some art [τινι τέχνῃ], I would condemn myself for the greatest foolishness. But in fact I believed that this capacity to help was granted me in connection with Alcibiades by divine dispensation [θείᾳ μοίρᾳ]. And nothing about that need cause surprise. For of the many sick people who get healthy also, some do so by means of human art and some by means of divine dispensation. Those who get healthy by human art do so by being treated by doctors. Those who get healthy by divine dispensation are led by their own impulse to that which is helpful; sometimes they are impelled to vomit, when this will help them, and sometimes to go hunting, when it will help them to exert themselves. But I experienced because of my love for Alcibiades just what the Bacchants experience. For the Bacchants, whenever they are divinely inspired [ἔνθεοι], draw milk and honey from springs where others cannot even fetch water. Thus did I, though I possess no knowledge which I might teach a man in order to benefit him [οὐδὲν μάθημα ἐπιστάμενος, ὃ διδάξας ἄνθρωπον ὠφελήσαιμ᾽ ἄν], yet believe that through accompanying Alcibiades I would improve him [βελτίω ποιῆσαι] because of my love. (fr. 12 Nestle)

In addition to confirming the account already given, this passage brings out one new point: Socrates recognizes, corresponding to his distinction between knowledge (or art), on the one hand, and divinely inspired capacities, on the other, a distinction between *teaching* and *improving*. Hence he claims in this fragment not to *teach* thanks to knowledge (οὐδὲν μάθημα ἐπιστάμενος, ὃ διδάξας ἄνθρωπον ὠφελήσαιμ᾽ ἄν᾽), but instead to *improve* (βελτίω ποιῆσαι) thanks to a divinely inspired capacity. This solves another puzzle which inevitably strikes the reader of Plato's *Apology* and other Platonic dialogues: the puzzle of how Socrates can consistently, on the one hand, deny that he has ever been a teacher or had pupils (33 A) or has ever promised to teach or taught (33 B; cf. his argument in the *Protagoras* for the unteachability of virtue), while, on the other hand, vigorously urging people to accept the right ethical views (28 B–D, 29 D–E, etc.) and indeed explaining his whole life as devoted to the task of morally improving people (29 D–31 B).[19]

---

[19] *Part* of the force of the contrast between teaching and Socratic improving is no doubt also that the latter, unlike the former, usually takes the form of *drawing*

14 *Michael N. Forster*

III

I would suggest that the Platonic texts discussed above also support certain further speculations about Socrates' position. In the *Apology* Socrates says that in the course of testing the oracle he asked the poets for the meaning of what they said in their poems ($\tau \acute{\iota}\ \lambda \acute{\epsilon} \gamma o \iota \epsilon \nu$), and that when he found that they could not answer this question, he inferred that 'they composed what they composed not by wisdom, but by nature and because they were inspired, like the prophets and oracle-givers; for these too say things many and fine [$\pi o \lambda \lambda \grave{\alpha}\ \kappa \alpha \grave{\iota}\ \kappa \alpha \lambda \acute{\alpha}$], but know nothing of what they say [$\H{\iota} \sigma \alpha \sigma \iota \nu\ \delta \grave{\epsilon}\ o \mathring{\upsilon} \delta \grave{\epsilon} \nu\ \mathring{\omega} \nu\ \lambda \acute{\epsilon} \gamma o \upsilon \sigma \iota$]' (22 B–C).

This passage seems to me most plausibly interpreted in the following way. As I argued in 'Socrates' Demand for Definitions', Socrates' request for the poets' meaning ($\tau \acute{\iota}\ \lambda \acute{\epsilon} \gamma o \iota \epsilon \nu$) was his notorious request for a definition of terms ($\tau \acute{\iota}\ \mathring{\epsilon} \sigma \tau \iota\ .\ .\ .;$). Moreover, as I argued there, Socrates believes the possession of definitions to be a necessary condition for understanding the terms one uses (hence, for example, his rhetorical question at *Theaet.* 147 B, 'Does anyone, do you think, understand the name of anything when he does not know what the thing is?' (cf. *Alc. I* 111 B–C; *Chrm.* 159 A)). It follows that the poets' failure to provide satisfactory definitions in response to his request was, in his eyes, a proof that they quite literally did not know the meaning of, did not understand, what they said (hence his extreme view in the *Ion* that when the poet composes, 'his mind is no longer in him [$\acute{o}\ \nu o \mathring{\upsilon} s\ \mu \eta \kappa \acute{\epsilon} \tau \iota\ \mathring{\epsilon} \nu\ \alpha \mathring{\upsilon} \tau \mathring{\omega}\ \mathring{\epsilon} \nu \mathring{\eta}$]', 534 B).

This enables us to interpret the above passage from 22 B–C more fully. In that passage Socrates is giving a highly compressed and

---

the correct view out of an interlocutor rather than *putting it into* him. The Aeschines fragment implies Socrates' employment of such a method in its use of the metaphor of the Bacchants drawing milk and honey out of springs to characterize Socrates' moral improvement of Alcibiades. There is also evidence that this was a characteristic Socratic method in sources as diverse as Plato's dialogues (e.g. the slave-boy example in the *Meno* and the midwife metaphor in the *Theaetetus*) and Aristophanes' *Clouds* (the episodes at 385 ff., 695–783). Moreover, at *Meno* 82 E, 84 C–D Plato actually depicts Socrates' use of this method as his ground for denying that he teaches (cf. *Ap.* 33 B; *Theaet.* 150 D). On the other hand, it seems unlikely that Socrates' use of this method is the *whole* explanation of his denial that he teaches, for it is pretty clear that his instruction was not *confined* to the use of this method (consider, for example, his use of exemplary passages of poetry and direct injunctions in the *Apology*, and his use of extended arguments of his own devising in the *Crito*). Hence we do need some further explanation, such as that offered above.

Socrates' Profession of Ignorance 15

easily overlooked *argument* for both the ignorance and the divine inspiration of the poets (an argument which, he implies, can likewise be used to establish both the ignorance and the divine inspiration of prophets and oracle-givers). He is arguing that because, by failing to provide satisfactory definitions, the poets proved to 'know nothing of what they say', namely in the strong sense of *not understanding* what they say,[20] this showed that they 'did not compose what they composed by wisdom'. And he is arguing that because, by failing to provide satisfactory definitions, they proved to 'know nothing of what they say', namely again in that strong sense, but yet made statements 'many *and fine*', this showed that their statements were instead the work of an inspiring divinity. (Analogously, he implies, the fact that prophets and oracle-givers such as the Delphic Pythia 'know nothing of what they say', namely in the strong sense of not understanding what they say, shows that they do not speak by wisdom, and the fact that they 'know nothing of what they say', namely again in that strong sense, but yet make statements 'many *and fine*' shows that their statements are instead the work of an inspiring divinity.)

Now if this *is* Socrates' argument for the conclusion that the poets compose not by knowledge but by divine inspiration, then we may, I suggest, plausibly infer that it is also his argument for the conclusion that true ethical belief is not knowledge but the result of divine inspiration. Two considerations support such an inference. First, the 'many and fine' statements which in this argument Socrates concludes the poets make not by knowledge but by divine inspiration are almost certainly *themselves* conceived by him to be mainly ethical truths.[21] After all, he is presumably questioning the poets in relation to ethical matters, since those are the matters he considers relevant to the oracle's message. And we know that he did consider poetry to be a source of important ethical truths, and was in the habit of quoting the relevant poetry in order to convey them. For at *Ap.* 28 B–D he quotes a passage from the *Iliad* in order to convey the ethical truth that one must do what one considers right, disdaining death; and at *Mem.* 1. 2. 56–9 Xenophon tells us that he made a practice of quoting poetry in order to convey ethical truths in this way.[22] Second, in so far as Socrates believed that

---

[20] Cf. *Meno* 99 D for the use of the expression in this strong sense.

[21] Cf. the ethical emphasis at *Rep.* 598 D–601 A.

[22] This evidence shows that the historical Socrates' attitude towards traditional

16   *Michael N. Forster*

people other than the poets—in particular, he himself—possessed
ethical truths, he must surely have been *driven* to apply just the
same argument to them as he applied to the poets. For, as we see in
the early dialogues, he found not only the poets but also everyone
else, including himself, to be at a loss for satisfactory definitions
of ethical terms.

We have, then, at least some reason to think that Socrates' argument for ethical insight being not knowledge but divinely inspired
true belief was the argument which he implies in the passage on the
poets: since possession of definitions is a precondition of understanding, people's lack of ethical definitions shows that they quite
literally do not understand their ethical claims. From this it of
course follows that their ethical claims cannot constitute knowledge. And furthermore, since many of these claims, despite not
being understood by those who make them, are yet clearly fine and
right, it follows that they must instead have a divine source.[23]

poetry must have been much less negative than it can appear from such Platonic
texts as the *Ion*, the *Protagoras*, the *Gorgias*, and especially the *Republic*. It seems
fairly clear that the historical Socrates did deplore large areas of traditional poetry,
especially tragedy (this can already be seen from Aristophanes' *Frogs* 1491–5), and
that he in particular objected to the false and immoral portrayals of the gods found
there (see already *Euthph.* 6 A–C). But the above passages show that he just as surely
saw other parts of traditional poetry as sources of ethical truth. Indeed, even in
the *Republic* he is still portrayed as approving of *parts* of Homer in this spirit (see
e.g. 389 E, 390 C–D), and a yet more striking and instructive example of the positive
side of his attitude to traditional poetry can be seen in his response, beginning
in bk. 1, to the poet Simonides' account of justice as 'rendering to each person
what is due to him' (331 E): Socrates assumes that Simonides is 'wise and divine'
(ibid.), and he accordingly proceeds in bk. 1 to run through a number of possible
interpretations of Simonides' account, dismissing those which would make it false
(very much as in the *Apology* he assumes the divine source and hence truth of the
oracle and accordingly sets out to dismiss interpretations of it which would make
it false—cf. M. Stokes, 'Socrates' Mission', in B. S. Gower and M. Stokes (eds.),
Socratic Questions: New Essays on the Philosophy of Socrates and its Significance
(London and New York, 1992), 26–81 at 37–8), never rejecting Simonides' account
itself, but on the contrary later in the work himself coming to a definition of justice
which he evidently conceives as capturing the real content of Simonides' account
(cf. T. H. Irwin, *Plato's Ethics* (Oxford, 1995), 173–4). The combination of positive
and negative attitudes towards traditional poetry which we see Socrates exhibiting
in all of this evidence should not really be surprising: Hesiod already tells us at
Th. 26–8 that the Muses convey both truths and falsehoods in poetry (albeit that
Socrates would differ from Hesiod in laying the responsibility for the falsehoods at
human doorsteps rather than divine).

[23] The interpretation developed so far prompts a question: *Why*, in Socrates'
view, do ethical terms and claims exhibit these peculiarities? *Why* are the grasp of
ethical definitions and hence the understanding of ethical terms, and hence also the

Socrates' Profession of Ignorance 17

The *Meno* supports these interpretative speculations. At *Meno* 97 D–98 A Socrates argues that the distinguishing mark of knowledge, as opposed to mere true belief, is that knowledge is anchored in the soul by a definition, an αἰτίας λογισμός (cf. *Phaedo* 76 B).[24] Hence, as I just inferred from the passage on the poets, it is because those who possess ethical insight cannot give definitions of their ethical terms that Socrates believes them not to possess knowledge. Moreover, Socrates indicates in the *Meno* that, as I just inferred from the passage on the poets, he believes the possession of ethical true belief to be literally 'without understanding [ἄνευ νοῦ]' (99 E; cf. 99 C–D).[25] He does not explicitly say *why* he takes this extreme view,

understanding and knowledge of ethical claims, unavailable to human beings, only available to gods, whereas in the case of non-evaluative subject-matters, by contrast, human beings do possess definitions, understanding, and knowledge? As far as I am aware, Socrates nowhere explicitly addresses this question. However, it seems likely that his answer to it would be roughly as follows: since ethical matters are 'the . . . matters of most importance' (*Ap.* 22 D), it is natural that the gods would preserve them as their own cognitive prerogative.

[24] The unusual expression αἰτίας λογισμός, literally an 'account of cause', is equivalent to more usual Platonic expressions for a definition such as λόγος or λόγος τῆς οὐσίας. That Socrates does mean a definition by an αἰτίας λογισμός is shown in the *Meno* by his statement at 98 A that he and Meno have agreed that arriving at an αἰτίας λογισμός is a matter of recollection, for this must refer back to 80 D–81 E, where Socrates had argued that discovering the definition of virtue is possible because the soul knows everything from a previous life and so need only recollect what virtue is, and to 86 B–C, where he had reiterated this position that defining virtue is possible through recollection after proving the theory of recollection to Meno by means of the slave-boy example (cf. *Phdr.* 249 C for the word λογισμός used alone in the sense of a definition). The full expression αἰτίας λογισμός is explained by the fact that Socrates understands the form or εἶδος which a definition describes (e.g. strength) to be in some sense the *cause* of a particular thing's possession of the corresponding quality (e.g. so-and-so's being strong). Hence at *Meno* 72 E a strong woman is said to be strong 'by reason of' (instrumental dative) the form of strength, and at 72 C virtue is said to be the form 'because of which [δι' ὅ]' particular virtues are virtues (cf. *Phaedo* 100 B–101 C, where forms are similarly characterized as causes; also *Euthph.* 6 D). (The question of the *nature* of the causation involved is of course a further matter.)

[25] Kraut says that 'in this passage to lack νοῦς is merely to lack knowledge or wisdom' (*Socrates and the State*, 302–3 n. 82). But this seems to me incorrect. The passages which Kraut adduces as evidence (*Meno* 88 B, *La.* 188 B, etc.) do indeed show that lack of νοῦς *can* mean no more than ignorance or stupidity. However, the passages which it is more relevant to consider here are the ones in the *Ion* which discuss the lack of νοῦς of the poets, prophets, and oracle-givers, for it is to these people that the *Meno* is comparing men who have ethical insight (99 C). The lack of νοῦς that is said to affect such people in the *Ion* is far more than a mere lack of knowledge; it is a complete lack of understanding (534 B–D). (On the other hand, Kraut seems to me correct to say that lack of νοῦς does not imply lack of *reasons* (*Socrates and the State*, 303 n. 82). The Socrates of the *Crito* presumably considers

18   *Michael N. Forster*

but it seems reasonable to infer that his ground for it is the mere true believer's lack of definitions. For, as has been mentioned, there is strong evidence that Socrates considers the possession of definitions to be a necessary condition for understanding (*Alc. I* 111 B–C; *Chrm.* 159 A; *Theaet.* 147 B).[26] If this *is* his implicit reason in the *Meno* for holding that ethical true belief is 'without understanding', then his full argument there for the position that ethical insight is not knowledge seems to be as follows: ethical believers lack ethical definitions; since definitions are a prerequisite for understanding, this shows that they literally fail to understand their own ethical claims; therefore these claims cannot constitute knowledge. In other words, we here again find Socrates relying on the first part of the argument to which the passage on the poets pointed.[27]

Similarly concerning the second part of that argument. At *Meno* 99 C–D Socrates in effect argues that if, like certain ethical believers, one has no understanding of one's ethical claims, and yet they are fine claims (correct and beneficial for action), then this shows that they must be the result of divine inspiration:

> SOC. And may we . . . rightly call those men divine who, having no understanding, yet succeed in many a great [μεγάλα] deed and word?

himself to possess his divinely inspired ethical beliefs concerning obedience to the laws without νοῦς, but he none the less has quite elaborate divinely inspired reasons in support of them.)

[26] The situation is complicated, though. While I do believe that the *Meno* is still implicitly relying on this consideration, I do not think that the work's failure to articulate it explicitly is merely an accidental omission. Rather, it occurs because the work is beginning to develop a new Platonic line of thought that is in sharp tension with this consideration, namely a line of thought (which I have discussed in 'Socrates' Demand for Definitions') to the effect that understanding comes in degrees, and that positive degrees of understanding can occur even without an ability to state a definition.

[27] It is, of course, a consequence of this interpretation that the historical Socrates considered human ethical insight to be at bottom an acceptance of uncomprehended true sentences. I can imagine someone being prepared to tolerate that as an interpretative possibility and yet balking at the further consequence that when Socrates is depicted as basing ethical insight on reasoning, as at the end of the *Apology* or in the *Crito* for example, he must consider such reasoning to be again a matter of intuiting logical relations between uncomprehended true sentences. However, I would suggest that such an asymmetry of response is in fact unwarranted, that if Socrates can accept the one consequence then he can just as well accept the other. Indeed, since it is part of the very nature of deductive inference that it is possible to recognize its validity without comprehending the non-logical vocabulary involved, to this extent at least one should actually find it *easier* to ascribe to Socrates a conception of uncomprehended reasonings than to ascribe to him a conception of uncomprehended beliefs.

Socrates' Profession of Ignorance

MENO. Certainly.

SOC. Then . . . we can say of the statesmen that they are divine and inspired, since they are under the influence and possession of the god when they succeed in speaking many great things, while knowing nothing of what they say.

On the reasonable assumption, once again, that Socrates' implicit ground here for holding that men have no understanding of their ethical claims is their lack of ethical definitions, we have here precisely a version of the argument for ethical insight being divinely inspired to which the *Apology*'s passage on the poets pointed: people who possess ethical insight have no definitions of their ethical terms; since definitions are a prerequisite for understanding, this shows that they do not understand their ethical claims; yet these are fine claims (correct and beneficial for action); therefore one must infer that they have a divine source.

Now there may be a temptation to object that this argument would involve either outright absurdity or vicious circularity, and in too crass a way for its attribution to Socrates to be plausible. The threatening outright absurdity: in identifying people as possessing ethical insight, or invoking the 'fineness' or 'greatness' of their ethical claims, in order thence to infer the divine source of those claims, would Socrates not himself have to be making ethical claims, ones which his demonstration that nobody possesses ethical definitions, and that therefore nobody understands his own ethical claims, invalidates? The threatening vicious circularity: in order to cope with that problem, would Socrates not have to be already assuming that certain ethical claims, in particular his own, had a divine source, and hence already assuming what he is setting out to prove? For, while it is indeed usually rational to react to a discovery that one fails to understand a claim one has made by retracting the claim, there will admittedly be exceptions in cases where one can rely on authorities (for example, the layman relies on the physicists' testimony that '$E=mc^2$'), but in this case human authorities are ruled out because human beings all lack ethical definitions and hence any understanding of ethical claims, so it looks as though, in order to avoid the outright absurdity that threatens, Socrates could only be appealing to divine authorities. However, there may in fact be an alternative way for Socrates to avoid the Scylla of outright absurdity *without* perishing on the Charybdis of vicious circularity. Suppose someone were to discover that nobody, including himself, under-

20   *Michael N. Forster*

stood some really central and indispensable area of discourse—such as ethics arguably is—but still felt strongly inclined to make certain claims and to deny others in it. Might it not be rational of him to make an exception to the rule of retraction in such a case too (i.e. even without any appeal to authorities)? If so, then Socrates could reasonably be making certain admittedly uncomprehended ethical claims (perhaps some of them without any deeper justification, but others justified in terms of their derivability from those ones, as in the *Crito*) without depending on any justificatory appeal to a divine source as an authority—and hence escape not only outright absurdity but also vicious circularity.

Nor does another consideration which might be thought to force his argument into vicious circularity apply. On a divine-command conception of morality (like that of Duns Scotus, for example), 'fine' or 'great' might actually *mean* (or at least *imply*) divinely commanded, in which case there would clearly be a vicious circle in arguing from a premiss that such-and-such ethical claims are 'fine' or 'great' to the conclusion that ethical claims have a divine source. However, there is in fact no question of a divine-command conception of morality being involved here; the oracle story in the *Apology* represents the god of the oracle as *knowing* ethical truths (not making them), and in the *Euthyphro* Socrates' refutation of Euthpyhro's definition of the pious as what is loved by all the gods takes it as axiomatic that what is pious is loved by the gods because it is pious, not pious because it is loved by the gods.

The *Meno* also shows that an additional argument supported Socrates' conviction that ethical insight was not knowledge but instead the result of divine inspiration. In effect, the argument is as follows: ethical insight is not teachable; men have no control over who does and who does not attain it (89 D–96 D).[28] But knowledge is of its very nature teachable (87 B–C, 89 C).[29] Therefore ethical insight is not knowledge (99 A–B). Moreover, since a person's attainment of ethical insight is not controlled by men (89 D–96 D), and it is not controlled by the person's inborn nature either (89 A–

---

[28] Cf. *Prot.* 319 A–320 B. Note also Diogenes Laertius' report that Socrates' followers Crito and Simon wrote Socratic dialogues with the titles *That Men are Not Made Good by Instruction* and *Of Virtue, that it Cannot be Taught* respectively (D.L. 2. 12–13). I agree with Kraut, *Socrates and the State*, 247 ff., that Socrates' denial of the teachability of virtue must be considered quite sincere.

[29] Cf. *Prot.* 361 A–B.

Socrates' Profession of Ignorance

B, 98 D–E),[30] one must infer that it is instead controlled by the gods: 'Virtue is found to be neither natural nor taught, but is imparted to us by a divine dispensation [θεία μοίρα]' (99 E).[31]

IV

If the account of Socrates' position given so far is broadly correct, then it is appropriate to ask how exactly he conceives the mechanisms and sources of the divine inspiration which lends him his ethical insights.

It is, of course, tempting to speculate that he regards his notorious δαιμόνιον as the *mechanism* responsible.[32] And the role of the δαιμόνιον in leading him to the insight that death is a good thing at the end of the *Apology*, together with its similar role in leading him to see that one should stay out of politics at *Ap.* 31 D–32 A, shows that there must be some truth in this.

However, I think it would be a mistake to exaggerate the role of the δαιμόνιον. For one thing, there is little or no textual evidence of the δαιμόνιον establishing further ethical principles for Socrates. For another thing, the case at the end of the *Apology* is peculiar in that it was the *inactivity* of the δαιμόνιον which did the work, not its activity. For yet another thing, several characteristics of the δαιμόνιον, as Plato and Xenophon describe it, make it seem a relatively unlikely source of ethical insights: as characterized by Plato, it only forbids but never enjoins (*Ap.* 31 D); in both Plato and Xenophon it always concerns some specific course of action rather than a general principle (at least in the first instance); in both it is almost always narrowly prudential and predictive rather than moral; and in both it is often concerned with rather trivial

---

[30] In some additional fragments from Aeschines' *Alcibiades* Socrates similarly argues that good judgement is not an inborn trait (P.Oxy. xiii, no. 1608, frr. 1–4).

[31] If the account given so far is correct, then we must revise even the judgement of one of the recent commentators who has been most hospitable to the religious side of Socrates' thought, McPherran, who writes of 'Socrates' and Plato's general disparagement of divine inspiration as a source of intellectual and moral guidance' (*The Religion of Socrates*, 196). Such a judgement is true enough of Plato, but not of the historical Socrates.

[32] Accordingly, at least one attempt has recently been made to interpret the δαιμόνιον as the mechanism responsible for his ethical inspiration: Brickhouse and Smith, *Socrates on Trial*, 242 ff.

22   *Michael N. Forster*

matters (for example, avoiding being bowled over in the street by a herd of stampeding pigs!).

This point is of some importance for the following reason (among others). If one assumed that Socrates normally identified the δαι-μόνιον as the mechanism of his ethical inspiration, then one would infer that he normally thought of his ethical inspiration as a *direct* communication from god to man, since he seems to understand the δαιμόνιον in that way (at Xen. *Ap.* 12 he refers to the δαιμόνιον as 'a voice of god [θεοῦ . . . φωνή]'; cf. Plato, *Ap.* 21 D). However, such a *direct* conception of his ethical inspiration may very well not be his usual one at all.

Thus, he certainly at least entertains the possibility of *indirect* ethical inspiration—that is, inspiration by a god via one or more persons acting as intermediaries—in the case of *other* people. That much is implied by his efforts to improve others by communicating his own divinely inspired ethical insights to them, as those efforts are depicted in such texts as Plato's *Apology* and Aeschines' *Alcibiades*. And in the *Symposium* it is suggested that ethical inspiration can occur at a still further remove from its divine source, that the inspiring power of Socrates' discourses entrances and possesses not only those who hear them from Socrates himself but also those who hear them from somebody who has heard them from Socrates: 'As soon as we hear you [Socrates], or your discourses in the mouth of another . . . we are entranced and possessed [ἐκπεπληγμένοι ἐσμὲν καὶ κατεχόμεθα]' (215 D). Indeed, Socrates probably thought it possible for people to receive indirect ethical inspiration via a fairly long human chain or tradition, just as long as that chain or tradition originated with direct inspiration by a divinity. For it is in this way that he envisages divine inspiration operating in the case of poetry in the *Ion*, and we have seen at least some reason to think that he regarded poetry as the mechanism of part of people's ethical inspiration. In the *Ion* he likens the poetic inspiration of the Muse to a magnet which

not only attracts iron rings, but also imparts to them a power whereby they in turn are able to do the very same thing . . ., and attract other rings; so that sometimes there is formed quite a long chain of bits of iron and rings, suspended one from another; and they all depend for this power on that one stone [the magnet]. In the same manner the Muse inspires men herself, and then by means of these inspired persons the inspiration spreads to others, and holds them in a connected chain. (533 D–E; cf. 535 E–536 A)

Socrates' Profession of Ignorance 23

Now, if this is the way in which Socrates envisages divine ethical inspiration operating in the case of *other* people, then it is, I suggest, at least a possibility that he may also understand some of his *own* ethical insights to have been inspired in an indirect way, that he may see *himself* as, on some ethical matters at least, a 'ring' at several, or even many, removes from the divine 'magnet'. None of the three texts in which he most explicitly invokes the inspirational model of ethical insight—the *Crito*, the *Meno*, and Aeschines' *Alcibiades*—contains any real obstacle to supposing that this may be his view. (Part of the significance of this point will become clear in the next section.)

V

If Socrates understood his ethical insight to be divinely inspired, then it also makes sense to ask whether he had any more precise conception of its divine *source*.

We know that he was especially devoted to one god in particular: Apollo. The evidence for this is abundant in both Plato and Xenophon. For example, Plato's *Phaedo* from beginning to end bears witness to Socrates' special devotion to Apollo, not least in Socrates' statement there that like the swans he is a servant of Apollo, consecrated to this god and imbued by him with a gift of prophecy (84 E–85 B).[33] And Plato's *Apology* of course explains Socrates' life as lived in obedience to a mission imposed on him by Apollo through the Delphic oracle. In addition, there are many further references in Plato and Xenophon to Socrates' deference towards Apollo's oracle at Delphi.[34]

More specifically, we know beyond reasonable doubt that Socrates devoted his life to philosophical activity because he understood this to have been ordained by Apollo, and we even know in some detail how he understood this command to have been communicated to him. In the *Apology* he tells us that Apollo commanded him to engage in his philosophical cross-examinations 'through oracles and dreams and in every way in which any man was ever commanded by divine power to do anything whatsoever' (33 C). As

---

[33] Cf. *Euthd.* 302 C–D.
[34] See esp. *Alc. I* 124 A–B; *Phaedr.* 229 D–230 A; Xen. *Anab.* 3. 1. 5–7; *Mem.* 1. 3. 1; 4. 3. 16–17; 4. 6. 24.

24   *Michael N. Forster*

to *oracles*, the *Apology* of course itself explains in detail the role of the message delivered to Chaerephon by Apollo through his oracle at Delphi. As to *dreams*, we learn in the *Phaedo* that Socrates repeatedly received dreams telling him to make 'music [μουσική]' and work at it, and that he understood these as commands to engage in philosophical activity (60 E–61 A). And lest there be any doubt as to his view of the divine source of these dreams, we are told that while in jail, just in case they after all meant 'music' in a narrower sense, he set about composing verses, first among them a hymn to *Apollo* (60 D, 61 B). As to other ways in which he received Apollo's command, it is, for example, pretty clear from a variety of sources that Socrates understood the maxim of the Delphic oracle 'Know thyself [Γνῶθι σεαυτόν]' as an injunction to philosophical cross-examination.[35]

In view of Socrates' special devotion to Apollo in general, and Socrates' understanding of his philosophical activity as commanded by and serving Apollo in particular, it would hardly be surprising if he understood this god to be the primary source of his own ethical inspiration. Indeed, it would be somewhat surprising if he

[35] The following evidence strongly suggests this. (1) Xen. *Mem.* 4. 2. 24–5: Xenophon has Socrates explain his subjection of an interlocutor to a demoralizing refutation (4. 2. 1–23) by reminding the interlocutor of this Delphic maxim. (2) Aristotle, as reported at Plut. *Adv. Col.* 1118 C: Aristotle says that 'Know thyself' seemed to Socrates the most divine of the Delphic maxims, and that it 'was the original source of Socrates' perplexity and search'. (3) Ar. *Clouds* 842: Aristophanes apparently makes a humorous allusion to Socrates' association of the duty to refute with this Delphic maxim when he has Strepsiades, newly instructed in Socratic learning, say to his son, 'Thou shalt know thyself, that thou art ignorant and dense [γνώσει δὲ σαυτὸν ὡς ἀμαθὴς εἶ καὶ παχύς]'. (4) At *Phileb.* 48 C–49 A Socrates interprets the maxim as including an injunction not to suppose that one has wisdom when one does not. (5) At *Chrm.* 167 A Socrates considers an interpretation of the maxim which equates knowing oneself with knowing what one does and does not know, and knowing what other people do and do not know, but merely believe they do, i.e. with just the sort of 'human wisdom' enjoined on him by the oracle's message to Chaerephon as related in the *Apology* (on the other hand, it is admittedly puzzling that in the *Charmides* Socrates fails to embrace this as his own position, and indeed criticizes it; perhaps Plato is using his literary mouthpiece 'Socrates' to test a position originally held by the historical Socrates?).

Since the maxim was traditionally interpreted as a warning that men should know and keep to their lowly place in relation to the gods, one can readily understand that Socrates must have interpreted its message as similar to that of the oracle given to Chaerephon: that, god alone being truly wise, human beings' wisdom is of little or no value (*Ap.* 23 A). And one can readily understand that, just as Socrates saw his refuting activity as standing in the service of demonstrating and disseminating this oracular message (23 B), so he must have seen it as standing in the service of demonstrating and disseminating the message of the maxim.

Socrates' Profession of Ignorance
25

did not (after all, he does say at *Ap.* 23 A that Apollo possesses the ethical knowledge which he and other human beings lack). And I would suggest that—especially when one keeps in mind the possibility raised in the previous section that he saw himself as at least to some extent *indirectly* inspired via a human tradition—there turns out to be a sufficiently striking congruence between his substantive ethical views and ethical views associated with one or another known Apolline milieu to bear out the suspicion that he believes Apollo to be the primary source of his ethical inspiration.

In order to see this, let us focus on three complexes of ideas central to Socratic ethics. The first such complex is the doctrine of the *Apology* that people should care for practical judgement ($\phi\rho\acute{o}\nu\eta\sigma\iota\varsigma$), truth ($\mathring{\alpha}\lambda\acute{\eta}\theta\epsilon\iota\alpha$), perfection of the soul ($\psi\upsilon\chi\acute{\eta}$), and virtue ($\mathring{\alpha}\rho\epsilon\tau\acute{\eta}$) before wealth, honour, reputation, and their bodies.[36] As Burnet emphasized, such a doctrine was far from being a commonplace at the date when Socrates advanced it.[37] None the less, its various parts were all strikingly anticipated by sources (both philosophical and non-philosophical) intimately associated with Apollo.

Consider, first, the positive side of the doctrine: the injunction to care for practical judgement, truth, perfection of the soul, and virtue (*qua* perfection of the soul). The most distinctive ideal here is that of perfecting one's soul. This ideal was no commonplace when Socrates advanced it. The very conception of the soul which it employs would probably still have seemed strange to most people: at a time when most of them probably still had a version of the Homeric conception of it as merely the insubstantial shade or ghost that left a man's body at death, Socrates was identifying it with the person and making it the possessor of the person's intellectual and moral qualities. Accordingly, Aristophanes could rely on a mere reference to the 'clever souls [$\psi\upsilon\chi\alpha\grave{\iota}$ $\sigma o\phi\alpha\acute{\iota}$]' of Socrates' Thinkery to raise a laugh among his contemporaries (*Clouds* 94). However, this conception of the soul and the ideal of perfecting the soul were not unprecedented either. Where did they come from? Tragedy con-

---

[36] That this doctrine is genuinely Socratic is confirmed by its attribution to Socrates, or repetition, in several other first-generation sources besides Plato. Concerning the whole doctrine, see e.g. Ar. *Clouds* 414–22, 439–42; Aeschines, fr. 29 Nestle; Antisthenes, at Xen. *Sym.* 4. 34–45 and frr. 57, 65, 72, 73 Nestle. On the central idea of care for the soul specifically, see e.g. Xen. *Mem.* 1. 2. 4; Aeschines, fr. 29 Nestle; Antisthenes at Xen. *Sym.* 4. 34–45 and fr. 65 Nestle.

[37] J. Burnet, 'The Socratic Doctrine of the Soul', *Proceedings of the British Academy*, 7 (1916), 235–59 at 243 ff.

26 *Michael N. Forster*

tains precedents for both.[38] But in all probability Socrates' main source for them was Pythagoras and his followers, with whom Plato closely associates Socrates in his ideas concerning the soul in the *Phaedo*.[39] Pythagoras seems to have been the first thinker to develop a conception of the soul somewhat like Socrates'.[40] And the ideal of perfecting the soul was developed by Pythagoras as well. Thus Diogenes Laertius ascribes to Pythagoras the view that 'the most momentous thing in life is the art of winning the soul to good or to evil. Blessed are the men who acquire a good soul' (D.L. 8. 32); and in an ode which Pindar wrote under Pythagorean influence early in the fifth century we read of the blessings enjoyed by 'those who . . . have . . . been courageous in keeping their souls pure from all deeds of wrong' (*Ol.* 2. 68–70). Moreover, Socrates' closely related ideas concerning the soul's afterlife and judgement, of which there is evidence not only in several Platonic dialogues but also in Aristophanes' *Birds*,[41] point in a similar direction. Once again these have precedents in tragedy,[42] but once again it is probable that they are mainly of Pythagorean provenance.[43] Now (and

[38] A conception of the soul rather like Socrates' already occurs fairly frequently in tragedy. And Aeschylus already implies the ideal of having a good soul: see A. W. H. Adkins, *Merit and Responsibility: A Study in Greek Values* (Chicago and London, 1975), 248–9.

[39] Cf. *Rep.* 600 A–B, where Socrates speaks approvingly of Pythagoras' way of life generally.

[40] *Pace* Burnet, 'The Socratic Doctrine of the Soul', 252. The most important evidence that Pythagoras abandoned the Homeric conception of the soul as a mere shade, identified it with the person, and ascribed mental functions to it is Xenophanes fr. 7, where Pythagoras, who believed in metempsychosis, is said to have told a man to stop beating a puppy because 'it is the soul of a friend of mine which I recognized when I heard its voice' (this evidence, overlooked by Burnet, is discussed by D. Furley, 'The Early History of the Concept of the Soul', *Bulletin of the Institute of Classical Studies*, 3 (1956), 1–18 at 4, 11).

[41] That the historical Socrates really did hold something like the suspicions about the soul's afterlife and judgement which Plato attributes to him in the *Apology*, the *Crito*, the *Gorgias*, and the *Phaedo* seems beyond much doubt in the light of *Birds* 1553–64.

[42] Aeschylus in particular had expressed such ideas (see Adkins, *Merit and Responsibility*, 143–4).

[43] It is indeed in connection with this particular aspect of Socrates' theory of the soul that we have what is perhaps the most explicit evidence in Plato that the theory was Pythagorean in origin. At *Meno* 81 A–B Socrates attributes the doctrine of the soul's immortality and judgement to 'certain priests and priestesses who have studied so as to be able to give a reasoned account of their ministry; and Pindar also', and he goes on to quote a passage from one of Pindar's Pythagorean-inspired poems on the subject. It is fairly certain that the priests and priestesses in question are the Pythagoreans, and the reference to and quotation from Pindar provide another

Socrates' Profession of Ignorance 27

this is the crucial point), it is well known that Pythagoras was intimately associated with Apollo.[44] In Diogenes Laertius alone we find reports that Pythagoras sacrificed only at the altar of Apollo, that he was said to have obtained most of his doctrines from the Delphic priestess, even that his followers thought he *was* Apollo.[45] The rest of the positive side of Socrates' doctrine—his injunction to care for practical judgement and truth—also has precedents with an Apolline background. For example, a saying of Pittacus, one of the seven wise men traditionally associated with Apollo, includes the prescription 'Love . . . practical judgement [φρόνησις], truth [ἀλήθεια] . . .'.[46]

Consider next the negative side of Socrates' doctrine, the side requiring subordination of concerns for wealth, honour, reputation, and the body. This is a version of Socrates' insistence on ἐγκράτεια, or the subordination and control of (bodily) desires—an insistence expressed by Plato's Socrates at *Rep.* 430 E ff., most heavily emphasized by Xenophon and Antisthenes,[47] and confirmed as genuinely Socratic by the earlier evidence of the comic playwrights.[48] Now, this feature of Socrates' morality is a version of the characteristically Apolline virtue of temperance [σωφροσύνη], which finds expression in the Delphic maxim 'Nothing too much [Μηδὲν ἄγαν]',[49] and in numerous sayings of the seven wise men traditionally associated with Apollo, such as 'Lack of self-control is a harmful

link to Pythagoreanism. The *Phaedo* of course furnishes additional evidence of a Pythagorean background here, again showing Socrates' account of the soul's afterlife and judgement in close association with Pythagoreanism.

[44] See W. K. C. Guthrie, *The Greeks and their Gods* (Boston, 1955), 197–8; H. W. Parke and D. E. W. Wormell, *The Delphic Oracle* (Oxford, 1956), 401.

[45] D.L. 8. 13, 37, 8, 11. Another thinker who may possibly have had some influence on Socrates' conception of the soul is Heraclitus, who at least broke with the traditional conception to the extent of ascribing intellectual and moral properties to it—as can be seen from fr. 118, where he says that a dry soul is *wisest* and *best* (cf. frr. 98, 107). Like Pythagoras, Heraclitus would bear out my point concerning the Apolline background of Socrates' views (Heraclitus' Apolline and Delphic commitments are evident in frr. 51, 92, 93, 101, 116).

[46] O. Barowski, 'Sieben Weise', in *RE* ii/4. 2242–64 at 2259.

[47] Xenophon's Socrates describes ἐγκράτεια as 'the foundation of all virtue' (*Mem.* 1. 5. 4; cf. Xen. *Ap.* 16). For Antisthenes' adoption of this ideal, see e.g. Xen. *Sym.* 34–45 and frr. 12, 13 Nestle.

[48] See e.g. Ar. *Clouds* 414–22, 439–42. The evidence is fully discussed by H. Gomperz, 'Die sokratische Frage als geschichtliches Problem', in Patzer (ed.), *Der historische Sokrates*, 184–224.

[49] Also, albeit less obviously, in the Delphic maxim 'Know thyself' (see *Alc. I* 131 B, 133 C; *Chrm.* 164 D).

28   *Michael N. Forster*

thing [βλαβερὸν ἀκρασία]' and several sayings which enjoin a care for virtue over pleasure.[50]

The second complex of Socratic ethical ideas which we should consider concerns laws, oaths, and authority. Socrates' profound respect for law is well attested. Plato and Xenophon both emphasize this aspect of his ethical outlook in recounting his behaviour during the trial of the sea generals after the battle of Arginusae (Plato, *Ap.* 32 B–C; Xen. *Mem.* 4. 4. 2 and *Hell.* 1. 7. 14–15); Xenophon in one place gives an extended illustration of Socrates' deep respect for law, citing in addition to his behaviour during the trial of the sea generals his refusal to obey the Thirty Tyrants by arresting Leon of Salamis and his refusal to flatter the jury during his own trial (*Mem.* 4. 4. 1–4); and Plato's *Crito* is of course from beginning to end devoted to illustrating and explaining Socrates' deep respect for law. Now, this ethical attitude is very characteristic of devotees of Apollo, since Apollo is the god most intimately associated with the giving and protection of laws.[51] This special association of Apollo with law, together with the fact that in speaking of 'the god [ὁ θεός]' in the *Apology* Socrates clearly means Apollo, makes it virtually certain that when at the end of the *Crito* Socrates says that 'the god' has guided his argument for obedience to the laws, that god is none other than Apollo. Moreover, we have further evidence that he attributed his respect for law to Apollo's inspiration in the form of a report by Xenophon that he used to follow, and counselled others to follow, a response of Apollo's oracle at Delphi, 'Follow the law of the state: that is the way to act piously' (*Mem.* 1. 3. 1; 4. 3. 16–17).[52] So, at least where this part of Socrates' ethical outlook is concerned, it seems almost certain that the hypothesis that he understood Apollo to be the source of his ethical inspiration is correct.

Related to Socrates' respect for law is his respect for oaths. This is prominent in his explanation at *Ap.* 35 C–D of why it would be wrong of him to beg his judges to acquit him; and again in his explanation at *Mem.* 1. 1. 18 of his behaviour during the Arginusae trial. It also lies behind his striking use in casual contexts of such

---

[50] Barowski, 'Sieben Weise', 2256, 2258.

[51] For an account of this function of Apollo, see Guthrie, *The Greeks and their Gods*, 183 ff. This function was especially associated with Apollo in Sparta, a state for which Socrates is known to have had a special affinity.

[52] Cf. *Rep.* 427 B–C.

Socrates' Profession of Ignorance

pseudo-oaths as 'by the dog' in place of oaths naming the gods. For such pseudo-oaths were used in order to avoid swearing by the gods, as a sign of deep respect for the gods and their oaths.[53] Now, it was again one of Apollo's special functions to watch over the keeping of oaths.[54] And concerning Socrates' avoidance of casually swearing by the gods in particular, it is recorded that among the precepts of Apollo's oracle at Delphi was one that read 'Use no oath [ὅρκῳ μὴ χρῶ]'.[55]

One should also consider here, as related to Socrates' insistence on respect for laws and oaths, his insistence on respect for authority. This is exemplified in the principle, which he states in the *Apology*, that it is bad to disobey a better, whether man or god (29 B; cf. 28 D– 29 A; *Crito* 50 E–51 C). It is also exemplified in his reported fondness for a famous Homeric passage which forcefully makes the point that one should obey one's betters, namely the Thersites passage from *Iliad* book 2 (Xen. *Mem.* 1. 2. 58; cf. *Rep.* 389 D–E). Now, insistence on respect for authority is once again a characteristic theme of Apolline ethics. For example, among the Delphic maxims are found 'Fear authority' and 'Bow before the divine'.[56]

Third and finally, consider the following Socratic religious doctrines intimately bound up with his ethical outlook: the doctrines of the *Apology* that the gods do not allow a good man to come to harm in life or after death (41 C–D), and that it is not divine law for a better man to be injured by a worse (30 D); and the closely related doctrine attributed to Socrates by Aeschines that it is a mistake to believe that 'good and bad men enjoy the same fortune, rather than that the gods grant a better fate to virtuous and more pious men'.[57] Views of this sort were at this period by no means the commonplaces that they are likely to sound to our ears today. However,

---

[53] A scholiast reports that such 'Rhadamanthian' oaths were used 'in order to avoid swearing by the gods' (see Plato, *Euthyphro, Apology of Socrates, Crito*, ed. J. Burnet (Oxford, 1924; repr. 1986), 173–4). That the intention was pious rather than the opposite, if not already sufficiently shown by Socrates' otherwise pious nature, is confirmed by the fact that Delphi encouraged such an avoidance of oaths (as my main text goes on to show), and also by Libanius' discussion of the matter in his *Apology*, which makes this point (*Ap.* (=*Decl.* 1) 109, v. 74 Foerster).

[54] K. Wernicke, 'Apollon', in *RE* i/3. 1–111 at 14. (This function also belonged to Zeus.)

[55] W. Dittenberger, *Sylloge inscriptionum Graecarum*, 4th edn. (Hildesheim, 1960), iii, no. 1268.   [56] Ibid.

[57] Fr. 9 Nestle. It seems likely that these religious doctrines were at least part of Socrates' grounds for his principle that virtue is necessary and sufficient for happiness (*Gorg.* 470 E ff.; cf. Antisthenes, fr. 12 Nestle; Aeschines, fr. 29 Nestle).

30 *Michael N. Forster*

they were already circulating in close connection with Apollo by the last decades of the fifth century. This can be seen from Euripides' *Ion*. Written during Athens' trials in the Peloponnesian wars, and in particular her bitter experience of the Delphic oracle's bias in favour of the Spartan cause, this play has sometimes been read as an indictment of Apollo. In truth, however, it is rather a reaffirmation of faith in the god: after apparently abandoning Ion and Creusa, Apollo in the end arranges things for their best advantage (just as, one may infer Euripides hoped, he would arrange things for Athens' best advantage after his apparent abandonment of her). The closing lines of the play express this reaffirmation of faith in Apollo, and in doing so ascribe to him a role as guarantor that good men and bad shall enjoy their respective deserts which is identical in spirit to the role ascribed to the gods by Socrates' doctrines: 'Hail Apollo, child of Zeus and Leto! He whose house is vexed by misfortunes ought to revere the deities and be of good courage! For at the last the good shall attain their deserts, but the bad, as their nature is, will never fare well' (Eur. *Ion* 1619–22).[58]

Reflection on these three complexes of Socratic ethical ideas shows, then, that they are strikingly congruent with ethical ideas associated with one or another known Apolline milieu. This fact— and perhaps especially Socrates' explicit attribution to Apolline inspiration of his ethical views concerning respect for the law— confirms the suspicion that he understands Apollo to be the primary source of the divine inspiration that gives him his ethical insight.

VI

Observe, finally, the striking coherence that this interpretation lends to the historical Socrates' philosophical life. Socrates learns that Apollo's oracle has said that no one is wiser than he. Puzzled because he knows that he is ignorant and yet knows that Apollo must be right, he sets out to discover the real meaning of the oracle by first of all refuting it in its apparent sense, and thereby confirming his suspicion that this is not its real sense. But when he

---

[58] It is just possible that Socrates is the *source* of these ideas found in the *Ion* rather than their *recipient*. If so, this evidence would provide even stronger support for my main point, namely the intimate association of Socrates' ethical doctrines with Apollo.

Socrates' Profession of Ignorance 31

looks for someone with wisdom to whom he might point in order to refute it in its apparent sense, he finds that those who at first seemed wise are in fact not, and he proves this on each occasion by refuting them—especially, by asking them for the meaning of the terms they use and then refuting the definitions which they give in response, thereby showing that they do not even understand their own claims. As he proceeds in this way, it gradually dawns on him that he is after all verifying the oracle in its apparent sense. And so eventually he realizes that the oracle is indeed meant in its apparent sense, and that its ulterior point must be that, unlike the god of the oracle, men have no ethical knowledge, he being the wisest of them who, like Socrates, recognizes his ignorance. And he infers that Apollo has sent him the oracle—along with encouragement in dreams and other signs (such as the Delphic maxim 'Know thyself')—in order to induce him to demonstrate and disseminate this insight to his fellow men, a task to which he henceforth consciously devotes his life.

This much we are told fairly explicitly in the *Apology*.[59] But it is really only half of the story. As Socrates tested men's ethical definitions and found that neither they nor he possessed any that were defensible, he was forced to the conclusion that men's ethical claims were made quite literally without understanding. Yet it seemed clear to him that in many cases these claims were nevertheless right and beneficial for action. How could this paradox be explained? The only solution was to suppose that these uncomprehended but right and beneficial claims were, like the uncomprehended but right and beneficial claims of the Pythia and her ilk, the deliverances of divine inspiration. And as Socrates reflected on certain further peculiarities of ethical endowment—how it appeared to be neither innate nor voluntarily communicated from one man to another like skill in the arts, but to have some other controlling source—this reinforced him in his conviction that its origin must be divine. And of course, once he was thus convinced of the divine origin of ethical insight, and in addition noted the Apolline character of the ethical principles which seemed right and beneficial, the whole situation was clear to him: Apollo was the divine source of ethical insight, and had sent Socrates on his mission in order to convince Socrates and other men not only of the negative point that, while Apollo had ethical knowledge, men had none, but also of the more positive

[59] For a fuller explanation, see my 'Socrates' Demand for Definitions'.

32 *Michael N. Forster*

point that men were dependent for whatever ethical insight they *could* achieve on Apollo's inspiration, and ought therefore to follow the ethical principles bestowed by this god.

I can think of no more, or equally, satisfactory explanation of what should otherwise strike one as the quite puzzling fact that in the *Apology* Socrates, after giving in the oracle story an elaborate explanation of his refuting activity as ordained by and standing in the service of Apollo, subsequently goes on to imply that he believes, not only his refuting activity, but also *his communication of a set of positive ethical principles* to have been ordained by and to stand in the service of Apollo.[60] If made the offer of being set free on the condition that he desist from philosophy,

I should say to you: 'Men of Athens, I respect and love you, but I shall obey the god rather than you, and while I live and am able to continue, I shall never give up philosophy or stop exhorting you and pointing out the truth to any one of you whom I meet, saying in my accustomed way: "Most excellent man, are you . . . not ashamed to care for the acquisition of wealth and for reputation and honour, when you neither care nor take thought for practical judgement and truth and perfection of your soul?" And if any of you argues the point, . . . I shall question and examine and test [ἐλέγξω] him, and if I find that he does not possess virtue, but says he does, I shall rebuke him for scorning the things that are of greatest value and caring more for what is of less worth. This I shall do to whomever I meet . . . For know that the god commands me to do this, and I believe that no greater good ever came to pass in the city than my service to the god.' (29 D–30 A)

VII

I turn now to a few concluding remarks. The Socratic position which I have described in this article is of course unlikely to be found philosophically attractive today. We have quite left behind the religious world-view that it presupposes. Moreover, as I argued in 'Socrates' Demand for Definitions', Socrates' notion that an ability to provide definitions is a precondition of understanding is fatally flawed—so that the main argument which we have here found undergirding his conviction that ethical insights are not known but divinely inspired is vitiated.

However, Socrates' position remains of considerable historical

[60] Concerning this puzzle, cf. Stokes, 'Socrates' Mission', 74–5 (who suggests a different solution to it, however).

Socrates' Profession of Ignorance 33

interest. And it is also important for the light that it promises to shed on Plato's position. For Plato's position can be fully understood only by seeing in which respects it agrees and in which it parts company with his teacher's.

In that connection, the lesson that emerges most immediately from the present enquiry is as follows: whereas Socrates' philosophical project involved a rather thoroughgoing dependence on divine inspiration, Plato was evidently uncomfortable with this, and increasingly eliminated it from his own position. That process is already at work in the *Apology*, where, although the dependence of the motivation of Socrates' *critical* project on divine inspiration is made clear (especially in the oracle story), his conception of positive ethical insight as divinely inspired is obscured. In subsequent dialogues Plato's suppression has an opposite emphasis: the dependence of the motivation of Socrates' critical project on divine inspiration (especially the oracle story) virtually drops from view, though there is a temporary rehabilitation of Socrates' conception of positive ethical insight as divinely inspired (in the *Crito* and the *Meno*). Eventually, however, Plato virtually eliminates this whole aspect of Socrates' position altogether.

This development is closely connected to another (which I merely sketch here, but hope to explain more fully in future work): the historical Socrates had a reasonably *unified* critical method, the elenchus, which, though dependent on the gods for its motivation (in particular, via the oracle), *did not itself depend on the gods*, whereas his positive philosophizing involved a *motley* of methods which *did depend on the gods* (including appeal to the δαιμόνιον, positive arguments such as those at the end of the *Apology* and in the *Crito*, the extraction of principles from an interlocutor by cross-questioning in the manner described by Aeschines' *Alcibiades*, and the discovery of principles in divinely inspired poetry). Plato evidently found the positive side of Socrates' philosophizing unsatisfactory both because of its reliance on the gods and because of its use of a motley of methods. He therefore attempted to solve both of these problems in one fell swoop by *turning the elenchus into a positive method*—something of which there is as yet no sign in the *Apology*, but which does occur in subsequent early and middle dialogues, indeed in about half a dozen different variants, including the following: the (unexplained) appearance of progress via successive applications of elenchus to attempts at a definition, as in the

34 *Michael N. Forster*

Euthyphro; the application of elenchus to theses selected in such a way that demonstrating their falsehood will also constitute a substantive positive result, as in the *Protagoras*; the use of elenchus as a positive method for discovering truth given a strong background assumption, not only that vulnerability to it is a sufficient condition of falsehood, but also that invulnerability to it is a sufficient condition of truth, as in the *Gorgias*; the theory of recollection in the *Meno* and the *Phaedo*, which *explains* why successive applications of elenchus can reasonably be expected to produce progress towards the truth; the positive method of hypothesis in the *Phaedo*, which incorporates elenchus as an essential part of itself; and finally, the positive method of dialectic in the *Republic*, which likewise incorporates elenchus as an essential part of itself.

University of Chicago

BIBLIOGRAPHY

Adkins, A. W. H., *Merit and Responsibility: A Study in Greek Values* (Chicago and London, 1975).

Barowski, O., 'Sieben Weise', in *RE* ii/4. 2242–64.

Beversluis, J., 'Socratic Definition', *American Philosophical Quarterly*, 11/4 (1974), 331–6.

Brickhouse, T. C., and Smith, N. D., *Socrates on Trial* (Oxford and Princeton, 1989).

Burnet, J., 'The Socratic Doctrine of the Soul', *Proceedings of the British Academy*, 7 (1916), 235–59.

Burnyeat, M. F., 'Socratic Midwifery, Platonic Inspiration', *Bulletin of the Institute of Classical Studies*, 24 (1977), 7–16.

Cornford, F. M., *Plato and Parmenides: Parmenides' Way of Truth and Plato's* Parmenides (London, 1939).

De Strycker, E., 'Die historischen Zeugnisse über Sokrates', in Patzer (ed.), *Der historische Sokrates*, 323–54.

Forster, M. N., 'Socrates' Demand for Definitions', *OSAP* 31 (2006), 1–47.

Furley, D., 'The Early History of the Concept of the Soul', *Bulletin of the Institute of Classical Studies*, 3 (1956), 1–18.

Gomperz, H., 'Die sokratische Frage als geschichtliches Problem', in Patzer (ed.), *Der historische Sokrates*, 184–224.

Grote, G., *Plato and the Other Companions of Sokrates* (London, 1865).

Gulley, N., *The Philosophy of Socrates* (New York, 1968).

Socrates' Profession of Ignorance 35

Guthrie, W. K. C., *Socrates* (Cambridge, 1971).

—— *The Greeks and their Gods* (Boston, 1955).

Irwin, T. H., *Plato's Moral Theory: The Early and Middle Dialogues* (Oxford, 1985).

—— *Plato's Ethics* (Oxford, 1995).

Kraut, R., *Socrates and the State* (Princeton, 1984).

McPherran, M. L., *The Religion of Socrates* (University Park, PA, 1999).

Nestle, W., *Die Sokratiker* (Jena, 1922).

Parke, H. W., and Wormell, D. E. W., *The Delphic Oracle* (Oxford, 1956).

Patzer, A. (ed.), *Der historische Sokrates* (Darmstadt, 1987).

Pauly, A. F., rev. G. Wissowa *et al.*, *Real-Encyclopädie der classischen Altertumswissenschaft* [*RE*] (Stuttgart, 1894–1980).

Penner, T., 'Socrates and the Eary Dialogues', in R. Kraut (ed.), *The Cambridge Companion to Plato* (Cambridge, 1999), 121–69.

Plato, *Euthyphro, Apology of Socrates, Crito*, ed. J. Burnet (Oxford, 1924; repr. 1986).

Ritter, C., *Sokrates* (Tübingen, 1931).

Robinson, R., *Plato's Earlier Dialectic* (Oxford, 1953).

Snell, B., *The Discovery of the Mind in Greek Philosophy and Literature* (New York, 1960).

Stenzel, J., 'Sokrates (Philosoph)', in *RE* ii/5. 811–90.

Stokes, M., 'Socrates' Mission', in B. S. Gower and M. Stokes (eds.), *Socratic Questions: New Essays on the Philosophy of Socrates and its Significance* (London and New York, 1992), 26–81.

Veresenyi, L., *Socratic Humanism* (New Haven, 1963).

Vlastos, G., 'Socrates' Disavowal of Knowledge', *Philosophical Quarterly*, 35/138 (1985), 1–31.

Wernicke, K., 'Apollon', in *RE* i/3. 1–111.

Zeller, E., *Socrates and the Socratic Schools* (New York, 1962).

THE DEVELOPMENT OF PLATO'S THEORY OF IDEAS AND THE 'SOCRATIC QUESTION'

FRANCESCO FRONTEROTTA

W. J. Prior's 'Socrates Metaphysician' undermines almost three decades of quasi unanimity in the English-speaking world on a certain interpretation of Plato's theory of Ideas with regard to the relationship between Plato and Socrates, and to the suggestion that this relationship evolved in various specific stages, corresponding to as many chronologically distinct groups of Platonic dialogues.[1] This reading, set out in its standard English-language version by Gregory Vlastos, actually excludes any reference to the metaphysical theory of Ideas from the early dialogues that were supposedly entirely devoted to the ethical search for virtue and its definition (as the historical Socrates would have exercised it), and confines the introduction of Ideas to the middle and late dialogues, the only ones to be truly Platonic in their content. By referring to R. E. Allen's important study on the *Euthyphro*, whose influence nevertheless seems to have been limited,[2] Prior argues that: (1) a theory of Ideas had been present since Plato's early dialogues; (2) this theory implies the existence of certain ideal entities that are not separated from sensible things, but immanent to them; (3) their function is

© Francesco Fronterotta 2007

Thanks to David Sedley for comments on an earlier draft of this paper.

[1] *OSAP* 27 (2004), 1–14. I use the term 'developmentalism' with reference to the thesis of those who acknowledge a development in Plato's thought, whereby the theory of Ideas is arguably absent from the early or 'Socratic' dialogues, only to arise more or less gradually in the middle dialogues. Although it is undeniable that some changes took place in Plato's thought (so that some kind of development has to be admitted), the argument I submit is 'anti-developmentalist' in so far as it acknowledges the presence of a progressively more accomplished theory of Ideas *since the early dialogues*, and ascribes to it certain philosophical traits that are not subject to development.

[2] R. E. Allen, *Plato's* Euthyphro *and the Earlier Theory of Forms* [*Earlier Theory*] (London, 1970).

38 *Francesco Fronterotta*

exactly the one Aristotle included among the purposes of Socratic enquiry, i.e. to serve as universal terms, thereby fulfilling the need for a definition—an issue Socrates' character often raises in the early dialogues (although it is not clear how an Idea that is immanent in something may at the same time work as a universal term that is predicated of that very thing and provides a definition of it). According to this interpretation, from the very first stage of his activity Plato was drawing up and endorsing an ontological perspective and a consequent metaphysical doctrine, at least in so far as he reflected upon the ontological status of certain truly existing entities, as distinct from physical objects. This, in a nutshell, is Prior's argument, hinging above all on the study of the *Protagoras* and the *Meno*, to which he applies the interpretation originally submitted by Allen for the *Euthyphro*. However, given that such issues have been debated in continental literature for a number of years,[3] I wish to take up the matter again to show: (1) that a closer reading of some of Plato's early dialogues may suggest elements additional to those put forward by Prior, endorsing the interpretation (originally suggested by Allen) that a theory of Ideas is present in these dialogues; (2) that even Allen's interpretation may be reprocessed in a more radical form, especially with regard to the inclusion or exclusion of the separation of Ideas in the early version of the theory; (3) lastly, that the standard interpretation, e.g. as proposed by Vlastos, perhaps hinges on an exegetic and historiographic bias, for which at least some clarification is needed.

1. The 'Socratic question' and the development of Plato's theory of Ideas

One can agree with Prior that out of the ten theses by which Vlastos distinguishes a Socrates$_E$ from a Socrates$_M$ (denoting the Socrates of the early and middle dialogues, respectively), the crucial ones for our purpose are undeniably the first two (although they may

---

[3] In addition to the titles cited in n. 5 below, recent examples are the short essay in German by M. Baltes: 'Zum Status der Ideen in Platons Frühdialogen *Charmides, Euthydemos, Lysis*', in *Plato:* Euthydemus, Lysis, Charmides, ed. T. Robinson and L. Brisson (Proceedings of the V Symposium Platonicum; Sankt Augustin, 2000), 317–23; in Italian, my *Methexis: la teoria platonica delle idee e la partecipazione delle cose empiriche. Dai dialoghi giovanili al Parmenide* (Pisa, 2001), 3–79 and 159–80; and, in French, appendix III to Platon, *Hippias majeur & Hippias mineur*, présentations et traductions par J.-F. Pradeau et F. Fronterotta (Paris, 2005), 231–42.

Plato's Theory of Ideas 39

actually be condensed into one): (I) Socrates$_E$ is a moral philosopher, while Socrates$_M$ is a moral philosopher, a metaphysician, an epistemologist, a philosopher of religion, science, language, education, politics, and more; therefore (II) unlike Socrates$_E$, Socrates$_M$ possesses a metaphysical theory of Ideas that are separated and exist apart from the sensible world, and which the human soul may grasp by virtue of recollection. According to this theory, the human soul must be (1) immortal and (2) ontologically homogeneous with Ideas. Wholly lacking such aims, Socrates$_E$ concerns himself with ethics and strives to attain universality in this context by way of an examination of his interlocutors' knowledge based on an in-depth analysis of their λόγοι.[4]

Indeed, comparing these two doctrinal cores, one may uncover the historical Socrates behind the features of Socrates$_E$ (portrayed in Plato's early or 'Socratic' dialogues), whereas Socrates$_M$'s doctrines (portrayed in Plato's middle dialogues) should actually be traced back to Plato's thought. It should not be difficult to see, then, that rather than the interpretation of Plato's dialogues, the foremost issue at stake here is the 'Socratic question', which (considering the form in which it is normally articulated) derives from these two cardinal assumptions: *since* (A) Plato's early and middle dialogues contain doctrines markedly unlike each other, and *since* (B) it is more reasonable to attribute to Plato the doctrines emerging in the middle dialogues, *then* (C) this considerable divergence must be explained, and a reasonable hypothesis is that (D) the doctrines of the early dialogues belong to the historical Socrates.[5]

---

[4] See Prior, 'Socrates Metaphysician', 1–2. As regards Vlastos, the reference is to the essays collected in the volume *Socrates: Ironist and Moral Philosopher [Ironist]* (Cambridge, 1991), esp. 45–131.

[5] The Socratic question dates back well before Vlastos, at least to the early nineteenth century: K. F. Hermann, *Geschichte und System der Platonischen Philosophie* (Heidelberg, 1839), had already advanced the hypothesis of a group of (early) Platonic dialogues, whose doctrines should be attributed to the historical Socrates; while H. Maier, *Sokrates: Sein Werk und seine geschichtliche Stellung* (Tübingen, 1913), is responsible for consistently laying down the Socratic question in the form that it later took on throughout the 20th-cent. debate. This position is almost unanimously shared in Socratic studies, as G. Giannantoni recalled in 'Il Socrate di Vlastos', *Elenchos*, 14 (1993), 55–63, and in *Dialogo socratico e nascita della dialettica nella filosofia di Platone [Dialogo socratico]*, ed. B. Centrone (Naples, 2005), 18–27 and 391; but this view also attracts a wide consensus in Platonic studies, as emerges, for instance, from the critical and bibliographical cadre traced by L.-A. Dorion in Platon, *Lachès & Euthyphron*, traduction inédite, introduction et notes par L.-A. Dorion (Paris, 1997), 208–13. A well-known recent exception is C. H. Kahn, *Plato and the Socratic Dialogue: The Philosophical Use of a Literary Form [Socratic Dialogue]*

40 *Francesco Fronterotta*

In spite of the fact that even if (A), (B), and (C) were granted, one would still have to consider for (D) the hypothesis that Plato himself developed different doctrines throughout various stages of his intellectual life, one must acknowledge that positing (A) as a premiss for this sort of methodological syllogism implies that an important demonstrandum is ultimately taken as a principle of the demonstration. As regards the interpretation of Plato's dialogues, this methodological syllogism produces a developmentalist interpretation that entails a radical shift in his conception of Ideas, from the early dialogues—where Ideas would merely constitute the universal terms of (Socratic) definition—to the middle dialogues—in which intelligible Ideas are finally established as the model and separate being of sensible things in the framework of a (Platonic) two-worlds theory. As stated above, I shall first seek to show that an anti-developmentalist thesis (like Allen's or more radical) is wholly plausible.

2. The 'definitional' dialogues

Turning to the dialogues where the main character is Vlastos's Socrates$_E$, which belong to what is generally regarded as Plato's early output, they show Socrates looking for the definition of something, by way of a question that he construes as follows: 'What is [$\tau\acute{\iota}$ $\acute{\epsilon}\sigma\tau\iota$] X?' The field may be narrowed down to four dialogues: *Charmides, Laches, Hippias Major*, and *Euthyphro*.[6] The search

---

(Cambridge, 1996), who disputed this traditional understanding of the relationship between Socrates and Plato, suggesting a new approach, on a historical and literary level, to the narrative form of the dialogue; still, Kahn does not include among his aims an examination of the problem of the development of Plato's theory of Ideas from the early to middle dialogues.

[6] I consider the *Hippias Major* to be clearly authentic, accepting the convincing arguments submitted by Pradeau, *Hippias majeur & Hippias mineur*, 15–22. Actually, other dialogues of the same period, such as the *Hippias Minor*, the *Lysis*, the *Ion*, and the *Euthydemus*, do not present a strictly definitional structure (since Socrates' examination does not go on to request a definition of something and subsequently analyse it), whereas definitional sections are to be found in the *Protagoras*, the *Meno*, and of course in the first book of the *Republic*. Unlike Prior, I would rather let these dialogues be, as I do not believe their content amounts to a relevant testimony of Vlastos's Socrates$_E$. As regards the Socratic question 'What is X?', the object 'X' in the dialogues I shall examine nearly always coincides with a moral quality (such as courage, temperance, or justice) or with virtue in general, or with an aesthetic quality (such as the beautiful or the ugly). Despite this limitation, I believe the

Plato's Theory of Ideas

for a definition normally ends with a negative outcome, since the definiens does not define the truly universal definiendum demanded by Socrates, namely because the definitions submitted by his interlocutors do not fully satisfy the requirements of his question, above all that of universality: more to the point, Socrates' interlocutors cannot explain what '*X*' is in general, but confine themselves to submitting a wholly particular and factual example of '*X*'.

This is exemplified in the *Charmides* by the definitions describing temperance as 'quietness' (159 B 1–160 E 1), 'modesty' (160 E 2–161 B 2) or the ability to 'do good' (163 D 1–164 C 6) that are all rejected by Socrates, who shows that the definiens fails to express its content *universally*, i.e. in a comprehensive form including all possible factual examples of temperance and all the possible cases temperance occurs in, since particular situations in which temperance cannot be equated with 'quietness', 'modesty', or the ability to 'do good' certainly arise. A similar situation occurs in the *Laches*, where the key specification that the object to be defined always remains the same, regardless of the circumstances it may find itself in (ἐν πᾶσι τούτοις ταὐτόν ἐστιν, 191 D 10–11), does not lead to a positive outcome of the search, because the submitted definitions of courage—such as 'remaining at one's post' (190 E 4–192 B 8) or an 'endurance of the soul combined with the faculty of judging' (192 B 9–193 E 5)—are once again easily refuted by Socrates, who merely observes the absence of the necessary condition, namely that of the universality of the definition. 'Remaining at one's post' indeed describes a most particular example of courage, and in a very restricted meaning; conversely, only in certain situations may

question could be applicable to any kind of object, as, for example, happens at *Meno* 72 A 8–B 2, where Socrates explains his request for a definition of virtue with the case of the bee, of which he asks 'What is the being?' (μελίττης . . . οὐσίας ὅτι ποτ' ἐστιν) in general, regardless of the different kinds of bee one could classify. Similar examples are suggested in the *Laches* (192 A 1–B 4) with the definition of speed (τάχος . . . τί ποτ' ἐστίν;), and again in the *Meno* (74 B 4–77 A 2) with the definition of geometrical figure (τί ἐστιν σχῆμα;) and of colour (περὶ χρώματος . . . ὅτι ἐστίν). The debate over the nature and structure of the Socratic method of enquiry has been raised again in recent decades by Vlastos (see especially 'What Did Socrates Understand by his "What is F?" Question?' (1976), in id., *Platonic Studies*, 2nd edn. (Princeton, 1981), 410–17, and 'The Socratic Elenchus', *OSAP* 1 (1983), 27–58, repr. in id., *Socratic Studies* (Cambridge, 1994), 1–33); useful general studies are R. W. Puster, *Zur Argumentationsstruktur platonischer Dialoge: Die 'Was ist X?' Frage in Laches, Charmides, Der größere Hippias und Euthyphron* (Munich and Freiburg, 1983); A. Longo, *La tecnica della domanda e le interrogazioni fittizie in Platone* (Pisa, 2000), 3–140; and Giannantoni, *Dialogo socratico*, 141–95.

42 *Francesco Fronterotta*

courage truly be conceived as an 'endurance of the soul combined with the faculty of judging', since one can quote an endless number of other situations in which this definition is manifestly found wanting. Yet, besides being universal the definition sought by Socrates must clearly be logically consistent, both in itself and towards the consequences that may be drawn from it: this requirement jeopardizes the last definition of temperance submitted in the *Charmides*, which makes it coincide with the Delphic precept of self-knowledge (166 E 5–169 B 5), and the last definition of courage submitted in the *Laches*, which describes it as knowledge 'of fearful and of hopeful things' (194 C 7–199 E 10). Both definitions turn out to fall into contradiction when under scrutiny.

The analysis carried out in the *Hippias Major* and in the *Euthyphro* is more complex. In the former, Socrates spells out his request—what is the beautiful ($\tau i \,\dot{\epsilon}\sigma\tau\iota\, \tau\dot{o}\, \kappa\alpha\lambda\acute{o}\nu$), or rather, to be precise, what is the beautiful 'itself' ($\alpha\dot{v}\tau\dot{o}\, \tau\dot{o}\, \kappa\alpha\lambda\acute{o}\nu$)?—with a number of examples: if it is right to say that what is just is just by justice ($\delta\iota\kappa\alpha\iota\sigma\sigma\acute{v}\nu\eta$), what is wise is wise by wisdom ($\sigma\sigma\phi\acute{\iota}\alpha$), and what is good is good by goodness ($\tau\hat{\wp}\, \dot{\alpha}\gamma\alpha\theta\hat{\wp}$), and if, moreover, justice, wisdom, and good are something that is ($\dot{\epsilon}\sigma\tau\iota\, \tau\iota\, \tau o\hat{v}\tau o$), as regards the beautiful, it will not be possible to say that it coincides with beautiful occupations and rich adornments, since the question is not 'What is beautiful?' ($\tau i \,\dot{\epsilon}\sigma\tau\iota\, \kappa\alpha\lambda\acute{o}\nu$), but 'What is *the* beautiful?' ($\ddot{o}\tau\iota\, \dot{\epsilon}\sigma\tau\iota\, \tau\dot{o}\, \kappa\alpha\lambda\acute{o}\nu$). The need for an objective reference for definition is here stressed in successive bouts (287 D 2–E 1, 289 D 2–5, 292 C 8–D 4, 294 B 6–C 2, 300 A 9–B 2), in so far as defining cannot merely imply an effective description of the definiendum, even in a universal form, that is solely based on a vague experience of the subject and on the interlocutors' agreement at a semantic and epistemological level. On the contrary, it must refer back to the proper nature of the relevant object, i.e. to that Form or Idea that, 'when added' ($\dot{\epsilon}\pi\epsilon\iota\delta\dot{\alpha}\nu\, \pi\rho\sigma\sigma\gamma\acute{\epsilon}\nu\eta\tau\alpha\iota\, \dot{\epsilon}\kappa\epsilon\hat{\iota}\nu o\, \tau\dot{o}\, \epsilon\hat{\iota}\delta o\varsigma$, 289 D 3–4) to anything, 'makes it beautiful': this 'Form' or 'Idea' ($\epsilon\hat{\iota}\delta o\varsigma$) is the 'beautiful itself' ($\alpha\dot{v}\tau\dot{o}\, \tau\dot{o}\, \kappa\alpha\lambda\acute{o}\nu$), and it is the cause (1) that produces the beauty of/in all the beautiful things or (2) by which all other beautiful things become beautiful. Actually, while at first claiming not to grasp the meaning of this distinction in full, Hippias starts submitting definitions pointing to 'things' in a proper sense, to objects possessing a certain ontological status, albeit with a certain crass simplicity. And that is why Socrates' refutation is itself aimed at this aspect, thus forsaking

Plato's Theory of Ideas

the formal assessment of the purely logical-semantic universality of the definition or at least greatly broadening its scope. A beautiful maiden (287 B 4–289 D 5), gold or another more fitting material (289 D 6–291 C 9), whatever is useful and beneficial (295 B 7–297 D 1), the pleasure proceeding from sight and hearing (297 E 3–303 D 10): barring the last two definitions, which appear inconsistent because they ultimately contradict the search assumptions, Socrates shows Hippias' mistakes by examining the ontological status of the objects of the sophist's definitions, thus proving that they do not coincide (nor could they do so) with the beautiful itself. From such a standpoint, the sole exception to this objective or ontological 'trend' is particularly revealing: the third definition submitted by Hippias—whereby beauty for a man consists in being rich, healthy, and honoured by the Greeks, and in being splendidly buried by his own offspring, at a ripe old age, after providing a beautiful funeral for his parents (291 D 1–293 D 4)—takes as its starting-point a set of traditional values, commonly accepted and acknowledged by the Greeks, and could perhaps come close to reaching a universal consensus on a shared concept of beauty.

Yet Socrates' critique chiefly focuses on its utter lack of ontological references: the beautiful itself, in fact, is not a belief borne by tradition, nor does it belong to the realm of social and family customs, honour, or public and private fame; the beautiful itself is a certain *quid*—a *quid* that, whenever added to any other thing, produces beauty in it. In the *Hippias Major* the shift of the enquiry from the analysis of the logical-semantic and, broadly speaking, epistemological conditions of the definiens to the study of the definiendum's ontological status is particularly clear in the rebuttal of the other submitted definitions. The definition that identifies the beautiful itself with a beautiful maiden is rebutted, as it designates an object that may be both beautiful and ugly (or beautiful for one and ugly for another, or beautiful in one respect and ugly in another), and whose status is therefore not truly universal as to its proper nature—as should conversely be the case with the beautiful itself. The definition that ascribes the cause of beauty to gold and its ornamental value misses the target completely, as it indicates an object that does not appear in each and every situation to produce beauty in the things containing it; an object, then, whose status is not truly universal as to its power of causation—as should on the other hand be the case with the beautiful itself.

44 *Francesco Fronterotta*

The definition that reduces the beautiful itself to 'that which is appropriate' or 'suitable' (τὸ πρέπον) also fails, because it points at an object that does not *make* beautiful the things containing it, but merely makes them *appear* beautiful; hence it is an object whose status, though universal (in that it *always* makes the things containing it appear beautiful), yields only a partial and merely apparent effect—quite unlike what should be expected with the beautiful itself. That is how, compared with the *Charmides* and the *Laches*, the truth requirement for the definitional question in the *Hippias Major* no longer consists in a form of 'extensional' universality (i.e. in the search for a universal definiens that *extensionally* embraces all the possible exemplifications of the definiendum), but in a form of 'causal-ontological' universality (i.e. in the search for a definiens which designates a definiendum, conceived as a universal reality producing the same effects in every single possible case):[7] an answer to the Socratic question 'what is *X*?' can now be given solely by indicating a unique and universal object—qualified by Plato as an 'Idea' or 'Form' itself—that is always unchangeable and identical to itself and yet 'present' in a multiplicity of particular things, to which, by virtue of its 'presence', it confers that same property whose true nature it embodies.

In the *Euthyphro* similar hallmarks are traceable in Socrates' request to his interlocutor that he be told what the pious and the impious are (τί . . . εἶναι) in any given situation: for the pious itself will be the same as itself in any case (ταὐτόν ἐστιν . . . τὸ ὅσιον αὐτὸ αὑτῷ), just as the impious itself, the opposite of the pious, will also remain identical to itself, thus possessing a certain unique form of impiety (τὸ ἀνόσιον αὖ τοῦ μὲν ὁσίου παντὸς ἐναντίου, αὐτὸ δὲ αὑτῷ ὅμοιον καὶ ἔχον μίαν τινὰ ἰδέαν κατὰ τὴν ἀνοσιότητα, 5 c 4– d 7). As in the *Hippias Major*, so in the *Euthyphro* the Socratic question evidently calls for a reference to the status of the object of the definition, which cannot consist in a verbal expression of what tradition or common knowledge claims to be the norm or concept of the pious, but must designate the intrinsically objective nature of the pious, i.e. its very being (τὴν οὐσίαν αὐτοῦ). Pursuant to Socrates' oft repeated intention (5 d 1–5, 6 d 10–e 6, 11 a 6–b 1), the aim of the analysis is the 'Idea' (ἰδέα) or the 'Form' itself (αὐτὸ τὸ εἶδος), always remaining identical in every case, regardless of any particular action or circumstance (ταὐτόν . . . ἐν πάσῃ πράξει), that

---

[7] On this distinction see Kahn, *Socratic Dialogue*, 172–8.

Plato's Theory of Ideas

by which pious things are pious ($\hat{\omega}$ πάντα τὰ ὅσια ὅσιά ἐστιν), the unique Idea of pious (μιᾷ ἰδέᾳ αὐτοῦ) by which pious things are properly designated as such. A new element here is the description of the Idea of pious as the universal 'model' (παράδειγμα), which must necessarily resemble all those things and particular circumstances of which piety can be predicated: that is why this model must be pious always and universally, and certainly not pious and impious at the same time, or pious in one respect and impious in another. The reference to the objective nature of the definiendum can also be inferred from the fact that Socrates' refutation tends to show primarily how the submitted definitions fail to grasp the proper being (τὴν οὐσίαν αὐτοῦ) of the object to be defined, merely capturing one of its affections (πάθος δέ τι περὶ αὐτοῦ) at best. All in all, Euthyphro does not reach beyond the ambit of purely extensional universality, whereas Socrates would rather identify the ontological status of the pious itself (finding out the definition expressing the unique nature or form of pious).

It is no coincidence that the second definition Euthyphro suggests (the pious itself is what is approved by the gods: see 6 E 10–8 A 12 and 9 D 1–11 B 1), which could perhaps attain a form of extensional universality, actually breaks down because it fails to identify that being representing the proper nature of piety: in fact, Socrates is not interested in learning which actions or things gain the gods' approval—since in his eyes this is a wholly accidental feature—but he wants to be told what the pious itself is, the very Idea of pious. Instead, the first definition, identifying the pious with Euthyphro's behaviour (the pious itself consists in prosecuting a murderer, whoever he may be: see 5 D 8–6 E 6), turns out to be wholly out of range, for it does not designate a universal being but just a particular sort of behaviour for which only a particular example is given; consequently, Socrates is once again forced to remind his interlocutor that the object he wishes to be shown is the nature or form of pious, the pious itself.

The third definition seems much more promising thanks to Socrates' suggestion (11 E 1–12 A 2), as it tries to understand the pious in relation with the just, as a part of it (11 E 4–15 C 10); yet, as soon as Socrates cross-examines Euthyphro by asking him which part of the just corresponds to the pious, the diviner hastily abandons the ontological ground so laboriously conquered by Socrates and reverts to the purely logical-semantic ambit of his previous defini-

46 *Francesco Fronterotta*

tions, stating that the pious is 'the part of the just concerned with the care of the gods' (12 E 5–8) and consists in sacrifice and prayer. By so doing, Euthyphro actually retreats to the indication of a body of customs and traditions, thereby missing every reference to the ontological status of the object to be defined, so that this definition falls victim to the same objections as the previous one as it establishes a semantic and epistemological ὁμολογία which, though possibly universal, does not show the very nature or being of pious.

What is clearly under way here is the search for an objective and universal ground on which to articulate the definition, an ontological ground which, by drawing from itself its own self-evidence and universality, may be opposed to the feebleness of common opinion and traditional knowledge, now shown up as ineffectual and inadequate.

3. The aim of the definition and the object of the Socratic search

It is not possible to examine here the form of the method Socrates deploys in these dialogues, in its interrogative (τί ἐστι X?) and refutative (ἔλεγχος) guises, which has been the object of many studies;[8] my aim now is just to consider the object of this method, so as to highlight the target of the Socratic search.

A widely shared thesis suggests that a search model devoted solely to attaining ὁμολογία between the interlocutors, typical of the historical Socrates' philosophical style and enquiry mode and widely present in Plato's early dialogues, ought to be set apart from a search model that is, conversely, aimed at catching the unchangeable nature or proper being of things, thoroughly developed in Plato's middle dialogues in the cadre of the theory of Ideas. The former, wholly independent of the introduction of Ideas, would place the criterion of truth for a definition in logical-semantic agreement among the interlocutors; the latter, intrinsically related to the admission of Ideas, would establish it in the perfect adherence to the objective and universal nature of intelligible beings.[9]

One can reject this interpretation because, first of all, ὁμολογία

[8] See n. 6 for some bibliographical references.

[9] In Socratic literature this thesis goes back to the works of G. Calogero (now collected in the volume *Scritti minori di filosofia antica* (Naples, 1984)); it was taken up by G. Giannantoni (see 'Socrate e il Platone esoterico', in Giannantoni *et al.*, *La tradizione socratica* (Naples, 1995), 9–37 at 20–7), and is shared by F. Wolff,

Plato's Theory of Ideas 47

among the speakers amounts to a fundamental criterion of Socratic διαλέγεσθαι as much in the definitional dialogues as in the dialectic of middle and late dialogues; it consequently does not represent an exclusive feature of the Socratic method that Plato would have dropped upon introducing the theory of Ideas.[10] Moreover, even in the context of the definitional dialogues, ὁμολογία among interlocutors can take place on at least three different levels:[11] at the lowest and simplest level, the ὁμολογία consists in a purely linguistic agreement on the meaning of words used to indicate the object to be defined. This agreement must obviously precede the start of the discussion, in that it presupposes an adequate clarification of the use of linguistic tools, which is a necessary condition for a constructive or simply intelligible dialogue (see *Gorg.* 448 E 6–7, 462 C 10, 463 B 7–C 5; *Sym.* 194 E 7–195 A 1; *Phdr.* 237 B 7–D 3). At a second level, the ὁμολογία depends on the knowledge of the object to be defined, which allows a satisfactory definition to be articulated. In this case the agreement among the speakers concerns the definition that fulfils the requirements listed by Socrates: whoever truly knows an object 'X' is also able to put forward a consistent definition embracing all the 'x' cases in which 'X' appears or is present. A principle of co-extensivity of definiens and definiendum is therefore admitted: by virtue of knowledge of the definiendum's nature and properties, it is possible to submit a definiens that extensionally (and universally) covers all the definiendum's particular instances. Actually, this kind of ὁμολογία, which is the target of the search for the definitions of temperance and courage in the *Charmides* and the *Laches*, is not attained in those dialogues in so far as the epistemological requirement remains unmet: the fact that the submitted definitions appear unfit indicates that they do not stem from a truly universal knowledge of 'X', and this means that the defining subject perhaps has some acquaintance with several particular exemplifications of 'X', but not a full acquaintance with its nature or proper being, so

---

'Être disciple de Socrate', in G. Giannantoni and M. Narcy (eds.), *Lezioni socratiche* (Naples, 1997), 29–79 at 48–9.

[10] An accurate examination of the occurrence of terms such as ὁμολογεῖν and ὁμολογία in Plato's dialogues, with regard to the rules of the Socratic dialogue and Platonic dialectic, has been carried out by F. Adorno, 'Appunti su ὁμολογεῖν e ὁμολογία nel vocabolario di Platone', in id., *Pensare storicamente* (Florence, 1996), 49–65; see also on this point Giannantoni, *Dialogo socratico*, 173–88.

[11] See Kahn, *Socratic Dialogue*, 93, 155–82, and, *contra*, Giannantoni, *Dialogo socratico*, 320–46.

48 *Francesco Fronterotta*

that he is unable to enumerate its properties, and to implement it correctly in such statements as 'X is y'.[12]

This leads even further towards a third and more demanding level of ὁμολογία which depends on the ontological status of the definiendum. In this case it is no longer sufficient to know the universal semantic extension of 'X', but it is necessary to grasp directly the very nature or proper being of 'X', its unchangeable Form or Idea that is always identical to itself throughout the particular circumstances, actions, or things in which it is present. That is why, in their successive attempts, Socrates' interlocutors in the *Hippias Major* and the *Euthyphro* perhaps come close to a definition that is capable of producing overall consensus around the object 'X', but Socrates suddenly extends the scope of the enquiry, suggesting the additional requirement of fixing the definiendum's ontological status: that is the fundamental premiss on which an epistemologically sound definition is now dependent. At this stage the ὁμολογία no longer depends on mere agreement over the use of the term 'X', nor on the interlocutors' actual familiarity with 'X', but on the true knowledge of the proper nature or Idea of 'X', a knowledge that does not deal with the (universal) semantic extension of 'X', but immediately concerns its ontological status: obviously, it is necessary to have knowledge of 'X' in order to define it, but with the proviso that the only true universal knowledge is that which is directed to certain objects marked by a peculiar ontological status, the unchangeable and ever identical Ideas or Forms. Thus the possibility of knowledge and definition depends on the ontological status of the objects to be known and defined, and Socrates' interlocutors' blatant inability to grasp this fundamental ontological dimension is the ultimate reason why the enquiry carried out in the definitional dialogues fails.

Bringing to light the target of definition leads to the next question: that of the gradual determination of the ontological status of

---

[12] See again Kahn, *Socratic Dialogue*, 157–64, 180–2. This conclusion highlights an epistemological priority of knowledge over definition, not to be confused with the paradox (groundless, in my opinion) of the *priority of definition*, detected by P. Geach, 'Plato's *Euthyphro*: An Analysis and Commentary', *Monist*, 50 (1966), 369–82, who has provoked many reactions: see e.g. J. Beversluis, 'Does Socrates Commit the Socratic Fallacy?', *American Philosophical Quarterly*, 24 (1987), 211–23; G. Vlastos, 'Is the "Socratic Fallacy" Socratic?', *Ancient Philosophy*, 10 (1990), 1–16, repr. in id., *Socratic Studies*, 67–86; H. Benson, 'The Priority of Definition and the Socratic Elenchus', *OSAP* 8 (1990), 19–65; and W. J. Prior, 'Plato and the Socratic Fallacy', *Phronesis*, 43 (1998), 97–113.

Plato's Theory of Ideas 49

the object to be defined. Since the *Hippias Major* and the *Euthyphro*, the objects of the 'τi ἐστι X?' question all possess an ontological status that makes their subsistence in some way distinct from their instances: the '$\tau\iota$' subject to analysis is a certain Idea (ἰδέα) or Form itself (αὐτὸ τὸ εἶδος) that does not appear in one manner now and in another later, but remains identical to itself for anybody, anywhere, and in any case, regardless of the many particular circumstances it appears in.[13] This Form or Idea represents the only proper being (οὐσία) of the multiplicity of things or instances in which it is present, or even the universal model (παράδειγμα) they must resemble as images or copies: for example, only what resembles (ὃ . . . ἂν τοιοῦτον ᾖ) the ideal model (παράδειγμα) of pious or beautiful may be said to be pious or beautiful. Likewise, the Idea of pious or beautiful is that which, when it is 'added' (προσγίγνεται) to a multiplicity of things or instances or is 'present' (πάρεστιν) in them, makes (ποιεῖ) them pious or beautiful: in other words, the Ideas are that 'by virtue of which' (ᾧ) a multiplicity of things or instances possess their properties; conversely, a multiplicity of things or instances possessing some properties 'have' (ἔχουσιν) or 'participate in' (μεταλαμβάνουσι) the Ideas corresponding to those properties.[14] The Ideas therefore represent, at the same time, the preferential object and the criterion of λόγος: being an unchangeable and self-identical model for their particular instances, only Ideas can be truly named and defined.[15]

The question raised in the definitional dialogues, emphasizing the need for a definition, leads to positing Ideas as the real beings one has to know beforehand, in themselves and in their relationship with the multiplicity of things or instances in which they are present, in order to put forward an appropriate definition: on these terms, it seems to me beyond doubt that one can legitimately speak of a 'theory of Ideas' in Plato's early dialogues.[16] The next step consists in taking a stand on the degree of being one can concede to Ideas, and on the kind of relationship (be it based on immanence or

---

[13] *H.Ma.* 286 c 3–E 4, 287 B 4–E 1; *Euthph.* 5 c 8–D 6, 8 A 10–12.

[14] *H.Ma.* 289 D 2–8, 292 c 9–D 4, 300 A 9–B 2; *Euthph.* 5 D 1–5, 6 D 9–E 6.

[15] *Euthph.* 6 E 3–6.

[16] Besides the studies by Allen and Prior which I have extensively cited, see also on this point the more cautious remarks by J. M. Rist, 'Plato's Earlier Theory of Forms?' ['Earlier Theory?'], *Phoenix*, 29 (1975), 336–57, by H. Gundert, 'Die ersten Spuren der Ideenlehre', in K. Döring and F. Preisshofen (eds.), *Platonstudien* (Amsterdam, 1977), 178–85, and by R. D. Mohr, 'Forms in Plato's *Euthydemus*', *Hermes*, 112 (1984), 296–300.

50   *Francesco Fronterotta*

transcendence) they are supposed to establish with the multiplicity of things or instances they are related to.

4. The ontological status of Ideas in the definitional dialogues

Classed as 'proper beings' in the *Euthyphro* (11 A 7–8), the Ideas are said to be 'in themselves' in the *Hippias Major* (286 D 8, 288 A 9, 300 A 9), where the beautiful itself is introduced, and again in the *Euthyphro* (6 D 10–11), where Socrates examines the 'form itself' of the pious and the impious. But what does it mean here to talk of something that is 'in itself'? The dialogues are unambiguous on this point: something can be said to be 'in itself' if and only if, despite appearing many times in different guises and in a multiplicity of particular things, actions, or circumstances, it nevertheless maintains its own nature and properties unchanged. This is the case with the Idea of beautiful in the *Hippias Major* (287 B 4–E 1), which is absolutely independent of all particular instances of beauty, even if it is that by virtue of which (ᾧ) all particular instances of beauty become beautiful: actually, the Idea of beautiful does not coincide with a single beautiful thing (τί . . . καλόν), for it is *the* beautiful, something that 'is' in itself (τῷ καλῷ . . . ὄντι γέ τινι τούτῳ). Likewise, in the *Euthyphro* (5 C 8–D 6, 6 C 8–D 11, 8 A 10–12) it is clear how the pious itself is that which remains the same in all pious actions (ταὐτόν ἐστιν ἐν πάσῃ πράξει τὸ ὅσιον αὐτὸ αὑτῷ), the Idea which does not appear pious and impious at the same time (αὐτὸ τὸ εἶδος . . . ⟨οὐ⟩ τυγχάνει ὂν ὅσιόν τε καὶ ἀνόσιον), but is constantly identical to itself (ταὐτόν).[17]

Yet a problem arises here: if in the early dialogues Ideas are kept distinct from the multiplicity of particular things, is it not

---

[17] A passage in the *Phaedo* provides further indications. At 64 C 4–8, in the context of the demonstration of souls' immortality, Socrates states that death is the 'separation' (ἀπαλλαγή) of the soul from the body: that is the moment when 'the body, separated from the soul, stands itself by itself' (χωρὶς μὲν ἀπὸ τῆς ψυχῆς ἀπαλλαγὲν αὐτὸ καθ' αὑτὸ τὸ σῶμα), just as 'the soul, separated from the body, stands itself by itself' (χωρὶς δὲ τὴν ψυχὴν ἀπὸ τοῦ σώματος ἀπαλλαγεῖσαν αὐτὴν καθ' αὑτήν). I infer from Socrates' argument that what is 'itself by itself' always subsists 'separately' from what is other than it (as in the case of body and soul), and I see no reason to believe that this equivalence is not also valid in the previous dialogues: the example of body and soul, in fact, establishes a linguistic equivalence that, being valid as much for formal as for sensible realities (such as soul and body, respectively), takes on a general meaning.

Plato's Theory of Ideas

paradoxical that they represent at the same time the proper being of that multiplicity and that, furthermore, the relationship between the Ideas and the particular things is conceived as the presence or the addition of Ideas *in/to* those things?[18] The matter is extremely difficult and we shall leave it at that: it is, however, noteworthy that Plato does not seem troubled by such a question, as in the middle and late dialogues he continues to describe participation of the sensible things in Ideas as the *presence* of separated Ideas in things that participate in them.[19]

If, as established above, the possibility of true definition depends on the assumption of Ideas as definienda, we should now be able to answer the Socratic question: from an ontological point of view, the 'What is X?' question (where 'X' = Idea) implies an ostensive and not a demonstrative reply, just pointing, so to speak, at 'X': whoever asks 'What is man?' should in theory be *shown* the Idea or Form of man.[20] Yet this kind of answer, rather doubtful in itself, would be utterly worthless if the interlocutor did not already possess a preliminary knowledge of 'X' (in our case, the Idea of man) and were therefore not able to recognize it by himself. From a linguistic point of view, the 'What is X?' question naturally suggests an answer grounded in a meaningful word combination, stating, for instance, that 'man' is a 'rational biped animal'. However, this cannot be a nominal definition, i.e. one that, setting aside its object's ontological status, just produces a consistent choice of words, so that its truth requirement consists in an abstract linguistic exactitude; indeed, if this were the case, as regards the definition 'rational biped animal', we should content ourselves with checking its logical-semantic consistency, but nothing could be said on man's real existence, nor on the objective truth of his definition, because the real existence of the definiendum and its objective truth

---

[18] *H.Ma.* 292 C 9–D 3, 300 A 9–B 2; *Euthph.* 5 D 1–5.

[19] *Phaedo* 65 D 12–E 1, 100 D 4–6, 101 C 2–4; *Rep.* 5, 476 A 4–7; *Phdr.* 247 C 6–D 1. Consider that the theory of resemblance between sensible images or copies and intelligible models, quite frequently adopted by Plato to explain the relationship between things and Ideas in the middle and late dialogues (*Phaedo* 76 D 7–E 4; *Rep.* 5, 476 C 9–D 3; 10, 597 D 1–598 D 6; *Phdr.* 250 A 6–251 A 7), also appears in the early works (*H.Ma.* 289 D 2–8; *Euthph.* 6 D 9–E 6). My conclusion is that this fluctuation between different conceptions of the relationship Ideas–sensible things remains an unresolved dilemma in Plato's thought.

[20] It is in this sense that Socrates ironically censures Euthyphro's reluctance to 'show' him the proper being' (τὴν οὐσίαν μοι αὐτοῦ . . . δηλῶσαι) of the pious at *Euthph.* 11 A 7–8.

52   *Francesco Fronterotta*

in a nominal definition depend on additional considerations that are arbitrary and impossible to settle. But with his 'What is *X*?' question, as it has been interpreted here, Socrates clearly requires a real definition, i.e. one that shows the very nature of the object to be defined, and that results from an immediate and objective knowledge of it: in fact, in Plato's view it is not the Ideas—i.e. the objects of thought and language—that depend on thought and language, but thought and language that must instead adhere to the universal and objective reality of their own content.[21] That is the sense of the enquiry on the pious, the beautiful, or any other Idea in itself, and that is why thought and language are not themselves able to establish the universality and objectivity of knowledge and discourse, but merely express them as a neutral vehicle of that universality and objectivity intrinsically belonging to Ideas.[22]

We can also reach the same conclusion from a different starting-

[21] I borrow the distinction between 'nominal' and 'real' definition from Allen, *Earlier Theory*, 79 ff., on which the analysis carried out here partly depends. The truth of the nominal definition results solely from the exactitude of the words used and the correctness of their combination in the sentence, certainly not from their correspondence to the real objects they designate, which remain out of the semantic context of λόγος. Consider the following example: that the centaur is 'a creature that is part man and part beast' is true; conversely, that the centaur is 'a creature that is part two-legged and part four-legged' is false. The truth or falsehood of such definitions derives only from the consistency or inconsistency of the words that constitute them. Yet it is clear that it is impossible in this context to know whether a definition is true, in that it corresponds adequately to a real object of this world, because the question of the actual existence of the definiendum is not even raised. However, if Ideas must serve as a universal and unchangeable model, as a criterion to guide thought, discourse, and behaviour, then knowledge and definition of Ideas must be objectively grounded, and no longer depend on a more or less broad agreement between the speakers on their consistency.

[22] The dialogues remain silent about a further implication of this perspective: if the answer to the 'What is *X*?' question is the proper being of '*X*' (the Idea of '*X*'), we shall dispose at first of a name, i.e. the name that designates the being of '*X*'. But to get a complex definition, one needs to assume that the Idea of '*X*' entertains mutual relationships with other Ideas, and it is by understanding these relationships that it will be possible to know which Ideas '*X*' does and does not communicate with, which Ideas it is and is not akin to, and which Ideas it embraces or is embraced by. This ontological map brings out the totality of predicates of the Idea of '*X*' in its definition. In the case of the quoted example, 'man' is first of all designated by its name, i.e. 'man itself' (or the Idea of man), but its definition is, let us say, a 'rational biped animal', because the Idea of man participates in the Idea of animal, though diverging from the genus of quadrupeds without reason and resembling the genus of rational biped animals. In short, the definition of '*X*' depends, on the one hand, on immediate and objective knowledge of the Idea of '*X*'; on the other, on tracing the map of its relationships with other Ideas: the definitional dialogues fall short on the first point, without even touching on the second.

Plato's Theory of Ideas

point. We have seen how the *Hippias Major* and the *Euthyphro* emphasize the causal function of Ideas that are held responsible for producing certain effects in the sensible world.[23] They are said to be universal causes that constantly produce the same effects, and are yet distinct from them because (1) the causes remain perfect, identical, and motionless, while their effects appear defective, relative, and merely apparent; (2) the causes 'produce' (ποιεῖν) their effects, so that they are *other* than their effects; and (3) to produce their effects, the causes must be 'added to' or 'placed beside' (προσγίγνεσθαι–παραγίγνεσθαι) those very things in which they produce them: indeed, what is 'added to' or 'placed beside' a sensible thing is not a particular property (e.g. beauty in a body or the colour blue in the sky)—so that one could say that it subsists nowhere but in the very thing wherein it shows itself—but, rather, it is the being itself that yields that property as its effect (i.e. the beautiful itself or the blue itself), which is 'added to' or 'placed beside' the thing in question (i.e. a body or the sky), and therefore exercises its own causal action, producing the effect of which it is the cause (e.g. beauty or the colour blue). But that which always produces a certain effect in something, being 'added to' or 'placed beside' it, as it precedes that effect in space and time, actually subsists separately from the thing in which it produces the effect (and separately from the effect itself), i.e. 'before' and 'outside' it. Therefore, if the universal power of causation of Ideas does not (merely) consist in a form of explanation, but properly in the production of certain effects, I believe that it cannot be construed in the intersubjective context of discourse or thought, because it depends on the objective nature of the causal action of Ideas, which are distinct from the multiplicity of particular things for their degree (for they are perfect compared with imperfect things), their being (for they are independent of what they produce, in so far as they produce it), for their ontological location (because, by subsisting 'before' and 'outside' what they

---

[23] The causal function of Ideas is introduced in these dialogues (1) by syntactical cases (the instrumental dative, in *H.Ma.* 287 C 2, C 5, C 8, 294 B 1–2, etc.; *Euthph.* 6 D 11–E 1; ὑπό+genitive, in *H.Ma.* 297 A 5–6, B 1–2; διά+accusative, in *H.Ma.* 288 A 9–11) or (2) by verbal forms (especially ποιέω, in *H.Ma.* 296 C 2–3, E 8, 297 A 5–8, 300 A 9, 303 E 11–12, or προσγίγνομαι–παραγίγνομαι, in *H.Ma.* 289 D 4, D 8) or ultimately (3) by qualifying the Idea as αἴτιον (in *H.Ma.* 269 E 9, 297 A 1–4, A 8, B 1–2, C 2) or as πατήρ (in *H.Ma.* 297 B 9), and its effects as τὸ γιγνόμενον (in *H.Ma.* 297 C 2).

54 *Francesco Fronterotta*

produce, they somehow exist 'elsewhere' in that they are separated from it).

The Ideas therefore exist independently of the logical and intellectual act of definition and knowledge by a subject, by being distinct, autonomous, and prior to the multiplicity of particular things of which they represent the proper being.[24]

5. The development of Plato's theory of Ideas

Let us now consider the developmentalist interpretations of the theory of Ideas in a more general context, leaving aside Vlastos's position from which we started. In its most traditional form, the developmentalist thesis states that Ideas in the early dialogues are represented as immanent beings that are actually present in the multiplicity of particular things, of which they constitute the proper nature (φύσις or οὐσία); from the middle dialogues on, conversely, with the establishment of a completely separated ideal 'world', the Ideas are instead conceived as transcendent and self-sufficient beings, existing apart from the sensible 'world', although to some extent related to it by virtue of a weak copy–model relationship.[25] However, an initial objection can easily be raised against this thesis, since the vocabulary of the theory of Ideas does not warrant such a strong distinction: indeed, as we have seen, expressions denoting at the same time the immanence and the transcendence of Ideas appear in the dialogues frequently and without important changes. Basically, as from the definitional dialogues, the Ideas are described (1) as immanent beings, for they are present in a multiplicity of particular things and so in relation with them, and (2) as transcendent models, for they are said to exist apart, in themselves and by themselves. Confronted with this contrast, scholars have proposed two alternative solutions.

The first one, held by the supporters of the developmentalist

---

[24] As I shall explain in what follows, on this point I go beyond Allen's conclusions shared by Prior.

[25] The classic form of the developmentalist thesis I am referring to here is the one originally submitted over a long series of articles by H. Jackson, 'Plato's Later Theory of Ideas', I–VII, *Journal of Philology*, 10 (1882), 253–98; 11 (1882), 287–331; 13 (1884), 1–40; 13 (1885), 242–72; 14 (1885), 173–230; 15 (1886), 280–305; 25 (1897), 65–82; but see also J. Burnet, *Greek Philosophy* (London, 1914), i. 254, and A. E. Taylor, *Philosophical Studies* (London, 1934), 28–90.

Plato's Theory of Ideas 55

thesis, implies that whereas the Ideas in the middle dialogues represent the standard models separated from sensible things, in the early works no theory of Ideas is actually deployed, so that the beings Plato refers to as ἰδέαι, εἴδη, or οὐσίαι ought merely to be regarded as the proper nature or structure of things, a certain distinguishing form or mark that always exists *together with* or *in* the sensible things and never *apart from* them.[26] These arguments are based on at least three assumptions that it is probably useful to look at briefly.[27]

(I) It has been argued that in Greek, and consequently in Plato's dialogues, the terms ἰδέα and εἴδος have first of all the generic meaning of 'outward appearance', 'aspect', or 'distinguishing form' of something; this would warrant the suggestion that Plato makes use of them in their technical meaning, with reference to the intelligible Ideas, *only* in middle dialogues.[28] However, I am keen to underline that even if there is actually no doubt as to the different meanings of the terms ἰδέα, εἴδος, or γένος—so that the introduction of the theory of Ideas in a dialogue cannot be inferred, *sic et simpliciter*, from their presence in a text—nothing warrants the hypothesis that in the early dialogues these terms *always* have a non-technical meaning, while in the middle dialogues they *always* refer to the theory of Ideas. In sum, the linguistic analysis does not produce strong enough arguments either to support or to reject the hypothesis of a theory of Ideas in the early dialogues.[29]

(II) It has been argued that Plato entirely overlooks the relationship between the distinguishing form or mark of things, which is the object of Socratic enquiry in the definitional dialogues, and the things themselves, whereas the participation of sensible things in intelligible Ideas represents one of the most de-

---

[26] Other scholars, however, while accepting the developmentalist thesis, conceive the Ideas in the definitional dialogues as pure linguistic terms, necessary to the definition of things, of their properties and relations, and therefore solely subsisting in the logical-semantic context of predication and λόγος: see e.g. J. M. E. Moravcsik, *Plato and Platonism* (Cambridge, Mass., and Oxford, 1992), 60–1.

[27] See the arguments set out by Dorion, *Lachès & Euthyphron*, 209–11.

[28] See e.g. Rist, 'Earlier Theory?', and Giannantoni, *Dialogo socratico*, 334–9.

[29] Developmentalist scholars omit to provide any indication about this distinguishing form or mark of things in the early dialogues, while it would be useful to specify at least whether it coincides with the thing itself or designates a to some extent independent property of it, thus possessing a certain ontological status.

56   *Francesco Fronterotta*

bated issues in his later works. However, this remark is partly wrong, because the relationship between things and Ideas is described in *all* dialogues either as 'presence' (παρουσία) of Ideas in the participating things or as likeness of participating things to the ideal 'models' (παραδείγματα: see above, n. 19). What is more, at least up to the *Parmenides*, Plato does not take a clear stand on the modalities of participation, and one is forced to admit that the problem is left unsolved even in middle and late dialogues.

(III) It has been argued that, upon surveying the properties belonging to Ideas and things respectively, it is *only* in the middle dialogues that some pairs of opposite terms are introduced, such as being and becoming, rest and change, eternity and time, and so on, pairs whose positive terms refer to Ideas while the negative ones invariably qualify sensible things: this would imply that *only* in these dialogues are Ideas finally conceived as properly metaphysical objects. Yet, the attribution of true and eternal being to Ideas is a direct consequence of their status (previously set in the definitional dialogues) of self-identical, universal, and perfectly accomplished entities, for such entities do not alter their state, nor are they subject to any change in space and time and are therefore eternal and fully being. Likewise, the reduction of sensible things to change and becoming is but a necessary consequence of their status (previously set in the definitional dialogues) of particular, material, and changing entities, for such entities are subject to generation and corruption: a changing and particular entity is necessarily involved in becoming, and therefore does not appear stable and motionless.

Hence, in this strong version, the developmentalist thesis does not possess a clear philosophical and textual basis.

The second alternative admits a continuity of the theory of Ideas in Plato's dialogues, especially as regards the reasons for the introduction of Ideas as universal models of a multiplicity of particular things. According to this interpretation, Ideas would already be conceived as existing entities, capable of establishing mutual relationships, and subject to participation by sensible things, as early as the definitional dialogues. Yet, as to the assumption of separation from the sensible, the ontological status of Ideas changes, for

Plato's Theory of Ideas

their separation (χωρισμός), while absent in the early dialogues, represents the most distinctive feature of Plato's middle dialogues, where a wide gap is opened between two absolutely different and rigorously separated worlds. Against this thesis, defended by Allen (one of the rare scholars who has nevertheless recognized a true philosophical meaning in the theory of Ideas in the definitional dialogues),[30] I would argue that the difference between Ideas and sensible things, in the early dialogues, *already* consists in a real and concrete separation between two kinds of beings. It is an indisputable fact that the clear distinction in the definitional dialogues between Ideas and sensible things never takes on the 'mythical' form of the juxtaposition between two separated worlds, typical of the middle dialogues: but this represents a narrative change at most, consisting in the enlargement of the same epistemological and ontological hierarchy of beings from a 'geographical' point of view, which does not actually change Plato's philosophical perspective, and in which the theoretical 'mechanism' leading to the introduction of Ideas in my view remains unaltered. For, if the object to be defined and known must be universal, unchangeable, and stable, it obviously cannot belong to the physical world and be subject to our experience, unless it is rid of all its sensible properties and its own material shape, thus escaping the cycle of perpetual becoming of the sensible world. Going along with this sort of intellectual abstraction, one gradually comes to grasp the 'something' that is left over from the sensible thing once it has been made free from the sum of its properties, i.e. its proper being (οὐσία), which, though initially belonging to the sensible world, is progressively determined by successive subtractions as a purely intelligible form. For instance, to define 'man' one needs to know its nature, namely the τί that is left of it (and of all the particular men) when, once this process of abstraction is complete, one finally grasps the universal, unchangeable, and stable being—now intelligible and no longer sensible—that Plato refers to as 'Idea of man'. I tend to believe that this onto-epistemological principle, which plausibly explains the introduction of Ideas, forcing their status to be separated from the physical world and justifying their set of functions, is on no account subject to development in Plato's thought.[31]

---

[30] See Allen, *Earlier Theory*, 129–64, esp. 154.
[31] For further details on this point, see my *Methexis*, 66–79, 159–63, 174–80.

58   *Francesco Fronterotta*

6. Socrates, Plato, and Aristotle: the origin of a methodological paradox

Once the question of the development of Plato's theory of Ideas has been stated in these terms, the necessary premiss (A) for the Socratic question, at least in the form in which it has been initially outlined in these pages, falls apart due to the close link binding the developmentalist interpretation of Plato to the Socratic question. I suggest that there is an implicit exegetical prejudice shared by many scholars, consisting in the dogmatic assumption that Plato's early dialogues represent a faithful portrayal of Socrates' philosophical activity. The reason for such an assumption is quite clear: indeed, if Socrates were not present in these dialogues—in other words, if the doctrines developed in them were attributable to Plato, for they are not unlike those developed in the later dialogues—how would it be possible to reconstruct his thought and traits? Certainly not solely through Aristophanes, who tends to portray Socrates as a comic figure and highlight his more paradoxical and ridiculous aspects; nor through Xenophon's writings, where Socrates is ultimately rendered as an honest thinker who dedicated his whole life to the *polis* (in any case as a much less interesting and complex personality than the one portrayed by Plato). Hence, one can look only to Plato's early dialogues, in which the young philosopher, while still under the influence of his recently executed master, is supposed to have faithfully portrayed his traits. But if this is really the case, all references to the theory of Ideas certainly have to be erased from these dialogues, otherwise, against all historical evidence,[32] Socrates would ultimately be credited with an ontological and metaphysical doctrine, or at least with its fundamental elements, broadening the extension of his thought, but drastically lessening Plato's. From this point of view, the only reasonable alternative is to make a clean cut between the early and middle dialogues, so marking Plato's detachment from his master, and thus assigning to the early dialogues the documentary aim of relating Socrates' doctrines, while consigning the introduction of the theory of Ideas to the middle dialogues.

Moreover, as regards Plato's dialogues, this exegetical outline implies a genetic interpretation of Aristotle's famous testimony on Socrates' activity and Plato's philosophical education: 'Socrates

---

[32] See only Aristotle, *Metaph.* M 4, 1078^{b}9–32; *NE* I. 4, 1096^{a}12–13.

Plato's Theory of Ideas

occupied himself with ethical matters . . . seeking the universal in them, and fixed thought for the first time on definitions; Plato accepted his teaching, but held that the problem applied not to sensible things but to things of another kind; . . . things of this other kind, then, he called Ideas, and sensible things, he said, are beside them and are all named after them'[33]—as if Aristotle were suggesting that Plato's dialogues can be classified according to a theoretical and chronological scheme 'early/late' (Socrates/Plato); in a word, as if Aristotle were stating that Socrates' search for the universal in ethics and Plato's doctrine of Ideas can be found in Plato's early and middle dialogues, respectively.[34] Unfortunately, a simple reading of the dialogues shows how the theory of Ideas progressively arises, starting from the definitional dialogues (i.e. from the *Laches* and the *Charmides* to the *Hippias Major* and the *Euthyphro*, and later on to the *Meno* and the *Cratylus*) in a uniform and consistent form, without any symptom of a clean break or a radical shift in Plato's thought. This raises the following question: how far is it possible to extend Socrates' influence, *in the dialogues*, and what, *in the dialogues*, may explain the introduction of the theory of Ideas, thus attributing a metaphysical dimension to Socrates' search in ethics and an ontological status to the universal he is said to seek?[35]

Now, without denying the unquestionable Socratic feature of Plato's dialogues (at this point, regardless of whether in all, most, or just some), notably in the setting, the method of enquiry, and even in the nature of the issues raised, I believe that Plato already inaugurates an original philosophical trend from the early dialogues, especially regarding the onto-epistemological framework of the theory of Ideas. This does not contradict Aristotle's testimony, according to which Socrates examined the universal form of definition in ethics, while Plato in turn placed this enquiry on a metaphysical level, identifying the Socratic universal with intelligible Ideas and first proposing a theory of Ideas, because Aristotle—it

---

[33] *Metaph.* A 6, 987^{b}1–10; see M 4, 1078^{b}9–32.

[34] This exegetical prejudice appears to be unanimously shared by developmentalist scholars, and, obviously, by all those who believe Plato's early dialogues to contain faithful evidence of the doctrines of the historical Socrates: see e.g. Vlastos, *Ironist*, 91–8.

[35] Vlastos, *Ironist*, 107–31, 271–5, 360–6, tried to explain this change in Plato's thought by resorting to Pythagorean influence (that would have arisen in addition to Socrates' teaching in the philosophical education of young Plato) and to Plato's ever greater interest in mathematics. This hypothesis, however, remains quite vague.

60 *Francesco Fronterotta*

is worth repeating once again—*never states or implies in any way* that this philosophical change is faithfully mirrored in the chronological succession of Plato's dialogues; on the contrary, I think one can rightly assume that Aristotle's testimony actually refers to Plato's early dialogues as a whole, where the theory of Ideas already emerges, but in a context that is still starkly influenced by the distinguishing traits of the Socratic method and style of enquiry.[36] This hypothesis does not exclude the search for traces of Socrates in Plato's writings, but, by narrowing the extent of this research, it provides a more consistent picture of Plato's thought throughout its various stages, granting the methodologically indisputable principle whereby the study of Plato's dialogues *can* and *must* be kept safe from any unjustified meddling with the Socratic question.[37]

7. Conclusion

I wish to make it clear that the arguments submitted here are not intended to refute the developmentalist interpretations of Plato's theory of Ideas, but merely to point out that they rest on controversial assumptions, to say the least. Likewise, I have not sought to demonstrate an anti-developmentalist thesis, but merely to highlight that it is entirely plausible. Finally, I have tried to show how developmentalist interpretations may depend on an exegetical prejudice related to the Socratic question, while the anti-developmentalist thesis does not in itself appear to be as systematic as has some-

[36] Moreover, it is most likely that Aristotle's testimony depends essentially on Plato, and this must warn against any incautious use by anyone assuming it implies a strict chronological order of dialogues. In other words, Aristotle certainly distinguishes Socrates' and Plato's doctrines, but this distinction, while allowing the reader to establish a comparison with the dialogues, certainly does not suggest that an analogous chronological scheme should be applied to Plato's dialogues.

[37] This conclusion is in agreement with Dorion's introduction to Xénophon, *Mémorables*, ed. L.-A. Dorion and M. Bandini (Paris, 2000), vol. i. Dorion actually goes further, stating that the Socratic question is groundless for at least three reasons: (1) each interpretation involves in this context a preliminary choice of testimonies to give credit to, and such a choice implies *a priori* a certain conception of Socrates' philosophy, thus generating a vicious circle; (2) the common elements in the description of Socrates between the two major testimonies, Plato and Xenophon, turn out to be entirely superficial as they are set in wholly different philosophical and historical contexts and are, ultimately, incomparable; (3) Plato and Xenophon certainly did not have the documentary aim of providing a historical testimony of Socrates' life but, rather, each in his own way sought to revive the Socratic model in the context of a certain literary genre, that of λόγοι Σωκρατικοί.

Plato's Theory of Ideas 61

times been alleged, since the only constant factor it supposes in the philosophy of dialogues is a certain onto-epistemological principle, which in my view does actually seem unfailingly present in Plato's thought.

Università degli Studi di Lecce

BIBLIOGRAPHY

Adorno, F., 'Appunti su ὁμολογεῖν e ὁμολογία nel vocabolario di Platone', in id., *Pensare storicamente* (Florence, 1996), 49–65.

Allen, R. E., *Plato's Euthyphro and the Earlier Theory of Forms [Earlier Theory]* (London, 1970).

Baltes, M., 'Zum Status der Ideen in Platons Frühdialogen *Charmides, Euthydemos, Lysis*', in *Plato:* Euthydemus, Lysis, Charmides, ed. T. Robinson and L. Brisson (Proceedings of the V Symposium Platonicum; Sankt Augustin, 2000), 317–23.

Benson, H., 'The Priority of Definition and the Socratic Elenchus', *OSAP* 8 (1990), 19–65.

Beversluis, J., 'Does Socrates Commit the Socratic Fallacy?', *American Philosophical Quarterly*, 24 (1987), 211–23.

Burnet, J., *Greek Philosophy* (London, 1914).

Calogero, G., *Scritti minori di filosofia antica* (Naples, 1984).

Dorion, L.-A. (trans. and comm.), Platon, *Lachès & Euthyphron*, traduction inédite, introduction et notes par L.-A. Dorion (Paris, 1997).

—— and Bandini, M. (eds.), Xénophon, *Mémorables* (Paris, 2000).

Fronterotta, F., *Methexis: la teoria platonica delle idee e la partecipazione delle cose empiriche. Dai dialoghi giovanili al Parmenide* (Pisa, 2001).

Geach, P., 'Plato's *Euthyphro*: An Analysis and Commentary', *Monist*, 50 (1966), 369–82.

Giannantoni, G., 'Il Socrate di Vlastos', *Elenchos*, 14 (1993), 55–63.

—— 'Socrate e il Platone esoterico', in Giannantoni *et al.*, *La tradizione socratica* (Naples, 1995), 9–37.

—— *Dialogo socratico e nascita della dialettica nella filosofia di Platone [Dialogo socratico]*, ed. B. Centrone (Naples, 2005).

Gundert, H., 'Die ersten Spuren der Ideenlehre', in K. Döring and F. Preisshofen (eds.), *Platonstudien* (Amsterdam, 1977), 178–85.

Hermann, K. F., *Geschichte und System der Platonischen Philosophie* (Heidelberg, 1839).

Jackson, H., 'Plato's Later Theory of Ideas', I–VII, *Journal of Philology*, 10 (1882), 253–98; 11 (1882), 287–331; 13 (1884), 1–40; 13 (1885), 242–72; 14 (1885), 173–230; 15 (1886), 280–305; 25 (1897), 65–82.

62 *Francesco Fronterotta*

Kahn, C. H., *Plato and the Socratic Dialogue: The Philosophical Use of a Literary Form* [*Socratic Dialogue*] (Cambridge, 1996).

Longo, A., *La tecnica della domanda e le interrogazioni fittizie in Platone* (Pisa, 2000).

Maier, H., *Sokrates: Sein Werk und seine geschichtliche Stellung* (Tübingen, 1913)

Mohr, R. D., 'Forms in Plato's *Euthydemus*', *Hermes*, 112 (1984), 296–300.

Moravcsik, J. M. E., *Plato and Platonism* (Cambridge, Mass., and Oxford, 1992).

Pradeau, J.-F., and Fronterotta, F. (trans. and comm.), Platon, *Hippias majeur & Hippias mineur*, présentations et traductions par J.-F. Pradeau et F. Fronterotta (Paris, 2005).

Prior, W. J., 'Plato and the Socratic Fallacy', *Phronesis*, 43 (1998), 97–113.

—— 'Socrates Metaphysician', *OSAP* 27 (2004), 1–14.

Puster, R. W., *Zur Argumentationsstruktur platonischer Dialoge: Die 'Was ist X?' Frage in Laches, Charmides, Der größere Hippias und Euthyphron* (Munich and Freiburg, 1983).

Rist, J. M., 'Plato's Earlier Theory of Forms?' ['Earlier Theory?'], *Phoenix*, 29 (1975), 336–57.

Taylor, A. E., *Philosophical Studies* (London, 1934).

Vlastos, G., 'What Did Socrates Understand by his "What is F?" Question?' (1976), in id., *Platonic Studies*, 2nd edn. (Princeton, 1981), 410–17.

—— 'The Socratic Elenchus', *OSAP* 1 (1983), 27–58; repr. in id., *Socratic Studies* (Cambridge, 1994), 1–33.

—— 'Is the "Socratic Fallacy" Socratic?', *Ancient Philosophy*, 10 (1990), 1–16; repr. in id., *Socratic Studies*, 67–86.

—— *Socrates: Ironist and Moral Philosopher* [*Ironist*] (Cambridge, 1991).

Wolff, F., 'Être disciple de Socrate', in G. Giannantoni and M. Narcy (eds.), *Lezioni socratiche* (Naples, 1997), 29–79.

PERSUASION AND THE TRIPARTITE SOUL IN PLATO'S *REPUBLIC*

R. F. STALLEY

A MAIN theme of Christopher Bobonich's *Plato's Utopia Recast*[1] is that there are important changes in Plato's political theory between the *Republic* and the *Laws* which are largely prompted by developments in the theory of the soul. In agreement with many recent commentators Bobonich argues that Plato in the *Republic* puts forward a view according to which the soul consists of three agent-like parts.[2] This does not mean merely that the parts are causes of action. Rather, each of them is like a person in the following respects (220):

(1) Each has its own desires ($\epsilon\pi\iota\theta\nu\mu\iota\alpha\iota$), and can wish and want ($\beta\omega\lambda\epsilon\sigma\theta\alpha\iota$ and $\epsilon\theta\epsilon\lambda\epsilon\iota\nu$).
(2) Each has conceptual and cognitive capacities:

© R. F. Stalley 2007

An earlier version of this paper was read to a colloquium on Plato's moral psychology organized by Antony Hatzistavrou at Edinburgh University in January 2005. I am grateful to those who took part in that colloquium for their criticism and advice and to David Sedley for his comments on the penultimate version.

[1] C. Bobonich, *Plato's Utopia Recast: His Later Ethics and Politics* [*Utopia*] (Oxford, 2002). The arguments I discuss in this paper were foreshadowed in Bobonich's article 'Akrasia and Agency in Plato's *Laws* and *Republic*' ['Akrasia'], *Archiv für Geschichte der Philosophie*, 76 (1994), 3–36.

[2] For other interpretations of the parts of the soul in the *Republic* as 'agent-like' or 'anthropomorphic' see J. Moline, 'Plato on the Complexity of the Psyche' ['Complexity'], *Archiv für Geschichte der Philosophie*, 60 (1978), 1–26, repr. with minor alterations as pages 52–71 and 74–8 of J. Moline, *Plato's Theory of Understanding* [*Understanding*] (Madison, 1981); J. Annas, *An Introduction to Plato's* Republic [*Introduction*] (Oxford, 1981), 109–53; T. Irwin, *Plato's Ethics* [*Ethics*] (Oxford, 1995), 203–42. For more cautious treatments see A. W. Price, *Mental Conflict* (London, 1995), 40–72; H. Lorenz, 'Desire and Reason in Plato's *Republic*' ['Desire and Reason'] *OSAP* 27 (2004), 83–116; id., 'The Analysis of the Soul in Plato's *Republic*', in G. Santas (ed.), *The Blackwell Guide to Plato's* Republic (Oxford, 2005), 146–65; id., *The Brute Within* (Oxford, 2006), chs. 2–4; M. Anagnostopoulos 'The Divided Soul and the Desire for the Good in Plato's *Republic*', in Santas (ed.), *The Blackwell Guide to Plato's* Republic, 166–88.

64 R. F. Stalley

    (i) each has beliefs;
    (ii) each has practical goals;
    (iii) each can engage in some forms of reasoning, including reasoning about what to do;

and

    (iv) each can communicate with the others: one part can persuade another and they can all agree.

  (3) Each has its own pleasures.

Bobonich offers some powerful arguments to show that this account of the soul as containing agent-like parts is fundamentally flawed. He sees two main difficulties in it. The first is that it leads to an infinite regress. One of the reasons for postulating that the soul has distinct parts is to provide an explanation of *akrasia*. But, if each of the lower parts can have not only desires but also beliefs about what is in its own best interest, it would seem that these could conflict and that there could therefore be *akrasia* within the part of the soul. To account for this we would have to further subdivide the part and so on (247–54). The second main difficulty is that if the parts are seen as agent-like we cannot account for the unity of the person. Instead of 'a single ultimate subject of all a person's psychic states and activities' we have three distinct 'sources of agency' each with its own point of view, its own beliefs, desires, and so on (254–7).[3]

A central claim of Bobonich's work is that Plato came to see the flaws in the *Republic*'s account of the soul and in his later dialogues moved towards a more satisfactory theory. The myth of the *Phaedrus* evidently presupposes the tripartite doctrine, but Bobonich plausibly interprets it as implying both that awareness of the forms is necessary for conceptual thought and that the lower parts of the soul are not aware of the forms (298–316).[4] This means that those elements cannot form beliefs, engage in reasoning, or

---

[3] Earlier commentators made similar points, usually with a view to arguing that the parts of the soul should not be seen as agent-like. See R. C. Cross and A. D. Woozley, *Plato's Republic: A Philosophical Commentary* (London, 1964), 124; B. A. O. Williams, 'The Analogy of the City and the Soul in Plato's *Republic*' ['Analogy'], in E. N. Lee, A. P. D. Mourelatos, and A. M. Rorty (eds.), *Exegesis and Argument: Studies in Greek Philosophy Presented to Gregory Vlastos* (Assen, 1973), 196–206 at 199. This argument is rejected by Moline, 'Complexity', 222–5; Annas, *Introduction*, 142–6.

[4] Bobonich, *Utopia*, 298–316, takes two main points from his reading of the *Phaedrus* myth:

  (1) Only those souls which have seen the forms can be reborn as men. The reason

The Tripartite Soul in the Republic 65

exercise rational persuasion on one another. In the *Timaeus* the appetitive element, at least, evidently lacks the power of reason and is incapable of responding to rational persuasion.[5] It thus lacks the cognitive and conceptual powers which, on Bobonich's account, it has in the *Republic* (316–28). In the *Laws* there is no explicit mention of the tripartite theory. Bobonich believes that Plato in fact dispenses altogether with tripartition and offers a more satisfactory unitary theory of the soul (260–7).

I have doubts about several elements in this story, but here I want to concentrate on the idea that in the *Republic* Plato sees the soul as having parts that are agent-like. Although Bobonich is by no means the first scholar to interpret Plato in this way, he has developed his view more fully than any of his predecessors and has explored more thoroughly its implications for Plato's moral and political philosophy as a whole. From the point of view of this paper his most important and distinctive claims are those listed under (2) above. Among these I shall give particular emphasis to the idea that the parts are capable of exercising persuasion on one another. This is in some ways the strongest claim, since persuasion, as Bobonich understands it, could be practised only by one agent on another.[6] It requires that the elements communicate with one another and that each possesses a degree of rationality. The lower elements and particularly the appetitive element have to be capable not only of forming opinions but of forming opinions about what is good for them and which are accessible to rational argument. Moreover, since, on this account, it is primarily through persuasion that the parts affect one another and influence the behaviour of the

> for this seems to be that those who have not seen the forms cannot engage in conceptual thought (249 B–C).
>
> (2) The horses, which evidently represent the lower elements in the soul, do not glimpse the forms. It is only the charioteer who raises his head high enough to catch sight of them (248 A).
>
> Taken together, these points suggest that because the lower elements of the soul have not seen the forms they are incapable of conceptual thought.

[5] The account of the appetitive element at 70 D 8–71 B 3 makes it explicit that this part does not understand reason. A further passage (77 B 5–C 3) describes it as totally devoid of belief and calculation. Thus the suggestion at 70 A that this element can at least sometimes 'willingly obey' reason cannot be taken to mean that it is capable of rational persuasion.

[6] There may be weaker ways of understanding the language of persuasion and obedience which do not carry any suggestion that the parts of the soul are to be personified. See e.g. Arist. *NE* $1102^{b}14-1103^{a}3$.

66   R. F. Stalley

person, their capacity to engage in persuasion seems to be central
to their agency.

It is, I believe, questionable whether Plato in the *Republic* did
think of the parts of the soul in this way, but before pursuing that
issue I want to make two methodological points. The first is that
when we describe what goes on within our minds it is almost impossible to avoid metaphorical language. Very often these metaphors
involve talking as though our minds are inhabited by separate per-
sonages which interact in much the same way that human beings
interact with one another.[7] They engage in conversation, quarrel,
seek to overpower one another, and so on. This tendency even
affects the language in which modern neurologists describe their
discoveries.[8] Clearly we cannot assume that the use of such language always involves a theoretical commitment to some view of
the mind as a collection of separate agents. In the *Republic* this kind
of personification may be more than a mere metaphor. Socrates
introduces the doctrine of tripartition in order to show that the account of justice and the other virtues that he has developed for the
city can also be applied to the individual. This is possible because,
in his view, the city and the soul share a common structure. The
same characteristics which are found in the city must also be found
in the soul (435 A 6–436 A 3). The fact that he uses his account of

---

[7] One of the best-known examples of this kind of language is Hom. *Od.* 20. 17–
18, quoted in the *Republic* at 390 D and 441 B, and in the *Phaedo* at 94 D. C. Gill,
Personality in Greek Epic, Tragedy, and Philosophy: The Self in Dialogue [Personality]
(Oxford, 1996), 183–9, discusses this passage in a chapter on 'The Divided Self in
Greek Poetry'. His other main examples are Hom. *Il.* 9. 645–8, Soph. *Aj.* 646–
92, and Eur. *Med.* 1021–80. The Sophocles passage does not explicitly suggest a
distinction between parts of the soul or personality. But those from Homer seem
to imply some kind of distinction between oneself and the 'heart' ($\kappa\rho\alpha\delta\acute{\iota}\eta$) seen as
the seat of emotion. A similar role is given to spirit ($\theta\bar{\nu}\mu\sigma$) in the *Medea*. For an
argument that such language should not be taken to deny the unity of the person
see B. A. O. Williams, *Shame and Necessity* (Berkeley, 1993), ch. 2.

[8] See e.g. A. Motluk, 'Particles of Faith', *New Scientist*, 189/2536 (28 January
2006), 34–6. Motluk discusses the work of the neurologist Vilaynur Ramachandran
on patients suffering from the condition called 'anosognosia', who deny obvious facts
about their bodies, such as that they are paralysed. She writes: 'Such observations
have led Ramachandran to suggest that in healthy brains there is a back and forth
between believing the old and accepting the new. The left hemisphere, he maintains,
tries to impose consistency, whereas the right hemisphere plays devil's advocate,
trying to get us to question our beliefs in the light of new evidence. In people with
anosognosia, he suspects that brain damage caused by the stroke somehow impairs
the right hemisphere's natural scepticism. The left hemisphere is left on its own to
uphold the status quo no matter what—even at the risk of becoming delusional.'
Here parts of the brain are personified but presumably this is not to be taken literally.

The Tripartite Soul in the Republic 67

justice in the city to cast light on justice in the soul means that much of what he says about the soul is couched in the language of politics. This political language is used not only in elucidating the nature of justice in the soul but in persuading us that justice is worthwhile. Since politics by its very nature involves the interaction of separate agents, it is inevitable that the parts of the soul are sometimes described as though they were human beings participating in the public life of a city. Clearly much of this language cannot be taken literally. Parts of the soul do not literally form factions, take up arms against one another, conduct wars against external enemies, exile their opponents, or seize a citadel.[9] An important task for the interpreter is to decide just how we are to understand this political language when it is applied to the parts of the soul.

It is also important to remember that the conversation between Socrates and his companions develops in quite complex ways. The doctrine of the tripartite soul appears and reappears in a number of different contexts, which may have a significant effect on what is said about it.[10] All of these passages can contribute to our understanding of Plato's doctrine, but clearly we cannot read them all in the same way as though they were intended as statements of literal scientific truth. It is particularly unfortunate that in discussing the tripartite soul scholars have sometimes taken passages out of context as though they had the same kind of status. We need, rather,

---

[9] 440 A 6–7, 440 B 3, 440 C 7, 440 E 2–4, 442 B 5, 559 E 4–560 B 9.

[10] (1) There are separate philosophic and spirited tendencies which need to be harmonized within the souls of the young Guardians: 375 A–376 C, 411 E–412 A. (2) The account of temperance in the city is based on the supposedly commonplace idea that there are better and worse elements in the soul: 430 C–432 A. (3) When Socrates raises the question whether there are parts in the soul corresponding to the classes in the city, he assumes that there are three broad kinds of individual: the spirited type, the lovers of learning, and the lovers of money. He sees it as likely that similar types will be found within the soul: 435 E–436 A. (4) Socrates argues that there are separate reasoning and appetitive elements: 436 B–439 D. (5) The spirited element is separated off from the appetite and from reason: 439 E–441 C. (6) Socrates shows that the virtues in the soul can be located in the same way that they were in the city: 441 C–444 B. (7) The tripartite soul underpins the discussion of the inferior cities and the corresponding kinds of individual in bks. 8 and 9: 553 A–580 C. (8) Bk. 9 classifies individuals according to the element that is dominant in their soul and argues that the philosopher is the most truly happy: 580 D–583 A. (9) At the end of bk. 9 the moral significance of tripartition is summed up in the image of the human being as a complex beast: 588 B–592 B. (10) The pleasures of the different parts of the soul are examined with a view to determining which is truest: 583 B–587 A. (11) In bk. 10 it is argued that illusions are the product of the lower part of the soul: 602 C–603 B.

68 *R. F. Stalley*

to look at the relevant passages in their context. To do that at all thoroughly is a major undertaking. In this paper I shall concentrate on the key sections in book 4 where Plato introduces the tripartite doctrine. These sections provide the clearest and most closely argued account of the doctrine, and are considerably less rhetorical than the passages in books 8 and 9 where Socrates seeks to convince his listeners that the life of the unjust man and of the unjust city is truly miserable.[11]

My second methodological point concerns what is sometimes called 'the principle of charity', the principle that one should, in general, try to read a philosopher in such a way as to make the best possible sense of what he says. In particular, one should not attribute to a philosopher a view that is obviously false if there is a reasonable interpretation of his writing that yields a more plausible view. This is particularly the case if we are going to argue, as Bobonich does, that Plato, at one stage in his life, put forward a theory with serious difficulties and then abandoned it for something better. Interpreting Plato in this way obviously raises the question why he did not see the difficulties in the first place. So if we are going to claim that the view of the soul's parts as agent-like really does get Plato into serious difficulties, we have to show not only that this view is *a possible* interpretation of what is said in the *Republic* but that it is the *only* reasonable interpretation. To put the point another way, if there are doubts about the meaning of what Plato says in the *Republic*, we should, if at all possible, resolve those in ways which leave him with a defensible position.

1. Reason and appetite

The argument for the separation of the reasoning and appetitive elements in the soul has the following structure:

---

[11] Annas, *Introduction*, 125 and 141, sees a discrepancy between the argument of bk. 4 and the treatment of the tripartite soul later in the dialogue. However she gives priority to the later passages primarily because she believes that 'Plato's actual argument for the distinctness of the soul's parts does not establish what the parts are which he needs and uses' for 'the main moral argument of the *Republic*'. I doubt if the main moral argument of the *Republic* does require a view of the parts as agent-like. In any case there are two problems with this view: (1) it relies on the selectively literal interpretation of passages which must be in large part metaphorical; (2) if Bobonich is right in suggesting that the agent-like view of the parts is unsustainable, then it implies that the *Republic*'s defence of justice is equally unsatisfactory.

The Tripartite Soul in the Republic   69

(1) The same thing cannot act or be acted upon in opposite ways at the same time, in the same respect, and in relation to the same object (436 B 8–9).

(2) Desire and aversion should be classed along with opposite ways of acting or being affected (437 B 1–C 10).

(3) Thirst is the desire for drink (437 D 2–6).

(4) So, if someone is thirsty and at the same time feels an aversion to drinking, there must be within him two distinct entities, one of which leads him to drink and the other of which draws him back from drinking (439 B 3–6).

(5) It does sometimes happen that people are thirsty and at the same time have an aversion to drinking (439 C 3–5).

(6) Therefore there must be separate entities within such people, one of which leads them to drink and one of which prevents them from doing so (439 C 6–8).

(7) That which leads them to drink stems from calculation while that which prevents them stems from passions and diseases (439 C 10–D 3).

(8) Therefore there must be separate calculative and appetitive elements within us (439 D 4–9).

Premiss 1 (sometimes called 'the principle of opposites' or 'the principle of contraries') is stated as an obvious truth in 436 B 8–9. Plato elucidates it by making Socrates consider two cases which might appear to be counter-examples. The first is that of a man who stands still while moving his arms. The second is that of a spinning top which stays in one place while revolving. Both might seem to be simultaneously moving and stationary and thus to be acting or being affected in opposite ways at the same time. Evidently we are supposed to deal with the case of the man by distinguishing different parts. The arms are moving but the legs and body are not. Thus we do not here have a case where one and the same thing is both moving and stationary. In the past it was commonly assumed that Plato means to deal with the top in the same way: he distinguishes different parts, the axis and the circumference, one of which remains stationary while the other moves. But if this is his view he is mistaken. Clearly the whole top revolves while remaining in a single location. Most recent interpreters have therefore taken him to mean that the top is stationary with respect to one kind of motion

70   R. F. Stalley

while moving with respect to another kind.[12] Here, therefore, we have a case where one and the same object is both stationary and moving at the same time and in relation to the same objects but does not violate the principle of opposites because it is not moving and stationary 'in the same respect'.

Premiss 2 is established in the following way:

'Well then,' I said, 'consider assenting and dissenting, seeking to take something and rejecting it, embracing something and rejecting it. Wouldn't you put all such things among those actions and affections which are opposed to each other—it doesn't matter which?' 'Of course,' he said. 'They are among the opposites.' 'What about these then,' I said, 'thirst and hunger and the desires in general, and then wanting and wishing. Wouldn't you put all these things among the classes we have just referred to? For example, won't you say that every time someone desires something his soul seeks after that which he desires or draws what it wishes to have towards itself? Or again, in so far as it wants to be provided with something doesn't it nod to itself in assent to that thing, as though answering a question from someone, and doesn't it reach out to be given it?'

'I agree.'

'What about not wishing, not wanting, and not desiring? Shall we put these into the category of its pushing something away and thrusting it from itself, that is, into the category of everything that is opposed to the things we have just mentioned?'   (437 B 1–C 10)[13]

It is notable here that Socrates does not say explicitly that desire and aversion are opposites. Instead he links them to three pairs of affections or actions in which the members of the pair seem very obviously to be opposed to each other. These pairs are carefully chosen. They each have an important psychological component, but in at least two of the cases the Greek terms also include rather more. Assent (ἐπινεύειν) is literally to nod one's head forward, while dissent (ἀνανεύειν) is literally to nod one's head back. Clearly one cannot do both these things at the same time. Similarly, embracing a thing (προσάγεσθαι) is literally drawing it towards one and rejecting it is thrusting it away (ἀπωθεῖσθαι). These may be seen as obvious examples of incompatible opposites only to the extent that they retain something of their literal senses. It is also striking that these terms could be applied literally only to embodied agents. Only a

---

[12] See e.g. R. F. Stalley, 'Plato's Argument for the Division of the Reasoning and Appetitive Elements in the Soul', *Phronesis*, 20 (1975), 110–28.

[13] Translations from the *Republic* are my own and follow the new Oxford text: Plato, *Res publica*, ed. S. R. Slings (Oxford, 2005).

The Tripartite Soul in the Republic

creature with a head can nod, and only one with a body of some sort can draw objects towards it or thrust them away.

Plato takes a good deal of time over premiss 3, largely because he finds it necessary to establish that thirst is a desire for drink as such, not for a good drink (437 D 7–439 B 1). This point plays no direct part in the argument for the division of the soul. Most commentators assume that Plato is fortifying his argument against objections based on the Socratic theory that all desire is for the good.[14] Someone who took this view might argue that, if all desires are for the good, the kind of conflict among desires which is presupposed by the argument for the division of the soul cannot occur. In particular, if the thirsty person desires a drink only in so far as it is good, there could be no conflict between the desire to drink and the desires of reason (which presumably seeks the good). So Plato has to make it clear that 'the soul of the thirsty man, in so far as it is thirsty, wishes for nothing except drink. It reaches for this [τούτου ὀρέγεται] and drives towards this [ἐπὶ τούτου ὁρμᾷ]' (439 A 9–B 1). Here again the terms used include ones which would make literal sense only if applied to an embodied agent.

Given premisses 1–3, one might expect Socrates to argue directly that if we find thirst and an aversion to drink within a soul, it must contain two separate elements, one of which is thirsty and the other of which is unwilling to drink. Instead he follows a more circuitous route. He argues at 439 B 3–C 1 that 'if anything ever pulls back the thirsty soul, it would be a different element from the one that is thirsty and, like a beast, draws it to drink'. Socrates illustrates this with the example of an archer. We should not say that the archer's hands pull and push the bow but rather that one pulls while the other pushes. If it has already been agreed that desire and aversion were opposites, there would, strictly speaking, be no need to introduce the idea that someone who is thirsty is being pulled towards drink while someone who is unwilling to drink is being pulled in the opposite direction. Possibly Plato put these words into Socrates' mouth to reinforce the idea that there are opposite forces at work within the soul of the person who is both thirsty and unwilling to drink and that these forces are of such a kind that they

---

[14] See N. R. Murphy, *The Interpretation of Plato's* Republic (Oxford, 1951), 28–9; T. M. Penner, 'Thought and Desire', in G. Vlastos (ed.), *Plato*, ii. *Ethics, Politics and Philosophy of Arts and Religion* (Garden City, NY, 1971), 96–118 at 106–7: Irwin, *Ethics*, 206–7. For a somewhat different view see G. R. Carone, 'Akrasia in the *Republic*: Does Plato Change his Mind?', *OSAP* 20 (2001), 107–48 at 116–21.

72   R. F. Stalley

must issue from different elements. But in this passage desires and aversions are pictured in a way that is significantly different from the way in which they were pictured earlier. Both passages use the language of pushing and pulling, but at 437 B 1–C 10 it was the desiring *soul* that drew the *object* towards itself while the unwilling soul thrust it away. Now it is the appetitive element which draws the *soul* to drink while reason pulls it back.

At 439 C 6–8 the conclusion is drawn that there must be at least two elements in the soul. But in drawing this conclusion Socrates complicates matters by introducing yet another way of describing what goes on in the soul of someone who is both thirsty and unwilling to drink. What we must say about such people is that there is an element in the soul commanding (κελεῦον) them to drink and another preventing (κωλῦον) them. The element which prevents them is distinct from the element which commands them and overpowers it.

In step 7 of the argument, whatever prevents the thirsty man from drinking is said to arise, when it does, ἐκ λογισμοῦ, 'from calculation', while whatever it is which draws the man to drink arises 'through affections and diseases' (διὰ παθημάτων τε καὶ νοσημάτων, 439 C 10–D 2). The conclusion (8) is that one of these may be described as 'that with which the soul calculates', λογίζεται, or as 'the calculative element', τό λογιστικόν, and the other as 'the part with which [the soul] loves, hungers, thirsts and is agitated by the other desires, the irrational and desiring [ἀλόγιστόν τε καὶ ἐπιθυμητικόν] companion of certain replenishments and pleasures' (439 D 5–8). The fact that a desire arises from a process of calculation is here taken to show that it stems from the rational element. This argument presupposes that the element in question is the sole element capable of calculation.[15] Similarly, when Socrates designates it as the calculative (λογιστικόν) because it is that by which the soul calculates (ᾧ λογίζεται), he is speaking generally. It is not just the element with which the calculation was done on this particular occasion but

---

[15] This point may appear controversial. Bobonich, *Utopia*, 244, like several other recent commentators, takes the description of the appetitive element as 'money loving' because 'it is chiefly through money that such desires are gratified' (580 E 5–581 A 1) to imply that the appetitive element must be capable of means–end reasoning. This claim is well criticized by T. Penner and C. Rowe, *Plato's Lysis* (Cambridge, 2006), 103 n. 16, and by Lorenz, 'Desire and Reason', 110–12 (= *The Brute Within*, 47–8). But it is, in any case, clear that 439 C 6–D 8 must imply the contrary. In other words, the claim that the appetitive element is capable of calculation is inconsistent with the main argument for tripartition.

The Tripartite Soul in the Republic 73

the element with which calculation is always done. Conversely the appetitive element is described as ἀλόγιστον with the apparent implication that it is devoid of calculative ability.[16]

Although the whole section 436 A–439 D is quite closely argued, it is surprisingly difficult to extract from it any very precise view about the nature of the parts of the soul, about the ways in which they interact with one another, or about how they influence our actions. For example, if Plato meant the parts to be seen as agents, one might expect him to make it clear that, strictly speaking, it is the parts that have wishes and desires. In other words, he could have made Socrates say explicitly that in the case of the man who is thirsty but unwilling to drink there is a part which desires to drink and a part which desires not to, but he does not do so. Throughout this whole section it is normally the human being or the soul that is the subject of psychological verbs such as 'desire' (ἐπιθυμεῖν) and 'wish' (βούλεσθαι).[17] The one exception is at 439 A 9–B 5, which reads as follows:

> 'The soul of someone who is thirsty, in so far as it is thirsty, wishes for nothing except to drink. It reaches for this and drives towards it.'
> 'That's clear.'
> 'Then if anything ever pulls back the thirsty soul it would be a different element from the one that is thirsty and, like a wild beast, draws it to drink?'

Here Socrates speaks of the part which draws the soul to drink as 'thirsty'. But it is in a context in which the soul is the subject of all the other psychological verbs. It is quite possible, therefore, to take the phrase 'the one that is thirsty' as a loose way of referring to the element which is responsible for the soul's being thirsty. We could then adopt a reading according to which it is the soul that has

---

[16] Moline, 'Complexity', 9–11, and *Understanding*, 59–61, counters this interpretation by arguing that τὸ λογιστικόν need not mean 'the sole calculative element' and that in calling this part ἀλόγιστον Socrates means that it is foolish or stupid rather than that it lacks all power of calculation. There is no doubt that ἀλόγιστον is most often used to describe a person who possesses some power of calculation but fails to use it, or uses it badly, and thus behaves in a foolish or thoughtless way. But it is far from clear that it bears this meaning when applied to a part of the soul. The adjective λογιστικός, on the other hand, always means 'calculative', never 'clever'. Thus when λογιστικός is opposed to ἀλόγιστος, the latter is naturally taken to mean 'incapable of calculation'. The present passage contrasts the element with which we calculate and the element with which we have desires, and characterizes the one as *the* calculative element and the other as non-calculative. So the natural way of taking the passage is to suppose that one element has and the other lacks the power of calculation.

[17] 437 C 1, D 8, 438 A 2–4, 439 A 9, B 3, C 3.

74 *R. F. Stalley*

desires. These are explained in terms of the actions of its different parts—actions which are described metaphorically either as pushes and pulls or as commands and prohibitions.

A closely connected question is whether the parts of the soul act upon the soul or on one another. The picture offered by Bobonich and many other recent interpreters suggests that, particularly in their supposedly persuasive function, the parts act on one another. But in the passage just cited the parts are represented as pulling the *soul* in one direction or another. They do not pull each other. It is explicitly the soul that is drawn back from drinking. Socrates sees this as being just like the case of an archer. We should not say that his two hands simultaneously push and pull the bow but rather that one hand pulls while the other pushes.[18] Similarly, when Socrates speaks of one element in the soul commanding us to drink while another prevents this, it is apparently the soul to which the commands are addressed and which is prevented from acting. One element is said to overcome another when it exercises a more powerful influence upon the soul.[19]

These points suggest the possibility of understanding the argument for the separation of reason and desire in a different way

---

[18] It is difficult to know what to make of the archer example. In reality the archer is an agent who uses his hands to push and pull the bow. This might suggest that the person is a subject who desires things with (or by means of) the different parts of his soul. Against this Bobonich, *Utopia*, 234, argues that the hands are thought of as subjects which do the pushing and pulling. But they are obviously not subjects in the sense of agents. Moreover, there has to be some single thing (the bow) which they are pushing and pulling. To preserve the parallel with the parts of the soul we have to suppose that they too are pulling and pushing some single thing (presumably the individual or his soul). So it is difficult to find any interpretation which avoids the suggestion that the individual is something over and above the parts of his soul.

[19] This point has often been blurred by commentators, presumably because speaking of the parts as 'pulling' the individual seems to imply that the individual or his soul is something other than its parts, or perhaps that there is a 'self' over and above the three parts of the soul. For similar reasons they have played down passages which suggest that the individual hands control over to one or other of the parts of his soul (443 C 9–444 A 2, 550 A 5–B 7, 553 B 7–D 7; cf. Bobonich, *Utopia*, 531 n. 27). The passage at 550 A–B is particularly interesting because it speaks both of the parts as pulling on the individual and of the individual handing over control to one or other of them. Although both forms of expression embody quite natural ways of describing our experiences, it is difficult to make sense of them if they are taken as statements of scientific truth. Since the same goes for the view of the parts as agent-like, the obvious implication is that we should avoid over-literal interpretations of any of the language in which Plato describes the inner workings of the soul. It is also worth noting that *Laws* 644 D–645 C describes both reason and the passions and desires as pulling on us like the strings of a puppet, while at the same time suggesting that we have some choice as to which of these strings we co-operate with.

The Tripartite Soul in the Republic 75

from that adopted by most commentators. Plato's language would be consistent with the view that this man wishes to drink because something within him draws him towards drinking and that he refuses to drink because something draws him away from drinking. Because drawing the soul towards an object and drawing it away from that object are opposites, these elements must be distinct from one another. On that model the desires of the soul would be explained in terms of the workings of its parts without suggesting that those parts can strictly be said to have desires of their own.[20]

Another issue concerns the way in which the activities of the three parts are described. Bobonich finds in this section two different ways of characterizing the conflicting desires. He notes that in 437 B 1–C 10 desires are described first in terms of assent and dissent and then as forces acting in opposite directions. The first way of characterizing them assimilates the relation of conflicting desires to the logical and psychological opposition between assent and dissent (236). Bobonich sees a similar significance in the passage at 439 C 6–8, which he takes to say that 'in the case of thirsty people who do not wish to drink there is a something in the soul that bids them drink and a something that forbids'. He takes these passages to imply that 'desires have conceptual or propositional content'

[20] It is significant here that desire and aversion are not explicitly said to be contraries. On many interpretations Plato's argument for the division of the soul could be summarized as follows:

(1) The same thing cannot act or be acted upon in opposite ways at the same time, in the same respect, and in relation to the same object.
(2) Desire and aversion are opposites.
(3) Therefore, if a person simultaneously desires the same object in the same respect, two different parts of the soul must be involved: one which desires the object and one which is averse to it.

An analysis on these lines would imply that the parts are the bearers of desires and aversions (a point argued by Bobonich, *Utopia*, 225–35). But an alternative analysis is in fact available:

(1A) The same thing cannot act or be acted upon in opposite ways at the same time, in the same respect, and in relation to the same object.
(2A) A soul which desires an object is drawn towards that object; a soul which is averse to an object is drawn away from that object.
(3A) Being drawn towards an object and being drawn away from it are opposites.
(4A) Therefore the same thing cannot be drawn towards an object and away from it at the same time by the same thing.
(5A) Therefore, if a person simultaneously desires and has an aversion to the same object in the same respect, two different parts of the soul must be involved: one which draws the soul towards the object and one which draws the soul away from the object.

76   R. F. Stalley

and 'can enter into interactions with other psychic items in virtue of their own content' (237). This in turn opens up 'the possibility that they can change in the light of new information and that the desires of one part could change in response to communication with another part' (237–8).

This looks very dubious. At 437 B 1–C 10 it is, as we have seen, the *soul* that assents or dissents. Bobonich takes this to imply that it is really a part of the soul that does so, but this is not obvious. If I am right in suggesting that the literal meaning of ἐπινεύειν and ἀνανεύειν as 'nodding forward' and 'nodding backward' plays a part here, we cannot assume that Plato means to focus on the conceptual content of desires in this passage. The talk of commanding at 439 C 6–8 may seem to suit Bobonich's case better since it is clear that the commands are issued by a part of the soul. But the recipient of the command is evidently not another part of the soul, but the person.[21] Moreover, Plato seems to go out of his way to play down any logical distinction between the commanding and force models. Commanding someone to drink is presented as parallel to leading him like a beast to drink. It is also significant that, while Plato uses κελεύειν, 'command', to describe the activity of appetite in leading the soul to drink, the verb he uses to describe the role of the reason in stopping it from drinking is κωλύειν, 'hinder' or 'prevent', which need not imply any kind of conceptual content. At 439 C 10–D 8 Socrates asks 'Is it not the fact that that which inhibits such actions [τὸ κωλῦον] arises when it arises from the calculations of reason, but that the impulses which draw and drag [τὰ ἄγοντα καὶ ἕλκοντα] come through affections and diseases?' Here κωλύειν is paired as an opposite with the verbs ἄγειν and ἕλκειν, which suggest a purely physical kind of pulling. This mixture of vocabularies suggests that any distinction between the command and force models is unimportant. So if Plato did see the terminology of assent and command as preparing the way for a view of the parts of the soul as communicating with one another, he took very good care not to advertise the fact.[22]

---

[21] 'There is in the soul of these people something which commands and there is also something which [tries to] prevent drinking' (439 C 6–7). A soul-part is just not the sort of thing that could be said to drink. So these commands must be addressed to the person rather than to a part of the soul.

[22] There may also be a kind of pragmatic contradiction in the suggestion that one and the same part of the soul simultaneously commands us to drink and drags us to drink. If the command is successful then there is no need to drag. If the dragging is

The Tripartite Soul in the Republic 77

One should also sound a note of caution about the suggestion that the use of the language of assent and command indicates that desires may change in response to information or to communication from other parts (Bobonich, *Utopia*, 237–8). If someone whose authority I accept gives me a command or assents to a course of action, that may give me a reason for action. But the command or assent does this, not by directly changing my opinions or desires, but by changing the situation in which I am operating. For example, if a soldier's dominant concern is to obey orders, then the command of a superior officer to clean the latrines constitutes a good reason for him to clean them even though he may detest doing so and regard the command as unreasonable. In this respect commands are different from advice or persuasion. The latter give us reasons for action either by changing our view of the situation or by changing our desires. It is important not to blur this distinction. So far we have seen nothing to indicate that the inner workings of the soul involve giving reasons in the sense of advice or persuasion.

Taken as a whole, the argument for the separation of reason and desire contains little, if anything, that requires us to see these parts as agents which have their own wishes and desires and beliefs and seek to exercise rational persuasion upon one another. Indeed, it contains some elements which seem incompatible with that view. What is, perhaps, most striking is that Plato systematically varies his language and uses a variety of different metaphors. Thus the passage does not suggest a single model for the activities of the parts or for ways in which the parts relate to one another. This would be a serious defect if Plato's aim in *Republic* 4 were to offer a systematic scientific psychology. But all he needs to do in the context is to establish that there are three parts of the soul analogous to the three parts he has distinguished in the state. For this purpose it is enough if he can establish that the conflicting desires to which human beings are subject must have their sources in different parts of the soul.[23] Like many writers who try to describe the workings of the human mind, he has to rely on metaphorical language. The

---

successful there is no need to command. If, on the other hand, I have neither enough physical strength nor enough authority to get my way, putting the two together will make no difference.

[23] This point is well made by Annas, *Introduction*, 124, who takes Plato to be 'insisting that there is complexity in a single person without saying too much about how that complexity may be realized'.

78 R. F. Stalley

fact that he uses a variety of different kinds of metaphor does not mean that he is confused. Rather, it suggests an awareness that the language he uses cannot be taken literally. We have to be careful not to over-interpret the text.[24]

2. Spirit

The section 439 E 1–441 C 4, which distinguishes the spirited element in the soul, is more loosely argued than the previous one. It aims to establish (*a*) that anger cannot be located in the appetitive part of the soul, (*b*) that anger generally comes to the aid of reason in its battles with appetite, and (*c*) that it is nevertheless distinct from reason. The argument for the first of these claims relies largely on the story of Leontius, who became angry with himself for looking at the dead bodies. This is taken to show that anger sometimes makes war with the desires as though it was distinct from them (439 E 5–440 A 7). This argument is very weak. There obviously are reflexive psychological attitudes: one can, for example, be ashamed of oneself just as one can love or hate oneself. These attitudes may be focused on one particular part of one's personality but need not be. One could be ashamed of one's whole character. So it is by no means obvious why a unitary being could not be angry with itself. What is not possible is literally to wage war against oneself, but this dubious metaphor can hardly bear the weight of the argument.

The fighting metaphor recurs with more elaboration in the argument that spirit generally takes the side of reason:

'. . . don't we often see, when desires force someone to act against calculation, that he reproaches himself and gets angry with the element within him that is doing the forcing, and that, just as when two parties engage in civil war, the spirit of a man like this becomes the ally of reason? But, so far as concerns associating itself with the desires when reason has decided that one should not oppose it, I don't think you would say that you have observed such a thing happening in yourself or in anyone else.' (440 A 9–B 6)

There is no hint here that either reason or spirit might seek to exercise persuasion over the appetites.

---

[24] As Bobonich, *Utopia*, 527–8, points out, there is no suggestion that the conclusion of the bk. 4 argument (that there are three parts in the soul) is metaphorical. However, it can hardly be denied that Socrates uses a good deal of metaphorical language in arriving at that conclusion and in describing the activities of the soul's parts.

The *Tripartite Soul in the* Republic 79

The claim that spirit scarcely ever takes the side of the desires against reason looks dubious, but Socrates has further arguments to support his claim of a natural affinity between spirit and reason. Suppose that someone acts unjustly. The nobler he is the less likely he is to get angry if he has to suffer at the hands of someone who punishes him justly. His spirit is unwilling to rouse itself against such a person. If, on the other hand, someone thinks that he has been unjustly treated, it will boil and get angry and ally itself with whatever seems just. Even if it suffers in consequence, it will not cease from its efforts until it achieves its goal, dies, or is called off and calmed by the reason like a dog being calmed by a shepherd (440 B 9–C 4). The metaphors here, if taken seriously, would suggest that the parts of the soul are agents. They are capable of fighting, forming alliances, and, in the case of reason, taking decisions. Spirit is capable of forming desires for vengeance and of getting angry. There is also an implication that they must be capable of communication. If spirit can ally itself with reason, one would suppose that it has some understanding of reason's decisions. Reason is capable of calming spirit down and calling it off. But there are obvious puzzles. Talk of parts of the soul as, for example, forming alliances and making common cause with one another suggests the personification of those parts. But, at the same time, the thoughts about justice and injustice are explicitly attributed to the man rather than to spirit. The comparison of spirit to a dog which goes on blindly attacking a supposed enemy until it is called off suggests that it lacks any rational judgements and simply responds to instinct or its master's orders.

The distinction between spirit and reason is argued in a perfunctory way. Glaucon points out that spirit is found in young children while the power of reasoning appears late, if at all, in most people. Socrates adds that even wild beasts have spirit and quotes from Homer the passage where Odysseus has to restrain his anger against the suitors.[25] He is described as beating his breast and reproaching his heart. Socrates takes this as showing how 'the element that has calculated [ἀναλογισάμενον] about better and worse reproaches the element that is irrationally [ἀλογίστως] angry as though it were a different thing' (441 B 6–C 2). Here again it is notable that, whereas reason is seen as judging good and bad, spirit is treated as an irrational animal element incapable of making its own judgements. The

---

[25] See n. 6 above.

80   R. F. Stalley

implication is that it cannot be persuaded by rational argument but
can be trained to obey.

3. *Akrasia*, reason, and desires

I shall digress here to say something about *akrasia*. It is sometimes
assumed that a major purpose of the division of the soul in *Republic* 4 is to provide an explanation of this supposed phenomenon.
At one level this is obviously wrong. Within the overall context
of the *Republic* the main reason for distinguishing three parts of
the soul is to show that the concept of justice which Socrates has
developed in connection with the city can also be applied to the
individual. Moreover, Plato seems to go out of his way to avoid
drawing attention to the possibility of *akrasia*. The argument for
the separation of reason and desire depends on the claim that people
are sometimes both thirsty and unwilling to drink. This is precisely
the kind of situation in which we might expect acratic actions to
occur—someone might drink even though they know that doing
so is bad for them. But in describing the case Plato makes it clear
that reason overcomes desire, in other words that *akrasia* does not
occur.[26] Similarly, when, in distinguishing spirit from reason, he
likens spirit to a dog, it seems to be an obedient dog he has in
mind. It continues to attack until it is called off. In the passage
from Homer Odysseus succeeds in restraining his anger.

The one place where we might see a reference to *akrasia* is in
the story of Leontius. The obvious interpretation of this is that
the reasoning element in Leontius' soul forbids him to look at the
bodies while his desires urge him to do so. When he gives way to
his desire he becomes angry with himself. If this is right, the story
does involve *akrasia* but that is not made explicit. The story is told
simply to show that we can be angry with our desires.

Although the possibility of *akrasia* is not explicitly thematized
in *Republic* 4, there is some justification for seeing the argument
for the division of the soul as having an important bearing on it.
As we have seen, that argument depends on the fact that human
beings can experience conflicting emotions. It is claimed that such
conflicts would not be possible unless there were distinct parts in

---

[26] Bobonich, *Utopia*, 539 n. 76, recognizes that the argument for tripartition does
not require that *akrasia* should actually occur, merely that it is possible.

The Tripartite Soul in the Republic   81

the soul. If we assume, as seems plausible, that acratic actions occur only when we have conflicting motivations, it follows that only an agent whose soul contained more than one part could act acratically. This implies that the division of the soul must play a part in any Platonic account of *akrasia*. On the other hand, it does not follow that the division of the soul is in itself sufficient to explain *akrasia*, nor even that it plays the major role in such an explanation.

Bobonich recognizes that the explanation of *akrasia* is not the only purpose of the division of the soul in the *Republic* (218) but does nevertheless make it the main focus of his account. In particular he recognizes that the way in which he develops the distinction between the command model and the force model could pose an important problem with regard to *akrasia*. It suggests that the thirsty man who is unwilling to drink has both a desire to drink and a belief that doing so would be bad for him. Thus the acratic situation involves a 'misalignment' between one's desires and one's opinion about what is best (241). However, seeing the acratic situation in this way threatens to make the division of the soul superfluous to the explanation of *akrasia*. Bobonich believes that, in Plato's view, all three parts of the soul have opinions about what is best for them as well as desires. This implies that misalignments between opinion and desire could, in principle, occur, not only between parts, but within each part. For example, my appetitive part might have a powerful desire to drink while also being of the opinion that satisfying that desire would be bad for it because it would frustrate the satisfaction of other appetites. So if the mental conflict that is the precondition of *akrasia* is one between opinion and desire, it could occur within a single element of the soul. Postulating the existence of distinct parts of the soul thus does nothing to solve the fundamental problem of *akrasia* (241).

Bobonich concedes that this criticism would be extremely damaging to his interpretation if it could not be answered. His response is, however, to suggest that 'Plato might think that such misalignment between strength and evaluation may only be possible if these two desires are in different parts'. The reason why Plato might think this is that 'partitioning may explain the origin or the persistence of the acratic desire itself or of the fact that it is stronger than the desire for what is overall best' (242). The point here is that 'the Reasoning part's desire not to drink because it is not best overall to do so, does not by itself destroy or reduce the

82 R. F. Stalley

strength of the Appetitive part's desire to drink. Only because of some further persuasion of the Appetitive part does such a change come about.' On the other hand, 'beliefs and desires within any one part, e.g., the Appetitive part, do tend to interact in more or less rational ways.' So if the appetitive part becomes aware that drink will interfere with the satisfaction of its long-term goals, this may lead to 'the loss (or diminishment of the strength) of the desire to drink' (246).

This account is admittedly speculative. It is offered as an account of what Plato *might* think without any evidence that he did actually think it. But, in any case, it looks inadequate to its purpose. Plato is supposed to recognize that there is a distinction between thinking something best and desiring that thing, i.e. that someone can be convinced that a course of action is best without having a strong desire to adopt that course of action. Conversely, someone can desire to do something while recognizing that it is not for the best. The fundamental problem is thus that of seeing how two quite different kinds of mental state, opinion and desire, might oppose one another. This problem cannot be solved simply by locating these states within the same part of the soul. If desire and opinion are not the sorts of thing that can interact, locating them within the same part of the soul is not going to help.

The theory is also unsatisfactory in another way. It just does not seem to be true that opinions and desires, which on this interpretation would be located within the same part of the soul, have a greater tendency to interact in rational ways than opinions and desires located in different parts. Suppose, for example, I realize that indulging my craving for alcohol this evening will prevent me from satisfying various other bodily desires. This presumably would be a case in which appetite's opinion of what is best for it is misaligned with the desire to drink. But I may still give way to that desire. What is more, even if I manage to resist the desire, it will not disappear. The craving will still be there. So the problem about the origin and persistence of desires that are misaligned with opinions about the good recurs whether or not the desire and the opinion are located in the same part of the soul. Bobonich's interpretation of the *Republic* can therefore be preserved only by supposing that Plato holds a seriously mistaken view, for which there is no evidence in the text and which he apparently abandoned in his later work.

It is important to recognize here that the problem with which

The Tripartite Soul in the Republic 83

we have been concerned in this section occurs only if we attribute to appetite opinions about what is good for it. It is this that opens up the possibility of a misalignment between opinions and desires within the same part of the soul. So if we deny that appetite has opinions about the good, the problem disappears. Of course, reason has opinions as well as desires but in its case there is no possibility of misalignment. According to Plato, the nature of the reasoning element is to seek the true and the good. So if reason is of the opinion that doing something would be good, it will necessarily form a desire to do that thing. In those who have been poorly educated that desire of the reason may well conflict with desires of the appetitive element. If the appetitive desires are stronger then the agent will act acratically. Thus there is a readily available interpretation which gives full weight to the distinction between opinion and desire and which does give the division of the soul an important role in the explanation of *akrasia*. However, we cannot adopt that interpretation unless we reject the idea that appetite can form opinions about its good.[27]

4. Justice and the tripartite soul

Between 440 C 6 and 444 D 10 Socrates uses the tripartite theory of the soul to show that the accounts of justice and the other virtues which he has developed in the case of the city can also be applied to the individual. In particular the individual is just when each part of the soul does its own work and does not interfere with that of others, that is, when reason rules with the aid of spirit and appetite obeys. The analogy with the city inevitably means that there is in this section a good deal of language which, if taken literally, would suggest personification of the parts of the soul. Verbs like πράττειν ('do' or 'act') and πολυπραγμονεῖν ('be a busybody'), for example, normally have a personal subject. There is an interesting variation of vocabulary between this section and the argument for the division of the soul which precedes it. When arguing that the soul has three parts Socrates spoke of one part 'overpowering' or 'being overpowered' by another (κρατεῖν and κρατεῖσθαι 439 C 8,

---

[27] See e.g. Moline, 'Complexity', 11; C. Kahn, 'Plato's Theory of Desire', *Review of Metaphysics*, 41 (1987), 77–103 at 86; Irwin, *Ethics*, 215–16, 218–20; Bobonich, 'Akrasia', 4 n. 3.

84   R. F. Stalley

440 A 2, βιάζεσθαι 440 B 1, 2). But in his account of the virtues the analogy with the state leads him to use more distinctively political metaphors. In particular, he makes extensive use of the language of 'ruling' and 'being ruled' (ἄρχειν and ἄρχεσθαι). The calculative part should rule because it is wise and exercises forethought on behalf of the whole soul. The spirited element should be its subject and ally (441 E 3–5). The musical and gymnastic training has harmonized these elements so that they can watch over the appetitive element and prevent it from filling itself with the so-called bodily pleasures. They will thus ensure that it does not abandon its proper role by trying to 'enslave and rule over what is not properly ruled by its class' (442 A 4–B 3).[28] Reason and spirit will 'provide the best defence on behalf of the whole soul and the body if the former makes decisions while the latter fights on their behalf, following the ruling element and by its courage accomplishing what has been decided' (442 B 5–8). So the soul will be courageous when the spirited element 'preserves through pleasures and pains the rational instructions that are passed on [τὸ ὑπὸ τῶν λόγων παραγγελθέν]'[29] about what is or is not to be feared' (442 B 10–C 2). The soul is wise by virtue of the part that rules and issues these instructions. It has knowledge about what is in the interests of the community composed of the three parts (442 C 4–7). The temperance of the soul consists in the friendship and harmony of the parts 'when the ruling and ruled elements agree that the calculative element ought to rule and do not rebel against it' (442 C 9–D 2).

Throughout this passage there is extensive use of political metaphors. The language used to describe the virtues of the state is applied directly to the soul. But a page or so later Socrates introduces another analogy—that with the body (444 C 6–E 2). The body is healthy when the different elements within it are in their natural condition as regards domination and subordination. In this it

[28] As Gill, *Personality*, 245–6, points out, we find here language suggesting that 'the rational part, supported by the spirited one, coerces recalcitrant desires into accepting its rule' in the same context as language which characterizes the temperate soul in terms of 'friendship and harmony'. As the reference to musical education makes clear, the friendship and harmony are created by forms of training which do not presuppose rationality on the part of the lower elements.

[29] This phrase is particularly difficult to interpret. A. Bloom (trans.), *The Republic of Plato* (New York, 1968), renders it literally but unintelligibly as 'what has been proclaimed by the speeches'. Shorey has 'the ruler's designs', which is more explicit than the text warrants (*Plato: The Republic*, trans. P. Shorey (Cambridge, Mass., and London, 1930)).

The Tripartite Soul in the Republic 85

resembles the just soul. In the unhealthy body and the unjust soul the elements rule and are ruled by each other in an unnatural way. Here the terminology of κρατεῖν and κρατεῖσθαι is combined with that of ἄρχειν and ἄρχεσθαι. The analogies with the state and with the body are both important for Plato but they push in different directions. Comparing the soul to the state suggests that its parts are like citizens who can communicate with one another in more or less rational ways. Comparing the soul to the body suggests that they should be seen as mindless constituents of a larger organism.

Two passages in this section have been cited as demonstrating that there must be persuasion among the parts.[30] The first is 442 B 10 ff., where the soul is said to be courageous when the spirited element preserves 'the rational instructions that are passed on about what is or is not to be feared'. This closely parallels the account of the courage of the auxiliaries (412 D 9–E 8) and of the city (429 B 7–430 B 8). It implies that there is communication among the parts to the extent that the spirited element is responsive to decisions taken by the reason. But the verb used to describe that communication is παραγγέλλειν, which is standardly used of passing on a message or command such as that issued by a military officer. It does not suggest rational persuasion.

The second passage is 442 C 9–D 2. There it is suggested that the temperance of the soul consists in the friendship and harmony of the parts 'when the ruling and ruled elements agree that the calculative element ought to rule and do not rebel against it'. Since a more literal translation of ὁμοδοξεῖν, the word I have translated 'agree', would be 'have the same belief (δόξα)' this may seem to suggest that, in Plato's view, all parts of the soul are capable of forming beliefs and indeed of sharing the same beliefs.[31] However, if 'belief' is taken to refer to the kind of belief that can be influenced by rational persuasion, this need not be the case. At *Phaedo* 83 D 4–E 2 ὁμοδοξεῖν is used to describe the agreement between soul and body which comes about when the soul gives itself over to bodily pleasures.[32] Moreover, in the only passage in the *Republic* where δόξα is explicitly attributed to the lower soul it is clearly not accessible to reason.[33]

---

[30] Bobonich, *Utopia*, 220, 242, 317, 555 n. 40. [31] Ibid. 526 n. 2.

[32] Bobonich, ibid. 486 n. 26, argues that Plato in the *Phaedo* does indeed see the body as capable of forming opinions, but this is highly implausible. The point is presumably that the body in desiring certain objects treats these as good. A soul which seeks the same objects may be said to agree with the body.

[33] At 602 C 7–603 A 8, where Socrates discusses illusions, the illusion that a straight

86   *R. F. Stalley*

In fact Socrates' use of ὁμοδοξεῖν in the description of the temperate soul recalls an earlier passage, 430 C 8–432 B 1, where he seeks to elucidate the temperance of the city by applying to it the idea that temperance is self-mastery. An individual is said to be master of himself when the better element in his personality is master over the worse. So Socrates suggests that his ideal city will be temperate because the desires of the many inferior people will be mastered by the desires and wisdom of the smaller and better class (431 B 9–D 2). He then adds that in his city the same opinion as to who should rule will be found both in the rulers and in the ruled (431 B 9–E 2). This is, of course, a different point from the previous one. However, when Socrates raises the question which of the virtues is most responsible for making the city good, he refers to temperance simply as the ὁμοδοξία, the sharing of opinion by rulers and ruled (433 C 6). There is a similar conflation of different accounts of temperance in the discussion of virtue in the soul. At 442 A 4–B 3 Socrates describes how in the just soul reason and spirit are set to watch over the appetitive element and to ensure that it does not grow so large and strong, as a result of over-indulgence in bodily pleasures, that it no longer does its own job but seeks to enslave and rule over the whole soul. This suggests a rather different view of the agreement between the parts, one according to which reason with the aid of spirit exercises a controlling influence over the appetites and shapes them so as to conform to its own judgements.[34] It is not the kind of agreement secured by discussion or persuasive argument but rather by a process in which the appetites are curbed by the restraining influence of the other elements. We should also notice that the agreement is simply an agreement as to who should rule. It does not imply that the lower parts form any kind of judgement about the value of particular kinds of action or ways of life. An agreement of this kind could be demonstrated simply by a habit of obedience to commands. It need not involve a judgement about the good.

---

stick placed in water is bent is described as a δόξα of the lower soul which is corrected by the judgement of reason. However, the fact that the illusion persists even after we have recognized it as such shows that δόξα here cannot refer to an opinion accessible to rational persuasion. See Penner, 'Thought and Desire', 101–3.

[34] Bobonich, *Utopia*, 548 n. 128, notes that 430 E 6–9 implies an account of temperance as something other than consonance of opinion, but does not seem to recognize that this could help to undermine his own interpretation of 442 C–D.

The Tripartite Soul in the Republic

5. Conclusion

If the arguments I have offered are correct, it is far from clear that Plato in the *Republic* commits himself to the view that the soul has parts which are agent-like. While there are, no doubt, passages which encourage that interpretation, a close examination of the arguments by which he introduces the tripartite theory of the soul in book 4 provides very little support for it. That argument certainly implies that conflicting desires must arise from different parts of the soul, but Plato avoids language which suggests that those parts have a will of their own. Equally there is very little to suggest that the lower elements, and in particular the appetitive element, have conceptual and cognitive capacities of the kind that would be required if they were to form their own conceptions of the good. Indeed, there are clear indications that only the reasoning part is supposed to have these capacities. Most importantly, there is little to suggest that the parts engage in communication, still less that they exercise rational persuasion on one another. There is, indeed, some evidence of a quite different way of thinking about the way in which they work—one which compares them to forces that pull the soul this way and that. The truth is that throughout this section Plato uses a variety of different images to describe the inner workings of the soul and is careful never to stay very long with any one of them. The obvious implication is that he does not mean any of these images to be taken in a literal sense. His fundamental point is that the conflicting emotions which we experience must have their source in different elements of the soul. He avoids committing himself to any particular account of the precise mechanisms by which those elements influence the behaviour of the soul as a whole.

Once we have conceded that the view of the soul-parts as agent-like is not central to the moral psychology of the *Republic*, there is obviously no basis for explaining developments in later dialogues by supposing that he has come to reject that view. The *Phaedrus* retains the tripartite doctrine but expresses it through a new image, that of the soul as a chariot team. This develops the idea that the parts of the soul are like forces which pull the soul in different directions. It also enables Plato to express in myth the point that the lower elements lack rational capacities—the horses, unlike the charioteer, do not see the forms. The context of the *Timaeus* is, of

88   R. F. Stalley

course, quite different since it locates the parts of the soul within the body. But it is significant that, while it recalls the *Republic* in using the language of command and obedience to describe the relations of the parts of the soul (70 A 4–8), it insists that appetite, at least, is devoid of intelligence and understanding (71 A 3, 77 B 5–C 3). Reason has therefore to influence it, not by rational persuasion, but by creating images, sometimes frightening, sometimes more pleasant, on the liver (70 A 3–D 4).

The *Laws* is different from any of these dialogues in that it does not, explicitly at least, claim that the soul has three parts. Bobonich sees it as offering a unitary theory of the soul. But it is notable that the image of human beings as puppets of the gods (644 D–645 B) which is given a central place in his interpretation has some features in common with the tripartite model. In particular, it implies that we have within us distinct sources of motivation and these are said to pull us in different directions. The picture of different motivations pulling on the soul recalls the *Republic*'s account of the conflict between reason and appetite.[35] There is certainly a difference in imagery here, but it is not clear that there is any difference in substance.[36]

University of Glasgow

BIBLIOGRAPHY

Anagnostopoulos, M., 'The Divided Soul and the Desire for the Good in Plato's *Republic*', in Santas (ed.), *The Blackwell Guide to Plato's* Republic, 166–88.

Annas, J., *An Introduction to Plato's* Republic [*Introduction*] (Oxford, 1981).

Bobonich, C., 'Akrasia and Agency in Plato's *Laws* and *Republic*' ['Akrasia'], *Archiv für Geschichte der Philosophie*, 76 (1994), 3–36.

—— *Plato's Utopia Recast: His Later Ethics and Politics* [*Utopia*] (Oxford, 2002).

---

[35] The verb ἀνθέλκειν 'pull against' is used in both passages. The similarities with *Rep.* 604 B, which recapitulates the argument for the division of the soul, are even closer.

[36] See also L. Gerson, 'Akrasia and the Divided Soul in Plato's *Laws*', in S. Scolnicov and L. Brisson (eds.), *Plato's* Laws: *From Theory into Practice* (Proceedings of the VI Symposium Platonicum: Selected Papers; Sankt Augustin, 2003), 149–54.

The Tripartite Soul in the Republic 89

Carone, G. R., 'Akrasia in the *Republic*: Does Plato Change his Mind?', *OSAP* 20 (2001), 107–48.

Cross, R. C.,, and Woozley, A. D., *Plato's Republic: A Philosophical Commentary* (London, 1964).

Gerson, L., 'Akrasia and the Divided Soul in Plato's *Laws*', in S. Scolnicov and L. Brisson (eds.), *Plato's Laws: From Theory into Practice* (Proceedings of the VI Symposium Platonicum: Selected Papers; Sankt Augustin, 2003), 149–54.

Gill, C., *Personality in Greek Epic, Tragedy, and Philosophy: The Self in Dialogue* (Oxford, 1996).

Irwin, T., *Plato's Ethics* [*Ethics*] (Oxford, 1995).

Kahn, C., 'Plato's Theory of Desire', *Review of Metaphysics*, 41 (1987), 77–103.

Lorenz, H., 'The Analysis of the Soul in Plato's *Republic*', in Santas (ed.), *The Blackwell Guide to Plato's* Republic, 146–65.

—— *The Brute Within* (Oxford, 2006).

—— 'Desire and Reason in Plato's *Republic*' ['Desire and Reason'], *OSAP* 27 (2004), 83–116.

Moline, J., 'Plato on the Complexity of the Psyche' ['Complexity'], *Archiv für Geschichte der Philosophie*, 60 (1978), 1–26; repr. with minor alterations as pages 52–71 and 74–8 of J. Moline, *Plato's Theory of Understanding* [*Understanding*] (Madison, 1981).

Motluk, A., 'Particles of Faith', *New Scientist*, 189/2536 (28 January 2006), 34–6.

Murphy, N. R., *The Interpretation of Plato's* Republic (Oxford, 1951).

Penner, T. M. 'Thought and Desire', in G. Vlastos (ed.), *Plato, ii. Ethics, Politics and Philosophy of Arts and Religion* (Garden City, NY, 1971), 96–118.

—— and Rowe, C., *Plato's Lysis* (Cambridge, 2006).

Plato, *Res publica*, ed. S. R. Slings (Oxford, 2003).

—— *The Republic*, trans. P. Shorey (Cambridge, Mass., and London, 1930).

—— *The* Republic *of Plato*, trans. A. Bloom (New York, 1968).

Price, A. W., *Mental Conflict* (London, 1995).

Santas, G. (ed.), *The Blackwell Guide to Plato's* Republic (Oxford, 2005).

Stalley, R. F., 'Plato's Argument for the Division of the Reasoning and Appetitive Elements in the Soul', *Phronesis*, 20 (1975), 110–28.

Williams, B. A. O., 'The Analogy of the City and the Soul in Plato's *Republic*', in E. N. Lee, A. P. D. Mourelatos, and A. Rorty (eds.), *Exegesis and Argument: Studies in Greek Philosophy Presented to Gregory Vlastos* (Assen, 1973), 196–206.

—— *Shame and Necessity* (Berkeley, 1993).

PLATO'S *PHAEDRUS* AND THE PROBLEM OF UNITY

DANIEL WERNER

1. Introduction

PLATO's *Phaedrus* is a protean text. In terms of subject-matter, it spans a very wide area, touching upon nearly all of Plato's major areas of interest: rhetoric, *erōs*, the soul, the theory of Forms, dialectic, sophistry, myth, the gods, and philosophy itself. In terms of literary style and tone, the dialogue is equally far-reaching, as Plato employs the resources of epideictic rhetoric, mythical narrative, dialogical conversation, and dialectical analysis—not to mention the variety of styles and motifs which he appropriates from Greek religion, literature, and culture. Indeed, as we read through the *Phaedrus*—particularly for the first time—the structure of the dialogue seems expressly designed to emphasize this thematic and stylistic diversity. Simply consider the basic action and sequence of events in the dialogue: Socrates and Phaedrus are taking a stroll through the countryside on a hot afternoon, and they begin to converse about various topics. After a brief introductory section, the dialogue proceeds with three monological speeches, each of which ostensibly deals with the topic of *erōs*. The third of these speeches—the so-called 'palinode', which is undoubtedly the most famous part of the *Phaedrus*—presents a truly cosmic vision, as it describes the nature of the soul, the fall and reincarnation of the soul, the prenatal vision of the Forms, as well as the nature of *erōs*. As soon as the palinode is over, however, we leave the rhetorical heights of myth and find ourselves immersed once again in the expected mode of Platonic philosophizing—one-on-one dialogue and elenctic cross-examination. This dialogical portion of the *Phaedrus* deals with the nature of rhetoric (in both its spoken and written forms), and in

© Daniel Werner 2007

92   *Daniel Werner*

particular, the way in which rhetoric *ought* to be practised in order to qualify as a true 'art' (*technē*).

With all of this thematic, stylistic, and structural diversity, the question naturally arises: just what is it that holds the *Phaedrus* together? Is this dialogue merely a hotchpotch of various ideas and themes, or is there some overriding concern or issue that binds it all together? How are we to read the dialogue, and what is its main focus—rhetoric, *erōs*, or something else altogether? These questions are the basis of the so-called 'problem of unity' of the *Phaedrus*: whether (and how) the dialogue has a unified coherence as a philosophical text. The problem of unity has in fact been voiced ever since antiquity;[1] and indeed it is made all the more pressing in so far as *within the dialogue itself* Plato explicitly makes structural unity and organic composition a *sine qua non* of good rhetoric (see 264 A ff.). The main difficulty involved in the issue of unity is essentially twofold. First, in terms of theme and subject-matter, the *Phaedrus* seems to be patently incoherent. Whereas the first half of the dialogue (the three speeches) deals explicitly and primarily with *erōs*, the second half seems to deal only with rhetoric; moreover, the two halves seem to have little or nothing to do with one another, as they have very little cross-referencing or cross-commentary. In particular, the soaring and cosmic vision of the palinode seems to drop completely out of sight at the end of the first half—it is hard to see how concerns regarding the Forms, the soul, reincarnation, and *erōs* fit into the more narrow concerns regarding rhetoric as a *technē*. Second, the problem of unity exists on a stylistic and methodological level: whereas the first half relies on set speeches and myth to make its point, the second half uses elenctic dialogue. There is, then, a rather abrupt change in tone, register, and intensity halfway through the dialogue.[2] Moreover, no attempt seems to

---

[1] This can be seen in the discussion of the issue by Hermeias (a Neoplatonist commentator on Plato), as well as in the plurality of subtitles that were given to the *Phaedrus* in ancient times; it was debated as to whether rhetoric, *erōs*, the soul, the Good, or Beauty was the main 'aim' or 'object' (σκοπός) of the dialogue. See G. J. De Vries, *A Commentary on the* Phaedrus *of Plato* [*Commentary*] (Amsterdam, 1969), 22, for the references.

[2] In keeping with contemporary literature on the *Phaedrus*, I speak as if there is an exact 'midpoint' in the text which neatly divides the dialogue into two equal 'halves'. Yet such terminology is misleading: the first 'half' (the introduction plus the three set speeches) actually constitutes some 58% of the total Greek text (30 Stephanus pages), whereas the second 'half' constitutes some 42% of the text (22 Stephanus pages). The palinode alone constitutes a full one-quarter of the text (13

Plato's Phaedrus *and the Problem of Unity*   93

be made to reconcile these two divergent approaches; Plato simply seems to have switched gears, but without explaining *why* he felt it necessary to do so.

In this article I shall examine the problem of unity, and consider some of the ways in which it might be solved. Indeed, scholars' attempted solutions to the *Phaedrus*'s unity have been as varied and multi-coloured as the dialogue which is the object of their discussion; not only is there disagreement as to textual and substantive issues in the dialogue, but there is disagreement as to just what 'unity' is supposed to mean—and consequently, just what the 'problem' of unity is supposed to entail. Accordingly, one of my aims in this article is classificatory: viz. to distinguish the *kinds* of approach that one can take towards the problem of unity. Broadly speaking, there are four such approaches:

(1) *The thematic approach.* Interpreters who take this view focus on the level of theme or subject-matter, and argue for one or more of the following claims: (*a*) there *is* a single, primary theme which encompasses the dialogue as a whole; (*b*) strong thematic links *do* exist between the first half and the second half, perhaps on a more implicit or subtle level; and (*c*) the thematic disunity of the dialogue is only superficial.

(2) *The non-thematic approach.* According to this approach, we must look *beyond* the level of theme and subject-matter in order to find the unity of the dialogue. There is, it is claimed, a variety of other levels on which Plato unifies the text: e.g. drama, form or structure, tone, verbal texture and imagery, and the interplay between word and deed.

(3) *The debunking approach* (*'questioning the question'*). The first two approaches accept the problem of unity on its own terms as a genuine difficulty, and suggest ways to resolve it. Interpreters in this third approach, however, deny the force of the 'problem' itself. They claim that strict unity is a requirement which modern commentators wrongly impose on Plato's text. The type of unity we are seeking is simply not to be found in the *Phaedrus*; instead, we must admit that the disunity of the text is real and ineluctable—though there are historical reasons as to *why* that is the case.

Stephanus pages). From the point of view of the dichotomous division, then, the *Phaedrus* is rather lopsided.

94 *Daniel Werner*

(4) *The strategic approach ('deliberate contrasts')*. Some commentators, though accepting the genuine force of the problem (in contrast to the third approach), do not attempt to resolve it by arguing for a deeper type of unity. Rather, they concede that the text *does* have disunity—or at least that it *appears* to be disunified. However, they see this not as a flaw of Plato's writing but as a *deliberate* manœuvre on his part: a philosophical and literary strategy designed to achieve certain ends (in particular, a certain response in the reader).

In what follows I shall examine each of these four approaches, and I shall consider some of the main arguments in support of each. I shall also discuss what I take to be helpful and/or problematic in each approach. I shall ultimately advocate a hybrid approach to the question of unity which combines important elements of the thematic, non-thematic, and strategic approaches (I shall not have anything to say in support of the debunking approach). I shall argue that, contrary to appearances—and to some extent *because of* those appearances—the *Phaedrus* is a deeply coherent and carefully organized text, and indeed that it well exemplifies the 'logographic necessity' of which Socrates speaks at 264 C. Hence the problem of unity *is* soluble—though a satisfactory solution requires a response that is as complex and multi-layered as the text at hand.

2. The thematic approach

(a) Thematic monism

As I noted above, there is disagreement among interpreters as to just what constitutes the 'problem' of unity. The most common approach, however, is to construe the question of unity as a *thematic* one—i.e. whether (and how) the *Phaedrus* is unified on the level of theme and subject-matter. Indeed, the majority of commentators on the *Phaedrus* simply tend to assume from the outset that the problem of unity is *entirely* soluble on a thematic level.[3] Accordingly, the issue is most frequently posed as follows: what is the main theme (or purpose, or subject) of the *Phaedrus*? Is it *erōs*, rhetoric, or something else altogether? Note the assumption

---

[3] As I shall argue later, this is an unwarranted assumption, in so far as it unfairly privileges the 'content' of Plato's dialogues over their 'form'.

Plato's Phaedrus *and the Problem of Unity* 95

underlying this formulation of the question: that it is proper for us to expect a Platonic dialogue to have a 'main theme', i.e. that there is *one* (and only one) main subject within each dialogue that will be 'primary' or 'most important' (with all other themes being 'subordinate' to that main theme).[4] I shall refer to this assumption as *thematic monism*, and later I shall question its correctness; for the moment, however, I wish to consider the ways in which it has been developed.

When posed as a question regarding the 'main subject', the task of solving the problem of unity thereby becomes that of identifying the focus of the dialogue—what is it all about? This is no simple question in the case of the *Phaedrus*. The first half seems to be about *erōs*, whereas the second half seems to be about rhetoric; moreover, the palinode seems to be about a great many other things: the soul, the Forms, the gods, and philosophy (just to name a few of its themes). Those who take the thematic approach to unity, therefore, must not only identify what they see as the main theme, but must also argue for its primacy over the other contenders.

Those who adhere to thematic monism in the case of the *Phaedrus* have tended to argue for one of several positions: viz. that either (i) rhetoric, (ii) *erōs*, (iii) philosophy, or (iv) some other theme is the main subject of the dialogue. I shall now consider each of these proposals in turn.

(i) *Rhetoric.* By far the most common proposal among commentators is that rhetoric is the main theme of the dialogue, and indeed support for this view runs quite wide.[5] Some commentators have also suggested that the main *purpose* of the *Phaedrus*—as dis-

---

[4] For a clear statement of this view, see R. Waterfield (trans.), *Plato: Phaedrus* (Oxford, 2002), xi.

[5] See W. H. Thompson, *The* Phaedrus *of Plato* (London, 1868), xiv; H. N. Fowler (trans.), *Plato*, i. *Euthyphro, Apology, Crito, Phaedo, Phaedrus* (Cambridge, Mass., 1914), 407; R. P. Winnington-Ingram, 'The Unity of the *Phaedrus*' ['Unity'], inaugural lecture delivered at King's College, University of London, 1953, *Dialogos* (*Hellenic Studies Review*), 1 (1994), 6–20 at 12; De Vries, *Commentary*, 23; A. Nehamas and P. Woodruff, *Plato: Phaedrus* (Indianapolis, 1995), xxviii, xxxviii; J. H. Nichols, Jr., *Plato: Phaedrus* (Ithaca, NY, 1998), 15, 18; J. V. Curran, 'The Rhetorical Technique of Plato's *Phaedrus*' ['Rhetorical Technique'], *Philosophy and Rhetoric*, 19 (1986), 66–72 at 71; D. C. Stewart, 'The Continuing Relevance of Plato's *Phaedrus*', in R. J. Connors, L. S. Ede, and A. A. Lunsford (eds.), *Essays on Classical Rhetoric and Modern Discourse* (Carbondale, Ill., 1984), 115–26 at 116–17; R. M. Weaver, 'The *Phaedrus* and the Nature of Rhetoric', in R. L. Johannesen, R. Strickland, and R. T. Eubanks (eds.), *Language is Sermonic* (Baton Rouge, La., 1970), 57–83 at 58; P. Friedländer, *Plato*, iii. *The Dialogues: Second and Third*

96 *Daniel Werner*

tinguished from the main theme—is to discuss and establish the principles of true rhetoric.[6] The only variation among all of these interpreters is the terminology which they employ: i.e. whether rhetoric is the 'central thema' (De Vries), the 'chief theme' (Fowler), the 'main subject' (Nehamas and Woodruff), the 'central theme' (Nichols), or the 'main purpose' (Taylor, Hamilton).

Notice that these views need not imply—rather implausibly—that rhetoric is the *only* theme of the dialogue. More broadly, thematic monism does not require that there be only *one* theme, but rather that there be only one *primary* theme. Indeed, it is a central feature of thematic monism that there be a hierarchy within a Platonic dialogue: a main subject on top, to which all the other subjects are subordinate in importance. In the case of the rhetoric-oriented view of the *Phaedrus*, this would mean that the discussions of *erōs*, the soul, the Forms, etc. would all be subordinate to the discussion of rhetoric.[7]

How sound is the rhetoric-oriented approach to the *Phaedrus*? That rhetoric is *a* central theme of the dialogue—as well as *a* unifying theme—is undeniable. The most compelling evidence for this is the simple fact that rhetoric truly is omnipresent throughout the *entire* dialogue—and not simply in the second half. That rhetoric is important in the second half of the dialogue is obvious, for in that half Socrates and Phaedrus examine the nature of the true *technē* of rhetoric. But what about the first half of the dialogue, which ostensibly deals with *erōs*? A careful reading of the text in fact reveals that the issue of rhetoric and *logoi* is central to that half of the text as well. Within the dramatic fiction of the *Phaedrus*, after all,

---

Periods, trans. H. Meyerhoff, 2nd edn. (Princeton, 1969), 241; P. Plass, 'The Unity of the *Phaedrus*' ['Unity'], *Symbolae Osloenses*, 43 (1968), 7–38 at 27, 33, 37.

[6] W. Hamilton (trans.), *Plato: Phaedrus and the Seventh and Eighth Letters* (Harmondsworth, 1973), 9; A. E. Taylor, *Plato: The Man and his Work* [*Plato*], 6th edn. (New York, 1956), 300. Cf. also G. Ryle's claim that the *Phaedrus* is intended as a kind of announcement or advertisement for the 'Academy's entry into the teaching of rhetoric' (cited in W. K. C. Guthrie, 'Rhetoric and Philosophy: The Unity of the *Phaedrus*' ['Rhetoric and Philosophy'], *Paideia* (1976), 117–24 at 117).

[7] Perhaps unsurprisingly, almost none of the commentators noted above have been sufficiently self-consistent as to state this implication explicitly; after all, when we first read the dialogue most of us intuitively regard the *palinode* as 'primary', and not the discussion of rhetoric. Nehamas and Woodruff are one exception: they bite the bullet and flatly declare that 'Plato is more interested in what the speeches show about the practice of rhetoric than in what they reveal about the nature of love' (*Plato: Phaedrus*, xxviii).

Plato's Phaedrus *and the Problem of Unity*   97

the genesis for the entire conversation is the fact that Phaedrus has just come from Epicrates' house, where the famous orator Lysias gave a public performance of speeches. Having departed from that performance, Phaedrus is now carrying with him a written transcript of one of Lysias' speeches. The entire drama of the *Phaedrus*, then, is indirectly instigated by Lysias, the master of rhetoric—and in this sense Socrates' reference to Lysias as the 'father' of a *logos* (257 B 3) is more than just a piece of irony. Other references to *logoi* abound in the opening scene. Socrates, for instance, describes himself as being 'sick for the hearing of words' ($\nu o\sigma o\hat{\nu}\nu\tau\iota\ \pi\epsilon\rho\grave{\iota}\ \lambda\acute{o}\gamma\omega\nu$ $\mathring{a}\kappa o\acute{\eta}\nu$, 228 B 6–7) and as a 'lover of words' ($\tau o\hat{\nu}\ \tau\hat{\omega}\nu\ \lambda\acute{o}\gamma\omega\nu\ \mathring{\epsilon}\rho a\sigma\tau o\hat{\nu}$, 228 c 1–2). A passion for words has in fact gripped both Socrates and Phaedrus—though for different reasons. Whereas Phaedrus' interest in *logoi* and speeches is almost entirely aesthetic—he takes delight in hearing new and strange things—Socrates approaches *logoi* as an opportunity to learn and to engage in enquiry. (In this way, the senses of *logos* as 'thing said' and as 'reason' merge in Socrates' case.) A passion for words, then—the stuff of rhetoric—has brought these two characters together in the first place, and has brought us the dialogue which we are now reading.

Hence the dialogue begins with a distinctly rhetorical orientation—and in truth it never really leaves this origin behind. After all, the first half of the dialogue consists of three *speeches*, that is to say, three *examples* of rhetoric. Moreover, the issue of rhetoric is present *within* the three speeches that Phaedrus and Socrates recite, both explicitly and implicitly. Simply consider the entire situation of the first two speeches: in each case, we have an older man attempting to *persuade* a younger boy that it is better to yield to a non-lover than to a lover. The imagined narrators of these two speeches, then, are *using* rhetoric to achieve their ends (just as Phaedrus and Socrates are using rhetoric to compete with one another). This suggests a more general point (to which I shall return later): all lovers are a kind of rhetorician, in so far as they necessarily engage in verbal 'intercourse' with one another.[8] The content of the speeches bears out this point as well. In Lysias' speech, for instance, the mere fact that two lovers are seen in *conversation* ($\delta\iota a\lambda\epsilon\gamma\acute{o}\mu\epsilon\nu o\iota\ \mathring{a}\lambda\lambda\acute{\eta}\lambda o\iota s$, 232 A

---

[8] Or as C. L. Griswold, Jr., nicely put the point, 'the desire to seduce requires rhetoric, whether one's purpose is to lead one's beloved into philosophy or into a sexual relationship' (*Self-Knowledge in Plato's* Phaedrus [*Self-Knowledge*], rev. edn. (University Park, Pa., 1996), 159).

98 *Daniel Werner*

8–B 1) is taken to be a sign of recently consummated (or soon-to-be consummated) sexual passion. Rhetoric and *erōs* are therefore fused from the very beginning of the *Phaedrus*.

Within the palinode too *logos* plays a pivotal role, particularly in the account of the philosophical lovers. On the one side of the erotic relationship, the lover seeks a kindred soulmate; and when he finds that soulmate, he then attempts to mould the beloved into a specific way of life—attempting, among other things, to *persuade* the beloved (πείθοντες, 253 B 6, presumably implying the use of verbal persuasion). On the other side, the beloved gradually comes to welcome the company and the *conversation* (λόγον, 255 B 3) of the lover, at least when such a relationship is fated to be. On both sides, the highest kind of *erōs* flourishes when the rational element of the soul (the charioteer) predominates, enlisting the help of the good horse and strictly controlling the bad horse. And part of what distinguishes the good horse is that it obeys the *verbal* command alone (κελεύσαντι μόνον καὶ λόγῳ ἡνιοχεῖται, 253 D 7–E 1). In the erotic vision of the palinode, then, *logos* is important within the relationship *between* the two lovers, as well as *within* the soul of each lover.

Finally, there seems to be an important connection between *logos* and the metaphysics of the palinode. In a crucial (and cryptic) passage Socrates states that the prenatal vision of the Forms is necessary prior to our incarnation as humans, in so far as 'a human being must understand speech in terms of general forms' (δεῖ γὰρ ἄνθρωπον συνιέναι κατ' εἶδος λεγόμενον, 249 B 6–7). Although the exact meaning of this passage is unclear, Socrates seems to be saying that the human capacity for language—and by extension, rhetoric— is dependent upon the metaphysical vision depicted in the mythical narrative.

The above evidence is enough to indicate, I think, that rhetoric and the issue of *logos* are by no means confined to the second half of the dialogue; in fact they are prominent in the first half as well, and are intertwined with the entire discussion from the beginning. This proves quite clearly that rhetoric is *a* recurring theme—and indeed *a* unifying theme—in the dialogue. But the above evidence proves no more than that. In particular, it does not yet prove that rhetoric is the *main* theme of the dialogue. On what basis, then, have so many commentators maintained the latter claim?

There are two arguments that are typically given in support of

Plato's Phaedrus *and the Problem of Unity* 99

this stronger claim. First, there is a formal or structural argument: viz. that rhetoric is the primary theme of the dialogue in so far as it is both *expounded* (in the second half) and *enacted* (in the first half). That is to say, in the second half of the dialogue Plato talks *about* rhetoric, and in the first half he provides three *examples* of rhetoric. In particular, it is frequently argued that the palinode is precisely an example of the 'true *technē* of rhetoric' which Plato delineates in the second half of the dialogue.[9] This kind of argument, however, does not prove all that it needs to prove. That rhetoric is both expounded and enacted—which is undeniably true—proves (once again) only that rhetoric is *a* central theme in the dialogue, and not that it is the *main* theme. To prove the latter, one would need to show that *no other theme* is as prominent or important in the dialogue, and that no other theme is treated both in word and in deed. Yet (as I shall later show) both of these claims are clearly incorrect.[10]

The second argument anticipates some of these difficulties, and attempts to provide a more clear-cut exclusion of alternative views. The argument essentially amounts to a disjunctive syllogism: either the main theme is *erōs* or it is rhetoric; but it cannot be *erōs*; hence it is rhetoric. The second premiss is generally supported on the (alleged) grounds that *erōs* plays little or no role in the second half of

[9] For the view that the palinode is the true *technē* of rhetoric, see Thompson, *The* Phaedrus *of Plato*, xvii ff.; Guthrie, 'Rhetoric and Philosophy', 121; W. K. C. Guthrie, *A History of Greek Philosophy*, iv. *Plato, the Man and his Dialogues: Earlier Period* (Cambridge, 1975), 415; C. J. Rowe, 'The Argument and Structure of Plato's *Phaedrus*' ['Argument and Structure'], *Proceedings of the Cambridge Philological Society*, 212 (1986), 106–25 at 108–10; id., 'Public and Private Speaking in Plato's Later Dialogues', in C. Eggers Lan (ed.), *Platón: los diálogos tardíos* (Sankt Augustin: 1994), 125–37 at 133–4; Nehamas and Woodruff, *Plato:* Phaedrus, xxviii–xxix, xxxviii; J. E. Smith, 'Plato's Myths as "Likely Accounts", Worthy of Belief', *Apeiron*, 19 (1985), 24–42 at 37–8; Curran, 'Rhetorical Technique', 69–70; E. Asmis, 'Psychagogia in Plato's *Phaedrus*' ['*Psychagogia*'], *Illinois Classical Studies*, 11 (1986), 153–72.

[10] I discuss the other recurring themes in the remainder of this section, and I also return to the notion of word–deed interplay in sect. 3. There is in fact an even deeper problem with this style of argument: namely, that there is good reason to doubt whether the palinode is in fact an example of the true *technē* of rhetoric. According to Plato, the true rhetorician must have knowledge of the subject-matter of his speech (260 A–262 C) as well as knowledge of the nature of the soul (270 B–272 B). But Socrates conspicuously *lacks* these two kinds of knowledge in the *Phaedrus*: with regard to the former, because neither he nor any other incarnate human could possibly have knowledge of the afterlife (the subject-matter of the speech); and with regard to the latter, because he explicitly disavows possessing psychological knowledge in the palinode itself (see 246 A). So by Plato's own standards, the palinode *cannot* be an example of the true rhetoric. (I say much more to develop this line of argument in my 'Rhetoric and Philosophy in Plato's *Phaedrus*' (forthcoming)).

100   *Daniel Werner*

the *Phaedrus*, and hence could not possibly be the main or unifying theme of the dialogue.[11] Consequently (it is claimed) we are left with rhetoric as the only reasonable option for the main theme of the dialogue as a whole. There are, however, some serious problems with this argument as well. For one thing, the first premiss—which tends to be assumed more often than it is argued for—seems to be a blatant case of a false dichotomy: why, after all, *must* we choose between *erōs* and rhetoric as the *only* possible options? Such a posing of the options immediately ignores the fact, for instance, that philosophy and myth (to take two examples) are also recurring themes in the dialogue as a whole. Moreover, no explanation is given as to why we must choose only *one* of the options.[12]

Yet even if we agree with the dichotomous posing of the available options, a deeper problem remains with the second major premiss of the argument. To appreciate this point, we must now take a closer look at the role of *erōs* in the *Phaedrus*.

(ii) *Erōs.* The above argument rejects the possibility that *erōs* is the main theme of the dialogue, on the grounds that *erōs* is 'forgotten' or 'disappears' in the second half. Yet this claim is clearly false. We may simply notice, for instance, the fact that love-related motifs, language, and imagery occur frequently throughout the second half of the dialogue. To cite a few examples: in discussing the cicadas, Socrates makes reference to Erato (the Muse pertaining to love (259 D 1); certain politicians are said to be those who are most in love (ἐρῶσι) with speech-writing and a leaving-behind of compositions (257 E 1–4); and Socrates calls himself a 'lover' (ἐραστής,

---

[11] See e.g. Nehamas and Woodruff, who claim that *erōs* is 'forgotten' (*Plato: Phaedrus*, xxvii) and is 'simply not discussed' (xxxviii) in the second half of the dialogue; R. B. Rutherford, who claims that 'love fades out of the limelight with surprising finality after the first half of the work' (*The Art of Plato: Ten Essays in Platonic Interpretation* [*Art of Plato*] (Cambridge, Mass., 1995), 262); Waterfield, who claims that 'there is evidently little about love in the second half of the dialogue' (*Plato: Phaedrus*, xliv); C. J. Rowe, who claims that 'there is nothing directly on the topic of love in the second half at all' (*Plato: Phaedrus*, rev. edn. (Warminster, 2000), 7); and F. E. D. Schleiermacher, who argues that if *erōs* were chosen as the main theme, the *Phaedrus* 'would appear deformed in a most revolting manner', with the second half appearing as 'an appendage strangely tacked on', since in the second half 'no return whatever is again made to the subject treated of in the speeches' (*Introductions to the Dialogues of Plato* [*Introductions*], trans. W. Dobson (New York, 1973), 49).

[12] That is to say, thematic monism is assumed but not argued for. I shall return to this issue below.

Plato's Phaedrus *and the Problem of Unity* 101

266 B 3) of collections and divisions.[13] In addition to these explicit references, there are several subtler allusions: for example, Socrates defines rhetoric as a 'leading of the soul' in both public courtrooms and private associations; however, the Greek term for 'associations' (σύλλογοι, 261 A 9) is a reference to the 'small intellectual meetings' with a 'more or less erotic character'.[14]

In addition to the recurrence of love-related motifs and language in the text, there are deeper ways in which Plato draws love into the discussion of the second half. Most prominent, perhaps, is the image of dialectical education which Plato describes in the course of the critique of writing (276 E–277 A, 278 A–B). The written word, according to Plato, is inherently flawed in so far as it can offer neither clarity nor certainty; more important is the living, oral word— in particular, the living word as it is spoken among dialectician-philosophers. Plato then describes philosophical education with an agricultural metaphor: the dialectician chooses a proper soul and 'plants' (φυτεύῃ) and 'sows' (σπείρῃ) discourse within that soul; such discourse, in turn, is not 'barren' (ἄκαρποι) but contains 'seeds' (σπέρμα) from which new λόγοι 'grow' (φυόμενοι), the seeds thereby becoming immortal. Plato also calls such seeds the 'legitimate sons' (ὑεῖς γνησίους) of the teacher. The sexual and erotic overtones of this passage are striking. On the one hand, the passage is a deliberate recall of the palinode, where the ideas of nourishment and growth are prominent—in particular, it recalls the graphic phallic imagery which Plato uses to characterize the psychological experience of *erōs* (see 251 B ff.). Yet it also points to something deeper: in the best of circumstances, the practice of philosophy involves intense interpersonal relationships (the type of relationship first described in the palinode). Hence the practice of dialectic is not passionless, and Socrates was not being ironic when he described himself as a 'lover' (ἐραστής, 266 B 3) of collections and divisions. As Helmbold and Holther nicely put the point, 'Philosophy is what the lover should be whispering to his beloved; and the conversation should

---

[13] In addition, if—as I am inclined to believe—φιλία can properly be taken to denote certain kinds of 'love', then the following evidence from the second half of the dialogue can also be adduced: the quality of 'love of honour' (φιλοτιμίας, 257 C 7) is discussed in connection with politics; Socrates refers to Phaedrus as a 'lover of the Muses' (φιλόμουσον, 259 B 5); and in the prayer which concludes the dialogue Socrates asks that his internal qualities be 'in friendly accord' with his external possessions (ἔξωθεν δὲ ὅσα ἔχω, τοῖς ἐντὸς εἶναί μοι φίλια, 279 B 9).

[14] Plass, 'Unity', 10.

102   *Daniel Werner*

be conducted in dialectic, so to speak.'[15] In this way, we again see that *erōs* is very much an integral part of the second half of the *Phaedrus*, for when Plato discusses dialectic and the philosophical way of life, so too does he indicate the role of *erōs* within that life.

Quite clearly, then, love—just as much as rhetoric—is a theme that recurs throughout the *Phaedrus* as a whole. One cannot therefore claim that rhetoric is the main theme of the dialogue on the grounds that *erōs* is 'forgotten' or that it 'disappears' in the second half. In fact there would seem to be just as much evidence to recommend *erōs* as there is to recommend rhetoric as the main theme. Strangely enough, however, I know of no modern interpreter who has argued that *erōs* is the main theme of the dialogue. Perhaps this is because the pre-emptive criticisms of such a view have already been put forward with great forcefulness, and with an apparent air of settling the matter.[16] Yet those criticisms—aside from being textually inaccurate—rest on a problematic charge that an *erōs*-oriented approach would render the *Phaedrus* blatantly 'deformed' or 'lopsided'. In fact the claim regarding lopsidedness or deformity applies with equal force to *both* the *erōs*-oriented *and* the rhetoric-oriented approaches: if *erōs* is chosen as the main theme, then one must 'explain' why rhetoric is so central to the dialogue; and if rhetoric is chosen as the main theme, then one must 'explain' why *erōs* is so central—and indeed, why it is chosen as the topic of the speeches at all.[17] (After all, if the purpose of the speeches

---

[15] W. C. Helmbold and W. B. Holther, 'The Unity of the "Phaedrus"' ['Unity'], *University of California Publications in Classical Philology*, 14 (1952), 387–417 at 407.

[16] See references in n. 11 above.

[17] Several commentators have attempted to address the latter question, but I find their proposals to be inadequate. J. I. Beare, for instance, argues that in order for Plato to explain how recollection works—which Beare sees as being one of the purposes of the palinode—he *had to* illustrate it with reference to Beauty, in so far as that is the only Form whose images are directly visible to the eye (and in so far as recollection begins from some perception). The *erōs*–Beauty theme, then, was necessary in order for Plato to give an intelligible account of recollection ("The *Phaedrus*: Its Structure; The ἔρως Theme: Notes' ['*Phaedrus*'], *Hermathena*, 17 (1913), 312–34 at 320–2). Yet Beare's argument founders given that images of the other Forms *are* visible to the eye as well—for example, we can see two equal sticks, and we can see an unjust man. So it is certainly open to Plato to use something *other than erōs*–Beauty in order to explicate recollection—which is precisely what he does in the *Phaedo* with the Form of the Equal.

Nehamas and Woodruff offer a different explanation for Plato's choice of *erōs* as the subject-matter of the speeches: Plato (they claim) has altered the view of *erōs* as it appeared in the *Symposium*, and thus wishes to announce that fact in the *Phaedrus* (Nehamas and Woodruff, *Plato: Phaedrus*, xxxix). Moreover, the use

Plato's Phaedrus *and the Problem of Unity* 103

were merely to provide an example of rhetoric, then presumably *any* subject-matter would suffice.)

Of course—and as I have already discussed in the case of the rhetoric-oriented approach—the fact that *erōs* is *a* recurrent and unifying theme of the text does not by itself prove that *erōs* is the *main* theme of the text. To prove the latter, one would need to exclude the other possible alternatives. Now it would be implausible to support an *erōs*-oriented approach merely on the grounds of the *frequency* of the theme; for as I argued earlier, rhetoric too—just as much as *erōs*—is important in *both* halves of the dialogue. So a rhetoric-oriented approach cannot be rejected on those grounds. Nor is it sufficient to argue that *erōs* is both discussed and enacted in the dialogue, since that (again) proves only that *erōs* is *an* important theme. (And, in any case, rhetoric *too* is both discussed and enacted.) Are there any remaining arguments, then, which might support an *erōs*-oriented approach to the dialogue?

One possible approach concerns the status of the palinode as a text-within-a-text. Most readers of the *Phaedrus* undoubtedly remember the dialogue for the brilliance of the palinode. And justifiably so: for within these thirteen or so Stephanus pages we have one of the truly unforgettable moments in all of classical literature. The language is gorgeous and the imagery is deeply moving; and in terms of subject-matter, the palinode treats of the highest of all human aspirations. It is very tempting, therefore, to view the palinode as being the 'most important' part of the *Phaedrus*, and as containing the 'main Platonic doctrines' of the dialogue—and a

of *erōs* has an instrumental role, in so far as it allows Plato 'to introduce various philosophical views that might otherwise not easily have found a place within the dialogue' (Nehamas and Woodruff, xl). Yet this kind of approach, by appealing to some extra-textual agenda or purported larger purpose, seems to me grossly to underestimate the *intrinsic* (and not merely instrumental) importance of *erōs* in the *Phaedrus*. Indeed part of Plato's point in the dialogue seems to be to suggest the importance of *erōs* in the life of the philosopher. It seems to me, then, that *erōs* is not merely 'an entry into the heart of Plato's philosophy' (as Nehamas and Woodruff claim, xl), but lies within that heart as well. (Similar remarks apply to G. R. F. Ferrari, who also sees *erōs* as playing an instrumental role in the dialogue: he argues that Plato selected *erōs* as the subject-matter of the palinode so as to be able to produce an epideictic speech that would have seemed maximally 'shocking' to the audience, and hence would show that Plato had beaten the professional orators at their own game. See Ferrari, '"The Unity of the *Phaedrus*": A Response' ['Unity'], *Dialogos (Hellenic Studies Review)*, 1 (1994), 21–5 at 24–5.)

All of this is a sign, I think, that the rhetoric-oriented approach—with its consequence that the presence of *erōs* is something that needs to be 'explained'—is problematic.

104 *Daniel Werner*

number of commentators have argued precisely that.[18] The sheer size and scope of the palinode only seem to reinforce this view, as does what many readers regard as the disappointing transition to the second half. In reading the palinode we are apt to feel as if we are gaining entry into a special world, and that by penetrating into the imagery we can somehow 'get at' the very truth of all Platonic philosophy. Notice that, if this line of thinking is correct, we have some justification for regarding *erōs* as the main theme of the dialogue: for if the palinode is the 'real' heart of the *Phaedrus*, and if the palinode itself is 'about' *erōs*, then Plato's entire purpose in writing this dialogue could very well be to say something about *erōs* and its value in human life.

Unfortunately, viewing the palinode as the 'most important' part of the text does great violence to the *Phaedrus* as a whole, and also contradicts some key evidence. For one thing, there is the rather obvious fact that Plato goes on to say a great deal in the second half of the dialogue, and that he handles topics (e.g. rhetoric and dialectic) which can hardly be said to be 'secondary' in importance. In particular, the second half of the dialogue introduces two topics which have *never* appeared previously in the earlier Platonic dialogues: the method of collection and division, and the status and value of the written word. If the palinode were truly intended to be the 'most important' part of the dialogue, then it seems unlikely that Plato would go out of his way to *avoid* talking about collection and division and writing within the speech. Moreover, there is evidence within the *Phaedrus* itself which suggests that, far from being the *raison d'être* of the dialogue or a wholly serious expression of philosophical truth, the palinode is in fact *limited* in what it can offer us. Socrates begins his description of the chariot image with a stern caveat: he will describe only what the soul is *like* (ᾧ δὲ ἔοικεν), and will not attempt to describe the sort of thing that it *is* (οἷον μέν ἐστι), in so far as the latter is attainable only by a god (246 A 3–6).

---

[18] The Renaissance Platonist commentator Marsilio Ficino saw the palinode as containing the 'principal mysteries' of the *Phaedrus* (as cited in Rowe, *Plato:* Phaedrus, 7). In a similar vein, J. Pieper declares that the first half is 'the most important', and that the palinode is 'the real content of the dialogue; it is also what makes reading the rest worth while' (*Enthusiasm and Divine Madness: On the Platonic Dialogue* Phaedrus, trans. R. Winston and C. Winston (New York, 1964), xiv, 42). Cf. also A. Lebeck, who claims that 'the myth forms a central point to which every idea in *Phaedrus* is related and should be referred' ('The Central Myth of Plato's *Phaedrus*' ['Central Myth'], *Greek, Roman and Byzantine Studies*, 13 (1972), 267–90 at 268).

Plato's Phaedrus *and the Problem of Unity*   105

The implication, then, is that we ought not to view the palinode as providing the literal Truth, and that we should be cautious about attaching *too* much importance to it. The status of the palinode is further demoted at 265 B–C, where Socrates declares:

We used a certain sort of image to describe love's passion; perhaps it had a measure of truth in it, though it may also have led us astray. And having whipped up a not altogether implausible speech, we sang playfully, but also appropriately and respectfully, a storylike hymn to my master and yours, Phaedrus—to Love, who watches over beautiful boys.[19]

Several aspects of this passage are noteworthy. First, Socrates says only that *perhaps* the palinode contained truth; and far from calling it a philosophical pearl of wisdom, here he merely describes it as 'a not altogether implausible speech' and a 'storylike hymn'. Second, he says that the speech was *playfully* done—and in a statement immediately after this passage, he declares that 'everything else' in the speech was 'spoken in play' (265 C 8–9). The motif of play vs. seriousness runs throughout the *Phaedrus*, culminating in the discussion of the written word. Like a written text, the palinode is a self-contained entity which seems to offer us great insight and certainty; yet such an appearance is spurious. We can gain philosophical knowledge only through the practice of dialectic, and not through the reading of a text (such as the *Phaedrus* itself) or the hearing of a set speech (such as the palinode). Those who view the palinode as the 'most important' part of the dialogue, then, have much explaining to do; for it now seems that in fact the palinode is itself placed—and places itself—in something of a *subordinate* role.

(iii) *Philosophy*. Thus far I have considered the possibility of either rhetoric or *erōs* being the main theme of the *Phaedrus*. Although there is good reason to regard each of these as *a* recurring theme in the text, there is (as of yet) no good argument which has emerged to show that either of these is the *main* theme of the dialogue. But perhaps the way in which the debate has been framed is misleading: perhaps there are other possibilities besides these two. Towards that end, philosophy has occasionally emerged in the scholarly literature as a 'third option' for the main theme.[20] Some commentators have also seen the unity of the dialogue as residing

[19] Translation taken from Nehamas and Woodruff, *Plato: Phaedrus*. Unless otherwise noted, all translations in this article will be taken from this version.

[20] Such a suggestion goes back at least as far as Schleiermacher, who claimed that

106   *Daniel Werner*

in its *purpose*—namely, that Plato's purpose was to affirm the value
of philosophy and vindicate the philosophical life.[21]

As in the case of rhetoric and *erōs*, I think it is undeniable that
philosophy is *a* recurring and unifying theme of the *Phaedrus*. In
fact philosophy is a unifying element of the dialogue in at least
two respects: on the level of theme or subject-matter, and on the
level of the structure or form. On a thematic level, philosophy is
omnipresent throughout the text—in both an explicit and implicit
sense—and it appears under multiple guises. Right at the start of the
dialogue, for instance, philosophy is central to the discussion when
Socrates suddenly reorients the conversation towards the issue of
self-knowledge. He asks: 'I am still unable, as the Delphic inscription
orders, to know myself . . . am I a beast more complicated and savage
than Typho, or am I a tamer, simpler animal with a share in a divine
and gentle nature?' (230 A). This question—particularly the reference to Delphi—reminds us of the *Apology*, in which the issue of
self-knowledge, construed in that text as an awareness of one's ignorance, is presented in connection with the philosophical way of life
(as exemplified in the figure of Socrates). In the *Phaedrus* Socrates
is again an exemplary figurehead for philosophy—someone who in
Plato's view holds the appropriate values and priorities. The imperative towards self-knowledge, then, turns out to be an imperative
towards the life of philosophy as a whole, for self-knowledge is a
central part of that life.

The *Phaedrus* thus begins with a reference to the entire philosophical way of life—and that very way of life lies in the foreground of

in the *Phaedrus* it is philosophy that Plato 'extols, independently and wholly, as the
highest of all objects, and as the foundation of every thing estimable and beautiful';
and hence that it is the focus on philosophy that gives the dialogue its coherence
(Schleiermacher, *Introductions*, 58; see 57 ff. generally). For a more recent view, cf.
G. E. Mueller, 'Unity of the *Phaedrus*', *Classical Bulletin*, 33 (1957), 50–3, 60–5
at 50–1.

[21] For instance, R. Hackforth claims that the 'dominant' and 'most important'
purpose of the *Phaedrus* is 'to vindicate the pursuit of philosophy' (*Plato's* Phaedrus (Cambridge, 1952), 9), and Winnington-Ingram similarly remarks that Plato's
purpose is 'to re-affirm what he had always taught; that philosophy, not rhetoric,
was the true culture of the soul' ('Unity', 14). Cf. also Guthrie: 'The *Phaedrus* is
not a manual of instruction in rhetoric . . . but a plea to abandon it for philosophy'
('Rhetoric and Philosophy', 123); and G. R. F. Ferrari, who identifies the 'major
philosophic concern' of the *Phaedrus* as 'the vindication of the philosophic life
against a life that seeks only its effects' (*Listening to the Cicadas: A Study of Plato's*
Phaedrus [*Cicadas*] (Cambridge, 1987), 222–3). Ferrari's claim regarding the 'major
philosophic concern' seems to undergird the entirety of his interpretation in *Cicadas*.

Plato's Phaedrus *and the Problem of Unity*   107

discussion throughout the remainder of the dialogue. The palinode, for instance, explicitly deals with the philosophical life. In a cosmic sense, the palinode describes the nature of the philosopher in relation to the soul's prenatal vision of the Forms; of all mortals, we are told, the philosopher has seen the most of the Forms, and has the highest type of soul. In a more earthly sense too the palinode draws a clear link between *erōs* and philosophy: the highest kind of love is a philosophical one, which brings to its possessors the possibility of a release from incarnation. The palinode, then, clearly valorizes philosophy as a way of life. The second half of the dialogue also continues to emphasize the importance of philosophy. Plato's description of true rhetoric, for instance, makes it clear that the best oratory has a philosophical basis, since a knowledge of truth and a knowledge of psychology are both prerequisites for such oratory. Moreover, the method which the orator is to use to attain truth is none other than philosophical dialectic (collection and division). Finally, the end of the *Phaedrus* again stresses the importance of philosophy as a way of life: what matters most, Plato says, is not the written word, which has only a specious appearance of clarity and certainty. Rather, true seriousness ought to be devoted to—and true fulfilment is to be derived from—the intimate relation between student and teacher in the practice of dialectical enquiry. Philosophy again stands on top.

In addition to these thematic linkages, philosophy is also present in the *Phaedrus vis-à-vis* the *structure* or *form* of the dialogue. A strong indication that this is so can be seen in Plato's use of the setting, and in particular, in his use of the cicadas (which are singing overhead during Socrates' and Phaedrus' conversation). At several crucial junctures in the dialogue—the opening scene (229 A–230 E), the midpoint (259 A–D), and the conclusion (279 B–C)—Socrates makes mention of the setting and the cicadas. Yet the cicadas, in turn, are explicitly associated with Calliope and Urania, the Muses that pertain to *philosophy*. Plato thus seems to be using the structure and setting of the dialogue to provide a distinctly philosophical orientation, reminding us, perhaps, of the ever-present need for philosophy (as symbolized by the ever-present cicadas in the background).[22]

Once again, however, we must ask whether there is any com-

---

[22] Ferrari provides an interesting discussion of 'background' vs. 'foreground' in the *Phaedrus*; see his *Cicadas, passim*.

108   *Daniel Werner*

pelling evidence for regarding philosophy as the *main* theme of the dialogue (and not merely *a* theme). Some interpreters have argued that the discussion of dialectical collection and division—which, as I noted earlier, had not appeared in any of Plato's previous dialogues—is the most important part of the *Phaedrus*;[23] and consequently, that dialectic—and by extension, philosophy—is the main theme of the dialogue. Yet this sort of view commits the same basic error as the view that the palinode is the 'most important' part of the dialogue. In both cases we wind up unfairly privileging one part of the *Phaedrus* at the expense of the other parts. And in both cases the result is still the same: a reading of the *Phaedrus* that is patently imbalanced. As a result, the very unity that we are seeking is compromised.[24]

(iv) *Other key themes in the dialogue.* Although the point is often lost in discussions of the unity of the *Phaedrus*, there are in fact a number of other themes—beyond the three that I have examined thus far—which recur throughout the dialogue as a whole and which help to unify the text. Most notable, perhaps, is *myth*. Indeed, the *Phaedrus* is the most 'mythical' of all of Plato's dialogues: not only are there four presented myths in the dialogue (Boreas–Oreithuia, the palinode, the cicadas, and Theuth–Thamus),[25] but there is also a good deal of discussion *about* myth (see e.g. 229 c ff., 265 b–c, 276 e). Moreover, far from being an adjunct to the dialogue, the mythical material is closely interrelated to its other themes. For instance, in so far as it is a form of speech or *logos*, myth is closely related the question of rhetoric; and in so far as it is an imagistic *logos* that makes a certain truth-claim—illegitimately, in Plato's eyes—myth is closely related to the question of philosophy.

---

[23] For an expression of this view, see Schleiermacher, who claims that the experience of reading the *Phaedrus* is one in which we reach progressively deeper levels of Plato's thought. Having moved through several speeches and other material, we finally reach the discussion of dialectic, which for Schleiermacher is 'the innermost soul of the whole work . . . for which all else in this dialogue is but preparation' (*Introductions*, 58). Hackforth makes the same claim, stating that 'the plan of the whole dialogue is centred upon' the discussion of dialectic, and that 'it is in the formulation of the new τέχνη that the formal relevance of the three discourses . . . is alone to be discovered' (*Plato's* Phaedrus, 136).

[24] I also take it that it is prima facie implausible that the entirety of the palinode is no more than 'preparation' (Schleiermacher's phrase) for the discussion of dialectic.

[25] Note that the myths are strategically placed at the beginning, middle, and end of the dialogue. I shall say more about this in sect. 3 below.

Plato's Phaedrus *and the Problem of Unity*   109

There are a variety of other themes—including self-knowledge,[26] politics,[27] education,[28] *psychagogia*,[29] and writing[30]—which have also been suggested as the 'main theme' of the *Phaedrus*. Space prohibits me from examining each of these views here, but I do think that a good case can be made to show that these themes genuinely recur throughout the whole dialogue. This then leaves us with the very question with which we began: just what is the *main* theme of the dialogue?

(b) *Thematic pluralism*

The assumption under which I have been operating thus far—the view which I have called thematic monism—equates unity with thematic unity; specifically, it requires that there be *one*, and only one, 'main theme' in the *Phaedrus* for the dialogue to be considered unified. I have argued that rhetoric, *erōs*, and philosophy—and other themes as well (such as myth)—are all recurring themes in the dialogue. If thematic monism is correct, then, the inevitable conclusion thus seems to be the following: *either* we must choose *one* of these available themes as 'primary' and regard the other themes as 'subordinate', *or* we must frankly admit that the plurality of good options is an indication that the entire problem of unity is insoluble. The problem with the first option is that (as I have suggested) none of the arguments advanced in favour of a 'pro-*erōs*' or 'pro-rhetoric' or 'pro-philosophy' view actually proves that the theme in question is 'primary'; and the problem with the second option is that it forces us to concede that the *Phaedrus* is disunified. Do we therefore have an unresolvable dilemma?

I think not. What we have here is a false dichotomy—a dichotomy, moreover, that is forced upon us by the assumption of the correctness of thematic monism. But why make that assumption in the first place? What if there is no such thing as a 'main' theme in a Platonic dialogue? What if Plato is *equally* interested in a *plurality* of themes in the *Phaedrus*, none of which can be said to be more

[26] See Griswold, *Self-Knowledge, passim*.

[27] Winnington-Ingram, 'Unity', 18.

[28] Waterfield, *Plato:* Phaedrus, xlvi ff.; H. Ll. Hudson-Williams, *Three Systems of Education: Some Reflections on the Implications of Plato's* Phaedrus (Oxford: 1954), 11.

[29] Asmis, 'Psychagogia', 154.

[30] R. Burger, *Plato's* Phaedrus: *A Defense of a Philosophic Art of Writing* (University, Ala., 1980), *passim*.

110   *Daniel Werner*

important than or subordinate to another? What if, in other words,
the question of unity—as I have been considering it thus far—has
been falsely posed?

I now wish to advocate an alternative approach to the issue of
thematic unity in the *Phaedrus*, which I shall call *thematic pluralism*
(in contrast to thematic monism). Rather than seek out *one* overriding theme in the dialogue, we should begin from the very fact
of the *Phaedrus*'s thematic diversity, and treat that diversity not as
a 'defect' to be smoothed over—through a hierarchy of subjects—
but as an intentional feature of the text. This is not to say that
we are thereby denying that the text has unity; quite the contrary,
I maintain that the dialogue *does* possess a strict internal unity—
and a strict thematic unity as well. I take it that *erōs*, rhetoric, and
philosophy—and other themes as well[31]—are *all* unifying themes of
the text, in so far as each of them recurs throughout the entire text
(i.e. in *both* halves) and each of them helps us to comprehend the
dialogue as a whole. Plato uses the entirety of the dialogue, in other
words, to comment on each of these subjects and to suggest their
interrelations, but without thereby 'subordinating' one to another.
What I am suggesting, then, is that we revise our notion of what
'thematic unity' itself means. The traditional assumption has been
to equate 'unity' with monism. By contrast, I would like to offer a
broader definition of thematic unity: a text possesses thematic unity
if it contains one *or more* themes which are an occasion for discussion throughout the entire text, and which the author uses to tie
together other (perhaps disparate) elements of the text. Thematic
unity, therefore, depends on whether a given theme effectively does
the job of knitting a text together—it does *not* depend on *how many*
such themes do the job.

There are several compelling reasons for adopting thematic pluralism as an approach to the *Phaedrus* (or for that matter, as an
approach to any Platonic dialogue). The first is that it is a more appropriate approach for the *dialogue form* than is thematic monism.
Indeed, the inordinate influence of thematic monism stems (at least
in part) from a failure to appreciate the uniqueness of the dialogue
form. When we read someone such as Aristotle or Kant, what we are

---

[31] Some of the other unifying themes are myth, the divine (or 'religion'), self-
knowledge, and writing. Space prohibits me from examining each of these; suffice it
to say that a close reading of the *Phaedrus* will clearly show that all of these themes are
present throughout the dialogue as a whole, and play more than an incidental role.

Plato's Phaedrus *and the Problem of Unity*   111

dealing with is fairly transparent: a treatise or essay that explicitly deals with a given subject in a systematic and sequential manner. Plato's dialogues do not function in this manner. Though the dialogues contain arguments and ideas that are just as sophisticated as anything in Aristotle or Kant, the *manner of presentation* of those arguments and ideas is utterly unique. The question of the dialogue form and the issues that form presents are too complex to examine here in any detail; suffice it to say that character, setting, irony, imagery, and other dramatic-literary elements are all integral to our understanding of a Platonic text. Moreover, such features of the form of Plato's writing cannot be divorced from the content of that writing. The upshot of all of this is that it is blatantly inappropriate to expect a Platonic dialogue to act like a Kantian treatise. Yet when we ask for a 'main theme' or 'primary purpose', we are doing just that—seeking black-and-white answers from a multi-coloured text. To seek a 'main' theme is to expect a tidy compartmentalization and hierarchization of ideas which do not exist in the dialogues; indeed, as Guthrie noted, the beauty of the dialogue form is that it enables Plato to *intertwine* several ideas which may be *equally* important to him.[32] (Just as, similarly, the dialogue form enables him to intertwine form and content.) Presumably Plato could have written treatises if he had wanted to; the fact that he did not do so compels us to ask why. It also compels us to read his texts in a manner that is appropriate to their genre.

In advocating thematic pluralism, I am in no way suggesting that the dialogues are somehow a jumbled hotchpotch of multiple ideas. Rather, it is part of Plato's genius that he is able to create multi-coloured and multi-thematic texts that *also* have a strictly controlled internal structure. In fact, the *Phaedrus* is by no means unique in being thematically pluralistic (and, hence, superficially 'disunified'); strict thematic unity, of the sort demanded by thematic monists, does not exist in *any* of Plato's dialogues.[33] For example, what could we possibly cite as the 'main theme' of the *Republic*—justice? politics? the soul? education? the philosopher? Selecting any one of these, to the exclusion and subordination of the others, would clearly give a skewed sense of the dialogue as a whole. Even the early aporetic dialogues can be said to be as much about

---

[32] Guthrie, 'Rhetoric and Philosophy', 117.

[33] Cf. De Vries, *Commentary*, 22–3. He well notes that 'Plato's thought is not departmental; but it is organized.'

112   *Daniel Werner*

method—proper definition—as about piety, courage, and so forth. We may grant that the *Phaedrus* is pluralistic to an extreme degree, and that it presents a much greater challenge to the reader. Yet it remains only a matter of degree and not of kind—for *no* Platonic dialogue has the strict thematic unity of a treatise.

In virtue of the dialogue form, then, I see good reason to abandon thematic monism in favour of a more nuanced and multi-coloured approach. There are also considerations arising specifically from the *Phaedrus* which favour such an approach. For example, one of the messages of the dialogue is that interpersonal relationships, persuasive speech, myth, and the written word all have a place within the philosophical life—although that place is also provisional, and subordinate to the practice of dialectic. It makes sense, then, for Plato to discuss a *plurality* of themes within a philosophical dialogue, given the plurality of activities and modes of discourse which he sees as part of the philosophical life itself.[34]

Moreover, Plato has good *philosophical* reasons for treating a plurality of themes—and not any one—as equally important. To wit: throughout the *Phaedrus* he draws numerous conceptual connections *between erōs*, rhetoric, and philosophy, thereby linking them in a most intimate manner. *Erōs* and rhetoric, for example, are closely interrelated in a number of respects. On the one hand, a lover— *qua* being a seducer who uses *words* to attempt to persuade the beloved—is necessarily a kind of rhetorician.[35] On the other hand, the converse is true as well: the rhetorician is a kind of lover. This is because Plato broadly defines rhetoric as a 'leading of the soul through words' (ψυχαγωγία τις διὰ λόγων, 261 A 8); consequently, all rhetoric involves intimate interpsychic contact, and an attempt to move—and indeed, to woo and to seduce—someone else's soul. (Rhetoric does so, moreover, in part by appealing to our *desires*.)

[34] I am *not* claiming, as some have, that the *Phaedrus* shows us a more 'tolerant' Plato who has become more accepting of erotic attachment and non-dialectic modes of discourse, and that in this dialogue he has moved away from the 'asceticism' and 'Socratism' of earlier dialogues. (For examples of this view, see G. Nicholson, *Plato's* Phaedrus*: The Philosophy of Love* [*Plato's* Phaedrus] (West Lafayette, Ind., 1999), 13–14; and M. C. Nussbaum, *The Fragility of Goodness: Luck and Ethics in Greek Tragedy and Philosophy*, rev. edn. (Cambridge, 2001), ch. 7.) I do not take the earlier Plato to be as 'ascetic' as is sometimes claimed, nor do I take the *Phaedrus* Plato to be as 'tolerant' as is sometimes claimed.

[35] As Nicholson eloquently asks, 'If we think of love, can we suppose that it would never be given expression in speech? Can we love without speaking to the one we love, and without speaking about love? Could we even experience love in the absence of language?' (*Plato's* Phaedrus, 124).

Plato's Phaedrus *and the Problem of Unity*   113

There are other connections between *erōs* and rhetoric as well: both have a connection to the divine, and require the divine in order to be fulfilled (*erōs* reminds us of the soul's discarnate 'divine banquet', and according to Plato the orator's true audience is not men but the gods (273 E)); both arouse all of the soul's powers and can powerfully lead the soul; both have higher and lower forms, depending on the *telos* which motivates the individual; and both are implicit in the activity of Socratic dialogue.[36]

Erōs and rhetoric, in turn, are both related to philosophy in a clear way: the best kind of *erōs* is the philosophical kind, as is the best kind of rhetoric. This is a perfect example of what we might call Plato's 'assimilation strategy': his consistent strategy of using commonly understood concepts and terms, but transforming their meaning so as to arrive at an opposite point; specifically, his strategy of assimilating all ordinary practices and activities into *philosophy*.[37] In the *Phaedrus* this assimilation strategy becomes fully clear at the end of the dialogue, where we find that philosophical *erōs* and philosophical rhetoric are to be found in the process of philosophical education and the practice of dialectic (wherein the dialectician 'plants' the appropriate *logos* within the soul of the student). The *Phaedrus* itself is only an imitation of such a process—not only because the dialogue is written (and hence falls short of the interactive nature of live dialectic), but also because the fictive conversation, even if it *were* live, does not rise to true dialectic (in large part due to the inadequacies of Phaedrus as a conversation partner).

So not only do *erōs*, rhetoric, and philosophy all recur throughout the text as a whole, but they are also conceptually and philosophically linked to one another; by no means are they unrelated themes which Plato has coincidentally discussed together in one dialogue. What we have, then, are no fewer than *three* main themes in the *Phaedrus*, and in my view the best way to accommodate

---

[36] I am indebted to Plass ('Unity') for these and other connections.

[37] As Guthrie insightfully puts the point, 'the fact is that, as many of the dialogues make plain, what Plato calls the "true" representative of every human art, science or practice turns into the philosopher and bears little resemblance to his counterpart in everyday life, be he called statesman, scientist, lover, poet, or rhetorician' ('Rhetoric and Philosophy', 120). On Plato's practice of 'assimilation', cf. also R. G. Edmonds III, *Myths of the Underworld Journey: Plato, Aristophanes, and the 'Orphic' Gold Tablets* (Cambridge, 2004), 167–9; and J. M. Redfield, who notes that 'for Socrates (as Plato represents him) all valid activities are one with dialectical philosophy and therefore can be included within it' (*Nature and Culture in the* Iliad: *The Tragedy of Hector* (Chicago, 1975), 44).

114 *Daniel Werner*

that fact is to adopt thematic pluralism as an approach to this dialogue. Such an approach is also more consistent with the reality of the dialogue form. Let us not feel compelled to choose *one* 'primary theme' from among the options; instead, it is more fruitful to think that a cluster of interrelated themes lies at the heart of the *Phaedrus*. The dialogue *does* indeed have strong thematic unity—we simply need a broader notion of 'thematic unity' to recognize that fact.[38]

3. Non-thematic approaches to unity

Thus far in this article I have been considering the thematic approach to unity—the approach which attempts to resolve the issue on the level of subject-matter (or what the dialogue is 'about'). Yet as I have been at pains to emphasize, the *Phaedrus* is a complex and multi-layered text. Consequently, in addressing the problem of unity, it is important to address a prior question: what, exactly, do we mean by 'unity' in the first place? Interpreters of the *Phaedrus* have not always asked this question, or have passed it over in silence;[39] the most common assumption is to equate 'unity' with 'thematic unity'. But such an assumption is unwarranted. The genre of the dialogue form compels us to employ multi-faceted and nuanced ways of reading; although theme and subject-matter are one element of a Platonic dialogue, there are a variety of other elements—such as structural, stylistic, and dramatic—which warrant our attention. Moreover, it would be a mistake to privilege theme or subject-matter as the 'most important' aspects of the text, for it is the entire *complex* of elements that provides meaning to a given dialogue. Accordingly, I now wish to look beyond the level of theme, and suggest some of the other levels on which the *Phaedrus*

---

[38] I take the above considerations to provide good grounds for adopting thematic pluralism. But I should also add, as further support, that I have not yet encountered any actual *arguments* in favour of thematic monism; it tends to be assumed as somehow self-evident. But (again) *why* make such an assumption? E. Black puts the point well: 'there is no binding fiat of literary activity nor any logical necessity demanding that a piece of writing, even a great piece of writing, and especially a dialectical enquiry, must have one and only one paraphrasable theme' ('Plato's View of Rhetoric', *Quarterly Journal of Speech*, 44 (1958), 361–74 at 363).

[39] Nehamas and Woodruff are one exception (see *Plato:* Phaedrus, xxxvii); Rutherford also pauses to give thoughtful consideration to the matter (*Art of Plato*, 261).

Plato's Phaedrus *and the Problem of Unity* 115

is unified. Doing so will provide a deeper understanding of the text at hand.[40]

(*a*) *Dramatic-literary unity*

Plass has made a very simple but important observation: the entire 'problem' of unity arises only when it is posed in philosophical terms, and not when it is posed in literary terms.[41] That is to say, it is largely because we expect an unbroken, tightly knit philosophical argument from Plato that we feel 'offended' by the *Phaedrus*'s apparent incoherence; yet if we view the dialogue purely as a literary text, there is nothing incoherent or disunified about it. Of course the *Phaedrus* is not *merely* a literary text, and we can no more treat it as such than we can treat it as a Kantian treatise with a bit of poetic adornment. None the less, the observation still stands: the dialogue *is* a unified literary work. Let me pursue this observation in greater detail.[42]

The dialogue has unity of *time*: it takes place on a single afternoon, and depicts a single conversation from beginning to end without any interruptions. It has unity of *place*: apart from some initial strolling, Phaedrus and Socrates remain immobile in one location throughout the entire conversation. The dialogue also has unity of *character*: Socrates and Phaedrus remain with us throughout the entire afternoon, and we learn a great deal about each man in the process. It also has unity of *action* or *plot*: we have a continuous, uninterrupted sequence of events, and each scene follows logically from the previous one. There is a clear beginning, middle, and end. Finally, the dialogue has unity of *tone* and *mood*: the tone is one of 'light irony', which is appropriate to 'a warm afternoon to be spent by the banks of a stream in pleasant company and delightful discourse'.[43] Taken together, all of this shows that the *Phaedrus* is a unified literary document. Now it may very well be that such literary unity is 'trivially' present, and that it does not do much to alleviate the general *feeling* or *impression* of dis-

---

[40] Note that—since neither form nor content can be privileged as 'primary' in a dialogue—there is no need to 'choose' between a thematic and a non-thematic approach to the problem of unity. Accordingly, I shall advocate a hybrid approach to the question which incorporates both thematic *and* non-thematic considerations.

[41] Plass, 'Unity', 7–8.

[42] I am indebted to Rutherford (*Art of Plato*, 261) for the following observations.

[43] Helmbold and Holther, 'Unity', 389.

116   *Daniel Werner*

unity. None the less, it is a dimension of unity which should not be ignored.

In fact, however, a good many of the dramatic and literary elements are by no means 'trivial', but afford us deeper insights into the dialogue as a whole. For example, the *setting* provides unity on a variety of levels. The fact that the dialogue takes place outside of the city is itself significant—and in fact this is the only Platonic dialogue that is set in the countryside. Socrates is literally ἄτοπος, 'out of place'—this Greek term recurs multiple times in the dialogue (see 251 D 8, 229 E 1, 229 C 6, 230 C 6)—since he rarely leaves the city walls. The entire dialogue is also figuratively ἄτοπος, since it leaves behind the 'civilizing' influence of the *polis*. And 'extraordinary' (another meaning of ἄτοπος) things do indeed happen on this afternoon, most notably the 'inspired' palinode of Socrates, which offers a supra-rational account from the most rational of men. (And let us not forget all the references to nymphs, potions, abduction, gods, and madness.) The 'inspirational' and 'mad' aspects of the setting are further reflected in the heat of the day: it is already quite warm when Phaedrus and Socrates begin their conversation (cf. 229 A ff.), and Socrates' recitation of the palinode coincides with the *hottest* part of the day, high noon.[44] Both the weather and the speech-making, therefore, reach an overwhelming climax at one crucial point, and the second half of the dialogue subsequently traces the gradual decline of the sun. With all of their energy spent, perhaps it is then inevitable that Socrates and Phaedrus return to the *polis* at the end of the dialogue. And this carries a philosophical implication: the extraordinary experience in the countryside cannot become a permanent condition; what is better is to lead the extraordinary life of the philosopher—a life which requires social interaction within the *polis*.

One further literary aspect also deserves comment: Plato's use of dramatic interludes. Each of the three speeches is bookended by a brief transitional moment; and far from being unimportant, these moments constitute one of the main structural techniques which Plato uses to cement together the overall dialogue. The introductory scene (227 A–230 E), for example, is not merely 'stage-setting'

---

[44] At 242 A, which occurs in the interlude between the first and second speeches of Socrates, Phaedrus states that it is *almost* (σχεδόν) high noon; this means that high noon—the climax or apex of the sun's reach—occurs *during* the recitation of the palinode.

Plato's Phaedrus *and the Problem of Unity*   117

but in fact encapsulates all of the major philosophical concerns of the dialogue as a whole: *rhetoric* (Phaedrus' arrival from listening to Lysias), *writing* (Phaedrus' written manuscript of Lysias' speech), *philosophy* (Socrates' reference to self-knowledge and the Delphic oracle), *memory* (Phaedrus' attempt to memorize the speech), *erōs* (the coy interplay between Socrates and Phaedrus, and Socrates' self-description as an ἐραστής of words), *myth* (the discussion of allegorization and Boreas), and *religion* (the mention of the altar of Boreas and the sacredness of the spot) are all broached in this scene. Similarly, the other interludes are not merely literary devices but are also structurally and philosophically significant. It is in the dramatic interludes, for instance, that the cicadas make their appearance: Plato first mentions them in the introductory scene (230 C), and then mentions them a second time in the transitional interlude from the palinode to the second half (259 A–E). On the one hand these dramatic references again help to cement together the dialogue as a whole; at the same time, they also provide crucial cues to the reader. Like Socrates and Phaedrus, we too (as readers) ought not to be negligent—lulled to sleep by the cicadas' song—but ought to remain vigilant in our approach to the text. Plato strategically returns to the cicadas just after we have heard the overwhelming palinode—alerting us, perhaps, not to be awed into submission by the soaring rhetoric but to remain keen philosophers.

I take it, then, that the *Phaedrus* has dramatic and literary unity in at least two senses. First, it possesses such unity on the most basic level of plot, character, mood, and so forth—i.e. in virtue of the fact that Plato creates a single 'story' that is self-contained. Second, the dialogue is unified through Plato's structural and philosophical *use* of those dramatic and literary elements. Both the setting and the transitional moments function in this manner, providing a global frame for the dialogue as a whole, and helping to join together disparate themes and concerns. That setting, in short, does not lie silently in the background; it permeates the action of the dialogue, fluctuates over time, and relates to the philosophical themes.

(b) *Verbal texture*

One particularly fruitful (though frequently ignored) approach to the question of unity is the examination of the recurrent motifs, imagery, and symbols of the *Phaedrus*—what Rutherford calls the

118 *Daniel Werner*

verbal texture of the dialogue.[45] This approach is different from the thematic approach to unity, in so far as it does not focus on the main subject-matter or 'topics' of the dialogue, but rather on the *language* through which that subject-matter is expressed and the enquiry is framed. After all, Plato is a master craftsman, and there is very little in the dialogues that can be attributed to mere whim or accident. And it is part of his craft of writing to use specific kinds of language and imagery to draw subtler connections, to reinforce the enquiry of a given dialogue, and to provoke the reader to engage in that enquiry in a more nuanced way.

Verbal and imagistic echoing and cross-referencing occur throughout the *Phaedrus*. Indeed, if we look at the dialogue as a whole, we find that certain motifs, words, images, and symbols are recurrent. These include:[46]

> light vs. darkness, brightness
> enthusiasm, possession, madness
> eyes, sight, blindness
> food, nourishment, feasting
> growth, reproduction, agricultural-organic metaphors, sowing, planting
> heat, warmth
> animals, animal-like behaviour, monsters
> simplicity vs. complexity
> health vs. sickness, medicine
> leading, guiding, path, way, route, track
> movement, motion
> leisure vs. work
> liquid, water
> memory, forgetfulness
> cure, potion, φάρμακον
> play vs. seriousness

---

[45] Rutherford, *Art of Plato*, 266. Rutherford takes her cue from Lebeck, whose seminal article 'The Central Myth of Plato's *Phaedrus*' showed how fruitful—and philosophically significant—results could be derived from an examination of the verbal texture of Plato's dialogues.

[46] Again, the seminal discussion for many of these motifs and images is Lebeck. For a comparison of Plato's use of some of these images with the ancient poet Theocritus, see C. Murley, 'Plato's *Phaedrus* and the Theocritean Pastoral', *Transactions and Proceedings of the American Philological Association*, 71 (1940), 281–95. W. W. Fortenbaugh has discussed the indebtedness of Plato's imagery to Sappho and Anacreon ('Plato *Phaedrus* 235C3', *Classical Philology*, 61 (1966), 108–9).

Plato's Phaedrus *and the Problem of Unity*   119

self-knowledge
wisdom
gold, statuary, votive offerings
freedom vs. slavery
victory, contest, honour
whip, goad
initiation, mysteries, sacred vision.

It is important to note that none of the motifs and images listed here occurs only in one isolated passage; rather, they are all genuinely *recurring* motifs, and arise in at least several different passages throughout the dialogue as a whole.

Plato's use of these recurring motifs and images in the *Phaedrus* is what we might call a technique of *verbal reminiscence*.[47] And this technique shows a further sense in which the *Phaedrus* is unified. For simply on a surface level, the repetition of language and imagery provides a kind of continuous thread that runs through the entirety of the dialogue. But there is more to the dialogue's unity than just a surface-level repetition of words. For Plato also uses the verbal texture to make a *philosophical* point. Plato has offered us a dialogue which has a plurality of philosophical topics (*erōs*, rhetoric, myth, dialectic, and so on) and a sequence of (seemingly) disjointed parts; but by simultaneously using a common verbal texture, he is implicitly encouraging us to seek out the *interconnections* among those various topics and parts of the dialogue, and to consider the philosophical implications of those interconnections.

As an example, consider Plato's use of the nourishment, agricultural, and organic motifs. In the palinode we are told that the soul's vision of the Forms is what nourishes the wings, and that—in this life—one way in which to regrow the wings is through an appropriate erotic relationship. Such is one use of these motifs. But the motifs recur again at the end of the dialogue, in the Theuth

---

[47] Such is Lebeck's phrase ('Central Myth', 289). She describes the technique well: 'As words and images recur they call up whole passages, major ideas. A network of association is created which continually expands the reader's consciousness' (289). As she notes, this technique is in perfect keeping with the dialogue's emphasis on *recollection*. Further levels of complexity and networks of interrelationship are created through the fact that Plato will often use the same word (such as 'perfect' or 'healthy') in more than one sense. Again, Lebeck makes a valuable insight: 'Plato, in a manner similar to the dramatists, uses thematic repetition as a means of keeping certain ideas before the reader . . . Since the word is employed in more than one sense, its repetition takes on a paronomasiac quality. That is, the theme meaning and the meaning uppermost in the context are not always identical' (272 n. 12).

120 *Daniel Werner*

myth and the critique of writing: we are told that dialectic is the true means of 'planting' a *logos* in an appropriate soul, that such a *logos* is one's true 'offspring', and that such a *logos*—by being 'sown' in other souls and by growing on its own—can give a kind of immortality. What we thus have is a single set of motifs being used in two different contexts, and in two different parts of the dialogue. Because the imagery is the same, however, the implication is that there is some sort of *connection* between the two contexts—in this case, between the palinode and the critique of writing. And such a connection indeed exists: the critique of writing is pointing us towards the practice of live, interactive dialectic as the means of attaining true 'growth' in the soul; but the content of that activity is fully appreciated only when we reflect back on the palinode, and in particular on the discussion of the philosophical lovers and the discussion of the divine banquet. The philosophical implication, then, is that dialectical activity is both social and Form-directed. So what at first seems to be a mere repetition of language in fact turns out to be a sophisticated means of suggesting thematic and structural connections among diverse parts of the text.[48]

The use of verbal texture, then, is another important way in which the *Phaedrus* is unified. Such a texture provides both a continuous thread as well as a provocation to seek out deeper connections among diverse topics and ideas—and hence is anything but 'superficial'.

(c) Formal-structural unity

When discussed in connection with the Platonic dialogues, 'structural unity' refers to a formal feature of a given text, i.e. some pattern or principle of organization among the various parts of a dialogue. In fact, as I noted earlier, in the *Phaedrus* Plato explicitly makes structural organization a *sine qua non* of good rhetoric. He insists that a good *logos* must possess 'logographic necessity' (ἀνάγκην λογογραφικήν, 264 B 7), i.e. a logical and consistent internal organization such that each part *necessarily* follows from the previous part. As Socrates famously puts the point:

Every speech must be put together like a living creature, with a body of its

---

[48] And it may be that Plato thinks that we do not fully *understand* the nature of *erōs*, rhetoric, etc. until we have grasped their interconnections. (Cf. M. M. McCabe, 'Myth, Allegory and Argument in Plato', *Apeiron*, 25 (1992), 47–67 at 53–5.)

Plato's Phaedrus *and the Problem of Unity* 121

own; it must be neither without head nor without legs; and it must have a middle and extremities that are fitting both to one another and to the whole work. (264 C)

There is no reason to think that this statement is not perfectly general: that is, the requirement of logographic necessity would seem to apply not only to oral speech-making but to any kind of *logos*, Platonic dialogues included. Yet this is precisely what has troubled so many readers of the *Phaedrus*; for given the thematic and stylistic diversity of the dialogue—and in particular the two seemingly 'disjointed' halves—it seems difficult if not impossible to discern any sense in which the *Phaedrus* is in fact an 'organic' *logos* whose parts are 'fitting' to one another and to the whole. So we must therefore ask: does the *Phaedrus* in fact possess the logographic necessity which it requires of other writers?

I think that it does.[49] Specifically, the dialogue has what we might call a *palinodic structure* (or *palinodic development*): that is to say, 'various points of view are presented as though they were final and are then purposely undercut to reveal a further, unanticipated meaning'.[50] In other words, Socrates' second speech (the 'backwards-ode' or παλινῳδία) is not the only instance of a *logos* which recants or moves beyond an earlier *logos*; there are in fact *multiple* palinodic discourses in the *Phaedrus*. Consider the basic sequence of events in the dialogue: we begin with Lysias' speech, which Phaedrus thinks supersedes all other Greek speeches on *erōs* (he considers it to be the greatest and most complete speech, 234 E); Lysias' speech is then superseded by Socrates' first speech (which Socrates offers in an attempt to 'outdo' Lysias); both of the earlier speeches—with their inadequate conception of *erōs*—are then superseded by Socrates' second speech, which is officially a 'recantation'; the palinode itself is superseded by the discussion of rhetoric and dialectic (in so far as *logos* and *technē* would seem to be superior to *muthos*); and that discussion—in so far as it is contained within a written dialogue—is superseded by oral, live dialectic. In each case, what initially appears to be a final and complete statement of the truth—a speech about *erōs*, a speech about the soul and the Forms, a discussion about rhetoric—is soon revealed to be *in*complete; and

---

[49] The account which I offer in this section is only a sketch; I present a much more extensive discussion of the structure of the dialogue in my *Myth and Philosophy in Plato's* Phaedrus (manuscript in preparation).

[50] Griswold, *Self-Knowledge*, 218.

122   *Daniel Werner*

so the *Phaedrus* as a whole takes on an onion-like structure, with a
series of layers built upon one another.[51] Put somewhat differently,
we might say that the *Phaedrus* has a kind of outward movement
or progression, as a series of retrospective and self-referential analyses broaden our awareness of the limitations of what has come
before.[52] In the end, the ultimate *telos* towards which the *Phaedrus* points—the continual 'other' or 'beyond'—is none other than
philosophy itself.

Notice that the myths of the *Phaedrus* play a central role in this
palinodic structure and development. It is a myth (Boreas) that
begins the dialogue, orienting us towards its major concerns; it is
a myth (the palinode) that moves us beyond the harmful ethos of
the first two speeches, and towards a broader conception of human existence; it is a myth (the cicadas) that moves us beyond the
palinode, and towards the discussion of rhetoric and dialectic; and
it is a myth (Theuth) that moves us beyond the *Phaedrus* itself,
and towards live, interactive dialectic. We thus see that, far from
being accidentally or randomly placed, the myths of the *Phaedrus*
are quite carefully and strategically located so as to help achieve
a palinodic effect in the dialogue as a whole. In other words, the
myths work together both *co-ordinately* (reflecting back on a previous λόγος) and *cumulatively* (building upon one another within the
overall progression of the dialogue), and play an essential role in
guiding our reading of the dialogue.

A variety of other proposals regarding the structure of the *Phaedrus* have been put forward, and I do not claim that my schematiza-
tion is the only possible one.[53] If we accept, however, that the *Phaedrus* has a palinodic structure—and I think that that is undeniable—

---

[51] Note, however, that in the *Phaedrus* we do *not* peel back various layers to arrive
at an inner 'core' (i.e. some final bedrock); if anything, the layers of the *Phaedrus*
are constructed so as to move us ever *outward*.

[52] In this sense I disagree with Ferrari, who suggests that—in so far as *both* myth
and argument are limited (and hence share a 'kinship of limitation')—each half of
the *Phaedrus* leads to the other (*Cicadas*, 34). Instead I am suggesting that the first
half leads to the second half, and that the second half leads to something else entirely.

[53] See e.g. Griswold, *Self-Knowledge*, 161–3; D. A. White, *Rhetoric and Reality in
Plato's* Phaedrus [*Rhetoric*] (Albany, NY, 1993), 172–3; Lebeck, 'Central Myth', 268;
Hackforth, *Plato's* Phaedrus, 136–7. Clearly we can reject Taylor's claim that 'in
structure the dialogue is of the simplest type' (*Plato*, 300). Some commentators claim
that 'mere' formal features are not enough to constitute unity (see e.g. Waterfield,
Plato: Phaedrus, xi; and Nehamas and Woodruff, *Plato:* Phaedrus, xxxvii). Such
a view, however, rests on the assumption of the correctness of thematic monism
(against which I have already argued).

Plato's Phaedrus *and the Problem of Unity*   123

then it is clear that the dialogue has a carefully planned and tightly controlled internal organization. More to the point, it also becomes clear that the dialogue does in fact possess logographic necessity.

(d) Word vs. deed

In addition to the verbal, dramatic, and formal kinds of unity, I wish to consider one final non-thematic approach: what I shall call (broadly speaking) the interplay between word and deed. I have already remarked that the uniqueness of the dialogue form—the fact that it functions on many levels—compels us to adopt appropriate reading strategies. Part of what this means is that content and form are inseparable in Plato, and hence that we will be unable to achieve a faithful interpretation of a dialogue if we focus solely on what is explicitly *said* in that dialogue. For in addition to the level of explicit *logos* or argument, we must also pay attention to the level of *action* or *deed* (*ergon*)—be it the action of a particular character, the dramatic context of a given argument, or the unspoken cues from Plato himself directly to the reader. In any given dialogue, then, there arises an interplay of word and deed, and it is through that interplay that (in part) the dialogue expresses meaning. In the case of the *Phaedrus*, this word–deed interplay is so prevalent throughout the dialogue as a whole—and is so important for the philosophical content—that it offers one more level of unity. For want of a better term, I shall call this 'unity of technique', since the word–deed interplay is essentially a device which Plato uses to make his point.[54] Let us consider some of the ways in which such unity is present.

I have already noted that Plato uses the opening scene of the dialogue to present—and indeed, to enact—all of its major themes. This kind of dramatic enactment occurs over and over again in the *Phaedrus* in relation to each of the central themes:

Erōs. While the three speeches talk *about erōs*, the interaction between Phaedrus and Socrates clearly has erotic overtones—and hence is an *instantiation* of the subject-matter. There is, for ex-

---

[54] It should be noted that the contrast of word vs. deed is also a *theme* of the text. As Ferrari notes, one of Plato's main claims in the *Phaedrus* is that explicit knowledge— i.e. a propositional knowledge of a set of codified rules—is not always sufficient for complete *understanding*. (This applies, for example, to both rhetorical and dialectical practice.) In addition to propositional knowledge, personal recognition or insight is often required. See *Cicadas*, 21–5.

124 *Daniel Werner*

ample, the coy interplay between the interlocutors in the opening scene and interludes; in addition, the dialogue can plausibly be read as an attempt by Socrates to 'seduce' Phaedrus into the philosophical life.[55]

Rhetoric. Whereas the second half is a discussion *about* rhetoric, the first half contains three *examples* of rhetoric (in *deed*).[56]

Myth. At several places Plato talks *about* myth (most notably in the opening scene), but he also provides us with several *examples* of myth (the palinode, the cicadas, and Theuth).

Psychagogia. The second half contains a discussion *about* 'the leading of the soul', but the dialogue also contains several *examples* of it: within each of the speeches, a lover leads a beloved; within the drama of the dialogue, Socrates attempts to lead Phaedrus; and through a self-reflexive myth about writing, Plato attempts to lead us (his readers) beyond his own dialogues.

Madness. In the palinode Socrates talks *about* madness—and identifies four kinds of madness (poetic, prophetic, telestic, and erotic)—but in the dialogue as a whole he is made to appear as if he *exemplifies* all four kinds.[57]

Dialectic. Whereas the second half offers a discussion *about* dialectic, Socrates' two speeches—at least according to his own self-analysis at 266 A–B—contain *examples* of collection and division. More broadly, the very act of opposing one speech to another is itself a 'dialectical' manœuvre.[58]

Philosophy. The dialogue is very much *about* philosophy, but so

[55] Some read the relationship between Socrates and Phaedrus as an instantiation of the *philosophical erōs* depicted in the palinode. (See e.g. J. Sallis, *Being and Logos: Reading the Platonic Dialogues*, 3rd edn. (Bloomington, Ind., 1996), 112–13.) I think this is unlikely, given that (among other things) they do not actually engage in dialectic, and given that Phaedrus seems very far from exemplifying the philosophically self-aware beloved of the palinode.

[56] Again, some view the palinode as an instantiation of the philosophical (ideal) *technē* of rhetoric; but as I have already noted, such a view seems to me to be implausible.

[57] (1) *Poetic*: before his first speech he invokes the Muses (237 A) and during the speech he nearly speaks in verse (241 E); (2) *prophetic*: at one point he calls himself a 'seer' (242 C), and at the end of the dialogue he 'prophesies' what will happen to Isocrates; (3) *telestic*: the act of recantation via the palinode is symbolic of telestic expiation; (4) *erotic*: he himself is a lover (of speeches, of wisdom), and speaks at length about *erōs*. (I am indebted to Rutherford for these references (*Art of Plato*, 262); cf. also White, *Rhetoric*, 61–2.) I emphasize that Socrates is only made to *appear* to exemplify madness, since there is probably a good deal of irony involved in all of this and since it is unlikely that he is literally 'out of his mind'.

[58] W. C. Helmbold and W. G. Rabinowitz, *Plato: Phaedrus* (Indianapolis, 1956),

Plato's Phaedrus *and the Problem of Unity* 125

too does it *depict* philosophy in action—for instance, in Socrates' actions (such as his recantations), as well as in the drama of back-and-forth conversation. It may be that, precisely because philosophy is fundamentally an *activity*, it can be learnt only through practice: hence the need to portray it (and not merely describe it).[59]

Writing. Socrates and Phaedrus talk *about* the written word, but of course the *Phaedrus* itself (not to mention the speech of Lysias which Phaedrus is carrying) is an inescapably written text.

Clearly, then, there is an interplay between *logos* and *ergon* which runs through the entirety of the *Phaedrus*. This provides yet another level of textual and philosophical unity to the dialogue.

4. The debunking approach

Thus far I have argued that the *Phaedrus* possesses unity in at least two ways: first, on the level of theme or subject-matter; and second, through a variety of non-thematic elements, including verbal texture, drama, form, and word–deed interplay. In making this argument, I have been assuming that the *Phaedrus* confronts us with a genuine textual problem—'the problem of unity'—that is (more or less) capable of solution. Yet not all commentators on the dialogue share this assumption. Rather, some question the very question itself, and claim that the alleged 'problem' of unity is unreal. On this view, strict unity is a demand which modern commentators wrongly impose on Plato's text, when in reality such unity is simply not to be found there. Instead, we must frankly admit that the disunity of the *Phaedrus* is real and ineluctable—though there are historical reasons as to *why* that is the case. I shall call this view the 'debunking approach', for its central claim is that we have been falsely conceiving of the scope and seriousness of the supposed 'problem' of unity. Rather than 'solve' the problem, then, we should dissolve it.

M. Heath has been the primary voice in support of the debunking approach.[60] The central assumption underlying Heath's argument is that 'there is a significant difference between Greek and our own

---

xii. Whether the speeches *actually* exemplify technical dialectic seems unlikely, and is perhaps just a convenient way for Socrates to analyse his own earlier *logoi*.

[59] Griswold, *Self-Knowledge*, 223.

[60] 'The Unity of Plato's *Phaedrus*' ['Unity'], *OSAP* 7 (1989), 151–73.

126   *Daniel Werner*

literary aesthetics' (162); specifically, there is a difference between
the type of unity that a Greek audience would expect from a text
and the type of unity that modern interpreters expect. We mo-
derns, according to Heath, expect a literary or philosophical text
to possess strong thematic unity; and it is the apparent failure of
the *Phaedrus* to possess such a feature that generates the entire
'problem' of unity. That 'problem', however, exists only for *us*—it
is non-existent for a Greek audience. The criterion of unity which
a Greek audience assumes is not theme-based, but what Heath
calls 'functional appropriateness' (163). That is to say, each genre
of writing—be it tragedy, comedy, or philosophy—has a *function*
or *end* that is appropriate to it; and (from the ancient Greek point
of view) a given text possesses unity if the content of that text is
appropriate to the relevant end or function. In the case of a philosophical text, the underlying function is that of 'instilling virtue
or promoting philosophical understanding' (172); thus, so long as
the content of the text serves that broader function—which is the
case in the *Phaedrus*—the text is thereby unified.[61] The upshot of
Heath's argument is that the supposed 'problem' of unity is merely
a result of anachronistic interpretation; in other words, we are guilty
of imposing inappropriate and unreasonable demands upon Plato's
text. From a *Greek* point of view, the dialogue *is* unified (in so far
as the content of the dialogue serves the function of the genre); but
we must also admit that, according to *our* (modern-day) criteria,
the *Phaedrus does* lack unity. Yet such disunity is almost irrelevant,
given the intentions and aesthetic sensibilities of the author.[62]

   Ferrari has also advocated a version of the debunking approach.[63]
Ferrari first addresses the issue of the abrupt 'change in register',
i.e. the shift in tone, language, and style from the first half to the

---

   [61] In this sense theme is subordinate to function, and Plato's main goal in writing
dialogues is not to explore a given topic but to achieve a broader end (172).

   [62] According to Heath, the *Phaedrus* does possess a basic unity of plot (what Heath
calls 'formal' unity), but no more than that. For Plato, however—and for any other
Greek—such plot structure is sufficient, for it 'provides a platform on which many
diverse, and perhaps divergent, material interests may be developed' (162). And so
long as those interests serve the broader end, the text is unified.

   [63] 'The Unity of the *Phaedrus*: A Response'. Although Ferrari considers the 1994
article to be a 'cooler, more historical response' (21) to the problem of unity than
that espoused in his earlier book on the *Phaedrus*, *Cicadas* already seems to advocate
the debunking approach. Consider the dismissive attitude of the final sentence of
Cicadas: 'Let us not struggle too hard, then, to unify the *Phaedrus;* for the real
struggle is elsewhere' (232).

Plato's Phaedrus *and the Problem of Unity* 127

second half. As we move from the soaring palinode to the drier second half, many readers are apt to feel disappointed; according to Ferrari, however, 'our sense of let-down may be a trick of time' (22). It is comparatively easy to feel moved and awed by the palinode—its language still speaks directly to us. By contrast, the discussion of rhetoric and the rivalry between Plato and Isocrates are far from our modern-day concerns; but for Plato's audience that rivalry *was* fresh and exciting, and so (according to Ferrari) they may not have felt any sense of 'let-down' at all when coming to the second half of the dialogue. The accusation of a 'change in register' is therefore anachronistic: what seems to be a change in excitement level to us was not so to a Greek audience.[64] Ferrari then addresses the question of thematic unity in a similarly historical manner. According to him, Plato's purpose in writing the *Phaedrus* was to 'outdo the rhetoricians (and especially Isocrates) at their own game' (24). The *Phaedrus* is therefore an epideictic piece (at least in part)—something which is intended to 'shock' its audience—and so must be disjointed in order to achieve that effect.[65] Ferrari concludes: 'The thematic disunity of the dialogue is a necessity of its genre. We must stop trying to explain it away' (25).

Although there is a certain cleverness in the debunking approach, I do not find the responses of Heath and Ferrari to be helpful as a means of actually *understanding* the text that lies before us. More to the point, their arguments face several key problems. For one thing, I am not yet convinced that there *is* a deep schism between Greek and modern aesthetic sensibilities; at the very least, much more needs to be done to *prove* that such a schism exists.[66] And even if there are *some* differences between Greek and modern aesthetics—which is trivially true—Heath and Ferrari then need to prove that the *extent* of those differences is as great as they claim. My own sense is that *any* reader of the *Phaedrus* would be struck by the thematic and stylistic contrast between the two halves. The debate

[64] One obvious problem with this argument is that it addresses only the question of intellectual 'excitement', and *not* the abrupt change in style, tone, and language. The latter would still have been noticeable to a Greek audience; why it occurs, however, is still unaccounted for in Ferrari's article.

[65] I have trouble following Ferrari's argument on this point.

[66] Ferrari merely *assumes* that the *Phaedrus* is intended to be epideictic ('Unity', 24), and without any evidence compares the Plato–Isocrates rivalry to our contemporary debate concerning political correctness (22). For his part, Heath tries to offer some evidence from Greek tragedy ('Unity', 161–2), but without stopping to consider the great disanalogy between philosophy and tragedy.

128 *Daniel Werner*

regarding the 'main theme', after all, goes back to antiquity: as I noted earlier, ancient commentators gave the *Phaedrus* a variety of subtitles.[67] At least some of the ancients, then, were deeply puzzled as to how to read the dialogue.

There is also good textual evidence which counts against the debunking approach. Both Heath and Ferrari claim that the dialogue *is* thematically disunified, and that we should simply accept that fact. If my earlier argument is correct, however, such a claim is false: the *Phaedrus does* possess strong thematic unity, albeit a unity of a complex and pluralistic type. Indeed, the underlying assumption in both Heath and Ferrari—and in most interpreters, for that matter—is that the sheer plurality of themes is proof positive of thematic disunity. If what I have been arguing is correct, however, thematic plurality is perfectly consistent with thematic unity. All we need is for one or more themes to recur throughout a text as a whole and to link together other (perhaps disparate) elements of that text. This is precisely what Plato does in the *Phaedrus*, and then goes on to show the interrelations *among* his chosen themes.

Finally, I consider the debunking approach to be unsound on broad methodological grounds. In this respect I find myself in wide agreement with Griswold, who in the introduction to his book lays out a helpful set of hermeneutical principles for reading Plato's dialogues. He suggests one central interpretative 'maxim': in approaching any text, we ought to assume that the author 'means to write both what and how he does write'.[68] He then justifies this assumption:

The point concerns . . . the logical precondition of the thesis that a text is coherent and possesses a unified meaning. The assumption is warranted at the very least on heuristic grounds, that is, relative to the reader's desire to be instructed. To deny the assumption is to begin study of the text with the prejudice that from a philosophical standpoint it is not worth the most serious study. (Ibid.)

But note what follows when we make this assumption: as a matter of charitable reading, we must begin by assuming that any textual 'problem'—e.g. a logical fallacy, an inconsistency, or (more to the point) apparent disunity—is *intentional* on the part of the author. By contrast, any appeals to external considerations—the chronology of the dialogues, Plato's intellectual development, Greekness

[67] See n. 1 above.   [68] Griswold, *Self-Knowledge*, 11.

Plato's Phaedrus *and the Problem of Unity*   129

or Greek culture, or carelessness of the author—ought to be made only as a last resort of interpretation, in those cases where no sense can otherwise be made of a text.[69] If this hermeneutical approach is correct, then the debunking approach to unity immediately becomes problematic. For what Heath and Ferrari do is to import historical and cultural considerations as the *basis* of their interpretation of the *Phaedrus*; it is far preferable, however, to begin by seeking reasons from *within* the text at hand. For one thing, appeals to external considerations are generally far more speculative in nature than appeals to the text itself. Moreover, it simply seems to me to be far more charitable to the author to seek a textual response to the problem of unity—looking, for example, for deeper levels of unity—rather than attributing the composition of the text to cultural or historical factors. Methodologically, then, the debunking approach seems to be a rather unsatisfactory way of reading Plato's dialogue.

5. The strategic approach

For the three above-mentioned reasons—the questionability of the supposed Greek–modern schism, the textual evidence in favour of thematic unity, and the methodological problem—I think there are serious problems with the debunking approach, and I do not find such an approach to be a fruitful way of reading the *Phaedrus*. In looking at the debunking approach, however, we have come across an important suggestion: that the apparent disunity of the dialogue and the contrasts between the two halves are *intentional* on Plato's part. This idea is the basis of the fourth and final approach to unity that I shall consider in this article, which I shall call the 'strategic approach' (since it claims that we are dealing with a strategic or intentional gesture on the part of Plato). Even if, as I have argued, the *Phaedrus* has unity on a variety of levels, it takes a certain amount of effort on the part of the reader to recognize that fact. This is because the deeper layers of meaning, interconnections, and structure can be uncovered only through successive readings of the dialogue, and because much of the *Phaedrus* can be understood only through the benefit of hindsight. One's first encounter with the dialogue, then, is likely to be a perplexing one, in which the

---

[69] Griswold, *Self-Knowledge*, 15.

130 *Daniel Werner*

text appears to be manifestly disjointed and disunified.[70] And even *after* multiple readings of the dialogue—even when we have come to recognize the deeper strata of unity—we are still likely to *feel* an abrupt change in moving from the palinode to the second half. This is where the strategic approach enters: it claims that Plato *intends* us to feel such a change. In other words (according to this view), Plato deliberately inserts the thematic and stylistic contrasts into the dialogue, using them as a means of making a philosophical point or achieving a certain end. Our puzzlement regarding the unity of the *Phaedrus*, then, is only natural—it is in fact intentionally encouraged by the author.

I think that this sort of approach is a sound one, and that it can provide another helpful perspective from which to address the problem of unity. The question that remains, then, is this: just *why* would Plato create a text which, on the surface, appears to be disjointed and disunified?[71]

I think that there are two general answers to this question. First, the apparent disjointedness and disconnectedness of the *Phaedrus* allow Plato to reinforce some of the philosophical themes of the dialogue. This can be seen most clearly with regard to Plato's treatment of the soul in the *Phaedrus* (a key recurring theme, to be sure). One of the main issues in the dialogue is the relation between madness and *sōphrosynē*, and between madness and philosophy; indeed, the palinode seems to extol erotic madness as a blessed and divine thing, and to suggest that philosophy itself is a form of madness.[72] The juxtaposition of the 'mad' (or 'excessive') palinode with the 'sober' discussion of rhetoric and dialectic serves to dramatize and further engage this very issue: as we question how the palinode is to be related to the second half, we are simultaneously questioning how madness (or the 'irrational' generally) is to be related

---

[70] Cf. Rutherford, *Art of Plato*, 265.

[71] When I refer to the 'appearance of disunity' in the *Phaedrus*, what I primarily have in mind is the (seeming) abrupt shift in *subject*, *style*, and *tone* from the first half to the second half: that is, the shift from an explicit and sustained discussion of *erōs* to an explicit and sustained discussion of rhetoric; and the shift from speech-making and mythical narrative to elenctic dialogue. In saying this, of course, I am not contradicting my earlier claims regarding the presence of *erōs* in the second half or the presence of rhetoric in the first half; rather, I am suggesting that it requires repeated and careful readings to *recognize* the presence of those themes.

[72] Just what 'madness' really means in this context, of course, is an exceedingly complicated issue which I cannot deal with here.

Plato's Phaedrus *and the Problem of Unity* 131

to the philosophical life.[73] More broadly, this engages the issue of human nature—i.e. the nature of the soul—and how the rational charioteer is to be properly related to the spirited and appetitive horses. Early in the *Phaedrus*, when Socrates posed the question of self-knowledge, he asked whether he was 'a beast more complicated and savage than Typho' or 'a tamer, simpler animal with a share in a divine and gentle nature' (230 A). The palinode provides a partial answer to this question: humans have a *complex* nature with *both* bestial *and* divine elements. Strict simplicity of nature— or, we might say, 'unity' of nature—is therefore an impossibility for humans (though perhaps it is an ideal worth striving for). The contrasting halves of the dialogue serve to reinforce this point, and to remind us of our complex nature. Just as the *Phaedrus* itself is not a wholly perfect or uniform text, so too does human nature contain discontinuities.[74]

The disjointedness of the *Phaedrus* is thus a deliberate reflection of, and commentary on, the psychology of the dialogue. Notice that it is the very abruptness of the transition between the two halves which helps make such meta-commentary possible. The apparent disjointedness of the dialogue also serves a second purpose: it provides a meta-commentary on the *dialogue itself* (and on Plato's writings more broadly). For one thing, the contrasting halves of the *Phaedrus* provide an occasion for reflection on the scope and limitations of the palinode. As we read through the dialogue for the first time, the palinode initially appears to be a complete statement of the truth—Socrates' 'final word', as it were (since, after all, it trumps the two earlier speeches). Yet this appearance is deceiving: the dialogue does *not* end with the palinode, as Plato soon has us move *beyond* it (in a literal sense). This manœuvre seems to me to be deliberate. For when the palinode abruptly ends, and we return to the sober level of dialogical conversation, we begin to think consciously *about* the myth; specifically, we begin to think about whether the speech is in fact 'the final word'.[75] Thus the abrupt transition from the first to the second half effects what the palinode alone cannot: reflection upon the very status of the palinode. The implication,

[73] Cf. Griswold, *Self-Knowledge*, 153.

[74] In addition to being a *reflection* of human nature, a disjointed dialogue is also *appropriate* for such a nature. For as Plato tells us, the true orator will offer a complex speech for a complex soul, and a simple speech for a simple soul (277 C).

[75] This is what Griswold calls the 'self-qualification' of the palinode (*Self-Knowledge*, 152 ff.).

132   *Daniel Werner*

I think, is that the palinode is conspicuously *in*complete.[76] More broadly, the abrupt transition from palinode to dialogue provokes us to reflect on the status of myth as a form of discourse, and on the relation of *muthos* to *logos*. Here again, the implication seems to be the *limitation* of myth, both in this case and more generally.[77]

In addition to provoking reflection on the status of the palinode (and of *muthos*), the seemingly disjointed structure of the *Phaedrus* also focuses our attention on the status of the dialogue as a *written* text. One of the main themes in the *Phaedrus*, after all, is the written word. For Plato, written texts are 'dead' *logoi* which lack the clarity and certainty of the 'living' *logoi* that are written in the soul; one therefore ought to be serious only with respect to dialectic, and regard writing as no more than a 'playful' activity. Once again, it is the seeming disjointedness of the *Phaedrus* that helps to remind us of this fact. That the *Phaedrus* appears as disunified reminds us that it, too, is an imperfect written *logos* that pales in comparison with the *logos* written in the soul. In this sense, the disunity of the *Phaedrus* could not be otherwise than it is: for Plato to have created a perfect, seamless text—which would in any case be impossible— would have been an empty achievement, and a sign that he had become one of the text-obsessed poets or speech-writers whom he condemns (278 D–E).

I conclude, then, that the contrasting halves of the dialogue are part of a strategic manœuvre on Plato's part to make broader points regarding the nature of the soul and the nature of the dialogue itself. One point is worth reiterating here. The strategic approach which I am here advocating is perfectly consistent with the claim that the dialogue *does* have unity. The strategic approach begins from the contrasts and diversity of the text, which are very real, and seeks to explain *why* they are present. Textual diversity, however, does not *ipso facto* imply textual disunity.[78] Indeed, it is perfectly consistent for Plato *both* to have placed certain con-

---

[76] This was hinted at in 246 A (in the palinode itself), but becomes fully clear in the myth of the cicadas and at 265 B–D. For a good discussion of the changing and dynamic role of the palinode in the *Phaedrus*, see C. Rowe's work on the dialogue (to which I am much indebted): 'Argument and Structure', *passim*; *Plato:* Phaedrus, 7–11; and 'The Unity of the *Phaedrus*: A Reply to Heath', *OSAP* 7 (1989), 175–88.

[77] As Ferrari well notes, though, part of the point of the interplay between the two halves of the dialogue is to show that *both* μῦθος *and* λόγος are limited (what he calls a 'kinship in limitation': *Cicadas*, 30 ff.).

[78] Helmbold and Holther, 'Unity', 388.

Plato's Phaedrus *and the Problem of Unity* 133

trasts in the text *and* to have simultaneously organized that text in a coherent way. From this point of view, the *Phaedrus* is indeed unified, but is also designed to *appear* as disunified. There is no contradiction here; what is required is simply acute attentiveness on the part of the reader to recognize the appearance *as* an appearance.

6. Conclusion

As a general principle of charity, I think that we owe certain assumptions to a writer as complex as Plato. In particular, we are justified in assuming from the outset that it is unlikely—though not impossible—that a text as complicated as the *Phaedrus* would be incoherent either accidentally or through authorial ineptitude. Consequently, the burden of proof must lie with those who claim that the dialogue is irredeemably incoherent. Conversely, the responsibility lies with the rest of us to take an acute look at the text and to *seek out* the ways in which it is unified. Only if we fail in that task ought we to bring a charge of textual defectiveness. Fortunately, if we genuinely approach the dialogue as attentive readers, we find (I submit) many levels on which it is an organized whole. Such is the main upshot of the analysis which I have offered in this article.

I began by considering the thematic approach to unity, and the main options that are available for the thematic monist. Rhetoric, *erōs*, and philosophy all emerged as solid contenders, with good textual evidence in favour of each. However, as I have argued, we need not choose from among these contenders—we can have our cake and eat it too. Both for hermeneutical reasons in general and philosophical reasons in this particular dialogue, thematic pluralism is the most appropriate way of approaching the text. Yet far from undercutting thematic unity, the pluralistic approach constitutes such unity; multiple themes are omnipresent in the dialogue, each of which is interrelated with the others. For these reasons, then, the *Phaedrus* is unified on a thematic level.

At the same time, the dialogue possesses unity on a variety of non-thematic levels. Specifically, it is unified through dramatic elements, verbal texture, structure or form, and the interplay between word and deed. In general, looking beyond the level of theme has a twofold advantage. First, it allows us to remain truer to the dialogue form and to the possibilities that are inherent in that form; and second, it puts into practice the hermeneutical assumption mentioned a moment ago—viz. that the burden lies with us to *seek out* unity. For when we begin to look at the level of drama, form, imagery, and word–deed interplay, we find a wealth of possibilities that would have been absent if we had merely dismissed the dialogue as incoherent. It is for this reason too that the debunking approach is (in my view) an unsound one. For, aside from being implausible on textual grounds, this approach underestimates the richness of the text and instead appeals to external considerations. To shoulder the burden of attentive readership, however, is to appeal to such considerations only as a last resort. Happily, in this case we need not find ourselves in such a dilemma.

I concluded, finally, by considering the strategic approach, which claims that the contrasts and changes of the dialogue are deliberately inserted so as to make a certain point or to achieve a certain end. This approach has proven to be especially fruitful, and one of its virtues is the hermeneutical discussion which it brings to the table. Again, however, we need not choose *between* the strategic approach and the thematic/non-thematic approaches. For it is perfectly consistent that Plato should give the *Phaedrus* a high degree of thematic, dramatic, and formal unity, and at the same time give it the *appearance* of disunity. One of the hallmarks of all Platonic philosophy, after all, is the distinction between appearance and reality, a distinction which applies as much to Plato's own dialogues as it does to his metaphysics. The implication is that the appearance of the *Phaedrus* is deceiving, but that if we are attentive readers—the sort of reader with an appropriately attuned philosophical soul—we need not be deceived ourselves. Though the contrasts and changes of the dialogue are real, through successive readings we can also come to recognize the deeper unity which is equally real.

On a broader level, then, we can again have our cake and eat it too—we can *simultaneously* pursue the thematic, non-thematic, and strategic approaches to unity. I conclude that a hybrid approach to the *Phaedrus* which includes all three of these methods is the soundest way to understand the text and its organization. We now have more than sufficient evidence to view the *Phaedrus* as anything

Plato's Phaedrus *and the Problem of Unity* 135

but incoherent. And we have learnt something much more general as well: Platonic authorship is a complex and multi-layered affair, and first impressions are not always to be trusted.

Wesleyan University

BIBLIOGRAPHY

Asmis, E, '*Psychagogia* in Plato's *Phaedrus*' ['*Psychagogia*'], *Illinois Classical Studies*, 11 (1986), 153–72.

Beare, J. I., 'The *Phaedrus*: Its Structure; The ἔρως Theme: Notes' ['*Phaedrus*'], *Hermathena*, 17 (1913), 312–34.

Black, E., 'Plato's View of Rhetoric', *Quarterly Journal of Speech*, 44 (1958), 361–74.

Burger, R., *Plato's* Phaedrus*: A Defense of a Philosophic Art of Writing* (University, Ala., 1980).

Curran, J. V., 'The Rhetorical Technique of Plato's *Phaedrus*' ['Rhetorical Technique'], *Philosophy and Rhetoric*, 19 (1986), 66–72.

De Vries, G. J., *A Commentary on the* Phaedrus *of Plato* [*Commentary*] (Amsterdam, 1969).

Edmonds, R. G., III, *Myths of the Underworld Journey: Plato, Aristophanes, and the 'Orphic' Gold Tablets* (Cambridge, 2004).

Ferrari, G. R. F., *Listening to the Cicadas: A Study of Plato's* Phaedrus [*Cicadas*] (Cambridge, 1987).

—— '"The Unity of the *Phaedrus*": A Response' ['Unity'], *Dialogos* (*Hellenic Studies Review*), 1 (1994), 21–5.

Fortenbaugh, W. W., 'Plato *Phaedrus* 235C3', *Classical Philology*, 61 (1966), 108–9.

Fowler, H. N. (trans.), *Plato*, i. Euthyphro, Apology, Crito, Phaedo, Phaedrus (Cambridge, Mass., 1914).

Friedländer, P., *Plato*, iii. *The Dialogues: Second and Third Periods*, trans. H. Meyerhoff, 2nd edn. (Princeton, 1969).

Griswold, C. L., Jr., *Self-Knowledge in Plato's* Phaedrus [*Self-Knowledge*], rev. edn. (University Park, Pa., 1996).

Guthrie, W. K. C., *A History of Greek Philosophy*, iv. *Plato, the Man and his Dialogues: Earlier Period* (Cambridge, 1975).

—— 'Rhetoric and Philosophy: The Unity of the *Phaedrus*' ['Rhetoric and Philosophy'], *Paideia* (1976), 117–24.

Hackforth, R., *Plato's* Phaedrus (Cambridge, 1952).

Hamilton, W. (trans.), *Plato:* Phaedrus *and the* Seventh *and* Eighth Letters (Harmondsworth, 1973).

Heath, M., 'The Unity of Plato's *Phaedrus*' ['Unity'], *OSAP* 7 (1989), 151–73.

Helmbold, W. C., and Holther, W. B., 'The Unity of the "Phaedrus"' ['Unity'], *University of California Publications in Classical Philology*, 14 (1952), 387–417.

—— and Rabinowitz, W. G., *Plato:* Phaedrus (Indianapolis, 1956).

Hudson-Williams, H. Ll., *Three Systems of Education: Some Reflections on the Implications of Plato's* Phaedrus (Oxford, 1954).

Lebeck, A., 'The Central Myth of Plato's *Phaedrus*' ['Central Myth'], *Greek, Roman and Byzantine Studies*, 13 (1972), 267–90.

McCabe, M. M., 'Myth, Allegory and Argument in Plato', *Apeiron*, 25 (1992), 47–67.

Mueller, G. E., 'Unity of the *Phaedrus*', *Classical Bulletin*, 33 (1957), 50–3, 63–5.

Murley, C., 'Plato's *Phaedrus* and the Theocritean Pastoral', *Transactions and Proceedings of the American Philological Association*, 71 (1940), 281–95.

Nehamas, A., and Woodruff, P., *Plato:* Phaedrus (Indianapolis, 1995).

Nichols, J. H., Jr., *Plato:* Phaedrus (Ithaca, NY, 1998).

Nicholson, G., *Plato's* Phaedrus*: The Philosophy of Love* [*Plato's* Phaedrus] (West Lafayette, Ind., 1999).

Nussbaum, M. C., *The Fragility of Goodness: Luck and Ethics in Greek Tragedy and Philosophy*, rev. edn. (Cambridge, 2001).

Pieper, J., *Enthusiasm and Divine Madness: On the Platonic Dialogue* Phaedrus, trans. R. Winston and C. Winston (New York, 1964).

Plass, P., 'The Unity of the *Phaedrus*' ['Unity'], *Symbolae Osloenses*, 43 (1968), 7–38.

Redfield, J. M., *Nature and Culture in the* Iliad*: The Tragedy of Hector* (Chicago, 1975).

Rowe, C. J., 'The Argument and Structure of Plato's *Phaedrus*' ['Argument and Structure'], *Proceedings of the Cambridge Philological Society*, 212 (1986), 106–25.

—— *Plato:* Phaedrus, rev. edn. (Warminster, 2000).

—— 'Public and Private Speaking in Plato's Later Dialogues', in C. Eggers Lan (ed.), *Platón: los diálogos tardíos* (Sankt Augustin, 1994), 125–37.

—— 'The Unity of the *Phaedrus*: A Reply to Heath', *OSAP* 7 (1989), 175–88.

Rutherford, R. B., *The Art of Plato: Ten Essays in Platonic Interpretation* [*Art of Plato*] (Cambridge, Mass., 1995).

Sallis, J., *Being and Logos: Reading the Platonic Dialogues*, 3rd edn. (Bloomington, Ind., 1996).

Schleiermacher, F. E. D., *Introductions to the Dialogues of Plato* [*Introductions*], trans. W. Dobson (New York, 1973).

Plato's Phaedrus *and the Problem of Unity* 137

Smith, J. E., 'Plato's Myths as "Likely Accounts", Worthy of Belief', *Apeiron*, 19 (1985), 24–42.

Stewart, D. C., 'The Continuing Relevance of Plato's *Phaedrus*', in R. J. Connors, L. S. Ede, and A. A. Lunsford (eds.), *Essays on Classical Rhetoric and Modern Discourse* (Carbondale, Ill., 1984), 115–26.

Taylor, A. E., *Plato: The Man and his Work* [*Plato*], 6th edn. (New York, 1956).

Thompson, W. H., *The* Phaedrus *of Plato* (London, 1868).

Waterfield, R. (trans.), *Plato:* Phaedrus (Oxford, 2002).

Weaver, R. M., 'The *Phaedrus* and the Nature of Rhetoric', in R. L. Johannesen, R. Strickland, and R. T. Eubanks (eds.), *Language is Sermonic* (Baton Rouge, La., 1970), 57–83.

Werner, D., *Myth and Philosophy in Plato's* Phaedrus (manuscript in preparation).

—— 'Rhetoric and Philosophy in Plato's *Phaedrus*' (forthcoming).

White, D. A., *Rhetoric and Reality in Plato's* Phaedrus [*Rhetoric*] (Albany, NY, 1993).

Winnington-Ingram, R. P., 'The Unity of the *Phaedrus*' ['Unity'], inaugural lecture delivered at King's College, University of London, 1953, *Dialogos (Hellenic Studies Review)*, 1 (1994), 6–20.

ARISTOTLE ON THE NECESSITY OF OPPOSITES IN *POSTERIOR ANALYTICS* 1. 4

RICHARD TIERNEY

1. Introduction

IN *Posterior Analytics* 1. 4 Aristotle defines two key senses in which one thing may be said to belong to another in-itself ($\kappa\alpha\theta'$ $\alpha\dot{v}\tau\acute{o}$).[1]

© Richard Tierney 2007

I am grateful for helpful suggestions from David Sedley, and for earlier guidance from Wolfgang Mann. A version of the paper was presented at the Marquette Summer Seminar in Ancient and Medieval Philosophy, and I have benefited from comments from the seminar participants, especially those of Robert Bolton and Owen Goldin. Work on the paper in its later stages was supported, in part, by a Graduate School Research Committee Award from the University of Wisconsin-Milwaukee.

[1] Aristotle defines the two senses as follows: 'One thing belongs to another in itself both if it belongs to it in what it is—e.g. line to triangle and point to line (for their substance depends on these and they belong in the account which says what they are)—and also if the things it belongs to themselves belong in the account which makes clear what it is—e.g. straight belongs to line and so does curved, and odd and even to number, and prime and composite, and equilateral and oblong; and for all these there belongs in the account which says what they are in the one case line, and in the others number' (*Post. An.* 1. 4, 73ᵃ34–ᵇ3). The intent of Aristotle's definitions, as I understand them, is that the reference of 'itself' in 'X belongs to Y in itself', for example, is Y. In the discussion that follows, however, I use the expression 'in-itself' as a technical term, which effectively blocks off the pronominal component. In most of its occurrences it functions grammatically either like 'essentially', or like 'essential', depending on the context. (Cf. Apostle's translation: H. G. Apostle, *Aristotle's* Posterior Analytics (Grinnell, 1981).) And I refer to the two senses of belonging in-itself as in-itself-1 and in-itself-2, respectively. On this usage, I take Aristotle's definitions to mean:

(1) X belongs to Y in-itself-1 iff X belongs to Y, and X occurs in what Y is (i.e. in the *what it is* (the $\tau\grave{o}$ $\tau\acute{\iota}$ $\dot{\epsilon}\sigma\tau\iota$) of Y).

(2) X belongs to Y in-itself-2 iff X belongs to Y, and Y occurs in what X is (i.e. in the *what it is* (the $\tau\grave{o}$ $\tau\acute{\iota}$ $\dot{\epsilon}\sigma\tau\iota$) of X).

Finally, I speak of 'in-itself attributes' to refer to the attributes that belong to a subject in-itself, and of 'in-itself predications' to refer to occasions where such attributes are predicated of a subject. In the latter case, there is no presumption that

140   *Richard Tierney*

He then draws a distinction between attributes that belong to their subjects in-itself, in either of these two senses, and those that belong to their subjects *accidentally* ($\kappa\alpha\tau\grave{\alpha}\ \sigma\upsilon\mu\beta\epsilon\beta\eta\kappa\acute{o}s$).[2] As it turns out, this division is intended to be exhaustive of the various different kinds of attribute that may be said to *belong* to something.[3] Later in the chapter Aristotle presents an argument, the apparent conclusion of which is that whatever belongs to things in themselves, again in either of the two senses, holds of them 'both because of themselves and from necessity' ($73^{b}18$). The argument is as follows (hereafter I shall refer to the argument as the 'necessity argument', and to the passage in which it occurs as the 'necessity passage'):

> In the case of what is understandable *simpliciter*, whatever is said to belong to things in themselves in the sense of inhering in the predicates or of being inhered in,[4] holds both because of themselves and from necessity. For it is not possible for them not to belong, either *simpliciter* or as regards the opposites—e.g. straight or crooked to line, and odd or even to number. For the contrary is either a privation or a contradiction in the same kind—e.g. even is what is not odd among numbers, in so far as it follows. Hence if it is necessary to affirm or deny, it is necessary too for what belongs in itself to belong. ($73^{b}16$–24)

This passage is central to Aristotle's major project in *Posterior Analytics* 1. 4, which is to ground the necessity of demonstrative propositions; for having already defined what it means for some-

---

the subject term is universal. For all translations of Aristotle I use *The Complete Works of Aristotle: The Revised Oxford Translation*, ed. J. Barnes (Princeton, 1984), with occasional slight variations.

  [2] '. . . and what belongs in neither way [neither in-itself-1 nor in-itself-2] I call accidental, e.g. musical or white to animal' ($73^{b}4$–5). I shall not be considering the third and fourth senses of $\kappa\alpha\theta$' $\alpha\grave{\upsilon}\tau\acute{o}$ discussed by Aristotle in the chapter, as these do not play a part in the argument with which I am concerned. Throughout the discussion I use the term 'attribute' rather broadly, to include anything that is said to *belong* to something, whether in-itself (in either of the two key senses), or *accidentally*.

  [3] See, in particular, *Post. An.* 1. 6, $74^{b}5$–12, where Aristotle concludes: 'for everything belongs either in this way [i.e. in-itself] or accidentally, and what is accidental is not necessary' ($74^{b}11$–12).

  [4] This is Aristotle's particularly awkward way of referring here to attributes that belong in-itself-1 and in-itself-2. What is not clear is whether he intends to refer to in-itself-1 and in-itself-2 attributes, respectively, or vice versa. For an explanation of the alternative assignments, see W. D. Ross, *Aristotle's* Prior *and* Posterior Analytics [*Analytics*] (Oxford, 1949), 522; R. D. McKirahan, *Principles and Proofs: Aristotle's Theory of Demonstrative Science* [*Principles*] (Princeton, 1992), 88–9; and J. Barnes (trans. and comm.), *Aristotle's* Posterior Analytics, 2nd edn. [*Posterior Analytics*, 2nd edn.] (Oxford, 1994), 117.

Aristotle on the Necessity of Opposites   141

thing to hold of *every case* (κατὰ παντός), and in-itself, Aristotle goes on to define what it means for something to hold *universally* (καθόλου), in a strict and technical sense of the term:

> Now let holding of every case and in itself be defined in this fashion; I call universal whatever belongs to something both of every case and in itself and as such. (73^{b}25–7)

And he observes that:

> It is evident, therefore, that whatever is universal belongs from necessity to its objects. (73^{b}27–8)

Universal propositions, defined in terms of the above concept of universality, constitute the primary principles of demonstrative science, and it is clear that their necessity—a fundamental requirement on demonstrative propositions, in general—is grounded in their being propositions concerned with what belongs to their subjects in-itself.[5]

The problem with which we are concerned here is that it is not clear exactly what Aristotle's necessity argument is intended to establish, or how it establishes it. In saying that whatever belongs to something in-itself holds of necessity, for example, does Aristotle mean to refer to what belongs to an *individual* substance in-itself, or does he mean to refer to what belongs to a *kind* in-itself? How we answer this question will obviously influence what we take the premisses of the argument to be, and how we view those premisses as purportedly establishing the conclusion of the argument, and thus what we take the conclusion itself to be. In addition to this is the difficult question of what role in-itself predications of the *second* kind—which are certainly included in the necessity passage—play in Aristotle's argument, and in his overall account of demonstrative science.

It is because of such questions that commentators on the *Posterior Analytics* have been led to a number of interpretations of the

---

[5] Cf. M. Ferejohn, *The Origins of Aristotelian Science* [*Origins*] (New Haven, 1991), 72: '. . . this intensional condition on demonstrative premises is addressed by subcondition (ii) on catholic [i.e. *universal*] predications, namely that their predicates apply καθ' αὑτό to their subjects. Clearly, this is what is supposed to ensure the necessity of such predications'; Barnes, *Posterior Analytics*, 2nd edn., 118: 'The rest of *A* 4 elucidates a singular sense of "universally" (*katholou*). This sense has three components: first, "of every case"; secondly, "in itself" (either in use (1) or in use (2): 73b30); and thirdly, "as such". It follows from this definition and the argument at 73b16 [the necessity passage] that what is "universal" is necessary (73b28)'.

142   *Richard Tierney*

necessity passage, and have adopted various different positions on
what the contained argument establishes, and how it does so.[6] Yet,
as I shall maintain, none of these interpretations is entirely satisfactory or true to Aristotle's intentions. In fact, no adequate account
of the argument has yet been given, and this is because all accounts
to date have worked on the assumption that Aristotle is presenting
an argument to *establish*, in one way or another, the necessity of in-
itself predications. In the following discussion I propose to show
that this is not the case and that Aristotle is actually presenting an
argument to a quite different (although related) conclusion, *based
upon* the claim that whatever belongs to something in-itself holds
of necessity. At the same time, however, the necessity passage is
indeed intended to provide a grounding for the necessity of *universal* propositions, but it does so in a way that does not draw on the
argument presented therein.

2. The orthodox view

Although there are a number of significantly different interpretations of the necessity passage, most of them share a common conception of certain key 'structural' features of the overall argument
involved. I shall refer to this common conception as the 'orthodox
view', and distinguish three central components of the view.[7]

First, the orthodox view takes the distinction being alluded to
between, on the one hand, what belongs to something in-itself
simpliciter and, on the other hand, what belongs to something in-
itself *as regards the opposites*, as pointing to, and in some sense
paralleling, the distinction between what belongs to something in-
itself in the first sense (in-itself-1) and what belongs to something
in-itself in the second sense (in-itself-2), respectively. As we shall

---

[6] Among the more recent and more thorough discussions of the necessity argument, and of the surrounding text, are Ross, *Analytics*; R. Sorabji, *Necessity, Cause,
and Blame: Perspectives on Aristotle's Theory* [*Necessity*] (Ithaca, NY, 1980); Ferejohn, *Origins*; McKirahan, *Principles*; Barnes, *Posterior Analytics*, 2nd edn.; and
R. Bolton, 'Aristotle on Essence and Necessity in Science' ['Science'], *Proceedings
of the Boston Area Colloquium in Ancient Philosophy*, 13 (1997), 113–38. See also
additional citations below.

[7] One notably different account of the necessity argument is that presented by
Ferejohn (*Origins*, 99–108), but even he follows the general structure of the orthodox
view in its broad details. For remarks on Ferejohn's position see below, nn. 30, 32.

Aristotle on the Necessity of Opposites   143

shortly see, however, this is not the only reading, and it is not obvious that it is the correct reading.

In addition, and perhaps in part as a result of embracing the first component, the orthodox view perceives that there are really *two* lines of argument present in the passage; the first to the conclusion that whatever belongs to something in-itself-1 holds of necessity, and the second to the conclusion that whatever belongs to something in-itself-2 holds of necessity.

Finally, it is usually thought that Aristotle takes his conclusion to be relatively straightforward in the case of that which belongs in-itself-1 (the first line of argument), but that in the case of that which belongs in-itself-2 (the second line of argument) something more of an argument is required, and is provided by Aristotle. It is this second line of argument that has been found most problematic by commentators, and with which we shall be most concerned.

(a)   The first line of argument—the definitional approach

Let us begin, however, with the purported first line of argument; that concerned with what belongs to something in-itself-1. One thing belongs to another in-itself-1, according to Aristotle, if it belongs to it in *what it is*. Given this definition, it is often observed that it is quite straightforward for Aristotle to conclude that whatever belongs to something in-itself-1 holds of necessity.[8] The implicit reasoning, sometimes attributed to Aristotle here, is something like the following: whatever belongs to something in-itself-1 belongs to it as a part (or as the whole) of the *definition* of the thing—for the definition simply is an account of the *what it is* of the thing[9]—and since definitions express necessary relations be-

---

[8] See e.g. Barnes: 'In I-predications A holds necessarily of B "either *simpliciter* or as regards the opposites". "*Simpliciter*" presumably refers to I1–predications, where it is taken as evident that necessarily every B is A' (*Posterior Analytics*, 2nd edn., 117); van Rijen: 'it is trivial that if X belongs *kath' hauto* to Y in the first sense, X belongs to Y as named by "Y" of necessity. So far there are no problems' (J. van Rijen, *Aspects of Aristotle's Logic of Modalities* (Dordrecht, 1989), 175).

[9] See e.g. *Post. An.* 2. 10, 93^{b}29. It is important to keep distinct, however, the notion of what belongs to something *in what it is* (ἐν τῷ τί ἐστι), which constitutes the substance (οὐσία) of the thing (73^{a}35–6), from the notion of what occurs in the *account of what it is* (λόγος του τί ἐστι), which gives a definition of the thing (cf. McKirahan, *Principles*, 80). I take the former to be a metaphysically primitive concept, for Aristotle, and as not restricted to just the γένος and the διαφορά, as such. For further explanation and discussion, see R. Tierney, 'Aristotle's Scientific Demonstrations as Expositions of Essence', *OSAP* 20 (2001), 149–70.

144 *Richard Tierney*

tween things, whatever belongs to something in-itself-1 must hold of necessity.[10] (Notice, by the way, how this reasoning indirectly introduces a commitment to the view that in-itself-1 predications must be predications over *kinds* of things, rather than over individuals, for only kinds are said to have definitions.[11] Yet such a commitment is not a part of anything that Aristotle himself has said in *Posterior Analytics* 1. 4.)

One way to understand the necessity being invoked here would be in terms of analyticity. If we construe the relevant definitions as articulating the meanings of the subject terms involved, then they may be held to express (semantically) analytic truths, and thus be said to be necessarily true in an analytic or conceptual sense of necessity.[12]

It is more generally acknowledged now, however, that for Aristotle the relevant sense of definition is that of a real definition, rather than a nominal definition, where a real definition is understood to articulate the metaphysical essence of a kind of entity. Thus, in speaking of what belongs to something in *what it is*, it is held that Aristotle is referring to attributes that are a part of the metaphysical essence of the thing, and it may then be observed that essential connections are metaphysically necessary. On this understanding the necessity being invoked in in-itself-1 predications is seen to be some sort of real or metaphysical necessity, rather than analytic or conceptual necessity;[13] but on either understanding, the necessity

[10] Thus, McKirahan: 'The application to per se 1 relations is clear. Bounded by lines belongs necessarily to triangle because it holds of triangle by definition, and relations asserted in definitions are necessary' (*Principles*, 90); see also Sorabji, *Necessity*, 188–9.

[11] Thus, Sorabji: 'When Aristotle talks of predicates attaching necessarily to their subjects, provided they attach definitionally, it is natural to suppose that the subjects he has in mind are *kinds* like triangle or man, not the *members* of a kind. For only *kinds* have definitions; individuals do not' (*Necessity*, 189–90).

[12] Such a view is attributed to Aristotle by Łukasiewicz, among others (J. Łukasiewicz, *Aristotle's Syllogistic from the Standpoint of Modern Logic*, 2nd edn. (Oxford, 1957)). More recently, Deborah Modrak has found this position in *Post. An.* 1. 4: 'In *Posterior Analytics* I 4, the favored definition of necessary predication makes necessity a consequence of definition. Demonstrative premises would be necessarily true, because true by analysis; their truth could be determined solely by appeal to the meanings of their constituent parts' (D. Modrak, *Aristotle's Theory of Language and Meaning* (Cambridge, 2001), 81).

[13] Sorabji describes the following modern interpretation, without attributing it to anyone in particular: 'Scientific definitions are, for Aristotle, statements which assign an essence to a kind, and it is just part of his *concept* of essence that a statement of essence is a necessary truth' (*Necessity*, 209). Bolton summarizes what he regards

Aristotle on the Necessity of Opposites 145

is seen to be grounded in the definitional connection (be it real or nominal) that exists between a *kind* and its in-itself-1 attributes.

Let us call this the *definitional approach* to the necessity of in-itself-1 predications.[14] There is, at least as far as I can see, no compelling reason to impute such implicit reasoning to Aristotle— nothing to suggest it appears in the necessity passage—and I shall argue below that Aristotle's reasons for holding that in-itself-1 predications are necessary are more direct than this. Indeed, if such reasoning was intended to be implicit in what he says, we might wonder why Aristotle needs the necessity passage at all; for he could just as well have immediately affirmed the necessity of the *universal*, based upon this implicit reasoning, without even introducing the necessity passage.

Moreover, as noted above, the reasoning presupposes that Aristotle intends the concept of belonging in-itself to be primarily applicable to kinds. I want to suggest, however, that when Aristotle initially introduces and defines the concept of belonging in-itself, he intends that concept to apply primarily to *individual* substances, rather than to kinds of substances. It is only through a later extension of the concept that it is applied to kinds, and then only in a secondary and derivative sense.[15]

---

as the currently prevalent view of Aristotle's position as follows: 'the first principles are necessary because they express or capture, in one way or the other, essential connections, or features, of the essences of the things they concern. Given this, the standard view now is that Aristotle's commitment to the necessity of scientific truth is based on his metaphysical essentialism and it stands or falls with that' ('Science', 116). Ferejohn sees both views in play: 'It was suggested in chapter 2 that in the *Posterior Analytics* [Aristotle] sees the necessity that attaches to definitional truths as grounded in analytic relations among general (natural) kinds, and in essentialistic connections between primary substances and their proximate species, but that he does not clearly recognize at that point that there are two different relations involved' (*Origins*, 100).

[14] I am intentionally *not* casting the present discussion in terms of the related *de dicto/de re* distinction (for example, *de dicto*: 'Necessarily, every human is an animal'/'$\Box(x)(Hx \to Ax)$'; *de re*: 'Every human is necessarily an animal'/'$(x)(Hx \to \Box Ax)$'. My reason is that I am concerned to argue that the definitional approach, broadly conceived in the sense that it views Aristotle as being concerned with the *definitions* (whether real or nominal) of *kinds*, in the necessity passage, is quite misguided. Aristotle may well have this concern elsewhere in the *Posterior Analytics*, but it is not this that is at work in the necessity passage. For further discussion of the *de dicto/de re* distinction in Aristotle, see R. Patterson, *Aristotle's Modal Logic: Essence and Entailment in the* Organon (Cambridge, 1995).

[15] The extension is first made explicit in *Post. An.* 1. 6 (75^a28–31), and then again in 1. 7 (75^a39–$^b2$), and in 1. 10 (76^b11–16).

146 *Richard Tierney*

For the majority of *Posterior Analytics* 1. 4, Aristotle is engaged in the process of setting forth the conditions for fully understanding the nature of demonstrative propositions, as being necessary and as exhibiting the right sort of universality. Thus, having argued that demonstration is deduction from what is necessary, he explains that 'we must therefore grasp on what things and what sort of things demonstrations depend' (73^a24–5). He then proposes to define 'what we mean by holding of every case and what by in itself and what by universally' (73^a25–7). This is the context in which the necessity passage is set.

But in defining what it means to hold of *every case* and to belong in-itself, and then in explaining that what belongs in-itself holds of necessity, Aristotle has not yet reached the point where he wants to, or even needs to, speak of what belongs to the *kind* in-itself. For him to do so would be to anticipate prematurely the use to which he puts these distinct concepts, in defining the further concept of belonging *universally*. If this is correct, then there will still be an additional step required before we can assert that whatever holds of the kind in-itself-1, holds of necessity.

(b) *The second line of argument—the definitional approach*

Let it be assumed for now, however, that the necessity of in-itself-1 predications *does* somehow lie in the fact that they express (real or nominal) definitional connections. And recall that the second line of argument, according to the orthodox view, is concerned with the necessity of in-itself-2 predications. Now, Aristotle says that one thing belongs to another in-itself, in the second sense, 'if the things it belongs to themselves belong in the account which makes clear what it is' (73^a37–8). Given the above assumption, one approach that the *second* line of argument might naturally be thought to take would be to hold that the necessity of in-itself-2 predications also derives from some such definitional connections. It is important to explain, then, that this cannot be what *grounds* the necessity of in-itself-2 predications, as in-itself-2 predications.

Let us again refer to this as the *definitional approach*, this time to grounding the necessity of in-itself-2 predications. In fact there are two possible directions that the definitional approach may take here, depending on whether we think in terms of what belongs in

Aristotle on the Necessity of Opposites   147

the definition of the subject, or in terms of what belongs in the definition of the predicate.

To understand the first direction, consider the example of odd and even, both of which belong in-itself-2 to number. With regard to these, it might plausibly be claimed that:

(1) Every number is either odd or even

expresses a definitional connection—for it is, arguably, a part of what number is that it be either odd or even[16]—and thus that:

(2) Every number is necessarily either odd or even,[17]

in virtue of this connection. This may or may not be so, but what we must immediately observe is that the resulting predication, in so far as *its* necessity is grounded in the definitional connection (however that is interpreted), is an in-itself-1 predication, and *not* an in-itself-2 predication.[18]

[16] In the sense that being either odd or even is a part either of the very meaning of, or of the essential nature of, number. Note that the example expresses the latter (*de re*) construal, but could have been rendered to express the former (*de dicto*) construal: 'Necessarily, every number is either odd or even'.

[17] It is not easy to identify an explicit proponent of this view (on either construal of the definition). Ross takes it that: 'disjunctive propositions such as "every number must be either odd or even"' should occur among the principles recognized by Aristotle (*Analytics*, 521–2), but he seems not to take 'such self-evident propositions' to be definitional (*Analytics*, 59). It does, however, seem to be a view that Sorabji explicitly attributes to Aristotle: 'the examples with which Aristotle illustrates the two possibilities [i.e. in-itself-1 predications and in-itself-2 predications] are probably meant to run: "a triangle is an arrangement of lines" and "numbers are odd or even". In the first, a triangle (the subject) is definable by reference to lines; in the second, oddness or evenness (the predicate) by reference to numbers' (*Necessity*, 188).

[18] Some commentators regard it as Aristotle's position that such *disjunctive* attributes are themselves the in-itself-2 attributes (or are at least among them). Part of their reason for believing this may be that they see no other way for Aristotle to ground the necessity of in-itself-2 predications. Apart from the passages from Ross and Sorabji cited above (n. 17), see also H. H. Joachim, *Aristotle on Coming-to-Be and Passing-Away* (Oxford, 1926), xxvi n. 3 and xxvi–xxvii n. 4. But this view surely cannot be right, for at least three reasons. (1) Virtually all of Aristotle's examples of in-itself-2 attributes are of single, non-disjunctive attributes. (Thus, apart from those cited in *Post. An.* 1. 4, 73^a38–$^b3$, we find, for example: at *Post. An.* 1. 22, 84^a11–25 odd to number, prime to number; at *Metaph.* Δ 11, 1018^b37–1019^a1 straight to line, smooth to surface; at *Metaph.* Z 5, 1030^b14–28 snub to nose, male to animal, equal to quantity, female to animal.) (2) Disjunctive attributes do not fit Aristotle's definition of in-itself-2 attributes; we cannot speak of the *what it is* of a disjunction, such that the subject to which the disjunctive attribute belongs occurs in the account of *what it is*. (Thus Bolton: 'it is doubtful that, for him, the predicate straight-or-curved is the sort of thing that has a real definition or essence in the scientific sense.

148   *Richard Tierney*

It is, of course, an interesting and important observation about this particular in-itself-1 predication that it involves a disjunction of attributes that individually belong to their subjects in-itself-2, but that fact, first, has nothing to do with the necessity of the predication; and second, does not thereby make the disjunctive predication an in-itself-2 predication. We cannot have it both ways: either the predication is (definitionally) necessary, in which case it is an in-itself-1 predication; or the predication is an in-itself-2 predication, in which case it is not (definitionally) necessary.

Moreover, if we *do* think the necessity of the in-itself-2 predication is somehow grounded in a definitional connection between the kind and the appropriate disjunctive attribute, we shall be left in the position of having to explain the relevance of the remainder of the necessity passage. If the *necessity* of the predication has been explained in virtue of the definitional connection, then what purpose, on this interpretation, does the argument in the second half of the passage serve? It would seem that the only available answer to this question is that the argument somehow attempts to distribute the necessity across the disjunction to the individual disjuncts; that is, so that we could conclude from 'Every number is necessarily either odd or even' that 'Every number is either necessarily odd or necessarily even'. This would certainly be a significant conclusion, but if it was Aristotle's intention to argue in this way he would commit a form of modal fallacy of which he was apparently aware, and which he explicitly rejects.[19]

(See *Metaph. Z.* 4, 1030a6ff.)' ('Science', 123–4). Cf. J. E. Tiles, 'Why the Triangle has Two Right Angles *kath' hauto*' ['Triangle'], *Phronesis*, 28 (1983), 1–16 at 8.) (3) The view effectively reduces in-itself-2 attributes to in-itself-1 attributes. If it is a part of the definition, or *what it is*, of number that it be either odd or even (and this is at least more plausible than that number occurs in the *what it is* of either-odd-or-even), then 'Every number is either odd or even' turns out to be an in-itself-1 predication.

[19] In *De interpretatione* 9 Aristotle recognizes that we cannot distribute the necessity across a disjunction of contradictory opposites: '. . . the same account holds for contradictories. Everything necessarily is or is not, and will be or will not be; but one cannot divide and say that one or the other is necessary. I mean, for example: It is necessary for there to be or not to be a sea-battle tomorrow; but it is not necessary for a sea-battle to take place tomorrow, nor for one not to take place—though it is necessary for one to take place or not to take place' (19ª27–33). Thus, from 'Every number is necessarily either odd or not-odd' we would not be able to infer that 'Every number is either necessarily odd or necessarily not-odd'. (And thus, even given that 'even is what is not odd among numbers', we could not then derive 'Every number is either necessarily odd or necessarily even'.) We may

The second direction that might be taken by the definitional approach to grounding the necessity of in-itself-2 predications is to note that, according to Aristotle's account, whatever belongs to something in-itself-2 has what it belongs to occurring in the account of *what it is*; that is, in *its* definition. Thus it might be proposed, for example, that the relevant in-itself-2 predication takes something like the following form:

(3) Every odd (thing) is necessarily a number,

since number occurs in the definition of odd.[20] But this approach reverses the order of the predication of the appropriate attribute to the appropriate subject: it is *odd* that belongs to number in-itself-2, not *number* that belongs to odd (things) in-itself-2. And we are once again left with the suspicion that the intended predication, in so far as it is necessary, is really an in-itself-1 predication, not an in-itself-2 predication. Again, we cannot have it both ways: either number occurs in the definition of odd, in which case the relevant *necessary* predication is an in-itself-1 predication; or odd is predicated in-itself-2 of number, in which case the relevant predication is not (definitionally) necessary.[21]

This exhausts the options available to the definitional approach for grounding the necessity of in-itself-2 predications. Note, then, that if these predications are indeed necessary, the necessity must have some other sort of grounding—the necessity involved must be different from definitional necessity. This may be a concern for those who hold that the necessity of in-itself-1 predications *does* lie in their definitional nature, for it would appear to require that we

presume that Aristotle would have recognized the same fallacy with regard to the necessity of contrary opposites, especially given his treatment of contrary opposites as contradictories within their kind (see below, pp. 153–4). In that case we could not directly derive: 'Every number is either necessarily odd or necessarily even' from 'Every number is necessarily either odd or even'.

[20] This appears to be the view held by McKirahan: 'If A belongs to B and "B" occurs in the definition of A, then A belongs per se 2 to B. If A is predicated of B and A belongs per se 2 to B, then B is predicated necessarily of A: all A's are necessarily B (all odd things are numbers)' (*Principles*, 90). Cf. P. H. Byrne, *Analysis and Science in Aristotle* (Albany, NY, 1997), 128; and Bolton, 'Necessity', 123.

[21] McKirahan acknowledges that the direction of necessity is reversed: 'if A belongs per se 1 to B and A is predicated of B, then all B's are necessarily A. If A belongs per se 2 to B and A is predicated of B, then all A's are necessarily B' (*Principles*, 90–1); but he fails to recognize or acknowledge that the resulting necessary predication is an in-itself-1 predication. And what does it matter that A is predicated of B in the second conditional?

150 *Richard Tierney*

acknowledge two distinct types of necessity at work in Aristotle's conception of a demonstrative science.

(c) The second line of argument—an alternative approach

The only obvious alternative for the second line of argument to adopt is to propose that, in the second half of the necessity passage, Aristotle is presenting an independent argument to establish the necessity of in-itself-2 predications. This alternative assumes that what belongs in-itself 'as regards the opposites' refers, in one way or another, to the attributes that belong in-itself-2 (that is, either as referring to a *disjunction* of opposite attributes as being the in-itself-2 attribute, or as referring to a disjunction of opposite in-itself-2 attributes), and it sees the second half of the necessity passage as establishing, independently of any apparent recourse to definitional connections, that the disjunction of opposite attributes holds of necessity of the appropriate kind.[22] On this alternative, Aristotle's purpose is to establish, for example, that:

(4) Necessarily, every number is either odd or even.

And he is thought to do so by way of an explicitly stated argument, rather than base his conclusion on purely conceptual or metaphysical grounds such as those given above on the definitional approach.

A number of commentators have suggested that it is possible to construct an argument to (something like) the above conclusion from what Aristotle actually says.[23] Having stated that whatever belongs to something in-itself, in the sense indicated by 'as regards

---

[22] This is the alternative that Barnes describes, while rejecting the definitional approach to the necessity of in-itself-2 predications. As Barnes observes, it is not the 'definitory link in them between subject and predicate' that grounds the necessity of in-itself-2 predications, and further: 'their necessity plainly does not depend upon the fact that their subject terms (in whole or in part) inhere in the definitions of their predicate terms' (*Posterior Analytics*, 2nd edn., 118).

[23] Barnes presents a version of the argument in the first edition of his commentary on the *Posterior Analytics* (J. Barnes (trans. and comm.), *Aristotle's* Posterior Analytics (Oxford, 1975), 119). He refines the argument, based on a minor textual emendation, in his second edition (*Posterior Analytics*, 2nd edn., 117–18)—see below, nn. 24 and 44. Certain remarks by a number of other commentators suggest at least an implicit acceptance of something like the argument. See e.g. G. R. G. Mure (trans.), *Analytica Posteriora*, in *The Works of Aristotle Translated into English*, ed. W. D. Ross and J. A. Smith, vol. i (Oxford, 1928), note to 73^b24; V. E. Wedin, Jr., 'A Remark on *per se* Accidents and Properties', *Archiv für Geschichte der Philosophie*, 55 (1973), 30–5 at 35; H. Granger, 'The Differentia and the *per se* Accident in Aristotle', *Archiv für Geschichte der Philosophie*, 63 (1981), 118–29 at 120;

Aristotle on the Necessity of Opposites 151

the opposites', holds of necessity, and having then given the examples of 'straight or crooked to line, and odd or even to number', Aristotle continues by explaining:

For the contrary is either a privation or a contradiction in the same kind—e.g. even is what is not odd among numbers, in so far as it follows. Hence if it is necessary to affirm or deny, it is necessary too for what belongs in itself [in the sense intended by 'as regards the opposites'] to belong. (73^b21-4)

The proposed argument then construes 'it is necessary to affirm or deny' as invoking some version of the Law of Excluded Middle; thus, to continue with our example:

(5) Necessarily, every number is either odd or not odd.

And it construes 'even is what is not odd among numbers, in so far as it follows', as somehow warranting the substitution of 'even' for 'not odd', to conclude:

(6) Necessarily, every number is either odd or even.

So construed, the argument appears to be relatively straightforward, but it cannot be what Aristotle really intended, for a number of reasons.[24]

First, unless the necessity is now thought to be distributed to the individual disjuncts, either (i) the in-itself-2 attribute, in so far as it

Tiles, 'Triangle', 7. Ferejohn rehearses the argument along the lines of Barnes's first edition (*Origins*, 101–5), although, like myself, Ferejohn denies that it is Aristotle's intended argument.

[24] What is being presented here is the overall gist of Aristotle's intended argument, as understood by the writers noted above. In his second edition, Barnes proposes a slight modification to the text, to allow the translation: 'For a contrary or privation is a contradictory in the same kind . . .' (deleting the ἤ before ἀντίφασις at 73^b21). He explains: 'It seems clear that Aristotle means to argue as follows: "Odd is contrary to, or a privation of, even. But contraries and privations are contradictories within their kind (i.e. if F and G are contraries within a kind K, then every element of K is either F or G). But of contradictories, necessarily one or the other holds. Hence of contrary pairs F and G, necessarily one or the other holds (within K)." The received text will not yield this argument; and I can see no other plausible argument in it. Hence I suggest a minor emendation' (*Posterior Analytics*, 2nd edn., 118). But the received text *does* seem to fit what Aristotle says about contraries in other contexts, where he frequently refers to them as privations. In *Metaphysics Γ* 6, for example, Aristotle explains that: 'If it is impossible that contradictories should be at the same time true of the same thing, obviously contraries also cannot belong at the same time to the same thing. For of contraries, no less than of the contradictories, one is a privation—and a privation of substance; and privation is the denial of a predicate to a determinate kind' (1011^b15-22). For further examples see *Metaph. Γ* 2, 1004^b27-9; *I* 2, 1053^b30-1; *I* 4, 1055^b14-15, $^b18$, $^b26-7$; *K* 3, 1061^a18-20; cf.

152 *Richard Tierney*

holds of necessity, *just is* the disjunction of the opposite attributes—which simply seems false for Aristotle, and certainly does not fit his usual examples of in-itself-2 attributes, nor does it fit his official account of what it is to belong in-itself-2;[25] or (ii) the genuine in-itself-2 attributes—i.e. each of the opposite disjuncts—have not been shown to hold of necessity in any sense at all (i.e. not in any sense established by the present argument).

It might be thought, perhaps, that the argument is not intended to establish the necessity of in-itself-2 predications *as* in-itself-2 predications, but only to establish the necessity of certain predications *involving* in-itself-2 attributes—i.e. those predications formed from the disjunction of opposite in-itself-2 attributes. But then it is not clear exactly what is thought to be going on in the argument, or why, for as it stands the proposed argument does not even rely on the nature of in-itself-2 attributes, as in-itself-2 attributes, in establishing its conclusion.

The same argument can be used, for example, to establish the necessity of *any* disjunction of opposite attributes holding of a kind, provided that those attributes belong exclusively to, and jointly exhaust, the members of the kind—and satisfying this requirement is not the domain of in-itself-2 attributes alone. By the above form of argument, then, we could establish both:

(7) Necessarily, every animal is either male of female,

and:

(8) Necessarily, every animal is either sick or healthy.

Yet whereas members of the first pair of opposite attributes belong in-itself-2 to animals, members of the second pair of opposite attributes only belong *accidentally* to animals (and hence not in-itself-2, according to *Posterior Analytics* I. 4 and I. 6). There is nothing about the fact that the opposite attributes belong in-itself-

---

Phys. 5. 6, 229[b]25–6. On the alternative interpretation of the passage that I later present, no emendation of the text is necessary to make sense of the argument. See below, pp. 161–3 and n. 44.

[25] See above, n. 18. It does fit the examples he uses in the necessity passage, but these are not examples of attributes predicated in-itself-2; they are, rather, examples of opposite pairs of in-itself-2 attributes. On this point, see below, pp. 157–8 and 161.

Aristotle on the Necessity of Opposites   153

2 that has contributed to the necessity of the disjunction of those attributes holding of the kind.[26]

Finally, the proposed argument is either trivial or invalid. In order to get from the Law of Excluded Middle to the desired conclusion, the argument must construe the second premiss: 'even is what is not odd among numbers, in so far as it follows', as asserting something like: 'every number is such that, if it is not odd, then it is even'. But in order then validly to infer the conclusion, as *necessary*, from the premisses, the second premiss must itself be necessary. If that is the case, however, then by a straightforward application of the principles of conditional exchange $[(p \supset q) \equiv (\neg p \lor q)]$ and double negation $[\neg \neg p \equiv p]$, we find that the second premiss is in fact equivalent to 'Necessarily, every number is either odd or even'—which is just the conclusion purportedly being derived from it. So either the second premiss is not itself necessary, in which case the argument is invalid, or it is necessary, in which case the argument trivially assumes what it sets out to prove.

In fact Aristotle elsewhere does assume the principle that for *any* pair of contrary opposites, specific to a kind, necessarily one or the other of the opposite attributes belongs to each member of the kind (call this the 'principle of contrary opposites').[27] This is something that he affirms on numerous occasions—specifically, within the context of articulating his more general conception of the nature of opposites—and may be understood as expressing the thought that contrary opposites are to be regarded as contradictories relative to the kind to which they naturally belong.[28] But

---

[26] Thus Barnes, again: 'it is hard to see what their status as I2–predications has to do with their necessity' (*Posterior Analytics*, 2nd edn., 118).

[27] Unless, of course, there are intermediates between the opposites, but then (according to Aristotle) necessarily one or the other of the opposites, or of the (finite number of) intermediates, belongs to each member of the kind. Thus: 'that which is neither white nor black has more claim to a name [than that which is neither good nor bad]. Yet even this has not one name, though the colours of which the negation is privatively predicated are in a way limited; for they must [ἀνάγκη] be either grey or yellow or something else of the kind' (*Metaph. I* 5, 1056^{a}27–30). I understand this to suggest that of the intermediate and contrary colours, necessarily one or the other must hold of each member of the relevant kind.

[28] On the principle of contrary opposites: 'Sickness and health naturally occur in animals' bodies and it is indeed necessary for one or the other to belong to an animal's body, either sickness or health; again, odd and even are predicated of numbers, and it is indeed necessary for one or the other to belong to a number, either odd or even' (*Cat.* 10, 12^{a}4–8), and more generally: 'With contraries between which there is nothing intermediate [odd/even, sickness/health, straight/curved, male/female,

154 *Richard Tierney*

it is not a principle that he argues for on any of those occasions; nor does it rest upon a solitary argument to be found in *Posterior Analytics* 1. 4—for, as we have just seen, that purported argument must trivially assume the principle. This is not to say, however, that Aristotle does not draw on the principle of contrary opposites to help establish some other conclusion in the necessity passage.

What, then, does the necessity argument successfully establish? An insight into this can be gained from considering a later passage, in *Posterior Analytics* 1. 6, where Aristotle again describes the relationship between belonging in-itself and holding necessarily:

> Now if demonstrative understanding depends on necessary principles (for what one understands cannot be otherwise), and what belongs to the objects in themselves is necessary (for in the one case it belongs in what they are; and in the other they belong in what they are to what is predicated of them, *one of which opposites necessarily belongs*), it is evident that demonstrative deduction will depend on things of this sort; for everything belongs either in this way or accidentally, and what is accidental is not necessary. (74^b5–12, emphasis added)

In the italicized portion of this passage, it appears that Aristotle is saying that one or the other of the opposite in-itself-2 attributes belongs necessarily to whatever object it is predicated of, rather than that the disjunction of those opposite attributes belongs necessarily. But if that is the case, and if the claim that they belong necessarily to their subjects is meant to be based upon the argument given at *Posterior Analytics* 1. 4, 73^b16–24 (the necessity passage), then somewhere along the way Aristotle would seem to have committed the very modal fallacy alluded to above, and which he himself explicitly rejects.[29]

The only way to reconcile this passage with the necessity passage, without having Aristotle commit this fallacy, I suggest, is to recognize that in the necessity passage Aristotle is actually arguing in essentially the reverse direction to that of the modal fallacy. That is to say, he is arguing from the fact that opposite in-itself-2 attributes belong necessarily to their respective individual members of a kind, to the conclusion that the disjunction of those necessarily belonging opposite attributes holds of the kind in general. In terms of our

---

etc.] it is necessary for one or the other of them always to belong to the things they naturally occur in or are predicated of' (*Cat.* 10, 12^b27–9).

[29] See above, n. 19. Cf. Ferejohn, *Origins*, 105.

Aristotle on the Necessity of Opposites   155

previous example, Aristotle is arguing *from*: 'Each number that is odd is necessarily odd', *and*: 'Each number that is even is necessarily even', *to*: 'Each number is either necessarily odd or necessarily even'.[30] This is what he means when he says that the opposites (i.e. the opposite in-itself-2 attributes) belong necessarily. In order to see this, we must consider the necessity passage more closely.

3. Reassessing the necessity passage

In the opening sentence of the necessity passage Aristotle asserts, in effect, that whatever belongs to something in-itself-1 holds of necessity, and that whatever belongs to something in-itself-2 holds of necessity. He then immediately continues: 'For it is not possible for them [i.e. the things that belong in-itself] not to belong, either *simpliciter* or as regards the opposites'.[31] As already noted above, the orthodox view takes the distinction between what belongs in-itself *simpliciter* and what belongs in-itself *as regards the opposites* to parallel the distinction between what belongs in-itself-1 and what belongs in-itself-2, respectively.[32] But it was also suggested that

---

[30] Ferejohn finds Aristotle reaching a similar conclusion, although he sees it as only an intermediate step on the way to the further conclusions that 'Some numbers are necessarily odd' and 'Some numbers are necessarily even' (*Origins*, 106–7). Ferejohn's understanding of what is going on in the necessity passage is quite different from that which I am about to propose, however, and appears to allow, for example, the false conclusion that 'Every animal is necessarily healthy or necessarily diseased', which Aristotle would clearly reject (see e.g. *Cat.* 10, 13^{a}20–1: 'For it is possible for the healthy to fall sick'). While I disagree with Ferejohn's reconstruction of Aristotle's argument, it is noteworthy that the conclusions he ultimately wishes to show drawn from it can be drawn directly from the presuppositions of the argument as I reconstruct it—that is, if we accept Ferejohn's understanding of Aristotle as invoking both *referential universals* and *referential particulars* (see *Origins*, 105–8).

[31] Aristotle does not actually say '*as regards* the opposites', but simply that it is not possible for them not to belong, 'either *simpliciter* or the opposites [ἢ ἁπλῶς ἢ τὰ ἀντικείμενα]' (73^{b}19).

[32] See e.g. Ross: 'ἁπλῶς applies to the attributes that are καθ' αὑτο in the first sense, τὰ ἀντικείμενα to those that are καθ' αὑτό in the second sense' (*Analytics*, 522); Barnes: '"*Simpliciter*" presumably refers to I1–predications, where it is taken as evident that necessarily every B is A. "As regards the opposites" then refers to I2–predications, and must mean that necessarily every B is either A or A′ (where A′ is the opposite of A)' (*Posterior Analytics*, 2nd edn., 117); McKirahan: '"Without qualification" refers to per se 1: if A is predicated in the definition of B, then A cannot fail to belong to B. The word for "without qualification" (*simpliciter*) implies a contrast with some kind of qualification. Here the qualification is "the opposites," which stands for the adverbial phrase "with the qualification that the attribute is one of a pair of opposites, one or the other of which must belong to the subject." This is meant to characterize

156 *Richard Tierney*

this is not the only reading, and that it is not obvious that it is the correct reading. Before presenting what I propose to be Aristotle's actual argument in the necessity passage, it is necessary to explain this point in fuller detail.

To belong in-itself-1 and to belong in-itself-2 are two distinct ways in which various different attributes may be said to belong to something in-itself, depending on how they are related to their subjects (if the attribute occurs in the *what it is* of its subject, then it belongs in-itself-1; if the subject to which the attribute belongs must be specified in giving an account of *what it* [the attribute] *is*, then it belongs in-itself-2). This being so, it is not immediately obvious that to belong in-itself-1 is to belong *in-itself* in an absolute or unqualified sense (i.e. ἁπλῶς), *in contrast to* belonging in-itself-2 as being a non-absolute or qualified sense of belonging in-itself. What is the relevant qualification? While it is certainly true that the mode in which in-itself-2 attributes belong to their subjects is significantly different from the mode in which in-itself-1 attributes belong to their subjects, the former mode is not in any obvious sense a qualification upon, or non-absolute sense of, the latter mode. Nor does it seem that belonging in-itself-2 in some sense involves a limitation on, or a restriction on, or an addition to, belonging in-itself-1; it is simply one of the two distinct ways in which an attribute may belong to a subject in-itself. There is, then, no apparent reason to suppose that Aristotle's reference to attributes that belong in-itself *simpliciter* should pertain exclusively to in-itself-1 attributes, rather than to both in-itself-1 attributes and in-itself-2 attributes.

Moreover, those attributes that belong to their subjects in-itself-2 are not disjunctive attributes, but simple, non-disjunctive attributes, such as: straight belongs to line, odd belongs to number, male belongs to animal, even belongs to number, etc.[33] It is, indeed, an important observation about these attributes that each of them is also one of a pair of mutually exclusive opposite attributes, and is such that one or the other of those opposite attributes belongs to

the per se 2 relation' (*Principles*, 89). Ferejohn sees the distinction being drawn as one between two distinct kinds of necessity (absolute necessity, and necessity in the manner of the opposites), but none the less regards the parallel with the two senses of in-itself as exact. Thus, according to Ferejohn, we have 'enough reason to surmise that the two distinctions in question are perfectly juxtaposed—that Aristotle thinks of type 1 per se attributes as "absolutely" necessary, and type 2 per se attributes as necessary "in the manner of opposites"' (*Origins*, 100).

[33] See above, n. 18 and pp. 151–2.

Aristotle on the Necessity of Opposites 157

each and every member of the relevant kind.[34] It will be true, then, that the disjunction of those (so related) opposite attributes will itself hold of *every case* of the members of the kind, but it is not the *disjunction* of attributes that belongs in-itself-2 to those members.

If the above two observations are correct, then the pairing of what belongs in-itself-1 with what belongs in-itself *simpliciter*, on the one hand, and the pairing of what belongs in-itself-2 with what belongs in-itself *as regards the opposites* (construed simply as the disjunction of opposite attributes), on the other hand, breaks down on both sides. An alternative explanation of what Aristotle intends is not only warranted, but necessary for a proper understanding of his argument.

Let us look once more at the first half of the necessity passage. Aristotle refers to those attributes that belong to their subjects in-itself-1, and to those that belong to their subjects in-itself-2, and says that it is not possible for them not to belong, 'either *simpliciter* or the opposites'.[35] Given the above remarks, it becomes plausible to read the '*simpliciter*' as applying *both* to what belongs in-itself-1 *and* to what belongs in-itself-2—that is, as referring to attributes of *either* kind, considered without qualification. Aristotle then immediately explains what he means by *the opposites*, by giving the following examples: 'straight or crooked to line, odd or even to number'; that is, disjunctions of opposite attributes that individually belong in-itself-2 to their subjects. But *'the opposites' refers to the members of the pairs of opposite in-itself-2 attributes that disjunctively exhaust the members of the kind, not to the disjunction itself—it refers to those attributes in their disjunctive opposition.* Aristotle's point is that it is not possible for the opposite in-itself attributes, so construed, not to belong.

When fully spelt out, then, Aristotle's necessity claim can be read as the following complex claim: (i) whatever belongs to something in-itself *simpliciter*, that is to say either in-itself-1 *simpliciter* or in-itself-2 *simpliciter*, holds of necessity, and (ii) *the opposites*, construed as referring to the members of pairs of opposite in-itself-2 attributes, in their disjunctive opposition, also hold of necessity.

---

[34] For further discussion of what underlies this observation, see R. Tierney, 'The Scope of Aristotle's Essentialism in the *Posterior Analytics*' ['Scope'], *Journal of the History of Philosophy*, 42 (2004), 1–20. Here I leave out of consideration cases involving intermediates, which can be accommodated through an extension of Aristotle's basic account (see above, n. 27).

[35] ἢ ἁπλῶς ἢ τὰ ἀντικείμενα. See above, n. 31.

158   *Richard Tierney*

Simply put: it is not possible for the *simpliciter* in-itself attributes
not to belong, nor is it possible for the *opposite* in-itself attributes
not to belong. This claim is, indeed, relatively straightforward in
the case of what belongs to something in-itself *simpliciter* (regardless of whether in-itself-1 *simpliciter* or in-itself-2 *simpliciter*) but,
as Aristotle recognizes, the claim requires further explanation and
elaboration in the case of *the opposites*.

Let us adopt this reading in considering the argument in the
remainder of the necessity passage, to see how it helps us in understanding that argument. In doing so we embark upon an entirely
different approach from that of the orthodox view, for in locating
both kinds of in-itself attributes on the side of what belongs in-itself
simpliciter, we can begin to see, and appreciate, that Aristotle is not
arguing for the necessity of in-itself predications, of *either* kind.[36]

In fact the ultimate justification for each of the two components
of Aristotle's complex necessity claim occurs relatively early in
the passage, and is deceptively simple—so much so that its nature
and importance have been easily overlooked: whatever belongs to
something in-itself holds of necessity, Aristotle explicitly tells us,
because it cannot not belong to it (οὐ γὰρ ἐνδέχεται μὴ ὑπάρχειν). This
is Aristotle's standard rendering of what it means for something to
hold, or belong, necessarily, but it should not be seen here as stating
a mere equivalence.[37] What Aristotle is claiming is that whatever
belongs to something in-itself is such that it cannot not belong to
that to which it so belongs, and it is because of this fact that it
belongs to it necessarily.

---

[36] This places the necessity claim for in-itself-2 predications on the same footing
as that for in-itself-1 predications, and it is indeed as straightforward as the claim
for in-itself-1 predications. There is no argument, as such, for the necessity of in-
itself-1 predications, and none intended by Aristotle; nor is there one for in-itself-2
predications (see discussion below).

[37] See e.g. *De int.* 13: 'if it is impossible not to be it is necessary for this to
be' (22^{b}6–7); *Metaph.* Γ 4: 'for this is what "being necessary" means—that it is
impossible for the thing not to be' (1006^{b}31–2); *Metaph.* Δ 5: 'We say that that
which cannot be otherwise is necessarily so. And from this sense of necessary all
the others are somehow derived' (1015^{a}33–6); 'demonstration is a necessary thing,
because the conclusion cannot be otherwise, if there has been demonstration in the
full sense; and the causes of this necessity are the first premises, i.e. the fact that the
propositions from which the deduction proceeds cannot be otherwise' (1015^{b}6–9);
NE 6. 3: 'We all suppose that what we know is not capable of being otherwise . . .
Therefore [ἄρα] the object of knowledge is of necessity' (1139^{b}19–23); and finally, in
closer proximity to our passage, *Post. An.* 1. 4: 'Since [ἐπεί] it is impossible for that
of which there is understanding *simpliciter* to be otherwise, what is understandable
in virtue of demonstrative understanding will be necessary' (73^{a}21–3).

Aristotle on the Necessity of Opposites 159

The mistake on the part of many commentators has been to think that the remainder of the necessity passage is intended to justify and support this necessity claim—at least with regard to in-itself-2 predications—whereas Aristotle takes it as (virtually) self-evident, and as not requiring any additional support, that whatever belongs to something in-itself cannot not belong to it, and so belongs to it necessarily. The remainder of the passage is intended to establish, rather, the necessity of opposites—that is, the *second* component of Aristotle's complex necessity claim—based upon this observation of the necessity of in-itself attributes belonging to their subjects (and, in particular, of the necessity of in-itself-2 attributes belonging to their subjects). Before considering this, it may help to add some further brief remarks concerning the first component of Aristotle's necessity claim.

In the case of attributes that belong to things in-itself-1, it should be clear that they cannot not belong to their subjects, and so hold of them of necessity. Whatever belongs to something in-itself-1, according to Aristotle's account, belongs to it in *what it is*. As such, it is a part of its subject's essential make-up, and so cannot not belong to it.[38] Thus, as we have already seen Aristotle explain in *Posterior Analytics* 1. 6: 'what belongs to the objects in themselves is necessary (for in the one case [i.e. in the case of what belongs in-itself-1] it belongs in what they are . . .)' ($74^b6–8$).[39] Aristotle's inference here is direct; the necessity is not grounded in some definitional connection between the attribute and the kind of subject to which the attribute belongs, but in the metaphysics of individual substances as substantial unities.

It may seem less obvious, to us, that whatever belongs to something in-itself-2 is also such that it cannot not belong to its subject, and so holds of it of necessity, but it is clear that this is what Aristotle intends. We must recognize that *Aristotle's* fundamental 'essentialist' distinction, as he presents it in the *Posterior Analytics*, is between what belongs to something in-itself and what belongs to it *accidentally*, and that it is *he* who defines what belongs in-itself as consisting both of what belongs in-itself-1 and of what belongs in-itself-2, in contrast to what belongs *accidentally*. Thus, as he

---

[38] And so, at *Post. An.* 1. 4, $73^a35–6$, Aristotle says of the subjects to which in-itself-1 attributes belong, that: 'their substance depends on these [ἡ γὰρ οὐσία αὐτῶν ἐκ τούτων ἐστί]'.

[39] Cf. *Post. An.* 2. 13, $96^b2–3$: 'we have made clear above that what is predicated in what a thing is is necessary'.

160 *Richard Tierney*

says: 'it is such things that I say belong in itself; and what belongs in *neither* way [neither in-itself-1 nor in-itself-2] I call accidental' (73^b3-4).[40]

Aristotle later explains that whatever belongs to something *accidentally* is such that it *can* not belong to its subject, and that it is for this very reason that such attributes cannot be shown to belong necessarily:

Of accidentals which do not belong to things in themselves in the way in which things belonging in themselves were defined, there is no demonstrative understanding. For one cannot prove the conclusion from necessity; for it is possible for what is accidental not to belong—for that is the sort of accidental I am talking about.[41] (75^a18-22)

What distinguishes *accidental* attributes from in-itself attributes is that the former *can*, whereas the latter *cannot*, not belong to their subjects. The fact that Aristotle includes in-itself-2 attributes with in-itself-1 attributes, in contrast to what belongs *accidentally*, makes it clear that he regarded such attributes as also being such that they cannot not belong to their subjects; they too are a part of the essential make-up of the individual substances to which they belong.[42]

---

[40] It is important to note that although Aristotle elsewhere refers to in-itself-2 attributes as belonging accidentally, this is *not* the sense of belonging *accidentally* that he explicitly contrasts with belonging in-itself, particularly in the passages from *Posterior Analytics* 1. 4 and 1. 6 with which we are concerned. For further discussion see n. 41 below, and R. Tierney, 'On the Senses of "*Symbebēkos*" in Aristotle' ['Senses'], *OSAP* 21 (2001), 61–82.

[41] The other sort of accidentals are the so-called 'in-itself accidentals' [τὰ καθ' αὑτὰ συμβεβηκότα], which (at least) include the in-itself-2 attributes (cf. *Post. An.* 1. 22, 83^b17-20). In-itself accidentals, in contrast to the *accidentals* described explicitly in *Posterior Analytics* 1. 4 and 1. 6, are such that they cannot not belong to their subjects. In *Physics* 1. 3 Aristotle again distinguishes *accidental* attributes from attributes that belong in-itself-2, there describing the former as 'separable': 'For an accident [συμβεβηκός] is either that which may or may not belong to the subject [i.e. a separable accident] or that in whose definition the subject of which it is an accident is involved [i.e. an in-itself-2 accident]. Thus sitting is an example of a separable accident, while snubness [an in-itself-2 attribute] contains the definition of nose, to which we attribute snubness' (186^b18-23). For further discussion of these distinctions, see Tierney, 'Senses' and 'Scope'.

[42] Aristotle's position, I maintain, is that whatever belongs to something in-itself-2 is 'entrenched' in the very make-up of the individual substance to which it belongs. Being male belongs to Socrates in-itself-2, for example. And this is something that cannot not belong to Socrates, because the attribute of being male (rather than that of being female) was actualized in the matter that was in the process of being worked up to become the individual substance, Socrates, before it existed as that individual substance. For further explanation of this claim see Tierney, 'Scope'.

Aristotle on the Necessity of Opposites 161

Herein, then, lies the metaphysical basis of Aristotle's necessity claim. Whatever belongs to something in-itself is essential to it in the sense that it is (at least partially) constitutive of the individual substance to which it belongs; it is because of this that it cannot not belong to it. Thus, whatever belongs to something in-itself *simpliciter*, whether in-itself-1 *simpliciter* or in-itself-2 *simpliciter*, cannot not belong to that to which it belongs, and so holds of necessity.

This explains why whatever belongs to something in-itself *simpliciter* holds of necessity, and (importantly) includes what belongs in-itself-2 *simpliciter*. But what now of the remainder of the necessity passage—what is the ensuing argument intended to establish, if not the necessity of in-itself-2 predications? The answer to this, as has already been said, is that it establishes the necessity of the opposites; that is, it establishes that the members of pairs of opposite in-itself-2 attributes also hold of necessity, in their disjunctive opposition.

By this it is not meant that the argument establishes that those attributes, taken by themselves, hold of necessity, for that has already been affirmed of individual in-itself-2 attributes (i.e. in the claim that whatever belongs to something in-itself *simpliciter* holds of necessity). Nor is it meant that it establishes that the disjunction of those opposite attributes holds of necessity (for, as we have seen, this is something that Aristotle presupposes as a part of his doctrine of contrary opposites).[43]

What is meant is that the argument establishes that those attributes belong necessarily *as opposites*: that is, as distributed disjunctively across their kind. This means that for each member of the kind, either that member necessarily has a particular in-itself-2 attribute, or it necessarily has the appropriate opposite in-itself-2 attribute. We already know from the first part of the necessity claim, for example, that each number that is odd is necessarily odd, and that each number that is even is necessarily even. But what we do not know, as yet, is that each number is either necessarily odd or necessarily even. This is something that would need to be established, and Aristotle recognizes the need to establish it.

We may now turn to the argument itself. Aristotle's argument for the necessity of the opposites, stated in general terms, is essentially the following. *Since* (i) each of the opposite attributes belongs

---

[43] See the discussion above, pp. 153–4 and nn. 27, 28.

162 *Richard Tierney*

necessarily to each member of the kind to which it does belong (because it belongs to each of them in-itself-2 *simpliciter*, and so cannot not belong to them), *and since* (ii) one or the other of the opposite attributes belongs to each and every member of the kind (assuming that it is necessary to affirm or deny, and that to deny one opposite is to affirm the other), *it follows that* (iii) one or the other of the opposite attributes belongs *necessarily* to each member of the kind. For example, it follows that:

(9) Each number is either necessarily odd, or necessarily even.

This conclusion (i.e. the general conclusion, of which (9) is an instance) is what Aristotle's argument in the second half of the necessity passage is intended to establish. The argument is not intended to establish that whatever belongs to something in-itself-2 holds of necessity, for this is something that it cannot establish; in fact, this is something that the argument presupposes. And it is in virtue of the above conclusion that Aristotle is able to assert the latter part of the claim, made in *Posterior Analytics* 1. 6, that: 'what belongs to the objects in themselves is necessary (for in the one case it belongs in what they are; and in the other they belong in what they are to what is predicated of them, *one of which opposites necessarily belongs*' ($74^{b}6$–10, emphasis added).

Finally, it is a conclusion that the argument successfully establishes. Given that whatever belongs to an individual substance in-itself *simpliciter*, whether it belongs to it in-itself-1 *simpliciter* or in-itself-2 *simpliciter*, belongs to it necessarily (because it cannot not belong to it), and given that it is necessary to affirm or deny (any one attribute of any one subject), and that to deny an attribute is to affirm the contrary opposite attribute (within the same kind),[44] it *does* follow, for in-itself-2 attributes, that either the one attribute

---

[44] At $73^{b}21$–2 Aristotle maintains that 'the contrary is either a privation or a contradiction in the same kind'—that is, it is what is *not* its opposite, within that kind. (Brown, for example, is not odd, but it is not the 'not-oddness' among numbers; that falls to the contrary of odd, even.) Thus, to deny an attribute is to affirm its contrary opposite (within the same kind). Barnes's emendation, then, is unnecessary in order to get a good argument out of Aristotle (see above, n. 24). Of course, the claim that the contrary is either a privation or contradiction in the same kind presupposes the principle of contrary opposites (that, of contrary opposites, necessarily one or the other belongs to each member of the kind), but this, as we have noted, is a presupposition that Aristotle *does* make, and is not one that renders the above argument trivial (although it does render Barnes's interpretation of the necessity argument trivial).

Aristotle on the Necessity of Opposites   163

necessarily belongs, or the opposite attribute necessarily belongs, to each member of the kind.

Not only is this a significant and non-trivial conclusion, it is one that is grounded in the concepts that Aristotle actually employs. On the above understanding of Aristotle's argument, the status of the relevant attributes, as belonging in-itself-2, is of central importance in establishing the conclusion, for it is because an attribute belongs in-itself-2 that it belongs necessarily. This is something that other interpretations of the necessity passage have been unable to incorporate satisfactorily into their understanding of the argument contained therein.

Why Aristotle actually wants to establish this conclusion is another and quite possibly contentious issue, raising the question of what role, if any, such predications might play in a demonstrative science. This, however, is a question that any interpretation of the necessity passage must address, with regard to whatever predications involving in-itself-2 attributes it sees as being at issue. Without going into the question, we may at least make one relevant observation, because we are now in a position to draw a distinction between two different kinds of predication involving contrary opposites. Aristotle's principle of contrary opposites, we have seen, admits both of the following:

(10) Necessarily, every animal is either sick or healthy,

and:

(11) Necessarily, every animal is either male or female.

But it is only with regard to the latter that we can derive the corresponding necessity of opposites:

(12) Every animal is either necessarily male or necessarily female.

This is because it is only in the latter case that the relevant attributes belong in-itself-2, and thus necessarily, to their respective subjects. On this basis, the latter such predications—at least in so far as they involve in-itself attributes that, in their disjunctive opposition, belong to every member of the kind—may be counted as *universal*, in a sense, whereas the former may not. Such predications may thus be regarded as *candidates* for demonstrative propositions (although they may be excluded on other grounds).

164 *Richard Tierney*

What is of greater importance is to recognize the manner in which the initial claim made in the necessity passage—that whatever belongs to something in-itself holds of necessity, because it cannot not belong—enables Aristotle to ground the necessity of *universal* predications which, I have maintained, is not grounded in their expressing the definition of a kind. Recall again that a *universal* predication, in Aristotle's strict sense, generalizes over whatever belongs to the members of a kind both in-itself and of *every case*, and that these conditions are especially satisfied by in-itself-1 attributes. What grounds the necessity of the *universal* predication, then, is the fact that the relevant attribute belongs in-itself-1, and so necessarily, to each of the individual members of the kind. The necessity, so to speak, distributes directly from the individuals to the *universal*.[45]

This is what the necessity passage importantly contributes to our understanding of the nature of the *universal*. In fact it appears that we cannot otherwise get to the *necessity* of the *universal* predication, unless we recognize that it is to individual substances that attributes belong in-itself, since it is in relation to the *individual* that those attributes cannot not belong. It is not clear, from a metaphysical point of view, what it could mean (at least for Aristotle) to say that an attribute cannot not belong to a kind, unless this is just to say that it cannot not belong to each of the members of the kind. It is significant to our overall understanding of the *Posterior Analytics* that Aristotle saw the need to ground the necessity of *universal* predications in this way, and that he had at his disposal the metaphysical concepts that would enable him to do so.

University of Wisconsin-Milwaukee

---

[45] This is the further step alluded to on p. 146 above. At one point Sorabji remarks that: 'Aristotle simply does not trouble to explain what justifies his moving from necessary truths about the kind to necessary truths about its members' (*Necessity*, 190). The claim being made here is that the transition, for Aristotle, goes in exactly the opposite direction—from the necessity of certain attributes belonging to individual members of a kind, to the necessity of those attributes belonging to the kind in general. This step does not need any justification—as Aristotle himself says: 'It is evident [φανερόν] . . . that whatever is universal belongs from necessity to its objects' (73^b27–8), presumably just because the *universal* generalizes over what belongs in-itself (and thus necessarily) to every member of the kind—but it is a step that none the less must be made if we are properly to understand the necessity of the *universal* predication.

BIBLIOGRAPHY

Apostle, H. G., *Aristotle's* Posterior Analytics (Grinnell, 1981).

Barnes, J. (trans. and comm.), *Aristotle's* Posterior Analytics (Oxford, 1975).

—— (trans. and comm.), *Aristotle's* Posterior Analytics, 2nd edn. [*Posterior Analytics*, 2nd edn.] (Oxford, 1994).

—— (ed.), *The Complete Works of Aristotle: The Revised Oxford Translation* (Princeton, 1984).

Bolton, R., 'Aristotle on Essence and Necessity in Science' ['Science'], *Proceedings of the Boston Area Colloquium in Ancient Philosophy*, 13 (1997), 113–38.

Byrne, P. H., *Analysis and Science in Aristotle* (Albany, NY, 1997).

Ferejohn, M., *The Origins of Aristotelian Science* [*Origins*] (New Haven, 1991).

Granger, H., 'The Differentia and the *per se* Accident in Aristotle', *Archiv für Geschichte der Philosophie*, 63 (1981), 118–29.

Joachim, H. H., *Aristotle on Coming-to-Be and Passing-Away* (Oxford, 1926).

Łukasiewicz, J., *Aristotle's Syllogistic from the Standpoint of Modern Logic*, 2nd edn. (Oxford, 1957).

McKirahan, R. D., *Principles and Proofs: Aristotle's Theory of Demonstrative Science* [*Principles*] (Princeton, 1992).

Modrak, D., *Aristotle's Theory of Language and Meaning* (Cambridge, 2001).

Mure, G. R. G. (trans.), *Analytica Posteriora*, in *The Works of Aristotle Translated into English*, ed. W. D. Ross and J. A. Smith, vol. i (Oxford, 1928).

Patterson, R., *Aristotle's Modal Logic: Essence and Entailment in the Organon* (Cambridge, 1995).

Ross, W. D., *Aristotle's* Prior *and* Posterior Analytics [*Analytics*] (Oxford, 1949).

Sorabji, R., *Necessity, Cause, and Blame: Perspectives on Aristotle's Theory* [*Necessity*] (Ithaca, NY, 1980).

Tierney, R., 'Aristotle's Scientific Demonstrations as Expositions of Essence', *OSAP* 20 (2001), 149–70.

—— 'On the Senses of "*Symbebēkos*" in Aristotle' ['Senses'], *OSAP* 21 (2001), 61–82.

—— 'The Scope of Aristotle's Essentialism in the *Posterior Analytics*' ['Scope'], *Journal of the History of Philosophy*, 42 (2004), 1–20.

Tiles, J. E., 'Why the Triangle has Two Right Angles *kath' hauto*' ['Triangle'], *Phronesis*, 28 (1983), 1–16.

166 *Richard Tierney*

Van Rijen, J., *Aspects of Aristotle's Logic of Modalities* (Dordrecht, 1989).
Wedin, V. E., Jr., 'A Remark on *per se* Accidents and Properties', *Archiv für Geschichte der Philosophie*, 55 (1973), 30–5.

ORGANIC UNITY AND
THE MATTER OF MAN

CHRISTOPHER FREY

1. Introduction

IF we assume, as many have, that Aristotle's discussions of arte-facts provide us with a characterization of matter and form that is applicable to hylomorphic composites outside the artefactual do-main, then a candidate for the matter of any composite must satisfy an important requirement:

(CS) *Contingent Specification.* For any hylomorphic composite with a given form, the matter of the composite must (1) be capable of being so formed, (2) be actually present in the composite, and (3) be identifiable independently of its hav-ing such a form.

Phys. 2. 1, 193ᵃ9 ff., offers the all too familiar illustration. The same bronze is present before, during, and after it has the form of a statue; that is, it persists as such through the statue's generation and destruction. Though the bronze has the capacity to take on the form of a statue, its identity bears no necessary relationship to that form.

The attribution of a unitary account is to be preferred in one's ex-egetical endeavours, but it is difficult to do so in this case.[1] For when we consider living composites, those composites whose form is soul (ψυχή), the obvious candidates for matter fail the CS test, specific-ally the condition that the identity of the matter of a composite be

© Christopher Frey 2007

I would like to thank James Allen, David Sedley, and Jennifer Frey for comment-ing on previous drafts of this work. I have also benefited from conversations with Ted McGuire, Jim Bogen, and the audience of a colloquium at the University of Pittsburgh.

[1] The *locus classicus* for this difficulty is J. L. Ackrill, 'Aristotle's Definitions of *psuchē*', *Proceedings of the Aristotelian Society*, 73 (1972), 119–33.

168 *Christopher Frey*

independent of that composite's form. This failure is manifest in Aristotle's application of the *homonymy principle* to the matter of living composites. An object is an *F* homonymously if it is called an *F* but differs from proper *F*s, either partially or completely, in its account/definition/essence/nature.[2] Aristotle is explicit that the candidates for the matter of a living composite—the body, the organs, and even the tissues—are not identical to any objects present in a corpse that we would ordinarily call by these names.[3] The body, organs, and tissues present when the composite is no longer alive, i.e. no longer ensouled (ἔμψυχος), are *not* the body, organs, and tissues except homonymously (πλὴν ὁμωνύμως).

The homonymy principle has an application here, commentators say, because it is applicable whenever something is identified, at least in part, by its function. And the matter of a living composite *is* identified, by Aristotle, in this way. The matter in such cases is 'a natural body which has organs' (*DA* 2. 1, 412ᵃ28), and to be an organ is to have the capacities necessary to perform a characteristic *ergon*—a work, job, or function:

What a thing is is always determined by its function: a thing really is itself when it can perform its function; an eye, for instance, when it can see. (*Meteor.* 4. 12, 390ᵃ10–12)[4]

Thus, for the matter of a living composite—an organic body—to exist, it must have the capacities necessary to work in a particular way. But the capacities that a body must be able to exercise in order to be organic are the very same capacities that constitute a body's being ensouled. So the matter of a living composite, an organic body, is necessarily ensouled. If this is correct, we must countenance at least two fundamentally different hylomorphic accounts—one for composites with contingently specifiable matter and one for composites with essentially informed matter.

But hope for a unitary account of hylomorphism in which artefacts retain their principal station has not entirely been extin-

---

[2] These variations need not trouble us at this stage of the argument.

[3] See e.g. *GC* 1. 5, 321ᵇ29–32; *Meteor.* 4. 12, 390ᵃ10–12; *DA* 2. 1, 412ᵇ12–13; 412ᵇ21–3; *PA* 1. 1, 640ᵇ34–641ᵃ34; *GA* 2. 1, 734ᵇ24–7; *Metaph. Z* 10, 1035ᵇ10–26; *Pol.* 1. 2, 1253ᵃ19–25.

[4] Except for minor changes, translations are from *The Complete Works of Aristotle: The Revised Oxford Translation*, ed. J. Barnes (Princeton, 1984); D. W. Hamlyn, *Aristotle's De Anima, Books I and II* [*Anima*] (Oxford, 1968); and C. J. F. Williams (trans. and comm.), *Aristotle's De Generatione et Corruptione* (Oxford, 1982).

Organic Unity and the Matter of Man   169

guished. Many have introduced, on Aristotle's behalf, a candidate for matter that, unlike an organic body, satisfies the CS requirement. On this account, what is present and persists as matter in a living composite is some 'structured physical thing' whose criterion of identity is not essentially tied to the form or the 'life-constitutive' functions of the composite.[5] This structured thing has on different occasions been called the BODY, remote matter, compositional flesh, and the non-organic body (which we shall use from now on), to name a few.[6] It is not an anachronistic amendment, they claim. For Aristotle has the resources to articulate the notion, and in fact does so in his physical and biological works. The task, then, for these commentators is to provide a more detailed account of the non-organic body and to explain the relation between this body and the essentially ensouled body that falls under the domain of the homonymy principle. Such an account, in its strongest form, will allow one to say that 'non-organic bodies exist before and survive the death of the organism. Just as the iron of an axe co-exists with axe matter, so the non-organic body exists while organic bodies exist.'[7] Let us call this interpretation the two-body thesis.

The ultimate aim of this essay is to undermine the attribution of the two-body thesis to Aristotle. Aristotle cannot take the matter of a living composite to be a second body that is actually present but not essentially ensouled. That no such body can play the role of matter is, it will be argued, a consequence of conditions that must be in place for an organic composite to be natural and for a natural body to be in *energeia*, that is, to be *actively*. This absence is not a failure; it is not a defect of Aristotle's account that living composites do not satisfy an artefact-oriented CS requirement. That insight can be obtained by jettisoning artefacts from their traditional position

---

[5] The phrase 'structured physical thing' occurs in B. Williams, 'Hylomorphism', *OSAP* 4 (1986), 189–99 at 193. The term 'physical' here cannot be Aristotle's, viz. φυσικός, since for Aristotle the psychological activities of humans are just as physical as the movements of inorganic bodies. One of the tasks of those who introduce bodies characterized in this way is the justification of this distinct use. Cf. A. Code and J. Moravcsik, 'Explaining Various Forms of Living', in M. C. Nussbaum and A. O. Rorty (eds.), *Essays on Aristotle's* De Anima [*Essays*] (Oxford, 1992), 129–45 at 130.

[6] The terms occur at S. M. Cohen, 'Hylomorphism and Functionalism' ['Hylomorphism'], in Nussbaum and Rorty (eds.), *Essays*, 57–73 at 69; T. Irwin, *Aristotle's First Principles* [*Principles*] (Oxford, 1988), 241; J. Whiting, 'Living Bodies' ['Living'], in Nussbaum and Rorty (eds.), *Essays*, 75–92 at 79; and C. Shields, *Order in Multiplicity* [*Order*] (Oxford, 1999), 137 respectively.

[7] Shields, *Order*, 152.

170 *Christopher Frey*

as the paradigm exemplars of Aristotelian change will, it is hoped, be demonstrated through the discussion that follows.[8]

2. Function and homonymy

Given the centrality of the homonymy principle in the above reasoning, we must re-evaluate one feature of this discussion that commentators almost universally accept before embarking on the positive project: namely, that the application of the homonymy principle to an object is ultimately a consequence of the object requiring a functional characterization. The following passages, by no means the only ones, reveal the tendency to relate homonymy and function when it comes to organs:

[The body] has organs which are defined by their functions, and therefore . . . it cannot exist in the absence of soul, without which these organs could not perform their functions.

Hands, feet, etc., . . . exist only when they fulfil their function: when the organism has perished these material parts are replaced by mere homonyms.

A dead hand . . . has lost its identity as a hand because that identity depends on a set of functions which it can no longer perform.[9]

This connection is understandable: whenever the homonymy principle is invoked, considerations of function are in close proximity. But *ergon* is not, for Aristotle, a single concept.[10] The way in which an organ has a function differs from the way in which an artefact has a function. Indeed, the simple bodies, inorganic bodies like copper and silver, and living composites—not just the organic body but *man*—are all said to have a function (*Meteor.* 4. 12) in a manner that differs from both organs and artefacts. In this section I shall

[8] Though the conclusions of this paper will bear on the debate over Aristotle's adherence to functionalism, this complicated issue will not be directly discussed.

[9] The quotes are from Whiting, 'Living', 77; Irwin, *Principles*, 241; and M. L. Gill, 'Aristotle on Matters of Life and Death', *Proceedings of the Boston Area Colloquium in Ancient Philosophy*, 4 (1989), 187–205 at 199–200, respectively.

[10] Though ἔργον is commonly translated as 'function', one should keep in mind its relation to the adjective ἐνεργός, which means 'at work, working, active, busy', and its relation to the noun ἐνέργεια, which, interestingly, can be translated either as 'actuality' or as 'activity'. One should also note that Aristotle sees a deep connection between ἔργον and ἐντελέχεια—'fulfilment' or 'completeness' (*Metaph.* Θ 1, 1035^{b}34). With these reservations in mind, I shall continue using 'function', noting the importance of these connotations when necessary.

Organic Unity and the Matter of Man 171

argue that the fundamental functional notion for Aristotle is that of a natural unitary function; the functions of organs, artefacts, and parts of artefacts are derivative. Once these distinctions are made, we can see the extent to which functional characterization justifies applications of the homonymy principle.

(a) The varieties of function

There are two orthogonal divisions among the bodies to which Aristotle attributes functions. There are the functions of parts and the functions of unities. There are also natural and artificial functions. Four classes of objects result—artefacts (unitary, artificial), parts of artefacts (part, artificial), natural unities (unitary, natural), and organs (part, natural):

	NATURAL	ARTIFICIAL
PART	heart, eye, flesh (?)	door, haft, blade
UNITY	man, silver, fire	house, axe

To attribute a function to an object is to attribute a capacity (*dunamis*) to display some character or perform some activity in a way that makes the end (*telos*) of the capacity explicit. In so far as an object succeeds in exercising such capacities, it will, to that extent, perform its function. There is a canonical method for making such attributions with respect to organs or parts. Minimally, a character or activity A is the function of an organ if and only if (*a*) A has the organ as its subject, (*b*) A is a consequence of the organ's being there, and (*c*) the organ came to be for the sake of displaying or doing A. The third clause allows one to distinguish accidental activities, e.g. the heart's making a thumping noise, from things that are more clearly candidates for being the function of an organ, e.g. the heart's pumping blood. Current accounts, focusing on biological cases, develop this condition by requiring that the character or activity be naturally selected for or confer some survival-enhancing propensity on the organism.[11] Of course, such elucidations are not germane to an Aristotelian framework.

Allan Gotthelf has proposed an analysis of this clause that an

---

[11] Cf. L. Wright, 'Functions', *Philosophical Review*, 82/2 (1973), 139–68, and J. Bigelow and R. Pargetter, 'Functions', *Journal of Philosophy*, 84 (1987), 181–96, respectively.

172   *Christopher Frey*

Aristotelian can countenance.[12] An organ comes to be for the sake
of doing A if and only if the generation of the organ is part of
the exercise of a capacity that is irreducibly a capacity to become
an individual with a form that requires an organ that does A. All
changes, according to Aristotle, are exercises of some capacity or
ability (in Gotthelf's terminology, an actualization of some potential), and these changes, according to Gotthelf, can be divided into
two fundamentally different kinds: those that can be explained by
citing only the exercises of the capacities of the simple bodies (earth,
water, air, and fire), and those that cannot (presumably because the
processes are so complex) and are, thereby, irreducibly exercises of
capacities for the exemplification of a form. Organic development
is among the latter and organs come to be because they (or something analogous) *must* come to be in order for an exemplar of some
organic form to come to be entirely—that is, for the capacity that is
irreducibly for an individual of that form to be entirely exercised.[13]
This 'must' exploits some character or activity of the organ, and
this character or activity is the organ's function.[14]

   Though I disagree with some of Gotthelf's analysis,[15] the fun-

---

[12] In A. Gotthelf, 'Aristotle's Conception of Final Causality' and 'Postscript 1986'
['Final'], in A. Gotthelf and J. Lennox (eds.), *Philosophical Issues in Aristotle's
Biology* (Cambridge, 1986), 204–42, esp. postscript III.

[13] The qualifier 'entirely' is meant to eliminate the positing of a natural good
not reducible to a specification of form. An organism can often exist without the
presence of some organs determined to be necessary in this way. For example, our
gut is convoluted because this delays excretion (PA 4. 1, 675^a19-^b23). We can come
to be, i.e. exist, without this, but we cannot flourish—we would have to replenish
ourselves much more often, limiting the leisure time needed to exercise our more
refined capacities. But if flourishing is complete exemplification of one's form, then
we do need a convoluted gut (or something analogous) to come to be *entirely*.
Exemplification of form is more than satisfaction of the minimal conditions for
existence.

[14] In some cases the organ must be present because it is included in the essence/
definition of the organism. In other cases, the 'must' is one of hypothetical necessity.
For a discussion of the distinction see GA 5. 1, 778^b16-17, and J. Cooper, 'Hypo-
thetical Necessity' ['Necessity'], in A. Gotthelf (ed.), *Aristotle on Nature and Living
Things* (Pittsburgh, 1986), 151–67, repr. in J. Cooper, *Knowledge, Nature, and the
Good* (Princeton, 2001), 130–47 at 131–2.

[15] For example, I do not think Aristotle requires a dual account of δύναμις. If a
simple body, say some small parcel of fire, in order to come to be in accordance
with its nature, required (essentially or by hypothetical necessity) a more complex
structure, the identity of its parts and the determination of the parts' functions
would depend on the nature of the simple body in the same way that organs depend
for their identity and function on the form of the organism. The capacities of all
natural bodies are on a par; they are all, in a broad sense, capacities for a form. That
this is so is one of the argumentative burdens of this essay.

Organic Unity and the Matter of Man 173

damental insight of this approach—the feature that it shares with current accounts—is important. The determination of an organ's function depends on the role the organ's coming to be serves in the coming to be of the organism to which it belongs.[16] The capacity whose exercise constitutes proper functioning for an organ is a capacity whose existence is explained by the role it plays in the development of a unitary organism, where the latter development is itself an exercise of a capacity whose end is the exemplification of a form.

This account of how the function of an organ or part is determined requires that there be objects with functions that are not themselves organs or parts. Let us call the functions of these wholes unitary functions. For example, the terrestrial simple bodies, inorganic metals, and organic composites all have functions (*Meteor.* 4. 12). As with organs and parts, to attribute a function to a unity is to attribute a capacity (*dunamis*) in a way that makes the end of the capacity explicit. The function of a parcel of fire, for example, is, in part, its characteristic movement towards the upper region and the ceasing of that movement upon reaching the upper region.[17] The principle that underlies this characteristic movement is a particular capacity/ability, the complete exercise of which, for fire, is rest at its natural place. Though environmental constraints or success in reaching the upper region may occasion the end of this characteristic locomotion, the simple body, in such cases, does not cease to be fire. It still possesses the ability to move towards its natural place of rest; it still has the same natural unitary function. So objects characterized by their natural functions 'are what they are in virtue of a certain capacity of action or passion' (*Meteor.* 4. 12, 390^{a}18).

But a simple body does not come to be and does not possess the capacities it does because of the development or structure of an encompassing system. This is not to say that fire's upward locomotive tendency or any other of its characteristic movements are caused or explained by an internal efficient principle. Indeed, inanimate bodies are not self-movers; their natural locomotive movements

---

[16] Cf. *PA* 1. 1, 640^{a}33–^{b}4, and *Metaph.* Z 10, 1035^{b}10–20.

[17] *Pace* Gill, 'Aristotle on Matters of Life and Death', and S. M. Cohen, *Aristotle on Nature and Incomplete Substance* (Cambridge, 1996), I accept the traditional reading that the terrestrial simple bodies possess natures that comprise a principle of movement *and* rest. See sect. 2 of I. Bodnár, 'Movers and Elemental Motions in Aristotle', *OSAP* 15 (1997), 81–117, for a persuasive argument against alternative interpretations.

174 *Christopher Frey*

are initiated by and require the activity of external bodies.[18] But to explain the function of a natural body one need not appeal to the form of any external body. As Aristotle says, 'to ask why fire moves upward and earth downward is the same as to ask why the healable, when moved and changed *qua* healable, attains health and not whiteness' (*De caelo* 4. 3, 310^{b}16–19). The explanation of natural unitary functions need not involve reference to any distinct form or nature. In contrast, as we have seen, the explanation and attribution of part functions require a reference to the form of the whole of which the body is a part, the *that for the sake of which*.

The discussion to this point has focused on examples that are natural. But much of what has been said so far is applicable, with small modifications, to artefacts. What is the function of a door? A door comes to be for the sake of entry to and egress from the home of which it is a part. Doors are made and are made to have the function that they have because they, or something analogous, are (hypothetically) necessary for a home to come to be. In addition, artefacts do not possess their functions because they are parts of a larger system; artefacts are functional unities. One need not appeal to anything beyond the form of an artefact in order to explain its characteristic activities. Houses shelter and axes chop in normal circumstances *because* they are houses and axes.[19] If the function of an artefact with form F is to ϕ, then an explanation of why the artefact ϕ's that goes beyond citing that the artefact exemplifies F seems out of place.

There remain, however, important differences between natural unitary functions and artificial unitary functions. The ground for such differences will not be fully described until Section 5(*a*), but a preliminary explanation of the primacy of natural unitary functions can be provided. One sense of primacy is ontological. The coming to be of a natural body is the outcome of the functioning of other natural bodies: either of individuals of like kind in the case of organic bodies, or of individuals of different but cyclically related kinds in the case of the simple bodies.[20] The forms corresponding to these natural bodies are eternal (ἀΐδιος) and collectively contain the principles required for production of new individuals with those

---

[18] *Phys.* 8. 2, 252^{b}21–3; 8. 4, 255^{a}10–15, 255^{b}29–31; *MA* 1. 6, 700^{b}6.

[19] Cf. W. Charlton, *Aristotle's* Physics *I–II* (Oxford, 1970), 89.

[20] Cf. *GA* 2. 1, 731^{b}21 ff.; *DA* 2. 4, 415^{a}22–^{b}8; *Metaph.* Z 7, 1032^{a}22–7; and *GC* 2. 4, respectively.

Organic Unity and the Matter of Man 175

forms. On the other hand, the coming to be of an artefact is the coming to be of an individual with a form that occurs in the soul of an artificer. Without the coming to be of natural bodies and the subsequent exercise of their natural unitary functions there would be no artefacts. A second sense of functional primacy follows from this ontological dependence. An artefact fulfils its function only in so far as the activity contributes, in part, to the flourishing of another individual.[21] A natural unitary function is that character or ability the display or exercise of which constitutes a stage in the development or flourishing of the very same object. When fire moves to the upper region, it is the fire that flourishes. When a man develops into a perfect exemplar of his form, it is the man that flourishes. But the flourishing of an artefact is, *ipso facto*, the flourishing of the artificer. Artefacts are the by-products of the exemplification of the form of natural unities and depend, both ontologically and functionally, on those natural unities.[22]

(b) Natural unitary homonymy

Though natural unitary functions are, for Aristotle, fundamental, it still might be the case that applications of the homonymy principle are not similarly prioritized. It is, as I have suggested, a goal of many commentators to apply a unitary account of matter and form to artefacts and natural organic composites. If applications of the homonymy principle can be explained by an account of function that is insensitive to the above distinctions, then such an assimilation gains support. This assimilation would favour a general hylomorphic account that satisfies the CS requirement, since there seems to be no impediment to countenancing both a functional and a non-functional level of matter for artefacts. Though one might, in certain circumstances, be inclined to say that it is doors and windows that are the matter of a house, at the most basic level the matter of the house is a collection of non-functionally specified objects—planks of wood, panes of glass, bricks, etc. Similarly, it will not be a natural body with functionally specified organs that is the matter of man. A non-organic body, however that is cashed out, will serve as matter for a living composite.[23] Three considerations,

---

[21] Cf. n. 13 for this generalized use of 'flourishing'.

[22] For an interesting development of similar considerations, see S. Kelsey, 'Aristotle's Definition of Nature', *OSAP* 25 (2003), 59–88.

[23] Cf. Shields, *Order*, 146 n. 34, in which the extension of homonymy to artefacts

176 *Christopher Frey*

however, suggest that homonymy attributions are sensitive to the primacy of natural unitary functions.

(i) *Local vs. terminal.* If an organ ceases to perform its function, this can be for two reasons. It can be a local malfunction, e.g. an eye of an otherwise healthy individual that can no longer see because of a deteriorative congenital condition or an injury. The non-functional organ stands at one extreme of a continuum of operative success. On the other hand, an organ may cease to function because the organism for the sake of which the organ came to be perishes. In such a case, the form that determines the identity of the organ and its function is no longer present. If the function of an organ is essentially for the sake of its contribution to the functioning of some encompassing organism, then the organ cannot play that role upon the death of that organism and thereby ceases to function.

This distinction mirrors one Aristotle finds in the notion of a lack (*sterēsis*):

Lack is said in many ways. For there is (1) that which simply does not possess, and (2) that which might naturally have it but has not got it, either (a) completely of that which might naturally have it but has not got it, or (b) when it is naturally suited to possess it, either in this way completely, or when in any degree it fails to have it. And in some cases, where things are naturally suited to possess, and fail to have it by force, we say they are lacking. (*Metaph.* Θ 1, 1046ª31–5)

Cases of local non-functioning arise when the lack occurs in that which should naturally have some function, but is no longer able to perform it, either partially or entirely, through internal defect or external violence. Terminal non-functioning is an instance of the first sort of lack; a severed hand does not naturally have the capacities that it lacks. The eye of a corpse does not have the ability to see in the same way that a rock does not have the ability to see.

Local non-functioning does not justify applications of the homonymy principle. An eye remains an eye if it is able to perform its function only half as well as it once did. And since the difference between fully functional organs, minimally functional organs, and non-functional organs is one of degree, an eye of an otherwise healthy individual will remain an eye even if it cannot perform its

is cited as a reason for accepting the two-body thesis (or at least for rejecting many arguments against it). Though the extension is made, the passage he cites as an example of this extension, viz. *DA* 2. 1, 412ᵇ12–13, is, we shall see, poorly chosen.

Organic Unity and the Matter of Man 177

function at all. Such organs retain their identities but are defective. Terminal non-functining, however, does justify applications of the homonymy principle. There are numerous instances of the homonymy principle that explicitly cite the death of the whole to which the part or organ belongs. A 'dead man', 'the hand of a dead man' (*Meteor*. 4. 12, 389^{b}31–2), 'a corpse', 'the parts of a corpse' (*PA* 1. 1, 640^{b}34–641^{a}34), and 'the face or flesh without soul in it' (*GA* 2. 1, 734^{b}24–7) are the objects to which homonymy applies. Applications of the principle are also introduced with such phrases as 'if the whole body be destroyed' (*Pol*. 1. 2, 1253^{a}19–25), 'If the soul were removed' (*DA* 2. 1, 412^{b}12–13), and 'if severed from the whole' (*Metaph. Z* 10, 1035^{b}23–4). The only citations that may be instances of local organ deterioration are that of a 'dead eye' (*Meteor*. 4. 12, 390^{a}12) and a 'dead finger' (*Metaph. Z* 10, 1035^{b}25). But given Aristotle's overwhelming tendency to place his remarks in contexts of organismic death and not local organ deterioration, even these applications seem to have as their subjects the eye and finger *of a dead man*. So it is true that the homonymy principle is applied to organs when they can no longer function, but only in circumstances in which the whole has ceased to function. It is the presence or absence of a unitary function that determines whether homonymy is applicable to the parts of an organism.

(ii) *Unitary vs. part.* Another important class of homonymy attributions appeals to material inadequacies. Aristotle speaks of hands made of stone, wood, or bronze (*Pol*. 1. 2, 1253^{a}19–25; *PA* 1. 1, 640^{b}34–641^{a}34), eyes made of stone (*DA* 2. 1, 412^{b}21–3), and face and flesh made of stone or wood (*GA* 2. 1, 734^{b}24–7) as being those objects only homonymously. In the artefactual domain, similar things are said of stone flutes and wooden saws (*Meteor*. 4. 12, 390^{a}10–12).

Aristotle often argues that some organ or artefact must have a particular material constitution. Schematically, the arguments take one of the following two forms.[24] Either:

(1) An object, *O*, has function *F* (or is for the sake of *F*ing).
(2) In order for *O* to *F*, *O* must have the character/property/ capacity *C*.

[24] Cf. J. Lennox, 'Material and Formal Natures in Aristotle's *De Partibus Animalium*', in id., *Aristotle's Philosophy of Biology* (Cambridge, 2001), 182–204 at 196–8, and Cooper, 'Necessity', 133.

178   *Christopher Frey*

(3) The material M is the only (or one of few) material(s) available from which O can come to be that displays C.

(4) So, O is made of M (or another material that displays C).[25]

Or, as a continuation of the above reasoning:

(5) In order for an O with character/property/capacity C to F, there must be another object, O', with function F'.

(6) Repeat (2–4) with O' and F'.[26]

So the reason these objects cannot function as the organs they purport to be is because their material constitution cannot satisfy the demands that need to be satisfied in order for the whole to come to be and exercise its unitary function. Again, it is the function of the whole that has the primary explanatory role in the application of the homonymy principle.

(iii) *Natural vs. artificial*. Cases in which Aristotle directly applies the homonymy principle to artefacts, and even cases where he applies it to the functionally specified parts of living organisms, occur under the counterfactual hypothesis that the objects are not artefacts, or mere parts, but natural or living unities. Phrases such as 'if an instrument, e.g. an axe, were a natural body . . .' (*DA* 2. 1, $412^{b}12$–13) or 'if the eye were an animal . . .' (*DA* 2. 1, $412^{b}21$–3) commence the relevant passages. This suggests that the applicability of the homonymy principle is intimately connected to the status, as natural, of the applicans.

The counterfactual hypotheses are not idle claims. The discussions that follow treat them as important qualifiers. Consider the first argument:[27] Aristotle assumes:

(1) An instrument, e.g. an axe, is a natural body.

On this assumption it follows that:

(2) (a) Being an axe [its essence] would be (b) its substance, and (c) this would be its soul,

[25] For example, at *PA* 3. 3, $664^{a}36$–$^{b}3$, Aristotle argues: (1) the larynx is for the sake of vocalizing; (2) in order for something to vocalize, it must be smooth and hard; (3) cartilage is smooth and hard; so (4) the larynx is made of cartilage.

[26] For example, at *PA* 2. 13, $657^{a}30$–5, after arguing that eyes must be made of a material that is fluid in character, Aristotle argues: (1) in order for an eye with a fluid character to see, there must be another object, an eyelid, to protect it; (2) in order to protect the eye, the eyelid must be solid . . .

[27] *DA* 2. 1, $412^{b}12$–16. This schema is James Allen's.

Organic Unity and the Matter of Man   179

and

(3) (*a*) Were this [its soul] separated, (*b*) it would not still be an axe, except homonymously.

Aristotle then makes a correction:

(4) But now it is an axe,

because

(5) It is not of such a body [an artefact] that the essence and the *logos* are the soul, but of such a natural body, having a principle of change and remaining the same in itself.

This argument has been a source of interpretative debate. Some take (4) to be a response to 3(*b*)—it would still be an axe. The correction would then either be to 3(*a*)—the soul, essence, or substance is not separated, so it is still an axe—or 3(*b*)—despite the fact that the (would-be) soul, essence, or substance is separated, it is still an axe. I follow Hamlyn, *Anima*, 86 and Cohen, 'Hylomorphism', 70, in reading the correction as a withdrawing of the counterfactual assumption—the axe is an artefact and not a natural body. This is the only way to understand Aristotle's justification of the correction. The soul can be the *logos* only of a natural body, not an artefact. Hence the conclusion that follows on the assumption, namely, that the homonymy principle applies to the axe, does not follow. Such homonymy depends on the object having a nature.

None of this undermines the importance of part functions in these debates. But these considerations do suggest that the non-functioning of a part is not the explanandum of the homonymy principle; the identity of a part/organ, the determination of an organ's function, and the applicability of the homonymy principle all have the same explanandum—the status of the unitary nature of a whole. It is for this reason that the homonymy principle and its connection to the functional characterization of organs/parts will not, as is traditionally the case, be the cynosure of the discussion that follows. What it takes for something to have a nature, what it is about natures that grounds functional explanations, and the relationship between natural unitary functions and applications of the homonymy principle will take centre stage. These questions will be resolved first with respect to two classes of natural objects that

180   *Christopher Frey*

are simpler than living bodies: the four simple terrestrial bodies—earth, water, air, and fire—and the homoeomerous bodies that result from the mixture of these. The lessons learnt from these investigations will then be brought to bear on living bodies. The resources needed to defeat the two-body thesis will be acquired *in ambulando*.

3. Inorganic unity

(*a*) *Simple bodies*

In order to clarify the relations between natures, functions, and homonymy with respect to our first example of natural unities, the simple bodies, we must highlight three features of Aristotle's account. The first thing to note is the familiar observation, though not always expressed in this terminology, that the simple bodies lack principles of individuation but have criteria of identity. Aristotle justifies these claims respectively by arguing that the simple bodies are not substances but are natural homoeomers.

It is sensible to ask if something before you is a parcel of earth and it is possible to distinguish a parcel of earth from a parcel of water. It does not make sense, however, to ask if the earth before you is one or many. 'Earth', 'water', and the like are not count nouns. Their semantic character is more like that of a mass noun. These linguistic observations reflect (meta)physical characteristics of the simple bodies and these characteristics explain why the simple bodies are not to be counted among proper substances. Aristotle says of the simple bodies that 'none of them is one, but they are like a heap before it is fused by heat and some one thing is made out of the bits' (*Metaph. Z* 16, 1040^{b}8–9). This is not to say that, like a heap of sand, a parcel of earth comprises numerous propinquous individual unities. For 'there is a lot of water, not many waters' (*Metaph. I* 6, 1056^{b}16). Rather, the analogy highlights that, like a heap, a parcel of earth *qua* earth is not *one thing*. To treat the simple bodies as countable unities is to impose on them an accidental unity (and a corresponding principle of individuation) that goes beyond any unity provided by the identity of the simple bodies as such.

That the simple bodies do have criteria of identity is clear from their having the status of homoeomers. A homoeomer is something 'such that we can apply the same name in the same sense to a part of

Organic Unity and the Matter of Man 181

it as to the whole' (*GC* 1. 1, 314ᵃ19–20). It is odd to speak of simple bodies as having parts, as 'part' is itself a count noun. If presented with a parcel of water, one cannot say how many parts it has until one has specified a principle of individuation to be conveyed by 'part'. Still, in so far as a parcel is divisible, it is sensible to say that no quantity of that parcel, once separated off, would cease to be water. So when Aristotle says that 'a part of water is water' (*GC* 1. 10, 328ᵃ10), he is claiming that any quantity of a simple body is divisible indefinitely into parcels that have the same *identity* as each other, namely, the identity of the whole from which they are separated.

Now in what does this identity consist? A clue is provided in a discussion of another homoeomer—gold. Aristotle, when talking about 'pieces of gold separated from one another', asserts that their 'nature is one' and clarifies this by saying that 'each piece must, as we assert, have the same motion' (*De caelo* 1. 7, 275ᵇ33–276ᵃ1). Aristotle continues and extends the claim to the simple bodies saying 'a single clod moves to the same place as the whole mass of earth, and a spark to the same place as the whole mass of fire' (*De caelo* 1. 7, 276ᵃ15). Thus, for a simple body to have an identity is for it to have a unitary nature.[28] And since 'a source of movement within the thing itself is its nature' (*De caelo* 3. 2, 301ᵇ17), the identity of the simple bodies is exhausted by this internal principle of movement (cf. *De caelo* 1. 3, 270ᵃ4–6). A simple body is not *one* nature, but it is one *in* nature (cf. *Metaph. I* 1, 1052ᵃ20).

The second feature of Aristotle's account that is important for our purposes is his more detailed analysis of these principles of movement. Strictly speaking, the simple bodies are not elements (*stoicheia*). Indeed, Aristotle contrasts his view with sundry Presocratic views that take the simple bodies to be elements (*GC* 2. 3, 330ᵇ7). The simple bodies are simple *qua* bodies; that is, they are the simplest material components of any composite body. But neither fire nor air nor any of those we have mentioned is in fact simple but mixed (*GC* 2. 3, 330ᵇ22).[29]

In *De generatione et corruptione* Aristotle focuses on two pairs

---

[28] Cf. 'the continuous by nature are more one than the continuous by art. A thing is called continuous which has by its own nature one [natural] movement and cannot have any other; and the movement is one when it is indivisible' (*Metaph.* Z 5, 1015ᵇ36).

[29] Cf. *GC* 1. 6, 322ᵇ1–2, 328ᵇ31, 329ᵃ16, 329ᵃ26; *PA* 2. 1, 646ᵃ13 for descriptions of the simple bodies as *apparent* or *so-called* simple bodies.

182 *Christopher Frey*

of contrary elements (*stoicheia*) from which the simple bodies are mixed: the hot and the cold, and the wet and the dry. Most commentators speak paronymously of the elements by predicating their adjectival forms to the simple bodies. James Bogen, for example, takes the elements to be abilities or powers *possessed* by the simple bodies.[30] Something is hot if it can aggregate like things, cold if it can aggregate all things regardless of similarity. Something is wet if it is not internally bounded but is easily bounded externally, dry if it is internally bounded but not easily bounded externally (*GC* 2. 2, $329^{b}26$–33). The simple bodies possess these abilities to the maximal degree. Alternatively, Mary Louise Gill takes the elements to be properties or differentiating features that the simple bodies possess essentially.[31] By assuming that the elements are metaphysically predicative, one can then appeal to Aristotle's account of contraries, which is worked out with predicates, to draw conclusions about the simple bodies. To say that two things are contrary to one another is to say that they are the extremes of a continuous spectrum each intermediate position of which represents a non-incidental change for objects of which the extremes can be predicated though not simultaneously. So while there may be six combinatorial possibilities for the elementary abilities/properties, the impossibility of there being a single metaphysical subject that simultaneously possesses contrary abilities/properties leaves us with only four pairings. The four simple terrestrial bodies are each associated with one of the possible pairings of extrema. Fire is hot and dry, air is hot and wet, water is cold and wet, and earth is cold and dry (*GC* 2. 3, $330^{b}1$–4).

These predicative accounts, however, leave an important aspect of Aristotle's discussion unexplained. The elements must occur in complementary pairs, or 'yokings'. Nothing can be hot or cold without also being wet or dry and vice versa.[32] If the elements are merely

---

[30] J. Bogen, 'Fire in the Belly', *Pacific Philosophical Quarterly*, 76/3–4 (1995), 370–405.

[31] M. L. Gill, *Aristotle on Substance* [*Substance*] (Princeton, 1989).

[32] Commentators who reify the elements seem to be at a loss to explain the phenomenon as well. For example, Furth simply claims that 'it is of the nature of the contrarieties to form pairwise "linkages"' (M. Furth, *Substance, Form, and Psyche* (Cambridge, 1988), 233). Some take the relation between the paired elements to be that of hylomorphic composition—the wet/dry is the matter and the hot/cold is the form. But in the transformation of air into water, it is the wet that serves as matter; in the transformation of water to earth, it is the wet that serves as form. There is nothing in the hylomorphic account that would prevent, in principle, a simple body that is wet/wet.

Organic Unity and the Matter of Man   183

predicable abilities or properties, why can they not be possessed in isolation as *white* and *musical* can? The resources available to Bogen and Gill, namely, that the abilities/properties are possessed maximally or essentially, apply individualistically to the elements and provide no ground for drawing connections between elements.[33]

The inability to explain the relation between the two pairs of contraries stems from thinking of them combinatorially: that is, from thinking of a simple body as a combination or conjunction of two metaphysically independent, but somehow complementary, elements. But the simple bodies are not constructed from below, as it were, out of independently determinable elements. One must instead take the complementation to be fundamental. One way to do this is to emphasize an important way in which Aristotle characterizes the elements. Aristotle says that the elements are principles (*archai*) of the simple bodies. Specifically, the two pairs of contraries, hot/cold and wet/dry, are said to be, respectively, the active and passive principles of change for the simple bodies.[34] Thus, the pair of elements *is* the nature of a simple body. And a nature is unitary, not a combination or conjunction of disparate principles.[35] Thus to say that a parcel of fire and a parcel of air share a feature, namely, the hot, is to say that the nature of the parcel of fire and the nature of the parcel of air manifest themselves similarly with respect to their active changes. When a parcel of fire is transformed into a parcel of air, the hot can serve as that which remains throughout the change so as to avoid Parmenidean worries of generation *ex nihilo* and destruction *in nihilum*; but for the hot to persist is not for there to be some autonomously identifiable element that at one time is paired with the dry and at a later time paired with the wet. It is, rather, for a unitary nature, hot/dry, to become a distinct unitary nature, hot/wet. Since it is natures that determine the identities of the simple bodies, having natures that are principles for simi-

---

[33] To be fair, Gill argues that 'actual tangibility demands features of both sorts (temperature and humidity)' (*Substance*, 81). Though tangibility and elemental pairing may be coextensive, I cannot find in the text a direct argument from tangibility to the pairing of elemental contraries, and Gill provides no citations for any such argument. I suspect that the tangibility of the simple bodies has the same explanandum as the elemental yokings and is not itself the explanandum.

[34] *GC* 2. 1, 329^{b}24–6; *Meteor.* 4. 1, 378^{b}10–25.

[35] On my reading, the notion of a body having only a principle of rest or a principle of motion is nonsensical. They are two sides of one nature, with rest being the privation of motion (*Phys.* 8. 1, 251^{a}27). Cf. above, n. 17.

184 *Christopher Frey*

lar movements makes elemental transformation possible without having to reify a unitary substratum (*hupokeimenon*).

The final feature of simple bodies that concerns us is the way in which they are subject to claims of homonymy. That homonymy is applied, by Aristotle, to the simple bodies is clear. For water and fire 'are not water and fire in any and every condition of itself' (*Meteor.* 4. 12, 390ᵃ7–9) and Aristotle considers what would follow 'if those elements are named homonymously' (*De caelo* 1. 8, 276ᵃ30 ff.).

There are two cases of homonymy of interest with respect to the simple bodies. The first is somewhat mundane. Much of what we point to and say 'that's fire' or 'that's some earth' is not, strictly speaking, *pure* fire or earth. They are aggregates of all sorts of different simple bodies and homoeomerous mixtures.[36] These aggregates often have the same appearance (*schēma*) as a parcel of isolated earth, air, water, or fire, but do not have a single identity, let alone one corresponding to the simple bodies in isolation.

The second case of homonymy requires that we further expand Aristotle's account of the simple bodies. I shall call the two pairs of elements, hot/cold and wet/dry, the primary, interactive, tangible contraries. They are primary because the other interactive, tangible contraries, e.g. viscous and brittle, hard and soft, etc., supervene on this pair (*GC* 2. 2, 329ᵇ32). They are interactive because they are said of things in virtue of those things affecting and being affected by other bodies (*GC* 2. 2, 329ᵇ20–4). And they are tangible because they are 'distinctive qualities of body, *qua* body' (*DA* 2. 11, 423ᵇ27–8). Aristotle focuses on interactive, tangible contraries in *De generatione et corruptione* because he is trying to explain, in that work, the processes of generation, corruption, growth, and mixture. A necessary condition for such processes is that the relata be in reciprocal contact with one another. Two bodies or magnitudes are in contact when 'they have their extremes together and are capable of moving, or of being moved by, one another' (*GC* 1. 6, 323ᵃ11). So the only capacities that one need appeal to in this context are those that are exercised when one body comes into contact with another and, in so doing, effects a change—the interactive, tangible contraries.

But this does not mean that a specification of the hot/cold and the wet/dry exhausts the nature of the simple bodies. There are the

---

[36] Indeed, there is some indication that Aristotle thinks that no bodies encountered in the sublunary sphere are simple (*GC* 2. 8).

Organic Unity and the Matter of Man 185

powers of these bodies to affect senses other than touch, say whiteness and blackness. But, given that the processes of generation, corruption, growth, and mixture can be explained by appealing solely to the tangible characteristics of the simple bodies, these features can be neglected as differentiae 'even if in fact [they are] prior by nature' (GC 2. 2, $329^{b}6-16$). There is, however, an important *tangible* contrary that is not reducible to the two primary, interactive, tangible element pairs, namely, the heavy and the light. The heavy and the light are 'not said of things in virtue of their acting upon something else or being acted upon by something else' (GC 2. 2, $329^{b}20$). That is, the heavy and the light are not reducible to and do not supervene on the primary, interactive, tangible contraries.[37] I shall call the heavy and the light the *non*-interactive, tangible contraries.

Attributions of heaviness or lightness to a body are attributions of a principle of natural locomotion. For Aristotle tells us to 'apply the term "heavy" to that which naturally moves towards the centre, and "light" to that which moves naturally away from the centre' (*De caelo* 1. 3, $269^{b}22-4$).[38] These principles of natural locomotion contribute to the natures of the simple bodies that manifest them.[39] And the locomotive aspect of a simple body's nature cannot be neglected when it comes to determination of identity, for 'one sort of movement is appropriate to each simple body, and we should be

---

[37] The following passage might lead one to think that the heavy and the light *are* so-reducible: 'perhaps it is better to speak of composition from the elementary capacities [δυνάμεων]; nor indeed out of all of these . . . For wet and dry, hot and cold form the material of all composite bodies; and all other differences are secondary to these, such differences, that is, as heaviness or lightness, density or rarity, roughness or smoothness, and any other such properties of bodies as there may be' (*PA* 2. 1, $646^{a}14-20$). This passage, however, is explaining the coming to be, *within animals*, of relatively complex structures, e.g. tissues and organs, from the simple bodies. This process need not appeal to the heaviness or lightness of the simple bodies. In general, the principles of natural locomotion that attributions of heaviness and lightness convey are often needed to bring parcels of simple bodies in contact with one another so that processes such as mixing and growth, which require the operation of the primary, interactive, tangible contraries, can occur. But the locomotion present in embryological development is caused by the principle of movement present in the semen of the male progenitor and is not reducible to the locomotive principles of the simple bodies that serve as matter. It is in this sense that wet/dry and hot/cold are the only contraries that 'compose' the more complex structures. Cf. sect. 4(*b*) for a more complete discussion of this.

[38] Cf. *Phys.* 8. 4, $255^{b}15-16$; *De caelo* 4. 1.

[39] '. . . the movement of each body to its own place is motion towards its own form' (*De caelo* 4. 3, $310^{a}35$).

186 *Christopher Frey*

compelled to identify it with one of the bodies which move in this way' (*De caelo* 1. 3, 369^{b}31–5).[40]

Homonymy can arise when the interactive tangible powers and the non-interactive tangible powers do not complement one another. This is clear in the following passage from *De caelo* in which Aristotle is contemplating 'whether there is any obstacle to there being other worlds [κόσμος] composed on the pattern of our own' (*De caelo* 1. 7, 274^{a}26–8):

Further, these worlds, being similar in nature to ours, must all be composed of the same bodies as it. Moreover, each of the bodies, fire, I mean, and earth and their intermediates, must have the same capacities [δύναμιν] as in our world. For if those elements are named homonymously and not in virtue of having the same form as ours, then the whole to which they belong can only be called a world homonymously. Clearly, then, one of the bodies will move naturally away from the centre and another towards the centre, since fire must be identical with fire, earth with earth, and so on, as the fragments of each are identical in this world . . . therefore, since the movements are the same, the elements must also be the same everywhere. The particles of earth, then, in another world move naturally also to our centre and its fire to our circumference. (*De caelo* 1. 8, 276^{a}30–^{b}14)[41]

If the simple bodies in this other world seem to move in the manner that the simple bodies in this world move, that is, if the foreign 'earth' moves to *its* centre and the foreign 'fire' moves to *its* periphery, then these foreign bodies will not be identical in nature to our simple bodies. For Aristotle, locations of natural rest determine the principles of locomotion for sublunary bodies, and these locations are not specified relative to a world but have absolute significance. So even if the foreign bodies interact with one another in a way that is identical to the manner in which our simple bodies interact, the classifications based on these principles of interaction alone will be homonymous.[42]

In sum: (1) For the simple bodies, natures determine identity.

[40] In a discussion clearly focused on locomotion, Aristotle says that 'the distinction of the elements depends upon the distinction of the movements' (*De caelo* 1. 8, 276^{b}9).

[41] The argument is a *reductio* of the claim that there is more than one world. So the homonymy that depends on this claim will never actually occur. Still, the argument shows the conceptual possibility of such homonymy. But compare: 'If one were to remove the earth to where the moon now is, the various fragments of earth would each move not towards it but to the place in which it now is' (*De caelo* 4. 3, 310^{b}2–5).

[42] Indeed, if an Aristotelian physicist were unknowingly taken from our world and placed this other world and if the interactions and local movements of the foreign

Organic Unity and the Matter of Man   187

(2) The identity/nature of a simple body is unitary. (3) This unitary nature is the principle of the characteristic interactive and non-interactive tangible contraries. (4) When the ends of these activities are made explicit, one has specified the natural unitary function of a simple body. (5) The homonymy principle is applicable to those bodies that are structurally/qualitatively similar but do not have the same nature.

These conclusions will serve as the core of a general account of natural unity. Once the (similar) account of mixtures is appended, we shall be in a position to assess the most complicated of natural bodies, the organic.

(b) Mixtures

The process of mixing (*mixis*) is *sui generis* among changes. It is neither a substantial change, nor one of the standard cases of movement (*kinēsis*): growth, alteration, or locomotion. That this is so is brought out by a tripartite *aporia* (*GC* 1. 10). It seems as if one of the following must occur in mixing:

(a) The ingredients of the mixture remain unchanged.
(b) One of the ingredients perishes while the other remains the same.
(c) Both ingredients perish.

If (a) is correct, then there is no mixture; what results is just an aggregate (*sunthesis*) of simple bodies, like barley and wheat shaken up in a bag. If (b) is correct, then there is no mixture; what results is the growth of one of the ingredients through the destruction of the other. If (c) is correct, there is no mixture; what results does not contain any of the prior ingredients, a paradigm case of generation and destruction. So the *aporia* demands of mixing that it (1) be different from generation and corruption—all the ingredients must be present in the product and must retain their identities—and (2) be different from aggregation—the product of mixing is homoeomerous and does not comprise distinct parcels of ingredients.

Aristotle's solution, in broad outline, is that 'it is possible for things after they have been mixed to be and not to be. Some other thing which comes to be from them is actually [ἐνεργείᾳ], while

bodies seem to be identical to her home bodies, then there would be no reason for her to not use the names of the simple bodies homonymously.

188   *Christopher Frey*

each of the things which were, before they were mixed, still is, but potentially [δυνάμει], and has not been destroyed' (*GC* 1. 10, 327ᵇ23–6). A complete analysis of this account would take us far afield, but a brief investigation will reveal many similarities between this account and that given of the simple bodies.[43]

Mixing differs from the generation of one simple body from another. In the latter transformations, one of the simple bodies occurs in greater quantity than the other.[44] This difference in quantity leads to the dominant body overpowering the smaller body and completely assimilating it. The other body does not have potential existence, or existence in capacity, in the product; it has been destroyed.[45] So one necessary condition for mixing to occur is that there be a balance of power between the two interacting bodies. When 'the two are more or less equal in strength, then each changes from its own nature in the direction of the dominant one, though it does not become the other but something in between and common to both' (*GC* 1. 10, 328ᵃ28–9). In mixture there is a mutual modification, whereas in generation the modification has a single direction.

The change that occurs when commensurate bodies interact is a mollification of excesses:

When one [of the contraries hot or cold] exists *simpliciter* in actuality [ἐντελεχείᾳ], the other exists in potentiality [δυνάμει]; when, however, it is not completely so, but as it were hot-cold or cold-hot, because in being mixed things destroy each other's excesses, then what will exisis neither their matter nor either of the contraries existing *simpliciter* in actuality [ἐντελεχείᾳ], but something intermediate. (*GC* 2. 7, 334ᵇ9–14)

So the mixture that results is neither, say, hot nor cold. It manifests one of the intermediate positions on that continuous spectrum of change.

---

[43] For a thorough discussion of mixing see K. Fine, 'The Problem of Mixture', *Pacific Philosophical Quarterly*, 76/3–4 (1995), 266–369. I disagree with important features of his analysis, e.g. his dependence on prime matter and his insistence that the *bodies* of the ingredients must be present in the mixture, but a detailed comparison of the views is beyond the scope of this essay.

[44] For when many of them are juxtaposed to few or large ones to small, then indeed they do not give rise to mixing, but to growth on the part of that which is dominant (*GC* 1. 10, 328ᵃ23–6).

[45] Instead of potential existence I shall often speak of existence in capacity. In sect. 4(*b*) this notion, and the corresponding notion of being in *energeia*, will be thoroughly discussed.

Organic Unity and the Matter of Man 189

But why is this not just an example of (c), a process in which two simple bodies are destroyed and a third body is generated? Since it is natures that ground all claims of identity for the simple bodies, these natures must persist in the mixture for the simple bodies to exist. But they must be present in a way that differs from their unfettered manifestation in isolation or they will completely exist in actuality.

This balancing might occur if both simple bodies continue to manifest their natures but do so simultaneously and antagonistically so as to cancel out each other's effects. But this suggests that a mixture results from the mere compresence of the natures of the ingredients, say hot/dry fire and cold/dry earth resulting in a mixture that is (hot/dry + cold/dry). In such a situation, the ingredients would actually exist compresently, an impossibility for Aristotle (e.g. *Phys.* 8. 1, 209ª6). Moreover, the resultant mixture actually exists and is homoeomerous. This requires that the mixture have a unitary nature.

Rather, a mixture is *composed* of its ingredients.[46] This composition results in a unitary nature that is produced by but is not eliminable in favour of the natures of the ingredients. To understand this relationship, it is helpful to note that it holds not just among the simple bodies, but is also manifest, Aristotle claims, in explaining colours. Bodies of many different colours are produced through the composition of black bodies and white bodies according to principles analogous to those active in the mixing of simple bodies (*De sensu* 3, 440ª31–ᵇ23). The relationship is not one of juxtaposition or superimposed compresence as suggested in the previous paragraph, but is rather a 'complete fusion'. The product, say a red body, depends both aetiologically and ontologically on black and white bodies. But it is homoeomerous with respect to colour and this colour is the manifestation of a single capacity. Red is a colour *sui generis* but it is not a primitive colour.

The same relation must hold between simple bodies and mixtures. A mixture of fire and earth results in a unitary nature, namely (hot-cold/dry-dry). This is not a substantial change resulting in a new primitive nature, say warm/dry. If it were, the process would

---

[46] '. . . since contraries admit of an intermediate and in some cases have it, intermediates must be composed out of the contraries' (*Metaph. I* 7, 1057ª18). Cf. *Phys.* 1. 5, 188ᵇ21–6.

190 *Christopher Frey*

be no different from generation or destruction. There must not only be an aetiological dependence but also an ontological dependence of the mixture's nature on the natures of the simple ingredients. Still, the natural activity of the resultant mixture is the result of a single unified capacity.[47]

So, like the simple bodies, inorganic mixtures are not substances. But they are natural and in this nature consists their identity. Despite their aetiology, they are 'continuous by nature', and this unitary nature is the principle of a mixture's characteristic interactive and non-interactive tangible contraries. When the ends of these contraries are made explicit, one has specified the natural unitary function of a mixture.

4. Organic unity

It is now time to apply these insights to the case that is most important for our purposes, namely, that of organic bodies. I have laboured to explain the unity of inorganic bodies because I think they, rather than artefacts, are paradigms of the unity present in organic composites. An organic body, say a man, is 'continuous by nature'. An immediate difficulty arises on this view. Organic composites and the organs they comprise, unlike the simple bodies and mixtures, are anhomoeomerous—no proper part of man or a hand is itself a man or a hand. This fact engenders a difficult *aporia*, the discussion of which will allow us to develop this hypothesis and provide us with the resources to defeat the two-body thesis.

---

[47] More will be said about being in capacity in sect. 4(*b*). Even after that discussion, the result may not seem like much of an explanation. But to request more is to ignore that mixture is a process *sui generis*. Mixing cannot be explained in terms of generation or alteration, and to show that it exists would be another example of one having 'to prove what is obvious by what is not; the mark of a man who is unable to distinguish what is self-evident from what is not' (*Phys.* 2. 1, 193^{a}5–6). That mixing exists is evident because, Aristotle contends, we observe that homoeomerous bodies result from the interaction of simple ingredients according to an effective rule of composition. Mixing allows one to countenance this phenomenon without having to posit an infinite number of primitive natures. Just as Aristotle must show that change is possible when confronted by Parmenidean arguments to the contrary but need not show that change occurs, Aristotle must only show that mixture is possible when confronted with the tripartite *aporia*.

Organic Unity and the Matter of Man 191

(a) An Aporia

Argument One. Organisms are paradigms of natural substances (*Metaph.* Z 7, 1032ᵃ18–19). As such, they are unities and individuals *par excellence.* Though there is much controversy among commentators as to how Aristotle accounts for a substance's unity of definition and for the metaphysical unity of its matter and form, one thing is clear. An individual substance cannot be composed of distinct individual substances. As Aristotle says, 'a substance cannot consist of substances present in it in actuality [ἐντελεχείᾳ]; for things that are thus actually two are never actually one' (*Metaph.* Z 13, 1039ᵃ4–6). The identity of an organ does not depend on the possession of its own unitary nature, but depends on the identity of the whole for which it came to be.

Argument Two. Organs are made up of tissues, e.g. flesh, bone, sinew, etc., and these tissues are homoeomerous mixtures of the simple bodies. For homoeomerous mixtures, there exists a route to identity that does not appeal to the role those tissues play as parts within an encompassing organism.

> (1) The ratio of simple bodies that serve as the ingredients of an animate tissue is sufficient to determine all of the mixture's interactive and non-interactive tangible differentiae. (Cf. *Meteor.* 4. 12, 390ᵇ3–19.)

Aristotle treats animate and inanimate mixtures on a par when he remarks that 'in flesh and wood and each thing of this sort, fire and earth are present in capacity [δυνάμει]' (*De caelo* 3. 3, 302ᵃ20).[48] So each tissue will have some natural temperature, some natural degree of heat, and some place towards which its locomotion naturally tends. Bone, for example, moves towards a point close to the centre of the sublunar sphere since earth predominates in its mixture.

> (2) A mixture that exercises natural interactive and non-interactive capacities possesses a unitary nature that is their principle.
>
> (3) A mixture's nature grounds its criterion of identity.
>
> (4) The *telos* of a body's unitary nature determines that body's natural unitary function.

---

[48] Cf. 'the mixture of the elements which makes flesh has a different ratio from that which makes bone' (*DA* 1. 4, 408ᵃ14).

192   *Christopher Frey*

So:

(5) Animate tissues have unitary identities/natures, and the ends of their natural capacities for change will determine their natural unitary function.

Corollary to Argument Two. A tissue of an animate body, *a*, and an inanimate mixture, *b*, can have identical tangible differentiae. If Argument Two is sound, then *a* and *b* will have the same unitary nature. But, for example, living bone and dead bone act very differently, as any corpse will testify. Only *b* seems to manifest the natural unitary function that is exhausted by its tangible differentiae. The only way to account for this difference in activity without denying that tissues have unitary natures is to attribute to the animating soul a power to constrain the nature of *a* violently so as to prevent it from exercising its natural unitary function.

If animate tissues possess unitary natures, the organs to which they belong will be aggregates of distinct natures, one corresponding to each of the parcels of homoeomerous tissue that compose it. A human being, say, would then be an aggregate of such aggregates. But not just any aggregate: a sack full of organs and tissues is certainly not a human. Each tissue would have to be arranged in such a way as to yield those organs (hypothetically) necessary for the exercise of the capacities distinctive of humans. The organs would have to be so organized as well. Since the natures of the tissues are, by Argument One, unitary, it makes little difference whether the natures of the animate tissues are identical to the natures of their inanimate correlates or not. In either case, the tissues would naturally move to some place of rest and would naturally interact in ways that would disrupt the required organization. Thus the soul *qua* organizing principle would be responsible for constraining the natural movements of its tissues.[49]

---

[49] Aristotle often writes in a way that suggests this picture. When discussing plants, he raises the question 'What is it that holds together the fire and the earth, given that they tend in opposite directions? For they will be torn apart, unless there is something to prevent them.' Though he hedges, he says 'if there is, then this is the soul' (*DA* 2. 4, 416ᵃ6–9). Moreover, this is not the popular *harmonia* account of soul that appears in Plato's *Phaedo* 85 E–86 C. In agreement with Aristotle, the proponent of this view can say that 'it is more appropriate to call health (or generally one of the good states of the body) a harmony than to predicate it of the soul' (*DA* 1. 4, 408ᵃ1–2).

Organic Unity and the Matter of Man

(b) *The solution and being in* energeia

The sympathies of two-body proponents lie with the second argument. When a man dies, bodies with identical tangible differentiae persist. But this assumes that such differentiae are sufficient to determine the identities of tissues regardless of the context of their coming to be. I shall argue that an enumeration of the tangible differentiae that mixtures manifest (if not constrained) is not always sufficient to attribute an internal principle of movement and rest to the body that is the subject of those differentiae.

An additional factor is required, and it becomes clear once we appreciate the distinction Aristotle makes between two ways of being: being in *dunamis*, i.e. being in capacity, and being in *energeia*, i.e. actually or actively being (*Metaph. Θ* 6). This distinction is orthogonal to the distinction among ways of being presented in the *Categories* (*Metaph. Θ* 10, 1051^{a}34 ff.). Our focus will be on the application of this distinction to the category substance (*ousia*). That is, we shall focus on two ways something can be an *F*—in capacity and in *energeia*.

To be an *F* in *energeia* is not simply to possess the set of capacities characteristic of *F*s. A house-builder, when watching television, has the capacity to build houses. This is one way to be a house-builder. But it is only when the art is being used in the production of a house that she is a house-builder in *energeia*. Being engaged in the process of house-building is a different way one can be a house-builder. Similarly, a sighted person with eyes shut becomes a seer in *energeia* only when her eyes open and the capacity for vision is being exercised.

But the distinction is broader than these cases suggest (*Metaph. Θ* 6, 1048^{a}35–^{b}9). Aristotle considers the relations between (*a*) matter (a block of wood) and that which is separable from matter (a statue carved out of the block) and between (*b*) that which is unworked (a pile of bricks) and that which is worked to completion (a house of bricks) to be analogous relations. In these cases, the relata are *one thing*, but they are that thing in different ways. A block of wood and a pile of bricks are, respectively, a statue and a house in capacity. I take it that this status, as in the above examples, consists, at least in part, in the various capacities these items possess. To be an *F* in capacity, something must possesses the tangible capacities

194 *Christopher Frey*

(hypothetically) necessary for an F to come to be.[50] The other relata, the statue and the house, are said to be such in *energeia*. If the analogy is to hold, this status must consist in the products being, in some sense, the exercises of the capacities just mentioned. Perhaps the tangible capacities are taken advantage of by the artificer and are exercised in an order that results in the relevant composite. For example, if bricks are a house in capacity because they have the strength to be laid upon one another to the height required for walls without toppling, then, when a house-builder arranges things so that this capacity can be exercised, the result is a house in *energeia*.

This account, whatever its merits, cannot be complete. It is given with respect to artefacts and seems to depend on the satisfiability of the CS principle for its plausibility. It is not bricks and a house that are related on this account; it is bricks and bricks. The bricks have being in two ways: before the artificer practises her art, they possess various capacities that are not being exercised; after she practises her art, the capacities are being exercised.

If we switch our focus to those beings that have natural unitary functions, the story must be altered significantly. Consider the mixture that results from a parcel of fire and a parcel of earth. These two parcels, before the mixing occurs, are the mixture in capacity. Our previous necessary condition will still hold—to be the mixture in capacity, the parcels must possess the appropriate interactive and non-interactive tangible differentiae necessary for the mixture to come to be. But this does not seem to be sufficient. To be an F in capacity and to be an F in *energeia* are two ways of being *the same thing*. In the artefactual case, this was satisfied by recognizing that the same bricks were present before and after the artificer employed her craft; to be a house in capacity and a house in *energeia* were two ways to be bricks. But this cannot hold for the simple bodies. Aristotle is explicit that the simple bodies that exist in a mixture do not have being in *energeia*.[51] So we are forced into the reading that is closer to the text but more difficult philosophically: the simple bodies are the mixture in capacity, the

---

[50] See sect. 2(*b*), item (ii).

[51] Perhaps the simple bodies, though existing only in capacity, are still the mixture in *energeia*. That this is not so will be argued in sect. 5(*b*). For now, note the dissimilarity between this case and the case of the bricks. The bricks exist in *energeia* both before and after the house is built.

Organic Unity and the Matter of Man 195

mixture is the mixture in *energeia*, and these are two ways of being *the mixture*.

Two questions must now be answered: (*a*) what further conditions must be met in order for the simple bodies *to be* the mixture in capacity? and (*b*) what is it for a mixture to be in *energeia*?

(*a*) Not just any parcels of fire and earth can be the mixture in capacity. There is an incredible number of mereological aggregates of parcels of fire and parcels of earth that have tangible differentiae sufficient to make such a mixture. In order to be a particular mixture in capacity, the parcels would have to be so situated that the changes that they would undergo through the exercise of their natures would necessarily result in the mixture if not constrained. In a related context, Aristotle says that 'the seed is not yet a human being in capacity (for it needs to fall into another and to change), but whenever it may already be of this sort through its own source, at that point will be this in capacity' (*Metaph.* Θ 7, 1049^{a}12–15). To be of a sort through one's own source is to be such that the exercise of the capacities that constitute one's nature *will result* in a product that is of that sort. The exercise can be interrupted and no product need result, but the conditions must allow that the uninterrupted exercise of natural capacities would result in the product in question.

(*b*) For a mixture to be in *energeia* is, if the analogy is sound, for it to be in the way that a house-builder is when she is pursuing her art. To be a mixture is, in an inorganic context, to have a unitary nature that is derived from but is not eliminable in favour of the natures of its ingredients. To have such a nature is to have some determinate interactive and non-interactive tangible capacities. Thus, to be a mixture in *energeia* is to be in such a way that those capacities are being exercised; it is to be in such a way that it is exercising its natural unitary function. To persist as such will require the continuous exercise of this function. This exercise need not result in a change. The mixture, for example, may reach its natural place of rest and cease to move. But to exemplify one's natural unitary function in its entirety is as much of an exercise of one's capacities as are the changes that must be undergone in order to exemplify one's form in its entirety.

Now a parcel of animate flesh and a parcel of inanimate flesh with the same tangible differentiae are not identical. This can now be seen by considering in turn the two manners in which something

196 *Christopher Frey*

can be. An account of being an *F* in capacity will include a description of the natural principles whose exercise is necessary in order for a complete exemplification of an *F* to come to be. An account of being an *F* in *energeia* will include a description of a unitary function the exercise of which results in persistence as an *F*.

The coming to be of an inorganic mixture with tangible differentiae that are identical to those of a living tissue can be explained in the same way as that of any inorganic mixture, e.g. gold or copper. This account has already been provided. If we assume that the simple bodies are arranged so that the exercise of their natural capacities will result in the mixture, then those simple bodies will be the mixture in capacity. Commensurate bodies will come into contact through their natural locomotion and mix with one another producing a homoeomerous body with a unitary nature that is the composition of the ingredient's natures. The entire process can be explained by appealing to nothing other than the natures of the ingredients.[52] The principles in virtue of which an inanimate mixture persists as such are also exhausted by an appeal to the mixture's tangible capacities. As argued above, these capacities exhaust the nature of inorganic mixtures.

This is not the case with the corresponding animate tissue. As Aristotle says, 'hardness and softness, stickiness and brittleness, and whatever other qualities are found in the parts that have life and soul, may be caused by mere heat and cold, yet, when we come to the principle in virtue of which flesh is flesh and bone is bone, that is no longer so' (*GA* 2. 1, 734[b]31–4). The tangible differentiae of the animate tissue can be explained by appealing solely to the ratio of the primitive contraries that compose them. But neither the natures of the ingredients nor anything which can be determined solely on this basis is the principle in virtue of which the animate tissue comes to be with those differentiae. Aristotle identifies this principle as 'the movement set up by the male parent, who is in actuality [ἐντελεχείᾳ] what that out of which the offspring is made is in capacity [δυνάμει]' (*GA* 2. 1, 734[b]34–5). It is not primarily the natural capacities of the simple bodies that are being exercised in the creation and organization of an animate individual, it is the capacities associated with the form of that animate individual itself that

---

[52] Perhaps one will have to appeal to the circular motion of the heavens or the influence of the unmoved mover, but these factors will apply universally to all sublunar bodies and will not be the source of discrepancies in identification.

Organic Unity and the Matter of Man 197

are being exercised when the semen of the individual's male progenitor interacts with the *katamēnia* within the female progenitor's uterus so as to produce the appropriate mixtures and their proper organization.[53] If one assumes contact, the explanation of mixing need only appeal to the interactive tangible differentiae of the interacting bodies. But that these bodies are brought into contact in the ratio and order (hypothetically) necessary for an organism to come to be requires the manifestation of a unitary nature whose natural unitary function has as its end the form of such an organism. It does not result from interactions consequent on rectilinear motions towards sublunar locations (cf. *Phys.* 2. 9, 200^{a}31–4). It is only in so far as they are subjects of a process that has as its end the generation of an organism that the simple bodies are that organism in capacity.

This developmental principle is the same principle that maintains the tissues as such once they are generated.[54] In nutrition, food is acted upon by that which is nourished in such a way that it is assimilated to the latter's nature. But the agent of nutrition is the human being, the 'ensouled body, *qua* ensouled' (*DA* 2. 4, 416^{b}10), not its organs or tissues. So in order for nutrition to be possible, the agent of nutrition must be of a unitary nature. It is only then that this 'first principle of the soul' can be 'an ability [δύναμις] such as to maintain its possessor as such' (*DA* 2. 4, 416^{b}18–19).

So organic tissues have material natures that are exhausted by their tangible differentiae but do not have internal principles of motion and rest. Like the organs that they compose, organic homoeomerous tissues depend for their identity on the coming to be of the whole organism to which they belong.

[53] Interpretative allies abound: 'Democritean necessity does not suffice to explain the coming to be of any fully-developed plant or animal: you cannot start from the presence of certain materials and trace a connected series of changes, resulting from nothing but necessities belonging to the natures and powers of the materials present, that leads up to the fully-formed living thing as its outcome' (Cooper, 'Necessity', 143), and 'the development of a living organism is *not* the result of a sum of actualizations of element-potentials the identification of which includes no mention of the form of the mature organism' (Gotthelf, 'Final', 213).

[54] Reproduction and nourishment are both functions of the nutritive soul. Cf. *DA* 2. 4, 415^{a}22, 416^{a}19; *GA* 2. 4, 740^{b}30–6.

198 *Christopher Frey*

5. The two-body thesis

So what, given the intricacies of inorganic and organic unity, is the fate of the two-body thesis? In what follows, two versions of the thesis will be described and assessed in the light of our conclusions.

(a) The artefact model

One way to uphold the two-body thesis is to deny that there is any significant difference between living and artefactual hylomorphic composites. I shall take Christopher Shields as the paradigm proponent of such an approach as his view culminates with the claim that 'non-organic bodies exist before and survive the death of the organism. Just as the iron of an axe co-exists with axe matter [i.e. iron shaped so that it can chop], so the non-organic body exists while organic bodies exist.'[55]

Shields is able to make this assimilation by ignoring factors that contribute to an object's identification. As I have argued, the identification of a body as an F must take into account the two ways in which something can be an F. In the case of organic unities, the principle in virtue of which some material can be an ensouled body in capacity is the very same principle in virtue of which the ensouled composite actively persists as such. It is not, as Shields claims, simply the case that 'an individual x will belong to a kind or class F iff: x can perform the function of that kind or class'.[56] On this principle of mere functional determination an artificial heart will be classified as a heart, a rock that happens to have a particular shape will be classified as a chair, and a spontaneously generated being, e.g. Davidson's swamp-man, will be classified as a human being. These class determinations ride roughshod over fundamental Aristotelian tenets.[57]

Even given the functional determination thesis, Shields's account is incomplete. Take his analysis of non-organic bodies:

Non-organic Body (NOB): x is the non-organic body of a human being iff: (i) x occupies space in itself (*kath' hauto*); (ii) at t_1 x can perform the functions of a human being; and (iii) at t_2 x cannot perform the functions of a human being. (Shields, *Order*, 137)

---

[55] Shields, *Order*, 152, explication added.   [56] Shields, *Order*, 33.

[57] This principle also blurs the distinction between local and terminal non-functioning.

Organic Unity and the Matter of Man 199

This assumes that there is one thing, x, which can exist at two different times despite its having different functional capacities at those times. There must be an independent way of identifying x that grounds the account, and none is provided that will satisfy our constraints.

The difference between artefacts and organic bodies is not, however, entirely obvious, and it is to this distinction that I now turn with the hope of clarifying the present account. An artefact, say a bed, is a product of *technē*. Though unlikely, it is conceivable that simple bodies could interact naturally so as to produce something that is indistinguishable from a bed. But this would *not* be an artefact; it would be an aggregate of homoeomerous mixtures—some wood, some iron, etc. There would be no artefactual unity. The artefactual unity accorded to an artefact is the result of its being an actualization of a form present in the mind of the artificer. The artificer takes natural bodies and moves them in ways contrary to their natures so as to create an object that instantiates a predetermined form. The product does not have any internal unity: that is, the whole does not possess an internal principle of movement and rest. Each of the natural components retains its nature; *qua* natural a bed is an aggregate. Thus a bed that is buried issues wood and not another bed (*Phys.* 2. 1, 193^{b}10). But the bed does possess an artefactual unity, and this unity depends on its being the actualization, through *technē*, of a unitary form. Artefacts are by-products of the natural actions of artificers. The fulfilment of an artefactual function is simultaneously the flourishing of a human being *qua* artificer.

But a human being, say, *is* a natural unity. It is the exercise of the natural unitary function of man in the semen that moves the simple bodies against their natures so as to create a human being, and it is this same natural unitary function that, when continuously exercised, maintains the human being as such through nutrition. The homoeomerous tissues have material natures, but they do not have natures in the sense of having local internal principles of motion and rest that ground identity and natural unitary functions. For 'nature is twofold, the matter and the form, of which the latter is the end' (*Phys.* 2. 8, 199^{a}30–3).

So while 'every sort of thing produced naturally or by an art is produced by a thing existing actually [ἐνεργείᾳ] out of what is that sort of thing in capacity [δυνάμει]' (*GA* 2. 1, 734^{b}21–2), those

200 *Christopher Frey*

things produced naturally are produced by something 'which is actually [ἐντελεχείᾳ] what the thing out of which the product comes is in capacity [δυνάμει]' (*GA* 2. 1, 734^{b}35), whereas artefacts are produced by something that is not actually what the thing out of which the product comes is in capacity. Nothing is actually a bed before the bed is produced.

The matter of an artefact and the matter of a natural unity are very different. The parts of artefacts are natural unities with autonomous natural unitary functions. The unity of the whole is a by-product of the activities of the artificer; an artefact does not come to be by the natural activities of something that possesses that unity. Natural unities, on the other hand, do not have parts that are autonomous natural unities. The organs and tissues come to be in virtue of the activities of something that actually exemplifies the relevant unitary nature. So the wood and iron of a bed can satisfy the CS requirement. The wood is actually present in the bed, is identifiable independently of its being the wood of a bed, and is not necessarily the wood of a bed. The same cannot be said of the organs and tissues of an organic composite.

(b) The mixture model

A more promising approach to the two-body thesis is proposed, in slightly different forms, by Jennifer Whiting and Frank Lewis.[58] They claim that the non-organic body is present below the level of an animal's organs and tissues: that is, the non-organic body is the totality of simple bodies that exist in capacity within the organic homoeomerous tissues.[59]

Each of these views is committed to the presence in an organic

---

[58] Whiting, 'Living', and F. Lewis, 'Aristotle on the Relation between a Thing and its Matter' ['Thing'], in T. Scaltas, D. Charles, and M. L. Gill (eds.), *Unity, Identity, and Explanation in Aristotle's Metaphysics* (Oxford, 1994), 247–77.

[59] Lewis also argues for a distinct thesis: an animal's form is essential both to the animal and to the animal's body, but the animal and the body are different. This is because the animal's form is an internal principle of behaviour for the animal, but, in the same way that heat relates to blood, the animal's form is an external principle of behaviour for the body (Lewis, 'Thing', 268–72). This independent thesis aims to provide a distinction between the proximate matter of an animal and the animal itself. Though not argued for in detail, I take the present account to be an analysis of hylomorphism that does identify the proximate matter with the organic composite, but does not appeal to the projectivism of W. Sellars, 'Aristotle's Metaphysics: An Interpretation', in id., *Philosophical Perspectives* (Springfield, Ill., 1967), 73–124 at 188.

Organic Unity and the Matter of Man 201

composite of something that can be entirely identified without appeal to (and can thereby exist without) a soul. For Lewis, there is the 'material basis for the flesh or bone, which comprises all the correct material parts, but which can exist independently of the animal's form or soul'. This material basis is the concurrent matter of the homoeomerous tissues, 'namely so much potential earth, air, fire, and water, each of which is *part of the* (*concurrent*) *matter* of the flesh but (since each is only potential earth, air, and the rest) *not* one of its *spatially determined parts*'.[60] For Whiting, a man and his corpse are both 'constituted by flesh and blood in the sense that the contraries are still present [in the corpse] in roughly those proportions causally necessary (but not sufficient) for the existence of functional flesh and blood'. Again, 'the elements survive in the homoeomerous parts and these elements have accidentally characteristics which belong primarily and essentially to the organic body and its functionally defined parts—in particular, the characteristic of being alive or ensouled'.[61]

I agree that an organic tissue and an inorganic body can have identical tangible differentiae. And in order to have identical tangible differentiae, two homoeomerous bodies must comprise identical ratios of simple bodies existing in capacity. But these ratios, in and of themselves, cannot determine the identity of anything, let alone the identity of something that could exist with or without a soul. In inorganic contexts, one can use tangible differentiae to determine the identity of a homoeomerous body because, in such a context, the body will possess a unitary nature that is the principle of those differentiae. It is this nature that determines the identity of the body. But this shortcut is not universally available, and the presence of bodies with identical ratios in living composites and corpses does not guarantee that the objects characterized by these ratios are identical.

But what about the simple bodies themselves? Are these not present, in capacity, in both a living composite and its corpse? Yes, but not in a way that would be satisfying to a two-body theorist. As we have seen, a mixture possesses a nature that depends both aetiologically and ontologically on the natures of the simple bodies. Without these dependencies, mixtures would not have the tangible differentiae that they do. But the characteristic activities of a mix-

[60] Lewis, 'Thing', 273 and 274 (emphasis original).
[61] Whiting, 'Living', 80 and 84.

202   *Christopher Frey*

ture have as their source a single unitary nature. The simple bodies
that exist in capacity and compose the mixture are not present in
a way that would make it sensible to think of them as constrained
by some external principle. If this were so, a mixture would not
have a unitary nature; it would be an aggregate of unitary natures
violently bound together.

6. Conclusion

The argument of this paper rests on two pillars: an account of what
it is for body to be natural and an account of the two ways in which a
body can be so natured—in capacity and in *energeia*. Given these accounts, it follows that there is nothing in an organic composite that
will satisfy the CS requirement. Neither the organs nor the tissues
will do: organic composites possess natures that are the principle
in virtue of which their organs and tissues come to be and persist
as such, and this must be appealed to in the identification of those
bodies. Nor will any sum of simple bodies do: the simple bodies
that serve as the ingredients of the homoeomerous tissues exist
only in capacity, and the natural unity of mixtures precludes the
simple bodies from serving as the contingently identifiable matter
of either organic or inorganic mixtures.

Asking for the matter of man is not like asking for the matter of a
bed or the matter of a bundle of sticks. Organic unities, despite their
complexity, are, first and foremost, *natural* unities. To ask for the
matter of man is more like asking for the matter of a parcel of earth,
or the matter of a homoeomerous mixture. When natural unities
are the subject, be they organic or inorganic, such enquiries will not
issue in an object identifiable independently of the unitary nature
of the whole. The matter of man is, essentially, the matter *of man*.

University of Pittsburgh

BIBLIOGRAPHY

Ackrill, J. L., 'Aristotle's Definitions of *psuchē*', *Proceedings of the Aris-
totelian Society*, 73 (1972), 119–33.
Barnes, J. (ed.), *The Complete Works of Aristotle: The Revised Oxford
Translation* (Princeton, 1984).

Organic Unity and the Matter of Man

Bigelow, J., and Pargetter, R., 'Functions', *Journal of Philosophy*, 84 (1987), 181–96.

Bodnár, I., 'Movers and Elemental Motions in Aristotle', *OSAP* 15 (1997), 81–117.

Bogen, J., 'Fire in the Belly', *Pacific Philosophical Quarterly*, 76/3–4 (1995), 370–405.

Charlton, W., *Aristotle's* Physics *I–II* (Oxford, 1970).

Code, A., and Moravcsik, J., 'Explaining Various Forms of Living', in Nussbaum and Rorty (eds.), *Essays*, 129–45.

Cohen, S. M., *Aristotle on Nature and Incomplete Substance* (Cambridge, 1996).

—— 'Hylomorphism and Functionalism' ['Hylomorphism'], in Nussbaum and Rorty (eds.), *Essays*, 57–73.

Cooper, J., 'Hypothetical Necessity' ['Necessity'], in A. Gotthelf (ed.), *Aristotle on Nature and Living Things* (Pittsburgh, 1986), 151–67; repr. in J. Cooper, *Knowledge, Nature, and the Good* (Princeton, 2001), 130–47.

Fine, K., 'The Problem of Mixture', *Pacific Philosophical Quarterly*, 76/3–4 (1995), 266–369.

Furth, M., *Substance, Form, and Psyche* (Cambridge, 1988).

Gill, M. L., 'Aristotle on Matters of Life and Death', *Proceedings of the Boston Area Colloquium in Ancient Philosophy*, 4 (1989), 187–205.

—— *Aristotle on Substance* [*Substance*] (Princeton, 1989).

Gotthelf, A., 'Aristotle's Conception of Final Causality' and 'Postscript 1986' ['Final'], in A. Gotthelf and J. Lennox (eds.), *Philosophical Issues in Aristotle's Biology* (Cambridge, 1986), 204–42; originally published in *Review of Metaphysics*, 30 (1976), 226–54.

Hamlyn, D. W., *Aristotle's* De Anima, *Books I and II* [*Anima*] (Oxford, 1968).

Irwin, T., *Aristotle's First Principles* [*Principles*] (Oxford, 1988).

Kelsey, S., 'Aristotle's Definition of Nature', *OSAP* 25 (2003), 59–88.

Lennox, J., 'Material and Formal Natures in Aristotle's *De Partibus Animalium*', in id., *Aristotle's Philosophy of Biology* (Cambridge, 2001), 182–204.

Lewis, F., 'Aristotle on the Relation between a Thing and its Matter' ['Thing'], in T. Scaltas, D. Charles, and M. L. Gill (eds.), *Unity, Identity, and Explanation in Aristotle's Metaphysics* (Oxford, 1994), 247–77.

Nussbaum, M. C., and Rorty, A. O. (eds.), *Essays on Aristotle's* De Anima [*Essays*] (Oxford, 1992).

Sellars, W., 'Aristotle's Metaphysics: An Interpretation', in id., *Philosophical Perspectives* (Springfield, Ill., 1967), 73–124.

Shields, C., *Order in Multiplicity* [*Order*] (Oxford, 1999).

Whiting, J., 'Living Bodies' ['Living'], in Nussbaum and Rorty (eds.), *Essays*, 75–92.

Williams, B., 'Hylomorphism', *OSAP* 4 (1986), 189–99.

Williams, C. J. F. (trans. and comm.), *Aristotle's* De Generatione et Corruptione (Oxford, 1982).

Wright, L., 'Functions', *Philosophical Review*, 82/2 (1973), 139–68.

THE UNION OF CAUSE AND EFFECT
IN ARISTOTLE: *PHYSICS* 3. 3

ANNA MARMODORO

1. Introduction

THE long history of philosophy has seen many formidable attempts at the analysis of causation. Necessary connection, counterfactual dependence, nomological subsumption, statistical correlation, and other core conceptions have been used in seeking to account for the relation between a cause and its effect. In view of the centrality causation has enjoyed in metaphysics on the one hand, and the immense amount of exegetical study that has been devoted to Aristotle's works on the other, it is surprising that Aristotle's unique analysis of causation has not been recognized as a chapter in the history of this concept. His analysis is fundamentally different from any other that has left its mark; and because his account has remained hitherto latent, it might even provide a promising new starting-point for us in tackling this elusive metaphysical notion.

Aristotle takes causation to be the occurrence of a complex entity. The entity comprises a physical process grounding two natures (e.g. building and being built). The two natures are ontologically interdependent, requiring a mutual process of realization. But the potentialities for the two natures belong, respectively, to two different substances, the agent and the patient, and so, in consequence, do the two natures themselves—it is the builder that builds, and it is the house (or its materials) that are being built. Thus, there is an underlying activity that grounds two natures, but there is no single subject that possesses both of these natures. Rather, they belong to

---

© Anna Marmodoro 2007

Previous versions of this paper were presented at conferences in Durham, Oxford, St Andrews, and Edinburgh. I am very grateful for the stimulating questions and feedback I received on those occasions from the audience. I warmly thank David Sedley for his valuable comments on the penultimate version.

206 *Anna Marmodoro*

two different subjects, but they are mutually interdependent in a complex and innovative way that bridges the ontological distinctness of the two substances. The interdependence of the two natures, which I shall explore in detail in what follows, is what explains the unity of the interaction between agent and patient, and the peculiar causal realism of Aristotle's account.

According to Aristotle, then, the property realization binds the substances together into a net of ontological dependencies that delineate the boundary of the causal entity. The distinctive element in his account is that the agent's potentiality is realized in the patient— which I shall call an 'ectopic' realization. Thus potentiality, actuality, and ontological dependence unite the two substances causally through a type of ontological overlap between them, without introducing any additional metaphysical causal cement to do the job.

Aristotle examines the relation between cause and effect by analysing the relation between mover and movable, in his discussion of *kinēsis* (change, motion) in *Physics* 3. Although his definition of *kinēsis* (see e.g. 201ᵃ9–10, ᵃ27–9, ᵇ4–5; 202ᵃ13–14) allows for a very wide span of instances to come under the mover–movable relation, including such cases as ageing or ripening, central to Aristotle's discussion are cases that we would readily treat as instances of causal relations, such as building, heating, curing, etc. I shall therefore talk of the relation of a mover to the movable as a causal relation, despite the fact that for Aristotle it also includes what we would consider untypical cases of such a relation.

Fundamental to Aristotle's search for an understanding of motion is the assumption that an ontological account of motion will not require a new, primitive category of being:

There is no such thing as motion over and above the things. It is always with respect to substance or to quantity or to quality or to place that what changes changes. But it is impossible, as we assert, to find anything common to these which is neither 'this' nor quantity nor quality nor any of the other predicates. Hence neither will motion and change have reference to something over and above the things mentioned; for there *is* nothing, over and above them. (200ᵇ32–201ᵃ3)[1]

This programmatic stance will play a role in directing Aristotle's account of the ontology of causation. In particular, instead of in-

---

[1] For this and other passages from the *Physics* I use the translation in *The Complete Works of Aristotle: The Revised Oxford Translation*, ed. J. Barnes (Princeton, 1984), sometimes lightly modified.

The Union of Cause and Effect in Aristotle 207

troducing new ontological items he will make use of his three principles: the form, the privation, and the substratum that remains through change. Furthermore, he will use his distinction between being in potentiality and being in actuality, which is a primitive distinction of ways in which things are. But even though he will not posit new metaphysical building-blocks, causation will introduce something novel in his ontology. For Aristotle the account of causation requires a new type of entity consisting of an *underlying substratum that grounds two natures*, each of which belongs to a different subject. This is a surprise in the context of Aristotelian substantial essentialism, where a substance is a composite of a material substratum and a single substantial form. But in causation we are not concerned with the metaphysics of substances as such, but with the metaphysics of the causal interaction between them.

The central undertaking of the present paper is to give an account of the metaphysical relations that Aristotle uses in explaining causation. Such a metaphysical investigation has not previously been undertaken in the exegetical tradition. For, the vast majority of the commentators, from late antiquity (Themistius, Philoponus, Simplicius) to the Middle Ages (Averroes, Aquinas)[2] on to contemporary commentators (Ross, Gill, Waterlow, Hussey), puzzled by the position Aristotle takes in *Physics* 3. 3, read the crucial passage as merely referring to two descriptions of one thing. But the textual evidence supports, in my view, the introduction of two natures, not descriptions, out of which the causal interaction is built.

Aristotle explores causation in terms of the modifications the mover and the movable suffer in the causal process. He uses his aporetic method in developing the metaphysical details of his account. In *Physics* 3. 3 he presents a dilemma regarding the actuality of the mover and the movable. This is a long and intricate argument, which I shall call the Actualities of Motion Dilemma (202^a21-^b5). In the course of the dilemma, Aristotle rehearses various candidate accounts of what happens to the mover and the movable in causal circumstances. He rejects some of these accounts, while introducing positions he will include in his own. I shall use the dilemma eclectically in this exposition, drawing from it the elements that are useful for configuring Aristotle's own account; his own final position does

---

[2] In a later commentary such as Zabarella's, the issue of the identity of the two beings that have one and the same reality is not even raised. See J. Zabarella, *In libros Aristotelis Physicorum commentarii* (Venice, 1601).

208   *Anna Marmodoro*

not result from this argument, but we can better understand him in view of various considerations he introduces in the course of it.[3] I provide an analysis of the reasoning in the dilemma in the appendix at the end of this article.

2. The Actualities of Motion Dilemma

In discussing the dilemma, I shall be concerned mainly with the way Aristotle understands the problem of the relation of a mover to a movable. I shall first identify the questions he thinks need to be addressed in giving a satisfactory answer to the problem, and then, in the following section, examine the solutions he gives, thereby developing his own theory of causation.

The starting-point of Aristotle's account is the cause of motion:

The mover will always transmit a form [$\epsilon \hat{i} \delta o s$], either a 'this' or such or so much, which, when it moves [$\kappa \iota \nu \hat{\eta}$], will be the principle and cause [$\dot{a} \rho \chi \dot{\eta}$ $\kappa a \dot{\iota}$ $a \check{\iota} \tau \iota o \nu$] of the motion; for example, the actual man begets man from what is potentially man. (202[a]9–12)

The core conception in Aristotle's account of causation is the transmission of the form from the mover to the movable, e.g. from the actual person to the potential one. During the causal interaction changes take place in the movable, but may also take place in the mover owing to its engagement in moving the movable.[4] But the causal interaction is the transference of the form from the mover

---

[3] Aristotle refers to the argument as an $\dot{a} \pi o \rho \dot{\iota} a$ $\lambda o \gamma \iota \kappa \dot{\eta}$. Interpreters disagree as to how to understand this characterization. The way I understand it is closest to Philoponus' reading: 'By "logical" he means one worthy of logical scrutiny' (Philoponus, *In Phys.* 376. 6 Vitelli, trans. M. Edwards, *Philoponus: On Aristotle, Physics 3* (London, 1994), 46). Aquinas' and Hussey's remarks are more descriptive than explanatory when they comment, respectively, that: 'the difficulty is dialectical, i.e. logical. For there are probable arguments on both sides' (Aquinas, *In Phys.*, trans. R. J. Blackwell, R. J. Spath, and W. E. Thirlkel, *Thomas Aquinas: Commentary on Aristotle's Physics* [*Physics*] (London, 1963), 157); and 'the arguments used are of a very general kind' (E. Hussey, *Aristotle's Physics, Books III and IV* [*Physics*] (Oxford, 1983), 67). The main alternative reading of $\lambda o \gamma \iota \kappa \dot{\eta}$ in the tradition, with which I shall find myself in disagreement, is reported first by Simplicius ('he calls this verbal . . . because its plausibility arises only from the words and it is not supported by the facts' (*In Phys.* 440. 21–2 Diels, trans. J. O. Urmson, *Simplicius: On Aristotle, Physics 3* (London, 2002), 58), and voiced among contemporary commentators, e.g. by Ross: 'the question is a superficial or dialectical one, turning on the verbal difference between $\pi o \dot{\iota} \eta \sigma \iota s$ and $\pi \dot{a} \theta \eta \sigma \iota s$' (W. D. Ross, *Aristotle's Physics: A Revised Text with Introduction and Commentary* [*Physics*] (Oxford, 1936; repr. 1979), 540).

[4] 'Every mover too is moved, as has been said—every mover, that is, which is

The Union of Cause and Effect in Aristotle 209

to the movable. Since causal efficacy consists in the transmission of the form, whatever happens to the mover in transmitting the form, the mover does not suffer its own causal agency, because the mover is not transmitting the form to itself; the causal efficacy of the mover impacts only on the movable.

The metaphysical mechanism of the transference of form is innovative and complex. To reach Aristotle's metaphysical innovation we need first to examine what occurs in the mover and what in the movable during the causal interaction. The mover moves in actuality, and the movable is actually moved. These two actualities are not casually coincident. The occurrence of the first requires the occurrence of the second, so their coincidence needs to be ontologically explained.

Aristotle explores the elusive relation between the two actualities (of the mover as a mover and of the movable as movable) in his dialectical puzzle about the Actualities of Motion. In brief, he considers two possibilities: that the two actualities are different, and that they are one and the same. If they are different, either both actualities occur in one of the two—either the mover or the moved—or one occurs in each. If both the actualities occur in one of them, then, first, one of them will not have its own actuality realized in it: for example, the actuality of the mover will occur in the moved, not in the mover; but how could that be? And secondly, whatever has both actualities in it will change in two different ways in relation to one form.[5] If, on the other hand, the actuality of the mover is in the mover, and the actuality of the movable is in the movable, then either the causal agency of the mover will impact on the mover itself, not on the movable, or it will impact on nothing, in which case it is not being a mover in actuality. Finally, if the actualities of the mover and the moved are the same, then we reach absurdity, since agency and patiency cannot be the same. I shall selectively discuss certain points in this argument which relate to important issues for the metaphysics of Aristotle's account of causation.

I shall begin by considering the role of the form (*eidos*) in Aristotle's account of causation. There are three interrelated subthemes.

capable of motion . . . To act on the movable as such is just to move it. But this it [the mover] does by contact, so that at the same time it is also acted on' ($202^a3–7$). This remark explains the motion of the mover as a reciprocal impact it suffers by the necessary contact with the movable.

[5] For example, it will become more and less hot at the same time.

210   *Anna Marmodoro*

First, there is the transmission of the form from the mover to the movable ($202^a 9$–12). Secondly, the actuality of the mover and the actuality of the moved are in relation to one form, the transmitted one.[6] And finally, these two actualities are of different types.[7] The form that is the principle and cause of the motion is the form that is transmitted from the mover to the movable. For example, the causal efficacy of fire consists in its transmitting the form of heat to the pot. It follows that the motion suffered by what is movable consists in the reception of the form that is transmitted to it. So the mover's being a mover and the movable being moved will be achieved in relation to one form. But since the mover transmits and the movable receives the form, their achievements are of different types,[8] because they relate to the same form differently. Thus the actuality of the mover as a mover *is* the transmission of the form, and the actuality of the movable as movable *is* the reception of that form.

The second issue that arises out of the Dilemma of the Actualities of Motion is the distinction Aristotle makes between the subjects the actualities occur in and the subjects they belong to. Here, as we shall see, Aristotle's metaphysical intuitions are tested to the extreme, and he finally opts for an account that opens new ground in the area of causation. Aristotle raises the issue of where the actualities *of* the mover as mover, the action, and *of* the movable as movable, the passion, are, i.e. whether they are *in* the mover or *in* the movable (ἐν τίνι; 'in what?', $202^a 25$). By asking *in what* the action *of* the agent and the passion *of* the patient are, he distinguishes in one and the same question two metaphysical relations: the one is

---

[6] This tenet is presupposed by the rhetorical question Aristotle asks: 'How will there be two alterations of quality in *one* subject towards *one* form?' ($202^a 35$–6). See **P (5.2)** in the dilemma in the appendix below.

[7] See *Phys.* 3. 3, $202^b 1$–5. Here Aristotle distinguishes teaching from learning, not because the content of the lesson is different, but because the one activity is teaching, and the other is learning, the same lesson. Contrast e.g. Themistius (*In Phys.* 78. 9–23 Schenkl), who in his interpretation confuses the content of teaching and learning and the common underlying substratum for both. Themistius talks about the very same theorem being taught and learnt as an example of the common substratum of teaching and learning, and assimilates it to the stretch of path for the routes from Athens to Thebes and from Thebes to Athens. But this mistakes what is common in the forms of moving and being moved with what underlies the activities of moving and being moved.

[8] 'It is contrary to reason to suppose that there should be one identical actualization of two things which are different in kind. Yet there will be, if teaching and learning are the same, and agency and patiency' ($202^b 1$–3). See **P 15** in the appendix below.

The Union of Cause and Effect in Aristotle 211

'belonging to a subject' and the other is 'occurring in a subject'.[9] We need to examine why this distinction arises here, and how it can be understood.

Let us first look at Aristotle's own attempt to justify the distinction. He says:

> Since, then, they are both [the agent's action and the patient's passion] motions, we may ask: in what are they? (202ᵃ25)

> It is not absurd that the actualization of one thing should be in another. Teaching is the activity of a person who can teach, yet the operation is performed in something—it is not cut adrift from a subject [the teacher], but is *of* one thing [the teacher] *in* another [the learner]. (202ᵇ5–8, emphasis added)

The first passage makes a general point, too broad to be illuminating in the present circumstances. It tells us that in relation to motions we can ask where they take place. Thus, my walk can take place in the park, and my tanning at the seashore. But in neither case am I doing something (at least in any way significant) to, or changing, that in which my motion takes place. My walk and my tanning are external to the park and the seashore. They are 'in' them in a local sense, which must not be what Aristotle means here, if he is not to conflate e.g. my tanning taking place at the seashore from its taking place in me, who tans.[10] The second passage gives us a clearer idea of the type of distinction that Aristotle has in mind. He concentrates on one of the two actualities, the agent's, and says that teaching is performed by the teacher in something. If this is to be more illuminating than the first passage, we must take Aristotle to be saying something other than that teaching takes place in a classroom. Indeed, he does tell us that teaching takes place in the learner. But how is this to be understood, and generalized?

A clue as to what Aristotle means by talking of where an action takes place can be found in a subargument in the dilemma (**P 9–12** in the appendix), in the following dialectical move:

> [Suppose] the agency is in the agent and the patiency in the patient.

---

[9] Being 'in a subject' in the context of *Physics* 3. 3 should not be understood along the lines of inherence in the *Categories*, as, for instance, red inheres in an apple. The reason is that the *Categories*' inherence in the substance entails belonging to that substance as subject; whereas here, as we shall see, heating something (for example) belongs to the fire but occurs in the pot.

[10] Contrast Hussey ad loc., who holds that 'there is nothing to suggest that anything other than a local sense of "in" is intended' (*Physics*, 65).

212   *Anna Marmodoro*

[Then] . . . the motion will be in the mover, for the same account will hold of mover and movable. Hence either *every* mover will be moved, or, though having motion, it will not be moved. (202ᵃ26–31)

The key ideas in this argument are that where the actuality of the mover as a mover is will also be where the motion is; and the thing the motion is *in* is set in motion. Aristotle's justification for the first claim, that motion follows the actuality of the mover as mover, is that the rationale here must be the same in the case of the movable. Because if, as per the initial hypothesis, the action of the mover moves the movable, then it must be that the action of the mover generates motion. But if the action of the mover is in the mover, the generated motion will, for that reason, also be in the mover. But then the mover will be in motion, for otherwise 'though having motion, it will not be moved', which is treated as absurd and closes this branch of the argument. So the motion is where the actuality of the mover as mover is, and where the motion is, it sets that thing in motion.

In that case we can interpret the question ἐν τίνι; ('in what?', 202ᵃ25) as asking '*Where* does the motion bring about the change?' Teaching is in a learner, as heating is in a colder object, because it is these objects that are set in motion by the movers. So the actuality of the mover as mover is in the patient, generating the motion in it. The way it is in the patient is like the way the form is in matter.[11] On the other hand, the actuality of the patient as patient is always in the patient because the patient always suffers the caused motion. The picture which emerges from the distinction of the two metaphysical relations, 'belonging to a subject' and 'occurring in a subject', is that there is a motion that is the coincidence of two activities, the agent's and the patient's, in the patient. We shall explore this metaphysical picture in the following section.

Before we come to this, a clarification is needed regarding whether the mover itself is in motion. Aristotle distinguishes the motion of the mover, due to necessary contact with the movable, from the motion in the movable due to the mover's causal efficacy. The first is in the mover and the second in the movable.[12] During the causal

---

[11] See *Phys.* 4. 3, 210ᵃ20–1.

[12] In the subargument of the dilemma examined above (p. 209) the falsehood that closes one of the branches is that 'every mover will be moved' (202ᵃ30). See **P (10.1)** in the appendix below. This follows from the assumption that the mover's actuality, as a mover, is in the mover itself. Then, owing to their self-inflicted causal efficacy,

The Union of Cause and Effect in Aristotle 213

interaction the mover and the moved become actually such without this involving an additional change in either of them besides the ones mentioned above.

3. Aristotle's account of causation

Immediately following the Actualities of Motion Dilemma, Aristotle denies three of its premises.

[1] It is not absurd that the actualization of one thing should be in another. . . . [2] There is nothing to prevent two things having one and the same actualization . . . [3] Nor is it necessary that the teacher should learn, even if to act and to be acted on are one and the same, provided they are not the same in respect of the account which states their essence . . . but in respect to that to which they belong [ᾧ ὑπάρχει ταῦτα], the motion. (202^{b}5–21)

This leads directly to the discussion of his own position, which he had already sketched, just before entering the dilemma, as follows:

The solution of the difficulty is plain: motion is in the movable. It is the fulfilment of this potentiality by the action of that which has the power of causing motion; and even the actuality of that which has the power of causing motion is not other than the actuality of the movable; for it must be the fulfilment of *both* . . . it is on the movable that it [the mover] is capable of acting. Hence there is one and the same actuality of both. (202^{a}13–18)

I shall first briefly outline Aristotle's solution to the problem of causation before discussing it in detail. Causal interaction consists in the transmission of a form from an agent to a patient. The agent's causal activity consists in transmitting the form, and the patient's activity, which is the causal effect, consists in receiving the form. So, causal interaction results in the actualization of properties in both objects: being the cause in the agent, and being the effect in the patient. The actualization of these potentialities is a physical process facilitating the transmission of the form, e.g. the movements

all movers would move, which is treated as a falsehood, and so it is denied that the mover's actuality is in the mover. But although 'every mover will be moved' is treated as a falsehood in the dilemma, Aristotle has earlier stated that 'every mover is moved' (202^{a}3). The difference between the statements is that the second ranges over movable movers only, while the first ranges over all movers, including god, who is immovable, which falsifies the statement. Of course this argument does not block the possibility of self-directed motion, as in the case of a doctor healing herself, where the mover and moved are the same.

of the sculptor's arms and chisel on the wood. This process is at one and the same time grounding the natures of the two actualized potentialities, the agent's as agent and the patient's as patient (e.g. sculpting and being carved into shape, heating and being heated, teaching and learning). So the process is both a causing and a suffering, which are different, interdependent, and asymmetrically realized. Their asymmetry lies in the fact that the activity of the agent is realized in the patient, producing the effect on the patient. It is a dislocated, or *ectopic*, realization of the agent's activity in the patient. The interdependencies of the two natures are multiple, binding them inextricably together into a complex whole which cannot be divided into distinct activities. This complex whole is generated by the mutual, interdependent actualization of properties of the two objects, which is their causal interaction. This is the causal 'bond' between the objects that could be more accurately understood as an overlap between the constitutions of the two substances, afforded by the ectopic realization of the potentiality of the one in the other.

We have already seen that causation is the transmission of form from the mover to the movable: 'The mover will always transmit a form . . . which, when it moves, will be the principle and cause of the motion' (202^a9-12). This is the core conception which explains further fundamental features of Aristotelian causation, such as its incompleteness and its asymmetry. The causal interaction begins with contact between the agent and patient (202^a5-7). The contact facilitates the transmission of the form from the mover to the movable. But the transmission is a process that takes place in time. While it lasts the transmission has not been completed. The unfolding of the stages of transmission marks the incompleteness of the causal process (e.g. building a structure). The process of the reception of the form by the patient is the causal effect. Once the transmission is completed, the causal interaction is not taking place any more. The agent is not acting on the patient, which now possesses the transmitted form. So the process of realization of the agent's capacity to transmit the form and the patient's capacity to receive the form is the causal process which lasts until the transmission is completed. The realization takes place through time, during which period the process is driven by the not yet entirely fulfilled potentialities of the agent to transmit the form and the patient to receive it. So the causal process of transmission is actual while these potentialities are

The Union of Cause and Effect in Aristotle   215

being realized, and only before they are fully realized. In that sense the causal process is actual only when the potentialities that drive it are incompletely actualized: 'motion is thought to be a sort of actuality, but incomplete, the reason being that the potential whose actuality it is is incomplete' ($201^{b}31-3$).

But more important than the explanation of the incompleteness of causation is the role that the transmission of the form plays in *selecting the cause*. We already saw that the agent is involved in different motions in the course of the causal interaction, owing to the contact with the patient which is necessary for the transmission of the form. All of these motions are required for the effect to occur— if not these particular tokens, at least their functional types. But although all of them can thereby be thought of as belonging to the causal field of this causal act, not all of them, or any arbitrary selection from them, are the cause. Some of what happens to the agent is only the means for the transmission of the form.[13] This distinction between the cause and the means towards its realization is already found in Plato's *Phaedo* (99 A 5–B 4).[14] But what Aristotle makes explicit here is the criterion that determines the cause, distinguishing it from the means. The form that is transmitted is the principle and the cause of the motion. Everything else that happens in the process, or even the conditions of its happening, is the means for the transmission of the form. Thus the heat from the fire, or from the match, or from the particle fission, is the cause of the explosion, while such factors as the presence of oxygen, or the striking of the match, or the uncovering of the reactor rods, are the means towards the transmission of the form, or even the generation of the form to be transmitted.

Since the causal interaction is the transmission of the form, at the

---

[13] A clarification needs to be made regarding the motion of the mover. One kind of motion is the one resulting from the mover's contact with the movable, which is required to transmit the form to it. But there is a further type of motion that may be required for the transmission of the form. It may be that to achieve contact at all, or to achieve the requisite contact, the mover needs to move itself, as e.g. in the case of a sculptor or a builder. These motions are neither the transmission of the form nor the result of contact with the movable, but the preparation for it. But this does not make them uncaused motions. They are motions that are for the sake of transmitting the form to the movable. They could be caused by chance motions, such as the falling of a tree, or be part of the mover's plan, if the mover is capable of planning, to engage in a more complex causal activity, e.g. hitting the ball in a game of tennis, which involves component motions. Aristotle does not set them apart here.

[14] See in particular 99 B 1–4: 'Imagine not being able to distinguish the real cause from that without which the cause would not be able to act as a cause.'

216 *Anna Marmodoro*

time of transmission the causal form must be present in the agent not only in actuality, but in a *transmissible state*. The teacher may possess knowledge, but this does not make her into a teacher until she embodies this knowledge in her lecture that transmits it to the students. The knowledge in her memory is the non-transmissible form, while that in her lecture is the transmissible one. (The memory knowledge is non-transmissible in the sense that the agent must come to posses the knowledge in a different form before it can be transmitted.)[15] But the mover need not possess the form in any way other than in a transmissible state at the time of the transmission. This is the least requirement of possession of the form by the mover. The mover may also possess the form in non-transmissible ways, but this is not necessary for it to be or become a mover. Moreover, even if it does possess the form in a transmissible state—for example, the teacher has prepared the lecture—it is not a mover until the conditions are such that they allow the form to be actually transmitted. And finally, even if it possesses the form in a transmissible way, it has to be transmissible for the type of patient at hand.

What metaphysics is involved in the *transmission* of the form from the mover to the movable? There is the actuality of the mover as a mover and the actuality of the movable as movable, both being realized in the transmission of the form from the mover to the movable, which is the motion caused and suffered. How are these actualities related? The metaphysical account of their relation is Aristotle's answer to the problem of causation. The challenge is to explain the nature of the special bond between two objects engaged in causal interaction. The challenge is made harder for Aristotle because he restricts himself to the ontology so far developed in his system, which does not make any provisions for such entities as necessary connections between objects, which later philosophers sought to find in causal interactions. But neither does he question or deny the existence of a type of connectedness between the interacting objects. So he has to build the connectedness from the materials of his ontological warehouse of substances and their properties, which they possess either actually or potentially.

---

[15] Of course, it is the memory knowledge that is transmitted, and in that sense it is transmissible too, but only by being the origin of the further, transmissible state of that knowledge, which the teacher comes to possess before transmitting it to the student.

The Union of Cause and Effect in Aristotle   217

Although I agree with Waterlow[16] that accounting for causation strained Aristotle's system, I disagree with her analysis of the problem and of Aristotle's solution in the following respect. According to Waterlow, the challenge for Aristotle comes from the fact that the world-view he operates with (and the language available to him) seemingly creates a need for a metaphysical justification of a bond between causes and effects that has no place in his metaphysics.[17] By contrast, in my view the challenge comes from the metaphysical problem of how to account for the union of cause and effect, which Aristotle assumes exists, without introducing ontological entities such as necessary connections.

Waterlow's interpretation of Aristotle's account of causation relies on the reading she offers of *Physics* 3. 3, which I shall discuss in detail below (pp. 221 ff.). For the moment I want to register in outline where our interpretations agree and where they disagree. There is agreement in understanding that Aristotle sees agent and patient as enjoying a special type of unity. There is disagreement in the understanding of Aristotle's account of that unity. For Waterlow agency and patiency have the same end and are from the same principle, and this is why they are one. But *contra* Waterlow, it is clear from the texts I have commented on so far that agency and patiency have different ends, one being the transmission of the form, the other its reception. Agency and patiency have different natures, being the realization of different potentialities which belong to different substances. Yet causation binds agent to patient through a complex entity.

[16] S. Waterlow, *Nature, Change, and Agency in Aristotle's Physics* [*Physics*] (Oxford, 1982).

[17] Waterlow attributes to Aristotle an 'anthropomorphic' view of causation and change, where 'the point of view of the voluntary agent is one from which the "halves" [sc. agent and patient] already present themselves as distinct' (*Physics*, 203), while in fact by his own metaphysical account there are not two distinct 'halves' to causation. See further points in her argument:

> Aristotle's retention of the language of agency and patiency has nothing to do with any postulation of a mystical (and mythical) transaction tying agent to patient or to its effect in the patient. (200) ... Why should we not regard the artifex and his material as forming, in the change, a concrete organic unity, as if the material were an extension of his own body? What happens in the one and what happens in the other have the same end and are from the same principle. (201) ... In the change as a concrete unitary event there are not different entities to be agent and patient. The active and passive of the verb, from this point of view, are used of the change itself only derivatively, on the basis of an actual distinction existing only *ante* and *post eventum*. (202) ... Since there are not two beings to connect, there can be neither problem nor solution about the nature and status of the connection. (202)

218 *Anna Marmodoro*

Substances move. Aristotle's solution to the problem of causal union is to make the motion of the causally interacting substances the same. Their motion, being one and the same but belonging to both substances, links the two substances together. But here a challenge emerges: how can the motion of the agent be the same as the motion of the patient?

> It is contrary to reason to suppose that there should be one actualization [ἐνέργεια] of two things which are different in kind. Yet there will be if teaching and learning are the same, and agency and patiency. To teach will be the same as to learn, and to act the same as to be acted on—the teacher will necessarily be learning everything that he teaches, and the agent will be acted on. (202ᵇ1–5)

Aristotle does not draw back from his solution in view of this problem, but is led to innovate. He will keep the oneness of the motion, but account for its twoness in a metaphysically novel way, which follows different principles from the essentialism established in his theory of substances.

Aristotle tells us that the motion that is in the movable, brought about by the mover,

> is the fulfilment of this potentiality [of the movable as movable] by the action of that which has the power of causing motion [the mover]; and the actuality of that which has the power of causing motion [the mover] is not other than the actuality of the movable; for it must be the fulfilment of *both*. (202ᵃ14–16)

The terms translated as 'fulfilment' and 'actuality' are *entelecheia* and *energeia* respectively, which are used interchangeably in this context.[18] Clearly, so described, the solution faces the prima facie objection we encountered above, that teaching will be the same as

---

[18] Gill offers a very informed discussion of the etymology of ἐντελέχεια, its possible translations, and the debated issue of its synonymy with ἐνέργεια. She devotes particular attention to the textual observation that 'Aristotle's argument . . . proves that the ἐντελέχεια of the agent and the patient is one, but in the argument Aristotle does not explicitly claim that motion is the ἐντελέχεια of both'. Gill finds it an 'attractive suggestion' to explain the textual observation thus: 'the claim would be that the ἐντελέχεια of the teacher and the learner is the same but what it is to be that ἐντελέχεια for the teacher is an activity, namely a teaching of the teacher in the learner, and a change in the learner, namely a learning of the learner by the teacher'. But she dismisses this as Aristotle's view in the light of 202ᵇ19 ff., because she finds no indication of an ontological asymmetry between agency as activity and patiency as change (M. L. Gill, 'Aristotle's Theory of Causal Action in *Physics* III 3' ['Causal Action'], *Phronesis*, 25 (1980), 129–47 at 134–5).

The Union of Cause and Effect in Aristotle   219

learning and that the teacher will learn what she teaches. So Aristotle proceeds to refine his answer by a series of examples. Before examining these, I should mention that it is only elucidation by example, rather than a change in the answer, that he offers. This is surprising in view of the fact that, as we shall see, we would have expected his answer to be given using different terminology in the light of the clarification he makes. But Aristotle does not change the terminology of his solution, despite the fact that he has the opportunity to do so when he repeats it (at 202^{b}5–9) immediately following the discussion of the prima facie objection. His solution, enriched by the examples, does avoid the objection, as I shall argue below. But one would have expected a fresh description of his solution that did not claim the (objectionable) sameness of the two actualities, a sameness which his solution does not require and is in fact misleading for the reader. As we do not get a fresh description, we need to conclude that Aristotle is using the terms *entelecheia* and *energeia* broadly here, to mean by 'actualization' the *activity* of the agent and patient, rather than the *natures* of their activities.

Aristotle gives four examples to elucidate his solution to causation. He sets up the problem by stating the explanandum: 'A thing is capable of causing motion because it *can* do this, it is a mover because it actually *does* it. But it is on the movable that it is capable of acting' (202^{a}16–17). The action of the mover can be realized only by acting on the movable. This requires Aristotle to explain how the mover's capacity is bound up with the movable. Immediately following his statement of the problem, he proceeds to offer his explanation by restating his solution and elucidating it with the first two examples:

Hence there is one and the same actuality [ἐνέργεια] of both [the mover and the movable] alike, just as one to two and two to one are the same interval, and the steep ascent and the steep descent are one. (202^{a}18–20)

The first example is ambiguous. On the one hand the interval from one to two can be taken to be *the same* as the interval from two to one, being either an arithmetical unit of value one, or a geometrical magnitude of value one. On the other hand, the two intervals can be taken to be *different*, such as vectors with opposite directions, or the positive and negative values of the number one. I take the example in the latter way because, as we shall see, the metaphysics

220 *Anna Marmodoro*

of the two intervals require them to have *different essential natures*, as opposite vectors do, or as the positive and negative unit values do; whereas taken in the former way the two intervals are one and the same, *described in two different ways*—from one to two, and from two to one.

The ancient and medieval commentators interpret this example in two ways, both of which belong to the one-entity-two-descriptions family of interpretations. They vacillate (often indiscriminately) between two readings within the one-entity-two-descriptions family: either one interval described in two different ways in terms of its end-points, or one relation described from the point of view of either relatum.[19] I believe that the reason for the commentators' vacillation between the two readings is that at 202^b17–19 Aristotle describes the example, speaking loosely, both as an interval (*diastasis*) between two points and as the relation of distance (*to dihistasthai*) of either point from the other, as if they were equivalent ways of formulating the example. The modern commentators do not fall prey to this possible confusion, yet most of them follow the one-entity-two-descriptions interpretation.[20]

The second example offered by Aristotle is also ambiguous, between the stretch of land being the same inclined road for both ascent and descent, and there being two routes, the route up and the route down, which, as any cyclist knows, are not only essentially, but dramatically different!

Aristotle proceeds to offer an explanation of the sameness involved in these examples:

---

[19] Reading the example as one interval described differently in terms of its end-points is found, for example, in Simplicius (446. 31–2 Diels); Philoponus (370. 7; 375. 26–376. 5 Vitelli); Aquinas (*Physics*, 147 Blackwell *et al.*). Reading the example as one relation that has two relata, and accordingly two descriptions (e.g. the relation of procreation, with father and son as the two relata, and 'being the father of' and 'being the son of' as the two descriptions), is found, for example, in Simplicius (439. 34*bis*–37; 448. 30 ff. Urmson; on this reading of Simplicius see also C. Luna, 'La relation chez Simplicius', in I. Hadot (ed.), *Simplicius: sa vie, son œuvre, sa survie* (Berlin, 1987), 113–48 at 126); Averroes (*Aristotelis De physico auditu libri octo. Cum Averrois Cordubensis variis in eosdem commentariis* [*Physica*], in *Aristotelis opera cum Averrois commentariis* (Venice, 1562–74; repr. Frankfurt a.M., 1964), vol. iv, fos. 92^v I–L, 94^r E, 95^r A).

[20] See e.g. Ross, *Physics*, 361, 362, 540; Gill, 'Causal Action', 140; 143; Waterlow, *Physics*, 182, 191; Hussey, *Physics*, 69–70. Waterlow and Hussey share the view that Aristotle has some insight into Frege's distinction between sense and reference. I shall come, at pp. 221–2, to the arguments they offer in support of their interpretation.

The Union of Cause and Effect in Aristotle 221

For these are *one and the same*, although their definitions [λόγος] are *not one*. So it is with the mover and the moved. (202ᵃ20, emphasis added)

This is important, but not complete. It is important because it blocks the objection that teaching would end up being the same as learning, by stating that they have different essential natures. But if they have different essential natures they are not one and the same entity described in two different ways. Whatever it is that is one and the same between the two intervals or between the ascent and descent must have two different definitions/natures.

Commentators who read *logos* as 'account/description' rather than 'definition' take the examples to be introducing a common single entity in each case, e.g. unit value one, or the inclined road (or the non-directional relation between the extremes). This view is held by the majority of the commentators, ancient and modern. I have already discussed the position of the ancient and medieval commentators, and I shall limit myself here to presenting two recent and very interesting accounts that have been offered for the same-entity view; one is by Waterlow (*Physics*, 180–2), the other by Hussey (*Physics*, 66).

Waterlow,[21] in analysing the analogous case of hearing and sounding, identifies the multiply described entity as a single event, a single change that is both teaching and learning:

His [Aristotle's] argument proceeds on the following assumption: the only reason anyone could have for supposing that being a changer (an actual changer) entails change in that changer, rests on a false view of the difference regarding these (in some given instance, such as teaching and learning) as different concrete events, that one could be misled into thinking that the changer as such undergoes a change. But once it is seen that these are different ways of describing the same event, the problem disappears, leaving only one change, which is to be located in the patient ... The point of crucial importance that Aristotle emphasizes again and again ... is that X's teaching is not a different concrete event from Y's learning. These are one and the same actuality under two descriptions. (*Physics*, 180–2)

Waterlow associates this single event that is the entity to which the two descriptions apply with

a neutral verb-stem determinable by active and passive voices ... we may say (a) that teaching is a predicate of Y as well as of X; and (b) that

---

[21] And also L. A. Kosman, 'Perceiving that We Perceive: *On the Soul* III, 2', *Philosophical Review*, 84/4 (1975), 499–519 at 514.

222 *Anna Marmodoro*

'teaching' applies to Y in a determinate form (the passive) which is perfectly consistent with the statement 'Y does not teach'. (*Physics*, 182)

My argument is that the ontology of causation for Aristotle is more complex than that of one event under two descriptions.

Hussey, who also holds the one-entity-two-descriptions view, considers that

Aristotle's positive argument to show that the changes [of the agent and patient] are the same . . . might be just that an operation must be something that *happens* over a period of time, and that if we look at the minimal case of change, in which the agent is completely unaffected, there *is* 'nothing happening' except the change(-intransitive) of the patient. Hence, the operation of the agent must be the change(-intransitive). (*Physics*, 66)

I do not agree that, because the agent's transitive change of the patient happens over time, within a small period of time the agent does not suffer any change. To put it in Aristotelian terms, some but not all of the form that is being transmitted will be transmitted within a short interval. According to the analysis I am developing here, the change is not one in so far as two essential natures are involved in its occurrence, agency and patiency. The change involves the transference of a form, and Aristotle finds this to be an irreducibly complex activity of give and take; there are not two distinct activities, nor only one: an indivisible physical process grounds two essential natures of action and passion. So even in the minimal case described in the quotation above, the agent transmits and the patient suffers the form. The changes in the agent depend on what is required in each instance for the form that will be transferred to be possessed by the agent in a transmissible mode, which is the causally active factor.

More generally, by contrast with the majority's view, my reading of Aristotle's examples and explanation directs me to take *logos* at 202^a20 to mean 'definition', and so I disagree with those which read the examples as involving one entity under two descriptions. Neither the complex of the two directional intervals and its respective ground nor the complex of the two routes and its respective ground constitutes any familiar type of entity of the Aristotelian ontology, although their components are. Aristotle is here engaging in a novel exploration of ontological dependence, not of matter and form or subject and property or potential and actual, but of two interdependent natures.

The Union of Cause and Effect in Aristotle   223

When Aristotle says that there is a single actuality (*energeia*) of both the mover and the movable (as there is between the two intervals or the two routes), he must be telling us that the mover and the movable are so related in their activity as to be *one* in some sense, but *not one* in the definitions that describe what each of them does or suffers. What makes the definitions of the vector lines two are opposite directions; but what is it that makes these vector lines one? It is the non-directional interval between one and two that is the same for both vector lines. The interval would not be the same, for example, between vector lines one to two and four to three (on a line). Similarly with the uphill and downhill routes: they are different because of their opposed directions but are both the same stretch of land, as opposed to two routes on different sides of the hill that share no common stretch of land. Although these examples and this explanation go some way towards accounting for what Aristotle means by claiming that the actuality of the mover and the movable is the same, his position is not as explicit as in the explanation we shall find in his next set of examples, to which I now turn.

After the dilemma Aristotle states his own position, resolving the puzzles encountered in the course of the dilemma itself. On the issue we are examining here, he says:

> Nor is it necessary that the teacher should learn, even if to act and be acted on are one and the same, provided that they are not the same in respect of the account [λόγος] which states their essence [⟨τὸ⟩ τί ἦν εἶναι] (as raiment and dress), but are the same in the sense in which the road from Thebes to Athens and the road from Athens to Thebes are the same, as has been explained above. (202ᵇ10–14)

The use of the technical expression, coined by Aristotle himself, for essence, ⟨τὸ⟩ τί ἦν εἶναι, settles the issue as to whether by 'account', *logos*, he means description or definition of nature.[22] This is further supported by his immediate example of things that have the same account, namely raiment and dress. 'Raiment' and 'dress' are one thing, under two names or descriptions, but with one definition which expresses its essence. At *Top.* 1. 7, 103ᵃ25–7, Aristotle says

---

[22] No doubt is recorded in the modern editions concerning the expression τί ἦν εἶναι at 202ᵇ12; only the two immediately preceding articles τὸν ⟨τὸ⟩ have a less firm transmission in the manuscripts, as Ross documents in the apparatus ad loc.: we find only τὸν in IJ; only τὸ in E; neither in F. It was easy for one or the other article to drop out by haplography during the copying process. Bonitz prints both articles τὸν τὸ as part of the text; Ross chooses to print ⟨τὸ⟩ as a supplement necessary to complete the sense.

224 *Anna Marmodoro*

that whatever is one in essence is one in the primary sense (*kuriōs*), and indeed we find there the very same example of 'raiment' and 'dress' to illustrate this type of oneness; this is not the case with the routes, but it would be if the descriptions were 'the road from Athens to Thebes' and 'the road we travelled on last week'. The route from Thebes to Athens differs in definition from the route from Athens to Thebes since they are not, as Aristotle tells us, like raiment and dress. The reference back to what 'has been explained above' in the last quotation is to the passage we just examined, 202ᵃ19–20, on the relation of the uphill route to the downhill one that differs in account, *logos*; hence there too Aristotle intends *logos* to be the definition of essence.

But there is further evidence that here *logos* is the definition of essence, and not a mere description. This comes in an unexpected metaphysical observation that Aristotle makes immediately afterwards. This observation also makes it evident that Aristotle's aim in the two passages we are examining, in which he says that mover and movable are 'one and the same', or that one 'actuality . . . must be the fulfilment of both', or that 'to act and to be acted on are one and the same',[23] is to introduce a sense of *qualified sameness*, a sense different from identity:

For it is not the case that all the same properties belong to [ταὐτὰ πάντα ὑπάρχει] those things which are in any way the same; rather, this is the case only for those things to be which is the same [τὸ εἶναι τὸ αὐτό]. (202ᵇ14–16, my translation)

The expression ταὐτὰ πάντα must be referring to attributes of substances, and not to the substratum underlying a substance; for it would be extremely unnatural for Aristotle to say that the underlying substratum belongs to (ὑπάρχει) a substance. Furthermore, although he talks only of things to be which is the same (literally, that have the same being, τὸ εἶναι τὸ αὐτό), I take it that he means things whose constitution is the same. One could take this to be limited only to forms, since their being exhausts their constitution, and so same being entails same properties. But one could take it more liberally to mean embodied being, so that substances whose embodied form is the same have the same properties.[24] There are

---

[23] ἐντελέχεια γάρ ἐστι τούτου [καὶ] ὑπὸ τοῦ κινητικοῦ. καὶ ἡ τοῦ κινητικοῦ δὲ ἐνέργεια οὐκ ἄλλη ἐστίν (202ᵃ14–15); μία ἡ ἀμφοῖν ἐνέργεια (202ᵃ18); οὔτε μίαν [sc. ἐνέργειαν] δυοῖν κωλύει οὐθὲν τὴν αὐτὴν εἶναι (202ᵇ8–9).

[24] Of course, if being picks out only the universal form, the entailment would not

The Union of Cause and Effect in Aristotle 225

other possible readings, but for our purposes the safe reading of mere forms gives us a clean contrast to the cases we are examining.

It is a cornerstone of Aristotelian substantial essentialism that if the essences are of different kinds, their substrata (at the same time) are different too, e.g. being a wolf and being a rabbit. But this is not the case with the causal agent and patient, which is why Aristotle is at pains to explain their unique metaphysics. What it is to be an agent is different from what it is to be a patient; their definitions are different (202^a20, $^b22$), and with them their kind (202^b1). But what makes the metaphysical situation of agency and patiency unique is that although the definitions stating their essence are different (202^b12), 'to act and to be acted on are one and the same' (202^b11).

But Aristotle's examples have already prepared us for understanding this statement. There is a kind of sameness that the route from Athens to Thebes has with the route from Thebes to Athens, because these routes are realized on the same road. The line from one to two is realized on the same interval as the line from two to one. In all such cases, their ground of realization is one and the same despite their essences being different in kind. Aristotle finally states this explicitly:

> To generalize, teaching is not the same in the primary sense [κυρίως] as learning, or agency as patiency, but that to which those belong [ᾧ ὑπάρχει] [sc. is the same for both], namely the motion [κίνησις]; for the actualization [ἐνέργεια] of this [teaching] in that [learning] and the actualization [ἐνέργεια] of that [learning] through the action of this [teaching] differ in definition. (202^b19-22)[25]

follow. Aristotle says in *Metaph. Δ* 6: 'Some things are one in number, others in species, others in genus . . . in number those whose matter is one, in species those whose definition is one . . . The latter kinds of unity are always found when the former are; for example, *things that are one in number are also one in species, while things that are one in species are not all one in number*' (1016^b31-6, emphasis added). So for our present passage, 202^b14-16, we need to assume embodiment if this is the particularizing principle, securing the numerical identity of the individuals. If one attributes to Aristotle a particularizing principle different from matter, then that principle can be understood to be evoked in the present passage.

[25] Since there is disagreement between interpreters on the translation of this passage, I report here the original text:

ὅλως δ᾽ εἰπεῖν οὐδ᾽ ἡ δίδαξις τῇ μαθήσει οὐδ᾽ ἡ ποίησις τῇ παθήσει τὸ αὐτὸ κυρίως, ἀλλ᾽ ᾧ ὑπάρχει ταῦτα, ἡ κίνησις·

As Hussey notes, there are two ways of understanding the passage:

(i) 'the change in which these things are present, i.e. of which it is true that it is an acting-upon and a being-acted-upon, is the same as the being acted upon';

226   *Anna Marmodoro*

The motion to which teaching and learning belong is the substratum of the two actualities. It is the exchange between the two substances which actualizes both the teaching and the learning. As such, the motion is the actuality of the agent's potentiality to teach and of the patient's potentiality to learn ($202^{a}13$–16), fulfilling both potentialities ($202^{a}16$, $^{a}18$). Since the two potentialities differ in kind, their actualities differ in kind too.[26] We are now faced

> (ii) 'but that in which these things are present, i.e. that of which it is true that it is both an acting-upon and a being-acted-upon, is the change' (*Physics*, 71)

The latter, (ii), is the way in which the majority of interpreters, including myself, read the passage (e.g. Philoponus 383. 21–2 Vitelli; Ross, *Physics*, 362; Gill, 'Causal Action', 137). Hussey, though, opts for (i) (*Physics*, 6), as does Charles (D. Charles, *Aristotle's Philosophy of Action [Action]* (London, 1984), 14). For, Hussey remarks, in (i) 'the extra point is made that the change is indeed the same in definition as the being-acted-upon (for change has been defined as an actuality of the changing thing)' (Hussy, *Physics*, 71). Hussey does not develop this point further, but Charles does, as he grounds on these lines his interpretation of the chapter, differing from that of the majority. I shall devote the discussion here to the arguments in support of, and against, translation (i), and discuss Charles's interpretation later in n. 28. Both Hussey and Charles acknowledge that on linguistic grounds readings (i) and (ii) of the passage are equally possible; the reasons why they prefer (i) to (ii) are mostly interpretative. Charles writes:

> I reject this translation [sc. the equivalent to Hussey's (ii)] because (a) it gives up the essential connection on which Aristotle elsewhere insists between the process and the suffering (202a14–6, b25–7); (b) it postulates a process which is non-directional (and non-relational) and thus conflicts with Aristotle's general view of the essences of processes as the realization of goal-directed capacities (201a16–8); (c) the grammar of 202b19–22 seems to require that the clause 'the process is the same in the primary sense' takes over both the notion in the primary sense from b20, and also the grammatical object with which it is the same in this sense: viz. the learning, suffering. (*Action*, 14)

In answer to (a), it is not true that by taking $\kappa\acute{\iota}\nu\eta\sigma\iota\varsigma$ as the ground of the instantiation for action and passion 'the essential connection . . . between the process and the suffering' is given up; rather, more than one essential connection is allowed, namely the relation to agency and also to patiency. In answer to (b), in my interpretation the nature of motion is to be found, not in the underlying physical activity, but in the two beings that this activity grounds, agency and patiency. Neither of its natures is truer of the motion than the other, any more than either direction of the route between Athens and Thebes is truer of the underlying road than the other. Aristotle's definition of change does not favour the one over the other. Change is no more the unfolding actuality of the potentiality of the patient as a patient than it is the unfolding actuality of the potentiality of the agent as an agent. In answer to (c), I defend my reading of the text on the ground that it is actually the most natural: it takes 'being one in the primary sense' to be retaining the same meaning throughout, and working as a predicate that has as its logical subjects on the one hand teaching and learning (as a pair) and action and passion (as a pair), and on the other hand 'that to which these things belong, namely the underlying process'.

[26] Because the agent's and the patient's capacities are *essentially different*, the

The Union of Cause and Effect in Aristotle 227

with three actualities, two of which are the third! The actualities of the two potentialities (for teaching and learning) are fulfilled in the interaction, the motion, which is their common actuality. No wonder Aristotle had difficulty expressing this; terminology let him down.

Teaching causes learning. Neither can happen without the other. The teacher is not teaching if the learner is not learning, and the learner (i.e. 'instructee') is not learning (being instructed) if the teacher is not teaching. These two potentialities can occur only together. Their interdependence is captured by the fact that they are actualized by one and the same activity, which cannot be separated into two. Both of them therefore characterize that activity, essentially, which in this case is an instance of teaching and learning. The activity bears the two forms in the way that matter bears the essential form in a substance, being en-formed by it. Except that here, the two forms come together in a package of interdependence; the activity is essentially both teaching and learning.

Neither oneness nor twoness can be sacrificed. The *oneness* of the activity reflects the interdependent actualization of the cause and the effect. The *twoness* of the activity preserves the polarity of the causal interaction; causes are born together with their effects. Is there a price to pay for this arithmetical versatility? What is lost is the unity of substance, or the autonomy of being a subject: neither teaching nor learning can stand on its own, the way substances do; they stand and fall together. Nor do we have quite two subjects, either, since neither is autonomous—changes in the internal properties of the one result in changes in the internal properties of the

---

one being the capacity of transmitting the form and the other being the capacity to receive the transmissible form, the realization of the two different capacities is also essentially different. Charles shows on the basis of an investigation of various passages of the *Physics* that

> A process is one in number only if it is one in essence . . . but the essence of each thing is defined when one says what it is to be that thing (1017b21–3). If so, processes are one in number only if the definitions of what it is to be that thing are identical. (*Action*, 10)

> Aristotelian processes are essentially realisations of given capacities of given subjects: their essential properties include the subject of change and the end point of the type of change (i.e. its goal). They are distinct if they do not share all essential properties. (ibid., 18)

> It follows that in III 3 teaching and learning must be numerically distinct processes since they differ in essence. (ibid., 18)

228 *Anna Marmodoro*

other, as would readily follow if the teacher taught a slightly different lesson. Together, they comprise a *new type of entity*, which has an ontological status of its own.

The new type of entity—call it a *two-in-one* entity—consists of two natures grounded on an underlying physical activity. The activity supports both natures together because of the relation that these two natures have to each other. They are interdependent in different ways, such as being coexistent and covariant, which is secured by their mutual dependence on the underlying activity.[27] And of course, the entity itself is further dependent on the two substances to which the two actualized potentialities belong. The one type of activity is the agent's actualized potentiality and cause, and the other type of activity is the patient's actualized potentiality and effect; the two are bonded together by interdependencies through their grounding on the underlying physical activity. Thus, for example, the physical movement of the carpenter's hands and chisel on the hard wood constitutes the carpenter's carving, and the log's being shaped into a statue.

Although the same type of dependencies binds together causal and non-causal complexes, e.g. teaching and learning but also the overlapping routes, there is a fundamental difference between them. Non-causal two-in-one entities are ontologically autonomous complex entities, such as two opposite overlapping vectors, while causal two-in-one entities, such as teaching and learning, are ontologically dependent on the substances which they causally unite.

Having examined the nature of the causal interaction between the two substances, I conclude by commenting on an explanatory remark Aristotle makes regarding the mutual actualization of the cause and the effect. In describing his own position on the oneness of the actualities of the agent and the patient (202^b8-22), where, as we saw, he explains that they share the same substratum, he introduces it by saying:

There is nothing to prevent two things having one and the same actualization (not the same in being, but related as the potential to the actual). (202^b8-10)

[27] Determining the details of the ontological interdependence of the two natures, through their relation to their underlying activity, would take us beyond Aristotle's text into metaphysical considerations which can be built on Aristotle's examples, but which are not to be found explicitly in the text. For an account of the metaphysical structure of the two-in-one entity see A. Marmodoro, 'It's a Colorful World', *American Philosophical Quarterly*, 43/1 (2006), 71–80.

The Union of Cause and Effect in Aristotle 229

Here he is making the same point with which he concludes this section, that what is common between two coactualized potentialities is not their respective actualities, which are different kinds of being (e.g. teaching and learning), but their substratum, the underlying process. The way Aristotle introduces this position is by the potentialities of the agent and the patient having one and the same actualization, not by becoming one thing, not even by realizing the same type of being, but by having one and the same process actualize both of them, underlying them both 'as the potential to the actual'. So the potentialities for agency and patiency are actualized in a common process which underlies their two actualizations, the activity of agency (teaching) and that of patiency (learning). This common grounding process underlies the beings of the two activities as potential to actual. For example, the physical process of the embroidering hands and needle on the material is related to the (realized being of) embroidering and to the (realized being of) the decoration of the material in the way that the wood is related to the statue of Hermes. Thus, although in the dilemma Aristotle objected to two potentialities having one and the same actuality because teaching would end up being the same as learning (202^b1–5), here he avoids this objection by saying that what is the same is only their *underlying actualization process, not their actuality*. They are two mutually bound potentialities in that they can be actualized only together in an actualization process that is one and the same in the sense that it cannot be divided into two processes, despite the two activity beings that it grounds, e.g. teaching and learning, or sculpting and being carved into shape. Because of the brevity of the description at 202^b8–10, different readings of it can justifiably be given, leading to alternative understandings of the relation between the potential and the actual. In particular, it can be read as saying that the actuality of the patient is the potential for the actuality of the agent, related to it as matter to form.[28] But I have argued that the

---

[28] This is the interpretation suggested by Charles on the ground of his and Hussey's translation of 202^b14–19 (see above, n. 25):

> Teaching and learning are numerically distinct, but are one in some sense because the teaching 'belongs to' the learning which 'underlies it'. Because Aristotle identifies the process strictly with the learning (the capacity of the patient: see also 202a14–16; b25–7), there is no non-directional process which underlies both teaching and learning . . . The learning is the underlying process which stands to the teaching in a relation akin to that of matter to form, because the latter 'imprints' on the learner the knowledge which he had possessed previously only

230 *Anna Marmodoro*

subsequent explanation Aristotle gives in the same passage, and his examples, support the common-underlying-activity interpretation.

University of Edinburgh

APPENDIX

The Argument in the Actualities of Motion Dilemma

In the structured representation of the argument below, the convention I follow is to indent under the conclusion the premises or the subarguments pertinent to the support of that conclusion. The premises justifying or objecting to a conclusion are grouped in the same level of indentation. I indicate in parentheses the premises I have supplied for completeness in addition to what is found in Aristotle's text.

C The realization of the agent's and the patient's capacities are neither the same nor different. (Supplied.)

> **P 1** Because it is impossible that the realization of the agent's capacity is different from the realization of the patient's capacity. (Supplied.)
>
>> **P 2** Because if the realization of the agent's capacity is different (in number) from the realization of the patient's capacity, one of the following disjuncts is true: **(2.1)** either both are realized in the patient; **(2.2)** or both are realized in the agent; **(2.3)** or one is realized in the agent and one in the patient: for example, the realization of the agent's capacity takes place in the agent and the realization of the patient's capacity takes place in the patient. (See 202^{a}25–7; **(2.2)** and **(2.3)** are supplied.)
>>
>> **P 3** But none of the disjuncts is true.
>>
>>> **P 4** Because **(2.1)** is impossible. Namely, it is impossible that the realization of the agent's capacity and the realization of the patient's capacity are both in the patient. (Supplied.)
>>>
>>>> **P 5** Because if the realization of the agent's capacity and the realization of the patient's capacity are both in the patient, then

potentially (202a9–12). (*Action*, 15)

Hussey finds the following in 202^{b}8–10:

Aristotle has in mind sophistic puzzles such as that about Socrates, who, at first unmusical, then becomes musical. The unmusical Socrates is potentially musical, the musical Socrates is 'operating' in respect of musicality. 'They' are one and the same man: yet different, incompatible things are true of the 'two Socrateses'. Accordingly, for Aristotle 'they' are not one in definition. (*Physics*, 72)

The Union of Cause and Effect in Aristotle   231

both consequences follow: **(5.1)** the agent's capacity will not be realized in the subject that has the capacity, the agent; **(5.2)** the same subject, the patient, will undergo the realization of two [opposite] capacities at the same time in relation to one form. (See 202^{a}33–6.)

P 6 But **(5.1)** is nonsense (202^{a}36).

P 7 And **(5.2)** is impossible (202^{a}36).

P 8 And *mutatis mutandis* for **(2.2)**. (See 202^{a}29–30.)

P 9 And it is impossible that the realization of the agent's capacity takes place in the agent, and realization of the patient's capacity takes place in the patient. (Supplied.)

P 10 Because if the realization of the agent's capacity and the realization of the patient's capacity are each in each, then one of the following disjuncts is true: **(10.1)** either every agent will also be acted upon; **(10.2)** or the agent, having causal efficacy, will not be causally efficacious. (See 202^{a}28–^{b}1.)

P 11 But **(10.1)** is false, and leads to infinite regress. (Supplied.)

P 12 And **(10.2)** is false. (Supplied.)

P 13 And it is impossible that the realization of the agent's capacity is one and the same with the realization of the patient's capacity (202^{a}36–^{b}2).

P 14 Because then agency and patiency would have the same actuality, and so acting and being acted upon would be the same thing. (See 202^{b}2–5 for the example.)

P 15 But agency and patiency are not the same actuality. (Supplied.)

P 16 Because agency and patiency are different in essence. (Supplied.)

P 17 Because the agent's capacity to act and the patient's capacity to suffer are essentially different things. (See 202^{a}20 and 201^{b}1.)

P 18 And the essence of an actuality is the same as the essence of its capacity. (Supplied.)

P 19 And it is nonsense that two things different in essence, e.g. the agent's acting and the patient's being acted upon, have one and the same actuality (202^{a}36–^{b}2).

P 20 Because the actuality of something is the instantiation of its essence. (Supplied.)

BIBLIOGRAPHY

Averroes, *Aristotelis De physico auditu libri octo. Cum Averrois Cordubensis variis in eosdem commentariis* [*Physica*], in *Aristotelis opera cum Averrois commentariis* (Venice, 1562–74; repr. Frankfurt a.M., 1964), vol. iv.

Barnes, J. (ed.), *The Complete Works of Aristotle: The Revised Oxford Translation* (Princeton 1984).

Blackwell, R. J., Spath, R. J., and Thirlkel, W. E. (trans.), *Thomas Aquinas: Commentary on Aristotle's Physics* [*Physics*] (London, 1963).

Charles, D., *Aristotle's Philosophy of Action* [*Action*] (London, 1984).

Edwards, M. (trans.), *Philoponus: On Aristotle, Physics 3* (London, 1994).

Gill, M. L., 'Aristotle's Theory of Causal Action in *Physics* III 3' ['Causal Action'], *Phronesis*, 25 (1980), 129–47.

Hussey, E., *Aristotle's* Physics, *Books III and IV* [*Physics*] (Oxford, 1983).

Kosman, L. A., 'Perceiving that We Perceive: *On the Soul* III, 2', *Philosophical Review*, 84/4 (1975), 499–519.

Luna, C., 'La relation chez Simplicius', in I. Hadot (ed.), *Simplicius: sa vie, son œuvre, sa survie* (Berlin, 1987), 113–48.

Marmodoro, A., 'It's a Colorful World', *American Philosophical Quarterly*, 43/1 (2006), 71–80.

Ross, D., *Aristotle's* Physics: *A Revised Text with Introduction and Commentary* [*Physics*] (Oxford, 1936; repr. 1979).

Urmson, J. O. (trans.), *Simplicius: On Aristotle, Physics 3* (London, 2002).

Waterlow, S., *Nature, Change, and Agency in Aristotle's Physics* [*Physics*] (Oxford, 1982).

Zabarella, J., *In libros Aristotelis Physicorum commentarii* (Venice, 1601).

ARISTOTELIAN INFINITY

JOHN BOWIN

ARISTOTLE begins his treatment of the infinite in book 3 of the *Physics* in an overtly systematic fashion. The *Physics*, he says, is a study of nature, and nature has been defined as a principle of change and rest. Change, in turn, is thought to be something continuous, and what is continuous is thought to be infinitely divisible. So the topic of the infinite falls neatly out of the topic of nature. It follows, then, that the student of nature must first investigate whether the infinite exists or not, and then, if it exists, enquire how it exists. It is clear that the infinite must exist in *some* sense, because if it did not, 'many impossible consequences' would result, such as a beginning and an end of time, and the existence of indivisible lines. It remains, then, to determine in what sense the infinite does exist, and in what sense it does not. Aristotle reminds us, at the beginning of his positive account of infinity in chapter 6, that to exist means either to exist actually or to exist potentially, so if the infinite exists, it must exist in one of these senses. The previous two chapters have established that the infinite cannot exist actually, so, by disjunctive syllogism, the infinite must exist potentially. In Aristotle's words, 'The alternative then remains that the infinite has a potential existence' (*Phys.* 3. 6, 206ᵃ18–19).

Jonathan Lear is right to point out that what is at stake, for Aristotle, in the rejection of the actual infinite is 'the possibility of philosophy—of man's ability to comprehend the world—[which] depends on the fact that the world is a finite place containing objects that are themselves finite'. In Aristotle's view, our ability to understand the world amounts to our ability to comprehend substances or actualities, and we could not do this if the definitions of

© John Bowin 2007

I would like to thank R. James Hankinson, Alexander Mourelatos, Paul Roth, David Sedley, Stephen White, Paul Woodruff, and especially Richard Sorabji for their comments on drafts of this paper.

234 *John Bowin*

these things were infinitely complex (*Post. An.* 82ᵇ37–9). What I wish to emphasize for the purpose of this paper, however, is that the rejection of the actual infinite also positions the concept of potentiality at the core of Aristotle's positive account of infinity in chapter 6. The only alternative in sight, at the beginning of this chapter, is that the infinite has a potential existence.

Of course, the force of this conclusion is that the infinite has *only* a potential existence, and never an actual one, since actual infinities have been categorically ruled out. Aristotle emphasizes this point in the following passage:

But we must not construe potential existence in the way we do when we say that it is possible for this to be a statue—this will be a statue, but something infinite will not be in actuality. (*Phys.* 206ᵃ18–21)[1]

As Aristotle proceeds to explain how the infinite exists potentially, however, his train of thought becomes less clear. The text continues as follows:

Being is spoken of in many ways, and we say that the infinite is in the sense in which we say it is day or it is the games, because one thing after another is always coming into existence. For of these things too the distinction between potential and actual existence holds. We say that there are Olympic Games, both in the sense that they may occur and that they are actually occurring. (*Phys.* 206ᵃ21–5)

At first sight, Aristotle seems to be telling us that the potential infinite exists as a process exists which may occur but is not yet occurring. Infinity, we are told, exists as a process does, and processes, like substances, are either potential or actual: they are potential when they may occur and actual when they do occur. We already know that infinity exists potentially, not actually, so infinity must exist potentially in the sense that a process exists potentially, viz. as a process which may occur but is not yet occurring. Twenty-one lines later at 206ᵇ13–14, however, we are told that infinity exists in actuality as a process that *is* now occurring—it 'exists in actuality [ἐντελεχείᾳ] in the sense in which we say "it is day" or "it is the games"'. If we are to save Aristotle from contradiction, we must revise our hypothesis of how the infinite's status as potential relates to its existence as a process. Clearly, if the ban on actual infinities is

[1] Translations of Aristotle in this paper are, with minor modifications, from *The Complete Works of Aristotle: The Revised Oxford Translation*, ed. J. Barnes (Princeton, 1984).

Aristotelian Infinity 235

to hold, then there needs to be a sense in which existing in actuality as a presently occurring process is also existing potentially.

Unfortunately, there is no explicit solution to this problem in the text. Instead, we get an account of how the infinite exists as matter exists, which seems to compete with the notion that the potential infinite exists as a process, rather than illuminate it. This, I believe, is the chief difficulty that we face in interpreting Aristotle's notion of infinity, and the chief reason why so much ink has been spilt on the subject by commentators. In the sequel, I shall give an account of how existing as processes do relates to existing potentially. I shall also show how, so far from conflicting or competing with each other, the concepts of existing as matter exists and existing as processes exist actually complement one another in Aristotle's account. Finally, I shall make use of Aristotle's claim that infinity is a *per se* accident of number and magnitude (συμβεβηκὸς καθ' αὑτό) at *Physics* 203ᵇ33 and 204ᵃ18–19 in order to reconcile the notion of potentially infinite processes with a passage in *Physics* 6. 10 that seems to rule them out, and with Aristotle's definition of change in *Physics* 3. 1 that conflicts with their lack of a *telos*. But first I need to deal with what I regard as a red herring.

I

The passage at the beginning of chapter 6 that I have been quoting continues as follows:

The infinite exhibits itself in different ways—in time, in the generations of man, and in the division of magnitudes. For generally the infinite has this mode of existence: one thing is always being taken after another, and each thing that is taken is always finite, but always different. Again, 'being' is spoken of in several ways, so that we must not regard the infinite like a 'this', such as a man or a horse, but must suppose it to exist in the sense in which we speak of the day or the games as existing—things whose being has not come to them like that of a substance, but consists in a process of coming to be or passing away, finite, yet always different. But in spatial magnitudes, what is taken persists, while in the succession of time and of men it takes place by the passing away of these in such a way that the source of supply never gives out. (*Phys.* 206ᵃ25–ᵇ3)

This passage claims that in the case of the infinite division of a magnitude, 'what is taken' persists, while in the succession of time

236 *John Bowin*

and of men it does not, a point that is reiterated at the end of chapter 8, in answer to an argument claiming that the infinite exists not only potentially but also actually as a 'separate thing':

> It remains to go through the arguments which are supposed to support the view that the infinite exists not only potentially but as a separate thing. Some have no cogency; others can be met by fresh objections that are true. . . . Time indeed and movement are infinite, and also thinking; but the parts that are taken do not persist. (*Phys.* 208^{a}5–23)

This passage is elliptical, but the main points are clear: someone (perhaps even Aristotle himself anticipating an objection) has suggested that time, movement, and thought are actually infinite (exist 'as a separate thing' rather than in potentiality). The reason Aristotle gives for these things not being actually infinite is that their *past* parts have passed out of existence. Hence, the reason why they were originally taken to be actually infinite must have turned on the number of their *past* parts. We know Aristotle held that there was no beginning of time, so, on this assumption, the past parts of time must have been infinitely numerous. We also know Aristotle held that the present cosmological order had existed in its present state for an eternity of past time, which requires, among other things, the existence of infinitely many past rotations of the celestial spheres. Hence, in the case of time and movement at any rate, it must have been these or similar infinities which were alleged to be actual.[2] The argument just reconstructed is the same, in substance, as the one raised by John Philoponus against the pagan Neoplatonist Proclus in the sixth century AD. Philoponus, in order to vindicate the Old Testament account of the creation of the universe, was trying to disprove the Aristotelian doctrine, adopted by the pagan Neoplatonists, that time and the world had no beginning. Philoponus argued that if the present cosmological order had existed in its present state for an eternity of past time, then time and the past generations of men and plants and the other individuals in each species would be actually infinite:

> If the world *had* existed from everlasting, it would be absolutely necessary for the number of things that have come into existence in the world from the beginning up until now—I mean men and plants and the other individuals in each species—to have become actually infinite as well. For should one

---

[2] Past thoughts may be infinitely numerous too, presumably, in the case of an immortal being.

Aristotelian Infinity 237

hypothesize that the number of men or plants or of individuals of any other kind that have come to be is finite, since each of them has had its existence in a finite time, it would also be necessary for the whole of time to be finite; for that which consists of finite [parts] is finite. So since, if the world is ungenerated, the time that has elapsed is also actually infinite, the individual things that have come to be in this infinite time must, I imagine, also be actually infinite in number. And so it will follow that, if the world is ungenerated, an infinite number actually exists and has occurred. (*De aeternitate mundi contra Proclum*, 9. 4–20 Rabe)[3]

Simplicius, a contemporary of Philoponus, answers this objection on behalf of the pagan Neoplatonists by drawing attention to the fact that Aristotle had already addressed this problem in the *Physics*: that is, past generations of men, for instance, escape being an actual infinity because they do not persist. Simplicius' preoccupation with this issue, however, causes him to offer a misleading gloss on Aristotle's distinction between existing as a substance and existing as a process. In *Physics* 206ª25–ᵇ3 Aristotle tells us that the latter mode of existence 'consists in a process of coming to be or passing away', while the former mode does not, and that processes involve 'one thing . . . always being taken after another'. Simplicius, however, claims that the gist of this distinction is that the parts of a substance exist 'all at once' ($\dot{\alpha}\theta\rho\dot{o}\omega\varsigma$ or $\ddot{\alpha}\mu\alpha$) while the parts of a process do not, and that time and the past generations of men escape being actual infinities *because* they do not all exist simultaneously.[4] This turned out to be a very influential reading. Aquinas adopts it without modification, as well as the claim that it solves the problem of past infinities,[5] and Kant argues for a similar distinction (without mentioning Aristotle) in his First Antinomy.[6] Clearly, it is true that the parts of a process do not exist all at once, in part because the past parts of a process do not persist. And by glossing the distinction in this way, Simplicius handily combines the notion of existing as a process with the claim that past times and generations of men do not persist. But there is a good reason to keep these issues distinct: for Aristotle, at least, the status of the past parts of a

---

[3] Trans. M. Share, *Philoponus: Against Proclus, On the Eternity of the World* 1–5 (London, 2004), 23–4.

[4] *In Phys.* 494. 14–495. 5 Diels; cf. 492. 26, 493. 10, 497. 15.

[5] *In Phys.*, lib. 3, l. 10, nn. 4–6.

[6] 'Demnach kann ein unendliches Aggregat wirklicher Dinge nicht als ein gegebenes Ganzes, mithin auch nicht als zugleich gegeben, angesehen werden' (Immanuel Kant, *Kritik der reinen Vernunft*, B 456).

238   *John Bowin*

process can have nothing to do with the way in which a process exists *potentially*, and, therefore, with the way in which infinity exists *potentially* as a process exists.

In *Nicomachean Ethics* 6. 2 Aristotle tells us: 'What is past is not capable of not having taken place; hence Agathon is right in saying "For this alone is lacking even to God, to make undone things that have once been done"' (*NE* 1139^{b}7–9); and in *De caelo* 1. 12 he says: 'No potentiality relates to being in the past, but always being in the present or future' (283^{b}13–14). I infer from these passages that no potentiality attaches to what has already happened, including the past phases of a process. Since this is the case, the status of these phases can have no bearing on the sense in which processes exist potentially and, therefore, on the sense in which the infinite exists potentially as a process does. Thus, the claim that the past generations of men escape being an actual infinity because they do not persist can have no relation to the claim that the infinite exists potentially, and if the central tenet of Aristotle's theory is that the infinite exists potentially, then the former claim must be wholly extraneous to that theory. This is one reason why invoking the non-persistence of past men and time sits poorly with the rest of Aristotle's discussion. Another is recognized by Simplicius himself, who notes that if the fact that men perish saves their number from being an actual infinity, it also saves them from being *any* sort of infinity, whether actual or potential, because the number of men at any time does not even tend towards infinity (*In Phys.* 506. 5 ff. Diels). But one of the motivations for positing a 'potential' infinity was to account for the prima facie infinity of the generations of men.

Clearly, what Aristotle has in mind is just that the process of generation and the advance of time go on and on without limit. Chapter 6 shows Aristotle entirely focused on this aspect of processes. He speaks of 'dividing *ad infinitum* [εἰς ἄπειρον]' (206^{b}5–6), which with the accusative implies a movement towards but not an arrival at infinity. When he claims that the infinite exists as processes do, such as days and Olympic Games, he says: 'one thing after another [ἄλλο καὶ ἄλλο] is always coming into existence' (206^{a}22). The examples of infinities Aristotle is trying to account for are disparate (e.g. time, generations of men, divisions of a magnitude), but he emphasizes that, even so, they all exist in the sense that 'one thing is always being taken after [ἄλλο καὶ ἄλλο] another' (206^{a}27–8). The problem that Philoponus raises, however, and which Aristotle re-

Aristotelian Infinity 239

cognizes himself in chapter 8, is not a problem about 'one thing always being taken after another'. It is a problem, rather, of one thing always preceding another. In other words, it is a problem of infinite *pre*cession rather than infinite *suc*cession. And as such, I think it caught Aristotle completely off guard, since his theory of the potential infinite was clearly devised to explain the latter. When faced with the prospect of admitting an actual infinity of past days and men, Aristotle had no choice but to opt for the *ad hoc* expedient of claiming that the past times and generations of men escape being an actual infinity because they do not persist. As we attempt to interpret Aristotle's notion of potential infinity, then, and in particular as we attempt to explain how existing as processes do relates to existing potentially, we can only regard this issue of persistence as a red herring, and must, at any rate, not conflate it with the relevant sense in which processes exist, which I shall now endeavour to describe.

II

To avoid saddling Aristotle with a contradiction, we must find a sense in which existing actually as a presently occurring process exists is also existing potentially, since the infinite was said to exist actually in this way. Sentences such as 'one thing after another [ἄλλο καὶ ἄλλο] is always coming into existence' (*Phys.* 206ᵃ22) seem to suggest the existence of an inexhaustible store of unfulfilled *future* possibilities for dividing, counting, etc. Perhaps presently occurring processes also exist potentially because they have these unfulfilled future potentialities. Charlton objects that this cannot be so.[7] If all there is to existing potentially (δυνάμει) is to have unfulfilled potentialities, 'we should all exist δυνάμει'. But since we are told that infinity exists as a process exists, this objection ignores a relevant difference in the way in which substances and processes have potentialities. Simplicius highlights this point in his commentary on chapter 6:

Just as the actuality of the changeable preserving the potential is change, so is the actuality of the unlimited. Just as things having their being in becoming lose their being in losing their becoming, so things whose being

[7] W. Charlton, 'Aristotle's Potential Infinites', in L. Judson (ed.), *Aristotle's Physics: A Collection of Essays* (Oxford, 1995), 129–49 at 145.

240 *John Bowin*

is in potentiality exist just so long as their potentiality exists. (*In Phys.* 493. 24–7 Diels)[8]

As Simplicius points out, Aristotle tells us at the beginning of book 3 of the *Physics* that a motion exists only in so far as, and as long as, it has the unfulfilled potentiality of being completed by the arrival of the moving thing at a goal state that is intrinsic to the motion. A motion is an actuality of a potentiality for a moving thing to be en route to a goal, but as long as the moving thing is en route, the motion is an actuality *qua* existing potentially since it is potentially, but not actually, completed.[9] Once this potentiality is realized, the motion no longer exists, but as long as it does exist, the motion has this unfulfilled potentiality. So one could say that a motion always has an unfulfilled potentiality, but this is different from saying that someone always has the potential to be a concert violinist. Substances, of course, always have unfulfilled potentialities, including potentialities to achieve states that are uniquely determined by their natures, but they do not exist in so far as, and as long as, they have these potentialities, as changes do.

Moreover, substances are not incomplete by virtue of having unrealized potentialities, whereas processes are. 'Change', says Aristotle, 'is thought to be a sort of actuality, but incomplete, the reason for this view being that the potential whose actuality it is is incomplete' (*Phys.* 201^{b}31–3). Aristotle refers back to this conclusion a number of times, at *Physics* 257^{b}6–9, *De anima* 417^{a}16–17 and 431^{a}6–7, and *Metaphysics* 1048^{b}29–30, but at *Nicomachean Ethics* 1174^{b}2–5 he gives the reason for this incompleteness, viz. 'the whence and whither give [changes] their form'. Change is not simply the actuality of a potentiality to be in any chance state, but rather, it is the actuality of a potentiality to be in a state that is the incomplete realization of a particular goal (i.e. the 'whither'). If manhood is the goal, for instance, change is the actuality of the potentiality to be en route to manhood. It is the actuality of the potentiality to be a teenager, for instance. But while the process of growth may be said to be incomplete, the teenager himself is not. He has the same form or species essence as the grown man, and none of his constitutive parts is missing.

A thing is incomplete if it has some of its constitutive parts miss-

---

[8] Trans. J. O. Urmson, *Simplicius: On Aristotle, Physics 3* (London, 2002), 116.

[9] As Aristotle puts it, 'change is the actuality of what exists potentially, *qua* existing potentially' (*Phys.* 201^{a}10–11).

Aristotelian Infinity 241

ing, and indeed there are always some temporal parts of a process that are not present. Commentators have often assumed that this is what Aristotle means when he says that the potential infinite exists as processes do and then describes it as incomplete, as he does in the following passage:

Thus something is infinite if, taking it quantity by quantity, we can always take something outside. On the other hand, what has nothing outside it is complete and whole. For thus we define the whole—that from which nothing is wanting, as a whole man or box. What is true of each particular is true of the whole properly speaking—the whole is that of which nothing is outside. On the other hand, that from which something is absent and outside, however small that may be, is not 'all'. Whole and complete are either quite identical or closely akin. Nothing is complete [τέλειον] which has no end [τέλος] and the end is a limit. (*Phys.* 207ª7–15)

But processes are not incomplete simply because some of their temporal parts are not present. Processes are incomplete because they are actualities that fall short of a goal state. What is unusual about processes that go on and on indefinitely is that they have no goal state. In the passage just quoted, Aristotle argues that what is incomplete always has something outside it, and 'nothing is complete [τέλειον] which has no end [τέλος]; and the end is a limit' (*Phys.* 207ª14–15). The absence of a goal or end, then, is a sufficient condition for a process always to have something outside of itself, which is, in turn, a sufficient condition for the infinite to be suspended in a perpetual state of potentiality. Thus, as Aristotle says about the process of dividing a continuous magnitude, 'the fact that the indefinitely extendable process of dividing never comes to an end ensures that this activity exists potentially' (*Metaph.* Θ 6, 1048ᵇ14–17).

III

At *Physics* 206ᵇ14–16 Aristotle says: 'the infinite . . . exists . . . potentially as matter exists, not *per se* [καθ᾽ αὑτό] as what is finite does'. He expands on this claim in the following three passages:

[The infinite] is in fact the matter of the completeness which belongs to magnitude, and what is potentially a whole, though not in actuality. It is divisible both in the direction of reduction and of the inverse addition. It

242 *John Bowin*

is a whole and limited; not, however, *per se*, but in virtue of something else. It does not contain, but, in so far as it is infinite, is contained. Consequently, also, it is unknowable, *qua* infinite; for the matter has no form. (Hence it is plain that the infinite stands in the relation of part more than of whole. For the matter is part of the whole, as the bronze is of the bronze statue.) (*Phys.* 207^{a}21–32)

The matter and the infinite are contained inside what contains them, while it is the form which contains. (*Phys.* 207^{a}35–^{b}1)

In the fourfold scheme of causes, it is plain that the infinite is a cause in the sense of matter, and that its essence is privation, the subject *per se* being what is continuous and sensible. All the other thinkers, too, evidently treat the infinite as matter—that is why it is ridiculous of them to make it what contains, and not what is contained. (*Phys.* 207^{b}34–208^{a}4)

In the discussion of place in *Physics* 4. 2 (209^{b}5–8) Aristotle identifies the spatial extension of a magnitude with its matter, and the magnitude itself with a form/matter composite consisting of a bounding surface and a spatial extension respectively. If this is the definition of a magnitude, and the infinite '*is* the matter of the completeness which belongs to magnitude', then the point of the passages just quoted appears to be that the infinite, understood as *what is* infinite, is to be identified with the material element or material cause of a form/matter composite. As matter, what is infinite is potentially but not actually complete and whole. It is complete and whole in so far as it is limited and contained by form, but only potentially so, because, as matter, form does not belong to it *per se*. Thus, what is infinite is unbounded, or ἄπειρος, in the sense that it is unlimited by anything *intrinsic* to it. The first passage also tells us that what is infinite, i.e. matter, is 'divisible both in the direction of reduction and of the inverse addition' (207^{a}22–3), which I take to mean *infinite* divisibility. Aristotle has told us at 206^{b}16–20 that divisibility in the direction of reduction, or the infinite in respect of division, is 'in a sense the same' as divisibility in the direction of the inverse addition, or the infinite in respect of addition. This amounts to the claim that the division of a magnitude according to an infinite geometric sequence such as $\frac{1}{2}, \frac{1}{4}, \frac{1}{8}, \ldots, \frac{1}{2^n}, \ldots$ ($n = 1, 2, 3, \ldots$), for instance, can also be viewed as the summation of the parts divided according to the infinite series $\frac{1}{2} + \frac{1}{4} + \frac{1}{8} + \ldots + \frac{1}{2^n} + \ldots$ ($n = 1, 2, 3, \ldots$), or rather, according to the sequence of partial sums $\frac{1}{2}, (\frac{1}{2} + \frac{1}{4}), (\frac{1}{2} + \frac{1}{4} + \frac{1}{8}), \ldots, (\frac{1}{2} + \frac{1}{4} + \frac{1}{8} + \ldots + \frac{1}{2^n}), \ldots$ ($n = 1, 2, 3, \ldots$). The infinite divisibility of a magnitude by reduction

Aristotelian Infinity

and addition relates to the potential completeness and wholeness of a magnitude in respect of the status of the material parts produced and added in this way. A magnitude is complete and whole if it has all of its material parts. But a magnitude has all of its material parts only potentially since new material parts may always be produced by additional divisions and added to the collection of material parts already produced. Thus, the infinite divisibility of a magnitude is the cause of its being complete and whole only potentially, and the material element, in turn, is the source of this infinite divisibility. Thus, potential infinity is a property that the material element of a form/matter composite (i.e. 'the infinite' understood as 'what is infinite') contributes to the form/matter composite, viz. its infinite divisibility, or conversely, its being filled out by a potentially infinite number of material parts.

At first sight, we seem to have competing accounts of potential infinity: one where infinity exists as a process, and one where it exists as matter. Recent commentators have tried to promote one of these accounts at the expense of the other. Hintikka, who favours the notion that infinity exists as a process, claims that the assimilation of infinity to matter is a remnant of a superseded earlier line of thinking.[10] Jonathan Lear takes the opposite extreme by locating potential infinity entirely in the 'structure of the magnitude', and demoting process to the role of merely 'bearing witness' to the potential infinite.[11]

Hintikka's chief reason for preferring the notion that infinity exists as a process exists is that it saves the 'principle of plenitude', or the doctrine that every genuine possibility is actualized in the fullness of time. In accordance with the principle of plenitude, claims Hintikka, actually infinite sets of objects *do* come to be in the fullness of time, just not simultaneously. They come to be successively as processes do. Lear points out that, while this might have some plausibility in the case of time, it loses all plausibility in the case of the infinite division of a magnitude because it seems to commit Aristotle to the view that there *will* be a magnitude that is endlessly divided.[12] But we need not feel obliged to accommodate the principle of plenitude at all costs since there is evidence that Aris-

---

[10] J. Hintikka, 'Aristotelian Infinity', *Philosophical Review*, 75 (1966), 197–218 at 207.

[11] J. Lear, 'Aristotelian Infinity', *Proceedings of the Aristotelian Society*, 80 (1979), 187–210 at 191. [12] Ibid. 190.

244 *John Bowin*

totle meant it to apply only within a restricted domain of objects. Sorabji has pointed out that in all clear cases where Aristotle accepts the principle of plenitude, it concerns everlasting properties of everlasting objects.[13]

Lear makes his case for favouring the notion that infinity exists as matter exists by emphasizing how Aristotle reduces the infinite by addition as well as the infinite extendability of the natural numbers to the infinite divisibility of magnitudes. Since Aristotle thinks the universe is only finitely large, he must say that magnitude is not indefinitely extendable by the addition of unit lengths (and, thus, is not even infinite potentially: *Phys.* 206^{b}12–13). Rather, a magnitude is indefinitely extendable only by the addition of parts according to a convergent infinite series—that is, only by adding parts resulting from the infinite division of a magnitude. Hence, Aristotle says, 'In a way the infinite by addition is the same thing as the infinite by division' (*Phys.* 206^{b}3–4). He then takes the further step of claiming that our ability to think of ever larger natural numbers also depends upon the infinite divisibility of magnitudes:

In the direction of largeness it is always possible to think of a larger number; *for* [γάρ] the number of times a magnitude can be bisected is infinite. Hence this infinite is potential, not actual: the number of parts that can be taken always surpasses any definite amount. (*Phys.* 207^{b}10–13)

All of this emphasis on the infinite divisibility of magnitudes does seem to focus Aristotle's account away from the case of time and towards the structure of magnitudes. But even so, Aristotle still talks about *processes* of division. For example, he says: 'For just as we see division going on *ad infinitum* [διαιρούμενον εἰς ἄπειρον], so we see addition being made in the same proportion to what is already marked off' (*Phys.* 206^{b}5–6). What Lear needs to do, in order to make his case that these processes only 'bear witness' to potential infinity, is to establish that infinite divisibility is a property that a magnitude can possess independently of any process of division. Lear thinks he has found his evidence in *Physics* 8. 8, where Aristotle claims that a magnitude has an infinite number of potential parts (*Phys.* 263^{a}28–9, 263^{b}3–9). Aristotle tells us at *De*

[13] R. Sorabji, *Necessity, Cause, and Blame: Perspectives on Aristotle's Theory* (London, 1980), 128–35. For a refutation of the claim that *Metaph.* 1047^{b}4–6 endorses the principle of plenitude without restriction see R. T. McClelland, 'Time and Modality in Aristotle, Metaphysics IX, 3–4', *Archiv für Geschichte der Philosophie*, 63 (1981), 130–49.

anima 430^{b}11 that an 'object has no actual parts until it has been divided', so clearly, the existence of a process is required for a potentially infinite (i.e. infinitely increasable) collection of *actual* parts. No process seems to be required, however, for the existence of *potential* parts, and indeed, it does not seem possible to change the number of potential parts of a magnitude through any operation. If we can equate having an infinite number of potential parts with being infinitely divisible, then, perhaps, it might seem plausible to say that processes just 'bear witness' to potential infinity.

The first problem I see with this account is that dividing a magnitude would bear witness to an *actual* infinity rather than a potential infinity. If a potential infinity is a quantity that can be increased without limit, and, as we just said, it is not possible to change the quantity of the potential parts of a magnitude, then the quantity of the potential parts of a magnitude will not be potentially infinite. Aristotle says that these parts constitute *some* sort of infinity, so it remains for them to be actually infinite. The process of division, then, would 'bear witness' to an *actual* infinity of potential parts. And if having an infinite number of potential parts is the same as being infinitely divisible, this process would bear witness to a magnitude being actually infinite by division. But Lear himself says: 'No actual process of division could bear witness to a length being actually infinite by division.' This may be a problem for Aristotle, however, as well as for Lear. Sorabji thinks Aristotle's admission of an actual infinity of potential parts in *Physics* 8. 8 is a mistake,[14] and I tend to agree, since it conflicts with his prohibition on actual infinities in book 3 and weakens his claim that past time is not an actual infinity. One can see, though, how this result might have seemed unavoidable: once one allows magnitudes to have potential parts, the question naturally arises of how many potential parts they have. It seems implausible that they should have a finite number of them, so they must have an infinite number of them, and they cannot have a potentially infinite number of them for the reason just stated. So the only alternative seems to be that they have an actually infinite number of potential parts. One way out of this difficulty might be to deny that having an actually infinite number of potential parts is equivalent to being actually infinite by division. Another alternative might have been to claim that the number of

---

[14] R. Sorabji, 'Infinity and the Creation', in id. (ed.), *Philoponus and the Rejection of Aristotelian Science* (London, 1987), 164–78 at 170.

246   *John Bowin*

potential parts is *indefinite* or *indeterminate* rather than infinite, but Aristotle chose neither of these options.

The second problem relates to how Aristotle construes the modal force of divisibility. Specifically, one must ask whether Aristotle distinguishes the divisibility of a magnitude from the possibility of its being divided. If Aristotle *does* distinguish these notions, then there is room for a type of divisibility within his philosophy that is conceptually separate from processes. If not, then we must say that divisibility requires at least the possible existence of a process of division. The test for this question is to ask whether, if no processes were available to divide a magnitude (e.g. in a motionless universe), it would still be infinitely divisible. The answer to this question, for Aristotle, would probably be 'No'. Aristotle does not distinguish countability from the possibility of being counted at *Physics* 4. 14, $223^{a}21-9$, where he claims that if there were no one to count the before and after in change, then there would be no time, because time is change *qua* countable. And at *Physics* $263^{a}25-6$ he makes the process of counting tantamount to the process of division in so far as they each mark off parts, so the cases of dividing and counting should be essentially equivalent. In any event, Sorabji points out that Aristotle conflates ϕ-ability and the possibility of being ϕ-ed in other instances as well and cites the fact that Aristotle does not distinguish perceptibility from the possibility of being perceived at *Metaphysics* 4. 5, $1010^{b}30-1011^{a}2$, and *De anima* 3. 2, $426^{a}15-26$.[15]

At least in Aristotle's mind, then, it does not appear that the infinite divisibility of a magnitude was conceptually separable from the process that divides it. Indeed, it appears that for Aristotle, the infinite divisibility of a magnitude is *defined* in terms of a possible process of division. What is more, existing as matter exists and existing as processes exist seem to complement each other in Aristotle's account, since the infinite divisibility of a magnitude depends on the possibility of an infinitely extendable process of division, and the possibility of an infinitely extendable process of division depends on the structure of the magnitude to supply it with an infinite number of points at which it can be divided. Thus, potential infinity is not predicated solely of a process or solely of a magnitude. It does not pertain only to the structure of a magnitude, or only to the nature of a process that divides it. There is a

[15] R. Sorabji, *Time, Creation and the Continuum: Theories in Antiquity and the Early Middle Ages* (London, 1983), 90.

Aristotelian Infinity 247

potential infinity of material parts and a potential infinity of acts of division. Or, perhaps a more accurate way to say it is that there can be an ever larger number of divided parts as well as an ever larger number of acts of division.

IV

I have suggested that potential infinity exists as a process exists, and in particular, as a process that has no goal or end. But this would seem to conflict with certain other texts. Aristotle argues in *Physics* 6. 10, for instance, that there can be no infinite or goalless changes (cf. *Phys.* 8. 2, 252^{b}7–12). In generation and corruption, alteration, and increase and decrease, contradictories or contraries form the natural limits of a change. The case of locomotion is more difficult, since 'it is not always between contraries', but

since that which cannot be cut (in the sense that it is not possible that it should be cut, the term 'cannot' being used in several ways)—since it is not possible that that which in this sense cannot be cut should be being cut, and generally that that which cannot come to be should be coming to be, it follows that it is not possible that that which cannot have changed should be changing to that to which it cannot have changed. If, then, that which is in locomotion is to be changing to something, it must be capable of having changed. (*Phys.* 241^{b}3–11)

The point seems to be that the definition of change includes completability within it, so saying that a change is not completable is to state a contradiction. This is consistent with *Physics* 3. 1, which defines change as such as something that involves a goal or *telos*, viz. as the actuality of a potentiality to be in a state that is the incomplete realization of a particular goal. Thus, the potentiality associated with a process is the potentiality to reach some specific goal, not the potentiality to go on and on indefinitely.

But perhaps the infinite 'processes' that do go on and on indefinitely can be classed as accidental changes and, as such, will fall outside the class of teleological change considered in the rest of the *Physics*.[16] Perhaps the procession of time owes its lack of teleology to the fact that time is at once a property of all teleological change,

---

[16] I take all natural change discussed in the *Physics*, even motions of the simple bodies, to be in some sense teleological, even though simple bodies are not said to move 'for the sake of' anything. Since nature is a principle of motion and rest, and

248   *John Bowin*

and thus lacks any teleology of its own. It is an accidental and goalless composite property of all of the changes in the universe. Likewise, the propagation of mankind as a species is perhaps the accidental sum of the teleological strivings of all individual men and women, and as such, it has no ultimate goal of its own either.

Another, and perhaps more promising, strategy might be to claim that this accidental character applies to the *goallessness* of certain processes, rather than to the processes themselves. The division of a magnitude according to a geometric sequence such as $\frac{1}{2}, \frac{1}{4}, \frac{1}{8}, \ldots,$ $\frac{1}{2^n}, \ldots$ ($n=1, 2, 3, \ldots$), for instance, is clearly a genuine, non-accidental change. But one will find, as a matter of fact, that any process of division will end after a finite number of steps. Perhaps, then, the potential infinity of the task is reflected in the *counterfactual* possibility that the task could have gone on longer. And perhaps one might generalize this to say that all genuine changes are, in fact, finite, but some of them are accidentally goalless, viz. it is just an accidental property of some of them that they could, counterfactually, have gone on indefinitely. This view finds support in *Physics* 3. 4 and 5, where Aristotle refers to the potential infinite first as a *per se* accident of number and magnitude ($\sigma\nu\mu\beta\epsilon\beta\eta\kappa\grave{o}s$ $\kappa\alpha\theta$' $\alpha\grave{\upsilon}\tau\acute{o}$) at 203^{b}33, and then, equivalently, as a *per se* affection of number and magnitude ($\kappa\alpha\theta$' $\alpha\grave{\upsilon}\tau\grave{o}$ $\pi\acute{\alpha}\theta os$ $\tau\iota$) at 204^{a}18–19 (cf. 204^{b}30). The concept of a *per se* accident or affection is introduced at *Metaphysics* 1025^{a}30–1, as 'what attaches to each thing *per se* but is not in its substance, as having its angles equal to two right angles attaches to the triangle'. A triangle is presumably defined as 'a three-angled figure', and this is its essence. But certain other properties not in the definition of a triangle may be deduced from this, which hold eternally and necessarily, e.g. that its angles sum to two right angles, and these properties are *per se* accidents or affections. Likewise, since Aristotle defines change in terms of definite goal states, the processes of dividing a magnitude and counting its divisions are, like all processes, essentially finite. But perhaps it is a *per se* accident or affection of some of these processes that they could, counterfactually, have gone on indefinitely. And perhaps it is the structure of the magnitude being divided that gives these processes this peculiar property.

Aristotle says that potential infinity is a *per se* affection of number

since motion is defined teleologically, I do not see how one can avoid ascribing at least some form of teleology, however etiolated, to everything that has a nature.

Aristotelian Infinity 249

and magnitude in a manner analogous to the way in which speech is incidentally invisible (*Phys.* 204^{a}14–17). Just as 'the invisible is not an element in speech, though the voice is invisible', so the infinite is not an element in number and magnitude, though number and magnitude are infinite. The invisible is not an element in speech in the sense that invisibility is not part of the definition of speech, yet speech is, of course, invisible, and necessarily invisible. Likewise, if it is in the essence of a magnitude to be a bounded extension, or a form/matter composite consisting of a bounding surface (form) and a spatial extension (matter), perhaps it is a *per se* accident or affection of a magnitude to have a potentially infinite number of material parts, i.e. a property which is not specified in the definition of magnitude, but is deducible from the mention of matter in its definition. Similarly, if it is in the essence of each and every number to be some finite and countable plurality of units, perhaps it is a *per se* accident or affection of each such number to be a member of the class of numbers (referred to generically as 'number', instead of 'a number') that can be increased indefinitely.

Thus, taking potential infinity as a *per se* accident or affection seems to explain the infinite increasability of number and the infinite extendability of certain types of changes. But given that infinity is a property of number and magnitude, and given the way that Aristotle defines these things, it is inevitable that infinity *must* be this sort of property. Aristotle clearly thinks that infinity exists as a property. *Physics* 3. 5 proceeds as a disjunctive syllogism: the infinite either exists as a substance or as a property; the infinite does not exist as a substance; therefore the infinite exists as a property (*Phys.* 204^{a}29–30), and, indeed, as a property of number and magnitude (*Phys.* 204^{a}18–19). Since number and magnitude are the sole members of the genus quantity (*Metaph.* 1020^{a}7–14), infinity is a property of quantity. Quantity is, by nature, measurable or countable because it is divisible into units by which it is measured or counted, viz. parts which are 'by nature a "unit" and a "this"' (*Metaph.* 1020^{a}7–32, 1057^{a}2–4). This is why Aristotle says that a quantity is always 'a particular quantity, e.g. two or three cubits; quantity just means these' (*Phys.* 206^{a}3–5). Since it is impossible to count an infinity of units, and since quantities are, by definition, measurable or countable, there is no infinite quantity (*Phys.* 204^{b}8–10, ^{a}28–9). But how can Aristotle claim that infinity is a property of number and magnitude if number and magnitude

250   *John Bowin*

cannot be infinite? To say that there is no infinite quantity is also to say that there is no quantity in whose definition the term 'infinity' appears, or as Aristotle puts it, 'if the infinite is not a substance, but an accident, then it cannot be, *qua* infinite, an element in things' (*Phys.* 204^{a}14–16). Infinity, then, must be a property of number and magnitude which does not appear in the definitions of number and magnitude, and it must be a necessary and eternal property, since it is a necessary and eternal fact that number does not give out in thought, and that continuous magnitudes are infinitely divisible. Infinity must be, in other words, a *per se* accident or affection of number and magnitude (*Phys.* 204^{a}29–30; cf. 204^{a}14, 28–9).[17]

University of California, Santa Cruz

BIBLIOGRAPHY

Barnes, J. (ed.), *The Complete Works of Aristotle: The Revised Oxford Translation* (Princeton, 1984).

Charlton, W., 'Aristotle's Potential Infinites', in L. Judson (ed.), *Aristotle's Physics: A Collection of Essays* (Oxford, 1995), 129–49.

Hintikka, J., 'Aristotelian Infinity', *Philosophical Review*, 75 (1966), 197–218.

Lear, J., 'Aristotelian Infinity', *Proceedings of the Aristotelian Society*, 80 (1979), 187–210.

McClelland, R. T., 'Time and Modality in Aristotle, Metaphysics IX, 3–4', *Archiv für Geschichte der Philosophie*, 63 (1981), 130–49.

Share, M. (trans.), *Philoponus: Against Proclus, On the Eternity of the World 1–5* (London, 2004).

Sorabji, R., 'Infinity and the Creation', in id. (ed.), *Philoponus and the Rejection of Aristotelian Science* (London, 1987), 164–78.

—— *Necessity, Cause, and Blame: Perspectives on Aristotle's Theory* (London, 1980).

—— *Time, Creation and the Continuum: Theories in Antiquity and the Early Middle Ages* (London, 1983).

—— *Philoponus and the Rejection of Aristotelian Science* (London, 1987).

Urmson, J. O. (trans.), *Simplicius: On Aristotle, Physics 3* (London, 2002).

[17] In the case of number, this also follows from the fact that numbers are either odd or even and that infinity is neither odd nor even (*Metaph.* 1084^{a}2–4). In the case of magnitude, this also follows from the alleged fact that there is no infinitely large body or collection of bodies of which an infinite magnitude can be a property (*Phys.* 204^{a}34–206^{a}7).

LISTENING TO REASON IN ARISTOTLE'S MORAL PSYCHOLOGY

GÖSTA GRÖNROOS

1. Introduction

ARISTOTLE's excellent, or virtuous, person must meet two requirements: he or she must strive for what is good, and be able to figure out how to achieve it. This means that the virtuous person must be motivated by sound desires, and have a well-developed power of reasoning. Virtue, therefore, is manifested both in the state of the desires and in the reasoning powers. Aristotle puts these two requirements on the excellent person in terms of two kinds of virtue: virtue of character and intellectual virtue. This twofold requirement has strong support in human experience. For it is easy to come up with examples of people with well-developed reasoning powers who still bring disaster upon both themselves and others. And in so far as the person acts voluntarily, it is the desires that lead the person astray, by pushing him or her into doing things that bring about misfortune (*NE* 6. 9, 1142^{b}17–20; 6. 12, 1149^{a}29–36). Hence, without a sound emotional constitution, virtue is not possible.

On the face of it, virtue is conditional on two different aspects of human nature: the potentiality to be a rational being, and an independent potentiality to be emotionally sound. However, it is a characteristic feature of Aristotle's view that virtue as a whole is a realization of human beings' rational nature, and hence that even virtue of character is a realization of that nature. Perhaps the contention can be explained along the following lines. To begin with, the two virtues are so intimately connected that they cannot be clearly separated from one another. For the relevant intellectual virtue, viz. practical wisdom (*phronēsis*), and virtue of character are dependent on one another, in the sense that the one cannot be had without the

© Gösta Grönroos 2007

252   *Gösta Grönroos*

other (*NE* 6. 13, 1144^{b}30–2; 10. 8, 1178^{a}16–19). Furthermore, Aristotle might simply incline to view the fusion of the two virtues in the light of practical wisdom, perhaps on the grounds that it squares better with his overall conception of human beings as rational.

However, Aristotle's contention that even virtue of character is a realization of the rational nature amounts to something else. For although dependent on one another, the two virtues are clearly separated, being virtues of different parts of the soul. That is, virtue of character belongs to the non-rational part, practical wisdom to the rational part of the soul (*EE* 2. 1, 1220^{a}4–12). And it is precisely by considering the nature of the relation between these two parts of the soul that Aristotle explains in what way virtue of character is dependent on practical wisdom. For he holds that virtue of character presupposes that the non-rational part follows reason's lead, i.e. the lead of the rational part of the soul (*EE* 2. 2, 1220^{b}5–6).[1] He puts this "following" (ἀκολουθεῖν) relation in somewhat different ways: the non-rational part has a kind of share in reason (μετέχειν λόγου) in virtue of listening to (κατήκοον), being obedient to (ἐπιπειθές, πειθαρχεῖν), or being persuaded by (πείθεσθαι) reason (*NE* 1. 13, 1102^{b}13–14, 31; 1. 7, 1098^{a}4; 1. 13, 1102^{b}26, 33). These metaphorical ways of putting the relation raise the question of what it amounts to, and of the precise nature of this capacity of the non-rational part of the soul.

To begin with, the non-rational part follows reason's lead in virtue of understanding its commands. For the rational part gives commands (ἐπίταγμα), and the non-rational part takes these commands in (*NE* 1. 13, 1102^{b}29–33; 7. 6, 1149^{a}25–32). But does this mean that the non-rational part of the soul is not, after all, entirely devoid of reasoning powers? The problem is that although it does not take much to understand a command, even this kind of cognitive capacity seems to presuppose a grasp of concepts and propositional thought. And if we grant that, then it is hard to resist the conclusion that the non-rational part is capable of more than merely understanding commands. In particular, it then seems that it must have some capacity for reasoning, such that it can understand not only the commands, but also considerations in favour of them.

However, such an anachronistic reading misses something crucial

---

[1] I take it that reason (λόγος) here refers to that part of the rational part of the soul which is responsible for practical reasoning, and of which practical wisdom is the virtue. Cf. *NE* 6. 1, 1139^{a}11–15; 6. 5, 1140^{a}24–8.

Reason in Aristotle's Moral Psychology 253

in Aristotle's conception of the relation between the rational and the non-rational part of the soul. For it seems that his starting-point is an entirely intuitive distinction. Consider the case of an individual, and his or her relation to other people. It is one thing to think a situation through for oneself so as to reach a considered and independent decision as to what to do, quite another to go by the authority of someone else. In the latter case, we need not have even the slightest understanding of *why* whatever we are told to do should be done; it is sufficient that we understand *what* we are to do.[2]

In what follows, I shall try to elucidate what the "following" or "listening" relation between the non-rational and rational parts of the soul amounts to in more detail, and what kind of cognitive capacity this implies in regard to the non-rational part. As we shall see, this relation holds regardless of whether the two parts of the soul belong to one and the same individual, or to two separate individuals, such as is the case when we go by the authority of other people.

I should acknowledge my indebtedness to J. M. Cooper's two seminal papers on the topic.[3] Two of his points in particular have guided my own explorations of the question. One is the idea that realizing virtues of character is in fact a realization of human beings' rational nature, precisely on the grounds that in the virtuous person the non-rational part follows reason's lead.[4] The other is his ground-breaking treatment of the part played by a particular kind of desire residing in the non-rational part, viz. spirited desire (*thumos*), both in moral education and in the fully developed virtuous person.[5]

However, I have some qualms about how Cooper portrays the non-rational part's "following" or "listening to" reason, and I shall challenge his view that listening to the rational part implies a capacity for reasoning, however limited, on the part of the non-rational

---

[2] This distinction may lie behind a few lines from Hesiod cited at *NE* 1. 4, 1095^b10–14, which run in a literal translation: "This is the altogether excellent: he, who figures out everything for himself | excellent too is the one who obeys the one speaking well. | But the one who neither figures out for himself nor, listening to another, | takes [the advice] to his heart—that is a useless man indeed" (*WD* 293–7).

[3] "Some Remarks on Aristotle's Moral Psychology" ["Aristotle's Moral Psychology"], *Southern Journal of Philosophy*, 27, suppl. (1988), 25–42, and "Reason, Moral Virtue, and Moral Value", in M. Frede and G. Striker (eds.), *Rationality in Greek Thought* (Oxford, 1996), 81–114.

[4] "Aristotle's Moral Psychology", 40; "Reason, Moral Virtue, and Moral Value", 83–4.

[5] "Reason, Moral Virtue, and Moral Value", 102–14. See also M. Burnyeat, "Aristotle on Learning to be Good", in A. Rorty (ed.), *Essays on Aristotle's Ethics* (Berkeley, 1980), 69–92.

254 *Gösta Grönroos*

part of the soul.[6] In particular, Aristotle's contention that the non-rational part can be persuaded by the rational part need not imply that the non-rational part, in addition to understanding the commands of reason, can understand the considerations in favour of them.[7] Instead, it will be argued that the "following" relation is a matter of directing the desires of the non-rational part towards values of reason itself by exposing them to those values through experience.

2. Divisions of the soul

In the final chapter of the first book of the *Nicomachean Ethics* Aristotle prepares for the distinction between intellectual virtue and virtue of character, by dividing the soul into a rational and a non-rational part.[8] The point, as mentioned, is that each of these parts has a virtue of its own. But virtue of character, it turns out, does not belong to the entire non-rational part. For having divided the soul into these two parts, he goes on to point out that a further division can be made of the non-rational part. For in addition to one part which is entirely beyond the reach of reason and virtue, viz. the nutritive part, there is another part, the appetitive and generally desiderative part. And although this latter part does not possess reason by itself, it nevertheless has a share in reason in virtue of its capacity to listen to it (*NE* I. 13, 1102^{b}29–31).

The point of introducing this reason-responsive part of the non-rational part of the soul is to prepare the ground for the contention that the non-rational part can be under the sway of reason. And importantly, in following reason's lead the non-rational part does not attend to any arguments or considerations, but obeys reason in authority. Hence, the non-rational part does not understand what speaks in favour of a certain course of action, but abides by the pre-

---

[6] "Aristotle's Moral Psychology", 32–4; "Reason, Moral Virtue, and Moral Value", 91.

[7] H. Lorenz makes a similar claim in regard to Plato, and as will be shown, his account of Aristotle, with some important exceptions, is akin to the one presented in this paper. See his *The Brute Within: Appetitive Desire in Plato and Aristotle* (Oxford, 2006), 2, 117–18, and 186–94.

[8] In what follows I shall speak of parts of the soul without taking a stand on the ontological status of these parts, or perhaps aspects, of the soul. At *NE* I. 13, 1102^{a}28–32, Aristotle himself points out that in this context the ontological questions make little difference.

Reason in Aristotle's Moral Psychology 255

scriptions of reason without questioning, as it were. In this respect, Cooper's interpretation is misguided.[9] For according to Cooper, the non-rational part can listen to and be persuaded by reason, in virtue of having recourse to the same conceptual framework as reason itself has. But what is more, he also holds that the persuasion of the non-rational part implies that it does not blindly follow the commands of reason, but that it can actually be brought to understand the reasons in favour of the recommended course of action. The problem with this suggestion is that the distinction between the two ways of having reason is blurred. For what are we to make of the point that only the rational part possesses reason by itself, if the non-rational part understands not only the commands of reason but also the considerations in favour of them? Besides, there is little support in the text for a distinction between understanding an argument, on the one hand, and producing it, on the other, and Cooper, at any rate, does not base his reading on that distinction.

The likely source of this problem is a certain fuzziness on Aristotle's part in drawing the distinction between the rational part, on the one hand, and the reason-responsive part of the non-rational part, on the other. In particular, having divided the non-rational part into two parts, he seems to make a further division of the rational part (*NE* i. 13, 1103[a]1–3). That is, even in the rational part there is one part such that it merely has a share in reason, without having it properly. On the face of it, it appears as if this further division collapses the basic division between the rational and the non-rational parts. For it now seems that the reason-sharing part of the non-rational part is merged with a similar part of the rational part, so that these two parts share a common part—an intersection, set-theoretically speaking.[10]

Apart from confusing the division between the rational and the non-rational parts, this intersection is also intolerable in that much of the point of introducing a part of the soul which can share in reason without itself possessing it is lost. For Aristotle is precisely

---

[9] Cooper, "Aristotle's Moral Psychology", 33–4.

[10] There is an implicit tendency towards this reading in scholarly commentators such as J. A. Stewart, *Notes on the* Nicomachean Ethics *of Aristotle*, i (Oxford, 1892), 167, and R. A. Gauthier and J. Y. Jolif, *L'Éthique à Nicomaque*, 2nd edn., ii/1 (Louvain and Paris, 1970), 97. A further, even more untenable, option is provided by F. Dirlmeier in *Aristoteles, Nikomachische Ethik* (Berlin, 1969), 292–3: the reason-responsive part too is divided into two parts, one belonging to the non-rational part, the other to the rational part of the soul.

256 *Gösta Grönroos*

concerned with explaining how even the non-rational part of the soul can come under the sway of reason. If the answer is that the non-rational part has a part in common with the rational part, then the explanation seems vacuous. For then it seems that the non-rational part, after all, has some reasoning powers in common with the rational part. And the other side of the coin, namely, that there is a part of the rational part which has a minimal power of reason, such that it has a share in reason without having it properly, is equally intolerable, and without backing in Aristotelian psychology.[11]

The problem arises from the phrase at 1103ᵃ1–2, εἰ δὲ χρὴ καὶ τοῦτο φάναι λόγον ἔχειν, διττὸν ἔσται καὶ τὸ λόγον ἔχον, which is standardly rendered "now if we must say that this [the non-rational part] too has reason, then the part which has reason should be double too". A possible way out of this problem is to accept a certain inconsistency in Aristotle's use of the expression 'the part which has reason' (τὸ λόγον ἔχον). That is, perhaps there is a shift in extension between its occurrences at 1102ᵃ28 and 1103ᵃ2, such that only the latter includes the reason-responsive part as well.[12] Considering the fact that there turns out to be a part of the non-rational part of the soul which has a share in reason, Aristotle at 1103ᵃ2 might just have chosen to reflect this insight by making an *ad hoc* variant division, without, however, abandoning the standard division, according to which the reason-responsive part belongs to the non-rational part.

Although my overall interpretation does not hinge on it, let me briefly consider a modest conjecture that would help us out. I suggest that we emend ἔχον to ἔχειν.[13] Now we get the sensible apodosis "then to have reason too should be twofold [that is, have two senses]".[14] In fact, the inferential force of the apodosis, strengthened by the future tense, makes much better sense if we adopt the conjecture. Neither the protasis nor anything else in the context

---

[11] Cf. Lorenz, *The Brute Within*, 186–8. Of course, there are other divisions to be made in regard to the rational part, such as that between the part of theoretical knowledge (τὸ ἐπιστημονικόν) and the calculative part (τὸ λογιστικόν), the latter of which is responsible for deliberation. Cf. *NE* 6. 1, 1139ᵃ3–15.

[12] So J. Burnet, *The Ethics of Aristotle* (London, 1900), 61, and (rather by implication) S. Broadie, *Ethics with Aristotle* (Oxford, 1991), 62, 69.

[13] The conjecture is possible on palaeographical grounds. Either a ligature such as ⟨ for ει has been mistaken for ο, or the common abbreviation of ἔχειν, i.e. ἔχ″, has been mistaken for the common abbreviation of ἔχον, i.e. ἔχ‵. I am grateful to Denis Searby for help with the palaeographical considerations.

[14] Aristotle elsewhere uses the expression διττόν for linguistic ambiguity. See *SE* 19 and *Post. An.* 1. 10, 77ᵇ24–6.

Reason in Aristotle's Moral Psychology 257

implies that the rational part should be double, whereas there is good backing for the conclusion that there must be two ways of having reason. What follows, τὸ μὲν κυρίως καὶ ἐν αὐτῷ, τὸ δ' ὥσπερ τοῦ πατρὸς ἀκουστικόν τι, gives the two senses: "to have it in the proper sense and in itself, on the one hand, and as something that listens to its father, on the other".

There is some support for the conjecture in the ancient commentators. Aspasius in the second century AD elaborates on the division of the non-rational part of the soul, and on the two senses of having reason, but does not so much as hint at a parallel division of the rational part.[15] A paraphrase, the authorship and date of which are uncertain, gives some support for emending the phrase in the way I have suggested.[16] To begin with, in elaborating on the two different ways of having reason, the paraphrast goes beyond Aristotle, and introduces a somewhat more elaborate scheme. As the examples show, the paraphrast first makes a distinction between the having of reason (τὸ λόγον ἔχειν) and the having of a share in reason (τὸ λόγου μετέχειν), such that the former is a matter of putting the capacity for attending to reason into actual use, whereas the latter signifies the mere potentiality to do so. The paraphrast's point, then, is that in regard to both of these a further distinction can be drawn: the non-rational part *has reason* in the way in which we listen to our father or our loved ones, whereas the rational part has it in the way in which we attend to the proofs produced by a mathematician. And in parallel to these two senses of having reason, the non-rational part *has a share in reason* in the sense of having the capacity to obey an authority, such as one's father, whereas the rational part has a share in it in the proper way and in itself, in virtue of having the capacity to understand arguments and proofs.

In other words, in the paraphrast's terminology the expression 'having a share in reason' comes to pretty much the same as Aristotle's 'having reason', in so far as the general capacity to attend to

---

[15] Aspas. *In EN* 35. 14–36. 21 Heylbut.

[16] [Heliodor.] *In EN paraphr.* 25. 7–14 Heylbut. On authorship and date, see Gauthier and Jolif, *L'Éthique à Nicomaque*, i/1. 106–1, and D. M. Nicol, "A Paraphrase of the *Nicomachean Ethics* Attributed to the Emperor John VI Cantacuzene", *Byzantinoslavica*, 28 (1968), 1–16. The only thing we are certain of is that the paraphrase is earlier than 1367. The suggested authors—Andronicus of Rhodes, Olympiodorus of Alexandria, the Byzantine Emperor John VI Cantacuzene, and the otherwise unknown Heliodorus of Prusa—give a time-span between the 1st cent. BC and the 14th cent. AD.

258 Gösta Grönroos

reason is at issue, regardless of whether it is a matter of attending to it in the proper way, or merely in the secondary way. Importantly, as the paraphrast turns to the two ways in which the having a share in reason is spoken of (in his terminology), he obviously has 1103^a1-3 in mind, to which the very phrasing and examples testify. And in what must be his somewhat loose paraphrase of 1103^a2, it is more likely that he read ἔχειν than ἔχον. For the paraphrase runs "in this way, having a share in reason too is spoken of in two senses [κατὰ τοῦτον τὸν τρόπον διπλῶς λέγεται καὶ τὸ λόγου μετέχειν]".[17]

3. Obeying in authority

Regardless of how we deal with the textual question, Aristotle's point is sufficiently clear. The soul is divided into a rational and a non-rational part, the latter of which, in a sense, can have a share in reason. The important thing now is that this kind of having reason must be distinguished from the rational part's proper possession of it. As Aristotle puts it, the non-rational part has reason in the sense in which we say that we have it from our father or our loved ones, and not in the sense in which we have it in mathematics (NE 1. 13, 1102^b31-3).[18] What he has in mind is the way in which we may take advice from other people on mere authority, without knowing the considerations in favour of the advice. In mathematics, by contrast, we are presented not only with the truths, but also with the proofs of them.[19]

---

[17] [Heliodor.] In EN paraphr. 25. 11–12 Heylbut. Eustratius' Byzantine commentary of the 11th/12th cent. on the Nicomachean Ethics, on the other hand, testifies to the text of the received manuscripts, the oldest of which is the codex Laurentianus of the 10th cent. For from the distinction between the two ways of having reason he concludes that the rational part (λογικόν) too is double. See Eustrat. In EN 120. 3–8 Heylbut.

[18] As far as having the λόγος of the father is concerned, Aristotle is playing on the idiomatic expression λόγον ἔχειν τινος "to have regard to someone". Cf. Stewart, Notes on the Nicomachean Ethics of Aristotle, 166.

[19] Cf. Aspas. In EN 36. 2–5 Heylbut. The expression τῶν μαθηματικῶν at 1102^b33 raises questions of both grammar and content. If the grammatical construction is analogous to that in the first part of the sentence, then mathematicians are intended. In that case, the point is likely to be that we have the λόγος from the mathematician in the sense that he or she demonstrates the claims in such a way that we can take part not only in the claim, but in the proof as well. However, the genitive here is most often taken to indicate the subject-matter of mathematics, thus suggesting that this way of having λόγος is the way in which λόγος is had in mathematics, allowing, without necessitating, the reading that it is the very producing of the proof that

Reason in Aristotle's Moral Psychology 259

What is more, in view of Aristotle's contention that "the non-rational part is in a way persuaded by reason, [as] is shown by admonition [νουθέτησις], and all sort of censure [ἐπιτίμησις] and encouragement [παράκλησις]", it seems highly unlikely that he has in mind being persuaded in the sense of understanding and accepting an argument, however primitively (NE 1. 13, 1102^{b}33–1103^{a}1). Instead, he seems to have in mind cases such as bringing up children, in which the child understands and accepts a command on mere authority without knowing the considerations in favour of it. This also explains why he qualifies the kind of persuasion by "in a way [πως]".[20]

Cooper's mistake mentioned above, I suspect, is that by articulating the capacity of the non-rational part in terms of conceptual capacities, he takes too much on board, cognitively speaking. It is more likely that Aristotle is dealing with the intuitive distinction between someone understanding, be it through education or by his own wits, why a certain thing should or should not be done, and someone relying on authority. Indeed, the very wording "to obey in authority" (πειθαρχεῖν) is suggestive of that.[21] In addition, Cooper overlooks the ambiguity of the notion of persuasion (πειθώ), and particularly the fact that we may be persuaded to do something without understanding why whatever we are persuaded about is to be done.[22]

This point is also brought home by Aristotle's remarks on the enkratic or self-controlled person. To begin with, it should be noticed that the non-rational part's having a share in reason is a universal feature of the relation between the two parts of the soul. Hence, the non-rational part of the enkratic person has a share in reason as well (NE 1. 13, 1102^{b}13–28).[23] Now, the point cannot be that the non-rational part of the enkratic person is brought

---

Aristotle has in mind. However, the point is more likely to be that this way of having λόγος amounts to being able to follow, rather than producing, the proof.

[20] Cf. Lorenz, *The Brute Within*, 189.

[21] LSJ has a persuasive list for this use in Sophocles (*Trach.* 1178), Aristophanes (*Eccl.* 762), Plato (*Rep.* 7, 538 C 6–E 4), and, not least, in Aristotle himself (*Pol.* 2. 4, 1262^{b}3).

[22] At *Gorg.* 454 E 3–455 A 7 Plato pinpoints a similar kind of ambiguity between two types of persuasion: one producing conviction without knowledge, the other providing knowledge as well.

[23] Thus, the non-rational part of the akratic person also has a share in reason. But for now I leave out this somewhat more complicated case, unnecessary for the point I am making here, and return to it in the next section.

260 *Gösta Grönroos*

to understand why something should or should not be done. The understanding takes place in the rational part, and the very characteristic of the enkratic person is that although his non-rational part strives in the opposite direction, his or her rational part is powerful enough to force the non-rational part into obedience, which requires only understanding of the command on the part of the latter. In other words, the non-rational part obeys the rational part without agreeing with it. If the rational part really managed to make the non-rational part understand why something should or should not be done, and thus made it agree with it, then that part would probably no longer strive in the opposite direction. In that case, self-control would be an inappropriate characterization of the enkratic person in the first place.

In regard to the non-rational part's having a share in reason, Aristotle describes the difference between the enkratic and the virtuous person by saying that the non-rational part of the enkratic person obeys reason, whereas the same part of the virtuous person obeys reason even more willingly, in the sense that it actually agrees with it and that no conflicts in the soul arise. But as we are about to see, this does not imply that the non-rational part of the virtuous person is made to understand why one should act or feel in a certain way, in virtue of a supposed power of reasoning. Instead, it is transformed in such a way that its desires agree with reason, and this transformation is not brought about through reasoning.

4. Spirited desire and reason

To become a virtuous person, then, the non-rational part of one's soul must agree with reason in such a way that no conflicts arise: it must chime in with reason (*NE* 1. 13, 1102^{b}28). The crucial point in Aristotle's account of how the desires of the non-rational part can be made to agree with reason is the idea that the non-rational part can be transformed to strive for values endorsed by reason itself. But since the non-rational part cannot be convinced through arguments, the transformation must be brought about in some other way. It is in this regard that one of the desires of the non-rational part, viz. spirited desire (*thumos*), plays a pivotal part.[24] For when it comes to the

[24] For the different kinds of desire see *DA* 2. 3, 414^{b}2; 3. 9, 432^{b}3–7; *MA* 6, 700^{b}17–18; *EE* 2. 7, 1223^{a}26–7; 2. 10, 1225^{b}24–6; *Rhet.* 1. 10, 1369^{a}1–4.

Reason in Aristotle's Moral Psychology 261

non-rational part's following reason's lead, it is in fact only spirited desire, not appetite (*epithumia*), that can do so (*NE* 7. 6, 1149^{b}1–3). What makes spirited desire suited to do this work on behalf of the non-rational part is the kind of objects, or values, it is set upon. For Aristotle distinguishes between the two kinds of non-rational desire by the kind of object each strives for: whereas appetite is always set upon pleasure (*hēdonē*), spirited desire is set upon an entirely different value, viz. what is fine and beautiful (*to kalon*).[25]

However, the desire of the rational part of the soul, i.e. wish (*boulēsis*), is set upon yet another value, the good (*to agathon*). The contention that the fine is a value endorsed by the rational part must therefore be qualified in some way, so that it does not imply that the rational part actually desires the fine. To begin with, the desire for the fine is a desire to become fine. In other words, spirited desire, in contrast to appetite, is concerned with obtaining and mainting a character. Since this character is developed and maintained through fine actions, spirited desire strives for actions that are fine, and is concerned with all aspects related to what makes a person, and his or her actions, fine. What is more, spirited desire is qualified not merely by its object, i.e. the fine, but also by its belligerence in defending the fineness of the person. By way of adumbration, we might say that the fine for Aristotle is a matter of pride, dignity, and self-esteem in regard to others as well as oneself, and in all aspects of life.

Before we consider what it is about the fine that makes it a value dear to reason, let us prepare the ground by piecing together a picture from the somewhat scattered remarks as to what spirited desire's susceptibility to reason's lead amounts to. A good start is the argument to the effect that the akratic person is more readily excused for being overcome by spirited desire than by appetite, precisely on the grounds that only spirited desire, in some sense at least, can listen to reason. For in that case the akratic person, in a way (*πως*), is overcome by reason itself (*NE* 7. 6, 1149^{a}25–^{b}3). The example is how we might be overcome by our feelings in the face of insults. The details will be explored shortly, but the idea, in outline, is that the non-rational part of the soul prompts a certain

---

[25] The aesthetic aspect of τὸ καλόν is important, but for convenience I henceforth render it as 'the fine'. The attribution of τὸ καλόν to spirited desire is far from explicit in Aristotle, but I find Cooper's arguments for this attribution, based on *NE* 2. 3, 1104^{b}30 ff., persuasive ("Reason, Moral Virtue, and Moral Value", 95–8). See also Burnyeat, "Aristotle on Learning to be Good", 79–86.

262 *Gösta Grönroos*

response to the insult solely in virtue of its sense of the fine, and not by reasoning about what course of action is fitting.[26]

On this point I depart from Cooper's account.[27] For he thinks that spirited desire, in contrast to appetite, is indeed involved in some kind of reasoning, such that, for instance, it puts together the evaluative view that insults are belittling and must be met with retaliation, with the factual information that an insult has taken place, so as to reach the decision to fight back. But the crucial textual evidence does not support this reading. As Aristotle puts it, spirited desire, on receiving the factual information that an insult has taken place, prompts action "as if having reasoned [ὥσπερ συλλογισάμενος]" that insults of this kind are a cause for going to war (*NE* 6. 6, 1149[a]32–[b]1). As the very grammar suggests, Aristotle does not think that spirited desire is involved in reasoning in a literal sense. On the contrary, since there is no reason to think that spirited desire has evaluative views to begin with, we need not conclude that it entertains any major premiss at all; it just seems as if it had reasoned.[28] Hence, Cooper ascribes too much cognitive power to spirited desire, and consequently to the non-rational part of the soul.

But what is more, the important point, to which I shall return shortly, is that Aristotle has no need for reasoning as a distinguishing mark of spirited desire. For all that matters is that spirited desire is susceptible to the fine, just as appetite is susceptible to pleasure, so as to motivate a particular course of action. In this regard, there is no important difference between the workings of spirited desire and those of appetite.

The question now is why reason values the fine. Indeed, why does it not value pleasure just as much, or just as little? Yet again,

[26] The example of how spirited desire rushes to action on the grounds of an insult is but one instance, and should not suggest that the responses of spirited desire are confined only to insults by others. For this very example is designed to explain how spirited desire can be responsible for ἀκρασία, and in that case it is a particularly belligerent and irascible kind of spirited desire that we are overcome by, viz. anger (ὀργή). Cf. *Rhet.* 2. 2, 1378[a]30 ff., for a definition of ὀργή.

[27] Cooper, "Reason, Moral Virtue, and Moral Value", 91; see also "Aristotle's Moral Psychology", 31–4. Broadie inclines in the same direction (S. Broadie and C. Rowe, *Aristotle*, Nicomachean Ethics (Oxford, 2002), 56–7).

[28] Lorenz suggests (*The Brute Within*, 192–4) that spirited desire obtains its evaluative view from reason, and thus in part reflects the evaluative view of reason itself. Although I am sceptical of the very idea of attributing evaluative views to the non-rational part of the soul, my own suggestion below of how the motivating values of spirited desire and reason, respectively, are related goes some way towards fleshing out in what way spirited desire is influenced by reason's own values.

Reason in Aristotle's Moral Psychology   263

Aristotle is not particularly explicit, but it is likely that the different attitudes reason has towards pleasure and towards the fine, respectively, come with the very nature of these values. Reason values what is good for human beings, viz. that which realizes someone's full potential as a rational being. The fine has a bearing on the human good in at least two ways. First, through spirited desire's drive for the fine, a reflective outlook on life and the self is developed. This reflective outlook, in turn, is indispensable if practical wisdom is to develop. For practical wisdom is conditional on the power of deliberation (*bouleusis*), i.e. the capacity to deliberate about what is good for oneself in general, in the sense that it contributes to well-being, or a happy life (*NE* 6. 5, 1140^{a}24–8). If such deliberation is to be successful, it is crucial that the self is taken stock of in the broadest possible perspective. And secondly, the fine character is also a prerequisite for realizing human beings' potential for theoretical knowledge (*epistēmē*) and reflection (*theōria*). Indeed, as Cooper suggests, spirited desire's striving for the fine in terms of order (*taxis*), symmetry (*summetria*), and determinateness (*hōrismenon*) in action prepares the soul for values that are pivotal for theoretical reason.[29] Spirited desire's sense of the fine thus has an important part to play in turning the soul towards the good.[30]

None of this implies that spirited desire itself is responsible for the reflective outlook, just that in virtue of the very value involved in spirited desire, which is more complex, and touches upon more aspects of life than pleasure, a more reflective outlook on life and the self is developed. The reflective outlook is a task for the rational part of the soul, but through the strengthening of spirited desire this part is nurtured and developed more than by appetite. This is not to say that pleasure is despised and to be avoided. The point is just that pleasure does not turn the soul towards the good, and that pleasure, to the extent that it is had at the expense of the fine, even constitutes an impediment to the good life. For the kind of pleasure

[29] Cooper, "Reason, Moral Virtue, and Moral Value", 113. He bases his interpretation here and at 105–6 on the interesting remark at *Metaph.* M 3, 1078^{a}31–^{b}6, that the fine and beautiful in terms of order, symmetry, and determinateness is found both in the sphere of action and among unchanging entities.

[30] The Platonic background is obvious. At *Rep.* 3, 401 D 5–402 A 4, Socrates pinpoints the importance of music and poetry in turning the young person towards the good in that they give him or her a sense of fine and beautiful things even before he or she can explain why they are so. I owe this reference to Eyjólfur Emilsson. For more on θυμός in Plato see J. M. Cooper, "Plato's Theory of Human Motivation", *History of Philosophy Quarterly*, 1 (1984), 3–21.

264 *Gösta Grönroos*

appetite strives for is intimately tied to the body, and these pleasures are a matter of momentary and isolated gratification, lasting no longer than the period in which the part of the body concerned is affected.[31]

Of course, in the case of appetite too a certain reflective outlook can be nurtured, such as figuring out schemes to maximize pleasure and minimize pain, which may indeed require complicated deliberations, as we can see in the Marquis de Sade's elaborate schemes for pleasure, but the scope of such reflection is narrower, and confined to the body. Generally speaking, the three kinds of desire differ in regard to their relative dependence on deliberation for their satisfaction. By and large, satisfying appetites requires less calculation than obtaining the fine does, let alone obtaining the good. Relatively speaking, for instance, it is easier to spot a partner for sexual pleasure than someone to be proud of, let alone someone to lead a happy life with.

5. Educating desires through habituation

In the virtuous person the desires of the non-rational part of the soul agree with reason, and spirited desire plays the crucial part in this regard. It now remains to flesh out the process or mechanism by which the non-rational part is made to agree with reason, without presupposing any amount of reasoning of the non-rational part of the soul. Aristotle puts the mechanism in terms of habituation (*ethismos*), and it can be likened to the training of a sense. By way of an analogy, it is an indispensable part of musical education to train the student's sense of melody, rhythm, and harmony. The way to train this sense is by exposing the student to pieces of music. This process must be allowed to take time, for the student must cultivate the sense by repetition and thus gradually learn to recognize different tunes, rhythms, and harmonies. The student cannot be

---

[31] Of course, in view of Aristotle's distinction between necessary and non-necessary appetites in *NE* 7. 4, this claim should be qualified. But in substance it is not affected. In fact, on the reading suggested here, there is a straightforward answer to the questions whether and why being overcome by spirited desire is more excusable than being overcome by any appetite, necessary or not. Being overcome by spirited desire is more excusable in both cases, because we are overcome by a value endorsed by reason itself. For discussion, see e.g. Cooper, "Reason, Moral Virtue, and Moral Value", 88–90, and Broadie and Rowe, *Aristotle,* Nicomachean Ethics, 56–7.

Reason in Aristotle's Moral Psychology   265

introduced to musical theory, such as harmonics, before he or she has a firm grasp of the phenomenon through the senses. And that grasp is gained through experience, not through reasoning.

Turning now to the ultimate sources of motivation in human beings, viz. the desires, the importance of habituation and the part played by spirited desire can be seen particularly clearly in the upbringing of the developing individual. For to the extent that children have no sense of whatever reasons there are for acting in a certain way, there are two ways of accustoming the child to proper conduct. The brute way is to persuade the child to act properly by promising it something pleasant, e.g. sweets, or to threaten it with punishment. This is to appeal to the child's sense of pleasure and pain; the child adjusts its conduct in order to achieve pleasure and to avoid pain. However, we may also encourage good behaviour by appealing to the child's sense of the fine. The child may not understand why honesty, for instance, is a good thing, but through being told that acting in an honest way makes him or her a better person, the child's spirited desire takes command and motivates honest behaviour. This is the point of exhortations such as "Be a good girl, and admit what you have done!"[32] Gradually, as the child's spirited desire is nurtured through habituation, its outlook on the world and its place in it will grow richer and more complex than if it had been trained merely to achieve pleasure and to avoid pain.[33]

The nurturing of the child's spirited desires is closely tied to, and dependent on, its sense of shame (*aidōs*). Since arguments, as Aristotle puts it, are not enough to make men good, and indeed out of place in the case of children, it is precisely through the sense of shame that we can correct bad behaviour and, ultimately, make the child a lover of the fine (*philokalon*) (*NE* 10. 9, $1179^{b}4–16$).[34] This is probably also what he has in mind when he points out that censure and encouragement show that the non-rational part of the soul, in a way, is persuaded by reason (*NE* 1. 13, $1102^{b}33–1103^{a}1$). For the

---

[32] Cf. Broadie, *Ethics with Aristotle*, 66, 107–10. However, Broadie does not single out spirited desire as doing the crucial work in this regard.

[33] I here disagree with Burnyeat's suggestion ("Aristotle on Learning to be Good", 80), developed further by H. J. Fossheim (*Nature and Habituation in Aristotle's Theory of Human Development* (Oslo, 2003), 170–7), that the spirited desire is brought about and developed through a learning process in which pleasures and pains are associated with fine things. Instead, I regard spirited desire as a basic, inborn desire (*Pol.* 7. 15, $1334^{b}22–5$), which requires only stimulation by means of exposure to the fine in order to be activated.

[34] See also Burnyeat, "Aristotle on Learning to be Good", 74–7.

266 *Gösta Grönroos*

point of encouragement is precisely that we appeal to the child's pride and self-esteem, whereas in censuring it for bad behaviour we are appealing to its sense of shame. By contrast, the less fortunate individuals who are not endowed in the first place with strong spirited desires do not obey the sense of shame, and do not avoid bad actions because they are base, but out of fear of punishment (*NE* 10. 9, 1179^{b}11–13).

The crucial point of accustoming the child to virtuous conduct is that the child acquires a taste for it, such that it will act virtuously not from mere habit, but from desire for such action. Here it matters a great deal what it has experienced in terms of satisfying its desires. Think of an analogy: the desire for delicious food or good wine can be satisfied to different degrees, depending on what we are served. But the very taste for food and wine can also be cultivated in such a way that our demands increase. The crucial first step in such cultivation is that we are exposed to delicious food and good wine, and it might even take some time to learn to appreciate them. In that case, our desire for delicious food and good wine is cultivated through experience. Reading studies in gastronomy, by contrast, will not do the trick.

Now, in the same spirit, the development of the child's character will be heavily dependent on what experience it has of satisfying its desires. To begin with, unless the child is introduced to fine conduct, it cannot develop a taste for this value. In that case spirited desire withers, as it were. Furthermore, it is through experience that the child comes to learn the difference between apparent and real instances of different values. This is crucially so in the case of reason's own desire, wish, and its object, the good (*NE* 3. 4). For we may err in regard to the good, and wish for what is merely the apparent good, by believing, for instance, that pleasure is the good (*NE* 1. 4). And as far as the child is concerned, it cannot be talked into changing its preferences; it must be exposed to real instances of the good. Once it experiences the real good, no arguments will be needed: for once it has experienced the real good, satisfaction of wish by means of the apparent good will no longer do. Extrapolating the case of spirited desire from wish, here too there is no guarantee that the child will end up with spirited desires that strive for the truly fine. To do so, the child needs to experience the difference between truly fine actions and those that merely appear so.

Finally, Aristotle's contention that only spirited desire can follow

Reason in Aristotle's Moral Psychology   267

reason's lead might leave us in doubt as to whether reason can have any bearing on the other kind of non-rational desire, viz. appetite. Aristotle does not say much about this question, but to hazard a conjecture, his theoretical framework seems resourceful enough to deal with it. To begin with, the question must be considered against the background of the gradual development of the individual's character through habituation. It is reasonable to say that the question of what impact reason has is irrelevant in the case of infants, and it is questionable anyway whether action should be attributed to infants in the first place. But at some point in one's development spirited desires can function as a moderating force *vis-à-vis* appetite, perhaps at about the same time that we begin to attribute action to children. For instance, in correcting excessive behaviour of even a fairly small child in regard to appetites, we can appeal to its sense of shame. This sense of shame with regard to appetites helps develop the power to resist excess, and thus is the beginning of moderation.

Some support for this conjecture can be found in Aristotle's account of moderation (*sōphrosunē*) (*NE* 3. 10–12). For he points out that in the moderate person the appetitive part of the soul is in harmony with reason in such a way that his or her appetites are ready to obey (εὐπειθές) it (*NE* 3. 12, 1119^{b}7–18). On the face of it, this seems to speak against the contention that only spirited desire—but not appetites—is capable of listening to and following reason's lead. However, Aristotle goes on to suggest that the moderate person's appetites are in harmony with reason in the sense that both the appetitive part and reason have a common goal, viz. the fine. His account here is sketchy, but it is tempting to think that it is precisely through spirited desire as a mediator that the appetitive part and reason are brought into harmony. For by forcing and moulding the appetites so that they do not put the fine at risk, spirited desire makes the non-rational part of the soul, including the appetitive part, more apt to follow reason's lead.

6. Virtue, the good, and community

The distinctive feature of Aristotle's conception of virtue of character is the idea that the rational part of the soul instils this virtue into the non-rational part by educating the desires of the latter. And it is an important fact about human nature that the first and

268 *Gösta Grönroos*

crucially constitutive steps of such education cannot be initiated by the rational part of the developing individual itself. For the proper development of the rational part of the individual requires that the non-rational part has reached a certain level of development in the first place. Therefore, guardians who can give the developing individual the proper lead are indispensable. This means that in respect of virtue, the individual is not self-sufficient; instead, the community introduces each of us to morality.[35] This, as we shall see, has some rather important bearings on Aristotle's conception of virtue, and on human nature as such.

The importance of community is not limited to the education of the non-rational desires. For even when it comes to the desire of reason itself, i.e. wish, and its object, the good, guardianship is crucial. To begin with, considering the fact that the good is the ultimate end of human activity, reason itself, in virtue of harbouring the desire for the good, is not just one source of motivation among others, but actually *the* source of motivation in human life. But since the good is the least apparent of the three values that the three different kinds of desire are respectively set upon, it takes more reasoning to hit the mark with regard to the good than with regard to the objects of the non-rational desires. Hitting the right mark with regard to pleasure, for instance, is more or less a matter of bodily instincts, and does not require much reasoning, if any.

This is not to say that a guardian can expose instances of the good to the developing individual in the same way that he or she can expose instances of the fine. For achieving the good is conditional on exercise of the reasoning power characteristic of practical wisdom, viz. deliberation (*NE* 6. 5, 1140ᵃ24–31).[36] But if the deliberative exercise is to have a point, then some grasp of the ultimate end is required. For however cumbersome it might be to figure out what course of action will contribute to the good life in the individual case, at least we must have some sense of what we are striving for. Thus, the ultimate end cannot be established through deliberation, for it serves as the starting-point for it. In this respect, there is a parallel between practical wisdom and theoretical knowledge: just as

[35] The city, as Aristotle puts it at *Pol.* 1. 2, 1253ᵃ18–29, is in nature prior to each of us just as an organism is prior to its parts.

[36] I here refrain from discussing the question whether deliberation is concerned with satisfying wish exclusively, as Cooper suggests ("Aristotle's Moral Psychology", 30 n. 4), but I agree with Broadie (*Ethics with Aristotle*, 106–7, 184) that Aristotle inclines towards the view that satisfaction of wish requires deliberation.

Reason in Aristotle's Moral Psychology 269

the axioms of demonstrative sciences cannot be demonstrated, but must be grasped through other means, in that case through induction (*epagōgē*), so the ultimate end of practical reason cannot be established by means of deliberation, but only through habituation.[37]

What is more, it should not be denied that the good can be articulated, or that conceptions of it can be justified dialectically in ethical enquiry. The point is just that such articulation and justification require that we already have a grasp of the good, and that that grasp must be established in some other way.[38] Aristotle's answer is that the grasp of the good is based on an inborn and uniquely human sense of this value (*Pol.* 1. 2, 1253^{a}9–18; 7. 15, 1334^{b}17–25). But just as in the case of spirited desire, it takes instruction and experience to cultivate this sense.

In regard to the good, guardians can merely get the individual started in the right direction. For since the good is conditioned by facts about ourselves and the particular circumstances in which we happen to live, to a great extent we will have to figure out for ourselves what to do, and learn from experience. Indeed, our deliberative skills will improve as we go along, and so will our grasp of the good. In regard to the first steps in such development, spirited desire has a particularly important part to play. For it is precisely by strengthening the desire for the truly fine that the grasp of the good is at the same time improved. That is, since to become truly fine is a matter of perfecting human nature as far as possible, and perfecting human nature is a matter of hitting the mark in regard to the good, spirited desire crucially prompts the rational part of the soul to figure out what the truly good is for the person in question.

By comparison, the person whose character remains uneducated, or is corrupted, risks achieving what is bad for himself, despite the fact that he might be good at calculating how to achieve his ends, because he is set upon what merely seems to be good. In these cases, one might suspect that things went wrong at the level of spirited desire. For to experience truly fine actions requires superiors who nurture and adjust the non-rational desires in such a way that they come to direct the person towards the truly fine. Only then can he or she start to develop the skills needed to hit the mark with regard to the good. In other words, only to the extent that the child is

[37] Cf. *EE* 2. 10, 1227^{a}5 ff.; *NE* 1. 7, 1098^{b}3–4.
[38] Cf. *NE* 1. 3, 1095^{a}2–13, and 10. 9, 1179^{b}4–31, which serve as the textual starting-point for Burnyeat's account in "Aristotle on Learning to be Good".

fortunate enough to have such superiors does it gradually, through experience, learn to appreciate and indeed even to take pleasure in truly fine and, in the end, virtuous action. Of course, not all human beings are equally fortunate in this regard, which also explains why some people never become virtuous.

Furthermore, it is a crucial tenet of Aristotle's conception of deliberation, or practical reasoning, that it is restrained by the desire of reason itself, i.e. wish for the good. For by directing man towards the good, the desire of the rational part of the human soul as it were provides the space of reasons within which practical reasoning may operate. For the very rationale of human activity is to accomplish what is good for human beings, and there is no point in practical reasoning unless it is restrained by that goal. Hence, with regard to the rational nature of human beings, the part played by human desires is not just a matter of providing practical reasoning with starting-points to work from. Rather, human desires are constitutive in this regard, and the part played by practical reasoning conditional on that. So, although the power of deliberation is a characteristic of man as a rational being, it is not basic in that regard.

Now, suggesting that virtue of character has a certain priority over practical wisdom, in the straightforward respect that unless the starting-points of the deliberative exercise are correct ones, nothing good can be accomplished, is not say that human virtue is basically a matter of perfecting human beings' emotional nature as opposed to their rational nature. First, although the beginning of virtue of character is developed through habituation, and not through exercises of deliberation, further development requires deliberation. For in view of the complexities and contingencies of human life, hitting the mark with regard to the good requires that the situation at hand is penetrated by means of deliberation before we can reach a sound decision as to what to do. Second, even though in the individual the beginning of virtue of character is not conditional on practical wisdom of that same individual, it is dependent on the practical wisdom of that individual's guardians.

It should also be borne in mind that for Aristotle, the values which motivate human beings are not beyond rational justification. Some values are right, others wrong, and the test lies in whether or not they contribute to the good for human beings. This is why virtue as a whole, comprised of both virtue of character and intellectual virtue, is a realization of the rational nature of human beings.

Reason in Aristotle's Moral Psychology 271

For to become fully rational, human beings must be motivated by values whose pursuit contributes to the good for them. And those are inborn values of human reason itself.

University of Stockholm

BIBLIOGRAPHY

Broadie, S., *Ethics with Aristotle* (Oxford, 1991).
—— and Rowe, C., *Aristotle,* Nicomachean Ethics (Oxford, 2002).
Burnet, J., *The Ethics of Aristotle* (London, 1900).
Burnyeat, M., "Aristotle on Learning to be Good", in A. Rorty (ed.), *Essays on Aristotle's Ethics* (Berkeley, 1980), 69–92.
Cooper, J. M., "Plato's Theory of Human Motivation", *History of Philosophy Quarterly,* 1 (1984), 3–21.
—— "Reason, Moral Virtue, and Moral Value", in M. Frede and G. Striker (eds.), *Rationality in Greek Thought* (Oxford, 1996), 81–114.
—— "Some Remarks on Aristotle's Moral Psychology" ["Aristotle's Moral Psychology"], *Southern Journal of Philosophy,* 27, suppl. (1988), 25–42.
Dirlmeier, F., *Aristoteles, Nikomachische Ethik* (Berlin, 1969).
Fossheim, H. J., *Nature and Habituation in Aristotle's Theory of Human Development* (Oslo, 2003).
Gauthier, R. A., and Jolif, J. Y., *L'Éthique à Nicomaque,* 2nd edn., vol. ii/1 (Louvain and Paris, 1970).
Lorenz, H., *The Brute Within: Appetitive Desire in Plato and Aristotle* (Oxford, 2006).
Nicol, D. M., "A Paraphrase of the *Nicomachean Ethics* Attributed to the Emperor John VI Cantacuzene", *Byzantinoslavica,* 28 (1968), 1–16.
Stewart, J. A., *Notes on the* Nicomachean Ethics *of Aristotle,* vol. i (Oxford, 1892).

PHRONĒSIS AS A MEAN IN THE *EUDEMIAN ETHICS*

GILES PEARSON

THE title of this paper might appear to suggest something absurd. Surely it is virtues of character that are means, on Aristotle's view, not intellectual virtues. That the latter could be means surely 'seems un-Aristotelian' (Broadie) and 'hard to believe' (Woods).[1] However, some well-attested texts suggest that Aristotle may at some point have considered *phronēsis*, at least, a mean, and it seems time to give them a run for their money. In *EE* 2. 3 Aristotle provides a catalogue of all the various character virtues and their two related vices. And the last virtue on the list, appearing alongside the vices of *euētheia* ('simplicity') and *panourgia* ('cunning'), is *phronēsis* ($1221^{a}12$).[2] In a subsequent gloss, a little later in the same chapter, Aristotle tells us:

© Giles Pearson 2007

Thanks to Gisela Striker and Jimmy Altham for thoughts on a very early version of this paper. A much later draft was read to the B Club at Cambridge in November 2005. Thanks to everybody who raised questions, and in particular Malcolm Schofield, David Sedley, Robert Wardy, and Catherine Osborne. Thanks also to Angela Chew for providing some penetrating written comments. Finally, thanks once again to David Sedley for comments on the version that was first submitted to this journal.

Translations are, unless otherwise stated, based on those in *The Complete Works of Aristotle: The Revised Oxford Translation* [*ROT*], ed. J. Barnes (Princeton, 1984), with a number of emendations of my own.

[1] S. Broadie, 'Commentary', in S. Broadie and C. Rowe, *Aristotle,* Nicomachean Ethics [*NE*] (Oxford, 2002), 309; M. Woods, *Aristotle:* Eudemian Ethics, *Books I, II, and VIII* [*EE*] (Oxford, 1982; 2nd, rev. edn. 1992), 106.

[2] The translations given in brackets are those in *ROT*. Woods, *EE*, translates *euētheia* as 'unworldliness' and *panourgia* as 'unscrupulousness'. Though the *ROT* translates *panourgia* as 'cunning' at $1221^{a}12$, it translates *panourgos* as 'rogue' at $1221^{a}37$, and *panourgia/panourgoi* as 'villainy/villains' in *NE* 6. 12. *Phronēsis* has also been variously translated; e.g. 'practical wisdom' (e.g. *ROT*; Woods, *EE*; R. Crisp, *Aristotle:* Nicomachean Ethics (Cambridge, 2000)), 'wisdom' (*ROT* (at $1221^{a}12$); C. Rowe, in his and S. Broadie's *NE*), and 'intelligence' (T. Irwin, *Aristotle:* Nicomachean Ethics (Indianapolis, 1985)).

274 *Giles Pearson*

the *panourgos* is after more [πλεονεκτικός] in every way and from every source, the *euēthēs* not even from the right sources. (1221ᵃ36–8)

No doubt for the reason mentioned, these lines have either been deleted or at best ignored by commentators, translators, and editors alike.[3] However, the starting-point of this paper is that getting rid of the lines or ignoring them on some such basis seems questionable. The prima facie case for reconsideration is straightforward and twofold. First, the lines are well attested in the manuscripts and come in two distinct places in the chapter. Second, there is a passage in the book that provides our most detailed account of *phronēsis* (*NE* 6 = *EE* 5) in which Aristotle again links *panourgia* and *phronēsis*.[4] He writes:

There is a capacity that is called 'cleverness' [δεινότης]; and this is such as to be able to do the things that tend towards the mark we have set before ourselves and to hit it. Now if the mark be noble, the cleverness is laudable, but if the mark be bad, the cleverness is *panourgia*; hence we call clever both *phronimoi* and *panourgoi*.[5] *Phronēsis* is not the capacity, but does not exist without this capacity. (*NE* 6. 12, 1144ᵃ23–9)

Both *phronimoi* and *panourgoi* can be called 'clever', but the *panourgos* is vicious, whereas the *phronimos* is virtuous.[6] At the very least, the juxtaposition of the two states in this entirely independent pas-

---

[3] F. Susemihl, in the Teubner edition of the text (*Aristotelis Ethica Nicomachea* (Leipzig, 1887)), Woods, *EE*, and *ROT* all place them in square brackets. (Though, interestingly, the new edition of the OCT, ed. R. Walzer and J. Mingay (Oxford, 1991), leaves them intact.) C. Rowe, 'The Meaning of φρόνησις in the Eudemian Ethics', in P. Moraux and D. Harlfinger (eds.), *Untersuchungen zur Eudemischen Ethik: Akten des 5. Symposium Aristotelicum* (Berlin, 1971), 73–92, ignores the lines.

[4] I shall generally follow common practice and refer to the long discussion of the various intellectual virtues as book 6 of the *Nicomachean Ethics*, but we should not think that in relating *EE* 2. 3 to *NE* 6 passages I am linking up two independent treatises by Aristotle. This is because the primary account we have of *phronēsis* exists in one of the common books, i.e. books common to *NE* and *EE* (*NE* 5–7 = *EE* 4–6), and we do not know whether these books belonged primarily to the *Eudemian Ethics* or to the *Nicomachean Ethics*, or (for example) were written afterwards for both. It could be that the primary locus of the common books was the *Eudemian Ethics* and that the passages in *EE* 2. 3 are meant to be in accordance with the only account of *phronēsis* we have from Aristotle. (I generally think that the primary locus was the *Eudemian Ethics*, but I shall not attempt to justify this here.)

[5] Reading καὶ ⟨τοὺς⟩ πανούργους.

[6] 'Cleverness' is described as a capacity 'to do the things that tend towards the mark we have set before ourselves and hit it' (6. 12, 1144ᵃ24–6). Since cleverness is characterized as a morally neutral executive capacity, a capacity for *doing* (πράττειν), Aristotle need not only be thinking about an ability one may or may not have in reason*ing* (though it will no doubt include this). When we have an end before us that

Phronēsis *as a Mean in the* Eudemian Ethics 275

sage suggests that we need to take seriously the idea that Aristotle may, at least at some stage in his thought, have considered *phronēsis* to be some kind of mean state. And it is this idea that I propose to develop.

For the sake of this paper, then, let me pursue the idea that the *EE* 2. 3 lines are genuine and refer to the *phronēsis* that we meet elsewhere in Aristotle's works. Accepting this would immediately raise a puzzle. Why would Aristotle list an intellectual virtue in a table of character virtues? Would it suggest that he thinks that *phronēsis* could be considered to be *both* an intellectual virtue *and* a character virtue? I shall argue it would not suggest this, but nevertheless the reason he might have been motivated to place the states on the list in the *EE* chapter turns out to be interesting, and to relate to a very important feature of his thought: namely, the relation between *phronēsis* and character virtue. I shall first consider the *EE* 2. 3 lines in greater detail (Section I), before turning to the puzzle just mentioned (Section II); in the final section I shall briefly consider the significance of the absence of the trio of states in the parallel list of character virtues in *NE* 2. 7.

I

In the first *EE* line, in which Aristotle simply lists the *phronēsis* trio, the ordering of the states relative to the others listed in the table tells us that *panourgia* is supposed to be the excessive state, *euētheia* the deficient one. In the first half of the subsequent gloss, Aristotle claims that the *panourgos* is characterized by *pleonexia*—that he is grasping or after more ($\pi\lambda\epsilon o\nu\epsilon\kappa\tau\iota\kappa\acute{o}s$)[7] in every way and from every source ($\pi\acute{a}\nu\tau\omega s$ $\kappa\alpha\grave{\iota}$ $\pi\acute{a}\nu\tau o\theta\epsilon\nu$). How should this be understood?

Pleonexia and its cognates $\pi\lambda\epsilon o\nu\epsilon\kappa\tau\iota\kappa\acute{o}s$ (adjective) and $\acute{o}$ $\pi\lambda\epsilon o\nu\acute{\epsilon}$-$\kappa\tau\eta s$ (the person with the state) are most frequently mentioned in

---

we want to achieve, cleverness will be the capacity to do the things that acquire for us that end. This capacity would have at least two aspects: first, a cognitive ability to *see* the things that need to be done to achieve a given goal; and second, an ability we may call 'know-how', knowing how to put into practice the things we see are needed to achieve our aim. Cf. Broadie, 'Commentary', 382.

[7] I shall sometimes translate $\pi\lambda\epsilon o\nu\epsilon\kappa\tau\iota\kappa\acute{o}s$ simply as 'after more'; on other occasions (especially in the context of particular injustice) I shall follow *ROT*, and translate it as 'grasping'. Nothing is meant to hinge on the translation, and I shall always supply the Greek if there could be some doubt as to what is being translated.

276 *Giles Pearson*

Aristotle in connection with his account of particular injustice (the πλεονέκτης is ὁ πλέον ἔχων, the man who has or claims more than his due). Recall, Aristotle claims that both (1) the lawless man (ὁ παράνομος) and (2) the grasping (πλεονέκτης) and unequal man are unjust (*NE* 5. 1, 1129ᵃ32–3). The kind of justice that corresponds to the first kind of injustice relates to complete virtue (ἀρετὴ τελεία), at least in so far as this concerns our relations to another (πρὸς ἕτερον) (*NE* 5. 1, 1129ᵇ26–7, 1130ᵃ12–13), since 'the law bids us practise every virtue and forbids us to practise any vice' (*NE* 5. 2, 1130ᵇ23–4; also 5. 1, 1129ᵇ19–24). On this specification, there is no characteristic motive that picks out unjust acts; they are simply vicious acts more generally. This is in contrast to the injustice that corresponds to the other kind of justice, which picks out one part of virtue (*NE* 5. 2, 1130ᵃ14). Aristotle contrasts the two as follows:

> while the man who exhibits in action the other forms of wickedness acts unjustly but not graspingly [πλεονεκτεῖ] (e.g. the man who throws away his shield through cowardice or speaks harshly through bad temper or fails to help someone with money through meanness), when a man is grasping [πλεονεκτῇ], he often exhibits none of these vices—and certainly not all together—but does exhibit wickedness of some kind (for we blame him) and injustice. (1130ᵃ16–22)

Aristotle thinks that this other kind of injustice is *a part* of injustice in the broad sense of contrary to the law (1130ᵃ23–4), and he here demarcates the unjust agent in this particular sense by reference to whether or not the agent is grasping (πλεονεκτικός). This, in turn, is explained by reference to whether or not the agent in question is motivated by gain:

> if one man commits adultery for the sake of gain [τοῦ κερδαίνειν ἕνεκα], and makes money by it, while another does so at the bidding of appetite [δι' ἐπιθυμίαν] though he loses money and is penalized for it, the latter would be held to be self-indulgent rather than grasping [πλεονέκτης], while the former is unjust, not self-indulgent. Clearly, therefore, [he is unjust] because [he acts] for the sake of the gain [διὰ τὸ κερδαίνειν]. (*NE* 5. 2, 1130ᵃ24–8)

Suppose Smith is obsessed about his boss's wife and in a quiet moment at an office party sets about seducing her. Then imagine that just as Smith is making headway, his boss wanders in and catches them in the act. In this scenario, career in tatters, Smith would be held to be self-indulgent (ἀκόλαστος), but, on Aristotle's account, he is not necessarily unjust in the narrow sense. Suppose, however,

Phronēsis *as a Mean in the* Eudemian Ethics 277

in another scenario, Smith has a female boss who is obsessed with him. Suppose also that this boss promises a treasured promotion will go Smith's way, not the way of his rival, if he has an affair with her. If this motivates Smith, he acts in order to gain something over and above the adultery itself, and this makes his act unjust in the narrow sense.[8] Now the gain, in this case, is financial, but Aristotle does not think that particular injustice is restricted only to financial gain. Particular injustice is said to be concerned with 'honour or money or safety—or that which includes all these, if we had a single name for it—and its motive is the pleasure that arises from gain [ἀπὸ τοῦ κέρδους]' (*NE* 5. 2, 1130^{b}3–4). Suppose Smith commits adultery with his boss, not for the money, nor for sexual pleasure, but for the prestige this would generate for him among his fellow workmates. This too would fall under particular injustice.[9] But though the motive underlying particular injustice is not simply financial reward, it is (like general injustice) restricted to our dealings *with others* (*NE* 5. 2, 1130^{b}1–2). This is represented through its being tied to the notion of 'gain', in so far as this seems to mean 'gaining at the expense of another' or 'gaining an unfair share' (cf. *NE* 5. 4, 1132^{a}6–14).[10] The upshot is that *pleonexia* seems tied to a particular motive in the injustice passages, and general and particular injustice are contrasted by reference to this motive. When a man acts viciously (with respect to another: πρὸς ἕτερον), he acts unjustly in the *general* sense, but he need not be grasping or after more; whereas when a man acts unjustly in such a way as to manifest the vice of *particular* injustice, his act must manifest *pleonexia*,

[8] Aristotle no doubt employs the conflict cases to make his point more perspicuous. But it clearly need not be the case that the self-indulgent agent *must* act in a way that is at odds with, say, financial gain. He follows his appetites without regard for such gain, and no doubt frequently this will be financially ill-advised. But he would still be self-indulgent if he somehow happened to earn money from the adultery. This is because even in some such scenario he only really chooses to pursue pleasure, and simply chances upon financial gain as well. The unjust agent, conversely, doggedly tracks the gain and chooses the action in question—which may or may not be pleasurable for him—only for the sake of this other end.

[9] On the third in the trio, safety, see B. Williams, 'Justice as a Virtue', in A. O. Rorty (ed.), *Essays on Aristotle's Ethics* (Berkeley, 1980), 189–99 at 198–9.

[10] Cf. *NE* 9. 6, 1167^{b}12–16: 'bad men cannot be unanimous except to a small extent, since they aim at getting a larger share [πλεονεξίας ἐφιεμένους] in what is beneficial, while in labour and public service they fall short of their share; and each man, while wishing for these advantages for himself, carefully examines his neighbour and keeps him in check [κωλύει], on the notion that unless they keep watch, the common good is ruined. The result is that they form into factions, putting pressure on each other to do the just thing, while not wishing to do it themselves.'

278 *Giles Pearson*

which here means: motivated by the prospect of the pleasure of gain (1130^a16–22).

Returning to *EE* 2. 3, it is clear that if *panourgia* is not simply to collapse into particular injustice, the use of *pleonexia* in connection with the *panourgos* should be somewhat different from that in which it is tied to this particular motive. In *NE* 6. 12–13 Aristotle makes it clear that *phronēsis* requires the possession of all the character virtues.[11] This means that it requires one to be prone to experience all the appropriate non-rational motivations. Similarly, in the passage quoted from *NE* 6. 12 in the introduction, in which Aristotle links *phronēsis* and *panourgia*, *panourgia* seems to represent one general way of going wrong. Aristotle simply states that if one is practically clever and yet wicked, one is a *panourgos*, and in so doing seems to indicate that he has no desire to distinguish between different forms of clever-wickedness.[12] *Panourgia* thus seems to represent one general pole of going wrong in contrast to the only way of going right, i.e. *phronēsis*. So in *EE* 2. 3 it is clear that if (1) we are to distinguish *panourgia* from the vice of particular injustice, and (2) *panourgia* on our table is meant to indicate a way of going wrong that is at the level of generality it has in *NE* 6. 12, then *pleonexia* in this context would have to be operating in a more general way than it is in particular injustice, in which it is tied to the specific motive of gain.[13]

But is there any indication that Aristotle here intends *pleonexia* to operate in some such more general way? In fact, there are a couple of textual considerations supporting this. First, the notion of *pleonexia*, in which it is tied to gain, is also present in the very chapter of *EE* in which our passage lies. For, besides the *phronēsis* trio, Aristotle also places particular justice in his table of virtues and vices. And he not only uses *pleonexia* in his characterization of the *panourgos*, he also uses it in his characterization of the unjust agent.

---

[11] See esp. 6. 12, 1144^a29–$^b1$; 6. 13, 1144^a31–2; cf. 6. 13, 1144^b36–1145^a2.

[12] The passages do not, however, rule out the possibility that some non-clever wicked states could also be *panourgia*. Aristotle simply writes: 'if the mark be noble, the cleverness is laudable, but if the mark be bad, the cleverness is *panourgia*; hence we call clever both *phronimoi* and *panourgoi*' (*NE* 6. 12, 1144^a26–8). Technically, this only implies that all clever-bad states are *panourgia*, not that all *and only* clever-bad states are *panourgia*. Either way, *panourgia* is still a very general sort of vicious trait.

[13] More like at the level of general *in*justice, which is 'vice as a whole towards others' (1130^b19–20). In fact, even broader than this, in so far as there would seem to be no good reason to think the *phronēsis* trio would have the 'towards another' restriction we saw applied to general injustice.

Phronēsis *as a Mean in the* Eudemian Ethics   279

He posits the just (δίκαιον) as a mean between gain (κέρδος) and loss (ζημία) (1221ᵃ4),[14] and in the subsequent gloss links *pleonexia* to gain:

the man seeking more from every source [ὁ πανταχόθεν πλεονεκτικός] is greedy of gain [κερδαλέος], the man who does not [seek enough] from any source [ὁ μηδαμόθεν], or only from very few, is ruinous [ζημιώδης]. (1221ᵃ23–4)

Since seeking more or being grasping is here said to be characteristic of the person seeking gain, this use of *pleonexia* seems likely to be the same as that in the injustice passages from *NE* 5. But the fact that this usage is here in *EE* 2. 3, it seems to me, suggests that the use of the term in reference to the *panourgos*, in which it is not specifically tied to gain, may be intended to be somewhat broader. In line with this, a second point concerns a small difference in the way Aristotle characterizes the *panourgos* in contrast to the *kerdaleos*, the man greedy of gain. The *kerdaleos* is said to be someone seeking more (πλεονεκτικός) from any source (πανταχόθεν), whereas the *panourgos* is said to be someone seeking more '*in every way* from every source [πάντως καὶ πάντοθεν]'. The insistence that the *panourgos* is someone who seeks more 'in every way' may be intended to indicate that this notion of *pleonexia* is operating in a more general way than the narrow notion in which it is tied to gain. If so, it suggests that the *panourgos* is after more of anything (he perceives to be valuable) that he can get access to, not just those things that would satisfy the pleasure he would get from gaining at another's expense.[15] And I suppose at this point it is worth remembering that a *pan-ourgos* is, literally, someone who will 'do everything' or 'stop at nothing'.[16]

We can attempt to fill out this specification somewhat by examining another passage that will also at the same time supply

---

[14] The fact that justice appears on the list of means is of course interesting in its own right, in so far as commentators have puzzled about Aristotle's attempt to make justice into a mean along the lines of, but somewhat different from, his other character virtues (see e.g. D. Bostock, *Aristotle's Ethics* (Oxford, 2000), 67 ff.; also Woods, *EE*, 106).

[15] The 'in every way' will presumably have to be qualified. Just as Aristotle claims in *NE* 2. 6 that the doctrine of the mean does not apply to all actions—some actions are just inherently bad, e.g. adultery, murder, lying, and so on (1107ᵃ8 ff.)—so too he might claim that some ends are inherently good and cannot be desired too much. But see n. 22 below on how the good man seeks to assign himself the greater share of what is noble.

[16] In the *History of Animals* Aristotle characterizes foxes as *panourga* (1. 1, 488ᵇ20).

280   *Giles Pearson*

independent evidence in Aristotle of a notion of *pleonexia* broader
than that in which it is tied to gain. In *NE* 9. 8 he writes:

> those that make self-love grounds for reproach call 'self-lovers' [φίλαυτοι]
> those people who assign to themselves [τοὺς ἑαυτοῖς ἀπονέμοντας] the greater
> share [τὸ πλεῖον] of wealth, honours, and bodily pleasures; for these are
> what most people desire [οἱ πολλοὶ ὀρέγονται], and busy themselves about as
> though they were the best of all things (which is the reason, too, why they
> become objects of competition). So those who are grasping [πλεονέκται]
> with regard to these things gratify their appetites [ἐπιθυμίαι] and in general
> their emotions and the non-rational part of the soul. ($1168^{b}15$–21)

Let me highlight two initial points about this passage. First, in so
far as Aristotle includes bodily pleasures on the list, this notion
of *pleonexia* is linked to a greater range of goods than it was in the
characterization of particular injustice (which, we saw, he restricted
to money, safety, and honour). Second, and most crucially, Aristotle
claims that those who are grasping (πλεονέκται) with respect to these
things gratify their appetites (ἐπιθυμίαι) and the non-rational part
of their soul. But if gratifying an appetite can now qualify an agent
as grasping or after more (πλεονεκτικός), then we have here a notion
of *pleonexia* that is not restricted to the specific motive of gain. In
NE 5. 2 ($1130^{a}24$–8) we saw that Aristotle claimed that if we are
motivated to commit adultery by an appetite we are self-indulgent,
not grasping; only if we act for the sake of gain are we grasping
and so unjust. But, on the above account, it seems, a person who
commits adultery through appetite *could* count as grasping. Thus
pleonexia must here be being used in a broader sense.[17]

But what does Aristotle mean in this passage when he claims that
these self-lovers assign themselves 'a greater share' (τὸ πλεῖον) in
wealth, honours, and bodily pleasures? Well, it could be that this
character is being imagined to have access to a set of these goods,
with an expectation on him to deal them out fairly, but he assigns
himself the 'greater share'. This is why CEOs in top companies
tend to get absurd bonuses, why civil servants tend to do well in the
New Year's honours lists, and why I tend to get rather a lot of wine
at dinner. On this interpretation, the non-rational desires of these
agents motivate them to assign themselves a 'greater share' of the

---

[17] A broader use of *pleonexia* is also present in Plato. See e.g. *Rep.* 2, 359 C 5, in
which *pleonexia* appears to represent a broad range of desires (*epithumiai*: 359 C 3),
typified by Gyges' activities when he discovers he has the magic ring (360 B 1–2).
See also *Gorg.* 483 C, and especially 490 A ff.

Phronēsis *as a Mean in the* Eudemian Ethics   281

divisible good in question. But I suppose Aristotle could also be understood to be claiming more simply that these self-lovers assign themselves more of these goods *than they should*. We might explain this idea by construing such agents as combining a number of the individual vices that Aristotle discusses in *NE* 3. 6–4. 9 and *EE* 3. 1– 7. They would assign themselves more wealth 'than they should', like the illiberal or stingy agents he describes in *NE* 4. 1 (esp. 1121^b12 ff.) and *EE* 3. 4, i.e. those deficient in giving and excessive in taking wealth. They would assign themselves more honours 'than they should', like the honour-loving or over-ambitious characters referred to in *NE* 4. 4, who aim at honour more than they should and from the wrong sources (1125^b8–10). (Each of these defects can also be considered on a 'grand scale' (*NE* 4. 4, 1125^b4), in which the illiberal man (ὁ ἀνελεύθερος) becomes a niggardly one (ὁ μικροπρεπής: *NE* 4. 2, 1123^a27–8; *EE* 3. 6, 1233^b2–4), and the character who is honour-loving (φιλότιμος) becomes vain (χαῦνος: *NE* 4. 3, 1125^a27– 8; *EE* 3. 5, 1233^a9–12).[18]) Finally, those who assign themselves more bodily pleasures 'than they should' would be like the self-indulgent agents (ἀκόλαστοι) referred to in *NE* 3. 10–12 and *EE* 3. 2, who are motivated to pursue bodily pleasure to a greater extent than they should. Self-lovers would then be people who are after more than they should in each of these ways.[19]

This latter reading of the *NE* 9. 8 text best suits the notion of *pleonexia* that I think is in play in *EE* 2. 3, in connection with the *panourgos*. Though even the first characterization extends beyond the domain of particular injustice, in so far as *pleonexia* is not tied to any specific motive, it nevertheless seems to retain the 'towards another' (πρὸς ἕτερον) qualification characteristic of *general* (in)justice. Aristotle claimed that general justice was 'virtue entire' in so far as that is exercised towards another, and refers to general injustice as

---

[18] I believe the same person could be both e.g. illiberal and niggardly. Cf. T. H. Irwin, 'Disunity in Aristotelian Virtue', *OSAP* suppl. (1988), 61–90; M. Pakaluk, 'On an Alleged Contradiction in Aristotle's *Nicomachean Ethics*', *OSAP* 22 (2002), 201–19; and S. Drefcinski, 'A Different Solution to an Alleged Contradiction in Aristotle's *Nicomachean Ethics*', *OSAP* 30 (2006), 201–10.

[19] Explaining these self-lovers by way of a combination of vices may be suggested by Aristotle's contrast with virtuous agents in the rest of the passage: 'if a man were always anxious that he himself, above all things, should act justly, temperately, or in accordance with any other of the virtues, and in general were always to try to secure for himself the honourable course, no one will call such a man a lover of self or blame him' (*NE* 9. 8, 1168^b25–8). Cf. also the way general justice is explained as a combination of virtues (*NE* 5. 1, 1129^b19–27), and general *injustice* is thought of as 'vice entire' (with the πρὸς ἕτερον restriction) (*NE* 5. 1, 1130^a8–13).

282   *Giles Pearson*

'vice as a whole' with the same qualification (*NE* 5. 1, 1130ᵃ8–13). And clearly, in so far as the first reading of *NE* 9. 8 involves one dividing up a good in one's favour (over the claims of others), it involves a 'towards another' component. But, if we are to have a notion of *panourgia* that operates at a parallel level of generality to *phronēsis* (as we noted, Aristotle thinks that *phronēsis* requires the possession of all the character virtues, and seems to mean this without restriction or qualification), and if we are to distinguish this vice from general injustice, then it should not have the 'towards another' restriction. Stuffing oneself full of cream cakes (i.e. 'more than you should'), even if this involves no 'towards another' component, could manifest one as grasping for or after more of bodily pleasure, on such an interpretation.

The suggestion, then, is that Aristotle's claim in *EE* 2. 3 that the *panourgos* is grasping or after more ($\pi\lambda\epsilon o\nu\epsilon\kappa\tau\iota\kappa\acute{o}s$) in every way and from every source could be understood in a way that means that following any non-rational motive can make the agent grasping— if it is indicative of that agent's general tendency to seek more of various core goods than he should.

Let me now turn to the other vicious state that Aristotle lists in his *EE* 2. 3 trio, *euētheia*. *Euētheia* literally means 'good-character', but in Greek it seems to have come to mean someone who was simple or stupid (see LSJ s.v.), somewhat similar to the way we may patronizingly say of someone who is foolish but good-natured that they 'mean well'.[20] In this respect, we may recall that Thrasymachus in Plato's *Republic* refers to justice as 'very high-minded simplicity' ($\pi\acute{a}\nu\nu$ $\gamma\epsilon\nu\nu a\acute{\iota}a$ $\epsilon\mathring{\upsilon}\acute{\eta}\theta\epsilon\iota a$: 348 C 12), and claims that injustice rules the 'truly simple and just' ($\acute{a}\rho\chi\epsilon\iota$ $\tau\mathring{\omega}\nu$ $\mathring{\omega}s$ $\mathring{a}\lambda\eta\theta\mathring{\omega}s$ $\epsilon\mathring{\upsilon}\eta\theta\iota\kappa\mathring{\omega}\nu$ $\tau\epsilon$ $\kappa a\grave{\iota}$ $\delta\iota\kappa a\acute{\iota}\omega\nu$: 343 C 6). Unjust agents, in contrast to the just, are said to show good judgement ($\epsilon\mathring{\upsilon}\beta o\upsilon\lambda\acute{\iota}a$) (348 D 2). (Indeed, the *Republic* passage just mentioned is significant in that in it, as in the *EE*

---

[20] A passage in *Republic* 3 is illuminating on the dual meaning of *euētheia*. In his discussion of the ideal education for the Guardians, Socrates elaborates on all the details of ideal and non-ideal music. After discussing which modes and metres are appropriate, he turns to words, and claims: 'fine words, harmony, grace, and rhythm follow *euētheia*; I do not mean this in the sense in which we use it for simple-mindedness [$\check{a}\nu o\iota a$], but I mean the sort of good [$\epsilon\mathring{\upsilon}$] and fine [$\kappa a\lambda\mathring{\omega}s$] character [$\mathring{\eta}\theta os$] that has developed in accordance with reason [$\delta\iota\acute{a}\nu o\iota a$]' (400 D 11–E 3). The use in reference to stupidity is, though, so prominent that Socrates not only has to ward off the interpretation here, but when he uses a cognate term slightly later, it is the stupid sense that is intended ('decent people appear *euētheis* and easily deceived by the unjust when they are young' (409 A 8–B 1)).

Phronēsis *as a Mean in the* Eudemian Ethics 283

passages, *euētheia* can be seen to be a parallel but defective version of *phronēsis*: just as, in Thrasymachus' perverted view, the just are simple, so the unjust are said to be '*phronimoi* and good' (e.g. at 348 D 3–4).) In *EE* 2. 3 the gloss about the *panourgos* runs into a parallel comment about the *euēthēs*:

the *panourgos* is after more [πλεονεκτικός] in every way and from every source, the *euēthēs* not even from the right sources. (1221ᵃ36–8)

One might understand this line to be claiming that the *euēthēs* is not *grasping or after more* (πλεονεκτικός) from the sources he *should be grasping* from. However, if this were the right way to read the line, it would have the uncomfortable consequence that *pleonexia* was not itself being considered a bad trait, but something that one can be right about. The *panourgos* would be defective in so far as he is grasping in every way and from every source, and the *euēthēs* would be defective in so far as he fails to be grasping even from the sources he should. This would imply that the *phronimos* would be grasping or after more in just the right ways and from just the right sources. However, I very much doubt that Aristotle would accept this. On all the notions of *pleonexia* we have seen, that in which it is employed in particular injustice, or the broader notions glossed from *NE* 9. 8 in which it is not tied to any specific motive, to be grasping or after more (πλεονεκτικός) seems to be a bad thing, and to be connected to seeking more than is appropriate. Recall also the origin of the term: the πλεονέκτης is ὁ πλέον ἔχων, the man who has or claims more than his due. But if *pleonexia* is always wicked, the mean would not be a virtue after all. Just as Aristotle claims in *NE* 2. 6 that it is not as if we can 'commit adultery with the right women, at the right time, and in the right way' (1107ᵃ16), so too I doubt he would allow that the *phronimos* is grasping or after more (πλεονεκτικός), but at the right time, and in the right way. Seeking to get more than one should, he would surely say, must always be wrong.[21] So rather than imagining the mean to be centred around having the right, excessive, or deficient amount

---

[21] At the end of *NE* 9. 8 Aristotle claims that 'in all the actions that men are praised for, the good man is seen to assign to himself the greater share [πλεῖον] in what is noble' (1169ᵃ34–ᵇ1). By this Aristotle means that the good man will be prepared to give up honours, offices, and even his life, if this is noble, since he chooses nobility before all else. But this suggests that nobility would be something that one could not seek 'more than one should', and so Aristotle would not have a reason to call the good man grasping or after more (πλεονεκτικός) even in this respect.

284 *Giles Pearson*

of *pleonexia*, we should probably construe Aristotle's compressed remark concerning the *euēthēs* as follows:

the *panourgos* is after more [πλεονεκτικός] in every way and from every source, the *euēthēs* is not even [after what he should be after] from the right sources.

And just as we explained the *panourgos* by reference to his tendency to manifest a combination of vicious traits, we might do something similar with the *euēthēs*. So, with respect to the goods we considered before, this agent would be prone to assign himself less wealth 'than he should', and would be like the prodigal or wasteful agent Aristotle describes in *NE* 4. 1 (esp. 1121^{b}8 ff.) and *EE* 3. 4, i.e. excessive in giving and deficient in the taking of wealth. Equally, he would assign himself fewer honours 'than he should', as does the under-ambitious character referred to in *NE* 4. 4, who fails to choose to be honoured even for noble reasons (1125^{b}10–11). (Each of these defects can also be considered on a 'grand scale', in which the prodigal man (ἄσωτος) becomes someone who manifests tastelessness and vulgarity (ἀπειροκαλία καὶ βαναυσία: *NE* 2. 7, 1107^{b}19; see also 4. 2, 1123^{a}19–27; *EE* 3. 6, 1233^{a}38–9), and the character who does not desire honour enough becomes unduly humble (μικρόψυχος: *NE* 4. 3, 1125–6; *EE* 3. 5, 1233^{a}12–16).) Finally, he who assigns himself fewer bodily pleasures 'than he should' would be like the insensate agent (ἀναίσθητος) referred to in *NE* 3. 11 (1119^{a}5–11) and *EE* 3. 2 (1231^{a}26–8), who fails to desire bodily pleasure to the extent that he should.[22]

In this way we can view the trio of states as varying with respect to whether one seeks more of such goods than is appropriate (i.e. is πλεονεκτικός), less than is appropriate, or as much as is in fact appropriate. Only the *panourgos*, on this account, is grasping or after more, since the *phronimos* seeks only what is appropriate (not more than it) and the *euēthēs* falls short of seeking that.

[22] If we add safety to the list of goods (cf. *NE* 5. 2, 1130^{b}2), we might also be able to consider the domain of courage covered. The *panourgos* would be cowardly in so far as he is driven by his non-rational desires to seek safety 'too much', the *phronimos* would be courageous, and the *euēthēs* could seem rash in so far as he would fail to be sufficiently concerned about his safety. Of course, Aristotle would normally refer to the coward as experiencing excessive fear, rather than as seeking safety too much. I see no reason why he should not also allow that the *panourgos* could be excessive in the sense of experiencing an emotion too much, though the gloss in *EE* 2. 3 ('after more from every source') more naturally fits a goods-based analysis of the *panourgos*.

Phronēsis *as a Mean in the* Eudemian Ethics   285

II

In some such way we might give some content to Aristotle's placing *phronēsis* on the list of virtues in *EE* 2. 3 and, if the lines are genuine, this could well be something like what Aristotle had in mind. I am not claiming that the characterization is trouble-free, but rather than attempt to clarify Aristotle's view still further or pursue specific problems with the detail of the account I have developed,[23] I would instead like to step back a little and consider a more general problem with the overall picture that has emerged. Doing so will help us to see why Aristotle could have been motivated to place the trio of states on the *EE* list in the first place and, as I see it, it is this motivational puzzle that actually turns out to be most interesting.

The problem I am referring to is the one I raised at the end of the introduction. By the time we reach *EE* 2. 3 Aristotle is meant to be discussing virtue of character. In *EE* 2. 1 he draws his distinction between virtues of character and intellectual virtues ($1220^a4–12$) and then immediately announces: 'After this we must consider character virtue' (1220^a13), which he then proceeds to do until the end of *EE* 2. 5 (after which he turns to voluntariness and choice (2. 6–11), before providing more detailed sketches of particular character virtues (3. 1–7)). It is character virtue that is said to be a mean (2. 3, $1220^b34–5$), and the table of virtues is provided to illustrate this. But what should we make of the fact that the *phronēsis* trio are listed in a table of character virtues and their co-ordinate vices? Are we now being invited to think that *phronēsis* can be considered *to be* some kind of (master) character virtue? In accordance with this, our understanding of the states in the last section suggested that Aristotle might be pointing to a

---

[23] We might wonder, for example, why Aristotle would want to single out just these two vicious characters, in contrast to the *phronimos*. Why should someone not, for example, combine an excessive desire for wealth with a deficient desire for bodily pleasure, or seek honour excessively but at the same time be a spendthrift? (A related problem applies on a smaller scale to Aristotle's accounts of individual virtues. Why should someone not, for example, be excessively afraid of some things but deficiently fearful of others? See R. Hursthouse on the 'fearless phobic' in 'A False Doctrine of the Mean', *Proceedings of the Aristotelian Society*, 81 (1980–1), 57–72; see also H. J. Curzer, 'A Defense of Aristotle's Doctrine that Virtue is a Mean', *Ancient Philosophy*, 16 (1996), 129–38; and G. Pearson, 'Does the Fearless Phobic Really Fear the Squeak of Mice "too much"?', *Ancient Philosophy*, 26 (2006), 81–91.) Perhaps Aristotle would view the combinations I mentioned, and the fearless phobic, as 'mixed' states (cf. *NE* 3. 7, $1115^b31–2$)?

286   Giles Pearson

non-rational basis for them: following the parallel passage in *NE* 9. 8, we suggested that following any non-rational motive can make the *panourgos* grasping—if it is indicative of that agent's general tendency to seek more of various core goods than he should (and *mutatis mutandis* for the *phronimos* and the *euēthēs*). But a non-rational basis to the states makes them seem equivalent to the other character states listed in the table, which in part involve being prone to undergo various non-rational motivations to act in certain ways. Again, we might think that the analysis suggests that *phronēsis* is here being considered *to be* some kind of (master) character virtue.

But the idea that it could be so, and yet at the same time still be the state that is referred to as *phronēsis* elsewhere (and, indeed, in the *NE* 6. 12 passage quoted in the introduction which juxtaposes *panourgia* and *phronēsis*), is problematic to say the least. Aristotle carefully distinguishes intellectual virtues from virtues of character in both ethical works. He does so on the basis of a division of the soul into two parts: a rational part, and a non-rational part composed of emotions and desires (*EE* 2. 1, 1219^b28–32, 1220^a8–11; *NE* 1. 13, 1102^a27–8).[24] The non-rational part, Aristotle claims, is capable of 'listening' to the part of the soul that has reason and so 'shares in reason in a sense' (*NE* 1. 13, 1102^b29–32; cf. *EE* 2. 1, 1219^b30–1, 1220^a10–11). In line with this, Aristotle in turn distinguishes between two types of virtue—virtue of character and intellectual virtue (*EE* 2. 1, 1220^a4–12; *NE* 1. 13, 1103^a3–5)—and in both works he then embarks on a discussion of character virtue. When we come to book 6 of *NE* (=book 5 of *EE*), Aristotle finally turns to intellectual virtue. And just as he had divided the soul in general into two parts (rational/non-rational) in *EE* 2. 1/*NE* 1. 13, so he now subdivides the rational part into two parts (*NE* 6. 1, 1139^a3–15). One part of the rational part, he claims, considers necessary and unchanging things, the other contingent and changing,[25] and Aristotle announces that his task is to 'learn what is the best state of each of these two parts; for this is the virtue of each' (6. 1, 1139^a15–16). It turns out that the virtue of the rational part that is concerned with necessary and unchanging things is wisdom

---

[24] I ignore the other non-rational part, the nutritive or vegetative part that Aristotle tells us is not important to his ethical investigation (*EE* 2. 1, 1219^b31–2, 36–9; *NE* 1. 13, 1102^a32–$^b12$).

[25] There is no third part of the rational soul considering contingent unchanging things; for in the Aristotelian cosmos anything that never will change never can change (see *De caelo* 1. 12).

Phronēsis *as a Mean in the* Eudemian Ethics   287

(σοφία),[26] and the virtue of the other rational part, that which is concerned with contingent and changing things, is *phronēsis*. Character virtue and *phronēsis* thus seem distinct. Virtue of character is virtue of the non-rational part of the soul, and seems to represent an agent's disposition to undergo appropriate action-prompting non-rational desires and emotions. *Phronēsis*, on the other hand, is the intellectual virtue of the rational part of the soul concerned with things that can be otherwise (*NE* 1. 13, 1103^{a}3–2. 1, 1103^{a}18; 6. 1, 1138^{b}35–1139^{a}16) and seems to represent something like an agent's ability to deliberate in a morally excellent way (*NE* 6. 5, 1140^{a}25–31).

In fact, though, the separation of *phronēsis* and character virtue is not as sharp as these passages make it seem. On the one hand, (1) Aristotle's definition of character virtue includes reference to choice (*EE* 3. 10, 1227^{b}8; *NE* 2. 6, 1106^{b}36), and so deliberation (*EE* 3. 10, 1227^{a}3–5; *NE* 3. 3, 1113^{a}2–12); and (2) virtue in the strict sense is said not just to be *in accordance* with *phronēsis* (κατὰ τὴν φρόνησιν) but actually to require its *presence* (μετὰ τοῦ ὀρθοῦ λόγου= μετὰ φρονήσεως: 1144^{b}27–8) (*NE* 6. 13, 1144^{b}16–17, ^{b}26–8).[27] And, on the other hand, just as character virtue involves an essential reference to *phronēsis*, so too Aristotle maintains that *phronēsis* is dependent upon virtue of character.[28] He writes:

> this eye of the soul [sc. *phronēsis*] acquires its formed state not without the aid of virtue, as has been said and is plain; for inferences which deal with acts to be done are things which involve a starting-point, viz. 'since the end, i.e. what is best, is of such and such a nature', whatever it may be (let it for the sake of argument be whatever we please); and this is not evident except to the good man; for wickedness perverts us and causes us to be deceived about the starting-points of action. Therefore it is evident

---

[26] Aristotle characterizes wisdom as 'comprehension [νοῦς] combined with knowledge [ἐπιστήμη] of the things that are highest by nature' (*NE* 6. 7, 1141^{b}2–3). This combines knowledge of what follows from basic principles with a true apprehension of those principles themselves. This is knowledge of e.g. being (esp. God) and the heavenly bodies (the latter are necessary and unchanging in Aristotle's schema).

[27] Indeed, in the famous *NE* definition of virtue of character (but not in the two proto-definitions in the *EE* (2. 5, 1222^{a}6–12; 2. 10, 1227^{b}8–10)), a reference to *phronēsis* is explicit in the definition: 'virtue is a state concerned with choice lying in a mean relative to us, this being determined by reason and in the way the *phronimos* would determine it' (*NE* 2. 6, 1106^{b}36–1107^{a}2).

[28] On the apparent circle here see e.g. N. O. Dahl, *Practical Reason, Aristotle, and Weakness of the Will* (Minneapolis, 1984), ch. 4, sect. 1; S. Broadie, *Ethics with Aristotle*, (Oxford, 1991), 265 n. 80; A. D. Smith, 'Character and Intellect in Aristotle's Ethics', *Phronesis*, 41 (1996), 56–74.

288   *Giles Pearson*

that it is impossible to be practically wise [φρόνιμον] without being good. (6. 12, 1144ᵃ29–ᵇ1)

'Being good', here, is equivalent to possessing the character virtues, as 6. 13 makes clear: '[it is impossible] to be practically wise [φρόνιμον] without character virtue [ἠθικὴ ἀρετή]' (1144ᵇ32). Now exactly how we are to understand these passages, and specifically the role of virtue in *phronēsis*, is a matter of dispute, and here is not the place to pursue the details of the debate.[29] But what cannot be disputed is that the passages assign a crucial role to virtue of character in *phronēsis*: *phronēsis* is not possible without virtue of character, because virtue of character is fundamental to our virtuous practical reasoning. And this is presumably because, at least in part, malign non-rational emotions and desires could interfere with the proper functioning of such reasoning.[30]

But although character virtue and *phronēsis* are not as independent as they might appear on the basis of the passages we first looked at, their interdependence does little to support the idea that *phronēsis* could be considered *to be* some kind of (master) character virtue. In fact, the first half of the interdependence (that character virtue requires *phronēsis*) strongly counts against it. For if, *ex hypothesi*, *phronēsis* were a character virtue, and yet virtues of character 'in the strict sense' are made 'in the strict sense' by the pre-

[29] The debate relates to how we understand Aristotle's claim in *NE* 6. 12 that virtue makes the aim right, and *phronēsis* the things leading to it (1144ᵃ8–9; cf. *NE* 6. 13, 1145ᵃ4–6); see e.g. W. W. Fortenbaugh, 'Aristotle: Emotion and Moral Virtue', *Arethusa*, 2 (1969), 163–85; D. J. Allan, 'Aristotle's Account of the Origin of Moral Principles', in J. Barnes, M. Schofield, and R. Sorabji (eds.), *Articles on Aristotle*, ii. *Ethics and Politics* (London, 1977), 72–8; R. Sorabji, 'Aristotle on the Role of the Intellect in Virtue', in A. O. Rorty (ed.), *Essays on Aristotle's Ethics* (Berkeley, 1980), 201–19; Dahl, *Practical Reason, Aristotle, and Weakness of the Will*, pt. I, esp. ch. 4; Broadie, *Ethics with Aristotle*, ch. 4, esp. sects. 10–11; W. W. Fortenbaugh, 'Aristotle's Distinction between Moral Virtue and Practical Wisdom', in J. P. Anton and A. Preus (eds.), *Essays in Ancient Greek Philosophy*, iv. *Aristotle's Ethics* (Albany, NY, 1991), 97–106; C. D. C. Reeve, *Practices of Reason* (Oxford, 1995), sect. 14; Smith, 'Character and Intellect in Aristotle's Ethics'; Bostock, *Aristotle's Ethics*, 88 ff.; S. Broadie, 'Philosophical Introduction', in Broadie and Rowe, *NE*, 49–50.

[30] However, as others have noted, this leaves the status of the enkratic agent problematic (and also the akratic, for that matter), in so far as the enkratic agent forms the correct *prohairesis*, but does not possess virtue of character; see e.g. M. Woods, 'Intuition and Perception in Aristotle's Ethics', *OSAP* 4 (1986), 145–66 at 150–1; and E. Telfer, 'The Unity of the Moral Virtues in Aristotle's *Nicomachean Ethics*', *Proceedings of the Aristotelian Society*, 90 (1989–90), 35–48 at 37–8. Surely we need to maintain that just as the enkratic agent does not possess virtue of character, so too he does not possess *phronēsis*; but then the issue is to understand in what sense his choice is right.

Phronēsis *as a Mean in the* Eudemian Ethics   289

sence of *phronēsis* (*NE* 6. 13, 1144^{b}16–17, 26–8), then it would seem that *phronēsis* 'in the strict sense' (as one character virtue) would be made 'in the strict sense' by the introduction of the presence of . . . *phronēsis*! And this looks to be viciously circular: a notion of *phronēsis* 'in the strict sense' suggests that there is a non-strict sense of *phronēsis* which does not possess the presence *of itself*.[31] So if *EE* 2. 3 and *NE* 6. 12–13 are supposed to be consistent, then *phronēsis* should not be in the table because Aristotle thought that (in the appropriate context) it could be thought of *as* a character virtue.

But what alternative is there, given the fact that it is placed in a table of character virtues, and that it seems likely that there is a non-rational basis to the states co-ordinate to it? Well, in fact, the other half of the interdependence highlighted above (that *phronēsis* requires virtue of character) suggests another possibility, and the one I want to propose. Since Aristotle thinks that *phronēsis* requires virtue of character, and yet also holds that virtue of character is essentially a mean (i.e. a mean state ($\mu\epsilon\sigma\acute{o}\tau\eta\varsigma$) that lies between two vices and involves hitting the intermediate ($\mu\acute{\epsilon}\sigma o\nu$) in passions and actions: see esp. *NE* 2. 9, 1109^{a}20–4^{32}), he might have inferred that *phronēsis* must 'inherit' the status of being a mean from virtue of character. This suggestion relies only upon the idea that *phronēsis depends on* character virtue, not that *it is* a character virtue, and so there is no new circularity problem arising with it.[33] Roughly, the idea would be as follows. *Phronēsis* requires an agent to be disposed to experience all the appropriate non-rational emotions and desires—i.e. possess character virtue—so that it can then function properly and direct the agent towards hitting the intermediate in action. But because character virtue in general is contrasted with

[31] The circularity is even more explicit with the *NE* definition of virtue (quoted above, n. 28), in so far as that makes explicit reference to the *phronimos*. However, I do not want to rely on this: the definitions of virtue in the *EE* do not directly incorporate this reference to *phronēsis*, and so it might be thought that there is shift from the *EE* to the *NE* in this respect (especially given that, as I shall discuss below, *NE* does not include the *phronēsis* trio of *EE* 2. 3 in its parallel list of virtues and their co-ordinate vices in *NE* 2. 7). However, as my main text makes clear, we do not need to rely on the *NE* definition of virtue to create the vicious circle; passages from *NE* 6 are sufficient. And *NE* 6 is a common book.

[32] On the doctrine of the mean, see esp. A. W. Müller, 'Aristotle's Conception of Ethical and Natural Virtue: How the Unity Thesis Sheds Light on the Doctrine of the Mean', in J. Szaif and M. Lutz-Bachmann (eds.), *What is Good for a Human Being: Human Nature and Values* (Berlin, 2004), 18–53.

[33] 'New', i.e. any more than the interdependence may be thought to generate a circularity problem anyway. See above, n. 29, for references to some discussion.

290 *Giles Pearson*

two vicious character tendencies (one excessive, the other deficient) (*NE* 2. 9, 1109ᵃ20–4), it might also seem that *phronēsis* itself should be contrasted with two defective states. Like *phronēsis*, these states would have an intellectual dimension to them; but just as *phronēsis* is dependent on virtue of character, the defective states co-ordinate to *phronēsis* would also be dependent on very general *vicious* character traits. And it is this character-state underpinning of all three states, I want to suggest, that would have motivated Aristotle to place them as a group in the table in *EE* 2. 3, and hence why, on my proposal, he there seems to point to a non-rational basis to *panourgia* and *euētheia*. Just as the *phronimos* has all the appropriate non-rational motivations, so too the *panourgos* is driven by his non-rational desires and emotions to be grasping or after more (πλεονεκτικός) in the very general way I specified, and the *euēthēs* has a set of non-rational motivations that make him deficient at seeking the core goods. Though both *panourgia* and *euētheia* presumably have intellectual dimensions as well (as the *NE* 6. 12 passage quoted in the introduction suggests for *panourgia*, and the name '*euētheia*', which connotes simpleness or stupidity, suggests for it), they are, I suggest, like *phronēsis*, placed in the table in *EE* 2. 3 with a view to the non-rational motivations that underpin them.

III

In Section I, I investigated the *EE* 2. 3 lines on their own terms; in Section II, I attempted to give some sort of explanation as to how those lines could fit into Aristotle's ethical architectonic. However, even if one grants me that the passages concerning *phronēsis* in *EE* 2. 3 are genuine, and should be understood in something like the way I have suggested, one might still try to undermine the significance of this by pointing to the fact that Aristotle does not refer to the trio of states elsewhere and, in particular, does not place them on the parallel list of character virtues in *NE* 2. 7. Thus, even if I am right about the *EE* passages, one might think that Aristotle must have given up on the idea and, therefore, that it is of little interest to us. To close, let me briefly consider this charge.

Our key locus for discussion of *phronēsis* is book 6 of the *Nicomachean Ethics*. But *NE* 6 is primarily concerned with providing a detailed account of the various intellectual virtues, virtues of the

Phronēsis *as a Mean in the* Eudemian Ethics   291

rational part of the soul. And with respect to *phronēsis*, Aristotle is chiefly concerned with the intellectual aspect of this virtue. For example, having claimed that *phronēsis* involves excellence in deliberation (6. 5, 1140ª25–31), he devotes a long chapter to considering exactly what excellence in deliberation is, distinguishing it from, among other things, knowledge, skill in conjecture, and readiness of mind (6. 9). From this perspective the character-virtue underpinning of *phronēsis* is less relevant. Nevertheless, it comes up at the end of the book and it is here that we get Aristotle referring to one of the states he listed in *EE* 2. 3 (sc. *panourgia*). Thus the fact that *phronēsis* as a mean is not prominent in the *NE* 6 discussion of *phronēsis* can be accounted for by the fact that Aristotle is there focusing on the intellectual dimension of the virtue and, on my account, it is not owing to this that he thinks the doctrine of the mean applicable to it.[34]

But what about the more specific absence of the states in the parallel list of virtues and vices in *NE* 2. 7? It is true that Aristotle does not *include* the *phronēsis* trio on this list; however, at the end of the list he postpones discussing both justice and the intellectual virtues in the following passage:

> with regard to justice, since it has not one simple meaning, we shall, after describing the other states, distinguish its two kinds and say how each of them is a mean; and similarly [ὁμοίως] also the rational virtues [περὶ τῶν λογικῶν ἀρετῶν]. (1108ᵇ7–10)

Sarah Broadie comments on the part about justice as follows: 'Some commentators think these words spurious, since justice in one of the two senses of book V (general justice) is not defined as intermediate.'[35] Admittedly, when Aristotle finally does discuss justice as a mean in *NE* 5, he seems to be concerned with the particular version of it (*NE* 5. 5, 1133ᵇ30–1134ª13), but the above lines need not be spurious on account of this alone. Aristotle does distinguish between two versions of justice in *NE* 5, as we have seen, and he devotes only a small discussion to particular justice as a mean. It is possible, since *NE* 5 is a common book (= *EE* 4) and may originally be from *EE* rather than *NE*, that when Aristotle wrote *NE* 2. 7 he

---

[34] It would surely be absurd to accept as a general principle the idea that if Aristotle mentions something only a couple of times then he did not believe it! I suspect that a fair bit of what is commonly taken to be core Aristotelian doctrine would fall by the wayside if this principle were adopted.

[35] Broadie, 'Commentary', 309.

292 *Giles Pearson*

planned to extend or rework his discussion of justice as a mean to say more clearly how both kinds are means.[36] Broadie comments on the line referring to the intellectual virtues as follows: 'Presumably the reference is to *NE* VI. But this sentence too is suspect. Its mode of designating the intellectual excellences occurs nowhere else in Aristotle. And any implication that these, too, are intermediates seems un-Aristotelian.'[37] The argument of this essay has suggested that it might not be un-Aristotelian to think that there is some sense in which *phronēsis*, at least, could be considered a mean. However, I have also consistently maintained that it is not *qua* intellectual virtue that *phronēsis* could be considered such, but only because it has a special relationship to virtue of character. Again, we have no reason to think that the other intellectual virtue, *sophia*, would also have this special relationship to character virtue (since it is not tied to action, but to contemplation); and, indeed, it is not on the list in *EE* 2. 3. So, even on my account, it is not the case that all the intellectual virtues should be considered means. But I suppose we might take the line about rational virtues in *NE* 2. 7 as a loose reference to the idea that *phronēsis* can be considered a mean. If so, we would again have to maintain that Aristotle never actually wrote the new version of *NE* 6, in which this was to be discussed, and that *NE* 6 was really written for *EE*, not for *NE*.[38]

At any rate, the suggestion that the *NE* 2. 7 line about the rational virtues is intended to pick out just *phronēsis*, and in the way we have examined, is surely, at the very best, highly speculative. However, even if the closing lines of *NE* 2. 7 are not genuine, but were, for example, added by a later editor of the corpus,[39] and we conclude

---

[36] He does, as I noted earlier, maintain that corresponding to general justice there is a notion of general *in*justice, which corresponds to 'vice entire' (*NE* 5. 1, 1130^{a}8–13).   [37] Broadie, 'Commentary', 309.

[38] Perhaps by the time he wrote *NE* he felt that it would be confusing to place it on the list of character virtues, when after all, even though it can be considered a mean, it is not so because *it is* a virtue of character, but because it inherits that status from character virtue. If so, he might have wanted to discuss it in a reworked version of book 6. (This motivation would fit with a general reason he might have for postponing discussion of *both* justice and *phronēsis* as means in *NE* 2. 7: namely, that both are *atypical* means.) All this is consistent with the fact that even though we *do* find the trio of states in *EE* 2. 3, there is still a general lack of references to the trio in *NE* 6 (assuming, for the sake of argument, that this is an *EE* book). This is because, as I mentioned above, in *NE* 6 Aristotle is primarily concerned with *phronēsis* as an intellectual virtue, and is not considering its character-virtue underpinning.

[39] Or perhaps, as C. C. W. Taylor suggests (*Aristotle:* Nicomachean Ethics, *Books II–IV* (Oxford, 2006), 122), the line about the intellectual virtues should be read

Phronēsis *as a Mean in the* Eudemian Ethics 293

that Aristotle changed his mind about characterizing *phronēsis* as a mean, that would not necessarily lessen the importance of the *EE* passages. We can still investigate what initially might have motivated him to place the states there. And this motivation, I want to suggest, relates to an issue that lies at the heart of Aristotle's ethical thought and seems to have caused him some concern: namely, the relation between *phronēsis* and character virtue. As we have seen, Aristotle seems compelled to maintain that there is a close interdependence between the two. Virtue of character in the strict sense requires the presence of *phronēsis*, and *phronēsis* in turn requires virtue of character. The latter half of this interdependence may have seemed suggestive to Aristotle: if *phronēsis* is singled out among the intellectual virtues as having an essential relation to character virtue, might it not also inherit their status as means? If so, he might have thought that *phronēsis* could sensibly be considered from two perspectives. On the one hand, it could be considered as an intellectual virtue, as it primarily is in *NE* 6, in which it amounts to excellence in deliberation. On the other hand, it might also be considered from the perspective of the non-rational motivations that it requires in order to exist. From this perspective, since it requires all the appropriate non-rational motivations, it could, he may have thought, sensibly be contrasted with other general ways in which such motivations might fail to be appropriate. Our investigation of the *EE* 2. 3 lines suggests that Aristotle considered both the *panourgos* and the *euēthēs* to be agents who consistently possess inappropriate non-rational emotions and desires (the former being motivated to seek the core goods more than is appropriate, the latter to seek them less than is appropriate). Now the absence of these states in the *NE* 2. 7 list may perhaps suggest that Aristotle was ultimately unhappy with that characterization, but even if he was, this would not, as I see it, diminish the importance of the attempt and its motivation. Before deleting well-attested lines in Aristotle we should consider every possible way to make sense of them. It may well be that in just such a situation we are best able to see Aristotle's ethical writings more as work in progress than as polished and published treatises. And that, I maintain, would be no bad thing.

Christ's College, Cambridge

more loosely as simply meaning that Aristotle will discuss them later, not that he will say how they are means.

294 *Giles Pearson*

BIBLIOGRAPHY

Allan, D. J., 'Aristotle's Account of the Origin of Moral Principles', in J. Barnes, M. Schofield, and R. Sorabji (eds.), *Articles on Aristotle*, ii. *Ethics and Politics* (London, 1977), 72–8.

Barnes, J. (ed.), *The Complete Works of Aristotle: The Revised Oxford Translation* [*ROT*] (Princeton, 1984).

Bostock, D., *Aristotle's Ethics* (Oxford, 2000).

Broadie, S., 'Commentary', in Broadie and Rowe, *Aristotle:* Nicomachean Ethics.

—— *Ethics with Aristotle* (Oxford, 1991).

—— 'Philosophical Introduction', in Broadie and Rowe, *Aristotle:* Nicomachean Ethics.

—— and Rowe, C. (trans. and comm.), *Aristotle:* Nicomachean Ethics [*NE*] (Oxford, 2002).

Crisp, R., *Aristotle:* Nicomachean Ethics (Cambridge, 2000).

Curzer, H., 'A Defense of Aristotle's Doctrine that Virtue is a Mean', *Ancient Philosophy*, 16 (1996), 129–38.

Dahl, N. O., *Practical Reason, Aristotle, and Weakness of the Will* (Minneapolois, 1984).

Drefcinski, S., 'A Different Solution to an Alleged Contradiction in Aristotle's *Nicomachean Ethics*', *OSAP* 30 (2006), 201–10.

Fortenbaugh, W. W., 'Aristotle: Emotion and Moral Virtue', *Arethusa*, 2 (1969), 163–85.

—— 'Aristotle's Distinction between Moral Virtue and Practical Wisdom', in J. P. Anton and A. Preus (eds.), *Essays in Ancient Greek Philosophy*, iv. *Aristotle's Ethics* (Albany, NY, 1991), 97–106.

Hursthouse, R., 'A False Doctrine of the Mean', *Proceedings of the Aristotelian Society*, 81 (1980–1), 57–72.

Irwin, T. H., *Aristotle:* Nicomachean Ethics (Indianapolis, 1985).

—— 'Disunity in Aristotelian Virtue', *OSAP* suppl. (1988), 61–90.

Müller, A. W., 'Aristotle's Conception of Ethical and Natural Virtue: How the Unity Thesis Sheds Light on the Doctrine of the Mean', in J. Szaif and M. Lutz-Bachmann (eds.), *What is Good for a Human Being: Human Nature and Values* (Berlin, 2004), 18–53.

Pakaluk, M., 'On an Alleged Contradiction in Aristotle's *Nicomachean Ethics*', *OSAP* 22 (2002), 201–19.

Pearson, G., 'Does the Fearless Phobic Really Fear the Squeak of Mice "too much"?', *Ancient Philosophy*, 26 (2006), 81–91.

Reeve, C. D. C., *Practices of Reason* (Oxford, 1995).

Rorty, A. O. (ed.), *Essays on Aristotle's Ethics* (Berkeley, 1980).

Rowe, C. J., 'The Meaning of φρόνησις in the Eudemian Ethics', in P. Moraux and D. Harlfinger (eds.), *Untersuchungen zur Eudemischen Ethik: Akten des 5. Symposium Aristotelicum* (Berlin, 1971), 73–92.

Smith, A. D., 'Character and Intellect in Aristotle's Ethics', *Phronesis*, 41 (1996), 56–74.

Sorabji, R., 'Aristotle on the Role of the Intellect in Virtue', in Rorty, *Essays on Aristotle's Ethics*, 201–19.

Taylor, C. C. W., *Aristotle:* Nicomachean Ethics, *Books II–IV* (Oxford, 2006).

Telfer, E., 'The Unity of the Moral Virtues in Aristotle's *Nicomachean Ethics*', *Proceedings of the Aristotelian Society*, 90 (1989–90), 35–48.

Williams, B., 'Justice as a Virtue', in Rorty, *Essays on Aristotle's Ethics*, 189–99.

Woods, M., *Aristotle:* Eudemian Ethics, *Books I, II, and VIII [EE]* (Oxford, 1982; 2nd, rev. edn. 1992).

—— 'Intuition and Perception in Aristotle's Ethics', *OSAP* 4 (1986), 145–66.

ARISTOTLE AND THE PROBLEMS OF METHOD IN ETHICS

MARCO ZINGANO

JOHN BURNET's thesis about the dialectical character of Aristotelian ethics seems nowadays to have become a common view, held by most if not all interpreters.[1] In addition, the dialectical method is now considered Aristotle's primary method of philosophical investigation: not only his ethics, but also his physics and its branches, and even his theology are taken to be fundamentally dialectical.[2] The sole exceptions recognized are mathematics and logic.

© Marco Zingano 2007

[1] J. Burnet, *The Ethics of Aristotle* (London, 1900), xvii: 'the Ethics is, and from the nature of the case must be, a dialectical and not a demonstrative work'. However, what dialectic means for him is less clear. On the one hand, 'the word *dialektikê* properly means nothing more than the art of dialogue or discussion—it signifies the theoretical formulation of the practice of Sokrates' (xxxix). However, this is too vague a notion of dialectic; moreover, according to this definition, dialectic will be particularly involved in *ad hominem* arguments, but as Hardie has remarked, 'for the most part Aristotle argues from premises which state his own views or views which he has made his own. Burnet, who held that the *EN* is "dialectical throughout" (p. v), exaggerates the extent to which Aristotle starts from the opinion of others, especially Plato and the Academy' (W. F. R. Hardie, *Aristotle's Ethical Theory*, 2nd edn. (Oxford, 1980), 39). On the other hand, the meaning of dialectic is defined according to the *Topics*, which Burnet cites on pp. xxxix–xlvi. A dialectical argument is, according to this second meaning, an argument whose premises are *endoxa*, reputable premises, accepted by all or most philosophers, including Aristotle. The latter meaning will be retained and considered throughout this paper.

[2] Authors with different perspectives accept this expanded version, even if some acknowledge that dialectic poses a threat to the status of truth in practical wisdom. Jonathan Barnes, in an outstanding article, accepts the expansion and identifies the problem, but tries to soften it owing to an optimistic finalism; he ends by saying: 'Yet Aristotle's practical philosophy is not, I think, seriously marred by his method', among other reasons because 'Aristotle's actual philosophising was not greatly affected by his reflexion on how philosophy ought to be conducted' (J. Barnes, 'Aristotle and the Methods of Ethics', *Revue internationale de philosophie*, 34 (1980), 490–511 at 510). Enrico Berti has strongly defended the expansion of dialectic in a series of essays (*Le raggioni di Aristotele* (Bari, 1989); see also 'Il metodo della filosofia pratica secondo Aristotele', in A. Alberti (ed.), *Studi sull'etica di Aristotele* (Naples, 1990), 23–63, and 'Does Aristotle's Conception of Dialectic

298   *Marco Zingano*

This expansion has been made at times with certain restrictions on the sort of dialectic considered,[3] but it has at other times been adopted without restriction.[4] I think that there are good reasons to resist such an expansion, particularly regarding physics, although in the present study I want to examine the dialectical thesis at its core, that is to say, in ethics.

My thesis is that Aristotelian ethics was initially dialectical in its method: *EE* systematically held that dialectic is the appropriate means of proof for morals. However, Aristotle himself abandoned such a view, and in *NE* the kind of proof required was no longer dialectical. This does not mean that, once abandoned in ethics, dialectic could not still find a place in other domains, such as physics, even if I think that unlikely. Nevertheless, I intend to show here only what happened with the method in ethics, from *EE* to *NE*, without regarding what might have happened in other domains.

I

I begin with three points and a caveat. First, (1) I shall determine what we are to call dialectic. In a broad sense, a dialectical argument is simply an argument that is disputed, but this sense is too general

---

Develop?', in W. Wians (ed.), *Aristotle's Philosophical Development* (Lanham, Md., 1996), 105–30).

[3] Adopted notably by Terence Irwin, whose book *Aristotle's First Principles* (Oxford, 1988) and several papers on Aristotelian ethics have been very influential. The main points of Irwin's strategy are: (1) to distinguish a strong from an ordinary dialectic, so that the problem of truth can be overcome by the former although not by the latter; (2) to take ethics as a non-autonomous discipline, dependent on metaphysics and psychology for its central theses, so that, even though a strict dialectical justification falls short of the ambitions of ethics, dialectic conceived of in a broad coherent sense can respond to such ambitions so long as it gains support from (1). Granted (1) and (2), Irwin pleads for ethics as 'dialectical throughout' (T. Irwin, 'Aristotle's Methods of Ethics', in D. J. O'Meara (ed.), *Studies in Aristotle* (Washington, 1981), 193–223 at 208). I think one can resist (1) and (2).

[4] Particularly by M. Nussbaum, *The Fragility of Goodness: Luck and Ethics in Greek Tragedy and Philosophy* (Cambridge, 1986), and 'Saving Aristotle's Appearances', in M. Schofield and M. Nussbaum (eds.), *Language and Logos: Studies in Ancient Greek Philosophy Presented to G. E. L. Owen* (Cambridge, 1982), 267–93. But see critical comments by John Cooper, 'Aristotle on the Authority of "Appearances"', in id., *Reason and Emotion: Essays on Ancient Moral Psychology and Ethical Theory* (Princeton, 1999), 281–91, and William Wians, 'Saving Aristotle from Nussbaum's Phainomena', in J. P. Anton and A. Preus (eds.), *Essays in Ancient Greek Philosophy*, v. *Aristotle's Ontology* (Albany, NY, 1992), 133–49.

Aristotle and Method in Ethics

to be useful here. Neither is the Platonic sense helpful, since, by contrast, it is too restricted. The Platonic dialectician makes divisions and establishes a strict internal agreement between Ideas, abandoning all links with the sensible world, and thus limiting his *dialegesthai* to too narrow a sense. For this and other reasons, he is unfit to argue Aristotelian ethical claims. The meaning of dialectic that I am proposing is rather the one provided by Aristotle himself when he writes at the beginning of the *Topics* that a dialectical argument is one whose premises come from reputable opinions (1. 1, 100^{a}29–30). Aristotle takes reputable opinions to be those that 'are accepted by everyone or by the majority or by the wise—i.e. by all, or by the majority, or by the most notable and reputable of them' (100^{b}21–3).[5] This is a well-known passage, but it would not be amiss to insist that, in the very determination of what is a reputable opinion, the notion of being 'reputable' reappears, in that a reputable opinion is the opinion of the most *reputable* wise. A premiss of a dialectical syllogism relies upon its reputability; and its reputability can be founded, in the last resort, on the reputation of whoever asserts it. If the opinion is accepted by everyone, or almost everyone, or by the wise and, among them, by almost all or by the most reputable, then this opinion is fit to be a premiss of a dialectical syllogism. A dialectical argument has other characteristics—for instance, it is produced for a dispute by means of questions and answers—but, so far as concerns our present enquiry, the nature of the premises is by far the most interesting feature: the premises of dialectical arguments are accepted or reputable propositions. If Aristotle's method in ethics is dialectical, the kind of proof used in ethics should be founded upon accepted or reputable premises in the sense we have just provided.

It is also necessary to consider (2) the purpose for which dialectical argument is to be used in ethics. The general recent positive revaluation of the role of dialectic in Aristotle's philosophy is closely linked to an approach according to which dialectic would function as the method of discovery in sciences, the one that, by enquiring from all points of view, would bring us to the threshold of rules and principles. Perhaps it would not grasp them directly, but none the less it would pave the way for the intellect (*nous*), which could then

---

[5] The translation is from *The Complete Works of Aristotle: The Revised Oxford Translation* [*ROT*], ed. J. Barnes (Princeton 1984). This translation will be used unless otherwise stated.

300 *Marco Zingano*

effect the apprehension of principles. In this sense, dialectic would play an intermediary role between the perception of particular cases and the intellection of principles. This heuristic role of dialectic also offers a highly plausible explanation of the fact that, despite the strictly deductive version of the sciences found in the *Posterior Analytics* (according to a method clearly inspired by mathematics), the science *en œuvre* that we find in Aristotle's treatises, notably the biological ones, rarely obeys the syllogistic and deductive scheme; instead, it is accomplished by much more flexible means, some of which are characterized by reputable opinions, making them similar or even identical to dialectical reasoning.[6]

This gap—or rather, abyss—between the deductive project of the *Posterior Analytics* and the science displayed in the physical treatises requires an explanation, and for this explanation one can reasonably expect to ascribe an important place to dialectic in the discovery of principles. However, regarding ethics, the gap—if it exists—lies elsewhere, for it is not between the dialectical ways of the enquiry and the rigorous deductive presentation of results. It lies, on the contrary, within the very presentation of results in moral matters, because, as we are about to see, dialectic is offered as a kind of proof of moral truths, and not just for the discovery of principles. Thus, one can momentarily put aside the problem of finding an explanation for the distance between the analytical project of scientific deduction and the profuse enquiry in the domain of theoretical sciences, since in practical matters dialectic is an element of the very presentation of moral rules. Consequently, investigating the nature of the dialectic used in practical proofs puts us in a privileged position for determining how far, and for what purposes, dialectical argument can be used.

Finally, (3) perhaps it is misleading to consider Aristotelian ethics as a unitary project. Perhaps one has seriously to consider whether

---

[6] To quote only one well-known paper by Paul Wilpert: 'sie [dialectic and induction] führen bis an die Schwelle, bereiten die Klarheit vor, die dann aber als Evidenz der Principien sich von selbst ergeben muss. Der Weg der Hinführung birgt noch nicht die Einsicht in die innere Begründung selbst. Und so scheiden sich Induktion und Dialektik als Wege des Aufspürens und der Nous als die Methode der Einsicht. . . . Episteme ist die in streng apodeiktischer Form gebotene Darstellung der Begründungszusammenhänge in der ausgebauten Wissenschaft, wie sie musterhaft die Mathematik darbietet. Dialektik aber ist der Weg der Forschung, der Prüfung des Für und Wider, die sich der induktiven Methode bedient, vom Wahrscheinlichen, noch nicht Gesicherten ausgehend' (P. Wilpert, 'Aristoteles und die Dialektik', *Kant-Studien*, 48/2 (1956–7), 247–57 at 255).

Aristotle and Method in Ethics 301

his ethics presents different approaches. There are three treatises on ethics: the *Magna Moralia*, *EE*, and *NE*. We can disregard the *Magna Moralia*, whose authenticity remains controversial, noting none the less that its style and theses are very similar to those of *EE*. The other two treatises, as is well known, have three books in common (*NE* 5–7 = *EE* 4–6).

An apparently prevailing consensus holds that *EE* was written before *NE*, the common books being part of *EE*, at least in their original version (which could have undergone revisions in order to be adapted to *NE*). However, it has also been insistently maintained that this chronological priority, even if accepted, is of no philosophical importance; for what would really be important in distinguishing these two treatises is the public to which each work is addressed. According to this interpretation, *NE* consists of lectures for young or would-be legislators (a learned public, but not strictly philosophical), whereas *EE* consists of lectures addressed to philosophy students (probably those of the Lyceum) with a typically philosophical background. According to this interpretation, discrepancies between the two treatises are best explained as due to the public to which they are addressed.

Such an interpretation may explain some differences between the two texts, but I do not think it grasps the essential point for explaining why there are two treatises. There are discrepancies between the texts which are due to philosophical changes, and which are not just superficial ones attributable to the diversity of the audience to which they are addressed. One could even imagine that *EE* is the first draft, whose problems and difficulties required a rewriting with a sharply distinct thesis. The outcome of this sort of revision is what we now know as *NE*.

Many clues make the thesis of a revision quite plausible, but I cannot develop them here.[7] In fact, I do not even need to argue

---

[7] Owen's thesis pointed to one fundamental element by showing how the absence of the notion of focal meaning for *good* and for *being* is an incompatibility between *EE* and the project of a single science of being, announced in book *Γ* of *Metaphysics*, whereas the corresponding version in *NE* is perfectly compatible with this project (G. E. L. Owen, 'Logic and Metaphysics in Some Earlier Works of Aristotle', in I. Düring and G. E. L. Owen (eds.), *Aristotle and Plato in the Mid-Fourth Century* (Göteborg, 1960), 163–90, repr. in Owen, *Logic, Science and Dialectic: Collected Papers in Greek Philosophy* (Ithaca, NY, 1986), 180–99). Closely linked to the notion of focal meaning, the changes made in the analysis of the three types of friendship, which is governed in *EE* by the notion of focal meaning, whereas in *NE* it is governed by the notion of resemblance, seem to indicate that *NE* is the more satisfactory—and

302 *Marco Zingano*

for it. I present it here merely as a hypothesis which will help me to make certain points more easily, without its being necessary for my argument. All that is necessary is that one accept the possibility of there being philosophically important differences between both treatises. I shall then endeavour to show that the problem of method is one of them. I want to suggest that, regarding the problem of method, *NE* assumes a thesis that is clearly distinct from that of *EE*, and that this difference is of strong philosophical import: as a result of this change, ethics becomes more satisfactory as a philosophical discipline. In my view, philosophical changes are central to explaining why Aristotle wrote two treatises, notwithstanding differences of style and public. As I hope to make clear by the end, such a difference in method can also serve as a clue for their historical relationship, but I shall not insist upon it. All that is necessary is the possibility that the two treatises are philosophically divergent, and that this divergence is relevant for ethics as a philosophical discipline. Hence, on the basis of this possibility, I shall examine separately Aristotle's two *Ethics*, intending to illustrate my case from the perspective of the problem of method.

Now the caveat: who is counted as dialectical? When we read passages such as *EE* 1. 6 (to be examined in the next section), the answer is: the philosopher who exercises *theōria* about practical matters, since the problems dialectic deals with are, for example, what bravery is and what happiness consists of, enquiry into which belongs to the philosopher, and not 'How should one act bravely here and now?' or 'Am I under such circumstances happy?', whose answer is provided by the prudent man. None the less, the prudent man is not very different, at least in *EE*. In *EE* the prudent man seems also to appeal to reputable opinions; as he builds on his practical syllogisms, he takes such opinions as his major premises and from them works out what he should do. What distinguishes him from other people who also appeal to reputable opinions is that he alone has a kind of moral perception that enables him to see the precise thing he has to do in the various circumstances in which he finds himself here and now. In formulating practical syllogisms, the prudent man shows his special ability properly not in the major premiss (which, as a reputable opinion, is in a way avail-

probably the later—version. There are other clues that point in the same direction; nevertheless, they would demand a minute analysis of the texts, which cannot be undertaken here.

Aristotle and Method in Ethics

able to everybody), but rather in the minor premiss, which applies a certain rule to the occurrence in question. Prudence thus operates fundamentally in the second premisses and is closely connected to perception, although it cannot be assimilated to a simple sensation.

In *NE*, on the other hand, we can see that the philosopher and the prudent man are more clearly set apart. They still have close connections, which ultimately are rooted in the way Aristotle conceives ethics as a philosophical discipline; for instance, the argument in book 10 about primary *eudaimonia* is carried out by the philosopher, although it has clear moral content since it determines what is the best life to live, and this kind of determination should be incumbent on the prudent man rather than the philosopher. However, the philosopher now enquires—or at least I claim he does—in a typical scientific pattern. As is said in *NE* 2. 2, the philosopher perceives that the agent *always* decides by considering the circumstances involved, and neither is this remark a reputable opinion (for it claims to be necessarily true), nor is its exactness—for it is expressed with perfect accuracy—in any way affected by the conditions of accuracy *NE* assigns to the moral decisions or advice of the prudent man, which do not take the form '*A* is always *B*'. As I shall try to show in this paper, in *NE* neither the philosopher nor the prudent man appeals in a relevant way to dialectic. This fact allows Aristotle to separate the philosopher from the prudent in a more satisfying manner than he did in *EE*, although I do not believe that he succeeds in distinguishing between them clearly. Aristotle continues to oscillate in *NE* between the philosopher and the prudent man. However, in this case too we can see that such blurring, because it obliterates clear demarcation of both roles, becomes almost harmless in *NE*, and I would like to suggest that this relative gain of clarity is largely due to a better understanding of the method applied in ethical subjects.

II

The passages concerning method in *EE* strongly support the use of dialectical method in ethics. In 1. 6 Aristotle writes:

About *all these matters* we must try to get conviction by arguments, using the *phenomena* as evidence and illustration. It would be best that all men should clearly concur with what we are going to say, but if that is unattain-

304 *Marco Zingano*

able, then that all should in some way at least concur. And this if *converted* they will do, for every man has some contribution to make to the truth, and with this as a starting-point we must give some sort of proof about these matters. For by advancing from true but obscure judgements he will arrive at clear ones, always exchanging the usual confused statement for more real knowledge. (*EE* 1. 6, 1216^{b}26–35)

This passage clearly represents dialectical debate, but it demands some explanations. First of all, the questions here referred to by 'all these matters' are ethical questions, such as the ones Aristotle mentioned previously: 'What is bravery?', 'What is justice?', or, more broadly, 'What is virtue, wisdom or happiness?' Secondly, when ascribing meaning to 'phenomena' (τὰ φαινόμενα) one may wonder whether these are empirical facts or opinions. It has been established in a very convincing manner that in ethical contexts the expression refers to opinions or sayings.[8] In the present passage, this is confirmed by the 'true but obscure judgements' of lines 32–3. I take 'this if converted [μεταβιβαζόμενοι] they will do' in line 30 as meaning that those who hold certain views change their formulation when required, and this also reinforces the dialectical nature of the passage. In *Topics* 1. 2, regarding the usefulness of the treatise for dialectical encounters, Aristotle says that when we make an inventory of the beliefs and opinions of other people we should not address them with theses alien to them, but with their own theses, making them sometimes reformulate what does not seem correctly formulated (101^{a}33–4: μεταβιβάζοντες ὅ τι ἂν μὴ καλῶς φαίνωνται λέγειν ἡμῖν). Aristotle does not say that we should make them reject the assertions that we do not accept,[9] but on the contrary that, regarding what they say in a confusing manner (μὴ καλῶς), we should make them reformulate their opinions so as to clarify them— yet these opinions should continue to be their own assertions, even

[8] G. E. L. Owen, 'Tithenai ta Phainomena', in S. Mansion (ed.), *Aristote et les problèmes de méthode* (Louvain, 1980), 83–103, repr. in Owen, *Logic, Science and Dialectic*, 239–51.

[9] *Pace* J. Brunschwig, who translates as follows: 'quand nous voudrons les persuader de renoncer à des affirmations qui nous paraîtront manifestement inacceptables' (J. Brunschwig, *Aristote: Topiques I–IV* (Paris, 1967)). Robin Smith's comments are very instructive: 'Aristotle has in mind the correction, or conversion, of others' opinions, not "shifting the ground" in an argument so as to defeat one's opponent. Compare 8. 11 161a29–36, and *EE* 1. 6 1216b28–35: the latter makes clear the role of this in leading others to philosophical understanding, claiming that we all have some understanding of the truth, on which philosophical education builds' (*Aristotle:* Topics *I and VIII* (Oxford, 1997), 52).

Aristotle and Method in Ethics 305

though reformulated thanks to our intervention. It is the same in our passage from *EE*: the idea is not to correct their assertions in the sense of making them accept our opinions and beliefs, abandoning their own, rather it means that they should reformulate their own confused opinions.

Finally, Aristotle says that, by proceeding in such a manner, one will provide *in some way* a proof about those opinions: δεικνύναι πως περὶ αὐτῶν (32). What exactly does this mean? Does it mean that one has *some sort of proof*, an attenuated or not so rigorous one? This is Solomon's translation in *ROT*, suggesting that one has a weakened demonstration—a proof, but not a rigid proof, probably due to the fact that it is carried out with a dialectical argument and not a demonstrative one. However, this is not the only interpretation the passage permits. The adverb 'in a way' can be linked, not to the demonstration, but rather to the elements of the proof: one has a proof of their opinions *in some respects*. According to this latter reading, it is not the deductive power that is weakened, but 'in a way' applies to the opinions that occupy the place of premises in the argument. It is proven, and one proves it perfectly, but, since some formulations have been changed because of our intervention, one proves it from *what is said in a certain way by them*: having as premises not exactly the beliefs and opinions held at the beginning, but reformulations of these, now expressed without the confusion they manifested at the beginning.

The dialectical proof is not viewed, according to this reading, as an impoverished proof. On the contrary, it is seen as a fully accomplished proof, which is different from demonstration only because of the nature of its premises—premises that can be reformulated within certain limits. Another passage confirms this interpretation: *EE* I. 3, 1214^{b}28–1215^{a}7. The beginning of this passage (1214^{b}28–1215^{a}5) has a history of textual problems, requiring a precise examination that I cannot carry out here. Fortunately, I want to consider only the last lines, 1215^{a}5–7, which have no transmission problems. Having declared that it is useless to examine every opinion (those of children and of the insane, for instance) or even the opinion of the majority of people when they talk idly about anything, Aristotle remarks that each discipline has its own difficulties: in regard to ethics, these *aporiai* concern the problems of the best life. He then continues:

306 *Marco Zingano*

It is well to examine these opinions, for a disputant's refutation of what is opposed to his argument is a demonstration of the argument itself. (1215ª5–7)

The context is again undoubtedly dialectical. These opinions engender special difficulties for ethics, notably the discussions regarding the best life. 'To examine' translates ἐξετάζειν, typical of the dialectical attitude, particularly of the Socratic one; 'refutation' translates ἔλεγχοι, a central term in the dialectical disputes. The most important point here is that, through the refutation of the objections, one obtains the demonstration of the opposite theses without any allusion to a weakening of the proof. As we shall see, Aristotle, in *EE*, typically proceeds through the use of dialectical proofs, according to the rules established in the *Topics*, without questioning the status of the proof, that is to say, without the weakening or diminution of its claims to demonstrate a point. He even writes that with it we arrive at ἀποδείξεις, 'demonstrations'. However, what he means is certainly that we obtain perfectly valid deductions, whose premisses, none the less, do not permit a demonstration in the precise sense of the term, owing to their not being necessarily true.

I would like to return to the *EE* 1. 6 passage mentioned above, since it contains an element that I have not examined yet. Aristotle says that 'every man has some contribution to make to the truth' (1216ᵇ31); he also mentions 'true statements' (1216ᵇ32), even if they are confusingly expressed. The theme of the truth may give us the hope of passing from the world of opinion into the domain of science, which would justify talking of 'demonstrations' now in a more rigorous sense. However, I fear that this hope will be disappointed. The opinions may be true, and the reputable opinions may have a stronger probability of being true than mere opinions; none the less, the premiss of a dialectical syllogism is not *necessarily* true. In scientific knowledge, on the other hand, premisses are not only true, but *necessarily* true. Extensionally, dialectic and science may coincide, but they differ radically. There is a gap no opinion can bridge or bypass, whatever dialectic's reputation: even if it is true, it is not *necessarily* true. The dialectical method is consistent with an effort to preserve other people's opinions, something that seems justified by such an epistemological optimism: if every man has some link to the truth, it seems reasonable to preserve everyone's

Aristotle and Method in Ethics 307

opinions, even when they are confusingly expressed, hoping that they may lead us to the truth. Such optimism, however, soon reaches its limits, for it is not possible through dialectic to have *de jure* access to the truth, even if, *de facto*, we have already that access.[10]

It is also important to understand that the Eudemian dialectical proof is fully compatible with a method of argument that proceeds by hypotheses. As long as these hypotheses are *endoxa*, the deduction may with perfect validity be made through suppositions such as 'Let A be the case', 'Suppose that B', etc. That is precisely what we find in *EE*. In this treatise, Aristotle uses arguments introduced by words such as 'Suppose', 'Take', 'Let it be', and 'Let's assume'. In a well-known article D. J. Allan strongly emphasizes this methodological feature of *EE*, coining the expression 'quasi-mathematical method' to refer to it.[11] Allan does not explain the reason for his 'quasi-'; in fact, he refers to this argumentative structure as if it were 'a mathematical pattern of deduction'.[12] However, he has good reasons to retain 'quasi-'. The proof is adequate as it is in mathematics and nothing prevents it from being formulated by way of hypotheses, as happens currently in mathematical sciences. Nevertheless, there is a characteristic that belongs only to ethical argument. In ethics, what is supposed or adopted as a hypothesis must come from reputable opinions; in mathematics, on the contrary, there is no such restriction. It is this difference that compels us to speak of a method which is not properly mathematical, but *quasi*-mathematical.

What particularly interests me here is that a hypothetical formulation is perfectly compatible with the dialectical structure that *EE* adopts for its proofs. Thus, in *EE* 2. 1, in order to conclude that happiness is an activity of a good soul ($1219^a34–5$), Aristotle *assumes* ($\dot{v}\pi o\kappa\epsilon\acute{\iota}\sigma\theta\omega$, 1218^b37) that virtue is the best disposition, state, or power of everything that has any use or work; *admits* ($\check{\epsilon}\sigma\tau\omega$, 1219^a8) that the best disposition belongs to the best work; reminds

---

[10] This is why Aristotle can write the following strong caveat against all who intend to produce scientific arguments based on reputable premisses, even if they are true: 'From this it is clear too that those people are silly who think they get their principles correctly if the proposition is reputable and true' (*Post. An.* 1. 6, $74^b21–3$).

[11] D. J. Allan, 'Quasi-Mathematical Method in the *Eudemian Ethics*' ['Quasi-Mathematical'], in Mansion, *Aristote et les problèmes de méthode*, 303–18. Allan remarks that this characteristic is 'the most singular feature of the method which the author actually uses' (307).

[12] Allan, 'Quasi-Mathematical', 307.

308 *Marco Zingano*

us that *it has already been assumed* (ὑπέκειτο, 1219ᵃ10) that the best end is the one for the sake of which all else exists; *declares* (λέγωμεν, 1219ᵃ19) that the work of a thing is also the work of its virtue, only not in the same sense (for virtue is the best work); *supposes* (ἔστω, 1219ᵃ24) that the work (function) of the soul is to produce living, from which he concludes that the virtue of the soul consists in making good living, which is, precisely, happiness. Formally, the argumentative structure adopts hypotheses and proceeds rigorously to conclusions, as 'the opinions common to all of us show that we have presented correctly the genus and the definition of happiness' (1219ᵃ39–40). We should not interpret 'opinions common to all of us' as meaning opinions internal to the Aristotelians, since these cannot function here as a guarantee of the results; it means rather external opinions, those shared by everyone, or most people, or by the sages and, among them, by all of them, most of them, or by the most reputable. This is why Aristotle immediately quotes Solon's famous saying: it is a widely held opinion. A mathematical proof makes no use of opinions, however reputable they may be, but ethical arguments cannot reach the formal structure mathematical proofs have except by appealing to the common nature of the opinions adopted as premises for the syllogisms.

When we turn our attention to the announcements of method in *NE*, the difference is striking. In the two most important passages on method, there is no reference to dialectical reasoning; there one finds, instead, a discussion about the conditions of exactness for ethical discourse. *NE* strongly stresses that it is necessary to abandon any intention of a *more geometrico* proof. In *NE* 1. 3, 1094ᵇ11–27, after noticing that ethical matters are indeterminate, Aristotle emphasizes that ethical proof must be limited to a rough outline (1094ᵇ20). This standard of *akribeia*, adapted to ethics in opposition to that of mathematics, is due to the nature of the practical object, human action (τὸ πρακτόν), since it takes place under circumstances whose moral value is indeterminate. Similarly, in 2. 2, 1103ᵇ34–1104ᵃ9, Aristotle insists again that moral reasoning must adapt itself to the conditions of its subject-matter, which means that it can neither be offered as a prescription nor adopt the routine production processes of arts and crafts; on the contrary, the agent's decision hinges dramatically on the circumstances in which action is produced, and one cannot assess in advance the moral worth of the circumstances. The hope of a rigorous proof, which would differ

Aristotle and Method in Ethics 309

from mathematical proofs only because of the nature of the premisses, is abandoned; in its place, one now finds a clear admission that ethical reasoning is closely linked to the indeterminate circumstances which bear on its moral value. Consequently, Aristotle even writes that ethics has no precision (1104^a6), but this is overstated; he certainly means that ethics does not have the *same* accuracy as mathematical sciences have, since it does not even have that of the crafts. Concerning method, then, there are two very different schemes: *NE* mentions no dialectical processes in its discussions of method; *EE* contains no reference to conclusions obtained roughly and in outline.[13] Even the Greek term 'in outline' ($\tau\acute{\upsilon}\pi\omega$), which expresses these new reservations about exactness in *NE*, is singularly lacking from *EE*.[14]

[13] As Daniel Devereux has pointed out ('Particular and Universal in Aristotle's Conception of Practical Knowledge', *Review of Metaphysics*, 29 (1986), 483–505). One can object that I am excessively dramatizing the point, since Aristotle also says in *NE* 1. 3 that 'in speaking about things which are only for the most part true and with premisses of the same kind [we must be content] to reach conclusions that are no better' (1094^b21–4). One finds here not only a verb expressing the idea of reaching conclusions ($\sigma\upsilon\mu\pi\epsilon\rho\alpha\acute{\iota}\nu\epsilon\sigma\theta\alpha\iota$, $^b22$), but also the idea that the virtuous man has at his disposition at least some rules expressed in a generalized form 'for the most part'; it is noteworthy that this register also plays an important role in the natural sciences, so that, in the end, it does not seem that there is so great a difference between reasoning in natural sciences and in practical matters. I cannot answer this objection thoroughly here but shall confine myself to just two remarks. (1) In *NE* 2. 2, which refers back to 1. 3, particularism in ethics is expressly and strongly restated, dramatically underscoring the fact that the agent should decide case by case, no mention being made of the 'for the most part' ethical rules. (2) I do not mean to deny that ethical reasoning contains generalized rules in the form 'for the most part'; however, what I do deny is that they are the basic expressions of practical decisions. I believe that the basic expression of moral decisions is deeply rooted in the particular circumstances within which the agent acts, which leads to a particularist pattern of ethics. From this sort of particular decision one can indeed generate rules that hold sway for the most part, but such rules are secondary and must always remain under the control of such a particularist perspective. These ethical generalizing rules cannot be assimilated to the 'for the most part' rules of natural sciences: they not only differ in their degree of contingency but are generated in a very different way as well.

[14] At the beginning of the treatise on justice (*NE* 5), which is one of the common books, Aristotle uses, none the less, the phrase $\dot{\omega}s$ $\dot{\epsilon}\nu$ $\tau\acute{\upsilon}\pi\omega$ (5. 1, 1129^a11). Since I consider the common books to have been originally written for *EE*, this seems to contradict what I have stated. However, here in *NE* 5. 1 the expression does not have the same value that it has in the discussion on method in *NE*. At the beginning of the treatise on justice Aristotle declares that he will follow the same method as used before (1129^a5–6). It is likely that he is thinking of the dialectical method, for the dialectical method is the method of ethics in *EE*. An indication of this is Aristotle's remarks that 'all men mean by justice that kind of state which makes people disposed to do what is just and makes them act justly and wish for what is just' (1129^a6–8),

310   *Marco Zingano*

Two points are called for at this juncture. First, there is one other passage on ethical method which I have not considered thus far: the well-known passage in *NE* 7. 1, 1145^{b}2–7, at the beginning of the treatise on *akrasia*:

> We must, as in all other cases, set the phenomena before us and, after first discussing the difficulties, go on to prove, if possible, the truth of all the reputable opinions about these affections or, failing this, of the greater number and the most authoritative; for if we both resolve the difficulties and leave the reputable opinions undisturbed, we shall have proved the case sufficiently.

This passage sounds perfectly dialectical; indeed, it is the declaration *par excellence* of dialectical method in ethics. Owen's analysis of the passage has shown, quite convincingly, that the 'phenomena' here are not empirical facts but reputable opinions, listed soon after and presented at the end of this chapter as 'the things that are said' (1145^{b}20). All of this is correct, but it is necessary to add a note: the passage appears in a common book (*NE* 7 = *EE* 6) and, most probably, the common books were written for *EE*. Thus, it is not surprising that the method of proof here is the dialectical method: *EE* in all of its books holds that proof in ethics occurs through dialectical arguments. Consequently, this passage is fully consistent with the rest of *EE*. According to the Eudemian dialectical method, as we have seen, one has to preserve all opinions; if this is not possible, then one should preserve most of them or the

---

and that injustice is the contrary of this (1129^{a}9–10), which are in agreement with the method of the *endoxa*. Aristotle writes just after: 'Let us too, then, first lay these things down as a *rough sketch*' (1129^{a}10–11). We find here our familiar expression 'Let's assume' or 'Let's lay down', which is also typical of the Eudemian dialectical context. However, what are 'these things' (ταῦτα), whose treatment shall be a 'rough sketch'? I do not think it refers to the just and the unjust, for they are to be considered *at length*, throughout this book; I take it to refer to certain conditions of the just and the unjust; that is, to what accompanies them as conditions of their voluntary or involuntary character, which permits the distinction between acting (un)justly and being oneself (un)just. These conditions are examined in 5. 8, 1135^{a}15–1136^{a}9; as Aristotle himself remarks at 1135^{a}23, this point has already been examined, more precisely in *EE* 2. 6–11, 1222^{b}15–1228^{a}19, in great detail. It is probably due to this that he declares that they will be reconsidered only *roughly* in book 5, that is to say, in a succinct manner. The term τύπῳ does not reflect on the accuracy of proof in ethics, but says that a part of what is being exposed will be considered succinctly because its detailed examination has already been carried out. This is also confirmed by the fact that in *EE* 2. 10, 1226^{b}37–1227^{a}3, a passage that refers to 5. 8, Aristotle writes that legislators have rightly distinguished between involuntary, voluntary, and premeditated passions, even if not with perfect exactness.

Aristotle and Method in Ethics

most reputable ones. Our passage asserts exactly that: the goal is to preserve if not all, at least most of the reputable opinions. The verb used is καταλείπειν, which means to let the beliefs stand without dispute—that is to say, to accept their contents. Our passage adds, however, that this will be achieved through the development of *aporiai*. Therefore, granted that the reputable opinions raise *aporiai*, they cannot be preserved as such. What needs to be preserved is the element of truth in each belief. The opinions will be preserved, but in a certain manner; that is why, despite the deductive power attributed to the dialectical method, Aristotle says that, having found the solutions to the difficulties, one has 'sufficiently' demonstrated: the beliefs must be reformulated in order to have their true content preserved. This passage partakes of the Eudemian dialectical mood. We must pay attention to this, for the passage is often advanced as evidence that *NE* is dialectical; but, as we have seen, *NE*, except for the common books, does not mention a dialectical method; instead, it contains a discussion regarding the exactness of ethical discourse, which is fundamentally different from the dialectical proof.

We also need to take into account another consideration. It is not clear, in this passage, what is meant by 'as in all other cases'. The first and more natural interpretation is 'other ethical cases'. However, when we look at the other Nicomachean discussions (excepting the common books), there is nothing *clearly* dialectical. In order to fulfil this expectation, many interpreters have been content to cite the presence of ambiguous phrases such as 'it seems that' (δοκεῖ), evidence which is far too vague and probably neutral as regards the question at issue.[15] This interpretation seeming doomed to failure, a natural alternative has been to use 'as in all other cases' as the basis for proposing an extension of the dialectical method into disciplines other than ethics. Granted that ethics is a philosophical discipline (κατὰ φιλοσοφίαν), one may think of extending this method into physics and into other philosophical

---

[15] One can easily find in *NE* passages in which opinions are listed. A good example is book 1: in 1. 8 Aristotle writes that we 'must consider it, however, in the light not only of our conclusion and our premisses, but also of what is commonly said about it; for with a true view all the facts harmonize, but with a false one they soon clash' (1098[b]9–12). From here until 1. 12 he compares his results with *reputable opinions*, the most famous being the saying of Solon, examined in 1. 10. However, here Aristotle uses the *endoxa* not for obtaining his own results, but for reinforcing them, and, what is more important, he strives to correct the received opinions under the guidance of his own results. Moreover, 'facts' here renders ὑπάρχοντα, which refers to data and not to sayings, τὰ λεγόμενα: cf. *Post. An.* 1. 19, 81[b]21–3.

312   *Marco Zingano*

disciplines, with the single exception of mathematics. I do not deny that there are dialectical contexts, even unambiguously dialectical contexts, in those other Aristotelian treatises that seem to support this expanded interpretation, but probably the kind of proof required for these philosophical disciplines is not *generally* a dialectical one, since they question not only the coherence of the beliefs, but also—and above all—the truth of the propositions.

However, let us keep our attention on ethics and its problem of method. When we relocate this passage to its probable original context, *EE*, the search for other cases in which the discussion is typically dialectical becomes fruitful. In fact, it cannot but be fruitful, since dialectical proofs are to be found everywhere in *EE*. When it is read in its original context, the most natural interpretation is that 'as in all other cases' refers to other ethical discussions, all of them clearly dialectical, as typically occurs in *EE*.

A second point needs to be considered. Having defined dialectical argument as deduction from reputable opinions, Aristotle does not forget to stress from the *Topics* onward the distance that separates scientific deduction from the dialectical syllogism. In *Topics* 1. 14, after proposing three sorts of premiss (ethical, physical, logical), Aristotle proposes that these questions 'must be treated, at the philosophical level, according to the truth, but dialectally according to the opinion' (105^b30–1). At the beginning of this treatise he has distinguished *endoxa*, reputable opinions, from primitive and true premisses (100^b1), the latter being premisses only of demonstrative syllogisms. He returns to this point when he writes in *Topics* 8. 13, regarding *petitio principii*, that 'the true account has been given in the *Analytics*; but an account on the level of opinion must be given now' (162^b32–3). Regarding the same topic, in *Prior Analytics* 2. 16 Aristotle ends the chapter by remarking that 'in demonstrations the point at issue is begged when the terms are really [κατ' ἀλήθειαν] related in the manner described, in dialectical arguments when they are believed [κατὰ δόξαν] to be so related' (65^a36–7). In *Prior Analytics* 1. 30, where he is enquiring into the search for the middle term, Aristotle writes that, 'in the pursuit of truth, ⟨one must start⟩ from an arrangement of the terms in accordance with truth [κατ' ἀλήθειαν], while if we look for dialectical deductions we must start from plausible [κατὰ δόξαν] propositions' (46^a8–10). In the *Posterior Analytics* he writes: 'Those who are deducing with regard to opinion and only dialectically [κατὰ μὲν οὖν δόξαν συλλογιζομένοις καὶ

Aristotle and Method in Ethics 313

μόνον διαλεκτικῶς] clearly need only enquire whether their deduction comes about from the most reputable propositions possible' (1. 19, 81ᵇ18–20). He concludes: 'But with regard to truth, one must enquire on the basis of what actually holds' (81ᵇ22–3: πρὸς δ' ἀλήθειαν ἐκ τῶν ὑπαρχόντων δεῖ σκοπεῖν). This is undeniably a clear expression of the abyss that separates true science from reputable opinion. Dialectical reasoning has premisses that may be true, but, if their criterion is their acceptability or good reputation, they are not necessarily true.

If proof in ethics is dialectical, as is held consistently in *EE*, does the abyss so clearly identified render all scientific claims on the part of ethics illusory? The answer is: yes. In *EE*, practical matters are expressed in terms of opinion. If we look at them closely, the keywords of *EE* are directly connected with opinion and its corresponding faculty. The virtuous or prudent man is the one who deliberates or chooses well. In *EE* 2. 10 Aristotle shows that choice can be identified neither with the three sorts of desire (θυμός, ἐπιθυμία, βούλησις) nor with opinion (δόξα). But this does not preclude choice from being essentially associated with opinion, and in fact, in the terms of *EE*, choice is a composite of desire and opinion (2. 10, 1226ᵇ4: 'consequently it results from both of them').

Soon after, at 1226ᵇ9, Aristotle declares that choice is made by a deliberative opinion (ἐκ δόξης βουλευτικῆς). Some lines after this, at 1227ª3–5, he notes that 'it is clear that choice is not simply wish or simply opinion, but opinion and desire [ἀλλὰ δόξα τε καὶ ὄρεξις] together when following as a conclusion from deliberation'. If the prudent man is the one who chooses well by means of deliberation, he is, in consequence, the one who *opines well*. In the treatise on prudence, another common book (*NE* 6 = *EE* 5), Aristotle writes that prudence is, along with cleverness, one of the two species of excellence of our opinion-forming part, τὸ δοξαστικόν (6. 13, 1144ᵇ14–15; cf. 6. 5, 1140ᵇ26). Ethics is deeply rooted in the world of opinion, so it is perfectly consistent with dialectical arguments, at least in *EE*. There is no gap between the claims of ethics and dialectical proof in *EE*: dialectic is the proper sort of proof in the domain of opinion.

Examining *NE*, one finds an altogether new world. Choice is no longer defined as a deliberative opinion, δόξα βουλευτική; on the contrary, it is now taken as a deliberative desire, ὄρεξις βουλευτική. This change seems to be trifling, but it is not. As he had already done in *EE*, Aristotle refused in *NE* the identification of choice with

314   *Marco Zingano*

one of the three sorts of desire or with opinion; nevertheless, in a significantly different manner from *EE*, he no longer assimilates choice to a composite of desire and opinion, but henceforth speaks of a deliberative desire belonging to our power of doing or not doing something. This new stance makes it possible to distinguish practical deliberation *entirely* from opinion.[16] In *NE* deliberation becomes the faculty that elevates the prudent man to the realm of the truth. He is no longer in the world of opinion; he is now a resident of the world of truth. In a passage of *NE*, which has no parallel in *EE*, Aristotle writes that the virtuous man is the one who 'judges correctly each action, and in each, the truth appears to him' (3. 4, 1113^a29–30). The virtuous man, once capable only of providing good opinions, now sees truth in each action. As soon as Aristotle makes such a change, he has to abandon the dialectical syllogism as the type of proof for ethics, for ethics is now in a place which opinion cannot systematically reach: the world of (practical) truth.

The Nicomachean virtuous man lives in the realm of truth, but this place is not quite so comfortable. He can be there only by diminishing his claims to accuracy in practical matters. This is why the central problem of method in *NE* is related to what kind of precision the moral discipline may claim. In *NE* 1. 3, 1094^b11–27, a passage we examined earlier, the virtuous man must abandon claims of reasoning by demonstrations, and be content with indicating the truth by means of a rough sketch. In Aristotle's own words, ethics may only 'indicate the truth roughly and in outline' ($\pi\alpha\chi\upsilon\lambda\hat{\omega}\varsigma$ $\kappa\alpha\grave{\iota}$ $\tau\acute{\upsilon}\pi\omega$ $\tau\grave{\alpha}\lambda\eta\theta\grave{\epsilon}\varsigma$ $\dot{\epsilon}\nu\delta\epsilon\acute{\iota}\kappa\nu\upsilon\sigma\theta\alpha\iota$, 1094^b20–1). Here 'indicate' contrasts with 'demonstrate'; this new ethical notion diminishes the claims

---

[16] In *NE* 3. 2, 1112^a11–12, after refusing any identification between opinion and choice, Aristotle writes that it is not the moment to discuss whether an opinion precedes or accompanies choice, for it suffices to know that they are not identical. According to Stewart, 'that opinion precedes (and accompanies) choice is undoubtedly Aristotle's opinion'; he refers to 3. 3, 1113^a4, 'the object of choice is that which has been judged upon as a result of deliberation', as well as to *EE* 2. 10, 1226^b9, and to other passages belonging to the common books (J. Stewart, *Notes on the Nicomachean Ethics* (Oxford, 1892), 250). Regarding *EE* and the common books, this is not surprising, for choice is seen there as derivative from opinion. None the less, so far as concerns *NE*, Aristotle has carefully *avoided* any talk about opinion, replacing it instead with 'what has been judged' ($\kappa\rho\iota\theta\acute{\epsilon}\nu$). The comments of Gauthier and Jolif seem to be more correct: 'Aristote, qui dans l'*Éthique à Eudème*, II, 10, 1226b9, consentait encore à donner à ce jugement le nom platonicien d'*opinion*, l'évite dans l'*Éthique à Nicomaque*' (R.-A. Gauthier and Y. Jolif, *L'Éthique à Nicomaque*, 2nd edn. (Louvain, 1970), ii/1. 197).

Aristotle and Method in Ethics

of ethics regarding scientific demonstrations, at the same time as it refuses to locate the practical man in the world of opinion. In place of demonstration, the prudent man aspires only to an 'indication'. However, despite this decreasing exactness, the virtuous man lives now in the domain of truth. He does not demonstrate, he only indicates, but what he indicates is the (practical) truth. The price of dwelling in the realm of truth is a reduction in accuracy; the advantage is that he is enduringly installed in the world of truth. *In this new world, dialectical reasoning is an inefficient manner of proving.*

Aristotle writes for his time. By 'indicating the truth' he is not proposing something that could not belong in a syllogism or argument, a sort of pointing to the world that would take the place of reasoning when reasoning is ineffective. Showing the truth means that the premises from which the syllogism occurs are true, and necessarily true, but they are different from scientific premises in a crucial way, and this crucial difference consists in their differing degrees of exactness. In the domain of science, the kind of proof *par excellence* is the syllogism Barbara, the one whose two premises are universal affirmative propositions: A belongs to every B; B belongs to every C; therefore A belongs to every C. Science can fall short of this high standard and deploy itself in 'for the most part' formulae, but it is precisely this pattern that governs the ideal of proof in scientific reasoning. Now, in practical matters, what the prudent man shows is that A is B in circumstances C for the agent S. There is a certain necessity: the necessity of duty, expressed in the imperatives of the prudent man. There is just one thing to be done, that thing that the prudent man ordains or wishes to be done. There is also a certain universality affecting every agent involved, but each practical decision is expressed case by case, owing to the circumstances in which they occur. We can hope to generalize these prudential determinations and then obtain practical 'for the most part' rules, as in 'we must for the most part return benefits rather than oblige friends, as we must pay back a loan to a creditor rather than make one to a friend' (*NE* 9. 2, 1164^{b}31–3), but the nature of ethical reasoning is such that the syllogism Barbara cannot be effective as a paradigm. On the contrary, ethics is rooted in the particular, and will perhaps never be able to escape it in a positive form.[17] Here we

---

[17] Moral decisions are similar to political edicts, which rule particular cases, and only at a secondary level are they similar to laws and constitutions, which are ne-

316 *Marco Zingano*

reach bedrock regarding the difference between ethics and the theoretical sciences. Ethics, even when generalized to the maximum, is always close to the particular; science inevitably universalizes, even though sometimes it contents itself with mere 'for the most part' generalizations. However, such a difference is not surprising. Science and ethics are both in the domain of truth, and both use the same rules of inference; what now distinguishes them can no longer be the gap between (theoretical) knowledge and (practical) opinion; instead, it is the accuracy of their respective judgements: that is, the register in which practical and theoretical truths are expressed. The scientific man demonstrates theoretical truth, taking as paradigm the syllogism Barbara; the virtuous man indicates practical truth, contenting himself with at most generalizations. For this reason they differ one from another, but both seek truth.

It is now time to consider an apparently strong objection. I have taken the common books as having been originally part of *EE*, and I believe that I have shown, among other things, that in the treatise on prudence, a common book, there were signs of the Eudemian doctrine according to which prudence is privileged with regard to opinion (for it is a good deliberative opinion). However, one cannot deny that, throughout book 6, Aristotle insists upon the notion of practical truth. Deliberation belongs to the calculative part (λογιστικόν: 6. 1, 1139^{a}12), not only to the opinionative part (as in 6. 5 and 13). Furthermore, choice is presented in this book as a deliberative desire (6. 2, 1139^{a}23), desiderative intellect, or intellectual desire (6. 2, 1139^{b}4–5). All this is in full accordance with *NE* and its locating of the prudent man in the domain of truth. Prudence itself is twice defined as a true practical disposition accompanied by reason regarding the good and the bad for man (6. 5, 1140^{b}4–6 and 20–1). Deliberative excellence is rectitude regarding the means to reach an end, 'of which prudence is the *true* apprehension' (6. 9, 1142^{b}33). In spite of the syntactical ambiguity of the

cessarily generalizations. In fact, nothing prevents prudential decisions from being generalized, as long as they have some provisos (for example, that the prudent man can always correct the law according to circumstances). The point is that generalizations either come from particular decisions (by way of certain abstractions) or have to be controlled by particular reconsiderations. There are also, in morals, universal rules, which do not depend on any circumstantial consideration (for example, murder is never morally acceptable). However, perhaps it is no accident that these rules are negatively expressed as *absolute interdictions*. See on this point my paper 'Lei moral e escolha singular na ética aristotélica', in M. Zingano, *Estudos de ética antiga* (São Paulo, 2004), 218–42.

Aristotle and Method in Ethics 317

pronoun 'which' in this last phrase, the fact is that *truth* is clearly indicated in the sentence. Finally, it is said at 6. 8, 1142^a1, that the prudent man is the one who knows ($\epsilon\imath\delta\omega s$) and concerns himself with his own interests; but knowing and expressing opinions are not identical. If book 6 is a book shared by both *Ethics* and belongs originally to *EE*, how can one explain the number of aspects connected to truth?

This objection may be countered in several ways. The first strategy would be to reply that, even if the common books were originally conceived for *EE*, nothing prevents them from having been revised partially in order to be included in *NE*—and a part of this revision could have consisted in emphasizing the theme of truth in contrast with that of opinion. In fact, there are traces of such an adaptation.[18]

A second strategy could attempt to soften the extent of the theme of truth in book 6. Prudence must fulfil two conditions simultaneously: (1) the correctness of the means to the end, which refers to the calculating part; (2) the correctness of the end, which must be morally good. Perhaps truth is connected to the latter condition. Aristotle remarks that temperance preserves prudence because it 'preserves that kind of apprehension' (6. 5, $1140^b12–13$), which seems to mean that it preserves the apprehension of ends. The end, however, belongs to moral virtue and not to prudence, which, being an intellectual virtue, must rather presuppose it. As regards 6. 9, 1142^b33 (leaving aside the syntactic ambiguity), prudence is true apprehension of the end because, one could say, it presupposes the end that is good. The same point is made in 6. 5, at $1140^b4–6$ and $^b20–1$: the truth for prudence is connected to the disposition, that is to say, to the condition of the moral end, and not to the correctness that is proper to the reasoning part, that of the means towards the end.[19]

---

[18] To give an example: in *NE* 2. 2, $1103^b31–4$, Aristotle writes: 'That we must act according to right reason is a common principle and must be assumed—it will be discussed later, i.e. both what it is, and how it is related to the other excellences.' This is a clear allusion to book 6, and can work as a sign of an actual or intended adaptation to *NE* at least so far as concerns that book.

[19] Against this, however, it is interesting to note that in 6. 5, $1140^b20–1$, one manuscript (Mb) reads ἕξω εἶναι μετὰ λόγου ἀληθοῦς, which links 'truth' to 'accompanied by reason' and not to 'disposition'. The same reading is found in Alex. Aphr. (*In Metaph.* 7. 22 Hayduck) for $1140^b4–6$. Susemihl follows Alexander and reads ἀληθοῦς in both passages; Bywater maintains the reading of the manuscripts. Bywater's text seems preferable, for there is only one manuscript that, in the second

318   *Marco Zingano*

Truth is a theme firmly present in *NE* 6, but the way it appears throughout this book is by courtesy of the notion of prudence. And what prudence is doing is to place in a favourable light what corresponds to truth in the irrational part, as its moral excellence. Prudence also stands in contrast to the theoretical intellect, as being rather a sort of special perception, always close to particulars, and one whose end is true or good.

These strategies, collectively or separately, do soften the objection, but I do not believe that they really amount to a solution. Choice is also presented in book 2 of *EE* as a deliberative desire (e.g. 2. 10, 1226[b]17), just as in *NE*. Moreover, Aristotle does not seem to abandon all claims to truth in *EE*. Even if this claim is not so central as it is in the Nicomachean books, it is not lacking in *EE*. Furthermore, there is no reason for it not to be present in it: an opinion may always be true. When Aristotle writes in *EE* 2. 10, 1227[a]4, that choice is both opinion and desire ($\delta\delta\xi\alpha$ $\tau\epsilon$ $\kappa\alpha\grave{\iota}$ $\check{o}\rho\epsilon\xi\iota\varsigma$), he immediately adds the condition under which the interconnection of desire and opinion produces choice: 'when following as a conclusion from deliberation' (1227[a]5). It is not any opinion, but an opinion mixed with desire and, above all, an opinion that is the result of a process of deliberation. What is obtained after deliberation seems to be able to assure, in relation to the conclusion, that it is not only an opinion, but also a *true* opinion.

Thus, truth is not absent from *EE*. However, it is present only in the form of a true *opinion*. That seems to be the answer Aristotle offers, in *EE*, to the fact that in moral matters there is always a greater variability, not only in quantity but also in quality, than the variability we find in nature when we consider things from a theoretical perspective. In order to provide an account of this phenomenon in the moral field, Aristotle proposes to restrict moral reasoning to that of opinion, admitting that the conclusions of deliberations become true opinions. Truth finds a place, indeed, but only as accompanying an opinion.

In *NE*, in contrast, the very same phenomenon—the greater variability of the moral world in contrast with nature—has another explanation. The prudent man is already in the domain of truth, and his assertions are not opinions, but propositions that are necessarily true, as are those of the theoretical scientist. Their difference

passage, has $\mathring{a}\lambda\eta\theta o\hat{v}s$ and, *pace* Alexander, every manuscript links 'truth', in the first definition, to 'disposition'.

Aristotle and Method in Ethics 319

consists in the degree of exactness that practical rules can obtain: always close to the particular, no sooner does it get generalized than it demands the intervention of equitable man to correct it. According to these degrees of exactness, practical and theoretical reason are not distinguished from one another as true opinion differs from knowledge; henceforth, both claim the truth inherent in knowledge, with the proviso that practical reason is content with an accuracy differing from that of theoretical knowledge.

These are two possible answers on behalf of moral reasoning: either to locate it in the field of opinion and give up on knowledge, or to rethink its accuracy in order to achieve knowledge. Again, it seems to me that the response brought in by *NE* is philosophically more satisfying.

III

I want to examine now three cases in which questions of method are neatly contrasted between *EE* and *NE*. I shall leave aside the common books, for it is not possible to find such a contrast here. Consequently, I shall examine three topics whose versions from *EE* to *NE* are distinct regarding their method. I shall begin with (1) friendship; afterwards, I shall examine (2) the argumentative structure concerning the well-known notion of human function; finally, I shall reconsider (3) the problem of the object of wish, βούλησις, examined in *EE* 2. 10, 1227^{a}18–31, and in *NE* 3. 4, 1113^{a}15–^{b}2.

(1) The two treatises define friendship as a conscious and reciprocal relation of benevolence, of a practical nature and with altruistic traits. Both treatises acknowledge three types of friendship according to their objects: virtue, utility, or pleasure. The most important difference consists in the manner in which Aristotle connects the three types of friendship to one another. In *EE*, he envisages a focal meaning that will relate one to another (probably advancing for the first time the notion of a focal (πρὸς ἕν) relation), according to which friendship for the sake of virtue has a central position, to which the other two types refer in their meaning. *NE* abandons focal meaning as a means of connecting the three types of friendship, and substitutes a resemblance-ruled relation. Friendship for the sake of virtue maintains its central and first place, but the other two species of friendship now relate to it by resemblance

320   *Marco Zingano*

($\kappa\alpha\theta$' $\dot{\delta}\mu o\iota\dot{\delta}\tau\eta\tau a$). I cannot examine here all the philosophical aspects involved in this change. What interests me is only the manner in which Aristotle vindicates the theses in each treatise from the point of view of method.

In *EE* the accent is clearly dialectical. The first chapter of the Eudemian treatise on friendship presents a list of typical opinions on the subject. Some think that like is friend to like, among them Empedocles (7. 1, 1235^a11), but others say that opposites are friends; here, Heraclitus is mentioned (1235^a25). For some, only morally good men may be friends; for others, among whom, curiously enough, Socrates is mentioned (1235^a37–9), only utility can ground friendship. Now all 'these' ($\tau a\hat{v}\tau a$) are opposed to one another, as we read at 1235^b2–3; by 'these' we must understand 'the phenomena' (the word appears in 1235^a31), that is to say, opinions and sayings. These opinions lead to *aporiai* (1235^a4–5) and the method, clearly dialectical, must account for them. Aristotle then writes:

We must, then, find a method that will best explain the views [$\tau\grave{a}$ $\delta o\kappa o\hat{v}\nu\tau a$] held on these topics, and also put an end to difficulties and contradictions. And this will happen if the contrary views are seen to be held with some show of reason; such a view will be most in harmony with the phenomena [$\tauo\hat{\imath}\varsigma$ $\phi a\iota\nuo\mu\acute{\epsilon}\nuo\iota\varsigma$]; and both the contradictory statements will in the end stand, if what is said [$\tau\grave{o}$ $\lambda\epsilon\gamma\acute{o}\mu\epsilon\nuo\nu$] is true in one sense but untrue in another. (7. 2, 1235^b13–18)

It is no longer necessary to highlight the dialectical accent of this passage and its agreement with the method presented in *NE* 7. 1 (*EE* 6. 1) with regard to the problem of *akrasia*. Whatever the results of the Eudemian treatise on friendship may be, the fact is that its manner of proof is typically dialectical. However, the treatment of friendship in *NE* differs radically in its method too. In *NE* 8. 1–2 Aristotle introduces the topic and remarks that 'not a few things about friendship are matters of debate' (8. 2, 1155^b32). As in *EE*, he mentions divergent opinions on the topic that produce *aporiai*, and he also mentions philosophers such as Empedocles and Heraclitus who hold this or that opinion. Furthermore, he explicitly refuses to study his topic in its natural or physical aspects (8. 1, 1155^b8). We might think that he intends to limit himself to opinions, as he has already done in *EE*. However, what he in fact does is limit the examination to the 'problems that are human and involve character

Aristotle and Method in Ethics

and feeling' (1155^b9–10). This is a remark on the subject-matter that is going to be examined, not on how it is going to be examined. Regarding the latter, Aristotle says a bit later that '[those subjects] perhaps may be cleared up if we first come to know the object of friendship [τοῦ φιλητοῦ]' (8.2, 1155^b17–18). *If we first come to know the object of friendship*: something that one will not obtain by examining opinions, but through examination of the thing itself, that is to say, by scrutinizing attitudes, relationships, and rapports friends have between themselves, which Aristotle calls the facts (ὑπάρχοντα) of friendship. Since there are three species of objects of friendship, namely virtue, utility, and pleasure (1155^b27), Aristotle takes them as basic for understanding the variety of actual friendships. They will be scrutinized not without an appeal to theses and opinions held by other philosophers, but what is important here is that the type of proof is not a dialectical argument, but an examination of the thing itself, which determines that the study of the types of friendship is to be guided by considerations about the three objects of friendship, themselves disclosed by a study of friends' attitudes and behaviour. Why these three types and not others? Because they are the ones revealed by studying friendly attitudes and behaviour. Whatever the results of the Nicomachean treatise on friendship may be, the fact is that its mode of proof is no longer dialectical, but appeals at its core to attitudes and behaviour between people.

(2) Another example is the argument concerning the proper function, or *ergon*, of man. It is well known that this argument plays an important role in the conceptual framework of Aristotelian ethics. In *EE* it appears in 2.1, 1218^b37–1219^b26, in a complex proof about what happiness is. The argument begins with the thesis that virtue is the best disposition, state, or capacity of each thing. As frequently in *EE*, such a starting-point is obtained by simply assuming a hypothesis (1218^b37: ὑποκείσθω, expressed in the vocabulary Allan named *quasi-mathematical method*). Next, it is taken for granted that the function of each thing is its end (1219^a8) and that the function is better than the disposition or the state of each thing (1219^a11–12). None the less, a thing's *ergon* is mentioned in two different ways: either as its product (a house, for instance, as the *ergon* of building), or as its use (for example, vision as the *ergon* of sight, and contemplation as the *ergon* of mathematical knowledge, 1219^a16–17). When *ergon* corresponds to the activity, it is necessarily superior to the disposition. It is then declared (1219^a19:

322 *Marco Zingano*

λέγωμεν) that the function of a thing and its excellence do not operate in the same manner. A pair of shoes is the *ergon* (here: the product) of the art of the cobbler, but the excellence of this art is such that its *ergon* (the product again) will not be a pair of shoes, but a good pair of shoes. It is then declared that the function of the soul is to produce living (1219ª23–4). From everything that has being agreed, it is deduced that excellence of the soul is a good life (ζωὴ σπουδαία, 1219ª27). However, a good life is nothing more than happiness; in the following lines, 1219ª28–39, Aristotle shows that, always in agreement with what has been supposed (1219ª28–9, ἐκ τῶν ὑποκειμένων), *eudamonia* means *to live well*, which is precisely the proper function of the human soul. Having stated this, Aristotle says that everything here is in agreement with 'common opinions' (1219ª40): he quotes Solon (1219ᵇ6); he mentions the practices of encomia (1219ᵇ8–16), and he concludes his argument showing why, during sleep, the prudent are no better than the bad (so long as there are no other activities than that of the vegetative soul, 1219ᵇ16–26). The unfolding of the argument and its vocabulary are archetypically dialectical.

In *NE* 1. 7, 1097ᵇ22–1098ª20, the argument about man's *ergon* also concludes with the claim that human happiness consists in an activity of soul in conformity with virtue or excellence (1098ª16–17). By way of his introduction it is shown that the function proper of man is to live in accordance with, or not without, a rational principle (1098ª7–8). It is not clear in that context whether 'rational' includes both theoretical and practical reason, or only the latter, so long as this is divided into a part that listens and another that commands. The framing of the passage seems to lend more support to the second perspective (1098ª4–5), but nothing prevents us from seeing in it a reference to reason in general, without distinction for both uses, or else seeing in it a complex expression with two branches, each referring to one of the uses of reason. Despite these obscurities, the aim of the argument is clear: its goal is to distinguish between living and living well, the latter being life in accordance with excellence, which includes a necessary reference to reason, be it practical or theoretical. This is exactly the same as the definition of happiness: so *eudamonia* consists in living well, and living well requires living in accordance with, or not without, the rational principle: QED.

What I would like to emphasize in this lengthy and complex

argument is how the notion of the function of man is introduced. We have seen that, in *EE*, the notion of *function* is simply taken for granted, and it can be easily supposed because it is one of the reputable opinions that are at hand. Now, in *NE*, the argument about the function of man is no longer supposed or assumed; on the contrary, it is supported by two analogies. According to the first analogy, presented at 1097^{b}27–30, given that every art or technique has a function, it would be very peculiar that man should not possess a certain function, but be by nature functionless (1097^{b}30). The second analogy comes into play at 1097^{b}30–3: considering that each part of the body has a function (e.g. the eyes, the hands, the feet), we are invited to infer that man too should have a certain function over and above those of his organs (1097^{b}32–3). It is not difficult to see that neither of these two analogies, either collectively or separately, allows us to conclude that man has a certain function—and not, for example, many functions, or even, as a whole, no function at all. That is true; but, as has already been said, the most important point here is that 'the idea that there is an *ergon anthrôpou* is not an assumption that Aristotle simply adopts without discussion'.[20] The analogies may not suffice to settle the point, but what is really important here is that they are now filling the vacuum left when the method of simply assuming reputable opinions was discontinued. For that method is absent from *NE*. The central point here is that, henceforth, it is necessary *to justify the theses adopted*, and not simply to assume them. The manner of justifying the theses consists in referring to the world and the nature of things: eyes, arms, feet, arts, techniques, and so on. In the present case, both analogies produced are too weak to prove the point fully. But they do introduce a different, and non-dialectical, means of proving a point.

(3) My final example is a decisive passage regarding the introduction of (practical) truth in *NE*. I am thinking of *NE* 3. 4, 1113^{a}15–^{b}2, where Aristotle writes that the good man 'judges rightly each action and in each the truth appears to him' (1113^{a}29–30). This last statement is the conclusion of an argument that may at first glance seem typically dialectical. This is surprising, not only because it occurs in *NE* but also because nothing corresponds to it in *EE*. The argument is as follows: on the one hand, the Platonists

[20] G. E. R. Lloyd, 'The Role of Medical and Biological Analogies in Aristotle's Ethics', *Phronesis*, 13 (1968), 68–83 at 70.

324 Marco Zingano

think the natural object of wish ($\beta o \acute{\nu} \lambda \eta \sigma \iota s$) is the good; if it is not in truth good, but a good only in appearance ($\phi \alpha \iota \nu \acute{o} \mu \epsilon \nu o \nu \ \dot{\alpha} \gamma \alpha \theta \acute{o} \nu$), it is not actually an object of wish (that is, of desire by the rational part of the soul), but is the object of an irrational desire (either of the appetite or of *thumos*). On the other hand, the sophists propose that what appears to be good for someone is actually good for him. Aristotle is not content with either of these arguments, and the solution he proposes aims to circumvent both obstacles. His solution declares that the real good is the object of wish in truth ($\dot{\alpha} \pi \lambda \hat{\omega} s \ \kappa \alpha \grave{\iota}$ $\kappa \alpha \tau$' $\dot{\alpha} \lambda \acute{\eta} \theta \epsilon \iota \alpha \nu$), but for each person it is the apparent good ($1113^a 22$–4). For the good man, what appears to be a good is actually the good in truth; for the base man, some other thing will appear to be good. Initially, it appears as if Aristotle has arrived at this thesis by preserving what is true in each of the theses that are opposed and rejecting what is false in them. If this is so, is he not then applying to it the Eudemian dialectical method, which would thus turn out to be exemplified in *NE*?

This is a strong objection, which threatens to undermine my arguments against the presence of dialectic in *NE*. Again, we could try to evade the objection with the consideration that, even though in *NE* the kind of proof is no longer dialectical, Aristotle might sometimes have occasion to use dialectical arguments. This answer, however, although not implausible, does not seem to me compelling. Aristotle could of course have used the dialectical method here, but has he in fact used it? I do not think so. At first glance, his solution does seem to conciliate between the disputed positions in the way required for a dialectical proof. However, is Aristotle's solution really conciliatory? The Platonists and the sophists share a common thesis. For both of them, it is a *sufficient* condition of anything's being an object of a wish either that it is in fact good (for the Platonists), or that it seems to be so (for the sophists). Aristotle's answer, however, makes no compromise: according to him, for anything to be an object of a wish, it is a *necessary* condition that it is taken as good, that is to say, that it appears to somebody to be so—in other words, that it is an apparent good ($\phi \alpha \iota \nu \acute{o} \mu \epsilon \nu o \nu \ \dot{\alpha} \gamma \alpha \theta \acute{o} \nu$). Nevertheless, this is in no case a sufficient condition for being good. Aristotle, in fact, rejects both positions unconditionally. The naturalness of the good is not contrasted with the conventionality attributed to it by the sophists in such a way as to preserve some truth in both. It is not a case of preserving one or another, or the truth of each. According

Aristotle and Method in Ethics 325

to Aristotle, the naturalness of the good is no longer tenable, for from now on what is good has to be taken as good by man. In other words, the good is directly connected to conditions of apprehension, whose expression is inevitably intensional. Intensionality in practical matters is something novel, which Aristotle discovers in the course of explaining practical statements. Although not fully aware of its consequences, he sees clearly its novelty, in that it does not rely on any point of agreement or of disagreement between the other disputants. *Such a thesis can be formulated in simultaneous opposition to those of the Platonists and sophists, and is not the outcome of preserving the truth of each of these.* An indication of its originality is the radically different meaning the expression 'apparent good' now conveys in Aristotle: it no longer means what has only the appearance of good without actually being good, but points to the necessity of something's being taken as a good in order for it to be an object of desire. All good is *bonum apprehensum*, to recall Aquinas' commentary on this passage: this is what Platonists and sophists ignore and what cannot be obtained by conflating their theses, although it can be explained by means of a contrast with their theses.

One can obtain the very same result if one compares this passage with another found in *EE*, which would have been the Eudemian parallel to the supposed Nicomachean thesis—if there were such a passage. In *EE* 2. 10, 1227ᵃ18–31, Aristotle writes that 'the end [τὸ τέλος] is always something good by nature' (1227ᵃ18) and that what is contrary to nature and by perversion is not the good, but only the apparent good (1227ᵃ21–2: παρὰ φύσιν δὲ καὶ διὰ στροφὴν οὐ τὸ ἀγαθόν, ἀλλὰ τὸ φαινόμενον ἀγαθόν). The cause of this perversion is to be found in the fact that, although certain things can be employed only towards their natural ends, there are others that can be employed in a manner differing from their natural ends: for example, as medical science is related to both health and disease. Conversely, sight can be used only for seeing, but science can be used for good or evil. Aristotle concludes: 'Similarly wish [βούλησις] is for the good naturally, but for the bad contrary to nature, and by nature one wishes the good, but contrary to nature and through perversion the bad as well' (1227ᵃ28–31). In this passage, two issues matter. Firstly, the thesis of the naturalness of the good is upheld. Secondly, such a defence is the dialectical outcome achieved by an opposition between the natural and the conventional character of the good.

326 *Marco Zingano*

According to this perspective, Aristotle is, on behalf of naturalness, accepting that to the perverted what appears good to them is only apparently good, owing to its perverted nature. However, they do *wish* these bad things as if they were good things, which is a partial acknowledgement of the conventionalist position. This perspective preserves something from both positions and is the outcome of a dialectical admixture of both. Such a thesis appears sporadically in Aristotle's works,[21] but, essentially, this solution is philosophically surpassed by a much more radical, and conceptually independent, thesis: the thesis of the inevitable intensional rooting of everything concerning the practical world, a thesis present not in *EE*, but only in *NE*.

IV

In conclusion, I would like to offer a final comment on the fate of the dialectical method in Aristotle's philosophy. I have examined it here only from the perspective of his studies in ethics, but I believe that one can show that its function as a kind of proof in the philosophical disciplines, including ethics, cannot but decrease after the clear distinction, introduced by the *Analytics*, between the necessary truth of the premisses of a scientific syllogism and the reputability of the premisses of a dialectical argument. Despite this, dialectic does not vanish completely—nor should one expect it to do so without leaving traces. In the *Physics* it is easy to find arguments containing dialectical strategies; the discussions on the nature of time and space are a good example of this. I cannot examine these aspects here, but I would like to mention two vestiges of the dialectical attitude that will play a very important role in Aristotelian scientific demonstrations. The first is the examination, preparatory to a discipline, of the difficulties and *aporiai* philosophers have encountered. *Aporiai* are often found in dialectical discussions, but they are neither essential elements of a dialectical argument nor found only in dialectical arguments. As we have seen, there is an epistemological optimism in Aristotle: each man contributes to the

---

[21] Particularly at *DA* 3. 10, 433ª28–9, where φαινόμενον ἀγαθόν has the sense of 'apparent good', i.e. 'false good', 'good only apparently'. This is surprising, for one of the few occasions on which we see in Aristotle an explicit acknowledgement of the logical feature of practical propositions (due to the fact of their being irremediably intentional) is found precisely at *DA* 3. 7, 431ᵇ10–12.

Aristotle and Method in Ethics   327

truth. Every art and technique has a history that one should not forget; furthermore, the chances of finding the truth and making a scientific advance are greater if we begin with results already acquired. Aristotle never tires of stressing the collective character of scientific research. To recognize the difficulties, to frame clearly the *aporiai* other scientists have encountered, is an appropriate device in this regard. Nevertheless, such a strategy does not mean that the argument in which it appears is dialectical.[22] In book 1 of the *De anima*, for instance, Aristotle presents the history of previous studies in psychology, then announces some difficulties and lists questions that remain unanswered; none of this, however, spoils the typically scientific argument with any of the dialectical aspects that he considers in book 2 regarding the nature of the soul. On the contrary, book 2 begins with a series of theses that are independent of everything that has been discussed before, but which are meant to dissolve the problems.

A second point, but no less important: there is a negative counterpart of the dialectical method used for discovering the truth. In certain contexts *logikōs* arguments (those made from, in Aristotle's terminology, a 'logical' point of view, λογικῶς) are purely verbal arguments, downgraded as proceeding in a 'vainly dialectical' way (διαλεκτικῶς καὶ κενῶς). In this sense, they are considered empty and deceptive conversations.[23] However, we may discover some useful features of a thing in the very manner in which we talk about it before scrutinizing the thing itself. In such cases, a *logikōs* argument has some advantages, for it can be a reliable guide when beginning a search in some fields, notably those of wide diversity. In this case, a *logikōs* argument can be followed by a proper scientific argument, or by *phusikōs*-led research, but nothing forces us to consider it idle

---

[22] A passage from *De caelo* illustrates my point well. In *De caelo* 1. 10 Aristotle wants to maintain the ingenerability and incorruptibility of the universe. At the beginning, he writes, 'Let us start with a review of the theories of other thinkers; for the proofs of a theory are difficulties for the contrary theory' (279^b5–7). This passage resembles *EE* 1. 3, examined above: 'It is well to examine these opinions, for a disputant's refutation of what is opposed to his arguments is a demonstration of the argument itself' (1215^a5–7). There certainly is a similarity, but also an important difference. In the Eudemian passage, the refutation of the objections amounts to a (demonstrative) proof; in *De caelo*, the demonstration of one thesis constitutes a difficulty for whoever wants to hold the contrary thesis. In the latter case, it is clearly reasonable to hear what the opponents have to say, but the sort of proof demanded is not (necessarily) a dialectical proof.

[23] e.g. *DA* 1. 1, 403^a2; *EE* 1. 8, 1217^b21. See also G. Mosquera, 'L'interprétation de l'argument *logikos* chez Aristote', *Études classiques*, 66 (1998), 33–52.

328   Marco Zingano

talk with no serious results. On the contrary: in *Metaphysics Z*, for instance, the *phusikōs*-guided examination of substance is preceded by *logikōs* analyses, and these latter prove to be very profitable for the scientific character of the enquiry.[24] Another example of the scientific interest of an analysis conducted formerly in a *logikōs* manner is one that occurs in *Posterior Analytics* I. 22 concerning the nature of predication.[25] The division of every proposition into subject and predicate, and the distinction between essential and accidental predication, reveal important elements of reality, and they are obtained through a *logikōs*-conducted enquiry. In no case do the *Analytics* use dialectical arguments, but this does not prevent them from introducing *logikōs*-guided arguments. The *logikōs*-acquired standpoint is a remnant of the former dialectical disputes, but it is a remnant that does not spoil the argument with dialectic.

One can now better understand the heuristic function of dialectical arguments, as well as their remnants and traces in Aristotle's scientific research. It is worth noting that Aristotle does not have the extremely promising empirical-experimental method of the natural sciences. He makes some observations and conceives some experiences, but he has never conceived of a clearly experimental method for natural sciences. It is not surprising, then, that some dialectical passages are found among scientific arguments, and it is even less surprising that some dialectical strategies (such as the locating of difficulties and the inventory of *aporiai*) play a positive role in a mode of reasoning henceforth scientifically governed and directed at the truth, but without a method of its own. In evaluating the strategies Aristotle adopts, some with dialectal

---

[24] The enquiry into the nature of quiddity, one of the candidates for substance, is conducted in Z 4, $1029^b 13$, by *logikōs*-guided remarks, beginning with the meanings by which something is said to be itself ($1029^b 14$). It is not so clear where that *logikōs*-guided investigation ends and where the *phusikōs*-guided examination begins; none the less, it is pretty clear that there is a positive value for the *logikōs*-guided enquiry (thus not to be mixed up with the *logikōs* declaration at $1030^a 25$ that non-being is, which is of no scientific use).

[25] The examination carried out in *Post. An.* I. 22 on predication—which appeals to fundamental elements of Aristotelianism (the distinction between essential and accidental predication, for instance)—is said to be a *logikōs* enquiry (I. 21, $82^b 35$). Proofs according to the *logikōs* manner are said to be sufficient to arrive at conviction ($84^a 7$–8); some considerations are then added of an *analutikōs* type ($87^a 8$), which corresponds, at the logical level, to the *phusikōs* proofs of the theoretical sciences. It is not easy to show where exactly the difference lies between the *logikōs* and the *analutikōs* examination; however, what is clear is that the *logikōs* argument is certainly not a dialectical argument.

origins and trends, one needs to take into account the absence of the empirical-experimental method.

Concerning moral matters, however, what could supplant the dialectical method? This is a question whose answer remains unclear. If we consider Aristotle's declarations in *NE* on the impossibility of pinpoint accuracy in ethical matters, it is highly unlikely that the experimental method could replace the dialectical method as successfully as it did in the natural sciences of late modernity. On the contrary, such a method seems entirely inconsistent with ethics, since Aristotelian ethics is wary of generalizations and is guided rather by the particular conditions or circumstances within which each action occurs. Nowhere in Aristotle is there a clear answer to this issue. We can see that his mature answer to a certain extent consists in valuing attitudes and feelings, but this has a great deal to do with opinions and judgements, which are likely to recall the dialectical strategies he intended to discard. Perhaps Aristotle has not provided us, in his extant writings, with a clear answer to this problem. But, by eliminating the dialectical method and its claim of a quasi-mathematical deduction in ethics, he has at least enabled us to formulate more clearly the questions that need to be asked about ethical method.

University of São Paulo

BIBLIOGRAPHY

Allan, D. J., 'Quasi-Mathematical Method in the *Eudemian Ethics*' ['Quasi-Mathematical'], in Mansion, *Aristote et les problèmes de méthode*, 303–18.

Barnes, J., 'Aristotle and the Methods of Ethics', *Revue internationale de philosophie*, 34 (1980), 490–511.

—— (ed.), *The Complete Works of Aristotle: The Revised Oxford Translation* [*ROT*] (Princeton, 1984).

Berti, E., 'Does Aristotle's Conception of Dialectic Develop?', in W. Wians (ed.), *Aristotle's Philosophical Development* (Lanham, Md., 1996), 105–30.

—— 'Il metodo della filosofia pratica secondo Aristotele', in A. Alberti (ed.), *Studi sull'etica di Aristotele* (Naples, 1990), 23–63.

—— *Le raggioni di Aristotele* (Bari, 1989).

Brunschwig, J., *Aristote: Topiques I–IV* (Paris, 1967).

Burnet, J., *The Ethics of Aristotle* (London, 1900).

330 *Marco Zingano*

Cooper, J., 'Aristotle on the Authority of "Appearances"', in id., *Reason and Emotion: Essays on Ancient Moral Psychology and Ethical Theory* (Princeton, 1999), 281–91.

Devereux, D., 'Particular and Universal in Aristotle's Conception of Practical Knowledge', *Review of Metaphysics*, 29 (1986), 483–505.

Gauthier, R.-A., and Jolif, J., *L'Éthique à Nicomaque*, 2nd edn. (Louvain, 1970).

Hardie, W. F. R., *Aristotle's Ethical Theory*, 2nd edn. (Oxford, 1980).

Irwin, T. H., *Aristotle's First Principles* (Oxford, 1988).

—— 'Aristotle's Methods of Ethics', in D. J. O'Meara (ed.), *Studies in Aristotle* (Washington, 1981), 193–223.

Lloyd, G. E. R., 'The Role of Medical and Biological Analogies in Aristotle's Ethics', *Phronesis*, 13 (1968), 68–83.

Mansion, S. (ed.), *Aristote et les problèmes de méthode* (Louvain, 1980).

Mosquera, G., 'L'interprétation de l'argument *logikos* chez Aristote', *Études classiques*, 66 (1998), 33–52.

Nussbaum, M., 'Saving Aristotle's Appearances', in M. Schofield and M. Nussbaum (eds.), *Language and Logos: Studies in Ancient Greek Philosophy Presented to G. E. L. Owen* (Cambridge, 1982), 267–93.

—— *The Fragility of Goodness: Luck and Ethics in Greek Tragedy and Philosophy* (Cambridge, 1986).

Owen, G. E. L., 'Logic and Metaphysics in Some Earlier Works of Aristotle', in I. Düring and G. E. L. Owen (eds.), *Aristotle and Plato in the Mid-Fourth Century* (Göteborg, 1960), 163–90; repr. in Owen, *Logic, Science and Dialectic*, 180–99.

—— *Logic, Science and Dialectic: Collected Papers in Greek Philosophy* (Ithaca, NY, 1986).

—— 'Tithenai ta Phainomena', in Mansion, *Aristote et les problèmes de méthode*, 83–103; repr. in Owen, *Logic, Science and Dialectic*, 239–51.

Smith, R., *Aristotle: Topics I and VIII* (Oxford, 1997).

Stewart, J., *Notes on the* Nicomachean Ethics (Oxford, 1892).

Wians, W., 'Saving Aristotle from Nussbaum's Phainomena', in J. P. Anton and A. Preus (eds.), *Essays in Ancient Greek Philosophy*, v. *Aristotle's Ontology* (Albany, NY, 1992), 133–49.

Wilpert, P., 'Aristoteles und die Dialektik', *Kant-Studien*, 48/2 (1956–7), 247–57.

Zingano, M. 'Lei moral e escolha singular na ética aristotélica', in id., *Estudos de ética antiga* (São Paulo, 2004), 218–42.

ENQUIRY AND DISCOVERY

A Discussion of Dominic Scott, *Plato's* Meno[1]

GAIL FINE

1. *Plato's* Meno is a beautifully written, sensitive, and elegant book that at the same time manages to be clear, analytical, and sensible: a rare combination. Dominic Scott pays careful attention not only to the dramatic setting and the nature of the interlocutors but also to the details of arguments, and he manages to illuminate both: another rare combination. This will surely be the standard book on the *Meno* for years to come, one that will be read with pleasure and profit by a variety of people ranging from undergraduates to professional philosophers. It serves as an excellent introduction to the dialogue; but it will also challenge and interest those who have worked intensively on it. Like the *Meno* itself, the book is a gem.[2]

2. Commentators have given different answers to the question of what the *Meno*'s central concern is; leading contenders are virtue, enquiry, and knowledge. Scott suggests that it is a mistake to search for a single main theme. Rather, the dialogue has a 'complex unity' (3): Plato 'offers us a dramatised conflict of interests. In a sense, the *Meno* is a dialogue that cannot quite decide what it is about, and that conflict is essential to the work' (214). For example, Socrates wants to define virtue, but Meno wants to talk about how virtue is acquired.

I agree that the *Meno* exhibits a complex unity, and that Socrates and Meno have conflicting interests. It does not follow that the *Meno* cannot quite decide what it is about. And to me, at any rate, it seems quite elegantly organized: Meno asks whether virtue can

---

© Gail Fine 2007

[1] D. Scott, *Plato's* Meno [*PM*] (Cambridge, 2006), pp. x+238.

[2] The *Meno* is so described by J. S. Mill, cited by Scott (3).

332 *Gail Fine*

be taught. Since Socrates thinks one cannot know the answer to that question unless one knows what virtue is, and since he also thinks that knowing what virtue is consists in knowing the definition of virtue, they try to define virtue. When they discover they cannot do so, they consider whether there is any other way in which they can make progress towards answering Meno's question, even if it will not yield knowledge in Socrates' demanding sense of the term. Moreover, since Socrates believes that virtue is knowledge, they naturally discuss the nature of knowledge and how to acquire it; and so they discuss the nature of enquiry, which is, or might be thought to be, a method of acquiring knowledge. These various themes fit together into a harmonious whole; there is no indecision, just a natural progression of related ideas.

It is, however, rather a lot of ground to cover in a relatively short work; so it is not surprising that, as Scott notes, many of the *Meno*'s arguments appear sketchy (3). Hence Scott naturally says that '[t]he main task of this book [i.e. of *Plato's* Meno] is to resolve the indeterminacies surrounding both the arguments and the conclusions that they are meant to support' (4). He accomplishes this by 'searching for premises that might be implicit and that would improve the quality of the argument; or, failing that, at least bringing out its interest and importance, whatever the flaws that remain' (4). Though not everyone appreciates this approach to Plato, I am wholeheartedly in favour of it. I also agree with much of what Scott says; and where I have disagreed, I have always learnt from trying to figure out why.

Scott argues that the dialogue contains four episodes in which Plato puts Socrates on philosophical trial (7): passages in which Plato raises a challenge to a Socratic claim—that is, to claims made by the historical Socrates as portrayed in Plato's early dialogues, claims that also appear at the beginning of the *Meno* itself.[3] The four Socratic views that Plato challenges are (i) his 'unitarian assumption', according to which 'whenever we apply the same term F to many different things, and say they are all F's, each one no less than the others, there is one unitary property, F-ness, that they have in common' (25; cf. 24–30); (ii) his view that 'the elenchus

---

[3] Scott assumes without argument that the Socrates of Plato's early dialogues (or of what are often taken to be his early dialogues) is the historical Socrates, in the sense that they represent his thought, though not *verbatim* (6). I too accept this view, but it is controversial.

Enquiry and Discovery

is beneficial and incites the interlocutor to further inquiry' (73; cf. 71–4); (iii) his view that we have a duty to enquire (87–91); and (iv) his view about philosophical method (140–2).

According to Scott, Plato replies to these challenges in different ways. Scott thinks that the *Meno*, like the early dialogues, accepts the unitarian assumption; but in contrast to earlier dialogues, it defends it. He also thinks that the *Meno*, like the early dialogues, values the elenchus and maintains that we have a duty to enquire. However, he thinks that the *Meno* challenges the view that we have a duty to enquire, by raising the possibility that we might not be able to acquire knowledge.[4] He thinks that Plato responds to this challenge by arguing that discovery is possible; hence the Socratic view that we have a duty to enquire can remain intact. But, Scott argues, in defending the possibility of discovery, Plato revises the foreknowledge principle accepted earlier in the *Meno*.[5] (The foreknowledge principle says that 'knowledge must derive from pre-existent knowledge' (84). I discuss it later.) Scott also argues that the hypothetical method, which is discussed towards the end of the *Meno*, involves an 'emendation' of Socrates' views on method (142), where this includes both the early dialogues and also views expressed earlier in the *Meno*. Thus, in the first and second trials the *Meno* defends the views of the early dialogues, as well as views accepted earlier in the *Meno* itself. But in the third and fourth trials there is some revision.

Scott interestingly argues that in each trial the *Meno* operates on two levels: on one level, Socrates tries to convince Meno of something; on another level, Plato speaks to a more sophisticated philosophical audience (30). Scott takes this to be a distinctive feature of the dialogue.[6] One of the most interesting and illuminating features of *PM* is its discussion of this strategy.

---

[4] He says there is 'no evidence to clinch the issue' (90) as to whether the historical Socrates thought knowledge attainable. So whereas the historical Socrates is clearly on trial in the first two cases, in this third case matters are 'not as straightforward' (89).

[5] Scott argues that the historical Socrates accepts foreknowledge at least 'in the specific case of knowing what something is before enquiring how it is acquired' (90). For a fuller discussion, he refers us to 141–2, where he says that the Socratic assumption is that 'we *should* achieve knowledge of the definition of virtue before we examine whether it is teachable' (141, emphasis added): a matter of preference rather than necessity. I discuss this in sect. 16.

[6] Cf. D. Sedley, *The Midwife of Platonism: Text and Subtext in Plato's* Theaetetus (Oxford, 2004), who defends a two-level reading of the *Theaetetus*, though the two levels he describes are different from the two Scott discusses.

334   *Gail Fine*

3. I shall explore each challenge in turn, beginning with the unitarian assumption. I agree that the early dialogues assume it and that the *Meno* defends it. However, the *Meno* also adumbrates the so-called Dialectical Requirement (DR), which Plato formulates twice over, once at 75 C 8–D 7 and once at 79 D. At 75 C 8–D 7 Socrates says, in part, that '[t]he more dialectical approach, perhaps, is to answer not just by speaking the truth, but also through things that the person questioned first agrees he knows'.[7] At 79 D he says, in part, that one cannot explain anything by appeal to what is 'not yet agreed and still under investigation'. According to Scott, there is a possible inconsistency in DR: in its first formulation, it seems to demand just 'a sense of familiarity'; in its second formulation, it seems to require 'a more exacting sense of knowledge' (37). Scott rightly resists the view that there are two different dialectical requirements (57). Rather, he argues, 'the requirement is indeterminate: it is a rule of dialectical engagement, but the sort of rule that can be applied flexibly' (58): 'the term "know" could be taken either as familiarity or as philosophical understanding' (57); first 'it is applied with a loose sense of "know"'; later it is applied 'more austerely' (58).[8]

---

[7] I have used Scott's translation. (I do so throughout, unless otherwise noted.) But there is a textual problem here that makes his translation uncertain. (Scott discusses this at 35–6 n. 6.) At 75 D 6 MSS B, T, and W have προσομολογῇ, and F has προσομολογεῖ; in either case, the sense is 'agree in addition'. Gedike proposed emending to προομολογῇ, 'agree in advance'; he is followed by E. S. Thompson, *The Meno* (London, 1901), and R. S. Bluck, *Plato's Meno* (Cambridge, 1964), though not by R. W. Sharples, *Plato: Meno* (Warminster, 1985). This is also the reading Scott favours, saying that it 'makes good sense of the procedure Socrates actually follows: before he gives his sample definitions, he carefully checks that Meno already understands the elements he is about to use in the definition'. On the manuscript reading of 75 D 6, by contrast, Socrates does not say that one must *first* agree to something. He says only that one must *additionally* agree, which allows *simultaneous* agreement. This is important, because later Scott appeals to at least the second statement of DR (at 79 D) as evidence that Socrates accepts the foreknowledge principle. On the manuscript reading of 75 D 6, the first statement of DR does not involve *fore*knowledge (or antecedent familiarity); if it does not do so, that may lessen the temptation to think that the second statement of DR does so.

As the foregoing perhaps makes clear, there are two distinct issues here. One is about what level of cognition DR requires: mere familiarity, or knowledge in a demanding sense. The other is whether one must have this level of cognition chronologically prior to engaging in enquiry. The textual difficulty concerns only the second issue. At the moment, I focus on cognitive level. I discuss chronological priority later.

[8] In his earlier *Recollection and Experience* [RE] (Cambridge, 1995), by contrast, Scott seems to think that satisfying DR always requires one to have high-level knowledge; see e.g. 28–9. Although 29 n. 3 explicitly says only that 79 D 1–4 requires high-level knowledge, Scott does not suggest that 75 D requires less than that; nor

Enquiry and Discovery 335

However, if, as Scott says, DR involves different *senses* of 'know', that violates the unitarian assumption that Scott rightly takes the *Meno* to defend.[9]

In addition to saying that DR involves different senses of 'knowledge', Scott also says that in 75 D DR requires just 'a relatively shallow *level* of knowledge', whereas in 79 D it requires philosophical understanding (57, emphasis added). Different *senses* of 'knowledge' and different *levels* of knowledge are quite different; indeed, speaking of the latter assumes that 'knowledge' is used univocally. So perhaps Scott's view is that DR uses 'know' univocally, but admits different levels of knowledge.[10]

Although this both renders DR consistent with the unitarian assumption and also allows us to say that there is just a single, univocal dialectical requirement, it raises a different problem. For, as Scott rightly thinks, as Plato understands knowledge in the *Meno*, it requires explanatory or philosophical understanding; anything short of that is at best true belief (20).[11] But then even the weak level of knowledge that Scott takes to be at issue in 75 D would have

does he say anywhere in *RE* that 75 D has a weaker sort of knowledge in view. At *RE* 215 Scott says that 75 D states foreknowledge, which he describes as the view that 'in an inquiry we should only proceed in terms of what we already know'; though he does not explicitly say what sense of 'knowledge', or level of knowledge, he has in mind, he seems to have high-level knowledge in mind.

[9] This would clearly be true if the unitarian assumption said simply that every term is to be defined in terms of a single unitary property; but Scott's formulation (cited above) is more nuanced than that. However, he thinks that genuine knowledge for Plato always requires philosophical or explanatory understanding; and that is sufficient for my main point.

It would have been interesting had Scott considered Plato's cognitive vocabulary. When he says that Plato uses 'to know' univocally for philosophical understanding, how many cognitive words are covered? Is it just ἐπίστασθαι that constitutes knowledge in this sense, or some or all of the following: φρονεῖν, νοεῖν, εἰδέναι, γιγνώσκειν? The answer might make a difference in spelling out precisely what various passages mean.

[10] L. Franklin, 'The Structure of Dialectic in the *Meno*', *Phronesis*, 46 (2001), 413–39, also suggests that 75 D requires just familiarity, whereas 79 D requires genuine knowledge which, in turn, requires understanding why something is so. However, Franklin thinks this is because 75 D concerns the beginning of enquiry, whereas 79 D concerns its completion. Scott, by contrast, seems to think that what level of familiarity is required depends not on what stage one is at in a given enquiry, but on what one is enquiring into: if one is enquiring how virtue is acquired, knowledge of what it is is required (or preferable); in the case of colour or σχῆμα (shape or, as Scott argues, surface), non-technical familiarity will do.

[11] Understanding and knowledge are sometimes opposed. But Scott rightly argues that for Plato, all knowledge involves understanding. He also rightly argues that this

336 *Gail Fine*

to involve explanatory understanding. Yet he says that to satisfy DR in 75 D 'Meno only needed to acknowledge a non-technical familiarity'; he did not need to have explanatory understanding. Hence moving to different levels of knowledge, all of which involve explanatory understanding (which is the one sense of 'knowledge' acknowledged in the *Meno*), leaves it unclear why Socrates thinks Meno satisfies it with respect to *schēma* (which is what is under investigation at that point).[12]

Perhaps, then, Scott thinks that DR requires different levels, not of knowledge, but of familiarity: sometimes the appropriate level of familiarity can be less than knowledge; but sometimes it must involve philosophical understanding. So understood, DR as such is broader than the foreknowledge principle, for the latter requires knowledge; mere familiarity will not do. But Scott thinks that 79 D 1–4 both states austere DR and is an 'application' of the foreknowledge principle (85 n. 15). So even if DR as such is broader than foreknowledge, there is a close connection between austere DR and foreknowledge.[13]

Scott thinks 79 D requires foreknowledge in two sorts of cases. First, 'where virtue is concerned, Socrates expects neither of them to be satisfied with a definition that fails a strict application of the dialectical requirement. The reason lies in his insistence that they achieve a philosophical understanding of the nature of virtue before they investigate how it is acquired' (58; cf. 131). Hence foreknowledge is required not just for acquiring (further) knowledge but also for engaging in at least some enquiries; in some cases, enquiry cannot proceed on the basis of mere familiarity. Secondly, '[r]ecalling the dialectical requirement, Socrates stipulates that one cannot explain anything by appeal to what is "not yet agreed and still under investigation", i.e. there must be no unresolved questions concerning the items that are to figure in the definition. Thus, if

---

is more continuous with modern epistemology than is sometimes supposed. See *PM* 184–5.

[12] On σχῆμα, see n. 10 above. In *RE*, by contrast, Scott takes σχῆμα to be shape; but he does not discuss the relevant issues there, since his concerns lie elsewhere.

[13] Interestingly, though *PM* distinguishes DR from foreknowledge as such (if not from austere DR), *RE* seems to identify them: on 215, for example, Scott says that 75 D (which is the first statement of DR) states foreknowledge. I am not sure whether *PM* identifies austere DR with foreknowledge, or merely thinks there is an intimate connection between the two; if the latter, I am not sure exactly how to spell out the connection.

Enquiry and Discovery 337

one is to define X by reference to a, b, and c, one must already have acquired knowledge of a, b, and c' (85 n. 15). So in order to know F (i.e. what F is), one must already know the terms mentioned in its definition.[14]

I agree with Scott that 75 D requires no more than familiarity.[15] I also agree with him that 79 D says that in order to know what F is, one must know the terms mentioned in its definition. But I am not convinced that 79 D says that one cannot *enquire* what virtue is like unless one already has philosophical understanding of what it is. Nor am I sure that it says that in order to know what F is, one must *antecedently* know the terms mentioned in its definition.

Let us look at the passage and its context. At 79 C 8–9 Socrates says: 'Do you think that someone knows what a part of virtue is when he does not know what virtue itself is?' As Scott agrees, this is an instance of the Priority of Definition (PD), which says that one cannot know either F's non-essential properties or whether something is an F unless one knows what F is;[16] hence, one cannot know that something is a part of virtue without knowing what virtue is.[17] Scott also agrees that PD involves just epistemological, not chronological, priority (56):[18] PD says that one needs to know what F is in order to know both F's non-essential properties and whether something is an F; it does not say that one needs to know what F is *before* knowing F's non-essential properties or whether something is an F. Perhaps there is joint illumination.

Socrates then says: 'And if you remember, when I answered you just now about surface, we rejected the sort of answer that attempts to proceed through what is still under investigation and not yet agreed' (79 D 1–4). Meno says he remembers, and Socrates then

---

[14] More precisely, one must know the items they refer to; but I shall for convenience speak of 'terms'. Scott uses 'X'; I use 'F', since it makes it clearer that a predicate (or predicable) is at issue.

[15] However, I am not sure that it requires *antecedent* familiarity: see n. 7.

[16] Scott thinks 71 B says that one must know what F is in order to know its non-essential properties; he calls this PDA, for the priority of definition over attributes. He does not think the *Meno* explicitly mentions the priority of definition over instances (PDI). But he thinks this latter sort of priority is assumed (20; 86–7). Although these claims are controversial, I think Scott is right to accept them. Rather than distinguishing PDA from PDI, I shall simply speak of the Priority of Definition (PD), meaning that to include both PDA and PDI.

[17] I take it that this sort of case is covered by PD.

[18] Cf. 132, where, however, Scott speaks of logical priority rather than of epistemological priority. That page, by the way, contains one of the very few typos I noticed: 'temporarily' should be 'temporally'.

338 *Gail Fine*

says: 'So while you are still investigating what virtue as a whole is, don't imagine that you will explain it to anyone by answering in terms of its parts or by saying anything else in the same way' (79 D 6–E 1). I agree with Scott that here, genuine knowledge is being required (not just familiarity, as at 75 D). But I do not think Socrates says or implies that one has to know what virtue is before one can enquire how it is acquired. He says only that if one does not know what virtue is, one will not be able to make its nature clear (δηλώσειν) to anyone by mentioning its parts. The idea seems to be that since no one knows what virtue is, no one knows what its parts are. Hence attempting to explain what virtue is by reference to its parts will not succeed in explaining what virtue is: that is, it will not provide an account that confers knowledge. If this is right, then 79 D allows one to enquire how virtue is acquired even if one does not already know what it is. It just says that if one does not know what virtue is, neither can one know what its parts are.

I am not sure whether 79 D also says, more strongly, that one has to know the terms mentioned in its definition *before* acquiring knowledge of what it is. If it does not, perhaps joint illumination is possible. But even if some sort of foreknowledge is required, it is not needed for enquiring how virtue is acquired, but only for knowing what virtue is.

What are the implications of saying that in order to discover what virtue is, one must already know the terms mentioned in its definition? One might think it implies that, in order to discover what virtue is, one must already know what it is. If that were so, one could not *discover* what virtue is; for one can discover only what one does not already know. As we shall see later, Scott seems to think this is indeed what 79 D commits Socrates to. However, this is not clearly the case. Suppose we grant that 79 D says that in order to discover what F is, we already need to know the terms mentioned in its definition. So long as the terms mentioned in the definition can be defined independently of F, it does not follow that we already need to know what F is.[19]

---

[19] Cf. T. Irwin, *Plato's Ethics* (Oxford, 1995), 153. Of course, one might argue that Socrates does not think that the terms mentioned in the definition can be defined independently of what is being defined; but that would take further argument. Irwin argues that at least the early dialogues assume independence.

Enquiry and Discovery 339

4. The second occasion of Socrates on trial that Scott discusses concerns Socrates' view 'that the elenchus is beneficial and incites the interlocutor to further enquiry' (72–3). Scott argues that the historical Socrates accepts this view; that Meno, in comparing Socrates to a stingray, challenges it; and that Socrates duly defends it in his discussion with the slave.[20] For during the course of this discussion, the slave enquires; and though he does not acquire knowledge, Socrates says that he has benefited from the discussion and is ready to enquire further. I can be brief about this trial: Scott is entirely successful in his defence of Socrates.

5. The third trial challenges the view that, as Scott rightly thinks the early dialogues assume, we have a duty to enquire. It does so by challenging the view that discovery through enquiry is possible. For it seems that if we cannot acquire knowledge through enquiry, we do not have a duty to enquire.

However, even if we cannot acquire knowledge through enquiry, we can come closer to that goal; and the fact that we can do so at least leaves open the possibility that we have a duty to enquire. Even if I cannot become good, I might have a duty to become as good as I can—to approximate to goodness in so far as is possible. Similarly, even if I cannot acquire knowledge, I might have a duty to come as close to doing so as possible by, for example, trying to acquire more justified and true beliefs, even if the total system of my beliefs falls short of constituting knowledge.[21]

I think this is one of the morals of Socrates' cross-examination of Meno's slave. For though the slave does not acquire knowledge, he is none the less benefited, by improving his cognitive condition and by realizing the extent of his ignorance. And that is at least compatible with his having a duty to enquire; he need not, in addition, be able to acquire knowledge.[22]

---

[20] Scott throughout talks of the slave boy, or of the boy. But παῖς can be used for a slave of any age; there is no implication that the slave is young. See Irwin, *Plato's Ethics*, 372 n. 12.

[21] If, as Socrates seems to think, virtue is, or at least requires, knowledge of the good, then, if I have these two duties, they in a way come to the same. At least, trying to become as good as I can be requires trying to acquire the relevant knowledge.

[22] It is true that Socrates says the slave can acquire knowledge, though he does not actually do so in the *Meno*. But he benefits and improves without achieving knowledge, and that seems sufficient for allowing him to have a duty to enquire.

340   *Gail Fine*

6. I now turn to some related questions about enquiry and discovery. Early in the dialogue, Socrates and Meno spend some time enquiring what virtue is. But they do not come up with a satisfactory definition; they do not discover what they were looking for. Frustrated by their inability to do so, Meno turns to the offensive:

(M1) And how will you enquire, Socrates, into something when you don't know at all what it is? Which of the things that you don't know will you propose as the object of your inquiry? (M2) Or even if you really stumble upon it, how will you know that this is the thing you didn't know before? (80 D 5–8)

Socrates reformulates Meno's three questions as follows:

I know what you want to say, Meno. Do you realize what an eristic argument you're bringing up—that it's impossible for someone to inquire into what he knows or doesn't know: he wouldn't inquire into what he knows, since he already knows it and there's no need for such a person to inquire; nor into what he doesn't know, because he doesn't even know what he's going to inquire into. (80 E 1–5)

Scott divides Meno's three questions into two, M1 and M2; and he collectively calls them 'Meno's challenge' (76). He calls Socrates' reformulation of Meno's questions 'the eristic dilemma', and he formulates it as follows (78):

S1. If you know the object already you cannot genuinely inquire into it.
S2. If you do not know it you cannot inquire, because you do not even know what you are inquiring into.
  [Implicit premise: S3. Either you know something or you do not.]
S4. Therefore you cannot inquire into any object.

Let us look first at M1 and M2. M1 asks how one can *begin* an enquiry if one does not know what one is looking for. Meno assumes that if one does not know what one is enquiring into, one cannot provide a specification of it. He also assumes that one can enquire into something only if one has a specification of it. Meno's first assumption rests on the view that if one lacks knowledge, one is, as Scott puts it, 'in a cognitive blank' about it (77). Scott calls this *the problem of inquiry*.[23]

M2, by contrast, focuses on *completing* an enquiry (77). Scott

---

[23] I agree with Scott's interpretation of M1. However, he seems to think that it is suggested by 'at all' (τὸ παράπαν) (76). But even if one does not know at all what F is, it does not follow that one is in a cognitive blank about F: having a mere true

Enquiry and Discovery 341

argues that it admits of two quite different readings. On one reading, it is continuous with M1:

if you are in cognitive blank about some object, you cannot make a discovery about it by means of inquiry. To make this point, Meno asks us to envisage a situation where you are attempting to assert that one thing (that you have just stumbled upon, x) is another thing (that you started out with, y). But this is impossible: you may be able to grasp x, but since you never had any specification of y, how can you make any sense of the statement 'x is y'? (77)

I shall call this *shallow-M2*. Like M1, it assumes we lack a specification of what we are enquiring into, and hence cannot enquire into it. None the less, it acknowledges that we might happen upon what we were in some sense looking for—we just would not have done so by enquiring into it. Still, even if we were to happen upon what we were in some sense looking for, we would not know it was what we were in some sense looking for, since we lacked a specification of it.

If M2 is so read, then, Scott reasonably thinks, it stems from the same worry as M1, and can be dealt with in the same way: by distinguishing between grasping a subject sufficiently to have a specification of it, on the one hand, and attaining full knowledge of it, on the other (83). A related response would be to distinguish true belief from knowledge: true belief falls short of knowledge; but if we have it, we are not in a cognitive blank.[24] Moreover, if we have relevant true beliefs, we can provide specifications of what we are enquiring into; knowledge is not needed.

Scott thinks that, though Meno intends shallow-M2, M2 can also be read as raising a different and deeper issue, which he calls *the problem of discovery* (83–4). I discuss it later. For now it will do to note that, according to Scott, the problem of discovery, unlike M1

belief about something does not involve knowing it at all (since, as Plato is at pains to emphasize in the *Meno*, true belief falls short of knowledge); but neither does it mean one is in a cognitive blank. Socrates omits 'at all' in the eristic dilemma, yet Scott rightly thinks it incorporates M1. Further, as Scott notes (77), when Socrates says at 71 A–B that he does not know anything at all about virtue (τὸ παράπαν occurs at 71 A 6 and at 71 B 3 and 5), he does not mean he is in a cognitive blank about it.

[24] I say 'related', because distinguishing knowledge from true belief is different from distinguishing *full* knowledge from a partial grasp. This is so in two ways. First, not all knowledge is full knowledge; there can be partial knowledge. Secondly, one could distinguish partial from full knowledge rather than distinguishing true belief from either knowledge or full knowledge. I shall focus on the distinction between true belief and knowledge.

342 *Gail Fine*

and shallow-M2, cannot be solved by distinguishing true belief from knowledge.

7. Let us now turn to the eristic dilemma. It captures M1. It does not, however, explicitly mention M2. However, Scott argues, the eristic dilemma, like M1 and shallow-M2, can also be solved by distinguishing true belief from knowledge. For armed with this distinction, we can say that, contrary to S2, one can enquire even if one does not know what one is enquiring into. True belief is not knowledge, but it is sufficient for enquiry.[25] Hence, though the eristic dilemma does not explicitly mention shallow-M2, an adequate solution to the dilemma satisfactorily answers shallow-M2. Thus, the fact that Socrates does not explicitly repeat M2 in formulating the dilemma might well be unimportant. Perhaps he fails to do so because his main concern is to show that one can enquire even if one lacks knowledge: after all, he has been emphasizing that he and Meno lack knowledge; none the less, they have been enquiring.

According to Scott, however, Socrates does not reply to the eristic dilemma at all or, therefore, to M1 or shallow-M2 (82, 83, 88). Rather, he replies only to a different problem, that of discovery. I find this very odd. Consider two views:

(i) Meno raises two questions. Socrates reformulates what Meno says in terms of the eristic dilemma, which explicitly captures the first question. Although the eristic dilemma does not explicitly mention the second question, Socrates replies to the dilemma in a way that answers both questions, in just the sense in which Meno intends them, by distinguishing knowledge from true belief—a distinction that is prominent in the dialogue not only at 97 A ff. but also in the discussion with Meno's slave, which is an important part of his reply. This distinction ably disarms the dilemma, and so also serves as an adequate response to M1 and shallow-M2.

(ii) Meno raises two questions. Socrates reformulates one of them. But rather than answering either of Meno's questions in the sense in which he intends them, or the eristic dilemma,

---

[25] At least, this is so if we have relevant true beliefs. If we distinguish partial from full knowledge, we can say that, if we have (relevant) partial knowledge, S1 is false: we can enquire even if we know what we are enquiring into, so long as our knowledge is partial; for we might then seek the knowledge we lack.

Enquiry and Discovery 343

Socrates instead replies only to a problem that, though it is suggested by what Meno says, is not what he had in mind. Prominent though the distinction between knowledge and true belief is in the dialogue, and adequate though it is as a solution to the eristic dilemma, Socrates does not intend it to reply to the dilemma. Although he has the perfect reply in hand, he does not use it, or any other reply, for that matter.

Scott favours (ii) over (i). Yet surely (i) is simpler, more satisfying, and more straightforward. Why does Scott none the less prefer (ii)? He seems to have three main reasons for doing so. First, he thinks that the eristic dilemma is so easy to solve that it is not worth dwelling on or taking seriously (83). Secondly, he thinks that Plato's answer to whatever problem concerns him is the theory of recollection. Yet, he thinks, the theory of recollection is neither necessary nor sufficient for solving the eristic dilemma, whereas it provides an elegant solution to the problem of discovery (80–2).[26] Thirdly, he does not think that Plato anywhere actually defends the possibility of enquiry; rather, Plato takes its possibility for granted, and spends his time defending the possibility of discovery instead (82–3 n. 10).

8. Let us consider these three reasons in turn.

First, the eristic dilemma is more worthy of serious consideration than Scott allows. For one thing, it is all too easy to confuse knowledge and true belief. If that does not seem true of us nowadays,[27] it might well have been true in Plato's day, when the distinction had not, until the *Meno*, been systematically and explicitly drawn.[28] It is one of the *Meno*'s enduring contributions to epistemology to have highlighted this distinction, and to display the confusion one can get into if one is not clear about it. We should not be surprised if the *Meno* considers a problem that highlights the importance of that distinction.

Further, though distinguishing knowledge from true belief is an

---

[26] In *RE*, by contrast, Scott thinks the theory of recollection is intended as an answer to the eristic dilemma: 33 n. 8.

[27] Though years of teaching Plato convince me that it is still true nowadays.

[28] Which is not to say that it was never implicitly assumed or relied on before. The early dialogues (except for the *Gorgias*—which, however, Scott controversially dates after the *Meno*) do not explicitly distinguish knowledge from true belief; but they assume and rely on the distinction. The *Meno* makes explicit what in earlier dialogues is largely implicit; in doing so, it explains and vindicates their procedure.

344 *Gail Fine*

important part of disarming the dilemma, it would be disappointing if Plato did no more than distinguish knowledge from true belief. For as Scott says, part of the point of M1 is that one needs a specification of what one is enquiring into: one needs to specify the target one is aiming at.[29] It is important to point out, as I think Plato does, that one can provide an adequate specification on the basis of true belief; knowledge is not needed. But not any old true belief will do. I might have the true belief that zebras are animals; that will not help me fix my target in enquiring into the nature of virtue. It is difficult, not easy, to say what criteria an adequate specification for fixing any given target must satisfy.[30]

Secondly, unlike Scott, I do not think Plato takes the possibility of enquiry for granted. Part of the point of Socrates' discussion with the slave is to show that enquiry is possible. He shows this by giving and commenting on an example of enquiry. This has the effect of showing those who doubt that enquiry is possible that they should not do so.

Thirdly, I agree with Scott that the theory of recollection does not provide a direct reply to the dilemma (81): the discussion with the slave does that, by showing that it is possible to enquire on the basis of true belief; hence knowledge is not necessary. But the slave does not just engage in enquiry: he improves his cognitive condition; he makes progress in enquiry. Socrates has a more ambitious aim, in replying to Meno, than showing that enquiry is logically possible; he also wants to show that we can improve our cognitive condition through enquiry. Merely distinguishing knowledge from true belief is not adequate to explain how we can do so. We will make progress in enquiry only if we not only have but also tend to rely on true rather than false beliefs. But what guarantees that we will do so? The theory of recollection explains that we once had knowledge, of some range of things, in another life. Though we have lost this knowledge, we retain tendencies to favour truths over falsehoods; this enables us to provide adequate specifications of the targets we aim at, and it makes it likely that we will tend to hit them. So while the theory of recollection does not provide a direct reply

[29] Cf. G. Matthews, *Socratic Perplexity* (Oxford, 1999), 58.

[30] Hence Matthews says that the Targeting Objection is hard to answer; by contrast, Scott says that M1 is easy to answer. In a way they are not disagreeing. For Scott focuses on what cognitive condition one needs to be in, in order to engage in enquiry, whereas Matthews focuses on what sorts of propositions are adequate for fixing targets aimed at.

Enquiry and Discovery 345

to the dilemma, it provides an indirect reply. The direct reply—the discussion with the slave—shows *that* enquiry, and progress in enquiry, are possible. The theory of recollection explains *how* progress in enquiry is possible.[31]

9. To say that Plato replies to the eristic dilemma is not to say that he does not also reply to Scott's problem of discovery: perhaps he replies to both. Let us, at any rate, now turn to the latter. Here is Scott's account of it (83–4):

Suppose that you do have an initial specification of the object. This allows you to start the inquiry. When you propose a candidate answer, you test it against the specification to see if the two match each other. (Again, we no longer have a problem about making sense of the statement 'x is y'.) But this means that the assumptions included in the specification play a crucial role in determining the direction and outcome of the inquiry; they constitute its premises. Yet, unless you already know that the specification is correct, how can you know that this proposed answer is the right one, even if it happens to be?

This problem, which I shall call 'the problem of discovery', can also be stated in terms of true belief and knowledge. Someone might launch a definitional inquiry with true beliefs about the object in question; it is also possible that they might find the right answer. Nevertheless, it might be said, all they can claim is that this answer matches their *beliefs* about virtue. But why should this amount to *knowing* that the definition is true of virtue? This new problem applies to the context of the *Meno* in a way the other reading of M2 [=shallow-M2] does not. For Socrates and Meno may well have some true beliefs about virtue from the very outset; they may have gathered others in the course of discussing the first three definitions [of virtue considered earlier in the dialogue]. All of these they can use to decide between future candidate definitions. Even so, it may be claimed, they will never get knowledge of what virtue is: they will always be trapped within a circle of belief.

Scott seems to describe two different problems of discovery. He begins by asking how one can know that one has found the right

---

[31] I discuss this in more detail in 'Inquiry in the *Meno*', in R. Kraut (ed.), *Cambridge Companion to Plato* (Cambridge, 1992), 200–26, repr., with minor modifications, in my *Plato on Knowledge and Forms: Selected Essays* (Oxford, 2003), ch. 2. I return to the theory of recollection below. Scott argues that the theory of recollection is meant to explain only how discovery—acquiring knowledge—is possible. On my view, it has a broader scope: it is also intended to show how progress in enquiry—even if the progress falls short of attaining knowledge, and so falls short of discovery—is possible.

346 *Gail Fine*

answer.[32] But he ends by asking how one can acquire knowledge of what (for example) virtue is. These are very different. The first asks how one can know that one knows the answer; the second asks how one can know the answer.[33]

Scott goes on to say (84):

What is distinctive about the problem is its underlying assumption that discovery or learning is a process of realising that one thing matches something that one already knows. . . . My claim is that Socrates takes the problem of discovery seriously. One reason he does so is that he shares the assumption that knowledge must derive from pre-existent knowledge, the 'foreknowledge principle', as I shall call it.

However, Scott argues, the foreknowledge principle (FP) is not sufficient for the problem of discovery to arise. Suppose I know what virtue is. I can then use that knowledge to discover whether virtue is acquired. The problem of discovery does not arise in this case. Suppose, however, that I want to know what virtue is. What is the relevant foreknowledge here? One cannot appeal to one's knowledge either of examples of virtue or of its non-essential properties. For as we have seen, Plato accepts the Priority of Definition (PD): in order to know F's non-essential properties, and whether something is an F, one needs to know what F is. Hence the only knowledge one can rely on, in enquiring what virtue is, is knowledge of what virtue is. But if one already knows what virtue is, one cannot *discover* what it is. In the case of definitional enquiry, then, FP coupled with PD leads to the problem of discovery.[34]

In addition to saying that FP and PD lead to the problem of discovery, Scott says that '[t]aken literally, the problem [of discovery]

---

[32] Both 'Yet . . . happens to be?' and 'But why should . . . virtue?' ask how one can know that a given answer is right.

[33] These two options come to the same if one can know that p only if one knows that one knows that p; this is the so-called KK thesis. Perhaps Scott assumes it; but he does not explicitly say so.

[34] For roughly this way of describing the problem of discovery, see *PM* 79, 129; cf. *RE* 29. In *PM* Scott speaks both of 'definitional enquiry' (87) and of 'definitional discovery' (87). One might think the conditions on engaging in enquiry differ from the conditions for discovery, i.e. acquiring knowledge; for one can engage in enquiry without succeeding in acquiring knowledge. Sometimes Scott seems to suggest that DR is a condition on (dialectical) enquiry, FP on discovery. However, since FP is so closely associated at least with austere DR, it seems to govern at least some enquiries. Hence it seems that the conjunction of PD and FP generates not just a problem of discovery but also a problem of enquiry. *RE* 215 takes satisfying FP to be a condition on enquiry.

Enquiry and Discovery 347

requires that the initial specification consist in knowledge of the very thing being sought' (85). These are not equivalent formulations. FP tells us that in order to discover what virtue is, one must already have some knowledge. PD tells us that if we do not already know what virtue is, the foreknowledge cannot be knowledge of virtue's non-essential properties or of its instances. It does not follow that the only foreknowledge available is knowledge of what virtue is. Suppose that F is defined as a, b, and c, where a, b, and c are neither instances nor non-essential properties of F. Suppose too that a, b, and c can be defined independently of F. I can then know a, b, and c without knowing what F is. I can then satisfy FP without violating PD; and the problem of discovery does not arise.[35]

I agree with Scott that Plato accepts PD. And I granted earlier that 79 D may involve some sort of foreknowledge, though I am not sure that it does. But even if it does, Scott's problem of discovery does not arise unless Plato is also committed to the further claim that one cannot discover what F is unless one already knows what F is. I am not convinced that he is committed to this further claim. Hence I am not convinced that he says anything, at the beginning of the *Meno*, that makes him vulnerable to Scott's problem of discovery.

Of course, even if Plato is not vulnerable to the problem of discovery that Scott describes, he might none the less consider and reply to it. After all, he considers and replies to the eristic dilemma but, as Scott rightly thinks, he is not vulnerable to it. However, though I think Plato considers *a* problem of discovery, I do not think it is the one Scott describes. The problem of discovery that Plato discusses asks, not how we can enquire if we already know what we are looking for, but how we can enquire if *do not* already know what we are looking for.[36]

10. In addition to thinking that Plato is vulnerable to the problem of discovery partly because he accepts FP, Scott also thinks that Plato's solution retains a (revised version) of FP.[37] The version that gives

---

[35] See sect. 3 above.

[36] Both Meno and Socrates wonder how we can acquire knowledge if we do not already have it. But their worries are based on different considerations. Meno wonders how we can achieve knowledge if our minds are, to begin with, complete blanks. Socrates wonders how we can achieve knowledge if we begin with mere beliefs.

[37] Given that Scott thinks that Plato accepts FP not only before considering the

348   *Gail Fine*

rise to the problem requires conscious explicit current knowledge of what one is searching for. In replying to the problem, Plato abandons that view. At the conscious level, we currently have just belief (87). 'But latently[38] there already exists within us knowledge that was once explicit. It is in virtue of this knowledge, as it gradually comes to the surface, that we are able ultimately to know that the answer we have hit upon is the right one' (87). The version of foreknowledge that solves the problem of discovery thus involves both conscious, explicit prenatal knowledge and also innate (hence also current) latent or unconscious (129) knowledge.[39] Or again: 'there must have been *knowledge* in the soul all along, otherwise he will not have answered the problem of discovery, based as it is on the foreknowledge principle. Throughout 85c–d, we find him assuming the foreknowledge principle to prove that the soul has always been in a state of knowledge' (117).[40] So in Scott's view, Plato responds to the problem not just by continuing to favour a version of *fore*knowledge but also by positing *current* knowledge:

problem of discovery but also as part of his solution to it, we might expect him to say that Plato abandons PD. After all, if FP coupled with PD leads to the problem, and Plato retains FP, we would expect him to abandon PD. However, Scott's view is rather that Plato initially accepts one version of FP, sees (or thinks) that, coupled with PD, it leads to the problem of discovery, and so revises FP.

[38] Scott seems to use 'latent knowledge' in two different ways in *PM*. Sometimes it refers to unconscious (129) knowledge, whether or not it is innate. So, for example, Scott says that Plato posits latent knowledge in steps (1)–(3) of his argument for immortality (which I discuss below); but he does not think these early steps of the argument assume the existence of innate knowledge. But on e.g. 108 he seems to use 'latent knowledge' for innate knowledge. These two uses of 'latent knowledge' differ in turn from how Scott uses the phrase in 'Innatism and the Stoa' ['Innatism'], *Proceedings of the Cambridge Philological Society*, 214 (1988), 123–53, and in *RE*. In these two works he uses it for the Leibnizian view according to which we have innate knowledge which, however, we have never been aware of. Since he thinks Plato takes us to have been aware of our innate knowledge prenatally, he says that Plato does *not* favour a theory of latent or implicit innate knowledge. In *PM*, by contrast, he says that Plato posits latent knowledge. This is a change in Scott's terminology, not in his view. In all these works he thinks Plato posits the existence of innate knowledge that we are not aware of in this life, but were aware of prenatally.

[39] It is worth noting that Plato does not himself speak of 'latent' or 'explicit' knowledge. He just asks whether the slave does, or does not, know. It is Scott who thinks some occurrences of 'know' refer to explicit knowledge, whereas others refer to latent knowledge. Cf. G. Vlastos, 'Anamnesis in the *Meno*', *Dialogue*, 4 (1965), 143–67 at n. 14; R. Dancy, *Plato's Introduction of Forms* (Cambridge, 2004), 226.

[40] The remark just quoted is odd, for it is one thing to say that the problem of discovery assumes foreknowledge, and quite another to say that Socrates asserts it in his solution. Even if the problem assumes it, Socrates might reply by rejecting it.

Enquiry and Discovery 349

'knowledge must pre-exist *and be present in him now*' (85, emphasis added).

I agree that in order to solve the problems that concern him, Plato posits prenatal knowledge.[41] I am less sure that he posits latent innate knowledge. I discuss this below. First, though, let us look in more detail at why Scott thinks Plato responds to the problem of discovery in the way in which he takes him to. Part of his reason is based on his careful and detailed reading of the text, which I consider below. But he also has other reasons for thinking that Plato's solution to the problem of discovery assumes some version of foreknowledge (construed broadly so as to include current knowledge as well).

One of his reasons is what we may call *the circle of beliefs objection*: if we began just with beliefs, we could never emerge from the circle of beliefs to the light of knowledge. Hence Scott says that, though the eristic dilemma can be solved by distinguishing knowledge from true belief, the problem of discovery cannot.[42]

However, foreknowledge is not needed in order to solve the problem of discovery. Suppose that (as Scott agrees Plato believes) knowledge is true belief tied down by explanatory reasoning. In that case, I know that p if and only if p is true, I believe that p, and I can explain why p is true. As Scott agrees (e.g. 179), Plato thinks that explaining why a proposition is true involves relating it to a suitable body of true beliefs, each of which, in turn, is properly explained. So I come to know what virtue is if and only if I come to believe a true account of what it is, and can integrate that account into a suitably large body of true beliefs about virtue, each of which is itself properly explained. We emerge from a circle of mere beliefs when we acquire a large enough circle of true, mutually supporting, and explanatory beliefs. We can do this by practising the elenchus in the way Meno's slave does. As Socrates says, if the slave practises the elenchus further, 'in the end, his knowledge will be as accurate as anyone's' (85 c 11–d 1). The slave begins with a mixture of true and false beliefs; gradually, over time, by enquiring systematically, he rids himself of his false beliefs and acquires more true beliefs. Eventually his belief system will constitute knowledge. Of course,

---

[41] I have already noted that Scott and I disagree about what problems concern Plato.

[42] See the passage cited in the last section, from *PM* 83–4. Though he does not explicitly say so, Scott seems sympathetic to the view that the problem of discovery can be solved only by positing some sort of foreknowledge.

350   *Gail Fine*

there is no mechanical way of guaranteeing that one will acquire knowledge. But given our tendency to favour truths over falsehoods, it is reasonable to think we are likely to acquire knowledge if we enquire in a systematic and open enough way.

11. Scott thinks Plato also has another reason for positing foreknowledge. In the demonstration with the slave Socrates shows how the slave, using his own resources, can acquire knowledge. Scott reasonably asks: '[H]ow does Socrates move from our ability to follow a proof [an ability the slave has been shown to have] to the thesis of latent knowledge?' (108). He replies (ibid.):

[The slave] will act as the judge, listening to the proposals made in the questions so as to make up his own mind whether to accept them. Now, in order for the boy to have this kind of independence, he must already have his own criteria by which to accept or reject any suggestion put to him. It is precisely these internal criteria that are lacking in someone who takes someone's word on trust—hence their cognitive dependence on the other party. In other words, the presence of internal criteria underlies the difference between merely being informed about propositions in a proof and perceiving their logical interrelations. According to Socrates, the existence of these criteria amounts to the possession of latent knowledge.

But surely one does not need to *know* anything in order to decide on one's own what suggestions to accept or reject: one can rely on one's *beliefs*. This seems especially so when we remember that (as Scott rightly says) for Plato all knowledge involves philosophical understanding. It is not clear why we need philosophical understanding in order to avoid relying on others.[43] Nor is it clear why the criteria need to be *innate*: why can one not acquire them over time?

Scott seems to think Plato posits innate *knowledge*, rather than innate *true belief*, because the latter is unstable, 'which makes it more likely that, having recollected a sequence of true beliefs, we shall sooner or later renounce some of them' 130); but, according to Plato, 'even though we may take many wrong turns, there is still something all along in our minds that can act to guarantee success' (130).[44] I am not sure, however, that Plato thinks any of

[43] If, on the other hand, latent knowledge does not involve philosophical understanding, we need to ask whether positing it is compatible with the unitarian assumption.

[44] Cf. 133: 'The only cognitive process that would have the stability to guide our inquiry reliably is knowledge.' However, here Scott is explaining why Plato's

Enquiry and Discovery

us is *guaranteed* to achieve knowledge; indeed, he thinks most of us never do so. He thinks each of us *can* achieve knowledge; but, in my view, he thinks this is because each of us had prenatal knowledge, not because we have innate knowledge.[45]

Although Scott does not challenge the assimilation of having one's own criteria and having latent innate knowledge (an assimilation I return to below), he agrees that positing latent innate knowledge is not the only alternative to relying on testimony: one could posit dispositional innatism instead. (Hence, though Scott seems sympathetic to the circle-of-beliefs objection considered in the last section, he is not as sympathetic to the view that we need to posit latent innate knowledge to avoid relying on testimony.) According to dispositional innatism, 'we are born with certain cognitive predispositions'; we are, for example, 'innately disposed (under appropriate conditions) to follow certain rules of inference, and assent to specific axioms' (108). On this view, according to Scott, what is innate is not knowledge, but just certain dispositions.

Although Scott seems to think that dispositional innatism is in fact a viable alternative to latent innate knowledge, he does not think anyone before the Stoics endorsed it (109 n.). I shall argue below that a more plausible case than Scott allows can be made for the claim that Socrates accepts a version of dispositional innatism. Be that as it may, I wish Scott had said something about why he thinks Plato rejects, or does not consider, dispositional innatism: is it just that the view, for whatever reason, did not occur to him? Or is it that he found the view unsatisfactory?[46]

---

preferred method requires knowledge, not why knowledge is *necessary*. I discuss method in sect. 16, and stability in sect. 17.

[45] I suggested this above; see also 'Inquiry in the *Meno*'. I discuss innate knowledge further below.

[46] In 'Innatism' Scott says that Plato would have little use for dispositionalism, for '[w]hat the dispositionalist has given up . . . is the claim that any *knowledge* is within us: what is innate to us are merely dispositions to know or form beliefs' (132). Here the thought is that since Plato *says* that knowledge is innate in us, he rejects dispositional innatism. But that does not address the question of *why* he says that knowledge is innate in us, rather than favouring dispositional innatism. Yet Scott goes on to say: 'So there are, after all, good reasons for Plato's not taking up . . . dispositional innatism' (132).

In *RE* Scott says that in the *Meno* 'the theory [of recollection] is at a tentative stage . . . and it would be a mistake to look for a determinate argument to show why recollection, as opposed to other varieties of innateness, is preferred in this dialogue' (215). Perhaps *PM* assumes the same view. (I myself would not say that recollection is a kind of innatism. It says that we once knew in a prior life, and that what we call

352   *Gail Fine*

Just as we can ask why Socrates posits latent innate knowledge (if he does: I ask about this below), so we can ask why he posits prenatal knowledge. According to Scott, 'the existence of latent knowledge . . . points to a prior state of awareness' (116). Yet as he is well aware, for the Leibnizian, at any rate, there is no such pointer: in the Leibnizian's view, we have latent innate knowledge, but no prenatal knowledge. Why does Plato think otherwise?

Scott's answer is that one cannot simply assert that we have latent innate knowledge (or, for that matter, that dispositional innatism is true); one needs to give an account of where the innate endowment came from (114). Innatists in the seventeenth century appealed to a benevolent deity. But, Scott thinks, 'Plato in the *Meno* would probably be very wary of this theological approach. On my interpretation he seeks to establish the existence of innate knowledge, not merely true belief. But given his views about the inability of testimony to justify knowledge, he would not be content with a theory that relied ultimately on divine providence' (114–15).

However, to say that god gives us innate knowledge is not to say that god does our knowing for us.[47] Rather, on this view, god gave us the ability to work things out for ourselves. This is so on both dispositional and latent innatism. On the former, god just gave us dispositions, and it is up to us to actualize them in such a way as to achieve knowledge. On the latter, god gave us latent knowledge, but it is up to us to bring it to consciousness; and so at least in this sense, we still do the knowing for ourselves. Moreover, we might be unaware of the fact that god gave us our innate knowledge; to say he gave it to us is not to say that we treat it *as* testimony. There is, as it were, an external guarantee of its reliability; but it is up to us whether to rely on it, and in that sense, we would not be relying on testimony.

There is also an *ad hominem* worry. According to Scott, Plato thinks we can know something only if we work it out for ourselves; that is why he does not think testimony gives us knowledge (101–5, 108, 115, 142–4; cf. 152–3).[48] However, Scott also says that, according to Plato, we did not acquire our prenatal knowledge but

learning is in fact recollecting the knowledge we once had. That, by itself, does not imply that we know now, and so it does not imply any sort of innatism.)

[47] Cf. *RE*: 'For Plato, however, it is as if the pre-existent knower cannot be anyone but the knower himself. There can be no knowledge by proxy; not even God can do our knowing for us' (216).   [48] Cf. 'Innatism', 132.

Enquiry and Discovery 353

simply had it all along (112–17). If we simply had it all along, we did not initially work it out for ourselves. But then it does not count as knowledge, as Scott thinks Plato conceives of knowledge. To be sure, if we had it all along, we did not acquire it by relying on testimony. But not relying on testimony and working something out for oneself are not exhaustive options.

12. Let us now ask whether Plato posits latent or unconscious innate knowledge.[49] Whether we should say that he posits innate knowledge of any sort depends in part on how we understand the notion. As we have seen, Scott says that 'the existence of these [internal] criteria amounts to the possession of latent knowledge' (108), where having these criteria involves more than having a disposition to come to know them.

Let us unpack this a bit further. First it will be useful to distinguish the cognitive condition of knowing from the content of knowledge. When we ask whether Socrates took himself to have knowledge, we are asking whether he took himself to be in the cognitive condition of knowing: whether he took himself to have true beliefs he could adequately explain. When we speak of the sum total of human knowledge, we are speaking of the content of knowledge: of what is known, rather than of the cognitive condition of the knowing person. Since the cognitive condition of knowing has content, anyone who is in that cognitive condition also has knowledge in the content sense. But there is a sense in which the converse is not true: one might be in a mental state that has content that is suitable for serving as the content of knowledge, even though it does not actually so serve. We might put this somewhat paradoxically by saying that knowledge can be in one even if one is not in the cognitive condition of knowing.[50]

Scott seems to think Plato posits innate knowledge in the cog-

---

[49] In 'Inquiry in the *Meno*' I briefly reject the view that the *Meno* posits innate knowledge. In *RE* Scott says that '[d]espite my agreement with almost everything else she has to say about recollection, I would take issue with her' on this point (16 n. 4). He proceeds to defend the view that the *Meno* posits innate knowledge; but his defence, like my denial, is very brief. I reply equally briefly in the introduction to *Plato on Knowledge and Forms*. In *PM* Scott defends his view in considerably more detail, and argues at some length against (what he takes to be) my alternative. I welcome the opportunity to pursue our debate further.

[50] Cf. Dancy, *Plato's Introduction of Forms*, 231–2. Though we differ in some ways, I am indebted to Dancy's discussion, which in some ways is very close to mine.

354 *Gail Fine*

nitive-condition sense.[51] However, positing innate internal criteria falls short of positing innate knowledge in the cognitive-condition sense. For internal criteria are propositions. If we have them, we have innate knowledge in the content sense: there are items in our minds that are suitable for serving as the content of knowledge.[52] It does not follow that we stand in the cognitive condition of knowledge with respect to them.

As we have seen, Scott distinguishes the sort of innatism he takes Plato to favour from dispositional innatism, saying that on the latter, all that is innate are dispositions, not knowledge. However, while it is true that some dispositionalists say that what is innate is not knowledge but just a disposition to know, other dispositionalists say that to have innate knowledge consists in having an innate disposition. On this view, innate dispositionalism and innate knowledge are not rival forms of innatism. Rather, the latter consists in the former.[53] Scott thinks Plato says we all have innate knowledge; he infers that Plato does not favour dispositional innatism. That is true as Scott defines dispositional innatism; but it is not true on all accounts of dispositional innatism. So even if,

[51] He says, for example, that 'we have latent knowledge of these principles' (i.e. of the internal criteria) (108)—that is, we stand in the cognitive condition of knowing them. He also contrasts latent with explicit knowledge (e.g. 109 ff.). The content is the same; what is different is our attitude towards it. Or again, he says that the slave 'has always been in a perpetual state of "having learnt"' (110); this too concerns cognitive condition. The slave 'already has knowledge of all disciplines' (111): that is, he is in the cognitive condition of knowing the propositions that constitute those disciplines. Many other passages might also be cited. Admittedly, there are also passages that seem to conceive of knowledge in the content sense. But perhaps this is because, if we know in the cognitive-condition sense, we also know in the content sense; it is just the converse inference that fails.

[52] Cf. *RE* 16. Alternatively, criteria could be conceived as abilities; if they are so conceived, having innate criteria amounts to having innate abilities. This is, or comes close to being, a version of innate dispositionalism.

[53] J. Barnes provides a nice description of the distinction between these two sorts of dispositionalism: 'Innate dispositions may appear in either of two guises. First, it may be supposed that among the dispositions natural to mankind are certain dispositions to know things. On this view P is innate in x's mind if x has an innate disposition to know that P. Secondly, it may be supposed that among the dispositions natural to mankind are certain dispositions that either constitute, or at least logically suffice for, the possession of some piece of knowledge. On this view P is innate in x's mind if x has an innate disposition to phi, and being disposed to phi is, or entails, knowing that P' ('Mr Locke's Darling Notion', *Philosophical Quarterly*, 22 (1972), 193–214 at 208). Scott understands dispositional innatism in the first way; I am now introducing the second way of understanding it. Barnes argues that classical innatists understand dispositional innatism in the first way, whereas Chomsky understands it in the second way.

Enquiry and Discovery 355

as Scott thinks, Plato says we have innate knowledge, we should not infer straightaway that he is not some sort of dispositional innatist.

I have identified three varieties of innate knowledge: Scott's view, according to which it involves being in the cognitive condition of having actual, though latent or unconscious, knowledge; a view according to which the content of knowledge is in us, though it is not there *as* knowledge; and the view that having innate knowledge consists in having an innate disposition. For convenience, I shall from now on call these latent innatism, content innatism, and dispositional innatism (hence I am using the latter phrase differently from Scott).

13. We can now finally turn to the relevant stretch of text, to see whether it posits any version of innate knowledge.

Socrates has been cross-examining Meno's slave, who, though he has improved his cognitive condition, has not yet achieved knowledge. He has, however, acquired some new explicit true beliefs. So, as Socrates says, 'the one who does not know has within himself true beliefs about the things he does not know' (85 c 6–7). He adds that, though the slave does not yet know, 'if he were repeatedly asked these same questions in different ways, you know that in the end his knowledge about these things would be as accurate as anybody's' (85 c 9– d 1): though the slave does not have knowledge yet, he can acquire it. Socrates proceeds to ask about this future knowledge (I insert numbers for ease of reference):[54]

(1) Won't he know without having been taught by anyone, but by being questioned, ἀναλαβών the knowledge himself from himself [αὐτὸς ἐξ αὐτοῦ]? (85 d 3–4)

(2) Isn't it the case that to ἀναλαμβάνειν knowledge oneself in oneself [αὐτὸν ἐν αὑτῷ] is to recollect? (85 d 6–7)

(3) Isn't it the case that he either acquired [ἔλαβεν] the knowledge, which he now has, at some time, or else always had [εἶχεν] it? (85 d 9–10)

(4) If, then, he always had it, he was always a knower.

(5) But if he acquired it at some time, it wasn't in this life.

(6) Or has someone taught him geometry? For he will do just the same with every part of geometry, and with all the other branches of know-

---

[54] Here I use my own translation. Below, I note some differences between it and Scott's.

356 *Gail Fine*

ledge [μαθήματα]. So is there anyone who has taught him everything? For I suppose you ought to know, since he was born and brought up in your household.

I certainly know that no one ever taught him.

(7) But does he have these beliefs, or not?

It is apparent that he must have them, Socrates.

(8) But if he didn't acquire them in this life, isn't it then clear that he had [εἶχε] them and had learnt them [ἐμεμάθηκε] at some other time?

So it appears.

Then is not this the time when he was not a human being?

(9) If, then, these true beliefs are in him both at the time when he was, and at the time when he was not, a human being, beliefs that, when stirred by questioning, will become knowledge, will not his soul for all time be in the condition of having learnt [ἆρ᾽ οὖν τὸν ἀεὶ χρόνον μεμαθηκυῖα ἔσται ἡ ψυχὴ αὐτοῦ]?

(10) For it's clear that for the whole of time, he either is or is not a human being.

So it appears.

(11) Then if the truth about beings is always in the soul, won't the soul be immortal,

(12) so that you must confidently undertake to enquire into, and recollect, what you do not in fact know now—that is, what you don't remember?

It seems to me that you're right, Socrates, but I don't know how.

(13) And I think so too, Meno. As far as the other points [τὰ ἄλλα] are concerned, I would not altogether take a stand on behalf of the argument. But that we will be better and more manly and less idle if we think one should enquire into what one doesn't know than if we think it is not possible to discover what we don't know and that we don't need to enquire into it—that is something I would certainly fight for to the end, if I could, both in word and deed.

In Scott's view, 'there is no getting away from the fact that 85d talks of latent knowledge' (110). Before assessing this claim, we should note that Scott translates (1), not as I have done, but as follows: 'So that without anyone having taught him, but only by being asked questions, he will recover for himself the knowledge within him' (106). And he translates (2), not as I have done, but as follows: 'recovering *knowledge that is in him* is recollection' (110, emphasis original). On Scott's translation, but not on mine, Socrates appears to say flat out that knowledge is in the slave. Hence it is not surprising that Scott interprets (1) and (2) as follows (110):

There can be no doubt as to what Socrates is saying here: first, that when

Enquiry and Discovery 357

the boy acquires explicit knowledge he will be recollecting; second, that recollection consists in the recovery of knowledge that is already in him. So at this future point, at least, there exists latent knowledge in the boy. Fine's suggestion that knowledge arises merely from the operation of tendencies to favour true over false beliefs cannot be right. Explicit knowledge emerges from knowledge already latent.

Although this is a natural interpretation of (1) and (2) as Scott translates them, his translation is difficult to get out of the Greek. In (1), Socrates does not explicitly speak of 'the knowledge within him'. Rather, he says that 'to ἀναλαμβάνειν knowledge oneself in oneself [αὐτὸν ἐν αὑτῷ] is recollection'. This might mean, not that knowledge is in the slave, but that the slave has the ability to work things out for himself, with no implication that the slave has any sort of knowledge: ἀναλαμβάνειν can mean, and is sometimes used by Plato to mean, 'to take up', in a sense that is compatible with learning for the first time.[55]

Moreover, if (1) is so understood, it follows quite nicely from the discussion with the slave so far. Socrates has been emphasizing that the slave has been working things out for himself; he has also emphasized that the slave does not have knowledge. He now simply adds that even when he eventually acquires knowledge, he will have done so by himself, using his own resources: his later, like his earlier, progress is *his* achievement.

To be sure, ἀναλαμβάνειν can also mean 'to recover', and that is how Scott translates it. But even if it is so understood here, it does not follow that the slave has knowledge. As Scott says elsewhere, 'The sense of "recovery" (ἀναλαμβάνειν) here is that of getting *back* (ἀνα-) something that had been there previously' (*RE* 216 n. 3). To say that knowledge *had been there previously* is not to say it is there *now*.[56] The knowledge could have been entirely forgotten, in such a way that one no longer knows at all.[57]

[55] LSJ, sv. ἀναλαμβάνω. For this point, see Irwin, *Plato's Ethics*, 132–6 and 372 n. 15.

[56] Indeed, in *RE* Scott emphasizes that what the slave is getting back is conscious awareness, and that *is not* in him now, even on Scott's view. That is compatible with the slave now having latent innate knowledge. But it does not say or imply that he has it.

[57] Forgetting what one once knew is sometimes compatible with still knowing it in some way; but it is also possible to forget what one once knew in such a way that one no longer knows it at all. Those suffering from severe Alzheimer's, for example, seem to me to have entirely lost the knowledge they once had; they do not have latent or unconscious knowledge.

358 *Gail Fine*

If (2) were to be translated as Scott translates it, the Greek should be (for example) τὴν ἐν αὐτῷ ἐπιστήμην. But it is not. In (2), as in (1), Plato speaks of the slave's ἀναλαμβάνειν knowledge; and this might just mean that he is working things out for himself.[58] To be sure, there is a new and startling move in (2): namely, that the fact that he can work things out for himself can only be explained (or is best explained) on the assumption that the slave is recollecting— in which case he had knowledge at some point in the past, since recollection involves the recovery of past knowledge. Socrates is now asking *how* the slave is able to work things out for himself. It cannot, in his view, be a brute fact. His suggestion is that the slave is able to work things out for himself in this life because he once knew—as it turns out, in a prior life. But, again, to say that the slave *once* knew does not imply that he *now* knows, even latently.

Perhaps (1) and (2)—even translated as I translate them—can be understood as Scott understands them. But it is less clear than his translation suggests that they should be so understood.

14. Let us now turn to (3). Here Socrates mentions 'the knowledge, which he [the slave] now has'. Scott says: 'On my view, having asserted that there is latent knowledge waiting to be aroused in the boy in the future [=(1) and (2)], Socrates further assumes that it is latent in him now as well' (111). Unlike Scott, I do not think 'now' is genuinely present tense. Rather, Plato is still thinking of the future time when the slave will acquire the knowledge he still lacks.

Scott gives three reasons for thinking that once we consider the whole sentence of which 'the knowledge, which he now has' is a part, we can see that the phrase should be taken to refer to current latent knowledge, not (as I think) to future explicit knowledge (111–12).[59]

First, Socrates asks whether the slave always had this knowledge or acquired it at some point. Scott thinks that if 'now' indicates future explicit knowledge, these two options 'come out of nowhere. By contrast, if Socrates has already assumed that the boy has latent knowledge now as well as in the future, it makes sense to ask just how long this knowledge has been in his soul' (111).

---

[58] (1) has ἐξ αὐτοῦ, whereas (2) has ἐν αὐτῷ, but I think both can easily mean just that the slave is working things out by or for himself, using his own resources.

[59] This is Scott's way of putting the contrast. As we have seen, he imports the terms 'latent' and 'explicit' into the text. What Socrates says, however, is simply that the slave will know: not that he will or does know explicitly.

Enquiry and Discovery 359

Secondly, Scott thinks that on my interpretation, one of the options Plato is considering is that the slave always has explicit knowledge; yet it has been emphasized that he does not. Why, then, mention this option at all? By contrast, if Plato first says that the slave will have latent knowledge, then that he has it now, it is natural to ask whether the slave has always had it.

Thirdly, Socrates mentions just two options (which Scott takes to be that the slave either always, i.e. for all time, has his latent knowledge or else acquired it at some point). But on my interpretation, he does not favour either of these options. Rather, he favours a third view: that the slave always has innate dispositions. But this option is not even mentioned.

Let me reply to these three arguments in turn. My replies all turn on the suggestion that the two options Scott describes are not the ones Socrates has in mind. Socrates has just said that the slave is recollecting. If so, he must have had knowledge at some time in the past, though it has been forgotten, so that he no longer knows.[60] Socrates is now asking just about the knowledge the slave once had: did he always have it (in the past, before he forgot it), or did he acquire it (at some time in the past, before he forgot it)?[61]

Bearing this suggestion in mind, I can now reply to Scott's three objections. To the first, I say that the two options Socrates mentions do not come out of nowhere: he has said the slave is recollecting, which implies that he had knowledge in the past. His question is then: did he acquire that earlier knowledge at some time in the past, or did he have it all along in the past? These are natural, indeed exhaustive, options to consider: either the slave always had his past

---

[60] As we have seen, he certainly does not have explicit knowledge, even on Scott's view. On my view, he does not have latent knowledge either.

[61] In support of this interpretation, notice that in (3) Socrates uses the aorist ($\check{\epsilon}\lambda\alpha\beta\epsilon\nu$) and the imperfect ($\epsilon\check{\iota}\chi\epsilon\nu$). If he were asking whether the slave always (for all time) has knowledge, we might have expected him to use the present tense. The fact that he uses the imperfect suggests he is not asking whether the slave always *has* knowledge, but whether he always *used to have it*—in the past, before he forgot it. At 85 D 9 Plato uses $\check{\epsilon}\chi\epsilon\iota$ (present tense), which, on my view, refers to the future time when the slave will acquire the knowledge he now lacks. The shift to the imperfect, $\epsilon\check{\iota}\chi\epsilon\nu$, in 85 D 10 suggests that Socrates is now asking, not about the knowledge the slave will have, but about the knowledge he used to have—the knowledge he is in the process of recollecting but does not yet have. Cf. 81 C 9, where Socrates speaks of recalling what one previously knew ($\pi\rho\acute{o}\tau\epsilon\rho\nu\nu$ $\check{\eta}\pi\acute{\iota}\sigma\tau\alpha\tau\sigma$, aorist). (Scott takes $\check{\epsilon}\chi\epsilon\iota$ to refer to the slave's current latent knowledge. Even if that is true—though I have argued it is not—the shift to the imperfect, $\epsilon\check{\iota}\chi\epsilon\nu$, suggests he is now talking just about a time prior to that, and so is not asking whether the slave has his (latent) knowledge for all time.)

360   *Gail Fine*

knowledge (until he forgot it, presumably on being born),[62] or he did not; if he did not, he must have acquired it at some point.

Secondly, on my interpretation Socrates is not considering the possibility that the slave always, for all time, has explicit knowledge. Rather, he is considering the possibility that he always had his past knowledge (until he forgot it, on being born).

Thirdly, since the two options mentioned in (3) concern just the slave's past knowledge, it is not surprising that they do not mention his current or future condition.

Before proceeding further, it is worth noting that Scott's alternative interpretation may face a difficulty. On his view, Socrates is asking whether the slave always (for all time) has his latent knowledge or acquired it at some time; and the answer is that he always has it. But it is important to Scott that prenatal knowledge be explicit. It is not clear how his interpretation leaves room for this crucial claim. All Socrates argues, on Scott's view, is that the slave always has latent knowledge.[63]

I think the rest of the argument for immortality can be neatly interpreted along the lines I have suggested (which is one reason to interpret it this way). But rather than defending that view, let me change tack. For though I do not think Socrates says the slave has any sort of innate knowledge, I understand the temptation to think he says this. So what I would now like to argue is that *if* we think he posits innate knowledge (though I do not), we should be reluctant to attribute to him the particular variety of innatism that Scott attributes to him.

Suppose, then, that we say that in (3) Socrates is referring to the knowledge the slave will have in the future, and is asking whether he has always had it or acquired it at some time; and suppose we also say that his answer is that the slave has always had it. Still, we need not infer that Socrates means that the slave has always had explicit knowledge: as Scott argues, that surely is not what Socrates means. We can say instead that he is asking about the knowledge that will be explicit in the future: did the slave always have it in

---

[62] Cf. *Phaedo* 74 D 9–76 D 6. Though this is not explicitly said in the *Meno*, I think it is assumed.

[63] Perhaps Scott thinks we can infer from present latent knowledge to conscious prenatal knowledge because, as we have seen, he thinks the latter 'points to' the former. But then it would be odd if Socrates' argument for immortality only shows the need for everlasting latent knowledge, ignoring explicit knowledge.

Enquiry and Discovery   361

some way or other (not necessarily explicitly), or did he acquire it at some point?[64]

This concedes to Scott that Plato posits innate knowledge (though it continues to say that 'now' is future-referring). But we need not concede that he posits latent innatism. Perhaps he instead means to endorse content innatism or dispositional innatism.[65]

15. Let me now defend this view. As Scott notes, in (7) Socrates suddenly starts talking about belief; then, in (11), he says that the truth is always in our soul. Why does he move from talking about knowledge, to belief, to truth? Scott suggests that Socrates retreats to a weaker claim about innate belief in order to prove immortality to those who are not convinced by the stronger claim that we have innate knowledge. 'Truth' 'smoothes over the difference between' innate knowledge and innate belief (120).

I think a more satisfying account can be given. Suppose we concede that Socrates speaks of knowledge being innate in us (though, again, in my view he does not do so). Still, we need not infer that it is in us *as* something actually known: that we are in the cognitive condition of knowing. Perhaps knowledge is always in us just in the sense that propositions that are suitable as the content of knowledge are always in us: knowledge in the content, not in the cognitive-condition, sense.

To make it clear that this is what he means, Socrates initially moves from talking about knowledge to talking about true belief. But since that too is ambiguous as between cognitive condition and content, he eventually says just that truths are in us. We may say, if we like, that knowledge is innate in us: but only if we are careful to be clear that what that means is just that propositions that are suitable as the content of the cognitive condition—certain truths—are in some sense in us. This would be content innatism. An alternative is that to have a truth, or knowledge, innately in the mind is just to be disposed to assent to it in the appropriate circumstances. This would be dispositional innatism (as I, rather than Scott, use the term).

I am not sure how (if, contrary to my view, Plato posits some sort of innate knowledge) to choose between saying that Plato is a con-

---

[64] Once again, it is worth noting that Socrates does not himself explicitly speak of explicit or latent knowledge; he just asks whether the slave does or does not know.

[65] For these labels, see the end of sect. 12.

362 *Gail Fine*

tent innatist and saying that he is a dispositional innatist (as I use the term). But to me, at any rate, both of these options seem preferable to saying that he favours latent innatism. For one thing, latent knowledge as Scott describes it does not seem to satisfy Plato's conditions on knowledge.[66] For example, it seems reasonable to think that Plato (reasonably enough) places an accessibility condition on knowledge: since the slave cannot readily explain why his beliefs are true, he does not count as knowing.[67] The fact that Plato does not explicitly say that the slave has latent knowledge, but does explicitly say that the slave does not know, also counts against positing innate knowledge.[68]

16. So far, I have addressed three occasions of Socrates on trial: his unitarian assumption; his views about the value of the elenchus; and his view that we have a duty to enquire. The fourth trial targets Socrates' views on method. Here Scott discusses the hypothetical method, which occupies *Meno* 86 c–87 c. It articulates a way in which one can enquire how virtue is acquired even if one does not already know what it is. (The method is applicable more widely; but this is the case Plato, and so Scott, focuses on.)

Scott argues that Socrates' willingness to use this method shows that he has revised his earlier views on method. That would be true if Socrates had said earlier that one *must* know what F is, in order to enquire how it is acquired. And as we saw in Section 3, Scott does sometimes say that Socrates initially holds this very strong view. However, he also sometimes seems to ascribe to Socrates just the weaker view that it is *preferable* to know what F is before enquiring how it is acquired. So, for example, he first says that

[66] Cf. L. Brown, 'Connaissance et réminiscence dans le *Ménon*', *Revue philosophique*, 4 (1991), 603–19 at 618. She none the less thinks Plato posits latent innate knowledge. Of course, there is a sense in which neither content nor dispositional innatism satisfies those criteria either. But I take it that Plato's criteria for knowledge are meant to govern the cognitive condition of knowing. In so far as neither content nor dispositional innatism involves knowing in the cognitive-condition sense, it is not surprising that they do not satisfy his criteria for knowledge. But it is a defect of latent innatism that it does not do so.

[67] Cf. T. Nagel, 'Linguistics and Epistemology', in G. Harman (ed.), *On Noam Chomsky: Critical Essays* (Garden City, NY, 1974), 219–28.

[68] See n. 39. One might argue that positing latent knowledge is the best explanation of what Plato has in mind. That might be so if he would otherwise be caught in contradiction. But contradiction can be avoided without positing latent knowledge. So, for example, (3) might be thought to contradict (12); but it does not if, as I have suggested, νῦν in (3) refers to the slave's future knowledge.

Enquiry and Discovery 363

'Socrates says that they *must* start with knowledge of the definition' (132, emphasis added); 'must' suggests that this is the only way one can enquire. But the next paragraph asks: 'If this is his *preferred* method . . .', which suggests it is not necessary, but just preferable, to begin with a definition.[69] If all that is true is that Socrates would *prefer* to begin with knowledge of what F is, using the hypothetical method does not involve any change of heart. The method may be an innovation (140, 141); but that falls short of saying that it is an 'emendation' (142).

Just as we can ask whether the hypothetical method involves a revision of what is said earlier in the *Meno*, so we can ask whether it involves a revision of what is said in the early dialogues. Scott suggests that Socrates in the *Meno* eventually allows one to enquire what F is like without knowing what it is, because the issue is of such practical importance (140). The same seems true in the early dialogues. In the *Crito*, for example, Socrates and Crito enquire whether it would be just for Socrates to flee; given the context, the enquiry is of considerable practical importance! Yet it is not said that they know what justice is, nor is any general definition offered even as a matter of belief. So it seems that in the early dialogues too, Socrates allows us to enquire whether something is an instance of a virtue (in this case, of justice) without knowing what that virtue is.[70] They may not do so via the hypothetical method; so, again, that method may be new. But it is not new to allow enquiry into what something is like in the absence of knowledge of what it is. If it is not new in the early dialogues, that may lead us to suppose that neither does the first part of the *Meno* hold that view. There, as in the early dialogues, Socrates would prefer to enquire whether virtue is acquired, or whether something is an instance of or kind of virtue, on the basis of knowledge of what virtue is; but he allows

[69] At 131–3 Scott several times speaks of Socrates' *preferred* method. On 140 he says that 'Plato is strongly attracted to a certain methodological purism: *where possible*, an inquiry should proceed on the basis of an explicitly known specification, or set of premises' (emphasis added). If methodological purism says only that one should begin with an explicitly known specification where possible, then it is not abandoned: Socrates is just focusing on cases where it is not possible given, as Scott emphasizes, the urgency of the case at hand.

[70] I take it that the same considerations that lead Scott to say that it is an innovation, or emendation of an earlier view, to allow that one can enquire how virtue is acquired even if one does not know what it is, would lead him to say as well that one can ask whether something is an instance of, or a kind of, virtue even if one does not know what virtue is.

364 *Gail Fine*

one to engage in these enquiries even if one does not already know what virtue is. The *Meno* gives us a more elaborate description of how one can do so; but it is a fuller description of a familiar practice, one that does not violate any Socratic assumptions.[71]

17. I close with a few brief comments on the scope of knowledge in the *Meno*, and on Plato's contrast between knowledge and true belief.

As is well known, Socrates says that one cannot know whether Meno is handsome or well born unless one knows who he is (71 B); and he illustrates the difference between knowledge and true belief by contrasting someone who knows the way to Larisa with someone who merely has a true belief about the way (97 A ff.). If these are literal examples of things one can know, then Plato admits knowledge of sensible particulars. But Scott dismisses both as analogies, and he seems sceptical as to whether Plato allows knowledge of empirical matters of fact. He argues against thinking that the way to Larisa is mentioned as an example of something one might know, as follows (182):[72]

[T]he text says that the person who merely has true belief has not travelled there and does not have knowledge (97b1–2); and this most probably means that he has not been there and *therefore* does not have knowledge, while the other person has knowledge *because* he has been there. In this case, therefore, first-hand evidence, rather than explanation, is sufficient to convert true belief into knowledge.

Scott thinks this conflicts with 98 A, which requires explanation for knowledge. However, one might say that travelling to Larisa

[71] Scott suggests at 141–2 that the *Laches* (190 B 7–C 2) and *Protagoras* (361 C 4–D 5) may say that one can enquire how virtue is best acquired only if one already knows what it is. *La.* 190 B 7–C 2 says: 'Then isn't it necessary for us to start out from knowing what virtue is? Because if we are not absolutely certain what it is, how are we going to advise anyone as to the best method of obtaining it?' This does not make knowing what virtue is a necessary condition of enquiring how it is best obtained. Rather, knowing what it is is a necessary condition of *advising* someone on how it is best acquired. I assume Socrates thinks that one cannot properly advise someone without knowledge; if so, the passage is an instance of PD, which, as Scott agrees, does not involve chronological priority. Nor does *Prot.* 361 C 4–D 5 seem to me to say that one must know what virtue is in order to enquire how it is acquired (whether, in particular, it is teachable). Rather, he says he 'should like' (βουλοίμην ἄν) to proceed in this way: this is his preferred method.

[72] Emphasis original. At 182 n. 9 Scott considers but rejects an alternative way of understanding the analogy (as Scott takes it to be). Though this alternative is rejected here, it is endorsed in *RE* 46.

Enquiry and Discovery 365

enables one to provide the explanation: perhaps only an experienced traveller is in a position to explain why this is the way to go. We need not oppose first-hand experience and explanation as sharply as Scott does: the former is a means that enables us to provide the latter; it is not a substitute for or in competition with it.

Scott also argues that, in Plato's view, we can achieve knowledge only through dialectic (152–3). In this case, either we need to use dialectic to discover the way to Larisa, or else we cannot know the way. Although Scott does not take a stand on the precise scope of dialectic (or recollection), he does not seem to think it covers things like the way to Larisa; so perhaps this is another of his reasons for doubting that it can be known. Again, however, I think Plato allows different routes to knowledge. Though dialectic may be necessary in the cases that most interest him—such as virtue—he thinks one can come to know the way to Larisa by repeatedly travelling it in an appropriately attentive way. If we open up the routes to knowledge, it becomes more plausible to think that Plato allows knowledge of empirical matters of fact. This is not to deny that, for Plato, all knowledge requires explanation. It is just to say there is more than one way of finding explanations. Certainly Plato's definition of knowledge allows for this possibility: for it defines knowledge, as Scott agrees, as true belief tied down by explanatory reasoning. It does not say that we can find the explanation only by doing dialectic.[73]

Socrates contrasts knowledge and true belief by saying that the former is stable in a way the latter is not. At first this might seem odd: are there not dogmatic people with mere true (or false!) beliefs, as well as modest knowers who will abandon what they know in the face of skilful reasoners? Scott rightly replies that it is not any old stability that distinguishes knowledge from true belief, but just stability reached as a result of explanatory reasoning (181). Retaining one's beliefs throughout one's life, come what may, is not sufficient for the sort of stability that is characteristic of knowledge; the right sort of stability needs to issue from explanatory reasoning in the right way. Hence retaining one's beliefs, come what may, is

---

[73] It is true that at 98 A 4–5 Socrates says: 'And this, Meno my friend, is recollection, as we agreed before'; and one might take this to mean that one can explain why p is so only if one engages in recollection. However, I do not think we need to take the passage in this way: see my 'Knowledge and True Belief in the *Meno*', *OSAP* 27 (2004), 41–81 at 59–60.

366 *Gail Fine*

not necessary for stability either: the relevant sort of stability is sensitive to the right sort of reasoning.

At least once, however, Scott says that the instability of true belief means that true beliefs *will* run away (144), and he takes this to be a reason for saying that teachers must have knowledge; for otherwise '[t]here would no longer be any asymmetry between them [teacher and learner] to justify calling one the teacher and the other the learner' (144). However, to say that mere beliefs are unstable is not to say they *will* run away, only that they are not sensitive to evidence in the way in which genuine knowledge is. Be that as it may, even if teacher and learner both have mere true belief, they need not be on a par: the teacher might have more true beliefs, or better-justified true beliefs, even if she lacks knowledge. Socrates takes himself to lack knowledge, but he seems to think he is cognitively better off than his interlocutors; one reason may be that he thinks his beliefs are better justified than theirs are, even if they are not justified enough to constitute knowledge. To be sure, Socrates does not take himself to be a teacher, and he does require knowledge for genuine teaching. The point is just that this requirement does not clearly stem from the thought that true beliefs *will* run away, or from the thought that there is no relevant cognitive asymmetry among all those who lack knowledge.

Cornell University

BIBLIOGRAPHY

Barnes, J., 'Mr Locke's Darling Notion', *Philosophical Quarterly*, 22 (1972), 193–214.
Bluck, R. S., *Plato's* Meno (Cambridge, 1964).
Brown, L., 'Connaissance et réminiscence dans le *Ménon*', *Revue philosophique*, 4 (1991), 603–19.
Dancy, R., *Plato's Introduction of Forms* (Cambridge, 2004).
Fine, G., 'Inquiry in the *Meno*', in R. Kraut (ed.), *Cambridge Companion to Plato* (Cambridge, 1992), 200–26; repr., with minor modifications, in Fine, *Plato on Knowledge and Forms*, ch. 2.
—— 'Knowledge and True Belief in the *Meno*', *OSAP* 27 (2004), 41–81.
—— *Plato on Knowledge and Forms: Selected Essays* (Oxford, 2003).
Franklin, L., 'The Structure of Dialectic in the *Meno*', *Phronesis*, 46 (2001), 413–39.
Irwin, T., *Plato's Ethics* (Oxford, 1995).

Enquiry and Discovery 367

Matthews, G., *Socratic Perplexity* (Oxford, 1999).

Nagel, T., 'Linguistics and Epistemology', in G. Harman (ed.), *On Noam Chomsky: Critical Essays* (Garden City, NY, 1974), 219–28.

Scott, D., 'Innatism and the Stoa' ['Innatism'], *Proceedings of the Cambridge Philological Society*, 214 (1988), 123–53.

—— *Plato's* Meno [*PM*] (Cambridge, 2006).

—— *Recollection and Experience* [*RE*] (Cambridge, 1995).

Sedley, D., *The Midwife of Platonism: Text and Subtext in Plato's* Theaetetus (Oxford, 2004).

Sharples, R. W., *Plato:* Meno (Warminster, 1985).

Thompson, E. S., *The* Meno (London, 1901).

Vlastos, G., 'Anamnesis in the *Meno*', *Dialogue*, 4 (1965), 143–67.

PHILOSOPHY, HISTORY, ANTHROPOLOGY

A Discussion of Bernard Williams, *The Sense of the Past*[1]

G. E. R. LLOYD

THERE was once a famous quarrel between philosophy and poetry, as to which of the two had the better claim to deliver wisdom. That is no longer a live issue. But a not too dissimilar battle continues to be waged between philosophy, history, and social anthropology. Which of these studies can contribute more to our understanding of the human condition? What should we expect from each and how easy is it to combine their insights? What methods should we use to resolve the question of what, on the one hand, is true of all human beings as the human beings we all are, and what, on the other, must be acknowledged to fall on the side of the culturally variable?

Of those three disciplines, the youngest or most recent, social anthropology, is perhaps the most straightforward both in its aims and in its methods, however controversial the results delivered remain. Its remit is the study of contemporary societies, in all their rich variety and complexity, from their kinship systems, economies, and technologies, all the way to their rituals and mythologies and, precisely, their views on the human condition. Modern ethnographic accounts alert us to the almost incredible diversity in belief systems and values. Yet that very variety poses severe problems of interpretation. Ethnographers are generally committed to understanding the societies they study in the societies' own terms in the first instance, using actors' categories, as the jargon goes, rather than their own observers' ones. Yet eventually each society's ideas have to be translated into the ethnographers' own terms. Faced with what

© G. E. R. Lloyd 2007

[1] B. Williams, *The Sense of the Past: Essays in the History of Philosophy*, ed. with an introduction by M. Burnyeat (Princeton, 2006), xxii + 393 pp.

370 *G. E. R. Lloyd*

seem irrational beliefs or practices, one school of thought maintains that there is no neutral vantage-point from which judgements of irrationality can be justified, and so notions of rationality itself have to be relativized to the culture concerned. But another insists that relativizing rationality in such a way is incoherent, as also is the idea that there are strictly incommensurable systems of belief. The threat that looms for the first position is that the exotic beliefs in question will have to be admitted to be unintelligible, leaving the ethnographer, and *a fortiori* other commentators, with nothing to say about the beliefs in question. Conversely, the second position always runs the risk that the interpretation offered will be irrevocably prejudiced by being translated into an alien conceptual schema.

The methods of the discipline of history evidently differ from those of the social anthropologist, and in one respect its aims are more problematic. The methods differ in that the historian cannot interview long dead subjects nor say anything about those who have left no trace in the literary or archaeological record—though no more can the social anthropologist investigate *every* member of a given society in the field. That immediately raises the spectre of bias. But there is an additional tension within the possible aims of history. On one view the goal is simply to report what actually happened, *wie es eigentlich gewesen*. But there is often another implicit or explicit goal, to draw lessons from the past for the present and even the future, where *historia* serves as *magistra vitae*, in the expression popularized by Koselleck. From one point of view the most accurate representation of the past may be thought to be a necessary condition for learning anything of any value from it. Yet the desire to extract lessons may and often does lead to distortions in the representation. Judgement is inevitable, in that no description can be theory-neutral, theory-free: but a similar problem dogs the historian as the ethnographer, that of securing a standpoint that will serve to minimize the tendentiousness of the judgements delivered. In both cases the otherness of the material under discussion is both a strength and a weakness, a strength since it gives access to aspects of human experience that are not visible in contemporary society, but a weakness since the hermeneutic problems of interpreting that otherness are massive.

At one time in the West, philosophy was the supreme intellectual discipline, claiming priority to all others in its delivery of understanding and wisdom. But that was in the days when philosophy's

Philosophy, History, Anthropology 371

role was understood as being to produce grand metaphysical, even theological, systems, resolving the problems of epistemology and in the philosophy of mind on the way to providing a secure basis for ethics and political philosophy. Those days are long past, but what has replaced that view, in the West, is a proliferation of ideas about the core concerns of philosophy, indeed remarkably narrow-minded and exclusive ideas in many cases. When I was an undergraduate at Cambridge in the 1950s and attended the lectures of John Wisdom, Richard Braithwaite, Casimir Lewy, and the rest, the history of philosophy was held to be of no importance, and large areas of contemporary Western philosophy—existentialism, phenomenology—were ignored.

Nowadays that is no longer true to anything like the same degree. But it is still the case that 'philosophy' is often treated as basically a Western phenomenon. For many it is problematic to claim that there *is* philosophy in any other than a hopelessly vague and wishy-washy sense in India, China, or Japan. The glib contrast between 'Eastern' wisdom and Western philosophy still serves the narrow-minded as an excuse for not considering other, non-Western, traditions and *a fortiori* for ignoring the differences between and within different 'Eastern' ones, between Confucius, say, and the Upanishads, or even between Confucius and Zhuangzi. Yet they and many others had important things to say about what makes a life worth living and why, and indeed about the roles and responsibilities of those who had important things to say about that, and on those grounds they should not, on the view I favour, be excluded from consideration. Nor should they be marginalized on the grounds of the modes of presentation of their ideas. There is plenty of robust argument in both Indian and Chinese philosophy, and we may go further: the way in which Zhuangzi subtly and tellingly debunks Confucius can be compared with how Plato gets Socrates to do the same to Protagoras in the *Protagoras* and the *Theaetetus*.

Bernard Williams was one of the sharpest British minds of the late twentieth century. He was trained in the Greats tradition at Oxford, not the most open-minded or ecumenical of all philosophical formations. Yet he came to be very dissatisfied with much academic philosophy in the English-speaking world, criticizing it as parochial and inward-looking and for ignoring the larger picture. In his later work, especially, he straddled philosophy in the analytic mode, the history of philosophy, and even anthropology.

372 *G. E. R. Lloyd*

Indeed, all three could and did, in his view, contribute to the general aims of philosophizing as he understood it. For that purpose he distinguished what he called ideal anthropology from regular ethnographic research in the field. The former addressed in general and abstract terms what can be said to be common to humanity as such, while recognizing that the latter threw up plenty of variation in its different cultural manifestations.

The way he combined those three main interests was certainly distinctive, maybe unique. He was not alone, to be sure, in treating the history of philosophy as a resource for philosophizing. He drew a distinction between the history of ideas, which is history, and the history of philosophy, which is primarily philosophical, while acknowledging that that contrast was not exactly a hard and fast one. It is interesting, in view of the considerable part of his career when he was based in Cambridge, that he spoke of the history of ideas as a discipline, when an earlier fashionable trend of Cambridge reflections on the issue would have insisted that strictly speaking ideas are not the kinds of item that can have a history: only people using them can.

Despite his disclaimer, in the book under review, to be only a part-timer in the field of the history of philosophy (147), his historical reflections provided him with essential arguments for the promotion of a particular style of philosophizing. The key tradition is the Greek, the prime exemplar of the philosophizing he most admired, Plato. So Williams famously claimed that 'the legacy of Greece to Western philosophy is Western philosophy' (3) and even that Plato 'invented the subject of philosophy as we know it' (148) or at least that he 'virtually' invented it (84). The chapter in which he makes the second claim ends with a passionate protreptic for philosophizing in the manner of Plato—though that is the Plato of, say, the *Theaetetus* rather than of the *Timaeus*, a work he does not mention in this collection.

'The dialogues', he writes,

are never closed or final. They do not offer the ultimate results of Plato's great enquiry. They contain stories, descriptions, jokes, arguments, harangues, streams of free intellectual invention, powerful and sometimes violent rhetoric, and much else. Nothing in them straightforwardly reports those theoretical findings on which everything was supposed to turn, and they never take the tone that now that you have mastered this, your life will be changed. There are theoretical discussions, often very complex,

Philosophy, History, Anthropology   373

subtle, and original. There are many statements of how our lives need to be changed, and of how philosophy may help to change them. But the action is always somewhere else . . . (178–9)

Then he concludes:

it is pointless to ask who is the world's greatest philosopher: for one thing there are many different ways of doing philosophy. But we can say what the various qualities of great philosophers are: intellectual power and depth; a grasp of the sciences; a sense of the political, and of human destructiveness as well as creativity; a broad range and a fertile imagination; an unwillingness to settle for the superficially reassuring; and, in an unusually lucky case, the gifts of a great writer. If we ask which philosopher has, more than any other, combined all these qualities—to that question there is certainly an answer, Plato. (179–80)

What Williams, in that remarkable passage, has to say about Plato admirably fits Williams himself. But that passionate sympathy for philosophy in Plato's style has certain consequences. First, the preference for dialogue over treatise inevitably means that systematic theory-building takes second place to the open-ended exploration of the issues. Williams has many intriguing insights to offer concerning Aristotle, but tends to see him as doctrinaire by comparison with Plato. Secondly, the strategy of leaving the reader to discover the answers on his or her own carries a certain risk.

Perhaps the best example of this is the alternative readings of the *Theaetetus* that emerged from the long dialogue on that work between Burnyeat and Williams. One line of interpretation of the first part of that work, the refutation of the thesis that knowledge is perception, sees Plato as building on his downgrading of the material world in such earlier dialogues as the *Phaedo* and the *Republic*. But an alternative reading, which Burnyeat generously ascribes primarily to Williams, has it that in the first part of the *Theaetetus* the discussion of flux is not an endorsement of that view, but part of a *reductio* undermining it. The examination of these two very contrasting interpretations in Burnyeat's book and in Williams's introduction to the dialogue produces sustained philosophical explorations of the highest order. But where the traditional view had Plato deliver a clear pedagogical message, the indeterminacies we are left with, on the two-possible-interpretations view, put the onus on us, the readers, who are given not just an example of philoso-

374 *G. E. R. Lloyd*

phizing, but a notable challenge to resolve the issues for ourselves. Heady, aporetic, Socratic stuff, but certainly harder work.

The twenty-five pieces collected in *The Sense of the Past* discuss a wide variety of philosophers. Plato has the lion's share, with seven essays devoted to him. But Hume, Sidgwick, Collingwood, and Wittgenstein each figure in one chapter, Descartes has three, and Aristotle and Nietzsche have four apiece. The collection opens with three more general pieces about aspects of Greek thought. The brilliant discussion of Collingwood's philosophy of history—which broaches many of the issues with which I started my remarks—has not been published before. The article on 'many kinds of eyes', i.e. many kinds of truths, in Nietzsche also appears here for the first time, and another of the Nietzsche pieces has previously been published only in German. On the other hand, four of the articles have been not just published before, but also reprinted already either in *Moral Luck*[2] or in *Making Sense of Humanity*.[3] The general idea for the volume was Williams's own, so we are assured by his wife Patricia and his editor Myles Burnyeat, who writes an introduction to the volume with many a moving, personal comment on his inspiring interactions with his mentor and colleague. This, together with the two other volumes of posthumously edited papers,[4] adds up to a formidable canon of work from what we may call Williams's later philosophy.

But if Williams had lived to see this volume through the press, he might perhaps have integrated the pieces more closely together. Several paragraphs of the discussion of the various positions represented by Gorgias, by Polus, and by Callicles in Plato's *Gorgias*, that figure in the article 'Plato against the Immoralist' (chapter 6 here, first published in 1997), are repeated more or less verbatim in chapter 8, 'Intrinsic Goodness' (originally published in 2003), and much of it appears again in substance in chapter 10 ('Plato: The Invention of Philosophy', from 1998). This is recognized in a note on page 118, where grateful acknowledgement is recorded for the use and adaptation of earlier material in what is here chapter 8. But the effect of this repetitiveness in the present collection is unhappy.

---

[2] *Moral Luck: Philosophical Papers, 1973–1980* (Cambridge, 1981).

[3] *Making Sense of Humanity, and Other Philosophical Papers, 1982–1993* (Cambridge, 1995).

[4] *In the Beginning Was the Deed: Realism and Moralism in Political Argument*, ed. G. Hawthorn (Princeton, 2005), and *Philosophy as a Humanistic Discipline*, ed. A. W. Moore (Princeton, 2006).

Philosophy, History, Anthropology 375

It is difficult, if not impossible, to attempt any general character-ization of Williams's work as manifested in these pieces, but some recurrent features stand out. First, there is the already noted pre-ference for open-ended discussion of the issues, which converts, on occasion, into a positive antipathy to theory. This spills over into his views of other philosophers. Plato, for instance, is said not to have a theory of Forms (154), so the question of whether he ever gave it up does not arise: a sympathetic point of view, no doubt, but one that risks tempting the unwary to cut corners. His discussion of Sidgwick on the ambitions of ethics ends with a personal statement, to the effect that there can be no coherent ethical theory:

No ethical theory can render a coherent account of its own relation to practice: it will always run into some version of the fundamental difficulty that the practice of life, and hence also an adequate theory of that practice, will require the recognition of what I have called deep dispositions; but at the same time the abstract and impersonal view that is required if the theory is to be genuinely a *theory* cannot be satisfactorily understood in relation to the depth and necessity of those dispositions. (295–6)

Again, the criteria adopted for what is to be a genuine theory are set so high that many tentative endeavours will fail.

A second recurrent theme that links many of the pieces together relates to Williams's views on the proper aims of doing the history of philosophy. On the one hand, he distances himself from the approach he describes as triumphant anachronism—the line taken by Ryle in a famous opinion (twice mentioned in this volume) that Plato's writings should be read as if they had just appeared in the most recent number of *Mind*. On the other, Williams rejects history for its own sake. The way to use it as a resource for philosophizing is to exploit the opportunities it provides for making strange what is familiar in our own assumptions (263). That might seem already to have an anthropological ring to it: but Williams is not on the lookout for the exotic. The continuation of the key phrase is important. What history of philosophy is to make strange, and to lead us to question, is precisely 'our own' assumptions. The project, which Williams carries through with remarkable subtlety and success, is to bring earlier, including ancient, philosophy to bear on our modern issues without falling into the trap of anachronism, though the collection is, to be sure, limited to Western thinkers, and other, non-Western traditions are not on the agenda.

376   *G. E. R. Lloyd*

There are some interesting comments, in this regard, on what Williams describes as Collingwood's paradox, namely that when the views of an earlier philosopher are understood correctly, they will turn out to be rational. That consequence is indeed a condition of our having understood the ideas correctly. Williams does not sign up to that principle himself, nor to a version of Davidson's recommendation of charity in interpretation, which Williams dismisses, rather too quickly I should say, as condescending. On the contrary, he is himself prepared, often enough, to diagnose confusion and error. Aristotle is wrong to link injustice with *pleonexia* (215), he is confused on the Good (chapter 12), and he is wrong to see ethics as connected with biology and his other enquiries in the way he does (197). Sometimes the criticism is that the philosopher has got it wrong on his own terms. But more often Williams argues that we have now moved on. One example is his comment that—as Burnyeat also maintained—we now have a more mechanical conception of life, which means that Aristotle's account cannot be accepted (222), another that modern developments make many of Descartes's ruminations on the subject of science inapplicable (239).

The fundamental issue that is expressed in so many words from time to time and that lies below the surface on many others is this: are there permanent cross-cultural human truths? To what extent are the views we accept the product of our own day and age? At what points, in other words, do we have to factor in cultural influences in our own self-understanding? Of course, Williams's own discussion in *Truth and Truthfulness*[5] did a masterly job of pointing out the flaws in the idea of a unique concept of truth, valid in all contexts. But even after that hatchet job has been completed, the problem of the nature of the justification that can be offered for beliefs, particularly those where other societies have taken different views, remains. It is characteristic of Williams's approach that he has rather different things to say about this Big Question in different contexts, and I shall come back, at the end, to where I think his perspective needs supplementing. But so far as his philosophical arguments on universals in human nature go, they are nothing if not tough-minded. Throughout, the exploration of the issues in this volume offers leads rather than conclusions, leaving the reader

---

[5] *Truth and Truthfulness: An Essay in Genealogy* (Princeton, 2002).

Philosophy, History, Anthropology 377

with the exhilaration of a challenge, not the closure of solutions, let alone of would-be definitive ones.

I cannot think of any collection of writings that better serve the purpose of introducing the reader to the real challenges of the history of philosophy. Yet of course not even Williams deals with every aspect of the problems with equal success. Let me point to one minor and one more important weakness. First, some of the pieces, naturally enough, have worn better than others. Some of the discussions of philosophy before Plato, the account of Empedocles and that of early Pythagoreanism, for instance, now appear dated. His remarks about the Babylonian contributions to science have, like many other general observations by non-specialists about that field, been totally superseded by the work of such scholars as Swerdlow, Rochberg, Robson, and Brown. By contrast, Williams's own explorations of Greek notions of agency not only have stood the test of time but remain the starting-point for most further work.

My more substantial criticism relates to the third arm of Williams's project. While the philosophy is superb, and the use of history intriguing, the anthropology strikes me as weak. Let me give two examples. At one point (80), when he says that all societies try to regulate enmity, what is missing in that over-general and superficial remark is due recognition of the differences between enmity within the group and enmity towards outsiders. On the latter subject the anthropology of war has brought to light very great divergences between different cultures. Here indeed Williams misses an opportunity to fulfil his own strategic aim of using the 'other' to make 'our own' assumptions strange.

Then in his discussion of understanding Homer, he throws out a challenge (67), with the claim that there is 'in the area of action and its ethical surroundings, a set of very basic ideas which, at the least, lay an extremely heavy burden of proof on anyone who claims to find a society in which these conceptions were not operative'. When he then specifies, with what he calls some banal examples, what he believes to be true 'everywhere', he includes the idea that 'people do things and are recognised by others as doing things'. Yet this remark skates over the extreme complexities apparent in the ethnographic reports concerning who exactly is counted as belonging to 'us', the 'people'. People are sometimes construed as stopping at the limits of the specific community, and sometimes animals are thought of

378 *G. E. R. Lloyd*

as persons as much as humans, indeed more than certain humans who belong to other communities.

This whole problem has recently been the topic of intense debate. Anthropologists such as Viveiros de Castro and Descola especially have brought to light the highly divergent views entertained on what Descola has called 'interiority' (roughly, the self) and 'physicality' (roughly, the body) across the world. While their particular contributions to the issues belong to the last couple of decades, the problems were opened up long ago by Lévi-Strauss, not to mention much earlier forays by some of the founding fathers of anthropology such as Boas. In his discussion of Collingwood, Williams remarks (358) on Wittgenstein's 'evasive' use of 'we', sometimes taken in an inclusive sense, sometimes referring to the 'we' of the here and now as distinct from other humans at other times and places. He continues, in a comment where he explicitly exploits that ambiguity for his own purposes, that 'it is a lively question, how far "our" understanding . . . of the ethnographically exotic, of cultural variation, and hence of the humanly universal, itself indelibly carries with it assumptions drawn from our cultural experience as historically understood'. Indeed a lively question, which surfaces also in some of the papers in *Philosophy as a Humanistic Discipline*. But it is one that takes more anthropology to come to terms with than Williams marshals in this book.

Given the ambitiousness of his project, it is in no way surprising that some parts of Williams's argument are stronger than others. But my criticisms should not be taken to detract from my judgement that this is a superb collection of philosophically acute historical discussions of many of the most important Western thinkers. As a model of the most productive and relevant history of philosophy, it is *sans pareil* and will surely be of enormous value to many who did not have the immense good fortune to have heard Williams in action as well as to all who did.

Needham Research Institute, Cambridge

INDEX LOCORUM

Aeschines of Sphettus
Alcibiades
fr. 12 Nestle: 1 n. 2, 13
P.Oxy. xiii, no. 1608, frr. 1–4: 21 n.
  30
Fragments, ed. Nestle
9: 29 n. 57
29: 25 n. 36, 29 n. 57

Alexander of Aphrodisias
In Aristotelis Metaphysica commentaria, ed. Hayduck
7. 22: 317–18 n. 19

Antisthenes
ap. Xen. *Sym.* 4. 34–45: 25 n. 36,
  27 n. 47
Fragments, ed. Nestle
12: 27 n. 47, 29 n. 57
13: 27 n. 47
57: 25 n. 36
65: 25 n. 36
72: 25 n. 36
73: 25 n. 36

Aquinas
In Aristotelis Physica commentaria
lib. 3, l. 10, nn. 4–6: 237 n. 5
147 Blackwell *et al.*: 220 n. 19
157 Blackwell *et al.*: 208 n. 3

Aristophanes
Birds
1553–64: 26 n. 41
Clouds
94: 25
135–9: 11
385 ff.: 12 n. 16, 13–14 n. 19
414–22: 25 n. 36, 27 n. 48
439–42: 25 n. 36, 27 n. 48
695–783: 13–14 n. 19
695–782: 12 n. 16
842: 24 n. 35

Ecclesiazousae
762: 259 n. 21
Frogs
1491–5: 15–16 n. 22

Aristotle
Categories
12^a4–8: 153–4 n. 28
12^b27–9: 153–4 n. 28
13^a20–1: 155 n. 30
De anima
bk. 1: 327
bk. 2: 327
403^a2: 327 n. 23
408^a1–2: 192 n. 49
408^a14: 191 n. 48
412^a28: 168
412^b12–16: 178 n. 27
412^b12–13: 168 n. 3, 175–6 n. 23,
  177, 178
412^b21–3: 168 n. 3, 177, 178
414^b2: 260 n. 24
415^a22–$^b8$: 174 n. 20
415^a22: 197 n. 54
416^a6–9: 192 n. 49
416^a19: 197 n. 54
416^b10: 197
416^b18–19: 197
417^a16–17: 240
423^b27–8: 184
426^a15–26: 246
430^b11: 245
431^a6–7: 240
431^b10–12: 326 n. 21
432^b3–7: 260 n. 24
433^a28–9: 326 n. 21
De caelo
1. 10: 327 n. 22
1. 12: 286 n. 25
4. 1: 185 n. 38
269^b22–4: 185
270^a4–6: 181
274^a26–8: 186

380   Index Locorum

$275^b33-276^a1$: 181
276^a15: 181
276^a30 ff.: 184
276^a30-^b14: 186
276^b9: 186 n. 40
279^b5-7: 327 n. 22
283^b13-14: 238
301^b17: 181
302^a20: 191
310^a35: 185 n. 39
310^b2-5: 186 n. 41
310^b16-19: 174
369^b31-5: 186
De generatione animalium
731^b21 ff.: 174 n. 20
734^b21-2: 199
734^b24-7: 168 n. 3, 177
734^b31-4: 196
734^b34-5: 196
734^b35: 200
740^b30-6: 197 n. 54
778^b16-17: 172 n. 14
De generatione et corruptione
1. 10: 187
2. 4: 174 n. 20
2. 8: 184 n. 36
314^a19-20: 181
321^b29-32: 168 n. 3
322^b1-2: 181 n. 29
323^a11: 184
327^b23-6: 188
328^a10: 181
328^a23-6: 188 n. 44
328^a28-9: 188
328^b31: 181 n. 29
329^a16: 181 n. 29
329^a26: 181 n. 29
329^b6-16: 185
329^b20-4: 184
329^b20: 185
329^b24-6: 183 n. 34
329^b26-33: 182
329^b32: 184
330^b1-4: 182
330^b7: 181
330^b22: 181
334^b9-14: 188
De interpretatione
ch. 9: 148-9 n. 19
19^a27-33: 148-9 n. 19
22^b6-7: 158 n. 37
De motu animalium
700^b6: 174 n. 18

700^b17-18: 260 n. 24
De partibus animalium
640^b33-^b4: 173 n. 16
$640^b34-641^a34$: 168 n. 3, 177
646^a13: 181 n. 29
646^a14-20: 185 n. 37
657^a30-5: 178 n. 26
664^a36-^b3: 178 n. 25
675^a19-^b23: 172 n. 13
De sensu
440^a31-^b23: 189
Eudemian Ethics
1. 3: 327 n. 22
1. 6: 302, 306
bk. 2: 318
2. 1: 285, 286, 307
2. 3: 273, 274 n. 4, 275, 278, 279,
281, 282, 283, 284 n. 22, 285,
289, 289 n. 31, 290, 291, 282, 292
n. 38, 293
2. 5: 285
2. 6-11: 285
2. 10: 313
3. 1-7: 281
3. 2: 281
3. 4: 281, 284
bks. 4-6: 274 n. 4
bk. 4: 291
bks. 5-7: 301
bk. 5: 274, 286, 313
bk. 6: 310
6. 1: 320
$1214^b28-1215^a7$: 305
$1214^b28-1215^a5$: 305
1215^a5-7: 305, 306, 327 n. 22
1216^b26-35: 303-4
1216^b28-35: 304 n. 9
1216^b31: 306
1216^b32-3: 304
1216^b32: 306
1217^b21: 327 n. 23
$1218^b37-1219^b26$: 321
1218^b37: 307, 321
1219^a8: 307, 321
1219^a10: 308
1219^a11-12: 321
1219^a16-17: 321
1219^a19: 308, 321
1219^a23-4: 322
1219^a24: 308
1219^a27: 322
1219^a28-39: 322
1219^a28-9: 322

Index Locorum

1219ᵃ34–5: 307
1219ᵃ39–40: 308
1219ᵃ40: 322
1219ᵇ6: 322
1219ᵇ8–16: 322
1219ᵇ16–26: 322
1219ᵇ28–32: 286
1219ᵇ30–1: 286
1219ᵇ31–2: 286 n. 24
1219ᵇ36–9: 286 n. 24
1220ᵃ4–12: 252, 285, 286
1220ᵃ8–11: 286
1220ᵃ10–11: 286
1220ᵃ13: 285
1220ᵇ5–6: 252
1220ᵇ34–5: 285
1221ᵃ4: 279
1221ᵃ12: 273, 273 n. 2
1221ᵃ23–4: 279
1221ᵃ36–8: 274, 283
1221ᵃ37: 273 n. 2
1222ᵃ6–12: 287 n. 27
1222ᵇ15–1228ᵃ19: 309–10 n. 14
1223ᵃ26–7: 260 n. 24
1225ᵇ24–6: 260 n. 24
1226ᵇ4: 313
1226ᵇ9: 313, 314 n. 16
1226ᵇ17: 318
1226ᵇ37–1227ᵃ3: 309–10 n. 14
1227ᵃ3–5: 287, 313
1227ᵃ4: 318
1227ᵃ5 ff.: 269 n. 37
1227ᵃ5: 318
1227ᵃ18–31: 319, 325
1227ᵃ18: 325
1227ᵃ21–2: 325
1227ᵃ28–31: 325
1227ᵇ8–10: 287 n. 27
1227ᵇ8: 287
1231ᵃ26–8: 284
1233ᵃ9–12: 281
1233ᵃ12–16: 284
1233ᵃ38–9: 284
1233ᵇ2–4: 281
1235ᵃ4–5: 320
1235ᵃ11: 320
1235ᵃ25: 320
1235ᵃ31: 320
1235ᵃ37–9: 320
1235ᵇ2–3: 320
1235ᵇ13–18: 320

Historia animalium
488ᵇ20: 279 n. 16

Metaphysics
bk. Γ: 301–2 n. 7
Γ 6: 151–2 n. 24
bk. Z: 328
Θ 6: 193
987ᵇ1–10: 59 n. 33
1004ᵇ27–9: 151–2 n. 24
1006ᵇ31–2: 158 n. 37
1010ᵇ30–1011ᵃ2: 246
1011ᵇ15–22: 151–2 n. 24
1015ᵃ33–6: 158 n. 37
1015ᵇ6–9: 158 n. 37
1015ᵇ36: 181 n. 28
1016ᵇ31–6: 224–5 n. 24
1017ᵇ21–3: 226–7 n. 26
1018ᵇ37–1019ᵃ1: 147–8 n. 18
1020ᵃ7–32: 249
1020ᵃ7–14: 249
1025ᵃ30–1: 248
1029ᵇ13: 328 n. 24
1029ᵇ14: 328 n. 24
1030ᵃ7 ff.: 147–8 n. 18
1030ᵃ25: 328 n. 24
1030ᵇ14–28: 147–8 n. 18
1032ᵃ18–19: 191
1032ᵃ22–7: 174 n. 20
1035ᵇ10–26: 168 n. 3
1035ᵇ10–20: 173 n. 16
1035ᵇ23–4: 177
1035ᵇ25: 177
1035ᵇ34: 170 n. 10
1039ᵃ4–6: 191
1040ᵇ8–9: 180
1046ᵃ31–5: 176
1047ᵇ4–6: 244 n. 13
1048ᵃ35–ᵇ9: 193
1048ᵇ14–17: 241
1048ᵇ29–30: 240
1049ᵃ12–15: 195
1051ᵃ34 ff.: 193
1052ᵃ20: 181
1053ᵇ30–1: 151–2 n. 24
1055ᵇ14–15: 151–2 n. 24
1055ᵇ18: 151–2 n. 24
1055ᵇ26–7: 151–2 n. 24
1056ᵃ27–30: 153 n. 27
1056ᵇ16: 180
1057ᵃ2–4: 249
1057ᵃ18: 189 n. 46
1061ᵃ18–20: 151–2 n. 24
1078ᵃ31–ᵇ6: 263 n. 29
1078ᵇ9–32: 58 n. 32, 59 n. 33
1084ᵃ2–4: 250 n. 17

382   *Index Locorum*

Meteorologica
4. 12: 170, 173
378^b10–25: 183 n. 34
389^b31–2: 177
390^a7–9: 184
390^a10–12: 168, 168 n. 3, 177
390^a12: 177
390^a18: 173
390^b3–19: 191
Nicomachean Ethics
1. 3: 309 n. 13
1. 4: 266
1. 8: 311 n. 15
1. 10: 311 n. 15
1. 12: 311 n. 15
1. 13: 286
2. 2: 303, 309 n. 13
2. 6: 279 n. 15, 283
2. 7: 275, 289 n. 31, 290, 291, 292, 292 n. 38, 293
3. 4: 266
3. 6–4. 9: 281
3. 10–12: 267, 281
bks. 4–6: 301
4. 1: 281, 284
4. 4: 281, 284
bks. 5–7: 274 n. 4
bk. 5: 279, 291, 309–10 n. 14
5. 1: 309–10 n. 14
5. 8: 309–10 n. 14
bk. 6: 9–10 n. 13, 274, 274 n. 4, 286, 289 n. 31, 290, 291, 292, 292 n. 38, 293, 313, 318
6. 5: 316
6. 9: 291
6. 12–13: 278, 289
6. 12: 273 n. 2, 278, 286, 288 n. 29, 290
6. 13: 288, 316
bk. 7: 310
7. 1: 320
7. 4: 264 n. 31
8. 1–2: 320
9. 8: 281, 282, 283, 283 n. 21, 286
bk. 10: 303
1094^b11–27: 308, 314
1094^b20–1: 314
1094^b20: 308
1094^b21–4: 309 n. 13
1094^b22: 309 n. 13
1095^a2–13: 269 n. 38
1095^b10–14: 253 n. 2
1096^a12–13: 58 n. 32

1097^b22–1098^a20: 322
1097^b27–30: 323
1097^b30–3: 323
1097^b30: 323
1097^b32–3: 323
1098^a4–5: 322
1098^a4: 252
1098^a7–8: 322
1098^a16–17: 322
1098^b3–4: 269 n. 37
1098^b9–12: 311 n. 15
1102^a27–8: 286
1102^a28–32: 254 n. 8
1102^a28: 256
1102^a32–$^b12$: 286 n. 24
1102^b13–28: 259
1102^b13–14: 252
1102^b14–1103^a3: 65 n. 6
1102^b26: 252
1102^b28: 260
1102^b29–33: 252
1102^b29–32: 286
1102^b29–31: 254
1102^b31–3: 258
1102^b31: 252
1102^b33–1103^a1: 259, 265
1102^b33: 252
1103^a1–3: 255, 258
1103^a1–2: 256
1103^a2: 256, 258
1103^a3–18: 287
1103^a3–5: 286
1103^b31–4: 317 n. 18
1103^b34–1104^a9: 308
1104^a6: 309
1104^b30 ff.: 261 n. 25
1106^b36–1107^a2: 287 n. 27
1106^b36: 287
1107^a8 ff.: 279 n. 15
1107^a16: 283
1107^b19: 284
1108^b7–10: 291
1109^a20–4: 289, 290
1112^a11–12: 314 n. 16
1113^a2–12: 287
1113^a4: 314 n. 16
1113^a15–$^b2$: 319, 323
1113^a22–4: 324
1113^a29–30: 314, 323
1115^b31–2: 285 n. 23
1119^a5–11: 284
1119^b7–18: 267
1121^b8 ff.: 284

Index Locorum

1121^{b}12 ff.: 281
1123^{a}19–27: 284
1123^{a}27–8: 281
1125–6: 284
1125^{b}4: 281
1125^{b}8–10: 281
1125^{b}10–11: 284
1129^{a}5–6: 309–10 n. 14
1129^{a}6–8: 309–10 n. 14
1129^{a}9–10: 309–10 n. 14
1129^{a}10–11: 309–10 n. 14
1129^{a}11: 309–10 n. 14
1129^{a}32–3: 276
1129^{b}19–27: 281 n. 19
1129^{b}19–24: 276
1129^{b}26–7: 276
1130^{a}8–13: 281 n. 19, 282, 292 n. 36
1130^{a}12–13: 276
1130^{a}14: 276
1130^{a}16–22: 276, 278
1130^{a}23–4: 276
1130^{a}24–8: 276, 280
1130^{b}1–2: 277
1130^{b}2: 284 n. 22
1130^{b}3–4: 277
1130^{b}19–20: 278 n. 13
1130^{b}23–4: 276
1132^{a}6–14: 277
1133^{b}30–1134^{a}13: 291
1135^{a}15–1136^{a}9: 309–10 n. 14
1135^{a}23: 309–10 n. 14
1138^{b}35–1139^{a}16: 287
1139^{a}3–15: 256 n. 11, 286
1139^{a}11–15: 252 n. 1
1139^{a}12: 316
1139^{a}15–16: 286
1139^{a}23: 316
1139^{b}4–5: 316
1139^{b}7–9: 238
1139^{b}19–23: 158 n. 37
1140^{a}24–31: 268
1140^{a}24–8: 252 n. 1, 263
1140^{a}25–31: 287, 291
1140^{b}4–6: 316, 317, 317–18 n. 19
1140^{b}12–13: 317
1140^{b}20–1: 316, 317, 317–18 n. 19
1140^{b}26: 313
1141^{b}2–3: 287 n. 26
1142^{a}1: 317
1142^{b}17–20: 251
1142^{b}33: 316, 317
1144^{a}8–9: 288 n. 29

1144^{a}23–9: 274
1144^{a}24–6: 274–5 n. 6
1144^{a}26–8: 278 n. 12
1144^{a}29–^{b}1: 278 n. 11, 287–8
1144^{a}31–2: 278 n. 11
1144^{b}14–15: 313
1144^{b}16–17: 287, 289
1144^{b}26–8: 287, 289
1144^{b}27–8: 287
1144^{b}30–2: 252
1144^{b}32: 288
1144^{b}36–1145^{a}2: 278 n. 11
1145^{a}4–6: 288 n. 29
1145^{b}2–7: 310
1145^{b}20: 310
1149^{a}25–^{b}3: 261
1149^{a}25–32: 252
1149^{a}29–36: 251
1149^{a}32–^{b}1: 262
1149^{b}1–3: 261
1155^{b}8: 320
1155^{b}9–10: 321
1155^{b}17–18: 321
1155^{b}27: 321
1155^{b}32: 320
1164^{b}31–3: 315
1167^{b}12–16: 277 n. 10
1168^{b}15–21: 280
1168^{b}25–8: 281 n. 19
1169^{a}34–^{b}1: 383 n. 21
1174^{b}2–5: 240
1178^{a}16–19: 252
1179^{b}4–31: 269 n. 38
1179^{b}4–16: 265
1179^{b}11–13: 266

Physics
1. 3: 160 n. 41
3. 1: 235, 247
3. 3: 207, 211 n. 9, 217
3. 4: 248
3. 5: 248, 249
3. 6: 233 ff.
6. 10: 247
8. 8: 244, 245
186^{b}18–23: 160 n. 41
188^{b}21–6: 189 n. 46
193^{a}5–6: 190 n. 47
193^{a}9 ff.: 167
193^{b}10: 199
199^{a}30–3: 199
200^{a}31–4: 197
200^{b}32–201^{a}3: 206
201^{a}9–10: 206

384   Index Locorum

201^{a}10–11: 240 n. 9
201^{a}16–18: 225–6 n. 25
201^{a}27–9: 206
201^{b}1: 231
201^{b}4–5: 206
201^{b}31–3: 240
202^{a}3–7: 208–9 n. 4
202^{a}3: 212–13 n. 12
202^{a}5–7: 214
202^{a}9–12: 208, 210, 214, 229–30 n. 28
202^{a}13–16: 226
202^{a}13–14: 206
202^{a}13–18: 213
202^{a}14–16: 218, 225–6 n. 25, 229–30 n. 28
202^{a}14–15: 224 n. 23
202^{a}16–17: 219
202^{a}16: 226
202^{a}18–20: 219
202^{a}18: 226
202^{a}19–20: 224
202^{a}20: 221, 225, 231
202^{a}21–^{b}5: 207
202^{a}25–7: 230
202^{a}25: 210, 211, 212
202^{a}26–31: 212
202^{a}28–^{b}1: 231
202^{a}29–30: 231
202^{a}30: 212–13 n. 12
202^{a}33–6: 231
202^{a}35–6: 210 n. 6
202^{a}36–^{b}2: 231
202^{a}36: 231
202^{b}1–5: 210 n. 7, 218, 229
202^{b}1–3: 210 n. 8
202^{b}1: 225
202^{b}2–5: 231
202^{b}5–9: 219
202^{b}5–8: 211
202^{b}5–21: 213
202^{b}8–22: 228
202^{b}8–10: 228, 229, 229–30 n. 28
202^{b}8–9: 224 n. 23
202^{b}10–14: 223
202^{b}11: 225
202^{b}12: 223 n. 22, 225
202^{b}14–19: 229–30 n. 28
202^{b}14–16: 224, 224–5 n. 24
202^{b}17–19: 220
202^{b}19–22: 225, 225–6 n. 25
202^{b}20: 225–6 n. 25
202^{b}22: 225

202^{b}25–7: 225–6 n. 25, 229–30 n. 28
202^{b}31–3: 215
203^{b}33: 235, 248
204^{a}14–17: 249
204^{a}14–16: 250
204^{a}14: 250
204^{a}18–19: 235, 248, 249
204^{a}28–9: 249, 250
204^{a}29–30: 249, 250
204^{a}34–206^{a}7: 250 n. 17
204^{b}8–10: 249
204^{b}30: 248
206^{a}3–5: 249
206^{a}18–21: 234
206^{a}18–19: 233
206^{a}21–5: 234
206^{a}22: 238, 239
206^{a}25–^{b}3: 235
206^{a}27–8: 238
206^{b}3–4: 244
206^{b}5–6: 238, 244
206^{b}12–13: 244
206^{b}13–14: 234, 237
206^{b}14–16: 241
206^{b}16–20: 242
207^{a}7–15: 241
207^{a}14–15: 241
207^{a}21–32: 241–2
207^{a}22–3: 242
207^{a}35–^{b}1: 242
207^{b}10–13: 244
207^{b}34–208^{a}4: 242
208^{a}5–23: 236
209^{a}6: 189
209^{b}5–8: 242
210^{a}20–1: 212 n. 11
223^{a}21–9: 246
229^{b}25–6: 151–2 n. 24
241^{b}3–11: 247
251^{a}27: 183 n. 35
252^{b}7–12: 247
252^{b}21–3: 174 n. 18
255^{a}10–15: 174 n. 18
255^{b}15–16: 185 n. 38
255^{b}29–31: 174 n. 18
257^{b}6–9: 240
263^{a}25–6: 246
263^{a}28–9: 244
263^{b}3–9: 244
Politics
1253^{a}9–18: 269
1253^{a}18–29: 268 n. 35
1253^{a}19–25: 168 n. 3, 177

Index Locorum

1262^b3: 259 n. 21
1334^b17-25: 269
1334^b22-5: 265

Posterior Analytics
1. 4: 139 ff.
1. 6: 152, 154, 160 nn. 40–1, 162
1. 22: 328
73^a21-3: 158 n. 37
73^a24-5: 146
73^a25-7: 146
73^a34-^b3: 139–40 n. 1
73^a35-6: 143 n. 9, 159 n. 38
73^a37-8: 146
73^a38-^b3: 147–8 n. 18
73^b3-4: 160
73^b4-5: 140 n. 2
73^b16-24: 140, 154
73^b16: 141 n. 5
73^b18: 140
73^b19: 155 n. 31
73^b21-4: 151
73^b21-2: 162 n. 44
73^b21: 151–2 n. 24
73^b25-7: 141
73^b27-8: 141, 164 n. 45
73^b28: 141 n. 5
73^b30: 141 n. 5
74^b5-12: 140 n. 3, 154
74^b6-10: 162
74^b6-8: 159
74^b11-12: 140 n. 3
74^b21-3: 307 n. 10
75^a18-22: 160
75^a28-31: 145 n. 15
75^a39-^b2: 145 n. 15
76^b11-16: 145 n. 15
77^b24-6: 256 n. 14
81^b18-20: 313
81^b21-3: 311 n. 15
81^b22-3: 313
82^b35: 328 n. 25
82^b37-9: 234
83^b17-20: 160 n. 41
84^a7-8: 328 n. 25
84^a11-25: 147–8 n. 18
87^a8: 328 n. 25
93^b29: 143 n. 9
96^b2-3: 159 n. 39

Prior Analytics
1. 30: 312
2. 16: 312
46^a8-10: 312
65^a36-7: 312

Rhetoric
1369^a1-4: 260 n. 24
1378^a30 ff.: 262 n. 26

Sophistici elenchi
19: 256 n. 14
183^b: 7–8: 1 n. 2

Topics
1. 14: 312
8. 13: 312
100^a29-30: 299
100^b1: 312
100^b21-3: 299
101^a33-4: 304
103^a25-7: 223
105^b30-1: 312
161^a29-36: 304 n. 9
162^b32-3: 312

Aspasius
In Aristotelis Ethica Nicomachea commentaria, ed. Heylbut
35. 14–36. 21: 257 n. 15
36. 2–5: 258–9 n. 19

Averroes
In Aristotelis Physica commentaria (Venice, 1562–74)
vol. iv, fo. 92^v I–L: 220 n. 19
vol. iv, fo. 95^r A: 220 n. 19

Cicero
Academica
1. 16: 2 n. 5
1. 44–6: 2 n. 5

Diogenes Laertius
2. 12–13: 20 n. 28
8. 8: 27 n. 45
8. 11: 27 n. 45
8. 13: 27 n. 45
8. 32: 26
8. 37: 27 n. 45

Euripides
Ion
1619–22: 30
Medea
1021–80: 66 n. 7

Eustratius
In Aristotelis Ethica Nicomachea commentaria, ed. Heylbut
120. 3–8: 258 n. 17

386   *Index Locorum*

[Heliodorus]
In Aristotelis Ethica Nicomachea
paraphrasis, ed. Heylbut
25. 7–14: 257 n. 16
25. 11–12: 258 n. 17

Heraclitus, 22 DK
B 51: 27 n. 45
B 92: 27 n. 45
B 93: 27 n. 45
B 98: 27 n. 45
B 101: 27 n. 45
B 107: 27 n. 45
B 116: 27 n. 45
B 118: 27 n. 45

Hesiod
Theogony
26–8: 15–16 n. 22
Works and Days
293–7: 253 n. 2

Homer
Iliad
bk. 2: 29
9. 645–8: 66 n. 7
Odyssey
20. 17–18: 66 n. 7

Kant
Kritik der reinen Vernunft
B 456: 237 n. 6

Libanius
Apology (=*Decl.* 1)
109, v. 74 Foerster: 29 n. 53

Philoponus
De aeternitate mundi contra Proclum,
ed. Rabe
9. 4–20: 236–7
In Aristotelis Physica commentaria,
ed. Vitelli
375. 26–376. 5: 220 n. 19
376. 6: 208 n. 3
383. 21–2: 225–6 n. 25

Pindar
Olympian Odes
2. 68–70: 26

Plato
Alcibiades I
111 B–D: 3
111 B–C: 14, 18
116 E–117 A: 12 n. 18
124 A–B: 23 n. 34
131 B: 27 n. 49
133 C: 27 n. 49
Apology
19 C: 1 n. 2
20 C: 1 n. 2
20 E: 1 n. 2
21 B: 1 n. 2
21 D: 1 n. 2, 3, 22
22 B–C: 14
22 B: 5
22 C–E: 3
22 C: 7
22 D–E: 3
22 D: 1 n. 2, 16–17 n. 23
23 A–B: 1 n. 2, 3, 11
23 A: 3, 9–10 n. 13, 24 n. 35, 25
23 B: 24 n. 35
28 B–29 A: 4
28 B–D: 13, 15
28 D–29 A: 4, 29
29 B: 4, 29
29 D–31 B: 13
29 D–30 B: 4, 5
29 D–30 A: 4, 32
29 D–E: 13
29 E: 9–10 n. 13
30 D–31 C: 5
30 D: 4, 29
31 D–32 A: 21
31 D: 21
32 B–D: 4
32 B–C: 4, 28
33 A: 13
33 B: 13, 13–14 n. 19
33 C: 23
35 C–D: 4, 28
36 C: 9–10 n. 13
38 E–39 B: 4
40 A–41 D: 8
41 C–D: 4, 29
Charmides
159 A: 14, 18
159 B 1–160 E 1: 41
160 E 2–161 B 2: 41
163 D 1–164 C 6: 41
164 D: 27 n. 49
165 B–C: 1 n. 2

Index Locorum

166 E 5–169 B 5: 42
167 A: 24 n. 35
Crito
48 B: 4
48 D: 4
50 A ff.: 9
50 E–51 C: 4, 29
54 B: 4
54 D–E: 8
Euthydemus
302 C–D: 23 n. 33
Euthyphro
5 B: 9–10 n. 13
5 C 4–D 7: 44
5 C 8–D 6: 49 n. 13, 50
5 D 1–5: 44, 49 n. 14, 51 n. 18
5 D 8–6 E 6: 45
6 A–C: 15–16 n. 22
6 C 8–D 11: 50
6 D: 17 n. 24
6 D 9–E 6: 49 n. 14, 51 n. 19
6 D 10–E 6: 44
6 D 10–11: 50
6 D 11–E 1: 53 n. 23
6 E 3–6: 49 n. 15
6 E 10–8 A 12: 45
7 B–C: 3
8 A 10–12: 49 n. 13, 50
9 D 1–11 B 1: 45
11 A 6–B 1: 44
11 A 7–8: 50, 51 n. 19
11 E 1–12 A 2: 45
11 E 4–15 C 10: 45
12 E 5–8: 46
Gorgias
448 E 6–7: 47
454 D: 8 n. 11
454 E 3–455 A 7: 259 n. 22
462 C 10: 47
463 B 7–C 5: 47
470 E ff.: 29 n. 57
506 A: 1 n. 2
509 A: 1 n. 2
512 D–E: 4
522 E: 4
523 A: 8 n. 11
524 A–B: 8 n. 11
526 D: 8 n. 11
527 C–D: 4
Hippias Major
269 E 9: 53 n. 23
286 C–E: 1 n. 2
286 C 3–E 4: 49 n. 13

286 D 8: 50
287 B 4–289 D 5: 43
287 B 4–E 1: 49 n. 13, 50
287 C 2: 53 n. 23
287 C 5: 53 n. 23
287 C 8: 53 n. 23
287 D 2–E 1: 42
288 A 9–11: 53 n. 23
288 A 9: 50
289 D 2–8: 49 n. 14, 51 n. 19
289 D 2–5: 42
289 D 3–4: 42
289 D 4: 53 n. 23
289 D 6–291 C 9: 43
289 D 8: 53 n. 23
291 D 1–293 D 4: 43
292 C 8–D 4: 42
292 C 9–D 4: 49 n. 14
292 C 9–D 3: 51 n. 18
294 B 1–2: 53 n. 23
294 B 6–C 2: 42
295 B 7–297 D 1: 43
296 C 2–3: 53 n. 23
296 E 8: 53 n. 23
297 A 1–4: 53 n. 23
297 A 5–8: 53 n. 23
297 A 5–6: 53 n. 23
297 A 8: 53 n. 23
297 B 1–2: 53 n. 23
297 B 9: 53 n. 23
297 C 2: 53 n. 23
297 E 3–303 D 10: 43
300 A 9–B 2: 42, 49 n. 14, 51 n. 18
300 A 9: 50, 53 n. 23
303 E 11–12: 53 n. 23
304 D: 1 n. 2
Hippias Minor
372 B: 1 n. 2
Ion
533 D–E: 22
533 E: 7
534 B–D: 17–18 n. 25
534 B: 7, 14
534 C: 7
534 D: 7
535 E–536 A: 22
536 C: 7, 8
Laches
186 B–E: 1 n. 2
188 B: 17–18 n. 25
190 B 7–C 2: 364 n. 71
190 E 4–192 B 8: 41
191 D 10–11: 41

388   *Index Locorum*

192 A 1–B 4: 40–1 n. 6
192 B 9–193 E 5: 41
194 C 7–199 E 10: 42
200 E: 1 n. 2
Laws
631 C: 9–10 n. 13
644 D–645 C: 74 n. 19
644 D–645 B: 88
Lysis
212 A: 1 n. 2
223 B: 1 n. 2
Meno
71 A–B: 340–1 n. 23
71 A: 1 n. 2
71 A 6: 340–1 n. 23
71 B: 337 n. 16, 364
71 B 3: 340–1 n. 23
71 B 5: 340–1 n. 23
72 A 8–B 2: 40–1 n. 6
72 C: 17 n. 24
72 E: 17 n. 24
74 B–77 A 2: 40–1 n. 6
75 C 8–D 7: 334
75 D: 334–5 n. 8, 335, 335 n. 10,
    336, 336 n. 13, 337
75 D 6: 334 n. 7, 338
79 C 8–9: 337
79 D: 334, 334 n. 7, 335, 335 n. 10,
    336, 337, 338, 347
79 D 1–4: 334–5 n. 8, 336, 337
79 D 6–E 1: 338
80 C–D: 1 n. 2
80 D–81 E: 17 n. 24
80 D 5–8: 340
80 E 1–5: 340
81 A–B: 26–7 n. 43
81 C 9: 359 n. 61
82 E: 13–14 n. 19
84 C–D: 13–14 n. 19
85 C–D: 348
85 C 6–7: 355
85 C 9–D 1: 355
85 C 11–D 1: 349
85 D 3–4: 355
85 D 6–7: 355
85 D 9–10: 355
85 D 9: 359 n. 61
85 D 10: 359 n. 61
86 B–C: 17 n. 24
86 C–87 C: 362
87 B–C: 20
88 B ff.: 9–10 n. 13
88 B: 17–18 n. 25

89 A–B: 20–1
89 C: 20
89 D–96 D: 20
96 E ff.: 10
97 A ff.: 342, 364
97 B ff.: 9–10 n. 13
97 B 1–2: 364
97 D–98 A: 12 n. 18, 17
98 A: 12 n. 18, 17 n. 24, 364
98 A 4–5: 365 n. 73
98 D–E: 21
99 A–B: 20
99 B–100 A: 10–11
99 B–C: 10
99 C–D: 17, 18–19
99 C: 7, 17–18 n. 25
99 D: 15 n. 20
99 E–100 A: 11
99 E: 17, 21
Phaedo
60 D: 24
60 E–61 A: 24
61 B: 24
64 C 4–8: 50 n. 17
65 D 12–E 1: 51 n. 19
69 A–C: 9–10 n. 13
74 D 9–76 D 6: 360 n. 62
76 B: 17
76 D 7–E 4: 51 n. 19
83 D 4–E 2: 85
84 E–85 B: 23
85 E–86 C: 192 n. 49
94 D: 66 n. 7
99 A 5–B 4: 215
99 B 1–4: 215 n. 14
100 B–101 C: 17 n. 24
100 D 4–6: 51 n. 19
101 C 2–4: 51 n. 19
Phaedrus
227 A–230 E: 116
228 B 6–7: 97
228 C 1–2: 97
229 A ff.: 116
229 A–230 E: 107
229 C ff.: 108
229 C 6: 116
229 D–230 A: 23 n. 34
229 E 1: 116
230 A: 106, 131
230 C: 117
230 C 6: 116
232 A 8–B 1: 97–8
234 E: 121

Index Locorum

235 C 3: 118 n. 46
237 A: 124 n. 57
237 B 7–D 3: 47
241 E: 124 n. 57
242 A: 116 n. 44
242 C: 124 n. 57
246 A: 99 n. 10, 132 n. 76
246 A 3–6: 104
247 C 6–D 1: 51 n. 19
248 A: 64–5 n. 4
249 B–C: 64–5 n. 4
249 B 6–7: 98
249 C: 17 n. 24
250 A 6–251 A 7: 51 n. 19
251 B ff.: 101
251 D 8: 116
253 B 6: 98
253 D 7–E 1: 98
255 B 3: 98
257 B 3: 97
257 C 7: 101 n. 13
257 E 1–4: 100
259 A–E: 117
259 A–D: 107
259 B 5: 101 n. 13
259 D 1: 100
260 A–262 C: 99 n. 10
261 A 8: 112
261 A 9: 101
263 A–B: 3
264 A ff.: 92
264 B 7: 120
264 C: 94, 120–1
265 B–D: 132 n. 76
265 B–C: 105, 108
265 C 8–9: 105
266 A–B: 124
266 B 3: 101
270 B–272 B: 99 n. 10
273 E: 113
276 E–277 A: 101
276 E: 108
277 C: 131 n. 74
278 A–B: 101
278 D–E: 132
279 B–C: 107
279 B 9: 101 n. 13
Philebus
48 C–49 A: 24 n. 35
Protagoras
319 A–320 B: 20 n. 28
344 B–345 C: 12 n. 18
352 C: 9–10 n. 13

361 A–B: 20 n. 29
361 C 4–D 5: 364 n. 71
Republic
bk. 1: 15–16 n. 22
bk. 3: 282 n. 20
bk. 4: 78 n. 24, 80
bk. 8: 67 n. 10
bk. 9: 67 n. 10
bk. 10: 67 n. 10
331 E: 15–16 n. 22
337 E: 1 n. 2
343 C 6: 282
348 C 12: 282
348 D 2: 282
348 D 3–4: 283
359 C 3: 280 n. 17
359 C 5: 280 n. 17
360 B 1–2: 280 n. 17
375 A–376 C: 67 n. 10
389 D–E: 29
389 E: 15–16 n. 22
390 C–D: 15–16 n. 22
390 D: 66 n. 7
400 D 11–E 3: 282 n. 20
401 D 5–402 A 4: 263 n. 30
409 A 8–B 1: 282 n. 20
411 E–412 A: 67 n. 10
412 D 9–E 8: 85
427 B–C: 28 n. 52
429 B 7–430 B 8: 85
430 C–432 A: 67 n. 10
430 C 8–432 B 1: 86
430 E ff.: 27
431 B 9–E 2: 86
431 B 9–D 2: 86
433 C 6: 86
435 A 6–436 A 3: 66
435 E–436 A: 67 n. 10
436 A–439 D: 73
436 B–439 D: 67 n. 10
436 B 8–9: 69
437 B 1–C 10: 69, 70, 72, 75, 76
437 C 1: 73 n. 17
437 D 2–6: 69
437 D 7–439 B 1: 71
437 D 8: 73 n. 17
438 A 2–4: 73 n. 17
439 A 9–B 5: 73
439 A 9–B 1: 71
439 A 9: 73 n. 17
439 B 3–C 1: 71
439 B 3–6: 69
439 B 3: 73 n. 17

390 · Index Locorum

439 C 3–5: 69
439 C 3: 73 n. 17
439 C 6–D 8: 72 n. 15
439 C 6–8: 69, 72, 75, 76
439 C 6–7: 76 n. 21
439 C 8: 83
439 C 10–D 8: 76
439 C 10–D 3: 69
439 C 10–D 2: 72
439 D 4–9: 69
439 D 5–8: 72
439 E–441 C: 67 n. 10
439 E 1–441 C 4: 78
439 E 5–440 A 7: 78
440 A 2: 84
440 A 6–7: 67 n. 9
440 A 9–B 6: 78
440 B 1: 84
440 B 2: 84
440 B 3: 67 n. 9
440 B 9–C 4: 79
440 C 6–444 D 10: 83
440 C 7: 67 n. 9
440 E 2–4: 67 n. 9
441 B: 66 n. 7
441 B 6–C 2: 79
441 C–444 B: 67 n. 10
441 E 3–5: 84
442 A 4–B 3: 84, 86
442 B 5–8: 84
442 B 5: 67 n. 9
442 B 10 ff.: 85
442 B 10–C 2: 84
442 C 4–7: 84
442 C–D: 86 n. 34
442 C 9–D 2: 84, 85
443 C 9–444 A 2: 74 n. 19
444 C 6–D 2: 84
476 A 4–7: 51 n. 19
476 C 9–D 3: 51 n. 19
483 C: 280 n. 17
490 A ff.: 280 n. 17
538 C 6–E 4: 259 n. 21
550 A–B: 74 n. 19
550 A 5–B 7: 74 n. 19
553 A–580 C: 67 n. 10
553 B 7–D 7: 74 n. 19
559 E 4–560 B 9: 67 n. 9
580 D–583 A: 67 n. 10
580 E 5–581 A 1: 72 n. 15
583 B–587 A: 67 n. 10
588 B–592 B: 67 n. 10
597 D 1–598 D 6: 51 n. 19

598 D–601 A: 15 n. 21
600 A–B: 26 n. 39
602 C–603 B: 67 n. 10
602 C 7–603 A 8: 85–6 n. 33

Symposium
194 E 7–195 A 1: 47
215 D: 22
216 D: 1 n. 2

Theaetetus
147 B: 14, 18
149 D: 12, 12 n. 16
150 B–C: 12 n. 16
150 C–D: 1 n. 2
150 D: 13–14 n. 19
151 C–D: 12 n. 16
210 B: 12 n. 16
210 C: 1 n. 2

Timaeus
70 A: 65 n. 5
70 A 3–D 4: 88
70 A 4–8: 88
70 D 8–71 B 3: 65 n. 5
71 A 3: 88
77 B 5–C 3: 65 n. 5, 88

Plutarch
Adversus Colotem
1118 C: 24 n. 35

Sextus Empiricus
Pyrrhoneae hypotyposes
1. 221–2: 2 n. 5

Simplicius
In Aristotelis Physica commentaria,
ed. Diels
439. 34*bis*–37: 220 n. 19
440. 21–2: 208 n. 3
446. 31–2: 220 n. 19
448. 30 ff.: 220 n. 19
492. 26: 237 n. 4
493. 10: 237 n. 4
493. 24–7: 239–40
494. 14–495. 5: 237 n. 4
497. 15: 237 n. 4
506. 5 ff.: 238

Sophocles
Ajax
646–92: 66 n. 7
Trachiniae
1178: 259 n. 21

Index Locorum

**Sylloge inscriptionum Grae-
carum,** ed. Dittenberger, 4th
edn.
iii, no. 1268: 29 nn. 55–6

Themistius
In Aristotelis Physica commentaria,
ed. Schenkl
78. 9–23: 210 n. 7

Xenophanes, 21 DK
B 7: 26 n. 40

Xenophon
Anabasis
3. 1. 5–7: 23 n. 34
Apology
12: 22
16: 27 n. 47
Hellenica
1. 7. 14–15: 28

Memorabilia
1. 1. 16: 3
1. 1. 18: 28
1. 2. 4: 25 n. 36
1. 2. 56–9: 15
1. 2. 58: 29
1. 3. 1: 23 n. 34, 28
1. 5. 4: 27 n. 47
4. 2. 1–23: 24 n. 35
4. 2. 24–5: 24 n. 35
4. 2. 40: 6 n. 8
4. 3. 16–17: 23 n. 34, 28
4. 4. 1–4: 28
4. 4. 2: 28
4. 6. 2–8: 3
4. 6. 24: 23 n. 34
6. 4. 9–10: 6 n. 8
Symposium
34–45: 25 n. 36, 27 n. 47

Notes for Contributors to Oxford Studies in Ancient Philosophy

1. Articles should be submitted with double or $1\frac{1}{2}$ line-spacing through-out. At the stage of initial (but not final) submission footnotes may be printed in small type at the foot of the page. Pages should be A4 or standard American quarto ($8\frac{1}{2} \times 11''$), and ample margins should be left.

2. Two identical printed copies, or a PDF attached to an e-mail, should be submitted to the editor. Authors are asked to supply an accurate word-count (*a*) for the main text, and (*b*) for the notes. The covering letter should provide a current e-mail address, if available, as well as a postal address. In the case of electronic submission, revised versions will not be accepted: the version first submitted will be the one adjudicated.

3. Typescripts will not normally be returned to authors. After all dealings have been concluded, typescripts will be disposed of and electronic files deleted.

The remaining instructions apply to the final version sent for publication, and need not be rigidly adhered to in a first submission.

4. Only one printed copy of the final version should be supplied, double-spaced and in the same typesize throughout, **including displayed quotations and notes**. Notes should be numbered consecutively, and may be supplied as either footnotes or endnotes. Any acknowledge-ments should be placed in an unnumbered first note. Wherever pos-sible, references to primary sources should be built into the text.

5. **Use of Greek and Latin.** Relatively familiar Greek terms such as *psychē* and *polis* (but not whole phrases and sentences) may be used in transliteration. Wherever possible, Greek and Latin should not be used in the main text of an article in ways which would impede comprehen-sion by those without knowledge of the languages; for example, where appropriate, the original texts should be accompanied by a transla-tion. This constraint does not apply to footnotes. Greek copy must be supplied in a completely legible and accurate form, with all diacritics in place both on the hard copy and in the computer file. A note of the system employed for achieving Greek (e.g. GreekKeys, Linguist's Software) should be supplied to facilitate file conversion.

6. For citations of Greek and Latin authors, house style should be fol-lowed. This can be checked in any recent issue of *OSAP* with the help of the Index Locorum.

7. In references to books, the first time the book is referred to give the ini-tial(s) and surname of the author (first names are not usually required), and the place and date of publication; where you are abbreviating the

394 *Notes for Contributors*

title in subsequent citations, give the abbreviation in square brackets, thus:

> T. Brickhouse and N. Smith, *Socrates on Trial* [*Trial*] (Princeton, 1981), 91–4.

Give the volume-number and date of periodicals, and include the full page-extent of articles (including chapters of books):

> D. W. Graham, 'Symmetry in the Empedoclean Cycle' ['Symmetry'], *Classical Quarterly*, NS 38 (1988), 297–312 at 301–4.
>
> G. Vlastos, 'The Unity of the Virtues in the *Protagoras*' ['Unity'], in id., *Platonic Studies*, 2nd edn. (Princeton, 1981), 221–65 at 228.

Where the same book or article is referred to on subsequent occasions, usually the most convenient style will be an abbreviated reference, thus:

> Brickhouse and Smith, *Trial*, 28–9.

Do *not* use the author-and-date style of reference:

> Brickhouse and Smith 1981: 28–9.

8. Authors are asked to supply *in addition*, at the end of the article, a full list of the bibliographical entries cited, alphabetically ordered by (first) author's surname. Except that the author's surname should come first, these entries should be identical in form to the first occurrence of each in the article, including where appropriate the indication of abbreviated title:

> Graham, D. W., 'Symmetry in the Empedoclean Cycle' ['Symmetry'], *Classical Quarterly*, NS 38 (1988), 297–312.

9. If there are any unusual conventions contributors are encouraged to include a covering note for the copy-editor and/or printer. Please say whether you are using single and double quotation marks for different purposes (otherwise the Press will employ its standard single quotation marks throughout, using double only for quotations within quotations).

10. Authors should send a copy of the final version of their paper on a compact disk (CD) or 3.5″ high density (HD) floppy disk (Macintosh or IBM format), indicating on the disk or in an accompanying note the program in which the text is written, including the system employed for achieving Greek (see point 5 above). This version must be in a standard word-processing format **and not a typeset file or PDF**, though an accompanying PDF version may be included. **NB. The version on disk must be the *exact* version which produced the hard copy sent in for printing.**